J. P. Benjamin

The Louisiana Purchase Bicentennial Series in Louisiana History

Glenn R. Conrad, General Editor

The Louisiana Purchase Bicentennial Series in Louisiana History

VOLUME IV

ANTEBELLUM LOUISIANA, 1830-1860

Part B

Politics

EDITED BY

CAROLYN E. DE LATTE

CENTER FOR LOUISIANA STUDIES
UNIVERSITY OF LOUISIANA AT LAFAYETTE
LAFAYETTE, LOUISIANA
2004

Front Endsheets:
Pierre A. B. Derbigny
Judah P. Benjamin

Back Endsheets:
Pierre Soulé
John Slidell

Library of Congress Catalog Number: 96-84494
ISBN Number: 1-887366-55-5

Published by the Center for Louisiana Studies
P.O. Box 40831
University of Louisiana at Lafayette
Lafayette, LA 70504-0831

CONTENT

PART III: ANTEBELLUM POLITICS, 1845-1861

PART IV: POLITICAL LEADERSHIP

PART V: SECESSION

ABOUT THE EDITOR

Carolyn E. De Latte is Professor of History at McNeese State University in Lake Charles, Louisiana. De Latte earned her Ph. D. from Louisiana State University. Her areas of specialization and interests include the Antebellum South, the Civil War, Reconstruction, and Louisiana History. De Latte is the author of *Lucy Audubon: A Biography* which was selected as an Honor Book by the Louisiana Literary Association. In addition, she has published widely in scholarly journals on subjects in her areas of specialization. She is a frequent book reviewer for state and national historical journals.

ABOUT THE SERIES

It was in the spring of 1992 that first thought was given to the matter of how best the Center for Louisiana Studies might commemorate the bicentennial of the Louisiana Purchase in 2003. For the next few months the Center's staff and members of its Advisory Council intermittently discussed the possible project, but no consensus was forthcoming. Perhaps the reason being that the Purchase looms so monumentally in United States history there are seemingly few memorials of proper proportion to commemorate the event's bicentennial.

Nevertheless, as time passed the outlines of a project began to take shape. To properly mark the occasion the Center for Louisiana Studies should produce a lasting tribute not only to the people who crafted the Louisiana Purchase but also to the people who, during the last two hundred years, have had a role in transforming that vast wilderness into the heartland of America. But the Center's focus is not mid-America for all practical purposes, it is Louisiana, the state that took its name from the Purchase territory. Therefore, the Center's project would concentrate on a Purchase bicentennial memorial that embraced the full range of Louisiana history.

There was another reason for this decision. In March of 1999 the Gulf Coast and the Mississippi Valley would mark the tercentennial of the founding of the French colony of Louisiana and the beginning of the region's historical era. Thus, if the Center's endeavor for the Purchase bicentennial was to be a history of Louisiana, then it should tell not only about the American experience in the area but also the Native American, French, Spanish, African, British and other influences that helped to lay the foundations for the present-day state.

Questions arose: Will the Center's Purchase bicentennial memorial be yet another history of Louisiana? If so, should it be another survey or should it be a more detailed account? Who would write this account of our times and those of our forebears? What interpretation would emerge from such a monograph? Who was expert enough to incorporate a harmonious blend of the political, economic, and social ingredients of our society?

Another year slipped by while we pondered these and other questions concerning the Center's memorial to the Purchase bicentennial and the tercentennial of the founding of the colony. After more discussion, there began to emerge a collective concept that was at once imaginative, exciting, and, above all, challenging. As a fitting memorial for the Louisiana Purchase bicentennial, the Center would organize and direct the publication of a major historical series. Marking the anniversaries, however, should not be the only reason for such an endeavor.

As discussion of the nature of the series evolved, it became obvious that there was an overriding reason for it. The series, to be known as the LOUISIANA PURCHASE BICENTENNIAL SERIES IN LOUISIANA HISTORY, would be a fine sampling of twentieth-century scholarship, particularly the scholarship of the last half of the century which embraced new methodologies leading to broader interpretations of the state's history. Here, in a multi-volume series the student of Louisiana history would be exposed to a wide range of scholarship reflecting multiple interpretations of historical events.

Thus, the decision was made; the Series would bring together in one place the very best articles, essays, and book parts that have been published about Louisiana in the twentieth century, particularly the latter half of the century. Its focus would be to inform scholars, teachers, students, and laypersons on far-ranging topics of Louisiana history drawn from a great reservoir of scholarship found in media ranging from scholarly to popular to obscure.

Most important to the development of such a series, however, was the person or persons who would select the "very best" to incorporate into the Series. The answer came quickly, only widely recognized experts, acting as volume editors, would determine from the broad spectrum of sources those essays which reflect the best in research, writing, and interpretation on topics in Louisiana history.

Initially, nineteen broad topics of Louisiana history were identified, and the Center plans to publish these nineteen volumes between 1995 and 2004. It should be noted, however, proper presentation of some topics in Louisiana history cannot be confined to a single book; hence, some volumes may incorporate several parts in order to present the full spectrum of scholarship on the subject. Finally, the volumes will not be published in sequential order, although Volume I, *The French Experience in Louisiana* was the first to appear. Each volume will be announced upon publication.

THE LOUISIANA PURCHASE BICENTENNIAL SERIES IN LOUISIANA HISTORY presents a great source of information for anyone interested in the history of the colony and the state. It stands as an appropriate memorial to the men and women who shaped the colony and state down to the dawn of the twenty-first century.

Glenn R. Conrad, General Editor

INTRODUCTION TO PART B

In many American states, citizens brag about the colorful political figures in their local history. They are proud to point to the honorable and noble politicians in their state, but will often speak in more eloquent terms about historic corruption, statehouse deals, city hall shenanigans and courthouse cronies. They may agree that such activities go on in every state and maintain that all of the states have a similar background in politics.

The Louisiana citizen will smile smugly at such remarks. This citizen KNOWS what state has had the most colorful political past. Historians agree that much of the talk is myth, but they will also add that the truth shows a political history that is more fascinating than the myths. Politics in antebellum Louisiana are often neglected, but they are as colorful as any other period in the state's history.

Antebellum Louisiana was a unique Southern state. On the one hand, was an urban state with the largest city in the South. In 1840 New Orleans was the fourth largest city in the United States. It was a great seaport and riverport rivaling New York in trade. The city had every sort of retail establishment one could imagine, and riverboats loaded with cotton lined the levee. Immigrants poured into New Orleans, giving the city a flavor of Irish and German as well as French and Anglo American. On the other hand, Louisiana was also a frontier state and a rural state. There were many small farmers in most sections of the state, while at the same time some of the largest cotton plantations in the South were located along the Mississippi. In the Southern part of the state huge sugar plantations flourished.

It was a state unique in the South with its large numbers of Catholics, the Irish of course, but also numerous descendents of the Acadians who lived along the bayous and on the prairies and of the French who had migrated from France or the West Indies and who continued to migrate. It was both a civil law and a common law state, unique, not just in the South, but in the nation with a complicated legal system that seemed foreign to many other Americans.

Louisiana was not unique in its attitude toward slavery. Like other Southern states it extolled the slave system. And like other Southwestern states the frontier areas attracted planters who dreamed of large fortunes made by exploiting the labor of the slaves. Almost all of the states political leaders owned slaves. These men were interested in wealth and prestige and slave ownership helped provide both. Many small farmers hoped to be able to buy more land and eventually be able to join the ranks of slaveowning planters.

In Part I Joseph G. Tregle, Jr. gives the background of the politics of the Constitution of 1812 and of the following years when French Louisianians were determined to keep control of the state. However, the Jacksonians demanded a more democratic document, and Judith K. Schafer discusses the Constitution of 1845 which was finally drafted when Jacksonian Democrats won at the ballot box. Wayne M. Everard explains the important features of the Constitution of 1852 including the unique feature which counted all slaves for apportionment in both the state senate and state house of representatives, thus providing the large plantation areas greater power in the legislature.

All of the selections in Part II are the work of Joseph G. Tregle, Jr. Dr. Tregle, a native of New Orleans, loves Louisiana. He has little patience with fantastic myths, rather he insists on the truth and is quick to point out that the truth of Louisiana's social and political history is much more fantastic than the myths. Historians throughout the state praise him as the outstanding Louisiana historian of our time.

The first five selections of Part II are from Tregle's well-known *Louisiana in the Age of Jackson: A Clash of Cultures and Personalities.* He examines the complicated political arena of Jacksonian politics in the state. He points out first that the animosity between French and American groups in the state were unique in American politics of the time. No other state had a passionate group of French politicians. Factions existed before there were national party groups in Louisiana. He traces the development of the Jacksonians and then the beginnings of the Whigs. Lest anyone assume that honesty was pervasive, Tregle in an article about corruption in the state certainly proves that corruption was alive and well during the antebellum period.

In Part III, the selections focus on Louisiana as a two-party state and indeed, Louisiana was a two-party state. William H. Adams describes the Louisiana Whigs who were a powerful party for twenty years in state and local government. John M. Sacher' s splendid article examines the entire history of the Whigs in the state and discusses them in relation and comparison with the Whigs in the nation and in the rest of the South. He finds that although slavery was a major cause of their downfall, another reason was because Louisiana Democrats had adopted most of the Whig economic programs and accepted Whig ideas about activist government, leaving the Whigs with no program that was solely their own.

In two articles James K. Greer discusses the Democratic party and the ascendancy of John Slidell and the struggle between Slidell and Pierre Soulé for control of the party. Slidell remained the dominant Democrat in the state. Dennis C. Rousey and Thomas K. Wharton look at the great amount of violence in New Orleans in the 1850s. One would expect violence in a seaport city, but the violence at election time was, if not more than in other large cities, as severe. Honest elections were few.

With the collapse of the Whigs, some Louisiana Whigs as well as some Democrats were attracted to the Know Nothing or American party. Leon Cyprian Soulé examines the early development of the Know Nothings in New Orleans, which was naturally where they were especially active in the state. The Know Nothings generally detested Catholics and immigrants. Members were not supposed to have any dealings with such people, but Louisiana, being Louisiana, was not a place where anyone was about to follow the rules. Thus, it was the only state where prominent members of the American party were not only people of foreign extraction, i.e., not Anglo American, but were also Catholic!

Part IV gives capsule biographies of important politicians in the state. The activities of most are discussed in other sections also. One aim of this volume is to provide the reader with information about every political leader in the state during the antebellum period.

Part V deals with the politics of secession. Waldo W. Braden discusses the 1860 Democratic convention where Pierre Soulé had given a speech in which he urged his fellow Southerners to support Stephen Douglas as "Secession Means Disunion." Many business leaders in New Orleans supported a moderate view. Although the state was carried by Breckinridge in the election of 1860, the city supported Bell and Douglas for president. Businessmen saw secession as ruinous to economic progress. Many were convinced that New Orleans could not survive secession.

However, the election of Abraham Lincoln caused great excitement across the South and the governor called for an election for a convention to discuss secession. When the convention met, it would not release the votes from the rural parishes leading some to believe that either the Co-operationists, i.e., the moderates who were against immediate secession, had won or that the vote was very close. The most influential New Orleans newspaper, the *Picayune* was a leader in the Co-operationist fight. Finally, some figures were released, but the complete tallies were not located for years. Charles B. Dew, who examined the "Long Lost Returns," has found that the election was very close between Co-operationist and secessionist delegates. Many in Louisiana were not at all certain about secession.

Haskell Moore discusses the famous sermon of Reverend Dr. Benjamin M. Palmer, a leading Presbyterian minister in New Orleans. The sermon was given in the period between the election of 1860 and the secession convention. Palmer delivered a speech centered on slavery and its importance to Louisiana and the need to defend the institution. He did not concentrate on the economic elements of slavery as much as the social and religious components. He pointed out that slaves were like children and were very happy with their lot. If slavery were abolished the South would soon witness horrors like the horrors of Haiti. God and religion supported slavery. Abolitionists were really atheists. The South had to defend the institution no matter what. The sermon was printed and distributed in pamphlet form and is credited with changing some views about secession. It was popular all over the South. It might be noted that Palmer was not alone in his thinking. The Catholic archbishop of New Orleans would have agreed completely with the sermon. Order in society must be maintained.

By the time of the secession convention the Co-operationists had little chance of success. Early in the month the governor had ordered state troops to seize the federal arsenal at Baton Rouge and the small fortifications on the lower Mississippi, Forts Jackson and St. Philip. Before the convention convened on January 23, 1861, five other states had announced the Union dissolved. Ralph A. Wooster looks at the members of the convention and finds that almost all were slave owners, that the ones who were dubious about secession tended to be from the sugar parishes and from the northern hill parishes and that those who wanted to discuss solutions other than secession were silenced. James G. Taliaferro, a lawyer from Catahoula Parish, gave an impassioned speech of protest in which he maintained that secession was illegal and that only ruin and anarchy could come to the state if the leaders tried to sever its ties with the Union. His speech was considered much too radical to be included in the proceedings of the convention. Other moderates wanted to let the Louisiana voters vote on secession, but that motion was defeated. With great enthusiasm the leaders of Louisiana jumped on the bandwagon to disaster.

Dolores Egger Labbé

SERIES EDITOR'S NOTE: Due to unforeseen and unavoidable medical circumstances, the editor of this volume, Carolyn De Latte, was unable to complete the introduction. At the series editor's request Dolores Egger Labbé agreed to contribute the introduction to this volume.

VOLUME IV

ANTEBELLUM LOUISIANA, 1830-1860

Part B

Politics

PART I
Antebellum Constitutions and Political Advantage

SKELETON OF IRON*

Joseph G. Tregle, Jr.

It was said of the Creoles, George Washington Cable tells us, that when the tricolor came down in the Place d'Armes in 1803, they wept.[1] Some have read into those tears a sign of despair at the termination of the brief reunion with a beloved France, but the greater likelihood is that they bespoke a different message altogether. There can be no question as to the native Louisianian's emotional attachment to the homeland of his forebears. He spoke its language, shared its loyalties and prejudices, reflected its manners and customs. To be separated from it again meant surely to offer the pangs of ending a treasured and binding relationship. But nothing in his reaction pointed to a rejection of his new status as citizen of the young and prospering Union to which he had been joined by the Louisiana Purchase. And so he wept and looked forward to a future brightened by the prospect of economic blessings and political empowerment which he had never known as a subject of European monarchy. But the mixed reaction evidenced by his behavior in the square that December morning gave clear signal that both he and his new fellow countrymen had embarked on an experience unique in the expansion of American democracy.

In truth, the assimilation of Louisiana into the United States in 1803 presented a tremendous challenge to all those engaged in the enterprise. With little preparation of any sort, provincial and sheltered Louisianians plunged into the confusing business of learning to govern themselves while striving at the same time to adjust to the swarm of newcomers who descended into their midst to become partners in the venture. The task weighed heavily upon them. Behind the Virginia of President Jefferson and the territory's new governor, W. C. C. Claiborne, there stretched decades of participation in self-government and even longer centuries of Anglo-Saxon traditions of freedom. Behind the Louisiana of the Creoles stretched nothing but the colonial rule of France and Spain, nations themselves destitute of any vital substance of political democracy. The Legislative

*First published as Chapter 4 in Joseph G. Tregle, Jr., *Louisiana in the Age of Jackson: A Clash of Cultures and Personalities* (Baton Rouge: Louisiana State University Press, © 1999), 54-78. Reprinted with the kind permission of the author and the publisher.

Assembly of Virginia had been almost one hundred years old, it is well to remember, when Bienville first planted New Orleans on the banks of the Mississippi.

Only twelve years bridged the gap in Louisiana from colony to full statehood in the American Union. Political immaturity and the clash of cultures and national groupings were not auspicious stars under which to begin a new life, but they were inescapable. How much, then, could be expected from the Constitution of 1812 under which Louisiana entered into statehood? Cumbersome, conservative, unbalanced, a patchwork of conflicting interests and designs, it remained in effect until 1845. To understand what went into its making is to begin to understand the political milieu of Louisiana's Jacksonian experience.

Sensing that time played to the advantage of the American invader, the native Louisianians in 1812 used their numerical strength to structure a state government favorable to their interests and almost impervious to change. They designed it specifically to freeze legislative power in those areas where they might hope to maintain dominance and then instituted property qualifications for officeholding and a tax-based suffrage system which severely limited political participation by those new to the land.

The constitution divided the state into fourteen senatorial districts, forever indivisible and allocated in a pattern which guaranteed that New Orleans and the sections above Red River where American numbers might grow would always have a voting strength less than that of districts along the coast and in the southern interior where Gallic influence almost certainly would remain paramount.[2] Even the addition of the Florida Parishes to the state shortly after adoption of the constitution, with a dubiously valid assignment of three extra senate districts to that area, failed to equalize regional representation in the upper house. With their great superiority of population and qualified voters, the Floridas and New Orleans had to content themselves with a senatorial voice no greater than that accorded the combined forces of the four least developed districts in the state. The single vote of the great metropolis counted no more than that of Pointe Coupée, with a fraction of New Orleans' population and voting strength.[3]

Composition of the lower chamber, too, though to a lesser degree, reflected this determination to preserve the status quo. Representation was apportioned among thirteen counties, subdivided into the unique parish units peculiar to Louisiana, to be "forever regulated and ascertained by the number of qualified electors therein," as determined by regular four-year census counts. Total membership of the house of representatives could never exceed fifty, thus placing a limit on the possibility of a significant shift of power by the rapid growth of any one area.[4]

Buttressing this already sturdy design, a series of qualifications limited those who might sit in these bodies or participate in the choice of their membership. In addition to the pro forma requirement that all legislators be free white citizens of the United States, senators had to be at least twenty-seven years of age, resident four years in the state and one year in their district, and possess landed property in that area valued at one thousand dollars or more. Representatives must have reached the age of twenty-one, with residence of two years in the state and one in their county, with a landed property holding of at least five hundred dollars according to the tax list.[5] Suffrage was limited to adult American citizens who had resided at least one year in their county and whose names had been enrolled on the state tax list during the six-month period immediately preceding an election.[6]

The same purpose which shaped these legislative and suffrage patterns also determined the constitution's provisions respecting the state's governorship. Election of the chief executive was by joint ballot of the two houses of the assembly, choice being limited to one of the two candidates standing highest in the returns from a general state election. To be eligible, a candidate had to be a citizen of the United States, at least thirty-five years of age, resident six years in the state, and possessed of landed property valued at five thousand dollars or more. Tenure was for four years, with succession in office prohibited. This peculiar indirect electoral process assured the Creole faction almost foolproof certainty of control over the choice of governors. Guaranteed a legislative majority by the constitution's apportionment schedules, and equally certain that at least one of the two leading candidates would be of their number, Creoles could await the popular returns and then snatch their man to the governor's chair even if he stood second on the poll.[7]

Having assured a Creole advantage in the gubernatorial election process, the constitution then placed extraordinary powers in the hands of the executive. In addition to the usual right to enforce the laws and command the state militia, governors received sweeping command of appointments, allowing them to name, with advice and consent of the senate, a secretary of state, all judges, the attorney general, all sheriffs, all justices of the peace, and all other state officers whose method of choice had not been specified.[8] In addition, they might veto proposed legislation, a right not generally accorded executives in most state constitutions of the period. State legislation eventually gave them additional power to name attorneys for the state's judicial districts, all surveyors, notaries, auctioneers, various state bank directors, coroners, regents for the central and primary schools in New Orleans, port wardens and harbormasters—creating, in effect, a vast gubernatorial patronage system.[9] The life terms of judges, surveyors, notaries, coroners, and several other lesser officers added considerably to this structure of aristocracy by tenure. As crowning testimony to their exalted position, Louisiana governors enjoyed a salary of $7,500 a year, higher by $2,500 than the closest similar payment by a sister state.[10] Legislative checks on executive power conformed to the typical American pattern. A two-thirds vote of each house might override a gubernatorial veto, and any executive misdemeanor in office could lead to impeachment.

The judicial system reflected much the same conservative temper, capped by a supreme court with appellate jurisdiction in civil cases involving sums over three hundred dollars. Administratively, the court functioned in two distinct districts, the eastern comprising the Isle of Orleans, the Floridas, the coast up to Red River, and the Lafourche area, the western embracing the prairies, Red River country, Ouachita, and Concordia.[11]

It met in regular session in New Orleans from November through July, then moved west for sittings at Opelousas and Alexandria during August, September, and October. Despite a usually crushing press of business, its membership remained at the minimum three justices required by the constitution until as late as 1839.[12]

District judges presided over seven judicial districts, hearing most criminal cases and possessing final decision in such matters—no appeal could lie to the high court in other than civil cases. The district court also tried civil disputes brought to it on appeal from the parish courts and justices of the peace, its judgments being final in all litigation involving less than three hundred dollars. Each parish had in addition a parish judge, whose jurisdiction extended to all civil matters in suits under three hundred dollars and to a criminal authority over abuse, assault or battery, and all crimes committed by slaves. Finally, justices of the peace throughout the state served as judges in lesser suits and functioned as general preservers of order in the community.[13]

Legislation established a system of local government based on parish divisions, with police juries in each empowered to regulate slaves, make and repair roads, bridges, dikes, and levees, control movements of cattle, establish ferries, police taverns and public houses, levy taxes for public works, and appoint treasurers and constables for the various units. The same qualifications as those which applied to the lower house of the state assembly governed eligibility in local elections, extending the constitution's conservative limitations down to the most basic level.[14]

As the single major urban community in the state, New Orleans enjoyed a considerable degree of self-government and exemption from many of the otherwise universal restraints imposed outside her limits. Executive authority vested in a mayor, required to be at least thirty years old, a resident for four or more years, owner of city property valued at no less than three thousand dollars, and with status as head of a family (a strange requirement with potential of various kinds of trouble). Chaired by an official called the recorder, a city council served as the legislative body of the municipality, its membership made of aldermen representing wards whose limits and relative delegate strength were fixed by the state legislature. Membership on the council required a two-year residence in the city and a landed property holding of one thousand dollars within its jurisdiction. Any adult citizen with a year's residence in the city and a listing on the state tax rolls might vote in municipal elections.[15]

The city government wielded broad powers of local control. Subject to the mayor's veto, which might be overridden, the council levied taxes on city property, licensed taverns, inns, drays, and carts, regulated building standards and wharfage space, and held complete police power over those within its bounds. A New Orleans parish court exercised concurrent jurisdiction with the state district tribunal over all civil cases arising in Orleans Parish, criminal cases being assigned to a third and completely distinct judicial unit. After 1825 a city court with five judges replaced justices of the peace to hear cases involving minor infractions of the law.[16]

Elections of a complete house of representatives and one-half of the senate took place every two years, with each fourth year given over also to the election of a governor. Constitutional edict scheduled balloting in these contests to begin on the first Monday in July and to last for three days, another sign of the foresight of the native Louisianians in fashioning this organic law. The political strength of the American faction dwindled significantly at that time of the year as many of its numbers fled the state in the sound conviction that the summer months could be a season of death for those not acclimated to its rigorous seasons.

State law made parishes the basic electoral units, combining them in senatorial balloting, however, when more than one parish made up a senatorial district. In either case, voting took place in the parish division, presided over by the parish judge, assisted by two justices of the peace chosen by him as commissioners of the election. The various parish commissioners in a multiparish senate district would meet subsequent to the voting and combine their returns, while house members were decided immediately on the parish level. The process worked somewhat in reverse in Orleans, which, although a single parish, made up two senatorial districts, one the city of New Orleans, the other the rest of the parish plus Jefferson. Each parish filed its returns in a gubernatorial race with the state legislature, which then met the following session to make the formal choice from the two highest candidates.[17]

Parish judges and commissioners chose the polling places in elections unless these had been otherwise fixed by special enactment, not uncommon when a parish was subdivided into electoral districts to make the polls more accessible to voters. In such cases respectable citizens served as poll commissioners, their returns subject to final accrediting by the parish judge. Each eligible citizen entered his vote for all candidates on a single ballot, which might be written or printed. At receipt of the ticket the judge called out the name of the voter and confirmed his residence in the district and his registration on the tax list. Absence of one's name from the roll could be rectified by producing a suitable tax receipt or by convincing the judge and commissioners by oath that the required tax had been paid and that the property on which it had been levied had not been received from another party simply to confer the right of suffrage, with the property to revert to the original owner following the campaign.[18]

Maintenance of order at the polls fell to the parish sheriff, subject to the lawful direction of the commissioners. Anyone offering more than one ballot lost his vote, and any attempt by unauthorized persons to read the deposited tickets made them subject to criminal prosecution. Sale of one's vote for any consideration, whether for money, food, or drink, credit or extension of debt, resulted in loss of that ballot and the possibility of fine and imprisonment, a penalty equally applicable to the bribe. During the three days of the poll, the ballot box remained securely fastened by three locks, each commissioner holding a different key.[19]

At the federal level, the counties of Orleans, German Coast, Acadia, and Lafourche made up the state's First Congressional District; Iberville, Pointe Coupée, and Feliciana, the Second; and Attakapas, Opelousas, Rapides, Natchitoches, Ouachita, and Concordia, the Third. Elections for these offices were held in the same manner and at the same time as those for the state assembly.[20] The legislature chose the state's federal senators by joint ballot of both houses on the second Monday of the January preceding expiration of an incumbent's term, with vacancies filled in the same way except when the legislature's being out of session required a gubernatorial appointment, valid until the assembly resumed its meetings.[21]

Consistent with the idea of limited suffrage and centralized power, state law kept the choice of Louisiana's five presidential electors firmly in the hands of the state legislature until after the disputed election of 1824. How change came to be introduced into this single aspect of the voting system of the state may better be told in the later narrative of the beginnings of the Jacksonian movement in Louisiana.[22]

Much of these governmental details depended on legislative enactment. But the great pillars of the edifice—representation and suffrage requirements, legislative and executive powers—rested on foundations cemented into the organic law and designed to keep Louisiana forever French and forever free of control by the American intruder. Having built to their pleasure, the original planners then made it practically impossible to change the design of the structure. Amendment of the constitution required a process so awkward and baffling as to frustrate any attempt at reform. If the legislature during the first twenty days of a regular session passed a measure listing specific changes to be made in the constitution, the proposal was referred to popular vote at the next election of representatives. Popular disapproval killed it, but a favorable reception required the next legislature to vote for a *second* referendum on the same question the following year. Ratification of a proposal by both of these popular votes bound the legislature at its next meeting to call for a constitutional convention to readopt, amend, or recast the fundamental law.[23] Not surprisingly, this first state constitution remained completely unaltered from 1812 to 1845.

The geographic patterns of Louisiana politics in the 1820s might best be compared to an enormous kaleidoscope, whose basic design regularly twisted into new shapes as perspectives and vantage points themselves shifted to reflect the multifaceted workings of a functioning governmental system. At first glance its fundamental composition seemed simple enough, formed naturally by the distinct geographic sections of the state. Almost like feudal domains they stood, each with its own interests, its own leadership and pride: the metropolitan center of New Orleans and its suburb parish of Jefferson; St. Bernard and Plaquemines below the city; then the Upper Coast, stretching along the banks of the Mississippi up to the Florida Parishes and Red River; Lafourche, following its spinal bayou down to the sea; Attakapas and Opelousas in the midst of vast prairielands; the Red River country of Avoyelles, Catahoula, Rapides, and Natchitoches, with its productive river bottoms and equally bountiful uplands; Ouachita and Concordia, resting on the rich alluvial gift of their waterways; and finally the Floridas, composite of seignorial plantations and petty farms.

Common interests linked various of these geographic districts together at one political level, only to yield to another set of objectives forging different alliances to compete in a second arena. The predominantly Creole communities along the coast and in the southwestern parishes, for example, united in unflagging Gallic antagonism against the equally combative American stronghold in Florida and the north-central districts beyond Red River, a division which consistently dominated sectional disputes over legislative apportionment and gubernatorial choice. But elections to the United States Senate split the state along entirely different eastern and western judicial district lines, each region jealously guarding its claim to one of the posts in the national chamber. Biennial campaigns to fill the three congressional seats generated combinations in yet a third configuration as well, and a final pattern, related to the entire scope of public policy, massed all of the rural sections, divided as they might be in other matters, into one solid bloc against the city of New Orleans. This was the crazy-quilt plain on which political leaders of early Louisiana fought their battles.[24]

Traditional historiography has regrettably gone astray in seeking to define the major issues and motives shaping Louisiana politics in the antebellum period. It centers on an assumption that the Constitution of 1812 and those who directed political life under it aimed primarily at fixing control in the hands of a slaveholding, commercial upper class, with intent to exclude from officeholding and voting all those outside that favored group. One such estimate claims flatly that the constitution "never admitted to the polls more than a third of the adult freemen," and "favored planters in the black belt at the expense of white people in New Orleans and on the frontier." Everything in the political activity of the early state is consequently represented as having its root cause in the determination of an undifferentiated "black belt" aristocracy to establish and maintain hegemony over "white belt" common folk.[25]

That such observations contain at least some truth can scarcely be denied. Suffrage requirements under the Constitution of 1812 did give undue influence to the older, rural, slaveholding regions. The state tax program rested primarily on the kind of property an agrarian slaveholder would of necessity own—real estate, slaves, cattle, horses, and mules. Towns and the sole city of New Orleans paid their share too, not only in taxes on real and slave property, but in a variety of other levies charged against merchants, retailers, brokers, auctioneers, taverns, and carriages, billiard tables, and corporation stock. But a surprisingly large number of city dwellers—clerks, laborers, draymen, barbers, tailors, mechanics, and even professional men—owned no such properties and paid no such taxes, causing them to be politically impotent. Many in the new American migration belonged to this category, and when one considers also that a large part of the rural population, French and American alike, remained landless or settled in fringe areas where clouded land titles, the practice of squatting, and a relatively lower incidence of slaveholding pared down the tax list, it is easy to understand how such a system gave undisputed political advantage to the more affluent segments of society.[26]

But the interpretation which sees class conflict as the primary moving force in this political system, pitting a slaveholding aristocracy against a lower class of yeoman farmers and unpropertied workers, stems from a failure to grasp how thoroughly that dynamic was actually energized instead by the ethnic and regional antagonisms described above. Any upper-class aggrandizement flowing from the governmental patterns established by the Constitution of 1812 came as a by-product of the Gallic formula for containing the American threat rather than as the galvanizing purpose of aristocratic policy. The factor of timing also requires attention. A number of state constitutions in 1812 contained restrictive aspects derived from an earlier, less democratic climate. It was Louisiana's fate to embrace these arrangements when the tides of change had already begun to sweep them away in other areas. Once accepted, the peculiar inflexibility of the 1812 document maintained them for decades, secure against any innovation which might upset the delicate political balance in a state torn between the forces of the past and those of the ever growing non-Latin future.[27]

Even given its undoubted restrictive consequences, the Constitution of 1812 never produced the degree of political exclusionism posited in the class-conflict interpretation. Despite an incidence of slaveholding less than that found in the southwestern black belt, for example, the Florida Parishes and those north of Red River in 1820 possessed 38.5 percent of the qualified voters of the state, a considerable margin over their 30.5 percent of white male Louisianians over age twenty in that same year. Property qualifications and all other difficulties encountered under the 1812 constitution did not keep the voting eligibility of this area below 58 percent of the adult male population of 1820, a figure not to be guessed from the assertion that the strictures of the organic law never admitted more than a third of Louisiana's freemen to the polls. In the region south of Red River, excluding Orleans and Jefferson parishes, 59 percent of the white adult males in 1820 had access to the ballot box.

Despite its 34.5 percent of the state's white male population, the Orleans-Jefferson metropolitan area in 1820 held only 17 percent of Louisiana's eligible electors, and only 23 percent of its adult white inhabitants possessed the right to vote—a dismal record compared with that of any other section of the state. Things improved not at all during the ensuing decade, the metropolitan area sending only 15 percent of its adult white males to the polls in the gubernatorial election of 1830, to cast a meager 15.3 percent of the total state vote. Many factors occasioned this seeming disfranchisement of the great commercial mart. As already noted, the tax requirement for voting proved particularly discriminatory against city dwellers not likely to own the kind of property subject to taxation. But an accurate estimate of the exact degree to which the metropolitan area's white male inhabitants lagged behind those elsewhere in enjoyment of voting rights is impossible to determine. Official lists of certified citizens of the United States simply did not exist in the state at that time, nor did census returns indicate place of birth of residents until the tabulation of 1850. Evidence on all sides, however, clearly indicated that the percentage of foreign-born in the New Orleans population far exceeded that to be found anywhere else in the state, just as experience supported the likelihood that the great proportion of that number had never been naturalized. No one could say, therefore, how many of the free white males of the metropolis were actually citizens, making it consequently impossible to determine precisely how much legitimate inequity is reflected in its paucity of legislative registration and voter strength as compared to its total population numbers. All in all, despite the dismal totals in the metropolitan area, at least 45 percent of adult white Louisianians had the right to vote in 1820, and as many as 34 percent of them did so in the gubernatorial election of 1830, figures which would be considerably higher if one were able to factor out the unquestionably large number of unnaturalized foreigners included in the total white male population count. (For more information on suffrage percentages and qualified electors, see Tables 1 and 2.)[28]

Table 1: Suffrage Percentages, 1830

Parishes	I	II	III	IV	V
Florida and North of Red River					
Ouachita	708		265		531 families, 218 hold slaves
Avoyelles	452		222		
Catahoula	415		176		
Claiborne	389				271 families, 61 hold slaves
Concordia	384		90		
E. Baton Rouge	984		399		
E. Feliciana	871		437		
Natchitoches	1,168		390		
St. Helena	633		366		480 families, 214 hold slaves
Rapides	671		274		404 families, 246 hold slaves
St. Tammany	360		143		
Washington	354		265		278 families, 113 hold slaves
W. Feliciana	710		282		487 families, 297 hold slaves
Totals	7,680	30%	3,315	39.4%	

Suffrage Percentages, 1830

Parishes	I	II	III	IV	V
South of Red River					
Terrebonne	268		85		
St. Landry	1,529		438		
St. John	441		195		196 families, 179 hold slaves
St. James	596		391		445 families, 333 hold slaves
St. Charles	233		94		190 families, 142 hold slaves
St. Bernard	219		157		

	I	II	III	IV	V
Lafayette	697		280		
Plaquemines	433		124		221 families, 140 hold slaves
Pte. Coupée	363		170		
Ascension	468		167		360 families, 150 hold slaves
Assumption	814		334		
Lafourche	751		303		620 families, 232 hold slaves
Iberville	694		265		
St. Mary	600		214		340 families, 252 hold slaves
St. Martin	676		281		545 families, 371 hold slaves
Totals	9,042	35.4%	3,708	44.3%	
Orleans and	8,203		1,241		
Jefferson	616		90		
Totals	8,819	34.5%	1,331	15.3%	

I: White Male Population over Twenty-one
II: Percentage of State Population over Twenty-one
III: Vote in 1830 Election
IV: Percentage of Votes Cast in 1830 Election
V: Slaveholding Incidence

As liberalization of suffrage and representation spread quickly in other states during the so-called Era of Good Feeling, demands for similar democratization of the Louisiana political system became more and more frequent during the 1820s and 1830s. But all such proposals shattered against the rock-hard determination of Gallic political leadership to maintain the advantages given its particular ethnic constituency by the Constitution of 1812. The New Orleans-Jefferson metropolitan area provided this faction its most readily exploited instrument for maintaining a status quo favorable to the Gallic interest. By continuing to link suffrage to tax liability, it kept a cap on any significant increase in American voting strength in the area most likely to experience steadily mounting immigration, a policy not nearly as limiting on the original population, possessed as they were of wider vested holdings in taxable property. In the rural parishes along the coast and in the southwest, this tactic had less importance, for in those areas American numbers never presented the same threat as that feared in the city, and there Gallic influence had the additional protection of the considerable preferential status accorded it by the legislative apportionment provisions of the constitution. The permanent division of the state into unchangeable senatorial districts gave these Latin country parishes 47 percent of the membership of the Louisiana senate. Against the 41.1 percent strength of Florida and the north-central parishes, the Gallic segment could also count upon sufficient support within the 11.7 percent controlled by Orleans and Jefferson parishes to assure an almost certain majority in the proceedings of the upper chamber, a margin which ensured, in effect, at least veto power over all state legislation. Much the same pattern prevailed in the composition of the lower house, where from 1820 to 1841 the indexes of relative delegate strength remained fixed at 16.6 percent for Orleans and Jefferson, 45.2 percent for the coast and southwestern parishes, and 38 percent for the Floridas and the area north of Red River (see Table 3).[29]

Table 2: Relative Electoral Strength, 1820

Parishes	*% of Total Louisiana Adult Population**	*% of Total Louisiana Electors*	*% of Own Population Eligible to Vote*
Florida and North of Red River	30.5	38.5	58
South of Red River	34.9	44.4	59
Orleans and Jefferson	34.5	17.0	23

*White male

Table 3: Representation Percentages, 1820

Parishes	*House*	*Senate*
Florida and North of Red River	38.0	41.1
South of Red River	45.2	47.0
Orleans and Jefferson	16.6	11.7

Time and time again representatives of American districts tried to breach this wall by proposals to amend the constitution, but just as regularly Gallic legislators from the city and the southwestern parishes combined to stem the attack. Ironically, these efforts frequently drew opposition even from some American rural areas, which would have most benefited from reform—so profoundly did they distrust any measure which might aggrandize the influence of the city. Conversely, many New Orleans legislators shied away from constitutional change which could have significantly improved the status of the metropolitan area, fearing that any such alteration might disrupt the status quo to the advantage of the American interest. Attempts to reform apportionment of the house of representatives met the same fate. Despite direct constitutional mandate directing reallocation of seats every four years on the basis of qualified electors, Gallic champions managed to defeat all new apportionment acts from 1823 to 1841.[30] Despite its limited delegate strength, the city nonetheless held the balance of power between the concentrated Gallic force in the southwest and the American in the Florida and north-central parishes. The sharp-eyed Henry Clay in his 1830 visit called New Orleans the pivot around which Louisiana legislative control revolved (see Table 3).[31]

All of these factors made for a political climate in constant agitation. Despite a clear advantage in the constitutional organization of the state, the French element could never relax, aware of American determination to overcome discrimination and gather strength from ever increasing numbers. They saw the growing influx of small farmers into the northern sections of the state and the constant flood of immigration into New Orleans as harbingers of a political reordering which might alter forever the ethnic and cultural substance of the state. To the Americans, the Gallic foe represented stultifying ignorance and backwardness rooted in European traditions at odds with basic precepts of democracy and progress. In a not overly dramatic sense, the battle which ensued might well be termed a struggle for the soul of Louisiana.

The epic contest which resulted summoned up a variety of political expedients and exploited a full measure of differing folkways, some of them commonplace throughout the nation, others with the stamp of a unique Louisiana culture. The French camp found its greatest prop in the paternalistic cast of the old population's society, which vested concentrated power in the hands of innumerable patriarchs throughout the state and bestowed upon politically ambitious natives a natural following difficult to minimize in a community so loyal to family ties. "Strong men" like Henry Schuyler Thibodaux in Lafourche, and Charles Olivier, Neuville Declouet, and Agricole Fusilier in the prairie parishes reputedly could marshal hundreds of voters to march to their command,[32] and the influence of Martin Duralde, son-in-law of Henry Clay, spread along family lines into so many parts of the state that his power as a clan chieftain won the begrudging respect and fear of his foes.[33]

The simplicity and cultural isolation of Creole life made such a deference to respected elders neither craven nor irresponsible, and no election plans or calculations in Louisiana could afford to ignore or minimize these block votes or the men who controlled them.[34] But their threat to American dominance lost much of its impact because of the general political inexperience and naïveté of the ancienne population as a whole. For many years after the Purchase, native Louisianians generally failed to recognize any tie between local and national political affairs,[35] confining their interest to the state because in that arena they clearly perceived the necessity of maintaining French control and everything that went with it—jobs, a way of life, and the sense of being master of their historic turf. Such an attitude made it relatively easy for the Americans to preempt the state's representation in national councils, an advantage compounded by their ability to monopolize federal appointments in Louisiana. Those jobs flowed from Washington, where the native Louisianian stood small chance of breaking the web of relationships and associations which tied the Americans to political influence in other parts of the nation. This ability to appropriate to themselves offices like those of collector of the customs, naval officer and surveyor at New Orleans, federal judge and district attorney, postmaster, land surveyor, and collector of public moneys added immeasurably to the American ability to survive the French concentration on state patronage.

Control of state and local positions lay in the hands of the governor and the mayor of New Orleans. The vast appointive powers of the chief executive gave him control of practically all important state jobs, creating in effect a kind of self-perpetuating circle, since many of these offices managed the very procedures by which governors were themselves chosen. Especially powerful in this respect, parish judges and sheriffs served as supervisors and police authorities at the polls, with almost unlimited right to decide suffrage eligibility under the tax law, to admit or reject ballots, to cast deciding votes, and to regulate activity around the polling places.[36] In New Orleans the police power of the mayor placed at his command a company of armed men so critical to the concerns of a multitude of owners of grog shops and coffee houses, to hack and dray drivers, and to countless others engaged in the complex life of the metropolis that they could generally be counted on to produce some three or four hundred votes for whatever candidate pleased the city administration.[37]

To be dominant in the city actually meant, moreover, to be custodian of the nerve center of Louisiana. Not even the peculiar devices which denied the metropolis a proportionate voice in the suffrage and representation could alter the natural primacy which New Orleans enjoyed by reason of its commercial importance, its access to credit and accumulated capital, and its ability to draw from its numbers political leaders of wide experience and ability. Despite their vocal and unquestionably sincere antagonism to the great urban community, rural political leaders seldom launched any extensive plans for political campaigns before laying a firm foundation in the capital and looking to city experts for advice.[38] This held true particularly in the Gallic faction, for much of its leadership and tactics, if not its numbers, depended upon the political skill of the foreign French, primarily city men to whom the patriarchs looked for leadership of a cause which they themselves could best serve by guaranteeing a following. Finally, as the center of government and headquarters of the legislature and chief executive, New Orleans enfolded the state's political life in the atmosphere of its amazingly variegated and seductive milieu. However much they might decry the wickedness of the city, legislators and civil servants flocked to the capital to frolic at balls, patronize theaters and coffee houses, gamble in sporting dens, and succumb to the pleasures of countless bagnios and brothels. Political persuasion could frequently be by other than vocal means.[39]

Try as they might, the Gallic and American factions never managed to realize complete unity of purpose within their own ranks, much of the effectiveness of their many ingenious tactics frequently dissipated by the sheer perverseness of human nature. Despite their realization of the danger of division in the face of the Americans, native Louisianians frequently weakened themselves by internal jealousies and quarrels, some of their number being known to vote against a measure vital to their cause simply to prevent praise being bestowed on a rival Creole who had introduced it. Clannishness had drawbacks as well as advantages, only too clearly revealed by frequent family dissensions among the French which spread disorder in the ranks.[40] Internal rivalries plagued their opponents as well, generated especially by the virulent hatred of New England Yankees felt by those of Southern stock, a passion which combined with notorious internecine squabbles in the Red River population to make many Americans despair of ever cementing a workable coalition among their followers.[41]

Ethnic and personal antagonisms so flourished in Louisiana that they may well have diminished controversy along other lines. Whatever the reason, dispute over the economic or professional status of those who filled its political leadership seldom occupied much of the state's attention. Throughout the 1820s and 1830s the state legislature consisted largely of planters and lawyers, and though occasionally someone grumbled in the press about the pretensions of this group and demanded a wider representation of the commercial community, such carpings seldom added much to the already bewildering complexities of the political scene.[42]

Not everything in the world of Louisiana politics departed from the national norm. Here as elsewhere in the Union a familiar pattern emerged in the process of nominating men to office and in molding the public opinion necessary to carry them into place, an indication, perhaps, of some essential common denominator in the equation of American democracy. Until the struggles of the Jacksonian period began to impose the additional factor of national group loyalties upon the older ethnic divisions of the state's politics, no formal party organizations figured as such in Louisiana's experience. Before 1830 nominations to all elective offices proceeded from supposedly spontaneous action on the part of interested citizens anxious to put before the public the names of candidates whose ability and integrity fitted them for public service. Just as on the national scene, by the 1820s the term caucus had fallen into disrepute, the practice which it identified being so tainted by political professionalism that Louisiana discarded it with little difficulty. Nominations of candidates generally originated in the columns of the local press, another long-standing custom, and since a current fashion seemed to favor the idea that a man should not seek the office, most proposals claimed to be the suggestions of friends and supporters or of anonymous sponsors who frequently pretended to no object other than the presentation of a worthy man to the consideration of his fellows. Rivaling these newspaper nominations in importance, widely publicized public meetings might also serve to launch a candidacy.[43]

Politics could hardly be that simple or spontaneous, even in those early days of the republic, and behind these reputedly unplanned proposals generally lurked clear and skillful maneuvering on the part of the office seeker and his supporters. Most commonly, especially in campaigns for important offices, managers engaged in wide canvassing of possible candidates throughout the state long before the day of election. When sufficient agreement had been reached among the principal leaders of a group, the agreed-upon candidate's name would then be offered in the press, usually well in advance of election day. Matters moved slowly in the months immediately following to allow for cautious checking of the reception of the proposal and to avoid any impression of trying to force a choice upon the people. If all went well, the nomination might then be pushed with greater fanfare as the election drew nearer. Not infrequently, peculiar circumstances of a particular campaign might upset such long-range planning and require the drafting of last minute candidates to fill a breach or thwart an opponent's move. Then as now, inevitably, some perennial candidates managed to get their names regularly before the public regardless of support or chances of success.[44]

By the 1830s the primitive beginnings of a convention system for nominations began to appear, made practical at last by the greater crystallization of party lines achieved during the Jacksonian era, but even then the older practices persisted. Indeed, it would take years before the party-meeting plan developed enough to dislodge the older procedures from their place of first importance.[45]

Actual political campaigning swept candidates and backers into a swirl of words and action so spirited and vigorous—and frequently so brutal and lusty—as to make modern techniques seem pallid indeed. Most of it found voice in the columns of what we today would consider an unbelievable number of newspapers (distinction between objective reporting and outright advocacy had few defenders). Several of the New Orleans publications in particular matched in quality and influence anything to be found in other parts of the nation.

The political arena of the Jacksonian era had little place for reticence and even less respect for privacy, truth, or the common sensibilities of those who entered it. Campaign propaganda frequently spilled over from newspapers into widely circulated pamphlets, almost always anonymous and filled with vicious attacks couched in prose designed to vilify and malign to such a degree that their creators seldom dared admit to their authorship.[46] The sheer number of legitimate newspapers made them all vulnerable to financial difficulties, and publishers often found relief from such stringency by simply selling their entire operation to one or another of the political factions eager to possess additional access to public favor, sometimes for remarkably modest sums. The long-established and influential *Louisiana Gazette* (New Orleans) changed owners in 1823 for as little as $2,783, and as late as 1833 a faction of the Jackson party acquired the *Louisiana Advertiser* (New Orleans) for a mere $8,000.[47] Even when an owner resisted pressure to sell, financial constraints might make him an eager partner in political strife. Much of the enthusiasm demonstrated by the press in critical elections could be traced back to judicious "gifts" from interested partisans or to pledges of support when the state legislature or national administration went about the selection of public printers.[48] Having incurred the expense of buying a favorable press, in one fashion or another, political leaders made certain that the papers did not go unread, frequently flooding the state with as many copies as could be afforded, even if this meant padding the mailing list with the names of persons who had never subscribed. This became especially commonplace in the 1830s, when complex national issues required wide circulation of such sheets as the *Washington Globe* and the *United States Telegraph*, which could be depended upon to speak with the voice of party authority.[49]

Despite the great influence of the press in political campaigning, no wise political leader could afford to ignore the many other outlets for his propaganda message. This prompted sponsorship of great public meetings, and especially lavish dinners, favorite devices for gathering audiences which might respond to florid bursts of oratory and join in the elaborately turned political expressions which accompanied a string of almost endless toasts. Much less formal but perhaps more subtle, nightly gatherings at the New Orleans coffee houses allowed for intense proselytizing from which not even the gaudy paintings distracted.[50]

The voting public demanded more than knowledge of a candidate's ideas, however. They insisted on knowing the man himself. No matter how exhausting and draining of time and money, no candidate could survive without travel through even the most inaccessible parts of the state where he was not familiar, to be seen and heard by those whose support he courted. There could be no evading of the responsibility, and the political correspondence of the period is replete with admonitions on this point.[51] The experienced office seeker could find many opportunities for making a "regular tour" without evidencing an unseemly grasping after office. Militia reviews, the innumerable racing events throughout the state, and especially the sessions of the Louisiana Supreme Court as it moved on circuit through the western district presented natural gathering places where a candidate might well exhibit himself to the public. Beyond this open field of political strife, indispensable as it was, lay other more secret but nonetheless critical battlegrounds. The private letter, the intimate conclave, and the wooing of the political strong men belonged to the weapons of a struggle generally hidden from public view. Who could say where the victory was really won?[52]

The three days given over to state elections often proved tumultuous and frequently violent, the very length of the voting period itself allowing for the accumulation of desperation as the final polling hours approached. Each faction prepared its own list of the eligible voters in a district, generally broken down into small numbers which became the special responsibility of individual workers. The most affluent and respected of these took up position at the polls to greet arriving voters and solicit their support, while others manned carriages to transport the tardy to the ballot boxes, even the sick and the lame being frequently bundled off to perform their civic duty. When persuasion failed, trickery might easily come into play. This worked on various levels to accommodate the particular astuteness or stupidity of the individual citizen. Some could be gulled by the simple device of putting into their hands counterfeit or rigged printed ballots, which incautious voters might fail to recognize as favoring candidates not actually of their choice. Others too wise to be taken in by such simple deception frequently found themselves at the mercy of hostile election commissioners who might turn away any voter imprudent enough not to have ensured that he had been rightfully entered upon the tax list; it was not uncommon for assessors to delay tax demands against those opposed to their political views and thus fail to register them officially as tax payers. For those of more venal character, whiskey and outright bribes sufficed. Employing one of the most effective techniques of all, Gallic protagonists regularly planted in their newspapers terrifying information of the visitation of yellow fever on the very eve of an election, in the sound expectation that many potential American voters would panic and flee for their lives.[53]

Despite these frequently sordid maneuverings, however, respect for the sovereignty of the public will, once expressed, seldom met with any challenge. Some elections were contested, to be sure, but only infrequently and rarely in any instance of importance. As high as political hatreds might run, no faction ever dared to attempt bypassing the popular choice for governor when the legislature met to exercise its constitutional right to select either of the two candidates who stood highest on the official ballot. American democracy had become at least this real in its newfound domain of Louisiana.

Notes for "Skeleton of Iron"

[1]George E. Waring and George W. Cable, *The History and Present Condition of New Orleans* (Washington, D. C., 1881), 32.

[2]Article II, Section 10, in Benjamin W. Dart, ed., *Constitutions of the State of Louisiana and Selected Federal Laws* (Indianapolis, 1932), 500.

[3]See, for example, Henry A. Bullard and Thomas Curry, eds., *A New Digest of the Statute of the State of Louisiana* (New Orleans, 1842), 544, and *Louisiana House Journal,* 1822, 26.

[4]Article II, Section 6, in Dart, ed., *Constitutions of Louisiana,* 500.

[5]Article II, Section 12, ibid., 500.

[6]Article II, Section 8, ibid., 500.

[7]Article III, Section 2, ibid., 501.

[8]Article III, Section 9, ibid., 502.

[9]Henry A. Bullard and Thomas Curry, eds., *A New Digest of the Statute Laws of the State of Louisiana* (New Orleans, 1842), 26, 30, 36, 37, 373, 464, 537, 796.

[10]*Louisiana Gazette,* June 14, 1821.

[11]Article IV, Section 3, in Dart, ed., *Constitutions of Louisiana,* 501.

[12]Bullard and Curry, eds., *New Digest of the Laws of Louisiana,* 176, 180.

[13]Ibid., 182-83, 208, 528.

[14]Ibid., 639, 640, 647.

[15]Ibid., 99-102.

[16]Ibid., 99-102, 192-93, 208, 213.

[17]Ibid., 390-91.

[18]Ibid., 389, 395, 386.

[19]Ibid., 386-93.

[20]Louis Moreau Lislet, ed., *A General Digest of the Acts of the Legislature of Louisiana Passed from the Year 1804 to 1827, Inclusive,* 2 vols. (New Orleans, 1828), 1:424-26.

[21]Bullard and Curry, eds., *News Digest of the Laws of Louisiana,* 378-79.

[22]Moreau Lislet, ed., *Digest of the Acts of the Legislature of Louisiana,* 1:449-50.

[23]Article VII, in Dart, ed., *Constitutions of Louisiana,* 506-7.

[24]*Louisiana Gazette,* January 12, December 29, 1824.

[25]The classic statement of this class conflict interpretation is that of Roger W. Shugg, *Origins of Class Struggle in Louisiana* (Baton Rouge, 1939). For a detailed analysis of the methodological and interpretative failures of this study, see Joseph G. Tregle, Jr., "Another Look at Shugg's Louisiana," *Louisiana History,* 17 (1976): 245-81.

[26]Bullard and Curry, eds., *New Digest of the Laws of Louisiana,* 700-01. John Sibley to Josiah S. Johnston, January 3, 1826, in Johnston Papers, Historical Society of Pennsylvania, Philadelphia, Penn. (hereafter cited as Johnston Papers); *Louisiana Advertiser,* August 25, 27, 1823. For an examination of the demographics of the antebellum state, see Tregle, "Another Look at Shugg's Louisiana," 245-81.

[27]See Fletcher M. Green, "Democracy in the Old South," *Journal of Southern History,* 12 (1946): 11-16.

[28]These computations are based on the unpublished federal census returns for Louisiana in 1820 and 1830, the census of eligible electors in the state taken in 1821 (*Louisiana House Journal,* 1822, 26), and the state election returns for 1830 (*Louisiana House Journal,* 1831, 7). These last returns were used instead of the state voter census taken in 1829 because though that survey was reported to the legislature, seemingly no copies were printed, nor are they extant in the archives of the Louisiana Secretary of State.

[29]For the apportionment laws, see *Louisiana Acts,* March 12, 1822, and April 7, 1826.

[30]*Louisiana House Journal,* 1828, 22; 1833, 69; 1835, 34; *Louisiana Senate Journal,* 1828, 62; 1833, 11.

[31]Henry Clay to Josiah S. Johnston, March 11, 1830, in Johnston Papers.

[32]Isaac Baker to Josiah S. Johnston, March 11, June 12, 1823, November 1, 1825, January 16, 1826, Henry A. Bullard to Johnston, April 19, 1824, Alexander Porter to Johnston, August 10, 1827, ibid.; *Louisiana Courier,* October 24, 1828, November 2, 1832; *La Fourche Gazette* (Donaldsonville), July 29, 1826.

[33]Alexander White to William S. Hamilton, July 22, 1826, in William S. Hamilton Papers, Hill Memorial Library, Louisiana State University, Baton Rouge, La. (hereafter cited as Hamilton Papers); Isaac L. Baker to Josiah S. Johnston, November 1, 1825, January 16, 1826, Alexander Porter to Johnston, March 10, 1830, in Johnston Papers; William L. Brent to Henry Clay, September 3, 1824, in Henry Clay Papers, Library of Congress, Washington, D. C. (hereafter cited as Clay Papers).

[34]H. B. Trist to Nicholas P. Trist, May 12, 1828, Robert Carter Nicholas to Nicholas P. Trist, October 22, 1831, in Trist Papers, Library of Congress, Washington, D. C.; H. B. Trist to Nicholas P. Trist, December 14, 1837, in Nicholas P. Trist Papers, Southern Historical Collection, University of North Carolina, Chapel Hill, N. C.; Alexander White to William S. Hamilton, July 22, 1826, in Hamilton Papers.

[35]Alexander Porter to Josiah S. Johnston, June 21, 1826, April 16, 28, 1828, April 13, 1830, in Johnston Papers.

[36]Isaac L. Baker to Josiah S. Johnston, September 2, 1823, May 19, 1825, ibid.; *Louisiana Journal,* September 7, 1826; *Baton Rouge Gazette,* June 17, 1826; *Louisiana Advertiser,* June 28, 1834.

[37]*New Orleans Argus,* August 29, 1826; *New Orleans Bee,* November 22, 1833, October 17, 1835.

[38]Thomas G. Morgan to Josiah S. Johnston, January 29, 1832, Henry Clay to Johnston, March 11, 1830, in Johnston Papers; Peter K. Wagner to William S. Hamilton, July 30, 1826, in Hamilton Papers.

[39]Sparks, *Memories of Fifty Years,* 404; *New Orleans Argus,* January 27, February 3, 1827.

[40]W. C. C. Claiborne to Henry Clay, May 23, 1830, in Clay Papers; Alexander Porter to Josiah S. Johnston, September 5, 1824, in Johnston Papers; *Louisiana Gazette,* May 6, 1822; *L'Ami de Lois,* February 1, 1823, January 20, 1824; *Louisiana Courier,* July 5, 1830.

[41]Archibald Haralson to William S. Hamilton, July 31, 1830, Peter K. Wagner to Hamilton, July 30, 1826, in Hamilton Papers; Isaac L. Baker to Josiah S. Johnston, January 16, October 5, 1826, in Johnston Papers; David C. Ker to Andrew Jackson, November 11, 1828, in Andrew Jackson Papers, Library of Congress, Washington, D. C.; *Louisiana Journal*, May 18, 1826.

[42]*Louisiana Gazette*, June 21, 1822; *Louisiana Advertiser*, December 22, 1823; *New Orleans Argus*, February 24, 1827.

[43]*Louisiana Gazette*, June 21, 26, 1822; *Louisiana Advertiser*, January 19, 20, 1824; *Louisiana Herald* (Alexandria), April 2, 1823; *St. Francisville Asylum*, May 20, 1823.

[44]L. S. Hazelton to Josiah S. Johnston, March 30, 1825, in Johnston Papers.

[45]W. L. Robeson to William S. Hamilton, March 21, 1830, in Hamilton Papers.

[46]Henry A. Bullard to Josiah S. Johnston, November 13, 1821, August 5, 1824, Charles T. Scott to Johnston, November 16, 1821, in Johnston Papers; John Sibley to S. F. Austin, July 8, 1824, in Eugene C. Barker, ed., *The Austin Papers. Annual Report of the American Historical Association for 1919. Vol. II* (Washington, D. C., 1924), 849; Isaac L. Baker to Andrew Jackson, March 21, 1825, in Jackson Papers.

[47]George Eustis to Josiah S. Johnston, October 31, 1827, Alexander Porter to Johnston, April 16, 1828, in Johnston Papers; *Louisiana Advertiser*, March 2, 1824; *New Orleans Bee*, February 12, 1834.

[48]H. B. Trist to Nicholas P. Trist, August 8, 1832, in Trist Papers; *Louisiana Gazette*, July 24, 1823; *New Orleans Mercantile Advertiser*, April 18, 1825.

[49]Hugh Alexander to Francis P. Blair, January 2, 1832, in Blair-Rives Papers; *Louisiana Journal*, September 28, 1826; *New Orleans Emporium*, October 5, 1832.

[50]*Louisiana Gazette*, June 26, 1822; *Louisiana Herald*, April 2, 1823; Alexander, *Transatlantic Sketches*, 2:16.

[51]Thomas W. Chinn to William S. Hamilton, April 21, 1822, Archibald Haralson to Hamilton, May 13, 1822, Isaac L. Baker to Hamilton, March 29, 1823, in Hamilton Papers; Baker to Josiah S. Johnston, July 26, 1822, Johnston to Baker, December 24, 1823, Philemon Thomas to Johnston, December 5, 1830, in Johnston Papers.

[52]Archibald Haralson to William S. Hamilton, May 13, 1822, Alexander Barrow to Hamilton, January 28, 1830, in Hamilton Papers; Isaac L. Baker to Josiah S. Johnston, June 12, September 2, 1823, in Johnston Papers; *Louisiana Courier*, September 18, 1828.

[53]Walter H. Overton to Josiah S. Johnston, July 10 1824, in Johnston Papers; Thomas F. Hunt to William S. Hamilton, July 30, 1826, in Hamilton Papers, HSP; *Louisiana Gazette*, July 7, 5820, June 15, 1822, August 1, 1823, July 7, 1824, November 30, December 1, 1825; *Baton Rouge Gazette*, April 10, 1830.

REFORM OR EXPERIMENT? THE LOUISIANA CONSTITUTION OF 1845*

Judith K. Schafer

By 1845, prevailing thought in Louisiana deemed the Constitution of 1812 to be outmoded and too aristocratic. In the popular mind, the Jacksonian principle of "equal ability of all" had shoved aside the Jeffersonian doctrine of "equal opportunity for all." The Democratic party had become the party of the "common man." Wealthy land owners and businessmen became staunch pillars of the opposition Whig party. The Constitution of 1845, reflecting Jacksonian values and the economic upheavals of the previous decade, sharply restricted the power of the state to lend money and forbade the state from becoming a stockholder of a corporation. It prohibited lotteries, dueling, legislative divorces, and the granting of monopolies, and it restricted the legislature's power to issue charters. The new constitution liberalized the suffrage, eliminated property qualifications for officeholders, and established total population (including slaves and voteless free blacks) as the basis of apportionment in the state senate. (The house of representatives continued to be apportioned on voter population.) It additionally created the office of superintendent of public education and directed the legislature to establish free public schools. The concept of "dedicated revenue" also made its initial appearance in a Louisiana constitution. Under the new charter, the organization and jurisdiction of the courts improved greatly. For the first time, felons under sentence of death or life in prison could appeal to the Supreme Court of Louisiana.

* * *

In *History of American Law*, Lawrence M. Friedman observed that "Louisiana takes some sort of prize for fickleness and inflation," having had more constitutions than any other state in the Union.[1] Friedman made his remark in 1973, one year before the passage of Louisiana's most recent constitution. One can only imagine how Friedman responded to news of yet another constitution for the Pelican State. Ten constitutions (or

*First published as Essay 2 in *In Search of Fundamental Law: Louisiana's Constitutions, 1812-1974*, eds. Warren M. Billings and Edward F. Haas (Lafayette, La.: Center for Louisiana Studies, 1993), 21-36. Reprinted with the kind permission of the author and the Center for Louisiana Studies.

eleven if the 1861 secession convention can be counted) is a staggering, but dubious achievement. Only Georgia comes close to achieving such an honor, with six.[2]

Louisiana's legal heritage of civil law based on Roman, French, and Spanish sources set the state apart, but the unique combination of historical influences did not isolate it from the constitutional trends in other states of the Union.[3] Although there was a great deal of diversity in other state constitutions, several common threads of constitutional craftsmanship are readily observable. In the decades before the Civil War, state constitutions grew longer and more complex as their creators were no longer content to provide a skeletal frame of government to be fleshed out by the legislatures. This development was born of a deep conviction that legislators could not be trusted to make suitable laws. Often this lack of faith was the result of bitter experience. An anonymous New Orleans pamphleteer expressed his suspicions this way in 1841, "the members of a Louisiana legislature, although they may have their morals purified and their intellects brightened . . . are by no means infallible—and at all events the safer course is to trust them as little as possible."[4] The Louisiana Constitution of 1845 was an embodiment of a national trend toward placing large areas of what was perceived as potentially harmful legislation out of the reach of these assemblies. Among other things, the framers of the Constitution of 1845 wanted to include in the document what Friedman has called "overriding superlaws;" that is, anti-laws which were designed to suppress legislative laws.[5]

Louisiana's colorful constitutional history began with the Constitution of 1812. Although the French-speaking majority may have been a people unaccustomed to self-government and crafting constitutions, they were quick to understand that they could use the state's first constitution to keep themselves firmly in control of the new state government. Despite their political inexperience, they created in the Constitution of 1812 a document designed to keep the "ancienne population" in power. By setting up residency and property qualifications for holding office, a franchise based on ability to produce current tax receipts, and a system of representation that favored the older parts of the state, the writers of the Constitution of 1812 strove to keep political power safely out of the hands of the Americans who flocked to the Pelican State after the Louisiana Purchase. Political unrest grew as the Americans increased in numbers and influence. Although the old constitution gave Franco-Louisianians almost unassailable control over state politics, the "ancienne population" saw the increasing strength of the Americans as a constant threat to their hegemony.[6]

One of the limitations of that constitution was the lack of a provision for amendment other than by the call of a new convention.[7] By 1841 a majority of the legislators expressed interest in revising the constitution. One New Orleans writer attempted to express the spirit of the time:

> The tendencies of the age are decidedly revolutionary. Change is the order of the day among nations. There is a strong and increasing desire throughout the world to simplify the action and regain the power of government, to secure effectually the political rights of

> the mass, and to introduce direct responsibility to the people, on the part of all who are entrusted with power.

Requiring a constitutional convention to amend the existing organic law was so cumbersome that it proved to be impossible until the turbulent economic and political conditions of the 1840s finally provided the impetus for change. As a result Louisiana lagged behind other states that had amended or rewritten their constitutions to meet demands for broader suffrage and more representative state governments.[8]

In the call for a constitutional convention, Louisiana legislators listed specific areas in need of reform. Among them were equal representation of all parishes, direct election of the governor, elimination of property qualifications for electors, expansion of the jurisdiction of the Supreme Court of Louisiana to include criminal appeals and greater administrative responsibilities, and redefinition of the boundaries of the state to incorporate the Florida Parishes.[9] On March 18, 1844, the legislature ordered a convention to meet at Jackson, Louisiana, in the parish of East Feliciana, on the following August, there to revise the Constitution of 1812.[10]

This first meeting of the convention was brief and unproductive. After electing officers and choosing a printer to publish its proceedings, the convention divided into committees to draft proposals for revising the legislative, executive, and judiciary articles as well as committees to make recommendations concerning public education and general provisions. The only accomplishment of the session was the adoption of the uncontroversial redefinition of the state boundaries so as to include the Florida Parishes.[11] After two weeks of inconclusive debates, the president of the convention, Senator Joseph Walker of Rapides Parish, entertained a motion to adjourn until January 9, at which time the delegates would resume their labors in New Orleans.[12] Walker was a symbol of what had become the new order in Louisiana. He was native born, the son of a French-speaking mother and an American father. Delegates on the floor of the convention used both languages.[13]

One of the major controversial themes of the entire convention surfaced during the debate on the resolution to adjourn. Delegates from the country parishes angrily accused their colleagues from New Orleans of secretly preferring the Crescent City for the deliberations. When some members argued that August was a period in which yellow fever was a threat, those who were eager to remain in Jackson countered that sickness could not be an excuse for adjournment because none of the delegates were sick. Walker offered proof of his assertion. "There is not," he said, "a man [here] who does not look ready and eager to take a hearty meal whenever the hour arrives for the customary repast." He also accused those who wanted to adjourn of letting "selfish dictates of personal ease and private convenience usurp devotion to the public good." And he hinted of dark consequences to follow should the convention adjourn; the authors of the resolution, he warned, "will lament it in sackcloth and ashes." This prophecy may have been fulfilled.

The next session was held during the season of Lent, although there is no evidence that any of the delegates were attired in that manner.[14]

One of the most vocal members of the Orleanians, Bernard Marigny, favored remaining in Jackson to complete the work of the convention. He asserted that in Jackson delegates could do in one month what it would take three to accomplish in New Orleans as his colleagues would be distracted by the carnival season and the session of the legislature, both of which would occur concurrently with the convention. He also stated his concern for the expense of meeting in the city, at least $25,000 in his estimation.[15] A member from Plaquemines Parish countered that argument by claiming the adjournment would actually save the state money because the delegates could reflect on the issues at no expense to the public and return with clear ideas. Another Orleanian, Pierre Soulé, appropriated a grievance against King George III contained in the Declaration of Independence to support his request for adjournment: "He [the king] has called together legislative bodies at places unusual, uncomfortable and distant from the depository of their Public Records, for the sole purpose of fatiguing them into compliance with his measures."[16] Soulé never identified the tyrant oppressing the delegates by compelling them to stay in Jackson, nor is there any evidence that his historicism impressed them; however, they voted 42 to 32 in favor of adjournment, and 46 to 29 to reconvene on the second Tuesday in January 1845 in New Orleans.[17]

The convention resumed on January 14 in the ballroom of the St. Louis Hotel. Rental of the ballroom cost $15 per day, and the proprietor informed the delegates that they would have to vacate on four dates because the room had been reserved for "society balls." Members requested that Royal, Chartres, and St. Louis streets be cordoned off to insure that their deliberations would not be disturbed by the noise of passing carriages.[18]

Bernard Marigny opened the debates by moving that the day designated for state elections be put forward from July to September, because by September what he called the "floating population" would be gone from New Orleans. He defined the floating population as being "those birds of passage who come to New Orleans for a limited season, and for some temporary purpose, and who are ready to quit any moment," especially during some outbreak of yellow fever. He assured the delegates that no true citizen of New Orleans was afraid of the dread disease, that on the contrary, yellow fever was a "baptism of citizenship . . . he that went through it offered some guarantee of devotion to the country." In the past the French faction had been known to plant stories warning of the beginning of a yellow fever epidemic just before election day to frighten American voters to quit the city without exercising their franchise.[19] Once again the different interests between the city and country were in conflict. F. B. Conrad argued that in September country people who lived far away from the polls would have to "brave the noxious influences of a September sun."[20] Delegates proposed other months, including June and November; some members expressed the fear that if state elections coincided with federal elections, the presidential race would lessen interest in the state contests. As was so often the case throughout the convention, this debate was long-winded, inconclusive, and it ended without agreement; at a later date the members decided upon the first Monday in November as state election day.[21]

Clashing interests of country and city came boiling to the surface once more over the issue of residency requirements for voters. The Constitution of 1812 mandated that qualified voters had to have held United States citizenship for at least two years and had to have lived in Louisiana a like period of time. Rural delegates feared the "tide of immigration flowing into New Orleans." Marigny assured them that those immigrants were "lost in the mass like drops of water in the ocean." Conrad proposed a five-year residency requirement, playing on the members' fears that immigrants from the North would cause problems for the state. He asked "can an inhabitant of Massachusetts who moves among us, regard slavery in its true light? Will he be tolerant of religions?" Marigny pointed out that people migrating from abroad could just as well be "tinctured with the doctrine of abolitionism." Isaac T. Preston of New Orleans pleaded eloquently and cogently for lowering the requirement to one year. Doing so, he claimed, would encourage settlers to come to Louisiana with their much-needed labor to drain swamps and to clear fields. If these newcomers were deprived of political rights, he contended, they would be equated with slaves; if given equal participation in government, the distinction made between immigrant and slave would "raise a wall of fire kindled from the united soul of free men . . . against the diabolical machinations of abolitionism." After a year in Louisiana, Preston continued, newcomers would have had sufficient time to observe "that the well regulated state of slavery in our State was indispensable to the happiness of the slave, the prosperity of the State, and the safety of the white population." A short residency rule would also draw wealthy planters and their slaves, which would benefit Louisiana. The delegates could not come to an agreement, and in the end, they retained the stipulations of the old constitution. Although the debate was never openly framed as such, it stemmed more from the city-country rivalry than from xenophobia. The majority of immigrants entering Louisiana in the 1840s came through New Orleans, where they tended to remain. Lowering the residency requirement would have swelled the numbers of enfranchised males, and would therefore have contributed to the city's political clout.[22]

A rare area of agreement was a decision to abandon the five-hundred-dollar property qualifications for holding office and the requirement that one had to have paid a state tax within six months of voting. Isaac T. Preston told his colleagues that the purpose of the convention was to extend rights and privileges to every white man in the state, and that property qualifications were a disgrace because they allowed the "whoremonger" to vote, while the poor man supporting a lawful wife was denied the franchise. His arguments were persuasive; the convention abolished the property requirement.[23]

The issue of slavery permeated many of the convention's deliberations and may have influenced the delegates in defeating the requirements for voting and holding office. Some saw white solidarity as a major consideration in establishing universal white male suffrage and as a defense against abolitionism:

> If the systematic efforts which are being made in some portions of this country and in England, to excite our servile population, and suddenly abolish our southern system of involuntary labor, should only be partially successful, the day may not be distant when the services of every man in the state will be required. It is a contingency to which all prudent men should look forward, and if the time ever come, how can the privileged voters of Louisiana consistently confide in the defence [*sic*] of the state in its extremity to men on whom they looked in days of quietness as unworthy of political existence; and how can we reasonably expect good service from that large portion of our people whom the present constitution places on a par with free blacks? The necessity of our position compels us to have two classes in the community, the white and the black; common sense dictates that every man should be used to unite the former by common interests and common feelings, in the support of the government.[24]

City and country members divided sharply over the issue of how to fix the basis of representation in the legislature. The choices were three; to count the whole population, including slaves or some portion thereof; to count just the totality of whites; or to count only qualified voters. Proportionately, there were more slaves in the rural parishes than in New Orleans, and although country delegates attempted to raise a smokescreen by introducing the spectre of abolition, claiming those who supported eliminating slaves from the population count were secret abolitionists, their real purpose was to reduce the political power of the city. The fight provoked the longest and most heated debate of the entire convention.

While it was true that some rural parishes contained so few whites that they might have been deprived of representation altogether if the slaves were not taken into account, a near-paranoid fear of the Crescent City was evident in their arguments. John C. Beatty of Lafourche Interior claimed "New Orleans is a corroding influence . . . dangerous to republican liberty;" with unintentional irony, he recommended safeguarding liberty by basing representation on the slave population. Isaac T. Preston countered that it should be grounded in the number of adult white males within the state. Furthermore, he contended that neither slaves nor women should be enumerated because women should have no direct power in any other government but what he called a "gynarchy." Women, he said, were quite properly represented by their "natural or selected protectors," and "their appropriate sphere," he concluded, was "the government of the fireside . . . daughters should be neat, plain, modest, and interesting; their sons intelligent, industrious, generous, and noble." Once again, slavery became a diversionary tactic when Bernard Marigny observed that the real danger to the state was "a class of men who call themselves Americans, who have the unblushing impudence to express themselves ready . . . to propagate amongst us the odious doctrine of absolutism, and even abolitionism itself."[25]

The debate continued intermittently in a like vein without resolution right up to the end of the convention. The *New Orleans Daily Picayune* observed that the convention moved at a "snail pace gait." Orleanians remained adamant in their insistence that slaves should not be counted, whereas the country delegates persistently pressed their claim that the very existence of slavery demanded special measures to secure "that species of property, and preserving it in a proper state of subordination."[26] Marigny thought it improper to consider slaves because they had no rights in American Louisiana. He reminded his colleagues how under Spanish rule slaves had the right of self-purchase as well as the liberty to own property. As slaves in American Louisiana had no rights, he argued they should not be counted. Doing so, he remarked, would be harmful to New Orleans, and he warned the convention, "you cannot act with such injustice to New Orleans without undermining the social fabric itself." Conrad speculated that were the representation of the city to be limited drastically, it would be impossible to get the new constitution ratified. He complained that the country delegates regarded New Orleans as a "monster whose ravenous appetite is never satisfied till we have swallowed up everything between the Balize [i. e., the mouth of the Mississippi] and the Sabine River, of course taking in the Red River and Ouachita country."[27]

At this juncture, the debate turned quite nasty. One of the most prominent delegates, and the person who first called for a new convention Solomon W. Downs of Ouachita, the "political spokesman of North Louisiana," alleged that a nameless Orleanian had claimed the country parishes were inhabited only by reptiles! James F. Brent of Rapides accused Cyrus Ratliff of East Feliciana of being an abolitionist merely because he favored representation based on free white voters. In the 1840s calling a political opponent an abolitionist was a common ploy calculated to wound an enemy.[28] Brent persisted, claiming Ratliff's speech was copied from the columns of the *Liberator* and the *Emancipator*. Enraged, Ratliff averred that he had never read any abolitionist newspaper; indeed, "he would hate to let the vile trash soil his fingers." He reminded his listeners how Mississippians and other Southerners used the white electorate as the basis of representation, and surely no one ever charged them with abolitionism. As the rest of the delegates competed to proclaim their orthodoxy on the subjects of slavery and abolitionism, some began to recognize the need of a compromise.[29]

One of the country delegates proposed fixing representation in the house of representatives on the number of voters. As to the senate, its size would be tied to the total population, but New Orleans would receive a maximum of one-eighth of the senators, thereby insuring that the city could not wield an excessive amount of power. Furthermore, each parish would receive at least one representative, no matter how few were its electors, while New Orleans would be divided into districts to dilute the influence of the delegation.

The proposition met with the general support of the country members. By contrast, a disgusted New Orleanian noted that "some strange things [have] taken place in this convention . . . there is a remarkable tendency to give power to people that are the furthest, the remotest from the city."[30] Bernard Marigny voiced strenuous objections, and as he did, he interjected another sub rosa rivalry—that of Creole versus American within the city itself. He pointed out that New Orleans was already divided into three cities, the First Municipality (the French Quarter), the Second Municipality (the American Sector), and the Third Municipality (downriver of the First Municipality). His impassioned speech was permeated with hostility for Americans:

> It [the Second Municipality] has struggled with herculean power to draw all the advantages from the old city . . . [there exists] a feeling of rivalry, which has reached a point where there is no identity of interests between them. Far from me to say or insinuate one word in disparagement of the inhabitants of the Second Municipality. They have advanced with great strides. I admire their energy and indomitable perseverance, and what I wish is, that the old population which is so fast receding, would only be stimulated by their example.

New Orleans, he argued, was a divided city; the inhabitants of the First Municipality danced and amused themselves on Sunday at the very time the people of the Second Municipality were attending church services. Another spokesman for French-speaking Orleanians, Pierre Soulé, stated that evidence of the sharp divisions within the city was the very fact that there were three municipalities in existence. "A law," he observed, "is nothing but the translation of the feelings, prejudices, and passions of those who called it into existence." Reminding the convention that only twenty-one of the seventy-seven delegates were Creoles, Soulé went on to say that the Creoles had become "strangers in this land of Louisiana." Furthermore, he asked whether "all the vengeance of the Convention [was] to fall upon New Orleans?" Soulé contended that restricting the number of city senators would be "to place the city at the mercy of the country, and we may well anticipate what that mercy will be!" The Creoles won this round, gaining two senatorial slots for the First Municipality, while the Second and the Third secured but one apiece.[31]

The question of the number of senators for New Orleans provoked one of the most hostile remarks of the entire convention. Cyrus Ratliff stated that while the committee report allotted four seats to the city, the New Orleans delegation had the temerity to seek five. "They are again trying to get the lion's share," he cried, "*turkey* for them all the time!!!" [*sic*] Although no evidence suggests the mixed metaphor influenced anyone, the convention sustained the committee report.[32]

In a desperate effort to stave off the political loss to the city, Marigny proposed exchanging an unrestricted number of senate seats for moving the capital away from New Orleans. Perhaps he gambled on the delegates' preferences for the city's comforts and pleasures. Earlier in the debates, he had reminded the convention how legislators had complained when they sat in Donaldsonville back in 1831. Then he had said "the legislature had scarcely assembled, ere they began to complain, and many even *cried* with bitterness and mortification at being cooped up in so small a place." Wadsworth of Plaquemines Parish replied, saying that no one would admit to being influenced by the charms of the city. Besides, he asked, "will any member of this body admit that any attempt has been made to seduce him with a plate of gombo [*sic*], or a stuffed turkey?" At this point Duncan F. Kenner of Ascension Parish attempted to place the discussion on a more honest footing. He argued the country delegates would seem more sincere if they plainly admitted that they did not want New Orleans to have as much power as the country parishes. Although he stated he did not believe the legislators in the past had "been affected by means of the stomach," he also reminded his fellow delegates that were the capital moved, "there will be no more fine dinners, no more fine wines, that can be brought to bear on the legislature." Whether Kenner's oratory persuaded, or whether fear of what another member termed "the dreaded lobby influence" of the Crescent City prevailed, the delegates chose to move the capital at least sixty miles away from New Orleans. They limited the city's representation in the senate to one-eighth of the total membership. As a sop to the Orleanians, the capital would not be moved until 1848. Their conviction that future legislatures could fall prey to the seductions of the city was evident in the stipulation that a return of the capital would require a four-fifths vote of the legislature, which was highly improbable given the limitations on the Orleans delegation and the proportional strength of the country parishes. In short, Marigny's gamble failed.[33]

Marigny now made a surprising suggestion, the adoption of a provision allowing the legislature to confer the rights and privileges of citizenship upon selected free men of color, provided they were native born. Evidently he was quickly suspected of ulterior ends, possibly of trying to include free blacks in yet another scheme to augment the representation of the city. Whatever explains his suggestion, he soon withdrew it, proclaiming the purity of his motives and stating his awareness that his colleagues opposed his idea.[34]

Undaunted by his lack of success in increasing the power of the city, Marigny next attempted to protect the interests of the Creoles. He offered a resolution to include in the constitution a stipulation that French and English be used on the floor of the legislature, and that anyone had the right to address members in either tongue. Marigny expressed his fear that in a few years the French language would no longer be heard in the legislature, and that out of respect for the "ancient population," he hoped the measure would be adopted. Some delegates protested that the use of French was too inconvenient, as many legislators were unable to understand the language. This issue was obviously a sensitive one, and members were careful to be conciliatory to the Creoles, perhaps because their number had declined to the point where others could afford to be magnanimous. For example, although Cornelius Voorhies of Attakapas spoke against the proposal, he was nevertheless careful not to offend the Creoles. He prefaced his complaint by saying he could remember "the time in Louisiana of the ancient virtue, when a man's word was his bond, and good faith needed not the spur of the law to be preserved inviolable, when bills, bonds, and notes were unknown." He tactfully based his objection upon the fact that this provision was not contained in the Constitution of 1812, rather than the French language. Marigny replied by saying the measure was not needed in 1812 because the Florida Parishes had not yet been included within the boundaries of Louisiana and nearly all the people of the state spoke French. He then proceeded to raise an even greater fear—that of the imposition of the common law upon the state:

> Let none be deceived by the covert character of the attack. The hostility to the French language is stimulated by the design to abrogate our civil system of law . . . I know that the Anglo-Saxon race are the more numerous, and therefore the strongest. We are yet to learn whether they will abuse the possession of numerical force to overwhelm the Franco-American population.

Following this eloquent threat, the measure passed. However Article 6, Section 15, of the constitution was not only retained but strengthened. That article required all laws and judicial proceedings to be written "in the language in which the Constitution of the United States is written." Article 103 of the Constitution of 1845 provided that "laws, public records, and the judicial and legislative written proceedings of the State" should be in English.[35]

Although the Constitution of 1845 contained some startling departures from its predecessor, only one other issue generated heated debate, that of whether the judiciary should be elected rather than appointed by the governor. Advocates of an appointive judiciary argued the necessity of winning elections would compromise the independence and dignity of the bench and the judiciary should be "free of the caprices of the popular will." Marigny presented a hypothetical example of whether a judge would risk convicting and sentencing a popular man of a crime. He proposed retaining an appointive judiciary, but limiting terms of office to allow for the replacement of incompetent judges without having to impeach them. Others argued for electing judges in order to reduce the governor's influence upon the Supreme Court of Louisiana, lest a judge become a "blind and passive instrument of executive will." The governor, maintained one delegate, should be shorn of all patronage. "It is a lamentable truth," he said,

> that there are hosts of individuals, who follow in the wake of the two great political parties, as sharks follow in the wake of a ship for the offal that is thrown overboard, or as thieves and banditti follow after the caravans of the east for the hope of plunder they may pick up in the rear.[36]

A New Orleans author had expressed similar sentiments in an 1841 pamphlet. He acknowledged that Andrew Jackson had rightly received criticism for his expansion of presidential patronage. He argued that opposing presidential appointments of political allies while at the same time supporting the extensive powers of the governor of Louisiana was "very much the same as 'straining at a gnat and swallowing a camel.' The patronage of the president is too great, but that of the governor exceeds it far. Every office in the state is his gift." However, the convention decided that the judiciary should remain appointive, although the terms of office were limited to eight years.[37]

There seemed to be general agreement that the jurisdiction of the supreme court should be extended to include criminal appeals (in the Constitution of 1812 the court was only permitted to take civil appeals). Delegates also accepted that the court should be enlarged to four members, a chief and three associate justices, to deal with the increased workload.[38] The discussion of how much the justices should be paid inspired some interesting remarks. Several delegates suggested paying the justices well to insure obtaining men of good quality. It was not unusual, they argued, to hear of attorneys who earned as much as $5,000 each year and occasionally much more. Zenon Ledoux, Jr., of Pointe Coupée Parish was appalled at the casual manner in which such figures were tossed about. He complained, "these gentlemen speak familiarly of fees of six thousand and then ten thousand as maids of thirteen do of puppy dogs." Another delegate told the convention that the highest paid supreme court justices in the United States were those of South Carolina and New York at $3,000 each, and that the justices of Rhode Island were paid only $650 per annum. The delegates decided not to fix the justices' salaries. They did set a minimum, however, of $5,500 for the associates and $6,000 for the chief.[39]

The Constitution of 1845, unlike its predecessor, contained a section concerning public education. Delegates were mainly in agreement that free public schools were a necessity and that higher education should be available within the state. Accordingly they approved the creation of free public schools funded by property taxes. Education was considered particularly important because of the existence of slavery. There was a strong feeling that white youths should be educated within the state because "Southern men should have Southern heads and hearts, with sentiments untarnished by doctrines at war with our rights and liberties." The "doctrines," of course, were those of abolitionism. When Louisiana children returned from the North, the delegates believed, they had to be re-educated to the proper orthodoxy about the peculiar institution. It is ironic that fear of abolitionism caused the delegates to agree that the only safety for freedom from the abolitionist taint was public education. On May 3, 1847, the Louisiana legislature passed an act to establish free public schools for "the white youths of this State, between the ages of six and sixteen years." A one-mill property tax funded the system, which required teacher certification and the teaching of French and English to those who wished to learn either language.[40]

The convention also authorized the establishment of a university in New Orleans, to be called the "University of Louisiana." It was to have four faculties: law, letters, natural sciences, and medicine. The faculty of the "Medical College of Louisiana" (the origin of Tulane University) was to become the medical faculty of the new university. Delegates believed that those who wanted their children to attend the university should pay for the privilege, and, accordingly, they wrote a provision into the Constitution of 1845 that the legislature "shall be under no obligation to contribute to the establishment or support of said university by appropriations."[41]

The Constitution of 1845 contained several innovations that inspired little or no dispute. A lack of controversy over those measure is as significant as its presence was in the more inflammatory issues. For example, the creation of the office of lieutenant governor was agreed upon with no contention. Apparently, the delegates accepted the creation of the office as a necessity. The Constitution of 1812 did not provide for such an office, but designated that the president of the senate assume the office of governor should a vacancy occur. This succession had caused great confusion in 1829 when Governor Pierre Derbigny died in a carriage accident. The president of the senate assumed the office, but the senators elected a new president three months later, and some demanded that the acting governor surrender his office to the newly elected president. Fear of an endless number of presidents resulted in a special election the following summer to choose a new governor. Not surprisingly, the members of the convention of 1845 agreed without debate on an orderly succession by erecting the office of lieutenant governor.[42]

The effort to limit the power of the legislature and to put large areas of legislation out of its reach is most apparent in the section of the Constitution of 1845 entitled "General Provisions." Distrust of the legislature is evident in the imposition of a limit of sixty days on the legislative session, after which time any measure became null and void. Although his mathematical skills left much to be desired, Lafayette Saunders of West Feliciana Parish expressed the sentiments of many of his colleagues: "We have had enough legislation to last us half a century. A body composed half French, half Spanish, and half Yankees could do no harm in a session of but 60 days." Suspicion of the legislature is also apparent in the adoption of a measure prohibiting the authorization of a lottery or granting divorces, which forced those applying for divorce to turn to the courts, rather than depending upon their influence with the legislature.[43]

One of the most radical provisions of the Constitution of 1845, the limitation on corporations and banking companies, also passed with little debate. Those restrictions had no precedent in the old document, and they show yet another side to the delegates' distrust of the legislature as well as reflecting the recent chaotic financial condition of the state. The financial Panic of 1837 had thrown the Pelican State into a deplorable situation. Between 1837 and 1845, state banks were chronically unable to make specie payments. Meanwhile, the state owed $75,000 to the banks in 1839, a debt that had grown to $850,000 by 1841. As of 1843, the obligation had risen to $1.2 million, plus an additional $200,000 in interest and back salaries. Furthermore, members of the legislature had borrowed $1 million in their private capacity from the state banks. On the eve of the convention, the exhausted state treasury had defaulted on interested payments on $1,273 million in state bonds. Accordingly members of the convention prohibited monopolies and forbade the state either to hold stock in corporations or to subsidize private businesses. They put a ceiling on the amount of debt the state could incur, and banks were totally abolished. Furthermore they authorized the legislature in the year 1890 to revoke all corporate charters that had not expired by that date, while they restricted the life of corporations to a term of twenty-five years. No one considered the requirements novel or extreme. On the contrary, they represented a determined attempt to reach legitimate legislative goals through what Lawrence Friedman has called "anti-legislation . . . closing whole areas of life to statutory change." The prohibition against corporations was copied in the Iowa Constitution of 1846. The Louisiana Constitution of 1845 also borrowed a provision out of the New Jersey Constitution of 1844 that required each statute to "embrace but one object." Other states subsequently adopted the measure, designed to prevent "log-rolling" legislation. Although prohibitions against banks, monopolies, and corporations disappeared from the next Louisiana constitution, the stipulation that a law should encompass a single subject was retained.[44]

Four months after the delegates began their deliberations in New Orleans, they completed their work. Nearly 150 days of consideration and debate, debates covering over thirteen hundred printed pages to report, produced a constitution that would last but seven years. Some members of the convention never were satisfied with their handiwork. George Eustis of Orleans Parish complained that, unlike the federal Constitution, which contained principles, the Constitution of 1845 was concerned with heterogeneous matters and was filled with "simple legislation;" he felt it should have been limited to principles. Judah P. Benjamin then asked the obvious question that no delegate chose to answer, "if you can't trust your legislature . . . whom can you trust?" Marigny stated that suspicion of the legislature had been used throughout the deliberations as a tool to convince the members of various points of view. In some debates, he said, they were told to "beware of the legislature." In other instances, delegates were persuaded to confide in the legislature, as "they [were] worthy of implicit confidence."[45]

On May 16, 1845, the convention concluded its labors. A few members remained unsatisfied with the resulting document, although the voters would approve it by a resounding margin of 12,227 to 1,385. W. C. C. Claiborne of Orleans voted against final passage because he believed it to be an experiment and not a reform. "We have," he said, "unnecessarily attacked too many feelings and interests." His observation proved correct. Undoubtedly, the Constitution of 1845 was a reform, but several of its most imaginative measures insured its speedy demise. The expanding economy of the state and the needs of the business community would not long be deprived of banks and corporations. The delegates to the next constitutional convention distributed favor to certain banking houses and railroad companies. One New Orleans newspaper commented that the delegates wanted banks to steal the people's money and railroads to cart it away.[46] Not surprisingly, Bernard Marigny had the last word. As he endorsed the Constitution of 1845, he remarked that it was the second time he had signed such a document, and "may God ordain it should be the last."[47]

Notes for "Reform or Experiment? The Louisiana Constitution of 1845"

[1]Lawrence M. Friedman, *A History of American Law* (New York, 1973), 303.

[2]Ibid., 102.

[3]Edward F. Haas, *Louisiana's Legal Heritage* (Pensacola, Fla., 1983), 1-6.

[4]Anonymous, *Remarks on the Propriety of Calling a Convention to Amend the Constitution of the State of Louisiana. By a Citizen* (New Orleans, 1841), 16.

[5]Friedman, *A History of American Law*, 303.

[6]Joseph G. Tregle, Jr., "Louisiana in the Age of Jackson: A Study in Ego Politics" (Ph.D. dissertation, University of Pennsylvania, 1954), 90-92.

[7]*Constitutions of the State of Louisiana, 1812-1898* (Baton Rouge, 1913); *West's Louisiana Statutes Annotated: Treaties and Organic Laws, Early Constitutions, U. S. Constitution* (St. Paul, Minn., 1977); *Constitutions of Louisiana of 1812, '45 & '52* (New Orleans, 1861). Hereinafter referred to as *Constitution of* (appropriate year). Constitution of 1812, article 7, section 1.

[8]William H. Adams, *The Whig Party in Louisiana* (Lafayette, La., 1973), 9-10; *Remarks on the Propriety of Calling a Convention,* 12; Tregle, "Louisiana in the Age of Jackson," 101-02.

[9]*Acts Passed at the First Session of the Fifteenth Legislature of the State of Louisiana, 1841* (New Orleans, 1841), January 30, 1841; *Journal of the Convention Called for the Purpose of Readopting, Amending or Changing the Constitution of the State of Louisiana Convened at Jackson, Aug. 5, 1844* (New Orleans, 1844), 1:15. Hereinafter referred to as *Journal.*

[10]*Acts Passed at the Second Session of the Sixteenth Legislature of the State of Louisiana* (New Orleans, 1844), March 18, 1844; *Journal,* 1:15.

[11]These parishes were not included in the definition of the state's boundaries at the time of the writing of the Constitution of 1812, although that constitutional convention accepted a resolution requesting that the new territory be added to the state. Constitution of 1812, preamble; Joe Gray Taylor, *Louisiana: A Bicentennial History* (New York, 1976), 51; *Journal,* 1:34.

[12]*Journal,* 1:92-93.

[13]Lewis William Newton, "The Americanization of French Louisiana: A Study of the Process of Adjustment between the French and the Anglo-American Populations of Louisiana, 1793-1860" (Ph.D. dissertation, University of Chicago, 1929), 195.

[14]*Journal,* 1:95.

[15]Ibid., 1:98-99.

[16]Ibid., 1:107.

[17]Ibid., 1:106.

[18]Ibid., 1:109; Tregle, "Louisiana in the Age of Jackson," 182.

[19]Tregle, "Louisiana in the Age of Jackson," 126-27.

[20]*Proceedings and Debates of the Convention which Assembled at the City of New Orleans, January 14, 1844* [*sic*] (New Orleans, 1845), 5. Hereinafter cited as *Journal,* 2:5.

[21]Constitution of 1845, title II, article 5.

[22]Constitution of 1812, article 2, section 3; *Journal,* 2:59, 62, 65-66; Constitution of 1845, title II, article 10; Bennett H. Wall, ed., *Louisiana: A History* (Arlington Heights, Ill., 1984), 125-27.

[23]Constitution of 1812, article 2, section 4; *Journal,* 2:64; Constitution of 1845, title II, article 10.

[24]*Remarks on the Propriety of Calling a Constitutional Convention,* 22-23.

[25]*Journal,* 2:150, 232.

[26]Ibid., 2:311, 314-15; *New Orleans Daily Picayune,* March 9, 1845.

[27]*Journal,* 2:320-21, 331, 337; *New Orleans Bee,* February 18, 1845.

[28]Adams, *The Whig Party in Louisiana,* 95, 142.

[29]*Journal,* 2:337, 349, 351, 356-57, 359, 361; Glenn R. Conrad et al., comps., *Dictionary of Louisiana Biography,* 2 vols. (Lafayette, La., 1988), 1:254-55.

[30]Constitution of 1812, article 2, section 6; Constitution of 1845, title II, article 8; *Journal,* 2:362, 367, 610, 638, 646.

[31]*Journal,* 2:603, 638, 646; Tregle, "Louisiana in the Age of Jackson," 183-85; Newton, "The Americanization of French Louisiana," 195.

[32]*Journal,* 2:523.

[33]Ibid., 2:325, 386, 390, 425; Constitution of 1845, title VI, article 112.

[34]*Journal,* 2:761, 831.

[35]Ibid., 2:835-36, 870; Constitution of 1845, title VI, article 104; Constitution of 1812, article 6, section 15; Constitution of 1845, title VI, article 103.

[36]*Journal,* 2:299, 292, 749; Constitution of 1845, title IV, article 65. For a detailed analysis of the reform of the judicial branch of state government by the Constitution of 1845, see Mark F. Fernandez, "From Chaos to Continuity: Early Reforms of the Supreme Court of Louisiana, 1845-1852," *Louisiana History,* 28 (1987): 19-31.

[37]*Remarks on the Propriety of Calling a Convention,* 12.

[38]Constitution of 1812, article 4, section 2; Constitution of 1845, title IV, articles 63, 64.

[39]*Journal,* 2:727-9; Constitution of 1845, title IV, article 76.

[40]Newton, "The Americanization of French Louisiana," 201.

[41]*Journal,* 2:904, 906, 909, 919; Constitution of 1845, title VII, articles 133, 134, 137, 138, 139; Ben Robertson Miller, *The Louisiana Judiciary* (Baton Rouge, 1932), 12-34; "An Act to Establish Free Public Schools in the State of Louisiana," Act of May 3, 1847, *Louisiana Acts, 1847,* 178-87.

[42]Constitution of 1845, title III, articles 38-46; *Journal,* 2:863; Constitution of 1845, title VI, articles 89, 130; Wall, ed., *Louisiana: A History,* 118; Tregle, "Louisiana in the Age of Jackson," 375-76; Adams, *The Whig Party in Louisiana,* 30-31.

[43]*Journal,* 2:481; Constitution of 1845, title VI, articles 116, 117; *Journal,* 2:840; Constitution of 1845, title II, article 26.

[44]*Journal,* 2:848; Constitution of 1845, title VI, articles 113, 114, 121, 122, 123, 124, 125; Friedman, *A History of American Law,* 108, 173 (note); Constitution of 1845, title VI, article 118; Friedman, *A History of American Law,* 312; Wall, ed., *Louisiana: A History,* 119; James Kimmins Greer, "Louisiana Politics, 1845-1861" (Ph.D. dissertation, University of Texas, 1927), 24-26.

[45]*Journal,* 2:655, 663, 717.

[46]Ibid., 2:942; Wall, ed., *Louisiana: A History,* 119; Greer, "Louisiana Politics," 40.

[47]*Journal,* 2:949.

LOUISIANA'S "WHIG" CONSTITUTION REVISITED: THE CONSTITUTION OF 1852*

Wayne M. Everard

In 1852, the continuing struggle between the common man and the aristocracy in Louisiana precipitated the adoption of a compromise constitution. The new document called for the popular election of numerous state officials—including all judges. It also created a board of public works to "exercise a diligent and faithful supervision of all public works in which the state may be interested, except those made by joint-stock companies." Under the Constitution of 1852, there were limits on state debts and the government was to distribute all tax revenue equally throughout the parishes. Maintenance of a state university became another governmental responsibility. The most significant constitutional change, however, embraced legislative apportionment. Total population, slaves included, subsequently determined representatives in both houses of the legislature, a provision that increased the power of large slaveholders and affirmed Louisianians' subscription to those Southern political tendencies that in 1861 would culminate in secession.

* * * *

On November 6, 1845, the voters of Louisiana ratified the state's new "democratic" constitution. Six years, five months, and six days later, they called for a convention to rewrite the document. Before another four months had passed, the 1852 constitutional convention completed its business, and on November 1, the electors gave final approval to a new fundamental law for the Pelican State.[1]

Although the previous constitution had been a great improvement upon its predecessor, it still contained features that were unsuitable to the political and economic milieu of antebellum Louisiana. In the political realm, for instance, illiberal elements survived in Articles 6 and 18 that retained or increased the lengthy 1812 residence requirements for

*First published as Essay 3 in the *In Search of Fundamental Law: Louisiana Constitutions, 1812-1947*, eds. Warren M. Billings and Edward F. Haas (Lafayette, La.: Center for Louisiana Studies, 1993), 37-51. Reprinted with the kind permission of the author and the Center for Louisiana Studies.

seats in the legislature. Article 39, moreover, required fifteen years' residence and citizenship in order to qualify a candidate for governor. The framers of the 1845 constitution had also stopped short of sanctioning the popular election of judges, one of the most widely acclaimed reforms of the era.[2]

Two additional features of that instrument saddled the state with potential obstacles to the effective operation of government. Article 64 set the number of the justices of the supreme court at four, which often left them evenly divided on appeals, thereby confirming by default numerous rulings of the district courts. Many critics argued that this article diminished the importance of the high court, while others warned of the likelihood that contradictory holdings would be affirmed because the justices could not reach a decision.[3] Randell Hunt, a New Orleans attorney who sat in the convention of 1852, commented at a political rally a year earlier, "it is, indeed, lamentable to reflect that the frequent contrariety of opinions has greatly impaired the moral power of the court over the sentiments of the people, and shaken the public confidence in the wisdom of that tribunal." Hunt went on to claim that the judiciary as it existed "has failed from a defect in its structure; it is incapable of settling principles and of establishing the law in cases within its acknowledged jurisdiction."[4]

The fundamental law of 1845 also limited the legislature to biennial sixty-day sessions. Reformers warned that the business of governing had become too complex to be conducted properly under that time constraint. Legislators were unable to give thoughtful consideration to the matters brought before them.[5] In 1848, for example, an extra session was necessary to enable the legislature to complete the implementation of a system of public education as the constitution had mandated.[6]

Commercial restrictions reflected an overreaction to the financial crises that followed the Panic of 1837. Banking and internal improvements were necessary components in the state's economic system, but the Constitution of 1845 forbade the creation, renewal, or extension of bank charters. At the same time, it practically eliminated Louisiana's ability to provide public assistance to railroads or other internal improvements.[7]

Those restrictions were detrimental to the state's economy because they made a complete recovery from the Panic of 1837 impossible. City merchants realized as well that the great port on the Mississippi was losing a significant share of business to eastern cities that enjoyed rail connections to western farm centers. They increasingly viewed railroads that linked New Orleans directly with those areas as essential to the competitive future of their city.[8]

The survival of the entire state was closely tied to the well being of the Crescent City. While obvious differences existed between the two, there was also an important degree of interdependence. Not only did city bankers and commercial factors provide the finances the planters needed to sustain their economic existence, but urban suppliers also kept country general stores and other commercial enterprises in business.[9] The port, moreover, served as a market for practically all of Louisiana's crops; most farmers had no alternative but to ship their produce to it. Unpredictable water routes, especially from the western section of the state, made the possibility of reliable railroad access to New Orleans attractive to those whose economic interests depended so heavily on the port.[10]

Banks helped to provide Louisianians with an effective money supply through their management of specie reserves. They also increased the amount of money in circulation through the issue of notes. If the banking system was not working to capacity, the money supply was constricted.[11] Farmers who marketed their crops in New Orleans then had to endure protracted delays in securing payment for what they sold.[12] Some observers also cited the currency deficit as a cause for the decline in cotton prices.[13] Owing to the distress among rural farmers and planters, several former enemies of banking in the country demanded permission to establish new banks. They soon allied themselves with urban Democrats who once opposed banks but who, by the 1850s, had come to realize their necessity for economic progress in the city and the state.[14]

Constitutional prohibitions against banking also adversely affected the capital available for the private financing of railroads at the very time state funding for such ventures was no longer possible. Without the investment of banks, internal improvements could not attract essential financial resources. Private investors, aware that only five banks were operating in the state, were reluctant to put their money into Louisiana projects.[15] The state desperately needed new capital, especially in light of the contractions in the money supply that had occurred during the 1840s, when so many banks lost their charters.[16]

Perhaps the most startling symbols of the flaws in the Constitution of 1845 were Articles 122 and 125; the one prohibited the creation of new banks while the other limited monopolies.[17] An unforeseen result was a constitutional anomaly. Even though Article 125 outlawed monopolies, Article 122 created one by permitting only the five banks that survived the crises of the 1840s!

As the decade of the 1850s opened, Louisianians faced the prospect of either living with an unworkable organic law or initiating constitutional reform. The amending process in the Constitution of 1845 was no solution. Amendment required a vote of a majority of three-fifths of both houses of the legislature, the approval of the governor, a simple majority vote by both houses in the following biennial session, and finally popular approval in the next general election. In other words any amendment took at least five years to accomplish.[18]

The legislature had already proposed amending the residency requirements and creating an elected judiciary.[19] Both Whig and Democratic commercial interests, however, feared that any change in the banking articles able to survive a gubernatorial veto would be insufficient to meet the complex needs of the Crescent City business community. That Gov. Joseph M. Walker had presided over the constitutional convention of 1845 and thus supervised the passage of the banking articles only heightened such fears.[20] Reformers also believed the number of other flawed articles was so great that piecemeal revision was not likely in one five-year amendment cycle.

The movement for constitutional revision started in the legislative session of 1850, when a Democratic senator and a Whig representative jointly introduced a bill calling for a constitutional convention.[21] Most Whig legislators backed the bill, but the Democrats split into two camps. One believed that a complete overhaul was preferable to amendments while the second held that amending the constitution was the only acceptable means of change. Democrats of the latter stripe warned that a convention would be nothing more than a means of subverting the existing banking regulations. They drew particular attention to an attempt at reviving the charter of the Citizens' Bank as evidence of the bankers' desires to extend monopoly banking in New Orleans.

Proponents of the revival rejoined by pointing out that the Citizens' charter remained in effect even though the bank had been inactive throughout the previous decade. The valid charter thus exempted the bank from constitutional prohibitions against new financial institutions. Moreover, a resurrected Citizens' Bank would not only add to the state's available credit by increasing the amount of active capital, but it would also relieve the state treasury of impending interest payments on bonds that the government had previously guaranteed.[22] A revitalized bank would care for the bonds itself, or so argued Isaac T. Preston, a Democrat from Jefferson Parish and a backer of the convention call who later sat on the Supreme Court of Louisiana.

Democratic opponents voiced concerns that the legislature had not previously debated the convention issue and that there had been no opportunity for members to study the question or to gauge the opinions of their constituents. Representatives from the Florida Parishes displayed considerable animosity to a convention which they suspected as little more than a ploy by Orleanians to move the capital from Baton Rouge back to its old seat in the Crescent City.

In the end, the convention bill passed the house of representatives by a margin of 52 to 32 with approximately 60 percent of members of both parties behind it. Party lines held firm in the upper chamber, though, where on a vote of 20 to 4 the senators voted to table. Despite Whig arguments that the bill did no more than put the issue before the voters, only one Democrat supported the measure.

Over the next year, the election contest for a new legislature provided an opportunity to air the question in a way that had not been possible in advance of the 1850 legislative session. Whig candidates for the house and senate quickly announced their commitment to a convention, and their party endorsed the proposition in its platform. The Democrats, owing to the split in their ranks, took no such stand. Democrats who wanted a convention urged the party to endorse the measure. Others opposed it merely because they considered it a Whig issue which they were bound to challenge for the sake of party purity. The anti-bank wing was against the convention as were those like Governor Walker who had written the Constitution of 1845.

Some observers claimed the Democrats, whom Zachary Taylor and the Whigs defeated in 1848, were reluctant to back a potentially divisive issue when they were in the midst of an effort to maintain unity and to regain strength for the presidential contest of

1852. The party's platform in 1851 gives credence to this contention. It focused on national issues and completely ignored the matter of constitutional revision.

Accordingly the combination of Whig solidarity and Democratic disunity assured the election of Whig majorities in both houses of the legislature. When the session convened in January 1852, those majorities guaranteed the passage of a call for a referendum on a constitutional convention. Opening the proceedings, Governor Walker informed everyone how he believed a convention to be both undesirable and unnecessary, although he ultimately came around to the idea. Despite skirmishing over details respecting the form of the call, an overwhelming majority of the house favored the enabling bill.

Support for the convention was virtually unanimous among the New Orleans delegation. Indeed such meager opposition as there was in both houses came from rural Democrats, whom the reformers anticipated would work to defeat the referendum itself. Urban Democrats meanwhile hoped to secure the party's official endorsement of the convention as a means of winning a share of delegate seats. Such a blessing never materialized, although several party leaders spoke in support of the measure.

The referendum was set for April 12, 1852. Voter turnout was light all across the state. Nine rural Democratic parishes voted no, but the remaining eighteen approved the call. Only one Whig parish stood in opposition.[23]

Elections for delegates to the convention followed in June. Democrats who backed constitutional revision now hoped the contest for seats would be nonpartisan. Their rivals within the Democracy urged the retention of party labels as a safeguard against the choice of candidates who favored the restoration of monopoly banking. Whigs also favored a partisan election because of their staunch stand on the issues that would come before the convention. They had no wish to risk the selection of anti-bank Democrats while they were themselves caught up in campaigning against independent candidates whose views matched their own.

Besides, some Whigs had already concluded that disunity among the Democrats demanded the election of Whig delegates. Now that the convention was a reality, support from the Democracy was no longer necessary; the Democrats were superfluous. The reforms the Whigs sought could only succeed if they controlled the convention, and so they mounted a full-scale partisan campaign. As part of their strategy, they played down the Democrats' role in bringing off the convention even as they sought to portray the Democratic party as an untrustworthy monolith that opposed change and should not have responsibility for writing the state's new fundamental law.

Democratic reformers ultimately decided to abandon their original call for independent candidates. They goaded their party into stating its objections to the 1845 document and into running a slate of candidates. Their late entry into the fray, however, put them at a distinct disadvantage because the Whigs ran on their consistent support of constitutional revision which made them much more likely to carry out the reforms the people demanded.

Rainy weather marked election day in New Orleans, but the Whigs managed to win twenty-seven of the twenty-nine seats allotted to Orleans Parish. Voters in the country parishes, by contrast, elected delegates from both parties in about equal proportions. Still the overall Whig majority, especially considering the strength of the city delegation, assured that the long-sought reforms would be embodied in the new fundamental law. Indeed, only three issues were expected to inspire much debate in the convention: the location of the capital, state support of internal improvements, and legislative apportionment. All three stemmed more from sectional antagonisms than from partisan ideals. The question of where to locate the capital pitted the country versus the city, whereas the issue of apportionment arrayed black belt parishes against predominantly white parishes, and despite the pressing need for internal improvements, rural delegates opposed state aid for such projects.

Deliberations opened on July 5, and after spending several days perfecting procedures and electing officers, the convention got down to the business of drafting the new constitution. Taking the Constitution of 1845 as their departure point, the delegates decided to read its articles seriatim, retaining, modifying, or rejecting each one in the process. Early on, it became clear that the Whig majority would not block political reforms as some had feared throughout the months leading up to the convention. Although Whigs resisted Democratic attempts to promote revisions more generous than those discussed prior to the election, they did vote for significant improvements upon the 1845 document.[24] For example they backed the creation of residency requirements for election to the General Assembly.

City delegates were especially determined to avoid any argument that could disrupt the debates. They saw harmony as essential to passage of provisions for banking and internal improvements which they hoped to get through the convention. Thus, when the resolution on the location of the capital came up for a vote, a majority of the Orleanians voiced no substantive opposition to it. Their votes in favor of internal improvements and banking, however, were nearly unanimous.[25]

Whereas a solid Whig majority consistently supported such issues, Democrats, by contrast, tended to oppose them. Nonetheless, between one-fifth and one-quarter of the Democratic delegates broke ranks and voted with the Whigs on the issues of banking and internal improvements.[26]

Legislative apportionment was perhaps the most bitterly debated revision to come before the convention. The 1845 constitution based representation in the house on the number of qualified voters in each parish, but it divided seats in the senate on the basis of total population. Reform-minded delegates preferred an apportionment in both houses according to qualified voters, but they never mustered a majority in support of their position, and the total population proponents prevailed.

This outcome distressed five rural Democrats, who made a joint declaration of the reasons for their opposition. They saw representation grounded upon total population as destructive "of the principles of Republican Government, and all political equality" and a subtraction of power from the electorate "into the hands of large slave holders, thereby stamping upon this Government the odious principles and character of an aristocratic government."[27] Despite their manifesto, it is noteworthy that 48 percent of their Democratic colleagues voted for change.[28]

While the decision on legislative apportionment distressed many, enough were sufficiently satisfied with the total product to vote overwhelmingly for adoption of the new constitution. It cleared the convention by a margin of 98 to 8, with three of the Democrats who protested the decision on apportionment in the majority. Perhaps R. A. Hargis, a Democratic delegate from Claiborne Parish, spoke tellingly for the supporters. "I vote yes," he declared, "not because I like the new Constitution in all of its details, but because I like it better than the Constitution of 1845."

On the other hand, some opponents of reapportionment remained adamant to the bitter end. As John R. Smart of Sabine Parish cast a futile vote against the new constitution, he acidly remarked that it "places the African and the white man on a level, so far as representation in the General Assembly is concerned."[29] His words were prophetic in that they were subsequently picked up and echoed by rural politicians and others who opposed ratification. The *New Orleans Daily True Delta* orchestrated the "Negro as good as a white man" argument to a fine pitch. Its appeal to racial prejudice masked its longstanding opposition to constitutional reform which the editor suspected of being little more than a thinly disguised agenda for the revival of "monopoly banking."

The referendum on the new constitution occurred on November 1, 1852, coincident with the presidential election.[30] Up to election day, rumors floated to the effect that Whigs would not vote for Winfield S. Scott, their presidential standard-bearer, if the Democrats would vote for the constitution. In truth such dealings were unnecessary because of the Democrats' own professed interest in constitutional revision.

Once again, the voters of New Orleans spoke loudly for reform. Joining them were almost 58 percent of their counterparts from the black belt, whereas voters in predominantly white parishes returned a 54 percent majority against the new constitution. All but two Whig parishes supported the document, while in the Democratic parishes the vote went twenty to eleven against ratification. Statewide, the constitution carried by a margin of slightly less than 3,200 votes.[31]

The campaign for ratification had sparked a variety of opposition as opponents seized on various features in the new instrument that were not wholly to their liking. Other anti-ratification arguments aside, however, it was the apportionment article that generated the most heat, and it indeed nearly doomed the constitution because it intensified intrastate rivalries.

An analysis of the convention's choice places it, as well as the entire document itself, in a clearer historical context. Fixing representation in the house upon the basis of the whole population was no radical idea for Louisiana politicians. After all, the concept governed the composition of the state senate under the old constitution. Even the federal Constitution counted three-fifths of a state's slaves in determining its representation in

Congress. Still, commentators have assumed that the alternative of counting only qualified electors was fairer and more democratic. In that view the convention's rule was seen as the way by which wealthy slaveholders got representation out of all proportion to their actual numbers. Thus black-belt parishes were aligned against white, with small farmers and laborers put at a decided political disadvantage. That reading is wrong on two counts.

First, census figures reveal that even in the black-belt parishes, more than half the adult white males owned no slaves. Accordingly, nonslaveholders stood to gain from the whole population rule.[32] Second, and of crucial importance to the actual outcome of the ratification contest, was the character of sectional divisions in the state during the 1850s. Rather than there being a simple split along black belt versus white belt, the state actually broke into three sections, black belt, white belt, and New Orleans.

Although whites made up a majority of its population, the city properly should be regarded as a section unto itself, rather than as one of the "white" parishes. After all, it accounted for nearly 36 percent of the state's entire white populace, it contained the largest number of slaves in absolute terms of any parish, and the value of its property, personal and real, equalled 25 percent of the total for all of Louisiana. Then too, considering its position as the chief economic rival of New York City, the Crescent City stood well apart from the rural portions of the Pelican State.

Under the old apportionment procedure, New Orleans would be entitled to a third of the house seats by 1854. Country delegates who favored its retention therefore tried to limit the city to a specified number of seats. Rather than acceding to such a diminution of power, the Orleanians opted for the new rule, by which the metropolis clearly stood to gain. A fast growing immigrant population and the largest number of free blacks in Louisiana would assure preeminence in future years.

The attempt to limit the number of city representatives was of a piece with traditional rural animosity toward New Orleans. That animus had manifested itself in the former constitution. Article 15 stipulated that no parish could elect more than one-eighth of the senate, whereas Article 112 specified the removal of the capital to a location no nearer than sixty miles to the metropolis. Such a "*cordon sanitaire*" served mainly to reinforce the feeling among Orleanians that the rest of the state was prejudiced toward them.[33]

Let us now turn from the what, how, and why of the constitutional convention of 1852 to an examination of the document itself.[34] The method by which the delegates revised the old constitution assured the reenactment of most of its articles with little or no substantive changes in wording or intent. For example, of the first 141 articles of the Constitution of 1852, fully 69 percent were essentially the same as those they replaced.[35] Conversely the convention broke with its predecessor when it modified the constitutional requirements for electors and officeholders, apportionment, legislative sessions, and the composition of the supreme court. Its provisions for banking, internal improvements, an elected judiciary, and a simplified mechanism for amending the constitution were among its other significant departures.[36]

Just as the convention took freely from the past, later redactors borrowed generously from the Constitution of 1852. Their degree of borrowing varied, to be sure, but in percentage terms, the range fell between a low of 2 percent of the articles in the 1879 instrument and a high of 36 percent of those in the 1921 document. Put another way, parts of more than three-quarters of the organic law of 1852 turned up in at least one of the constitutions that succeeded it.

Among provisions that were changed in the later documents, several merely brought the state's fundamental law up to date by purging matters no longer relevant to the political realities of post-bellum Louisiana. The convention of 1864, for example, dropped the requirement that only free white males were liable for service in the militia. References to duelling in the oath of office were deleted as was the mandate to publish the statutes in both English and French. Even though the Constitution of 1852 provided for the creation of banks either by special charters or by general law, none was ever formed except under the free banking act of 1853. Accordingly the convention of 1868 dropped the special charter clause once and for all.[37] Other modifications broke patterns set in 1852. Terms of legislators and state officials rose from two to four years, as did the age requirement to run for governor. The Constitutions of 1864 and 1868 abolished the elected judiciary, though that novel idea reappeared in the Constitution of 1879. Similarly, the elected board of public works provided for in 1852 gave way in the Constitution of 1864 to an appointive state engineer. Lotteries, meanwhile, though expressly forbidden in 1852, were sanctioned in succeeding charters until they were again prohibited by the Constitution of 1898.

In general, though, the later instruments tended toward congruence with rather than a sharp turn away from the Constitution of 1852. Thus it represented more of a link between the past and the future than the break with tradition that some observers have argued for. Its most controversial feature, Article 8, the apportionment article, was retained in each of the subsequent constitutions, except that of 1864. Of course the implications raised by the existence of slavery disappeared after the Civil War, and the idea of basing representation on total population became less troubling. Indeed that concept had not been altogether foreign to antebellum Americans; the constitutions of ten Northern and three Southern states included it in one form or another.[38]

Just as the apportionment question was more or less in the American, if not quite the Southern mainstream of constitutionalism, so were the suffrage provisions. Article 10 granted the franchise to all free adult white male citizens of the United States if they were residents of the parish and state six and twelve months, respectively. Fourteen state constitutions contained more restrictive provisions. Six demanded payment of a poll tax, while in North Carolina property ownership was required. The New York constitution was unique in that it extended a limited franchise to free men of color.

Regarding the qualifications for officeholders, the Constitution of 1852 was actually more generous than most of its contemporary counterparts. One had to live longer in other states in order to run for a seat in their legislatures. Then too a candidate had to meet a higher age requirement to be a senator or a representative, as he did if he sought the governor's chair. South Carolinians, meanwhile, could not vote directly for their governors, and in New Hampshire only Protestants could legally hold state offices of any sort.

An elected judiciary had been a key goal of the Louisiana constitution makers. Although the idea drew support from Whig and Democratic delegates alike, Louisianians were actually rather slow in adopting the reform. Mississippians, by contrast, had incorporated it twenty years earlier. As of 1852, it had been written into thirteen other state constitutions, but eleven still retained an appointive judiciary, whereas another six provided for a mixed system of election and appointment.

Banking regulation was of greater importance in Louisiana than in most other states merely because New Orleans existed as one of the nation's vital commercial and financial centers. Eleven state constitutions contained no regulatory articles. An additional three prohibited banks altogether, while several others limited banking to a specified number of institutions or required referenda on whether or not banks should be allowed to operate. In the Constitution of 1852, the banking article bore similarities to a provision in the New York constitution. The major difference between the two was that the Louisiana version contemplated the creation of banks either by special charter or general law, whereas the New York constitution forbade the legislature from chartering them individually.

Internal improvements were also an issue of consequence to Louisianians, especially Orleanians who struggled to keep or to expand the city's share of trade with the rest of the South as well as the West. A similar concern did not manifest itself in the nine constitutions that contained no articles to govern the matter. In four additional states, the organic law either prohibited state expenditures on improvements or kept the degree of state involvement in such projects to a bare minimum. Another five documents merely paid lip service to them, and six more prohibited their states from pledging full faith and credit. Clearly, then, the provisions in the Constitution of 1852 were among the most advanced in the nation.

As in Louisiana, constitution makers elsewhere in the United States grappled with the touchy business of where to locate the state capital. Possibly because it was no longer an issue, thirteen constitutions were silent on the matter. Ten more specified a means by which relocations might occur. Four documents promised rather more imaginative solutions. The Connecticut document required alternating the seat of government between Hartford and New Haven, but in Rhode Island, the legislature would sit twice yearly, once in Newport and once at alternating sites about the state. In Missouri, the constitution put the responsibility of site selection into the hands of a special commission. The solution in Texas was the calling of a state-wide vote to decide where to put the capital.

In education, the Constitution of 1852 stood with the leaders. It was one of but seven documents to provide for a state superintendent of education. Only nine others called for the establishment of a comprehensive system of schools. Four more called for funding schools with a special tax, though an additional sixteen dedicated the interest from permanent funds to schools. Elsewhere there were more general commitments as in Massachusetts, where public and grammar schools were "cherished." Constitutional statements such as these render the Louisiana provisions the more remarkable, at least on paper. Even though what the convention of 1852 did merely tracked the wording from the 1845 constitution, its action manifestly argues the delegates' intention of extending rather than diminishing the commitments of their predecessors.

Ease of amendment had been a primary consideration for the convention, and the delegates succeeded in streamlining the process under the new constitution. After 1852, Louisianians faced fewer hurdles in the path toward constitutional reform than twenty-six of the other states.

The Constitution of 1852 differed from its counterparts in one significant respect. It lacked a bill of rights, a distinction it shared with the charters of South Carolina and Michigan. Moreover its general provisions article incorporated only four of the twenty-two guarantees contained in the "average" bill of the time. There had been an attempt to rectify this disparity in the convention, when a New Orleans Whig, Henry St. Paul, moved consideration of a bill of rights. St. Paul got nowhere; his resolution was tabled, and the citizens of Louisiana remained without explicit protection of their civil liberties until 1868.[39]

Comparing the length of American state constitutions in the period, the 155 articles placed the Constitution of 1852 somewhat above the national average of 137. The shortest charter was that of South Carolina with but 60 articles, while the longest was that of Michigan with 246. If quantity correlates with modernity or complexity of government, then Louisiana's approached the norm of the times.

It should be obvious that the analysis of the Constitution of 1852 presented here controverts the interpretation offered by Roger W. Shugg in his now classic *Origins of Class Struggle in Louisiana*. That study, which has profoundly influenced more recent histories of the state, is replete with inaccuracies and insubstantial conclusions. Among the most notable are those in Chapter Five, "Government by Gentlemen," where he analyzes the call for the convention and its workings.

First Shugg asserts, "only the mercantile interests of New Orleans remained dissatisfied" with the Constitution of 1845, insisting that economic concerns drove the movement for constitutional revision in 1852.[40] In doing that he denigrated the wishes of both the politicians and the voters for reform, a desire that clearly moved the convention to regulate the banks, to refashion the judiciary, to sanction internal improvements, and to provide for public education.

Conceding the existence of the reformist tendency, Shugg turned it aside with the dismissive conclusion that it was "stolen by the Whigs as a popular cloak for their own desires."[41] He then went on to quote a statement from a Whig newspaper, "we now have it in our power to place Louisiana beyond the reach of locofocoism and to retain its government in our hands for years to come—there will be no excuse if we do not."[42] From this, he inferred a palpable admission by the Whigs that they intended to use the convention to gain control of the state at the expense of the Democracy. He failed, however, to include the line which preceded his quotation. It reads, "the Whigs have an awful responsibility to work and to present to the people a Constitution, liberal in its provisions, and worthy of the great State of Louisiana and the Whig party."[43] Clearly, that sentence casts an utterly different meaning to the quotation Shugg selected, especially if one identifies locofocoism with the radical anti-bank wing of the Democratic party.

Shugg's insistence on styling the Constitution of 1852 as the "Whig constitution" is quite misleading. After all, the reform movement began in a spirit of bipartisanship as early as 1850, and it gathered significant Democratic support throughout the convention and the ratification campaign. Shugg argues that Judah P. Benjamin and his party brought about "changes in representation that might perpetuate the power of Whiggery," referring to the change in the basis for legislative apportionment.[44] If that revision was solely to benefit the Whigs, why then did nearly half the Democratic delegates support it?

Not only was Shugg's "explanation" of the Whigs' motivation erroneous, but so was his basic understanding of the effect of changing the method of apportioning the legislature relative to the political strength of the Whigs. In 1852, Whigs sat in fifty-six of the seats of the house of representatives; that is, they controlled 57.7 percent of the total number of places. If the parishes that sent Whigs to the house in 1852 also returned Whigs in 1855—the first year under the new apportionment rule—then the party would have held only fifty seats, for a majority of 56.8 percent of the total. In short, counting the whole population as the basis of representation hardly can be said to have augmented the Whigs' power.

Lastly Shugg's assessment of the economic features of the Constitution of 1852 was deficient. His contention that the new organic law removed any "limitation of the state's capacity to borrow money" was incorrect.[45] No such prohibition existed in the constitution it replaced. Moreover, he claimed the convention specifically exempted the Citizens' Bank of New Orleans from requirements it imposed on banks that might incorporate after 1852.[46] In truth, the exemption was consistent with existing statutory banking laws and it applied to the five other chartered banks that remained in business after 1845.[47]

Joseph G. Tregle, Jr., in his article, "Another Look at Shugg's Louisiana," published in 1976, called for someone to lay bare the shortcomings of Shugg's analysis. While this essay is not the final answer to that need, perhaps it can serve to point in the direction of a reexamination of antebellum politics. *Origins of Class Struggle* has muddled the interpretation of Louisiana's antebellum political history for over fifty years now. A new standard of interpretation is certainly overdue.[48]

Notes for "Louisiana's 'Whig' Constitution Revisited: The Constitution of 1852"

[1]For a more detailed study of the constitutional reform movement in the 1850s, see Wayne M. Everard, "Louisiana State Politics and the Constitution of 1852" (M.A. thesis, Louisiana State University in New Orleans, 1972).

[2]See Benjamin Wall Dart, ed., *Constitutions of the State of Louisiana and Selected Federal Laws* (Indianapolis, 1932).

[3]Ibid., 508-11.

[4]William Henry Hunt, ed., *Selected Arguments, Lectures, and Miscellaneous Papers of Randell Hunt* (New Orleans, 1896), 116-17.

[5]*New Orleans Daily Delta,* March 26, October 29, 1851.

[6]See Charles E. A. Gayarré, *History of Louisiana,* 4 vols. (1903, reprint ed.; Gretna, La., 1974), 4:672.

[7]Dart, ed., *Constitutions,* 517-18.

[8]*New Orleans Daily Delta,* March 15, 1851; Hunt, ed., *Selected Arguments,* 107-12.

[9]George D. Green, *Finance and Economic Development in the Old South: Louisiana Banking, 1804-1861* (Stanford, 1972), 15.

[10]Marshall Scott Legan, "Railroad Sentiment in North Louisiana in the 1850s," *Louisiana History,* 17 (1976): 128.

[11]Green, *Finance and Economic Development,* 17.

[12]Abraham Kelly to G. Burke and Co., February 16, 1851, Glendy Burke and Co. Papers, Department of Manuscripts and Archives, Howard-Tilton Memorial Library, Tulane University, New Orleans, La.

[13]*Alexandria Red River Republican,* April 5, 1852.

[14]*New Orleans Daily Courier,* April 28, 1851.

[15]Steven A. Caldwell, *Banking History of Louisiana* (Baton Rouge, 1953), 83.

[16]Green, *Finance and Economic Development,* 27, 59, 132.

[17]Dart, ed., *Constitutions,* 518.

[18]Ibid., 519.

[19]*Acts passed by the 4th Legislature of the State of Louisiana . . . 1852* (New Orleans, 1852), 14-15.

[20]*New Orleans Daily Delta,* October 14, 1851.

[21]Louisiana *Senate Journal,* 3 Leg., 1 Sess. (1850), 37; Louisiana *House Journal,* 3 Leg., 1 Sess. (1850), 44. The following description of the events leading up to the convention, its deliberations, and the ratification referendum derive from Everard, "Louisiana State Politics."

[22]Green, *Finance and Economic Development,* 132.

[23]Parochial political allegiance is derived from the vote of each parish in the 1849 gubernatorial election as recorded in the *Senate Journal* (1850), 15. The official report on the convention referendum, as published in the *New Orleans Bee,* May 18, 1852, omits returns for four parishes, all Democratic.

[24]A majority of the Whig delegates voted to table a Democratic resolution that would have reduced the residency requirement from twelve to nine months. *Journal of the Convention to Form a New Constitution for the State of Louisiana* (New Orleans, 1852), 45. Hereinafter cited as *Journal.*

[25]Ibid., 39, 73, 79.

[26]Ibid., 73, 79.

[27]Ibid., 66.

[28]Ibid., 65-66.

[29]Ibid., 99-100.

[30]Ibid., 100.

[31]The political identities of parishes are based on the votes cast in the 1850 gubernatorial election as recorded in Perry H. Howard, *Political Tendencies in Louisiana: 1812-1952* (Baton Rouge, 1957), Table 1 on page 48.

[32]Everard, "Louisiana State Politics," 129-30.

[33]Dart, ed., *Constitutions*, 510-17.

[34]The following comparison of the Constitutions of 1845 and 1852 is based on Dart, ed., *Constitutions*, and Huey P. Long, comp., *Constitutions of the State of Louisiana* (Baton Rouge, 1930).

[35]The remaining articles set forth the schedule for implementation of the new charter. By definition the schedule articles in each constitution differed from one another.

[36]Dart, ed., *Constitutions*, 523, 526, 533-35.

[37]Green, *Finance and Economic Development*, 23.

[38]This and other comparisons between the Constitution of 1852 and those of the other states is based on the texts in Francis Newton Thorpe, comp., *The Federal and State Constitutions, Colonial Charters, and Other Organic Laws of the States, Territories, and Colonies Now or Heretofore Forming the United States of America*, 7 vols. (Washington, D. C., 1909).

[39]*Journal*, 12. A reporter was not appointed to record the debates until later, and he did not begin his work until July 12.

[40]Roger W. Shugg, *Origins of Class Struggle in Louisiana* (Baton Rouge, 1939), 134.

[41]Ibid., 136.

[42]Ibid.

[43]*Baton Rouge Gazette*, July 10, 1852.

[44]Shugg, *Origins of Class Struggle*, 136.

[45]Ibid., 137. Article 111 merely provided that the creation of any debt over the amount of one hundred thousand dollars could only be contracted by specific statutory authorization that also contained a repayment schedule. The article was essentially the same as article 114 of the Constitution of 1845.

[46]Shugg, *Origins of Class Struggle*, 137.

[47]Shugg continues his comment on the Citizens' Bank by observing, "small wonder that farmers believed the Whig merchants wanted banks to steal the money of the people, and . . . railroads to run away with it." His source for this quotation was the *New Orleans Daily Delta* of October 24, 1852. That reference is actually a report of a Democratic meeting held in the city. Thus what Shugg cites as evidence of the feelings of farmers really represented the point of view of a New Orleans Democrat, Capt. F. Leech. The *New Orleans Daily True Delta* report, moreover, notes that "the joke produced a greater effect" than the address it followed. Not only does Shugg imply the quotation stated the position of the *Daily Delta*—which was in reality pro-bank, pro-improvements, and pro-constitution—but he elevates what was the humorous end to a spirited meeting to the level of representing the attitude of the state's farmers. Shugg's misjudgment is repeated in the most recent history of the state. See Bennett H. Wall, ed., *Louisiana: A History* (Arlington Heights, Ill., 1984), 119. There the attribution is to the *New Orleans (Daily) Delta* rather than to Captain Leech.

[48]Joseph G. Tregle, Jr., "Another Look at Shugg's Louisiana," *Louisiana History*, 17 (1976): 245-81.

PART II
Antebellum Politics in the Jacksonian Era

BOTH THEIR HOUSES*

Joseph G. Tregle, Jr.

Long before national parties or issues attained any degree of importance in Louisiana, the deep and divisive antagonisms pitting Creole versus American overwhelmingly preoccupied the concerns of its citizens and provided the principal issues around which the political life of the state would take shape. That fact complicated tremendously the emergence of a Louisiana counterpart to the common national political party dichotomy familiar in other sections of the country, the state's peculiar local loyalties having no relevance to national issues or candidates. Who could vote for a French president? And of what use were traditional parochial prejudices and divisions in any evaluation of the tariff or the Second Bank of the United States? Nonetheless, despite her newness to the Union, Louisiana had no intention of avoiding her responsibilities or losing her rights in the national political arena.[1]

The rise of the Jacksonian movement, or perhaps one should say the intensification of national politics in the late 1820s, developed in Louisiana as a foreign addition to an already existent order with totally different dynamics and orientations. National political allegiances could not be superimposed on the older local factions, to rest as a separate structure on an earlier foundation. Instead it was necessary to immerse them in the turbulent waters of Louisiana's prior and continuing conflicts, to mix them with those deeply flowing currents in all the ways perceivable to shrewd political intelligence. As a result, no national party emerged in Louisiana based on one ethnic or geographic faction as against a second organization based on the other; no Jacksonian army of Americans poised against a Whiggery completely French. Rather would there be national parties exploiting each in its own way the traditional divisions in the state and finding with an irritating frequency that national attachments often broke before the demands of older gods. The intensity and persistence of these original rivalries make it necessary, therefore, to understand more clearly their substance.

*First published as Chapter 5 in Joseph G. Tregle, Jr., *Louisiana in the Age of Jackson: A Clash of Cultures and Personalities* (Baton Rouge: Louisiana State University Press, © 1999), 131-173. Reprinted with the kind permission of the author and the publisher.

The triple division of the Louisiana population—Creole, foreign French, American—unquestionably presented the most formidable challenge to those attempting to create national party units in the state. The long battle for internal control which these factions had been waging since 1803 had a vigorous life of its own, not possible to suspend so that men might turn their attention to the war between Clay and Jackson. Leaders of the national parties in the state could be satisfied, however, with nothing less than unquestioning allegiance to the party candidate in every campaign, those of a purely local character as well as those which sent their winners to Washington.[2] Clearly, they needed to exploit old issues when profitable and to keep them submerged when they might fragment hard-won unity. That such an assignment proved impossible to accomplish reflects less on the quality of their leadership than on the vitality of Louisiana's traditional hatreds.

No political movement in the state, on whatever level, could ignore, for example, the still smoldering resentments against the United States felt by a large number of the ancienne population. Whatever else might be said of the Louisiana Purchase, it certainly engendered a variety of responses, and the Louisianians never forgave what they considered to be bad faith on the part of the United States in its interpretation of that document. No treaty in all history, their champions charged, had been more clear or more unworthily violated.[3] They had been especially infuriated by the Act of 1804, which broke the new American acquisition into the two territories of Orleans and Louisiana in complete defiance to the native insistence that the treaty had guaranteed the integrity of the whole Purchase area and its immediate admission into the Union as a state possessed of all the rights common to the signatories of the Constitution. Persistent claims by Jefferson and his appointees that Louisianians lacked proper preparation for self-government struck them as a gross insult, and they generally refused to collaborate with a territorial government which they professed to find more arbitrary and confining than anything they had known under France or Spain. They added to these general complaints specific protests against the 1804 act forbidding the introduction of Negro slaves from abroad and the federal decision that the treaty did not grant unique trading privileges to France in her onetime colony, measures which the Louisianians denounced as malicious and punitive disregard for the rights preserved to them in the 1803 compact.

In reality, much more than disagreement over particular provisions of a treaty created this breach between disaffected partners. Equally productive of tension, Louisiana suddenly found itself required to submit to a new and vigorous government, whose edicts could not be trifled with as had been possible under the inefficient and anemic rule of a Spanish colonial system already suffering the death pangs of dissolution. Prompt application of strict revenue laws, for example, and immediate American steps to wipe out smuggling and piracy in the Gulf introduced Louisianians to a governmental policy so threatening to long-established freedom from supervision that many saw it as the hand of oppression.[4]

The Americans who flocked to Louisiana after the Purchase brought with them no soothing balm to ease these injured feelings. Most of these newcomers seem to have been unbelievably lacking in tact, and with the brashness perhaps symptomatic of youth and nascent nationalism, they rushed in to claim as their own the full slate of offices created to govern the new Territory of Orleans. They dismissed any suggestion that some of these might go to natives of the area with blunt pronouncements that ex-colonials had no understanding of republican principles and thus lacked any ability to serve. As late as 1814, one visitor to Louisiana remarked, Creoles were still being advised "not to interfere with Government, as that is a subject peculiar to ourselves. They have even been told that in purchasing the Country we purchased them also, at no higher price than 50 cts. pr. head."[5]

Conferring of statehood in 1812 did much to ease these early tensions. Marriage into a Creole family and genuine charity toward refugees of Saint-Domingue who settled in Louisiana finally made W. C. C. Claiborne acceptable enough to the old population to win him the first governorship of the new state in 1812, a victory hardly to be predicted during his tempestuous administration of the Territory of Orleans. This apparent relaxation of ethnic tensions signaled a native willingness to support a compromise rotation of the executiveship between the two populations, with the Louisianians looking forward to their turn in the office in 1816. But the wounding behavior of Andrew Jackson during the trying days of the British attack on New Orleans did much to disturb this still uneasy reconciliation. That doughty son of the frontier made no secret of his doubts as to the loyalty of the French-speaking Louisianians and their willingness to defend the city whatever the cost. His fears led him to a rigorous enforcement of martial law, a dissolution of the suspect state legislature, and defiance of the rulings of a federal judge attempting to free a French Louisianian accused of inciting disobedience to his commands. Typically, Jackson made no effort to justify his actions until after danger had passed and he had submitted once again to civil authority, but many Louisianians saw in his behavior yet another confirmation that they still had not been accepted as Americans. Others in the Gallic community, however, acclaimed him as a true and deserving patriot, defender of their soil, and protector of the chastity of their wives and daughters. For the rest of his life the Hero of New Orleans would continue to be loved and hated in the Louisiana which he had saved.[6]

Amelioration of these ethnic antagonisms abated considerably during the term of the state's first Creole governor, Jacques Villeré, who succeeded Claiborne as governor in 1816, presumably in implementation of the rotation compromise. This venerable favorite of the old population had little genius or political skill but much innate charity and good will, which he expended liberally in a sincere attempt to dissipate ethnic hostilities in the community.[7]

But the antagonisms ran too deep to be so readily suppressed. By 1820, stimulated by the growing leadership of the foreign French, many of the Gallic group began to feel more secure in their American citizenship and to yearn for that greater dominance which they felt to be rightfully theirs. Villeré's support of the gubernatorial rotation policy ensured election of a Virginian, Thomas B. Robertson, to the governorship in 1820, but only at the price of rising opposition in his own faction. For their part, the Americans too grew more and more impatient for a trial of strength. To the native Louisianians they held out the invitation to join them in an American fusion, to study under them the lessons of true republicanism, while they put away the seductive blandishments of the foreign French who knew and understood only the repugnant doctrines of European aristocracy and tyranny.[8]

The Creoles, however, understood full well that in such a venture they would be junior partners and suspected that by *republicanism* might well be meant the renunciation of their character as a culturally distinct group. These "strangers in the land,"[9] Marigny fumed, "want to take all and share nothing,"[10] and any persistence in Villeré's "extreme kindness and condescension for the new population," he warned, would lead to shameful slavery: "Virginia will exhaust itself before a Louisianian is made governor in his country!"[11] Aware of this deep attachment to a traditional Gallic way of life, the foreign French kept alive Creole fear of the Americans, content to forswear the governor's chair for one of their own while they moved behind the seats of power and gave strength and guidance to the battle against the "outsiders." But their own supercilious and scornful dismissal of Creoles as crude country bumpkins proved almost as infuriating to native Louisianians, who frequently toyed with the idea that it might be well to wish a curse on both French and American outsiders and thus prevail in their own homeland by steering a course between these two extremes.[12] It was a beguiling thought—but then would come the realization that without their French-speaking ally the old population stood vulnerable indeed to the wiles of the American.

The election of Robertson in 1820 ushered in a time of troubles, during which ethnic controversy brought the state perilously close to civil war. Dissatisfaction with Villeré's concessions to the Americans burst into flaming anger when Robertson began to employ his wide appointive powers in a fashion which the already aroused French faction accepted as proscription against their part of the community.[13] When the usual early political explorations revealed some Americans already plotting to make yet another Virginian Robertson's successor, the state plunged into a tempest of ethnic conflict.

The storm raged around those divisions which had never been bridged and which now loomed more than ever as symbols of the war between disparate ways of life which refused to be reconciled. Creole attack concentrated against the hated system of the common law which had been brought into their midst by the American lawyers and judges after 1803. They denounced this "monstrous English code . . . this confused mass of edicts handed down by the most ferocious despots"[14] as a devilish device meant to despoil the original settlers of their property and lead them into a slavery like that imposed upon the hapless Creoles of Missouri, snatched from their beloved Louisiana by the treacherous Territorial Act of 1804.[15] In their most exaggerated fantasies, they perceived defenders of these barbarous English customs as plotters who hoped one day to subvert American freedom through the courts and return the nation to the bondage of British colonialism.[16] They found especially vile and humiliating what they conceived to be the trickery by which they had been innocently led to accept as part of the Constitution of 1812 a provision making English the legal language of Louisiana, a maneuver which they now discovered made illegal the use of their own tongue in such intimate documents as the *procès verbal* of family meetings or the awards of arbitrators.[17] And where, they demanded, could one find any justice in a system which allowed a Louisianian to be at the mercy of a judge whose language he could not understand and whose judgments derived from traditions and customs alien to his ways and hidden from his knowledge? Jury trials in federal courts they looked upon as rigged to the same pattern of American favoritism and persecution; the federal marshal selected panels at his discretion from larger pools chosen by lot, a procedure which they claimed led to unequal voice being given to the more literate American segment of the community.[18] Not even the advent of changes such as legislation in 1822 which permitted the use of French in most legal business,[19] the congressional measure promoted by Edward Livingston which fixed selection of Louisiana federal juries completely by lot,[20] or the great Louisiana Civil Code of 1825, quieted fears that their legal rights remained forever in jeopardy. Convincing them of the legitimacy of their concerns, American reaction to their plaints consisted generally of accusations that they represented nothing but typical Gallic attempts to subvert justice.[21]

The passage of years did little, moreover, to lessen the Creole conviction that the swarm of Americans in their midst had come to despoil their land in search of quick fortunes which might be carried away to support lives of ease in the North at some future date. Each summer's migration by those who feared to tarry in the yellow-fever zone called down from the native population strident denunciation of these "Yankee Buzzards" and "birds of passage."[22] Americans naturally bitterly resented this blanket condemnation and ridicule, not unreasonably, for after more than a decade of tenure in New Orleans in which he had probably given more than he had taken, James Caldwell, for example, still heard himself derided as a bird of passage by one of his more moderate French-speaking rivals.[23]

Few areas of Louisiana life escaped the corrosive effect of this pervasive ethnic discord. In an almost pathetic plaint, the Creoles began to talk of those halcyon days of the past "when neighbor was not required to bespatter his neighbor with dirt, or perhaps blood as the *douceur* for which he was to receive a petty office—when Shylock jurisprudence was unknown" and the frauds of banks and paper money had yet to be born.[24] In short, when the American was still foreign to the land. More and more the American seemed to menace every social and cultural form precious to those of Gallic ancestry. Never a particularly religious people, the native Louisianians reacted with disbelief and repugnance to the puritanical impress upon so much of the American culture to which they were introduced. The endless attempts to establish sabbatarianism in their midst particularly outraged them, threatening as it did their passionate dedication to dances, bear baitings, cockfights, and general patronage of ubiquitous places of good cheer on their favorite day for relaxation, and they winced to see appended to advertisements of a Sunday ball the earnest New England admonition to "Remember the sabbath day to keep it holy!" On their side, American Protestants girded themselves with sincere determination to reform a society which did violence to their every precept of Christian morality, flooding the legislature with petitions to ban desecration of the Sabbath, which they claimed gave "iniquitous advantage over all those who are disposed to keep that day holy."[25] Having little success, they charged persecution of Protestantism,[26] blasted at "priestcraft,"[27] and demanded of those resistant to sainthood, "will it not be more tolerable for Sodom in the day of judgment than for you!"[28] They found particularly reprehensible the *ménages de couleur* in which Gallic New Orleanians set up handsome quadroon women as mistresses of second households,[29] and when the legislature received a request to allow a Louisianian to marry his niece, nothing more remained, said one shaken American, than for the state to be asked to legalize incest. Gallic tradition saw in these attitudes little of honesty and nothing of virtue, frequently making the legitimate point that as much as Protestant divines might decry dalliance with dusky beauties and patronage of gaming halls and brothels, they seemed notably unsuccessful in making it unpopular among their own countrymen.[30]

Even matters of considerably less import generated other levels of misunderstanding. Management of public receptions and functions frequently foundered in the face of rival concepts of protocol and places of honor.[31] Americans charged that French ignorance and backwardness continued to blight the educational hopes of the community, only to be answered that American pride and arrogance had caused the death of the Collège d'Orléans.[32] Champions of the rival French and American theaters lashed their opponents with ridicule and often vulgar derision,[33] and differing burial practices and competing cemetery rights came under regular cross fire from both factions.[34]

Furious arguments raged over Napoleon Bonaparte, a hero dear to the French heart and a conqueror in whom the Creole found a vicarious pride, one thing at least to which he could cling without fear of being bested by the American. Americans could, however, express disgust at the adulation bestowed on an emperor called "the Man," the "Great Man," or the "Greatest of Mortals,"[35] and then go on to proclaim that perhaps little else could be expected of those who mourned the death of Louis XVIII, amused themselves with bull baiting and cockfighting, visited unmerciful cruelty upon mules and horses,[36] and kept alive the debauchery of the masked balls of New Orleans, that "rotten relict of European degeneracy."[37] In the face of such barbarism, they asked, who could condemn those who felt it necessary to import "our house materials, our workmen, and our society."[38]

These quarrels ramified throughout the whole state but always flared with greatest intensity in New Orleans, where the three population groups were packed so closely together and responded so quickly to the exhortations of their leaders. Much of the violent dispute also had origins in clashes local to the great metropolis. Gallic leadership always dominated the city, providing the mayor and a majority of the members of the council, an arrangement which worked obviously to the advantage of those parts of the municipality which retained their old population character. As the American section of New Orleans grew in commerce and wealth, fattening on the ever increasing stream of trade down the Mississippi, those who spoke for her interests began to demand fairer representation in the city governing body. Nothing but expansive reform, they insisted, could protect them from neglect and the effects of Gallic inefficiency and corruption.

They pointed to the city's dismal record in such matters as street paving and the erection of wharves and dock space, protesting what they called deliberate attempts to cripple the American section and force trade unnaturally into those precincts where the older population prevailed. Such misguided policy, they warned, would make it impossible for New Orleans to offset growing competition from eastern ports for control of the great western commerce.[39] The extent of such Gallic stupidity, they charged, could be clearly gauged by that faction's support of quarantine regulations drafted and enforced by a French-dominated Board of Health not to protect the city from disease, as they pretended, but to make entry into New Orleans so troublesome and vexing as to cut off the stream of new American settlers into the city.[40] They pointed to waste and favoritism encouraged by the council, saw corruption in city purchases of useless property at exorbitant prices,[41] criticized as incredibly wasteful the tax farming system of collecting city revenue,[42] and decried the carefree manner in which the council released its favorites from any monetary obligation when the city treasurer for whom they had given bond absconded with sixty thousand dollars of the city's money.[43] French venality or incompetence even jeopardized their lives and homes, they fumed, on one occasion actually relaxing fire ordinances to allow an old and feeble man to build a forge in a wooden building.[44]

Gallic leadership replied to these charges with complaints of their own, equally fiery and impassioned. What community anywhere, they demanded, would be so fatuous as to improve suburbs while the "bosom of the city" withered and decayed?[45] Control of the council must be retained by the Gallic sections, Marigny warned, or the Faubourg Ste. Marie would turn the old quarter into a colonial appendage, shamed and degraded in the eyes of the world.[46] No better summary of these fears could be found than in the philippic of another champion of the original city, Joseph Rodriguez, who climaxed his prophecy of destruction with the cry, "Such is the grand plan of the Vandals of the West, *delenda est carthago*! And passersby, surveying with pity all this debris and ruin, will read, *hic Troja fuit! Ici exista la Nouvelle Orléans!*"[47] In such contrasting ways did the citizens of New Orleans fear for their city's safety.

It was in 1823 that this ethnic bitterness came closest to plunging the state into actual armed conflict. For some time the French had realized that the most ominous threat to their control of Louisiana lay in the growing strength of the Florida Parishes. They listened in rising anger and fury to continued demands in the legislature that the state capital be removed from New Orleans to the interior, which they understood rightly to mean a shift to the Florida area. The arguments presented in favor of such a change flowed from a strategy designed to exploit the rural conviction, pervasive even in Gallic parishes, that New Orleans had no legitimate claim to the seat of government, being a notorious sinkhole of iniquity where official business went ignored in a riotous round of dissipation and where the excesses of party feeling kept alive hatreds racking the state.[48] In addition, removal of the capital from the city, the argument ran, would end the dominance exercised over state affairs by the foreign power concentrated in its Old-World milieu.[49]

New Orleans Creoles and foreign French rushed to the defense of the metropolis and pleaded with their country brethren to recognize this attack as but one more of the insidious plans by which the Americans hoped to enslave all those not part of an Anglo-Saxon tradition and to "wrest forever from the Louisianians control over their own affairs."[50] The intensity of their anxiety even generated recriminations among their own number, Marigny lashing at those of his compatriots who had refused to heed his jeremiads in 1812 that to submit to the annexation of the Florida Parishes would be to betray the French people of Louisiana.[51]

To frustrate these threats against their capital required not only vigor but skill, and here, as usual, the foreign French stepped in to show the way. Late in January 1823, Louis Moreau Lislet threw the Louisiana senate into confusion with the demand that the Florida members be ousted from their seats for the simple reason that their districts were unknown to the Constitution of 1812 and had never been legally incorporated into the state. The French press of New Orleans overflowed with praise for this move, and *L'Ami des Lois* expressed amazement "that a question of such great interest to the Louisianians, had not been agitated sooner." "Let honor be given to the Senator faithful to Louisiana," they proclaimed, "to the statesman who is aware that to defend the Constitution, is to defend our liberties, our property, and *National Independence!*"[52] Recovering from their shock, the Florida delegation soon demanded immediate expunging of all mention of the Florida Bill from the records of the senate, blasting it as an insult to their constituents and a threat to republican government in Louisiana as guaranteed by the Constitution of the United States. Legislative decorum promptly collapsed. A cry went up from Arnaud Beauvais that the motion of the Floridians should be spread upon the records so that all might see the shameful extent to which some men could push party feeling,[53] and for days the New Orleans papers kept the argument going at white heat. Sentinels stood guard, and patrols roamed the city at night to preserve order, while one American editor proposed that "if they were on the watch for *traitors*, we imagine they could sooner catch them, at noonday, in the [Senate] house."[54]

American anger flared through the state, and in the Florida Parishes men talked of taking up arms to defend their rights.[55] Even Moreau Lislet began to grow uneasy at the tempest he had blown up; it is clear that he had hoped only to force the Floridians to give up their moves against New Orleans as the price for ending the challenge to their place in the senate.[56] Feeling that his main objective had been won, he steered a conciliatory measure through the upper chamber admitting the senate's lack of power to inquire into the right of the Florida delegation to its seats,[57] and technically the battle was over. But no easing of tension followed, for the Florida Bill had opened the way to a series of enflaming controversies.

The times themselves engendered suspicions, charges, and counterattacks. A conservative temper and the force which most people called the Holy Alliance hovered over Europe, menacing and unpredictable, triggering fear and conjecture in Louisiana to a degree probably unknown in other parts of the Union. Reacting uneasily to the nebulous intentions of the allied European powers, the American faction in the state had no reluctance to question whether Creoles and especially the foreign French could be trusted to remain loyal to the United States in the event of foreign invasion. Proclaiming the existence of a "foreign faction" in Louisiana, masterminded by the foreign French but spread through the whole Gallic community in the state, they warned that the national security could be guaranteed only by vesting complete political control in the hands of those whose Americanism traced back through long generations. Now the real objective behind the attempt to keep French influence paramount in Louisiana had been made clear, went the American charge, predicting that when the Holy Alliance felt free to move it would find an agent in Louisiana to throw open the door to invasion of the Western Hemisphere. Bred to the traditions of European aristocracy and tyranny, the Americans claimed, this foreign faction hoped to incite Louisiana to treason.[58] The French readily agreed that treason indeed stalked the land, but it did so, they proclaimed, not so much in New Orleans as in the Floridas, where Hartford Convention Yankees busily spawned hate against those who loved their homeland, spreading alarms designed to paralyze the state with fear of a foreign faction while they made ready to push the whole Gulf area into the hands of British warlords already grasping at Cuba and the islands of the Caribbean.[59]

How much of all this noise reflected sincere alarm for the safety of Louisiana and how much had no real purpose but to inflict damage on an old foe is difficult to determine. But that it constituted something more than mere political bombast finds ample demonstration in the fierce struggle which ensued for control of the militia companies in New Orleans. Late in 1822 tension began to mount when the Americans made it clear that the Louisiana Legion, largest of the military units in the capital, had become suspect because of the large number of foreign French who held commissions in its ranks without being citizens of the United States. What could present a more alarming danger, they asked, with the nation's safety imperiled by tyranny from abroad, than to have the defensive forces of the state under the command of men who still owed allegiance to the "imbecilic Louis XVIII?" What clearer sign could be found than this to prove the evil purpose of the foreign faction, the American press demanded, once more raising the ghost of supposed French and Creole treachery in the desperate days of the Battle of New Orleans. In this hour of threat from France and the Holy Alliance, they asked again, who could trust men who would have surrendered their homes and their women to the depraved seekers after "Booty and Beauty," men who even now insisted that American citizens should submit themselves to the orders of aliens who admitted no loyalty to the state or nation?[60] The necessity of choosing a new major in the Legion in December 1822 brought a stiffening of battle lines, plaguing the city for a while with sporadic brawls between the contending militia factions.[61]

For the American companies, the election of Pierre A. Cuvillier came as an insufferable insult. Major Cuvillier had taken no steps toward naturalization, though a resident of Louisiana for more than five years. He admitted having fought as a mercenary soldier for the British during the American Revolution, and worst of all, he was the law partner of the archconspirator Moreau Lislet. What man worthy of the name, bristled the Americans, would take orders from such "vile mercenary wretches?" "Let them manufacture anathemas against the proud sons of America—but let these shameful things be done under the flag, and in the name of Louis XVIII, *their master!*"[62]

Hopes of peaceful reconciliation collapsed on January 8, 1823, when the Louisiana Guards under Capt. Edward Fenno refused to obey Cuvillier's command to join the Legion in the Battle of New Orleans celebration[63] and filed demands with the legislature that all alien officers be read out of the Louisiana militia,[64] a move which the French condemned as being intolerant and in violation of the Militia Act of 1815.[65] Prompt steps to court-martial Fenno faltered when proof emerged that the charging officer, Brig. Gen. Pierre Lacoste, had never taken the oath of office and allegiance required by the state constitution,[66] but Cuvillier then brought separate complaints against the rebellious captain and made ready to dismiss him from his command.

At daybreak on Sunday, August 24, Cuvillier marched his Louisiana Legion through the city streets, arranged them in a hollow square in the Place d'Armes, and read out the order to strip Fenno of his rank. One irate American youth threw himself through the military cordon with drawn poignard, only to be repulsed unharmed. The next day as Fenno and the Guards marched in defiance to the decree, armed rowdies gathered in the public square and only good fortune averted certain bloodshed as bricks hurled from the watching crowd whistled harmlessly past the parading color guard.[67] By this time General Lacoste had taken his proper vows and, fearful that the city might be plunged into factional violence, had countermanded Cuvillier's action against Fenno. The major promptly resigned and tempers relaxed.[68]

The relief from tension proved to be little more than a truce. Near panic seized New Orleans on November 13, when Mayor Joseph Roffignac hastily called out the Legion and the Guard, paraded them in full battle garb past city hall and then shipped them by steamboat four leagues up the coast. Roffignac's absolute refusal to comment upon whatever danger might be threatening the metropolis extended even to keeping Commodore Patterson of the United States Navy in the dark, and wild fears spread over the city. The next day the troops straggled back to New Orleans, exhausted and slimy with the mire of the swamps, obviously having met no enemy.

The American papers exploded with mingled anger and boisterous glee when they finally learned that an anonymous letter reporting a band of one thousand runaway slaves on the outskirts of New Orleans had impelled Roffignac to launch this grandiose and fruitless campaign. They exploited the comic aspects of the march of the "Grand Army" to the fullest, delighting especially in the supposed dejection of Roffignac and the French because of their lost opportunity to strut as lesser Napoleons. Their touchy Gallic targets found nothing at all amusing in the event, and when the *Louisiana Advertiser* published *Nigraud*, a burlesque poem ridiculing the Legionnaires as effeminate city boys, discord burst once again over the city. One section of the *Advertiser's* piece particularly infuriated the Gallic community. It ran:

Peut on marcher quand on a peur
J'en appelle aux timides.
Enfin les voilà nos bourgeois
A battre la Cyprière
Dans la boue et l'eau je les vois
Plongez jusqu'au derrière.

Can one march when afraid,
I called out to the timid ones.
Finally there were our city boys
Battling the cypress grove
Plunged in mud and water
Up to their behinds.

A boisterous crowd at Elkin's Coffee House threatened to mob James Beardslee, editor of the *Advertiser*, and in the city council, Alderman P. A. Rousseau, up to then rather friendly to the Americans, bellowed that with the help of twenty men like himself he would have marched on the offender's plant and destroyed his presses.[69]

And so it went. Throughout 1824 the quarrel continued, the French complaining of insults against their troops and still grumbling at the refusal of the American companies to rejoin the Legion,[70] the Americans busying themselves with a successful fight to win legislative prohibitions against aliens holding state militia commissions.[71] Then in December of 1824 the legislature elected William L. Robeson as brigadier general of the 1st Brigade to succeed Lacoste, promoted to major general,[72] and the French officers in their turn refused submission to superiors of the rival faction. The visiting Lafayette did everything in his power to restore amity in the midst of these ruffled tempers, but to no avail.[73] The Legion insisted it did not belong to the 1st Brigade and ignored Robeson's orders, whereupon the latter called Maj. Bartholomew Grima before a court martial, in ironic reversal of the 1823 Cuvillier-Fenno quarrel. Furious debate raged over the trial proceedings, and although Grima remained under arrest, he received orders from Lacoste to lead the Legion in the July 4 parade. The continuing clash between Grima and Robeson plunged the city and state into another angry affray, with the sharpest intensification of the American charges of a foreign faction yet seen, and with the French employing the full talents of their redoubtable defenders.[74]

R. D. Richardson of the *Louisiana Gazette* took the lead in assailing what he called the vicious intrigue of the faction, and did much to arouse American demands for a division of the city into independent sections based on ethnic groupings.[75] The French gave blow for blow, none so satisfying, perhaps, as the offer by Benjamin Buisson, editor of the *Journal of Commerce* and ex-soldier of Napoleon, to pay five dollars to anyone who contrived to knock out Richardson's brains.[76] A thoroughly outdone Governor Henry Johnson finally managed to restore some semblance of order by allowing Grima to retain his command upon submission to Robeson. Designation of the Legion in 1826 as a separate regiment of the 1st Brigade under Roffignac as colonel brought eventual equilibrium to the militia question,[77] but the basic antagonisms had by no means disappeared. Chances of actual ethnic warfare grew more remote with the passage of the years, but Jacksonian politics could never escape completely from the shadow of these abiding hatreds.

The clash between New Orleans and the rural parishes proved less enervating but no less real. In part this animosity sprang from the deeply held American conviction that the capital was the Medusa head with which the French party froze into immobility any movement aimed at weakening their hold on the political life of the state. But even traditionally Creole parishes shared the general rural resentment aroused by the city's economic hegemony over the agrarian countryside. New Orleans controlled access to capital funds and to the marketing of crops, and no argument that this undisputed fact derived form the immutable nature of the economic system could persuade the planting interests that the city did not exact from them more than it had a right to demand. A major complaint charged New Orleans banks with deliberately frustrating every legislative attempt to make easy credit available through country branches[78] and with engaging in speculation responsible for needless fluctuation in cotton prices.[79] Planter animosity centered as well on the city's many commission houses as an integral part of an insatiable profit-seeking "monied aristocracy" bent on making "overseers of the backbone and sinew of the country."[80]

The stringencies of the economic depression of the early 1820s so severely affected Louisiana that the planting interest moved to attack what seemed to them their most obvious and vulnerable enemy. Attempts to weaken the New Orleans monopoly by removing the capital to the interior received widespread rural approval, only to be blocked not only by skillful city tactics such as Moreau Lislet's assault upon the senators of the Florida Parishes, but just as effectively by failings in the rural ranks as well. Paralyzing rivalries made it impossible for the rural strength to be united behind any one of the many locations competing to replace New Orleans, and immobility intensified by stubborn refusal of some rural legislators to abandon a capital which afforded them the means of caring for their own business affairs while they made laws for the state.[81] Even when success crowned these efforts and the capital moved to Donaldsonville in 1830, the inconvenience and boredom of that small community drove the legislators quickly back to the hateful but alluring precincts of the metropolis.

Some independence from the city's economic hegemony came in 1827 with the creation of the Consolidated Association of Planters of Louisiana, which pioneered the principle of using land for banking collateral, but the fiery demands in 1823 for a usury law to cripple the so-called shaving and extortion practices of the New Orleans money lenders failed to push the measure past the veto of Governor Robertson, who resisted firmly what he considered unconstitutional and harmful limitations to the rights of private property.[82] By the turn of the decade many rural spokesmen saw no hope except in trying to bypass New Orleans altogether. Alexander Porter regularly lectured his friends on the wisdom of selling directly to northern houses,[83] and the whole Attakapas region seriously explored ways by which to exploit its outlets to the Gulf as avenues to direct trade with New York and Philadelphia.[84]

Such animosities no doubt reflected age-old town and country antagonisms, ancient then and persistent even to the present day. Mixed with the bitterness of ethnic rivalries, they made up profound and lasting issues in Louisiana politics. With them would pro- and anti-Jacksonians alike have to contend.

Notes for "Both Their Houses"

[1]The *St. Francisville Asylum* of February 13, 1823, voiced a conviction common to many Louisianians during the 1820s and 1830s: "To have a firm, upright and impartial Governor, is of more importance to Louisiana, than the choice of President of the United States."

[2]See, for example, the *Louisiana Advertiser*, May 18, 1830, which carries a demand for support of the Jacksonian gubernatorial candidate.

[3]*L'Ami des Lois* (New Orleans), January 10, 1822.

[4]Ibid.; J. W. Windship to William Plumer, Jr., November 1, 1813, in Everett S. Brown, "Letters from Louisiana, 1813-1814," *Mississippi Valley Historical Review*, 11 (1924), 575.

[5]J. W. Windship to William Plumer, Jr., April 2, 1814, in Brown, "Letters from Louisiana," 575.

[6]Marquis James, *The Life of Andrew Jackson* (New York, 1940), 232-33, 250-62.

[7]*St. Francisville Asylum*, July 3, 1824; Bernard Marigny, *Memoire Addressed to His Fellow Citizens* ([Baton Rouge?], 1939), 36.

[8]*Louisiana Gazette* (New Orleans), April 14, 1824; *Louisiana Advertiser* (New Orleans), April 27, May 7, 1824.

[9]Baron de Montlezun, *Voyage Fait dans les Années 1816 et 1817 de New York à la Nouvelle-Orléans*, 2 vols. (Paris, 1818), 1:336.

[10]Bernard Marigny, "Reflections on the Campaign of Gen. Andrew Jackson in Louisiana in 1814 and '15," *Louisiana Historical Quarterly*, 6 (1923): 76.

[11]Marigny, *Memoire Addressed to His Fellow Citizens*, 36.

[12]*New Orleans Argus*, April 19, 1824.

[13]*Louisiana Gazette*, July 24, 1821, December 17, 1823; *Louisiana Courier* (New Orleans), February 11, 1824.

[14]*L'Ami des Lois*, February 8, 1823.

[15]Ibid., October 7, 1822.

[16]Ibid., February 7, 1823; *Louisiana Gazette*, October 29, 1822.

[17]Henry A. Bullard to Josiah S. Johnston, February 2, 1822, in Johnston Papers, Historical Society of Pennsylvania, Philadelphia, Penn. (hereafter cited as Johnston Papers).

[18]*L'Ami des Lois*, October 14, 1822.

[19]Henry A. Bullard and Thomas Curry, eds., *A New Digest of the Statue Laws of the State of Louisiana* (New Orleans, 1842), 451.

[20]*Louisiana Advertiser*, January 20, 1826; George Eustis to Josiah S. Johnston, January 17, 1826 (Alexander Porter file), Letters of Application and Recommendation During the Administration of John Quincy Adams, 1825-1829, in Record Group 59, General Records of the Department of State, National Archives, Washington, D. C.

[21]Eustis to Johnston, January 17, 1826 (Alexander Porter file), ibid. Important for any understanding of the confused legal system of Louisiana in this period are Eberhard P. Deutsch, "Jury Trials Under the Federal Rules and the Louisiana Practice," *Louisiana Law Review*, 3 (1941); Gordon Ireland, "Louisiana's Legal System Reappraised," *Tulane Law Review*, 11 (1937); John H. Tucker, Jr., "Source Books of Louisiana Law," *Tulane Law Review*, 6-9 (1931-34); and John H. Wigmore, "Louisiana: The Story of Its Legal System," *Southern Law Quarterly*, 1 (1916).

[22]*Louisiana Gazette*, June 29, 1821, October 30, 31, 1822; *L'Ami des Lois*, February 18, 1823.

[23]*Louisiana Advertiser*, April 10, 1834.

[24]*Louisiana Gazette*, May 1, 1824.

[25]*Louisiana Advertiser*, February 8, 1824.

[26]Ibid., December 27, 29, 1823.

[27]Ibid., July 24, 1834, March 23, 1835.

[28]Ibid., June 12, 1826.

[29]*L'Ami des Lois*, January 18, 1823.

[30]Ibid., February 4, 1823; *New Orleans Argus*, July 7, 1825; *Louisiana Advertiser*, February 7, 1824; *New Orleans Observer*, February 28, 1835; *Louisiana Courier*, May 28, 1827, December 1, 1830.

[31]*Louisiana Courier*, August 15, 1826; *Louisiana Gazette*, August 8, 1826.

[32]*New Orleans Argus*, December 18, 22, 23, 1826, January 17, February 2, 1827; *Louisiana Gazette*, April 18, 1826.

[33]*Louisiana Gazette*, February 28, 1821, March 24, 1823; *Louisiana Advertiser*, March 28, 1823.

[34]*Louisiana Gazette*, November 15, 1822, October 29, 1823; *Louisiana Advertiser*, March 24, 1823.

[35]Helen Parkhurst, "Don Pedro Favrot, a Creole Pepys," *Louisiana Historical Quarterly*, 28 (1945): 729; *Louisiana Gazette*, November 22, 1822; *Louisiana Courier*, November 5, 8, 1834.

[36]*L'Ami des Lois*, January 1, 1824; *Louisiana Gazette*, December 9, 1825.

[37]*Louisiana Gazette*, January 7, February 11, 1825.

[38]James Pearse, *Narratives of the Life of James Pearse* (Rutland, 1825), 17.

[39]George Kernion, "Samuel Jarvis Peters, The Man Who Made New Orleans of Today and Became a National Personality," *Publication of Louisiana Historical Society*, 7 (1913): 72; *Louisiana Advertiser*, July 14, October 11, 1823; *Louisiana Gazette*, February 11, 1823, July 29, August 3, 5, 10, 15, 17, 19, September 9, 1825.

[40]*L'Ami des Lois*, January 31, 1823; *Louisiana Advertiser*, May 24, June 19, 26, July 8, 1823.

[41]*L'Ami des Lois*, May 24, 30, June 13, 1823; *Louisiana Advertiser*, May 5, 6, 20, 21, 24, 26, 17, 28, 1823; *Louisiana Gazette*, May 9, 19, 22, 23, 24, 26, 28, 29, 30, 31, 1823.

[42]*Louisiana Gazette*, February 25, 1823; *Louisiana Advertiser*, August 9, 1823.

[43]*New Orleans Argus*, March 23, 1830; *New Orleans Bee*, September 10, 1834.

[44]*Louisiana Advertiser*, October 1, 1831.

[45]*Louisiana Gazette*, August 3, 10, 1825; *New Orleans Argus*, September 27, 1826.

[46]Marigny, *Memoire Addressed to His Fellow Citizens*, 8-9.

[47][Joseph Rodriguez], *Défense Fulminante contre la Violation des Droits du Peuples* (New Orleans, 1827), 35.

[48]*L'Ami des Lois*, June 26, 1822.

[49]*Louisiana Gazette*, June 25, 1822.

[50]*L'Ami des Lois*, October 16, 1822, January 18, 1823.

[51]Marigny, *Memoire Addressed to His Fellow Citizens*, 16.

[52]Quoted in *Louisiana Gazette*, January 22, 1823.

[53]*L'Ami des Lois*, January 24, 1823.

[54]*Louisiana Gazette*, January 23, 1823.

[55]Isaac L, Baker to Josiah S. Johnston, January 21, 1823, Alexander Porter to Johnston, February 16, 1823, in Johnston Papers.

[56]Alexander Porter to Josiah S. Johnston, February 16, 1823, ibid.; *L'Ami des Lois*, January 28, 1823.

[57]*L'Ami des Lois*, January 31, 1823.

[58]*Louisiana Gazette*, July 13, 1822, July 22, 1823; *L'Ami des Lois*, February 7, March 22, 1823; *Louisiana Advertiser*, August 28, 1823.

[59]*L'Ami des Lois*, January 27, 1823.

[60]*Louisiana Advertiser*, March 8, August 25, 1823.

[61]*Louisiana Gazette*, December 10, 1822.

[62]*Louisiana Advertiser*, August 27, 1823; *L'Ami des Lois*, February 26, 1823.

[63]*Louisiana Gazette*, January 10, 11, 1823.

[64]*Louisiana Advertiser*, March 3, 1823.

[65]*L'Ami des Lois*, March 3, 1823.

[66]*Louisiana Advertiser*, March 8, 1823.

[67]Ibid., August 27, 1823; *Louisiana Gazette*, May 15, 1824.

[68]*Louisiana Advertiser*, August 28, 1823.

[69]Ibid., October 31, November 15, 18, 20, 21, 22, 27, 1823.

[70]*Louisiana Gazette*, September 15, 18, November 15, 18, 20, 21, 22, 27, 1823.

[71]*Louisiana Advertiser*, February 7, 1824.

[72]*Louisiana Gazette*, December 22, 1824.

[73]A. Levasseur, *Lafayette en Amérique, en 1824 et 1825*, 2 vols. (Paris, 1829), 2:218.

[74]*Louisiana Gazette*, July-October 1825; *Louisiana Courier*, July 20, August 17, 22, 1825.

[75]*Louisiana Gazette*, July 29, August 3, 5, 19, 15, 17, 19, September 9, 1825.

[76]Ibid., August 3, 1825.

[77]*Louisiana Advertiser*, July 3, 1826.

[78]*Baton Rouge Gazette*, November 1, 1826.

[79]Henry Johnson to Josiah S. Johnston, January 17, 1826, in Johnston Papers.

[80]*Baton Rouge Gazette*, June 14, 1828; *Louisiana Courier*, January 5, 1823; *New Orleans Bee*, October 5, 1833; Alexander Porter to Josiah S. Johnston, February 14, 1832, in Johnston Papers.

[81]John Sibley to Josiah S. Johnston, February 26, 1822, in Johnston Papers; *Louisiana Gazette*, November 6, 1822; *Louisiana Herald*, April 21, 1824; *La Fourche Gazette*, February 11, 18, 1826.

[82]James Brown to Josiah S. Johnston, April 11, 1823, in Johnston Papers; *L'Ami des Lois*, January 17, March 3, 6, 8, June 12, 1823; *Louisiana Advertiser*, March 18, 1823; *St. Francisville Asylum*, May 13, 1823.

[83]Alexander Porter to Josiah S. Johnston, February 14, 1832, in Johnston Papers.

[84]*New Orleans Mercantile Advertiser*, October 16, 1829.

BIRTH OF A CAUSE*

Joseph G. Tregle, Jr.

Edward Livingston recognized Andrew Jackson as a prime presidential possibility as early as 1815. Anyone in the Tennessean's presence felt immediately the force of his personality and authority, but the sharp-eyed Louisianian sensed that the stunning victory over the British at New Orleans transcended all these qualities and transformed Old Hickory into a national hero with an open road to the White House. Livingston had grown up in an ambience with those in places of power, and in 1815 he saw on Jackson the stamp of future greatness.

Not everything seemed so clear only a short time earlier. The Livingstons had been somewhat perturbed in the days before the arrival of the backwoods warrior to take over the defense of their city, troubled by what might lie in store for them. Word of Jackson's temper and violence preceded him, creating among the ladies visions of all kinds of unpleasantness when common courtesy might force them to introduce this lion into their social circles. Some had even worried that he might gouge their floors with hobnailed boots. Jackson, it turned out, proved to be anything but the savage. His great personal dignity, his openness to close personal relationship, and the compelling charm which fell over anyone in his company worked upon those whom he met in New Orleans as they worked upon others in the years to come—to the perplexity and dismay of his enemies. Mrs. Livingston and her coterie were at first unbelieving, then captivated. Livingston watched and pondered.[1]

Seldom far removed from Jackson during the Louisiana campaign, at his own request Livingston became the general's aide-de-camp and military secretary, a spot he had sought even prior to the commander's arrival in New Orleans.[2] Jackson soon found himself surrounded by Livingston associates: Davezac as his judge-advocate; young Lewis Livingston, the jurist's son, as a commissioned captain in the engineers; and John R. Grymes as a member of his staff.[3] Through the whole crisis of the British attack, Livingston made himself invaluable to Jackson, and even after the enemy's withdrawal the gen-

*First published as Chapter 7 in Joseph G. Tregle, Jr., *Louisiana in the Age of Jackson: A Clash of Cultures and Personalities* (Baton Rouge: Louisiana State University Press, © 1999), 131-73. Reprinted with the kind permission of the author and the publisher.

eral depended on the able legal advice of his aide in defending his martial law restraints on Judge Hall and the suspect Louisiana legislature. With his usual flamboyance, Davezac played an equally conspicuous role, prominent in almost every aspect of the celebrations attendant upon Jackson's remarkable victory.[4] When Rachel Jackson arrived to join her husband, Mrs. Livingston took pains to tutor the plain frontier wife in the rules of social behavior, making her own home a retreat in which the weary and beset Jackson could find what few moments of relaxation opened to him in New Orleans.[5] Before the general departed for the Hermitage, he heard carefully dropped hints from his aide that perhaps Jackson's services might one day be required in the presidency, to which the victorious soldier gave nothing but vocal disbelief.[6] But the suggestions could hardly have lowered Livingston in the eyes of an already grateful recipient.

"Je chante ce guerrier qui sauva notre ville," the citizens of New Orleans sang in Jackson's praise,[7] their enthusiasm for the champion who had delivered the "Booty and Beauty" of Louisiana from unspeakable danger magnified by the fact that the enemy he had crushed was their traditional foe, the British.[8] In him, moreover, the Louisiana French saw a duplicate of another great hero, Napoleon, and the aura of military glory which surrounded Jackson's name guaranteed the constancy of their affections.[9] No less appreciative, the American segment of the community celebrated the New Orleans campaign as a testimony to the vitality and endurance of their young nation. The United States had offered no reassuring picture in the winter of 1814, with the Louisiana capital feeling particularly abandoned and distressed. "But oh! The Guardian Spirit of our country watched over us," these Americans could recall in later days, "in the despair, and the darkness of the hour when consternation and destruction sounded, a genius appeared to reanimate our expiring hopes, and to brave the threatening horrors of the storm: The heroic Jackson spoke, and all was calm!"[10] As Livingston himself once explained, others might read of Jackson's great gifts and be told of the frightful terrors from which he had delivered them, but Louisianians knew at first hand who he was and what he had done.[11]

The innumerable close personal friendships which tied Jackson to so many leading figures in the state buttressed this already broad base of gratitude and affection to provide a strong foundation of future political support in Louisiana. Like Davezac, who admitted that from his first meting with the general he fell under "the power of an irresistible spell,"[12] many others retained warm memories of their wartime association with a valiant commander and were willing to pledge to him their support in his every undertaking. Gen. Jean B. Plauché, one of the most beloved and respected of the Creole citizens of New Orleans, was so overcome with gratitude to the general during the victory celebration in the Place d'Armes in 1815 that he threw down his sword and astonished the Americans, Jackson most of all, by kissing his hero soundly on both cheeks.[13] He later urged his son to pattern his life upon that of the general and stood ever ready to prove his loyalty by acts of generosity in times of Jackson's need which reflected the obvious sincerity and selflessness which motivated them.[14]

Like Livingston, Grymes, and Davezac, Abner L. Duncan, another Jackson aide in 1814-1815, also understood the advantages to be won in keeping memories of Chalmette alive. He and his friends took pains over the years to apprise Jackson of their continuing fight against old enemies like Thomas B. Robertson and Fulwar Skipwith, whom Jackson continued to believe guilty of trying to surrender New Orleans to the British.[15] Jackson also knew that even more than Livingston, Duncan continued to be assailed politically as his principal adviser in the Louisiana Legislature dispute of 1814-1815, and few things bound Jackson more closely to another than the suffering of attack in his cause. Thus Duncan became a valued friend and political sponsor of the general in Louisiana, host to his relatives or associates on their visits to New Orleans, and frequent supplicant for aid in acquiring whatever federal office might attract him.[16]

Isaac Baker's relationship with Jackson also reflected much more than simple political allegiance. A close friend of Andrew Jackson Donelson in his youth, Baker had himself been in some fashion or other a protégé or ward of the general. From his home in St. Martinville he made frequent pilgrimages to the Hermitage to visit with Jackson and report on the latest maneuvers of their common enemies.[17] "In my progress through life," he once wrote his benefactor, "I may safely say that after my father I owe you more obligations than to all other men living and, you cannot be ignorant, feel great solicitude for any and everything which regards you."[18]

Similar personal ties stretched from Jackson to many others in Louisiana. Lafayette Saunders had not only fought under him at New Orleans, but he had also married Mary Smith, daughter of Rachel Jackson's niece, in a ceremony at the Heritage. And Clark Woodrooff had followed up his military service at Chalmette with an 1819 honeymoon of several weeks at the Jackson home in Nashville.[19]

Gen. Walter H. Overton, for his part, had connections to Jackson not only through their shared military backgrounds, but also through membership in the family of John Overton of Tennessee, one of the old soldier's closest and most cherished friends. In like fashion, Thomas Butler's regard for the Hero of New Orleans stemmed from more than an impersonal attachment to his political principles. His brother, Adj. Gen. Robert Butler, had been the general's chief of staff at New Orleans, and both he and Jackson had enjoyed the hospitality of the Cottage on their way home from the great battle.[20] Another Floridian, the effusive John B. Dawson, prided himself on having been born in the Hero's own town of Nashville and found in the old warrior a personality which appealed to his own notions of emotional leadership. Jackson "sums up all my ideas of human perfectibility," he gushed to William S. Hamilton, "Intelligent, Brave and magnanimous. . . . Huzza for Jackson! In war, the spirit of the mountain storm, and in peace, the Widow's Friend, and the Orphan's Father."[21]

Less demonstrative, perhaps, but certainly as sincerely devoted to their commander, Isaac T. Preston, Maunsel White, and W. L. Robeson had all served under the general at one time or another, Robeson winning considerable renown as the leader of the company in the forefront of Jackson's successful attack against Pensacola. They remained steadfast in loyalty to the general, White matching Plauché in the generosity of his personal assistance during many of Jackson's not infrequent financial crises.[22] Alfred Hennen, too, had renewed an old acquaintance with Jackson during his Louisiana campaign, and he and his wife kept this association alive in the years which followed.[23] All in all, the list of Jackson's close personal friends in Louisiana—Livingston, Davezac, Duncan, Grymes, Baker, Preston, Overton, White, Hennen, Robeson, Butler, Saunders—reads like a roll call of the eventual Democratic chieftains of the state. Jackson had, in effect, an already constituted cadre of leadership in Louisiana the moment he gave his consent to be entered in national politics and certainly before it could be well understood what political principles, if any, he might champion.

There could have been no better time for Jackson to look for political support in Louisiana than the early 1820s. The state lay almost helpless in the grip of despair and bewilderment, anxious for its future and searching for someone who might recognize its plight and crush the evils which had given it birth. Aggravating the effects of the national depression of the 1820s which hit hard in Louisiana, a series of floods, broken levees, heavy rains, and rot struck the lower Mississippi valley, wiping away more than two-thirds of the area's crops for two or three years. Capital sources dried up, banks curtailed, and the state looked on incredulously as many of its oldest and heretofore soundest businesses began to close their doors. By the beginning of 1824, even the Mississippi itself seemed to waver, its water stage so low that the usual torrent of trade from the vast western interior diminished to scarcely a trickle.[24] Hard-pressed planters cursed the New Orleans factors and commission merchants and pushed through the legislature a state usury law clamping a 10- to 12-percent limit on interest rates. None of the leading men of the community rallied to continue the fight, however, when Governor Robertson vetoed the measure as an unwise and arbitrary extension of government power, and despite these real hardships, no strong demands emerged in the state for stay laws or replevin acts. Even the bitterest critics of Robertson, such as Isaac Baker, applauded his stern refusal to abandon what they considered the basic rules of sound economy.[25] A compromise of sorts finally calmed planter anger by creating the Bank of Louisiana, designed specifically to provide funds to the agrarian group, but the stopgap measure brought only partial relief at best.[26] Moreover, what little help the bank did give could not offset the effects which even the limited talk about usury and stop laws had generated. Capital became more closely guarded than ever, and many Northern and Eastern investors began cautiously to pull their funds from the state.[27]

As trying as these economic tensions might be, experience led to a general acceptance that in the normal workings of the economic system things would eventually get better. No such optimism attached to those problems most Louisianians identified as having origins in the simple lack of knowledge about the state and indifference to its concerns which existed in Washington. With memories of the British attack in 1814 still fresh in Louisiana, its citizens found it inconceivable that even after the lessons of that terrible crisis the United States in the 1820s had still made not a single effort to provide the state the defenses necessary for its security. A state legislative committee issued a nervous warning in 1823 that Louisiana might well be considered "the Achillean Heel of these confederated States; for, from its geographical position, as well as from its scattered and spare white population, it is more accessible to the evil designs and actual inroads of a foreign foe, than any other state of the Union."[28] Governor Robertson filled his annual messages to the legislature with like sentiments, pointing out in 1822 that the state at that moment remained "as much exposed to invasion as it was seven years ago, when it experienced its horrors." Why does the United Stated build defenses at Mobile, he asked, while "New Orleans could be taken by a *coup de main*?" Because, he answered, (ours) is unfortunately the only portion of the Republic, not only always unrepresented in what is termed the cabinet, but unknown by personal observation, as well to all its members, as with few exceptions indeed, to all the legislators of the nation." The following year Robertson reported that his pleas had gone unanswered, and in words shaped more by the recognition of helplessness than by bitterness, he advised the assembly that Louisiana simply lay "too far from the center of power to be regarded at Washington—distance seems to operate on them like time; and events which occur a thousand miles off, are like those which happened a thousand years ago."[29]

Public sentiment vented similar outrage over the marauding pirates in the gulf, who terrorized the approaches to Louisiana and forced commercial insurance rates higher and higher because the federal government did nothing to provide adequate protection to American vessels in those waters. Repeated demands called for a naval squadron to patrol the seas off Cuba, and Robertson added to his complaints by questioning "the wisdom of the policy which has sent our naval force to Africa, whilst our own coasts, particularly those of the Gulf of Mexico, have been permitted for years to exhibit scenes of blood and rapine, unequalled in atrocity in the annals of the world."[30]

Mail service to Louisiana was primitive at best; the lack of a direct national road from New Orleans to Washington necessitated a twenty- to twenty-five-day journey to move correspondence from one of these cities to the other.[31] The whole state west of the Mississippi had serious need of federal improvements to the navigable streams which provided the region with its sole linkage to the outside world.[32] Not even in the vital function of the administration of federal justice did the central government show any concern for the interests of the state. The Judiciary Act of 1807 failed to create a federal circuit court for the Western area of the United States, leaving Mississippi, Alabama, Indiana, Louisiana, Illinois, and Missouri with nothing but district judges, though the number of their federal cases exceeded those of the Eastern states. These western district courts could try only those disputes involving sums in excess of five hundred dollars, an amount considerably higher than the fifty-dollar qualification in their eastern counterparts. Nor could the Western states send on any appeals to the Supreme Court in criminal matters or in civil cases involving sums under two thousand dollars.[33]

Such restrictions convinced many in the West that an Eastern conspiracy operated to strangle their growth, with some insisting that even the great Jackson had scarcely been able to survive a similar jealousy in his military career.[34] Caught up in much the same belief, Governor Robertson attacked the Adams-Onis Treaty in 1819 as one by which "our title to a province . . . has been most wantonly thrown away" to satisfy East Coast interests.[35] The level of resentment occasioned by these affronts did not always match the seriousness of the offenses. New Orleans editors raged against a New York counterpart, for example, who had claimed that the mayor of their city jailed theatrical performers who muffed their lines. Was there no limit, they asked, to the absurdities which men would believe about their state?[36]

Nothing plagued Louisiana more than its inability to bring the vast acres of its public lands into private ownership. Therein, said Robertson in 1824, could be found "the principal cause of all the evils" besetting the state,[37] and the complexity of the situation made most men despair of any early solution. In part, the difficulty traced back to the confusion surrounding the status of private land claims in the state. The treaty of 1803 vested in the United States ownership of all soil in the Purchase territory not legitimately held by private title, and shortly after the transfer Congress passed legislation requiring all land titles in Louisiana to be registered in order to distinguish public from private holdings.[38] Lacking registration, no unrecorded title could be used as evidence in any court proceedings, but even this stringent measure did little to hasten entry of claims by the Louisianians. Many failed to register under the impression that the law did not apply to already established clear titles, an opinion held even by many attorneys,[39] while others lagged because most entries had to be made in New Orleans, requiring costly and time-consuming trips to the capital not only by the claimant but by his witnesses as well.[40] Some, especially the French-speaking residents, simply paid no attention to these mysterious pronouncements by their new masters, confident in their belief that ownership of property which they and perhaps their ancestors had held for decades could never be questioned.[41] Faced with the obvious fact that to adhere rigidly to the time limit set for private entries would cause real and widespread injustice, Congress repeatedly extended the period for registration, and the Louisianians continued to make few attempts to meet the new deadlines.

Complicating this already confused picture immeasurably, a great number of claims presented to the United States clearly lacked credible authenticity, many of such vast extent that they tied up literally whole sections of the state in dispute. In the Ouachita area the federal government refused to accept the claims of those holding under the Maison Rouge and Bastrop grants of the late Spanish period, placing hundreds of thousands of acres in question when claimants continued to press their suit against the ruling. Some of the relatively few actual settlers in the area had purchased titles from the large-grant claimants, others from the United States, while the remainder hoped eventually to be able to buy from the government under preemption rights. Congress found itself caught squarely in the middle of pressure from all these interests, with one group supporting the Spanish grants and another assailing them as fraudulent schemes to deprive the small settler of his proper rights.[42]

The Florida Parishes faced equally baffling and disturbing problems, for there the Spanish had denied that the Purchase included West Florida and maintained possession until 1810, with many corrupt officials carelessly issuing or selling fraudulent land claims during the last seven years of their control. Unfortunately, even many patents and grants legitimately conferred during the period of uncontested Spanish authority had never been entered or registered because of incompetent or careless clerks, adding immensely to the confusion.[43] On a smaller scale, similar problems could be found in practically every part of the state.

This persisting inability to guarantee land ownership had a devastating impact on Louisiana settlement. Few persons could be induced to purchase land for which a variety of claimants might show bogus Spanish titles, and the federal government could hardly open public lands to sale before determination of just what was and what was not public property. Confusion and inadequacy in the operation of the federal land office in Louisiana only deepened the problem, with agents making little effort to perfect surveys and plats for expansive areas incontestably owned by the government.[44]

As a consequence, the United States sold not a single plot of land in Louisiana until 1821, and as late as 1829 only 185,000,000 acres had been transferred to private ownership.[45] This count fell far below that of other states during the same period, understandably stimulating increasing demands for some change which would allow the region to share in the growing flood of western migration.[46] Adding to its disabilities, since Louisiana could collect no taxes from federal lands within her borders, construction of badly needed roads and bridges came to a virtual halt, the state refusing to improve property over which it had no control and from which it could expect no revenue. With settlers avoiding these federal acres, Louisiana watched helplessly as its sister states forged ahead in population and congressional representation. "The tide has passed [us] by," a state legislative committee reported sadly in 1824, lending support to Governor Robertson's repeated outburst against the unchanging grievance.[47] "Louisiana is in the situation of a colony," he once protested. Is it nothing, he demanded, to permit the United States "to hold possession and exercise sovereignty over more than half the soil of our independent State? Ask the Virginians, who contend that the [United] States do not own soil over which a post road runs, or, on which a post office stands in the ancient dominion."[48] From countless others in the state echoed the cry, "Send us people to settle!"[49]

It is only natural in such a situation that men would turn to Andrew Jackson as a possible savior, for who more than he identified with the salvation of the state? A toast at a New Orleans dinner in 1823 spoke eloquently to the point: "The next President—may he be a man who knows that there is such a state as Louisiana, and that there has been such a day as the 8th of January!"[50] Even those outside the state looked upon Jackson as an obvious champion of its interests. John C. Calhoun reported to Governor Villeré in 1820, relative to a request upon the national government, that "the subject has been referred to Gen. Jackson whose local knowledge—and zeal to promote the interests of Louisiana—will dispose him to give to it the attention it merits."[51] Reflecting much the same conviction, a plea sent to Jackson by New Orleans mayor Augustin Macarty in 1819 asked for aid in speeding the sale of United States lands in the city. "It would be deemed a fault, toward you, Sir," said Macarty, "to aim at any advancement without your participation."[52]

But not everyone in the state looked upon Jackson with the admiration and gratitude felt by Plauché, White, Baker, and those who sang his praises as the savior of New Orleans. The whole state might agree on the existence of problems which cried out for solution and complain against the neglect and injustice suffered at the hands of the federal government, but many saw the General as a false friend in whose custody the interests of the community would not be secure. The wounds which Jackson had inflicted upon French pride in Louisiana during his campaign against the British still stung in any number of important households. Louis Louaillier, for example, jailed by Jackson during his martial-law rule in 1815, was active in the 1820s recounting the insults and injuries he had suffered by command of the Hero of New Orleans. Others, such as Mazureau, found in Jackson the very distillation of everything they hated in Americans, and the Ajax of the Gallic forces never forgot that his own military advice had been unceremoniously disregarded by a backwoods soldier during the crisis of the invasion. He once entertained Edward Everett in New Orleans with "astonishing anecdotes of the ignorance of General Jackson relative to tactics,"[53] and later in his life he told Henry Clay, "I glory to have been engaged from the beginning of the struggle against Dirtocracy," by which he meant, of course, Jacksonianism.[54]

To countless Louisianians, indeed, Clay rather than Jackson deserved to be the champion which everyone agreed the state so desperately needed. A westerner like the Tennessean, he could be relied upon to understand the needs and problems of the newer societies. Even more important, he had personal ties to Louisiana even stronger, perhaps, than those of Andrew Jackson. A brother, John Clay, had long been active in the business world in New Orleans, and two of his daughters made their homes there as well, one the wife of Martin Duralde, the great favorite of the Creoles, the other the spouse of John Erwin, one of the best known slave traders of his day. To these extensive family alliances Clay added a host of private friends such as Alexander Porter, James Brown, Josiah Stoddard Johnston, and Etienne Mazureau, and like Jackson, he was himself no stranger to the streets of New Orleans.[55] Clay, moreover, had already by the 1820s made a clear record of his political ideas. His support of internal improvements and the protective tariff appealed strongly to the sugar-growing regions of interior Louisiana, while his championing of Clay's "American System" and the Second Bank of the United States made him a favorite with many of the commercial and business leaders of New Orleans.[56]

No one else in national life offered serious competition to the popularity and support enjoyed in Louisiana by the two westerners. Among the numerous "Down East" settlers in the Floridas and in the Ouachita area, John Quincy Adams did have a considerable following, but one based almost completely on his New England origins, which called down upon him the full force of the anti-Yankee sentiment so strong in Louisiana.[57] In addition, his dominant role as secretary of state in the crafting of the Adams-Onis Treaty of 1819 exposed him to the charge that he had ignored Southern interests by surrendering American claims to Texas in that agreement with Spain,[58] and his supposed hostility to the Louisiana Purchase still rankled in the minds of many of the ancienne population.[59] Support for the political advancement of William H. Crawford of Georgia or John C. Calhoun of South Carolina attracted only a limited number of independent thinkers such as Thomas B. Robertson, who seemed to be drawn to Crawford primarily because he found so much to oppose in all the other major leaders of the day.[60]

Louisiana participated in only three presidential elections prior to 1824, all in the placid calm of the Era of Good Feeling which discouraged development in the state of any major factions grouped around contending national leaders. Its citizen had passively watched the legislature give their electoral votes to Madison and Monroe in 1812, 1816, and 1820, and then rushed once again into the consuming competitions of their local political scene, with all the unique ethnic and cultural tensions which made it practically a world apart from the rest of the Union. National politics seemed remote from Louisiana in the early 1820s, and whatever might have been said about Washington's neglect of the state could have been affirmed with equal justice of its own lack of concern over national political affairs except as they tended to impinge directly on its own interests. "In Louisiana," United States senator James Brown remarked in the spring of 1822, "our bales of cotton and hogsheads of sugar absorb all other considerations."[61] And Lafayette Saunders reported much the same thing to Jackson in 1823 when he wrote from his new home in the Florida Parishes that "In this Country, Politics as well as all other considerations, yield in a great degree, to the cultivation of cotton and sugar."[62]

This political indifference generated spirited criticism in the local press,[63] perhaps unjustly, given the peculiar circumstances of the community. Except for those in the metropolis, few native Louisianians knew anything at all about national affairs. They seldom read newspapers, content to allow their chieftains to manage the esoteric problems of political maneuvering.[64] Both amused and irked by the appalling ignorance of the outside world exhibited by his Creole neighbors, Browse Trist regularly passed on to his brother Nicholas tidbits of their storehouse of misinformation.[65]

The state's continuing choice of presidential electors by legislative ballot added to a widespread feeling that national contests concerned only the political leaders of the state. Even those at that level seemed to give but little thought to federal elections. They clearly recognized the magnitude of the state's problems, particularly those involving unguarded frontiers and unsettled lands, but these had not become party questions. It appeared certain, at any rate, that in Louisiana Henry Clay would be the only major candidate to succeed James Monroe in the White House, and as much as any man in active politics he might be expected to defend its interests in the national councils. As late as 1822 most thought that Jackson had no intention of offering himself for the presidency, and with little serious competition to Clay in sight, the state tended to ignore the approaching campaign. In April of that year James Brown wrote to Clay from New Orleans that the Kentuckian remained "the only candidate for the P[residency] known here, and the only one having warm personal friends," so that his hope for Louisiana's five electoral votes seemed assured of realization.[66]

Nothing in the congressional campaigns in 1822 had any reference to the approaching presidential race except for a brief comment by William S. Hamilton in his opposition to Henry H. Gurley in the Second District. Fully aware of the hatred felt toward Yankees by many in his neighborhood, Hamilton attacked what he called a "new party . . . collecting the scattered forces" of Federalism to "overwhelm the South and the West," implying that Gurley, a New Englander, might be expected to assist Adams in the building of this Northern despotism.[67] But Hamilton's thrust clearly aimed more at defeating Gurley than at affecting the presidential election, and it proved ineffective in any case, the Yankee experiencing little trouble in retaining his seat.[68] The battle in the western district between the incumbent Josiah Johnston and William Brent developed into a vicious struggle revolving almost completely around personal issues, with Brent finally wining a close victory by circulating anonymous pamphlets on the very eve of the canvass linking Johnston to attempts to guarantee the large grants at the expense of small settlers. Neither candidate had taken a stand on the presidential race.[69] At the same time, Mazureau had managed to line up such concentrated strength in New Orleans behind Livingston's try for the First District seat that no opposition offered, and the ex-New Yorker could now make ready to enjoy the rewards of his long fight in the French cause.[70] Whatever else had cemented the relationship between these two men, they certainly shared no agreement over the attractions of Andrew Jackson.

The general simply did not seem to be an issue in 1822. He had passed through New Orleans the previous year on his way to serve as governor of Florida and received a magnificent welcome, with celebrations at the theaters, specially composed poetry proclaiming his fame, and brilliant transparencies commemorating his 1815 victory. But he must have left his friends with the firm belief that he would never seek the presidency, for even in late 1822, months after the Tennessee legislature had brought his name forward in July, his Louisiana admirers remained convinced he would not make the race. The dedicated Isaac Baker sadly accepted the fact and wrote to Hamilton that De Witt Clinton had now become his first choice for the White House: "I have so much gratitude and good feeling for Old Hickory," he assured the colonel, "that I would deem it a species of treason to abandon his standard beneath which I have always found promotion . . . and the kindest protection." But the general, Baker insisted, had no intention of becoming a candidate.[71]

In early 1823, however, everything changed. Jackson's reply to the Dauphin Committee in Tennessee confirmed his entry into the campaign, and as the publication of this correspondence began to appear throughout Louisiana, the presidential race immediately assumed an entirely new configuration.[72] Not even the bitterness of the ethnic quarrel which had erupted in January with Moreau Lislet's Florida Bill and continued into the Fenno-Cuvillier militia dispute of the next several months, or the violent debate over usury and depression, could hide this fact from Mazureau, Duralde, and the other Clay champions who had for so long been sanguine in their expectations of delivering the state to Clay practically by default. Henceforth they had the general to contend with, and they entertained no doubts as to the magnitude of his threat. Now they faced the possibility that all their golden dreams of influence and patronage through Duralde's father-in-law in the White House could be totally blasted by this hated Tennessean with whom they had no alliances and whose friends in Louisiana had always been their most inflexible enemies. Fear made them rash, and early in February one of their spokesmen gave formal notice in the state legislature that he planned to call for a recess so that the assembly might caucus and nominate a successor to James Monroe. Obviously the Clay leaders wished to commit the state to their candidates as early as possible, hoping to convince Louisianians that Jackson should not be considered a serious aspirant to the presidency and that he had offered too late in any case. But they had moved too soon. Many of the members of the assembly felt it unwise to bind the state to any man so early in the campaign, preferring to hold out in hopes of profiting from a long courtship for their votes. At best, the Clay forces had failed to assess the assembly's probable reaction, and they retreated ingloriously from their call.[73]

Baker wrote immediately to inform Jackson of these developments. For their part, the general's adherents preferred to delay any Louisiana Legislative pronouncements. The "opinions of the present members are so difficult to get at," Baker told Jackson, "that we think it rather unwise to risque a caucus until we see our way more clearly . . . Clay's friends are in despair and talk with less confidence than two weeks ago."[74] Adhering to this original plan, Baker and his associates turned immediately to prepare the way for a move of their own, hoping to give "the voice of the people a chance of being heard" and thus build up a strong force of public opinion which would avoid the charge of trying to dictate a popular choice. Especially did they hope for a pro-Jackson pronouncement from one of the large states, which would give their cause a sound prospect of success and ease the common fears that Jackson could make little headway against the more experienced candidates in the field.[75]

In mid-March the Clay faction moved once more to the attack, and again they blundered. What had been intended as an assembly caucus on the night of March 15 turned into a heated debate between Mazureau on one side, pleading for a vote endorsing Clay's candidacy, and Baker and Davezac on the other, demanding that no caucus be declared in session at all. Fearing another defeat, the Clay men hurriedly produced a list of resolutions in support of their favorite and allowed the meeting to disband without a formal vote of any kind. Within a few days they began to give wide circulation to their proposed caucus resolutions, now bearing the signatures of thirty-four of the slightly more than sixty members of the legislature, the preponderance of French names in the list testifying to the effective influence of Mazureau and Duralde.

The resolutions, themselves, however, did nothing to advance the Clay cause. The preamble's shaky defense of caucus nominations carried little conviction, and in the desire to win over those who still might not give credence to Jackson's candidacy, the resolutions themselves bestowed glowing praise upon the general, whose claims "upon his country," they conceded, "cannot be effaced." The assurance that Jackson himself would not "desire the suffrage of his fellow-citizens of Louisiana, when given at the hazard" of defeating the only westerner with a chance to win did little to erase the fact that the resolutions failed to enumerate the virtues of Clay or any other candidate and only provided a blanket endorsement of the Kentuckian. As Samuel Overton wrote in glee to Jackson, his enemies had played into his hands. "Louisiana cannot gainsay these declarations," he rejoiced, "and must ultimately give you an unanimous vote."[76]

The next year and a half buzzed with intrigue and ever mounting campaign propaganda. But most of the political agitation in Louisiana had nothing to do with the presidential campaign. In July of 1824 Louisiana had to elect a governor to succeed Robertson, and the passions aroused by this contest overwhelmed all other topics of public concern. Inevitably, the basic issues related to the now highly inflammatory ethnic antagonism in the state, so local in their content that they pushed matters of national concern into the background.[77]

The insensitive and highly pro-American policies of the Robertson administration had inflamed the always smoldering ethnic controversy into the most dangerous domestic crisis known to the community since statehood. Economic depression, the Florida Bill, militia disputes, fear of the Holy Alliance, and Gallic conviction that the Americans had conspired to monopolize the public affairs of the state combined to make the 1824 gubernatorial election one of unprecedented virulence and ill temper. The French insisted that the established rotation tradition demanded choice this time of a Gallic governor, and long before the end of Robertson's term some proposed bringing old Jacques Villeré back to the chief executive's chair.[78] But still jealous of Villeré's popularity and furious at what he termed the ex-governor's capitulation to American control, Bernard Marigny returned from France in 1823 to seek the governorship for himself, throwing the Gallic forces into turbulent and raucous confusion. Adding fuel to the flames, Marigny condemned Villeré as a tool of Mazureau, a strange tactic indeed, joining together supposed pro-American principles and the reputed field marshal of the Gallic troops.[79]

Only a comparable disunity in the American camp held out any hope for eventual French success. There a three-man split had developed, with Henry Johnson, Philemon Thomas, and Thomas Butler all in the field, a fragmentation clearly to be laid at the door of Johnson. His Senate term expired in 1823, and although he had given repeated indications that he had every intention of offering for governor in 1824, he did not relish retirement into private life while waiting for Robertson's tenure to end. Several of his American colleagues grumbled at Johnson's voracious appetite for office, however, and put it to him bluntly that he should decide for one post or the other, his seat in the national Senate or the governorship, and leave the way open for someone else to win the remaining honor. Both Philemon Thomas and Thomas Butler eagerly awaited the chance to make the race for Robertson's place in 1824, and when Johnson indicated that he would prefer to keep his Senate seat, the Florida leaders interpreted this as a surrender by him of all gubernatorial ambitions. Thus they gladly gave him their support when he won reelection to the Senate over Judge Martin in January 1823, expecting in this way to rid themselves of a dangerous competitor for the governorship.[80]

By the fall of that year, however, Johnson's actions made it obvious that he had every intention of remaining in the gubernatorial race, something which had been rumored in the press for months, and in September he released his formal announcement, despite the fact that Butler and Thomas had already entered the field.[81] The outraged protests of the followers of the two Florida candidates gave Johnson little pause. The *Louisiana Advertiser*, backing his campaign, charged that Butler and Thomas had entered the race primarily to block Johnson's victory, their hatred of him so great that they would even suffer the governorship to fall to the French if in the process they might humiliate their rival.[82] The consummate professional, Johnson surveyed the state with an eye long accustomed to discerning the political lay of the land. Confident of a considerable vote in New Orleans, the Floridas, and along the coast, plus the backing of H. S. Thibodaux in Lafourche, he assured Josiah Johnston in October 1823 that "It is to me a matter of no consequence, whether Judge Butler and General Thomas withdraw from the contest or not."[83] He was already certain of success.

In December, Governor Robertson once again energized the Gallic community into bitter opposition by the deviousness of his policies. He announced that Mazureau could not be renamed attorney general at the expiration of his appointment unless he resigned his seat in the legislature, leading the Frenchman to accept this as a pledge of the governor's continued support. When he stepped down from his legislative position, Robertson promptly placed Isaac T. Preston in the attorney general's office, and French accusations of perfidy swirled through the state.[84] Mazureau immediately made a successful bid for his old assembly place and then moved to stimulate Gallic forces to even greater exertions in the governor's race.[85] Working closely with Davezac and Grymes, who had other objectives in mind, he also pushed Livingston's claim to the United States Senate seat vacated by the appointment of James Brown as American ambassador to France, but his involvement greatly angered the American wing of the assembly. Aided by rural French representatives who rebelled against sending a city man to Washington, they turned against Livingston and gave the Senate post to Josiah S. Johnston.[86]

This defeat further aggravated the decline in French unity and morale which continued in the raucous fight between the adherents of Villeré and Marigny in the gubernatorial campaign. With Mazureau properly perceived as the driving force behind the Villeré candidacy, Marigny summoned every means at his command to prevent the success of that partnership, for he had long been unable to decide which he hated most, the Americans or the foreign French. While Henry Johnson continued to win French support in rural areas aghast at the internecine Gallic fight in the city, the two Creole candidates practically ignored the other contenders to wage their private war. Marigny announced publicly that he would use any means, even deception, to defeat his Creole rival.[87]

The *Louisiana Advertiser* did everything in its power to keep the feud boiling, printing glowing accounts of Marigny to balance the campaign propaganda in the city's two French papers controlled by Villeré and Mazureau, the *Louisiana Courier* and the *Argus*.[88] Johnson's backers killed all Gallic attempts to convene a legislative caucus proposed to unite French strength around a single candidate,[89] and Marigny's suggestion to end the division by a pulling of lots came to naught.[90]

The intensity and vulgarity of this all-French battle made the performances of the American contestants seem insipid indeed and climaxed late in June 1824 with the appearance of a heated exchange in the columns of the *Louisiana Gazette*. "A Citizen" submitted a note reading:

> The editor of the *Courier*, C. de St. Romes, a man of universal talent, a writer, orator, soldier, horseman, distinguished swordsman, and marksman, Reared in the Grand Opera of Paris, inventor of the new and graceful step in dancing called '*Le Fendu*' which is performed by first loosening the suspenders and then with the activity of a harlequin bringing the posterior in contact with the floor and again vaulting into the air. This great man accuses Mr. Marigny of not speaking his language correctly. He ought to remember that it is not known that his candidate Mr. Villerie [*sic*] can speak at all; he once attempted to make a speech to both houses of the Legislature when he commenced by opening his mouth and ended with a gape. We have yet to look for a specimen of his writing.[91]

St. Romes replied the following day:

> We read this morning in the *Louisiana Gazette*, a very mean paragraph, from a very mean writer, Bernard De Marigny, *candidate for ever and ever* for the office of Governor, which he shall never get, notwithstanding all his journeys, and the handsome Spanish songs and *Boleros*, with which he treated the voters of the upper Fourche, his promises to some, and his threats to others, in short, those delicate means which excited a feeling of pity in the mind of every one . . . we have often said and we still say, that Mr. de Marigny does not know two words of French.[92]

In such fashion did the Gallic host so divide itself that Johnson's sanguine predictions of success proved completely well founded in the July elections. He carried every Florida parish, but Thomas's own East Baton Rouge and piled up a sufficient vote even in the interior French country to outdistance Villeré and Marigny in the total count. Butler and Thomas trailed very far behind. So Louisiana was to have two American governors in succession, and the French could look with sorrow and growing wisdom at the final tally. Their combined vote had exceeded that of the Americans by 3,115 to 3,071.[93]

If nothing else, the gubernatorial election of 1824 highlighted the ideological emptiness of Louisiana politics of the period. No issues had been decided; indeed none had been discussed. The all-consuming concerns remained the old ones of ethnic dominance and personal ascendancy within the contending factions. Nor had national interests been reflected in the campaigns. The *Louisiana Courier* and the *Argus* both supported Villeré, though the first backed Andrew Jackson and the second championed Henry Clay. The Jacksonian *Louisiana Advertiser* endorsed Henry Johnson, whose national loyalties probably lay with John Quincy Adams,[94] and the pro-Adams *St. Francisville Asylum* served as the principal organ of the pro-Jackson Thomas Butler. Mazureau, who loathed Jackson, had thrown all his strength behind the senatorial bid of Edward Livingston, a pronounced champion of the General, primarily because Livingston had long served the French cause, which Mazureau headed in Louisiana. An intimate friend of Clay, Josiah Johnston profited in the same race from the aid of such staunch Jacksonians as John B. Dawson, Martin Gordon, Isaac Baker, and Walter H. Overton,[95] none of whom liked Livingston and all of whom detested Mazureau. These same men during the same time span aligned in different combinations to contest the presidential election, but as yet no clear-cut national political affiliation had emerged in Louisiana comparable to that which developed over the course of the next decade. Even during the later period of greater devotion to national party identity, there would be not infrequent returns to the ethnic and personality loyalties so obvious in the governor's race of 1824, a tendency which kept Louisiana politics particularly unpredictable in the Jacksonian era.

Despite the intensity of the gubernatorial contest, the presidential campaign had not been completely forgotten. The uncertainty surrounding Jackson's candidacy until early 1823 inhibited somewhat any vigorous campaigning by adherents of the various nominees, and even such committed champions of Jackson as Livingston, Grymes, and Duncan held back from active participation in the General's cause until its prospects of success could be clarified.[96] But by midsummer Jackson's chances seemed far more favorable,[97] the campaign picked up speed, and the press began to devote greater attention to the claims of the various aspirants. Even then, however, interest remained largely concentrated in New Orleans and, to a lesser degree, in St. Francisville, the greater part of the rural section of the state, remaining relatively placid during the whole contest.[98] James Beardslee, editor of the *Louisiana Advertiser*, acknowledged as the principal American paper in the state, took the lead in sponsoring Jackson's candidacy. P. K. Wagner of the *Orleans Gazette* and James M. Bradford of the *Louisiana Journal* (St. Francisville) joined him in vigorous support of the General, with intermittent and rather pedestrian assistance from J. D. de St. Romes, the foreign-French editor of the *Louisiana Courier*. Clay's chief advocacy came from R. D. Richardson of the *Louisiana Gazette* and Manuel Cruzat of the *Argus*, who had the distinction of being one of the rarities of the day, a Creole newspaper editor, while John Quincy Adams won the backing of Joel K. Mead in the *Mercantile Advertiser* and George Bissett in the *Asylum*.

In Louisiana elsewhere the campaign concentrated its greatest attention on the individual strengths and weaknesses of the candidates, although it did give substantial recognition to a variety of sectional and political problems which transcended this competition of personalities. Despite the large New England backing which gathered around him, for example, Adams' backers had to combat the fierce anti-Yankee sentiment so common in Louisiana and vigorously deny that his conversion to Jeffersonianism represented only a transient phase in a long political career, an interlude which would soon give way to the resurgence of the inborn Federalist tenets normal to a man bearing the Adams name. That charge severely damaged Adams, representing him as a threat to the western states, a deceiver whose opposition to the acquisition of Louisiana exposed his real intent to maintain a New England and Eastern supremacy which amounted to nothing less than Federalism in new garb.[99] Not even the common admission that his illustrious career made him unquestionably the man best trained for the presidency could overcome these fears among the mass of the people,[100] allowing opposition spokesmen to claim that his candidacy found support only among a "few yankee pedlers and school masters stuck in every one of our villages, political priests, and federal lawyers."[101]

Crawford had so few personal contacts with Louisiana that his candidacy never attracted any sort of following in the state. At first there had been some rumors that Governor Robertson and William L. Brent might attempt to organize a faction in his support, but the folly of such a course became so quickly obvious that they both abandoned any such plans and rallied behind Clay.[102] The congressional caucus of February 1824, which pronounced in Crawford's favor, produced little response in Louisiana except from those who seized it as an opportunity to denounce politicians who "have set themselves up as being better judges of the 'people's candidate,' than the people are themselves."[103] The Georgian's candidacy, nationwide as well as in Louisiana, did little more than kill the caucus as a nominating device for the presidency.[104]

In Louisiana, Clay and Jackson in effect had the field to themselves, backed by those bands of friends, relatives and associates who expected so much from the political success of their favorite. Clay benefited particularly from the growing Creole impatience with a national policy which had never seen fit to confer a federal political office of any significance on a native Louisiana, their expectations being that Duralde's influence would certainly change all that with Clay in the White House.[105] Jacksonians, in turn, never tried in their reiterations that the immense debt owed by Louisiana to Jackson for having saved its people from British slavery compelled it to support the Hero of New Orleans. The "very houses we occupy proclaim their choice of Jackson," they said,[106] adding the warning that only his attachments to Louisiana could be relied on to reverse the shameful neglect the state had suffered at the hands of an uncaring nation.[107]

The Clay forces early on adopted as a favorite tactic the ridiculing of Jackson as a political naïf totally devoid of governing skills, a "man on horseback" who might plunge the nation into tyranny or war,[108] at the same time praising the "statesmanship" of the great Kentuckian and the profound political wisdom he would bring to the presidency.[109] They also branded the general as a notoriously sadistic and despotic militarist, known to have inflicted cruel punishment on men in his command for minor infractions of his arbitrary discipline. Jacksonians answered that these charges reflected the same perverse judgment which justified criticism of Jackson's martial law rule in Louisiana at the time of the British invasion. His actions, they claimed, always matched the seriousness of a particular crisis, just as his military rule in New Orleans had been absolutely necessary for the salvation of the city.[110] They added the additional jibe that men who opposed Jackson because of his military service did violence to the memory of Washington.[111]

The constant demeaning of Jackson's political skill and experience struck his admirers as especially wrong headed because they saw in that aspect of his record precisely the point which made him so attractive as a presidential candidate. The long political vacuum of the Era of Good Feeling seemed to them a contrivance of professional hacks designed to lull the public into a lassitude during which they might establish themselves in a perpetual circle of political control. They saw Jackson as a plain and straightforward nonprofessional who would protect the interests of the producing classes of the society and expel the conniving office gluttons from their long-held positions. Compared to Jackson, Dawson insisted, the "other candidates seem to be scientific, skillful politicians, untrammelled by principle,"[112] and Isaac T. Preston made this same point his most telling argument in the major Jacksonian rally of the campaign in New Orleans:

> Since the days of Washington, an usurpation has grown up, in our Government, which if not crushed by the power and virtue of the people will soon destroy the republic. . .
>
> The people have presented *Jackson* as their candidate, and he must and will succeed. . . . Plain farmers! he is one of you! Industrious mechanics! Enterprising high minded merchants! he encourages industry and noble enterprize—Hardy seamen! you are his favorites. All these will unite for *Jackson*. And who fears his election? Not the brave, not the honest; he loves honesty, and makes no distinction among men but that of virtue; not the faithful public servant; he is the most faithful; not the Christian, he is one. No—it is the enemies of his country—the faithless public servant—those who prey on the vitals of the people. Let these, and these alone, shake and quake like Belshazzar of old for their time is come.[113]

Thus Jackson appeared in the eyes of his contemporaries as anything but a radical or an innovator. Soldier of the Revolution, Hero of New Orleans, he seemed to them a corrective force, the one man able to restore the nation to *old* ways, to the virtuous republican path made clear by Jefferson and Madison in 1798 and 1800. Class conflict, economic liberalism, or doctrinaire philosophies of any kind simply did not figure in this Louisiana campaign of 1824. Except as imported issues generated elsewhere, they would remain unknown in the state throughout the Jacksonian era.

Only with respect to the tariff did economics play much of a role in the campaign of 1824. Hatred of protective duties on imports flourished throughout Louisiana, not only in the cotton-growing sectors such as the Floridas and the Red River country, but also in New Orleans and the western interior as well. Brent denounced the Tariff of 1824 despite its continued support of duties on imported sugar, railing against the act's reaffirmation of protection and condemning it as "that unjust and unequal burthen upon the Southern States," and the *St. Francisville Asylum* labeled the same enactment an "odious and pernicious measure" ruinous to the whole nation but especially so to Louisiana.[114] His famous, or notorious, championing of the protective doctrine stimulated most of the attacks on Clay, raising charges that he would sacrifice the whole South to the "hemp growers in Kentucky, and the iron manufacturers of Pennsylvania."[115] Jackson's position on the tariff went practically unnoticed, though he also had voted for the 1824 act as a senator from Tennessee. His backers kept this vote hidden as much as possible, and to those such as William S. Hamilton who found this part of Jackson's past disturbing, defenders such as Dawson could write, "I want you to forgive the old fellow's vote upon the Tariff," with clear implications that it amounted to nothing but a minor oversight on the General's part, an indiscretion which sprang from his unfamiliarity with the devious ways of politicians.[116]

Clay at least had the advantage that his protariff stand made him also a champion of the protective duties on sugar, and in a bizarre twist of logic which persisted in Louisiana for years, the sugar planters of Louisiana managed to defend high import rates on their own product while they condemned them on everything else. Clay represented to them a symbol of economic security, and this, plus his support of internal improvements and his many family connections, made him always a favorite in the sugar parishes of the state.[117] He exploited this situation to the fullest in the 1824 campaign, advising Duralde and other friends how to demonstrate that he had done more than anyone else to save the sugar duty in the last Congress while at the same time publicizing Jackson's protariff vote.[118]

As the campaign moved deeper into 1824, the strategies of the opposing camps tended to narrow around clearly defined themes. The Jacksonians reviled the attempted legislative caucus endorsement of Clay as an aristocratic technique clearly demonstrating the determination of professional politicians to keep power out of the hands of people, and to counter it they introduced in the state house of representatives a bill conferring the choice of presidential electors upon the voters. The Clay faction rejected such a measure as unthinkable. It would constitute nothing less than a repudiation of the legislative resolutions favoring their candidate, and even had they not feared the untested strength of the general's partisans in the state, they well knew that French legislators, among whom Clay had his greatest influence, would certainly oppose surrender of any of the paternalistic power so much a part of their tradition. They accordingly took an adamant stand against the proposed measure and sent it down to defeat. There could be no question of where the responsibility lay, for anyone could match the names on the pro-Clay resolutions with those recorded against the electoral bill. The Clay forces had lost another round in the battle for public approval.[119]

Having been balked in their proposals for a change in the electoral law, the Jackson leaders, sure of their strength in the city, hit upon a device by which they hoped to prove Jackson's standing as the true choice of the people. In mid-May a self-appointed committee made up of Jean B. Plauché, Bartholomew Grima, J. B. Labatut, W. C. Withers, and Isaac Preston wrote to all New Orleans candidates seeking election to the legislature in the approaching July canvass and asked for an expression of their feelings on the presidential contenders. They explained that the committee proposed drawing up an all-

Jackson ticket, so that friends of the general might cast their ballots for men pledged in turn to cast their votes for him in November.[120] Assurances of loyalty flooded in from the Jackson candidates, and Davezac's reply set the tone in its praise for the "greatest services ever rendered to a whole nation by a man."[121] On June 5, Preston presided over an enthusiastic meeting in one of the most popular meetinghouses in New Orleans, Davis's Ball Room, where Davezac and General Ripley joined the chairman in rousing speeches honoring their favorite, following which the company resolved not to "support any candidate for the legislature, who would, if elected, act in opposition to the will of a majority of the people."[122] A second meeting on June 22 adopted a Jackson legislative ticket made up of Labatut, Davezac, John R. Grymes, C. G. de Armas, P. A. Rousseau, and Alonzo Murphy, and appointed committees of ten to work in each of the city's wards to get out the vote for their nominees.[123]

The anti-Jackson forces immediately protested this "unauthorized" attempt by the general's "pretorian cohorts" to "dictate to the whole community," and protagonists of the opposing factions joined to repudiate the efforts to bind the legislative candidates to any pledge so early in the campaign. They insisted that they too had every intention of obeying the public will in the presidential question, but to make this the whole test of a man's fitness for an assembly seat, they maintained, would minimize the consideration due many other responsibilities perhaps even more important to the local interests of the community. Professing their great admiration and love for General Jackson, they then went on to assail his claims to the White House, with special emphasis on his violence and "insatiable ambition," and finally called a public meeting of their own, at which they adopted an "Independent" legislative ticket, composed of two Adams men, Thomas Urquhart and George Eustis, and four who favored Clay, Etienne Mazureau, J. J. Mercier, Felix Grima, and Charles Maurian.[124]

While all of Louisiana sweltered through the most blistering June in memory,[125] these opposing forces swept the community with gales of continuous political controversy. Upset by the vigor of the Jackson leaders and disturbed by confidence in the enemy's camp that its candidate would poll a vote large enough to win without sending the election into the national House of Representatives,[126] the Clay men increased their emphasis on what they had come to consider one of the general's greatest weaknesses, his supposed lack of support outside Louisiana and Pennsylvania. Jackson's persistence in remaining in the race, they argued, could accomplish nothing except a division of the western states, which would weaken Clay sufficiently to keep him out of the House and deliver the presidency to Adams or Crawford.[127] The "prospect of Gen. Jackson's election," Richardson warned in his *Louisiana Gazette*, "however dazzling in the eyes of his admirers . . . [is] baseless, as illusive, and as evanescent as a soap bubble." The state, he argued, should not "allow the legitimate influence of Louisiana, on a decision of a most important national question, to be thrown away, on a chimerical and quixotic project of giving a public and irrefragable testimony of its gratitude."[128]

The July elections gave the Jacksonians four of the six legislative seats assigned to New Orleans, a result which the adherents of the general greeted as a sure harbinger of success in November. But the victory came at the price of stirring up new personal animosities which promised possible discord and dispute in the future. Marigny had thrown his considerable strength behind the Jackson ticket on the second day of the election, in exchange for a commitment that Davezac, a foreign Frenchman, would be put aside, and the latter bitterly resented his consequent exclusion from the assembly. Mazueau, too, had gone down to defeat, and he in turn denounced the ingratitude of Davezac and Livingston, complaining that after he had labored to give them political power, their first use of it had been to promote the "Jacksonian pledge" in the legislative campaign which helped bring about his own defeat.[129] Elsewhere in the state the elections essentially ignored the presidential preferences of the candidates,[130] but results suggested that adherents of Clay had won a solid majority in the legislature.[131]

The congressional races, run concurrently with the state canvass, managed to proceed without a single question being raised as to the presidential preferences of the men who would be called upon to cast the state's vote if, as many thought, the election would devolve upon the House. No one offered against incumbents Henry H. Gurley in the Second District and Edward Livingston in the First,[132] though Livingston might well have had opposition had news of his recent activities in Washington not been delayed in reaching New Orleans. They involved repeated efforts to place Davezac in the recently vacated federal district judgeship in Louisiana, an appointment guaranteed to horrify a good portion of the community. "It was certainly a most shocking insult to the feelings of society," Judge Porter confided to his friend Josiah Johnston. "People said the candidate wanted only two of the qualities necessary for the station—Integrity and Knowledge."[133] But the news came only after the election, and Livingston, like Gurley, received practically the unanimous vote of his constituency.

The only real congressional contest of the year produced a stormy fight between William L. Brent and Henry A. Bullard, who had come forward at the solicitation of his friends to punish the incumbent for his slanderous campaign against Johnston two years earlier. Even though Johnston had now moved up to the Senate, Isaac Baker vented his psychopathic hatred of Brent by convincing Bullard that the detractor of their friend must be turned out, and in the optimism of his passion led the politically naïve Alexandria lawyer to believe that the whole western district shared his determination to oust the incumbent. Brent remained in Washington during the campaign, pleading illness in his family, while Bullard toured the parishes in exhaustive exertion. The turning point came when the impressible Baker overplayed his hand in publishing a pamphlet so violent in its attacks upon Brent that it aroused the public to his defense. Bewildered and hurt, Bullard finally wrote Johnston that all had miscarried, leaving Brent successful once again and the world indeed awry.[134]

As the summer months slipped away, the campaign grew wearisome in its repetitions. Despite the exertions of the press, public interest in the race began to lag, but behind the scenes political managers of the various factions filled their days with elaborate consultation and planning. The Clay camp expended the greatest energy, desperately looking for some way to boost its candidate's strength in the East. Crawford seemed certain to carry Virginia and Georgia, Adams dominated New England, and Jackson held the lead in the middle-Atlantic states. Clay had to pick up at least a few votes in these areas to get to the House. Once there he was safe, conventional wisdom being that congressmen would give their Speaker an overwhelming victory. Josiah Johnston spent the last months of the campaign scouring the eastern seaboard for Clay support, finally managing to strike an agreement with the Adams men of New York. Contingent upon Clay's carrying Louisiana, Thurlow Weed pledged to divert seven of his state's electoral votes from Adams to the Kentuckian, a move which would push Clay ahead of Crawford, keep the Georgian out of the House, and humiliate the New Yorker's pro-Crawford rivals such as Martin Van Buren.[135] It remained now for the Clay men to make sure of Louisiana.

Within the state, confusion and indecision mounted on all sides. Both the Jackson and Clay camps resounded with confident predictions of certain victory, but everyone recognized such talk as sheer bluster. Even old hands like Alexander Porter and John Linton, one of New Orleans' busiest and best-informed factors, admitted their inability to fathom what the legislature's choice would be.[136] When the assembly convened in mid-November the state watched in fascination as the battle for votes raged among the members, who found themselves wined and dined and solicited by tenders of political honors.[137] When the issue finally came to rest, the Clay forces had been undone.

Much the smallest of the three contending camps, the Adams faction held the balance of power between the other two groups, and they had long recognized the possibility of using this advantage to win at least a part of Louisiana's five votes.[138] Their eleven legislative members, however, could not agree among themselves as to a preference between Jackson and Clay, and as late as November 18 they had not decided which of the two to support as a second choice. Clearly that determination would rest upon what offers came to them from the Clay and Jackson men.[139] Aware of Johnston's agreement with Weed and thus of their need for all five Louisiana votes, the Clay leaders were less willing than the Jacksonians to accede to the granting of the two votes which the Adams men demanded in exchange for their backing. They tried desperately to track down and round up five absentee legislators who would give them a clear majority in the assembly vote and thus an uncompromised victory. Those reinforcements could never be found, and on November 22 six Adams men joined the twenty-four Jacksonians to outvote the Clay ticket thirty to twenty-eight, giving three electoral votes to Jackson and two to Adams.[140]

Behind the result many saw a mass of intrigue. John Clay raged against what he called this "dirty Bargain" as the secret work of Gov. Henry Johnson,[141] who had long been rumored sympathetic to Adams though he had given a personal pledge of support to Clay.[142] No one ever satisfactorily explained why five members of the assembly simply failed to appear on the day appointed by law for the balloting, but in one case, at least, there is much to ponder. Placide Bossier, a strong Clay partisan, had remained home in Natchitoches to accept a challenge to a horse race tendered him by a known Adams sympathizer. As John Sibley wryly summed up the outcome to his expectant son-in-law, Josiah Johnston, "Bossier lost the Race & Clay the Election."[143]

The effect of the Louisiana vote on the New York balloting remains highly problematic. Weed insisted at a later date that the failure of Clay to carry the state released his group from its pledge to divert seven votes to the Kentuckian,[144] and Clay came out of the New York contest with but four of the total promised him. It seems impossible for Weed to have known of the Louisiana results at the time of the New York ballot, however, and the Clay camp most likely had simply been hoodwinked, for Weed must have realized the folly of allowing the Speaker to move ahead of Crawford and into a House vote, which he certainly would have won against the New Yorker's candidate, Adams.[145] As it was, the loss of Louisiana's five votes, even had Weed been true to his pledge, put Clay fourth highest on the electoral tally, trailing Jackson, Adams, and Crawford, and his name could not therefore be presented to the House when it met to resolve the deadlock in this election which had produced a majority for none of the contenders. Looked at in another way, the electoral count which gave Crawford forty-one votes and Clay thirty-seven would have read Clay forty-two and Crawford forty-one had the Kentuckian's majority held fast in the Louisiana legislature. Dr. Sibley's wry comment carried more truth than perhaps even he understood—Clay *had* lost the election in Louisiana, and now the nation could await the House choice from among his rivals. In Louisiana, as elsewhere, the result would be explosive.

"In the name of God and the Love of your Country prevent his Election!" John Clay pleaded with Josiah Stoddard Johnston as the House of Representatives made ready to choose the next president of the United States.[146] Like many others, he found the prospect of Andrew Jackson in the White House repellent and frightening.

But in Louisiana, Jacksonians delighted in the assurance that their candidate's plurality in the electoral vote of 1824 would finally bring him the rewards he so richly deserved. Even if the state had been forced to split its vote, they felt that the result saved them from the disgrace of ingratitude to its greatest benefactor. None exulted more extravagantly than James McKaraher, a Pennsylvania Irishman who had long been a loud and contentious part of the New Orleans scene. Sometime professor at the Collège d'Orléans,[147] McKaraher purchased the *Louisiana Gazette* from R. D. Richardson late in the presidential campaign and transformed that Clay sheet into the brashest and most fanatical of the pro-Jackson journals in the state. His wisdom now vindicated, on the morning following the choice of the Louisiana electors he proclaimed to his readers: "The market has been rummaged, and the wine cellars called, presses have been bought, and writers hired to bring upon the State of Louisiana the contempt of her sister states, yet all have filed and *Jackson* is *Triumphant.* From New York to the Gulf of Mexico—Justice is done to the Hero of Orleans."[148]

In practically every subsequent issue, McKaraher kept up the flood of self-congratulation and thanksgiving, hailing this "triumph of the people" over evil politicians and giving wide circulation to a common Louisiana impression that the election was over. He labeled the procedures of the coming House choice mere formalities, bound to confirm Jackson as unquestionably the choice of the majority of the citizens of the republic.[149]

Much of the force of this argument in Louisiana could be traced to the peculiarities of her own constitution, for inevitably the function of the House in the coming presidential choice would be seen as comparable to that of the State's assembly when it regularly balloted in the official election of Louisiana governors. That the legislature picked from the two highest names on a list while the House would choose from three seemed no real difference at all. And everyone knew that no legislature had ever failed to name as governor the man with the highest number of votes—why should not the same respect be given to the public will in this presidential contest? The sanctity of this obligation had only recently been reaffirmed, when a brief attempt to bypass Henry Johnson for Jacques Villeré in the legislative gubernatorial election a few weeks earlier failed decisively, smothered under protests against any such shameful defiance of the people's will.[150] For McKaraher no doubt existed—the House was bound in honor to follow a similar course, and Jacksonians over the state agreed. Isaac Baker spoke for them all in his observation that "according to our Louisiana notions about pluralities the old general must be president."[151] In high spirits, they could hardly wait for the Hero to come into his own.

But wait they must, and once again attention turned to more localized political manipulations. Henry Johnson's resignation from the Senate to become governor required the selection of his successor in the opening days of the legislative session in November, and for the first time the full effect of Marigny's strategy during the July election could be measured. His efforts encouraged the Creoles to demand a great share of national offices, and their full strength now gathered behind Dominique Bouligny for the Senate post. Livingston's disappointment at being passed over by his French friends found solace in their pledge that if he did not oppose Bouligny they would assure him of their complete backing against Josiah Johnston when he stood for reelection. Bouligny won the seat, and Johnston found himself on notice that he faced a major challenge to his own in January of 1825.[152]

With so much attention centered on the coming showdown for the presidency, it is surprising to find that in neither of these senatorial elections did questions of national factional loyalties play any part. Once again the ethnic issue pushed all other considerations aside. Livingston and the Clay enthusiast Bouligny had no difficulty in cementing their alliance, the eminent lawyer remaining thoroughly acceptable to the Gallic population because of past services and his ties to them by marriage. At the same time avowals came to Johnston of support from Jacksonian and anti-Jacksonian Americans alike. He needed every bit of aid he could get, so skillfully did the Livingston forces manage their campaign. Marigny scampered to their side when told that a Johnston victory would make the senator a powerful favorite to succeed Henry Johnson as governor; old General Thomas willingly acceded to suggestions that he contest the seat, opening dangerous inroads into Johnston's American backing; and Florida legislators began to receive a flood of reports that the incumbent had been the major voice at Washington defending the hated Orleans Navigation Company, which monopolized commerce through the Canal Carondelet and forced the lake trade between New Orleans and the north-shore parishes, to pay what many considered exorbitant fees and tolls.[153] Brent and Gurley, longtime personal enemies of Johnston, did what they could from Washington to oust Clay's great friend in favor of Livingston, Brent filling Ouachita and the Red River parishes with renewed tales of how the incumbent championed large land claims and defended the hated tariff, while Gurley added supposed confirmation of the senator's subservience to the Orleans Navigation Company.[154]

It required all the energies of Johnston's friends to save him from defeat. Livingston felt so certain of victory that Davezac was already in the field to succeed him in the national House.[155] But the phalanx behind Johnston proved too deep and strong. The French support which Livingston so much relied upon could not withstand the counter-pressures exerted by Duralde and Henry Clay, and Philemon Thomas shifted his own votes to Johnston after the first ballot in the state senate. Meanwhile, Governor Johnson, W. H. Overton, and Isaac L. Baker, as well as others, vigorously denied all rumors unfavorable to Johnston, even when they had no knowledge of the facts giving Martin Gordon, president of the Orleans Navigation Company and an ardent Jacksonian, time to amass in secret the backing of stockholders grateful to the Clay incumbent. The fact that Livingston's election would give New Orleans three of the state's five members of Congress also weighed heavily on Johnston's side. He won reelection by a thirty-two-to-twenty-seven vote,[156] causing that staunch Jacksonian, W. H. Overton, to exult, "Mr. Livingston will never be a Senator in Congress."[157] As in the gubernatorial campaign of the preceding July, tempers had run high in both senatorial elections, but certainly not because of rivalry between Clay and Jackson men. Once again ethnic loyalties and sheer personal antagonisms had determined the outcome. It would be the last time they enjoyed such complete supremacy.

As the House election of a president in February drew closer, excitement in Louisiana mounted beyond anything felt in the days of the regular campaign. Crowds milled in post offices every mail day for news, and the uncertainty began to irritate even the most phlegmatic.[158] The Jacksonians strove to keep up their confidence with constant assurances of final success and celebrated the January 8 victory anniversary in New Orleans as a prelude to the promised festivities of the general's inauguration.[159] But through the press and in the circles of private conversation, clear hints and speculations began to suggest that all was not right in Washington. Rumor had it that Brent and Gurley would never cast their votes for Jackson, that Clay had been bought by the Adams party, and that corrupt alliances meant to divert the House from its duty.[160] McKaraher denounced such stories as shear fantasy, promising that if any Louisiana congressman, "knowing as he does that nine-tenths of his constituents are in favor of Gen. Jackson," should nonetheless "vote against the General, he will receive, as he will merit, the contempt and detestation of those whose interest he may betray."[161]

The long winter weeks stretched out, with extensive time for gossip and conjecture on all these moot points. Rain poured down in endless torrents from November to March, and roads almost merged with the swampland. There was little to do but sit and talk and wonder.[162] By mid-February the frosts had gone for good, and though the rains still pelted the countryside, men could look forward impatiently to spring. Those interested in public affairs, however, found little time to contemplate the vagaries of nature, for on February 28 the news from Washington finally arrived—Adams was to be president, and with the vote of Louisiana registered in his favor.

That morning McKaraher draped the *Louisiana Gazette* in black. Skulls and crossbones headed the dreary announcement and studded the paper's columns. "It may be as well for us," the story ran, "to record our own disgrace. To be the Heralds of our own infamy. Louisiana has, in the persons of her representatives, bound herself by a sacred compact to honor and obey his Excellency, J. Q. Adams. The deed is past and recorded, it must be, strictly, complied with." This submissive note recognizing the legality of the election behind him, McKaraher then burst with rage. He pronounced mighty curses on Clay and reviled Brent and Gurley, who had cast their votes for Adams while Edward Livingston proved loyal to Jackson. They were, said McKaraher, guilty of "shameful treachery, unparalleled in history . . . Treachery! Treachery! Treachery!" As for the two ingrates, the shameless subverters of the people's will, "Their funeral will take place as soon as a proper stage can be erected for their *elevation*."[163]

McKaraher's indignation mirrored a Jacksonian fury which swept across the nation. From Philadelphia the general received a passionate letter which very likely reflected his own brooding thoughts: "Louisianians! Degraded—Ungrateful Men!! To vote against you! Who under God, they are indebted for the possession of their soil!—The Protector of the chastity of their wives and daughters!! You saved them from the brutal lust of a mercenary soldiery! . . . The heart sickens at the thought." Isaac Baker hastened to assure Jackson that Brent and Gurley had damned themselves forever: "I scarcely think Brent will ever return to Louisiana," Baker wrote, and he went on to predict that the people would rise up to crush "Clay & Co." in 1828. Jackson unquestionably agreed. Andrew J. Donelson urged Louisiana followers of the general to launch immediate attacks upon Brent and Gurley, and Baker reported with great gusto the appearance in New Orleans of a doggerel poem entitled "A Defence of Col. William Lovetruth Bluster," obviously aimed at Brent.[164]

In some other quarters news of the Adams election brought joy and unanticipated elation. The *Argus*, the *Mercantile Advertiser*, and the *Asylum* congratulated the people on their escape from the clutches of the violent soldier into the custody of the statesman, and ridiculed the emotionalism of McKaraher.[165] Like the *Natchitoches Courier*, they insisted that Adams had been the second choice of Clay's backers in the state and that

Brent and Gurley had thus truly reflected the popular will of Louisiana.[166] Such refusal to recognize the state's betrayal added to the Jacksonians' already towering anger, and they found in Clay's soon-announced appointment as secretary of state proof of Cong. George Kremer's charge that the Kentuckian had indeed sold himself to Adams.[167] McKaraher and St. Romes of the *Courier* threatened physical violence against C. W. Duhy, editor of the *Mercantile Advertiser*, for his defense of Clay and Adams, only adding to the troubles of Duhy, who had already been challenged to a duel by a furious Jackson sympathizer.[168]

Nothing incensed Louisiana followers of Jackson more than the torrent of blame and ridicule which now poured down upon the state from all quarters of the nation, and though it must have made McKaraher writhe, he printed it all for the enlightenment of his readers. In Philadelphia a birthday banquet for the general toasted him with a typical sentiment: "Louisiana—Saved from British pollution by the valor of Jackson, to be a Harlot, in the hands of a Western Gambler. Her black ingratitude will call down the vengeance of Heaven!"[169] No wonder that friends reported Brent fearful that he might be killed should he ever return to the state.[170]

Despite their protestations of innocence, the votes of Brent and Gurley clearly ran counter to their previous commitments. Brent, especially, had pledged in May of 1824 to "vote the sentiments of those I represent" should the election go to the House,[171] and Gurley maintained immediately after the fateful ballot that he had wavered until the last moment and voted for Adams only when it appeared that it was impossible for Jackson to win.[172] It is clear, however, that as early as September 1824, both Brent and Gurley had already decided to abandon Jackson in the House, no matter what the electoral vote in Louisiana turned out to be.[173] Unable to prove this, Louisiana Jacksonians nonetheless remained convinced of Clay's perfidy and found it therefore easy to believe the worst of their representatives, especially since Brent figured prominently as a defender of the Kentuckian in all aspects of the controversy.[174]

In such fashion did the Jacksonians see all their dark forebodings of the previous months crystallize into reality. The professional politicians had been victorious over the people; dishonesty, bargain, and corruption had robbed the sovereign citizens of their republican birthright and plunged the nation back into the grip of the hated principles which had prevailed before Jefferson killed the evils of Federalism. Now again the aristocrats held sway—not the aristocrats of wealth, perhaps, but the aristocrats of irresponsible power. Jackson's close friend John Eaton vented his anger in the observation that "Corruption stalks thro our land—our politicians like the monks of old, claim to have everything of govt. science in their hand, & of right, apart from the people, an authority to rule." Those sentiments found echo in McKaraher's judgment:

> From this time forward; at least as long as the "*Era of correct principles*" shall prevail; let the shoemaker seal up his mouth with his own wax; the hatter not presume to intrude his smutty face into public concerns; the carpenter confine his sinewy arms to their proper sphere, the work bench; and let the blacksmith beware that his bellows does not blow opinions that are seditious, for the "*era of correct principles has commenced.*" Let the

people cease to think, and the printer to propagate their opinions—for who will respect them when their own representatives treat them with contempt.[175]

The Jacksonian cause had been born.

Notes for "Birth of a Cause"

[1]Marquis James, *The Life of Andrew Jackson* (New York, 1940), 257; Charles Hunt, *The Life of Edward Livingston* (New York, 1864), 197-98.

[2]Edward Livingston to Andrew Jackson, September 21, 1814, in Andrew Jackson Donelson Papers, Library of Congress (hereafter cited as Donelson Papers). John S. Bassett, *The Life of Andrew Jackson* (New York, 1916), 1:154.

[3]William B. Hatcher, *Edward Livingston* (Baton Rouge, 1940), 215.

[4]Ibid., 215-25; *A Letter to Edward Livingston, Esquire, Delegate from Louisiana to General Congress at Washington City, on the subject of the Speech Delivered by Him, at Washington, at the Late Celebration of the Anniversary of the 8th of January, 1815* (Natchez, Miss., 1828), 9-11. Livingston seems to have played a brave role in the 1814-15 campaign, though his arch foe, Vincent Nolte, insists that he left the battleground after December 23 and spent January 8 in a dressing gown anxiously pacing his gallery while the battle progressed. The same charge is made in the anonymous pamphlet cited above, which may well have been written by Nolte.

[5]James, *Andrew Jackson*, 257.

[6]James Parton, *The Life of Andrew Jackson*, 3 vols. (New York, 1860), 2:350. Parton offers no evidence for this statement, but there is little reason to doubt its accuracy.

[7]Ruby Caulfield, *The French Literature of Louisiana* (New York, 1929), 71.

[8]*New Orleans Argus*, June 21, 1828.

[9]Ibid.; *Louisiana Advertiser*, September 20, 1828.

[10]*Louisiana Gazette*, January 10, 1824.

[11]Ibid., June 2, 1826.

[12]Auguste Davezac, "Fragments of Unpublished Reminiscences of Edward Livingston," *United States Magazine and Democratic Review*, 8 (1840): 369.

[13]*New Orleans Argus*, November 15, 1827; J. B. Plauché to Andrew Jackson, June 8, 1822, in Andrew Jackson Papers, Library of Congress (hereafter cited as Jackson Papers).

[14]Vincent Nolte, *Fifty Years in Both Hemispheres* (New York, 1854), 210; J. B. Plauché to Andrew Jackson, June 8, 1822, in Jackson Papers; Andrew Jackson to William B. Lewis, January 15, 1842, in William B. Lewis Papers, New York Public Library (hereafter cited as Lewis Papers).

[15]James Gadsden to Andrew Jackson, April 30, 1820, Jackson to John McLean, March 22, 1824, in Jackson Papers; Thomas B. Robertson to Fulwar Skipwith, May 7, 1820, in Personal Miscellaneous Papers, Library of Congress; James Monroe to Fulwar Skipwith, September 15, 1823, in James Monroe Papers, New York Public Library (hereafter cited as Monroe Papers).

[16]James Gadsden to Andrew Jackson, April 30, 1820, James Scallan to Jackson, December 18, 1820, Andrew Jackson Donelson to Jackson, March 3, 1821, Abner Duncan to Jackson, December 12, 1821, A. P. Hayne to Jackson, October 7, 1823, in Jackson Papers.

[17]Andrew Jackson Donelson to Andrew Jackson, March 3, 1821, Jackson to J. C. Bronough, January 10, 1822, ibid.

[18]Isaac L. Baker to Andrew Jackson, February 18, 1821, ibid.

[19]Elrie Robinson, *Early Feliciana Politics* (St. Francisville, La., 1936), 53-54, 103-108.

[20]Louise Butler, "West Feliciana: A Glimpse of Its History," *Louisiana Historical Quarterly*, 7 (1924): 103.

[21]John B. Dawson to William S. Hamilton, June 29, 1824, in William S. Hamilton Papers, Department of Archives, Louisiana State University, Baton Rouge, La. (hereafter cited as Hamilton Papers).

[22]Maunsel White to Andrew Jackson, April 7, 1827, in Jackson Papers; *Louisiana Gazette*, December 20, 1824.

[23]Alfred Hennen to Andrew Jackson, November 8, 1825, in Jackson Papers.

[24] *Louisiana Gazette*, November 6, 1822, July 8, 1823, January 8, 1824; *St. Francisville Asylum*, August 23, 1823; Josiah S. Johnston to Eliza Johnston, April 29, 1823, John Linton to Johnston, April 12, 1824, John H. Overton to Johnston, May 20, 1824, Walter H. Overton to Johnston, April 22, 1824, all in Johnston Papers, Historical Society of Pennsylvania, Philadelphia, Penn. (hereafter cited as Johnston Papers); Nathaniel Cox to Stephen Austin, August 6, 1824, in Austin Barker, ed., *The Austin Papers. Annual Report of the American Historical Association for 1919, Vol. 2* (Washington, D. C., 1924), 872.

[25]*Louisiana Advertiser*, June 3, 11, 12, 14, 19, 1823; Isaac L. Baker to William S. Hamilton, March 29, 1823, in Hamilton Papers; James Brown to Josiah S. Johnston, April 11, 1823, in Johnston Papers. For a discussion of different developments in a similar situation in Kentucky, see Arthur M. Schlesinger, Jr., *The Age of Jackson* (Boston, 1945), 31-32, 36.

[26]*Louisiana Gazette*, April 7, 1824; Alexander Porter to Josiah S. Johnston, April 3, 1824, in Johnston Papers.

[27]Dicks, Booker, and Company to William S. Hamilton, March 27, April 20, 1823, in Hamilton Papers.

[28]*Louisiana House Journal*, 1823, p. 103. See also, the *Louisiana Gazette*, January 3, June 28, December 20, 1821, June 3, 1822.

[29]*Louisiana Gazette*, January 10, 1822.

[30]Ibid.; Alexander Porter to Josiah S. Johnston, January 12, 1821, Thomas B. Robertson to Johnston, December 24, 1822, in Johnston Papers.

[31]*Louisiana Gazette*, July 28, September 19, December 15, 1824.

[32]Ibid., September 19, 1824; *Louisiana Journal*, June 15, 1826.

[33]Curtis Nettels, "The Mississippi Valley and the Federal Judiciary, 1807-1837," *Mississippi Valley Historical Review*, 12 (1925): 203-206. *Louisiana Courier*, January 12, 1832.

[34]*Louisiana Gazette*, May 2, 1822.

[35]Ibid., January 10, 1823.

[36]*St. Francisville Asylum*, August 30, 1823.

[37]*Louisiana Gazette*, January 8, 1824.

[38]For these early land laws in the Territory of Orleans, see Clarence Carter, ed., *The Territory of Orleans* (Washington, D. C., 1948), 408-14, Vol. 9 of Clarence Carter, *The Territorial Papers of the United States*, 26 vols. (Washington, D. C., 1934-1962).

[39]Henry Clay to ______, February 16, 1831, in Thomas Clay Papers, Library of Congress.

[40]H. Lavergne to Josiah S. Johnston, December 11, 1830, in Johnston Papers.

[41]Alexander Porter to Josiah S. Johnston, January 19, 1831, ibid.

[42]*St. Francisville Asylum*, August 22, September 19, 1822; *Washita Gazette* (Monroe), October 24, 1825; *United States v. The Mayor, Aldermen, and Citizens of the Cities of Philadelphia and New Orleans*, 609 ff. See also the many letters of D. W. Coxe to Josiah S. Johnston in defense of his Maison Rouge claim, in Johnston Papers.

[43]Carter, ed., *Territory of Orleans*, 967-69; Henry Flower to Josiah S. Johnston, January 14, 1825, in Johnston Papers.

[44]*L'Ami des Lois*, May 14, 1822; *Natchitoches Courier*, February 21, 1825; K. McCrummen to Josiah S. Johnston, February 1, 1824, Thomas B. Brashear to Johnston, December 10, 1825, John Sibley to Johnston, January 3, 1826, in Johnston Papers.

[45]*Debates in Congress*, 20th Cong., 2nd Sess., 46; 24th Cong., 1st Sess., appendix, 61-62.

[46]See, for example, Henry Boyce to Josiah S. Johnston, February 1, 1824, Henry Bryce to Johnston, November 5, 1824, in Johnston Papers.

[47]*Louisiana House Journal*, 1826, p. 79.

[48]*Louisiana Gazette*, January 10, 1823; Thomas B. Robertson to Josiah S. Johnston, November 7, 1821, in Johnston Papers.

[49]Henry Boyce to Josiah S. Johnston, February 1, 1824, in Johnston Papers.

[50]*Louisiana Courier*, January 10, 1823.

[51]John C. Calhoun to Jacques Villeré, November 25, 1820, in Jackson Papers.

[52]Augustin Macarty to Andrew Jackson, December 30, 1819, ibid.

[53]Edward Everett Diary, May 5, 1829, in Edward Everett Papers, Massachusetts Historical Society.

[54]Etienne Mazureau to Henry Clay, February 6, 1841 (Louis Hermann File), Letters of Application and Recommendation During the Administration of Martin Van Buren, William Henry Harrison, and John Tyler, 1837-1845, in Record Group 59, General Records of the Department of State, National Archives, Washington, D. C.

[55]James Brown to Henry Clay, April 26, 1822, in Henry Clay Papers, Library of Congress; D. W. Coxe to Josiah S. Johnston, March 10, 1824, in Johnston Papers; H. B. Trist to Nicholas P. Trist, March 31, 1828, in Nicholas P. Trist Papers, Library of Congress.

[56]Joseph G. Tregle, Jr., "Louisiana and the Tariff, 1816-1846," *Louisiana Historical Quarterly*, 25 (1942): 48.

[57]*St. Francisville Asylum*, April 17, 1824; T. S. Slocum to Josiah S. Johnston, December 8, 1824, in Johnston Papers.

[58]*Louisiana Gazette*, January 3, 1821, January 10, 1823; *St. Francisville Asylum*, May 29, 1822.

[59]*L'Ami des Lois*, January 17, 1823.

[60]Andrew Jackson to J. C.. Bronough, January 10, 1822, Isaac L. Baker to Jackson, February 14, 1823, in Jackson Papers.

[61]James Brown to Henry Clay, April 26, 1822, in Henry Clay Papers.

[62]Lafayette Saunders to Andrew Jackson, July 28, 1823, in Jackson Papers.

[63]*Louisiana Advertiser*, August 4, 1823.

[64]Alexander Porter to Josiah S. Johnston, January 19, 1831, in Johnston Papers.

[65]H. B. Trist to Nicholas P. Trist, May 12, 1828, in Trist Papers.

[66]James Brown to Henry Clay, April 26, 1822, in Henry Clay Papers.

[67]*St. Francisville Asylum*, May 29, August 22, 1822.

[68]*Louisiana Gazette*, July 9, 1822.

[69]Isaac L. Baker to Josiah S. Johnston, July 26, November 11, 1822, in Johnston Papers; *Louisiana Herald*, June 9, 1824.

[70]*Louisiana Gazette*, July 4, 1822; Samuel R. Overton to Andrew Jackson, June 9, 1822, in Jackson Papers; Alexander Porter to Josiah S. Johnston, July 8, 1824, in Johnston Papers.

[71]Isaac L. Baker to William S. Hamilton, December 26, 1822, in Hamilton Papers.

[72]Lafayette Saunders to Andrew Jackson, July 28, 1823, in Jackson Papers.

[73]Isaac L. Baker to William S. Hamilton, February 14, 1823, ibid.; Alexander Porter to Josiah S. Johnston, February 16, 1823, in Johnston Papers; *St. Francisville Asylum*, February 13, 1823.

[74]Isaac L. Baker to Andrew Jackson, February 14, 1823, in Jackson Papers.

[75]Isaac L. Baker to Andrew Jackson, February 26, 1823, ibid.

[76]Isaac L. Baker to Andrew Jackson, May 3, 1823, Samuel R. Overton to Jackson, June 27, 1823, ibid.; *Louisiana Courier*, March 19, 1823; *Louisiana Advertiser*, March 18, 22, 1823.

[77]Hatcher's statement in *Livingston*, 318, that "the national election was practically the sole issue in the 1824 state campaign" has no merit. Even a cursory reading of the newspaper comments of the period reveals that the presidential race went virtually unmentioned in the gubernatorial contest. Moreover, Hatcher says that the "Jackson forces made the mistake of dividing their support between the two [Marigny and Villeré]." Besides the error in assuming that there *was* a "Jackson force" in this election, Hatcher mistakes the position of Villeré, who was, if anything, a Clayite.

[78]*Louisiana Courier*, February 5, 1824; *St. Francisville Asylum*, February 27, August 16, September 6, 1823; Isaac L. Baker to William S. Hamilton, December 26, 1822, in Hamilton Papers.

[79]*Louisiana Gazette*, November 28, December 5, 1823; *Louisiana Courier*, January 17, 21, February 9, March 23, May 1, 29, 1824; *L'Ami des Lois*, February 16, 1824; *New Orleans Argus*, April 26, 1824; Ferdinand de Feriet to Janica de Feriet, November 21, 1823, in Feriet Family Papers, Howard-Tilton Memorial Library, Tulane University, New Orleans, La.

[80]Isaac L. Baker to William S. Hamilton, December 26, 1822, January 14, 1823, in Hamilton Papers; *Louisiana Gazette*, March 13, 16, 17, 31, April 20, 29, 1824; *Louisiana Courier*, March 5, 1824; *Louisiana Herald*, February 18, 1824.

[81]*Louisiana Advertiser*, September 5, 1823.

[82]Ibid., August 15, October 1, 1823.

[83]Henry Johnson to Josiah S. Johnston, October 24, 1823, in Johnston Papers; *Louisiana Herald*, September 17, 1823; *Louisiana Gazette*, November 7, 1823.

[84]*L'Ami des Lois*, December 15, 26, 22, 1823; *Louisiana Gazette*, December 16, 17, 19, 23, 1823; *Louisiana Advertiser*, December 5, 15, 19, 23, 1823.

[85]*Louisiana Advertiser*, January 1, 1824.

[86] Isaac L. Baker to William S. Hamilton, January 16, 1824, in Hamilton Papers; Joseph Walker to Josiah S. Johnston, January 5, 1824; Johnston to Eliza Johnston, January 15, 1824, in Johnston Papers; *Louisiana Advertiser*, January 8, 13, 14, 1824; *Louisiana Courier*, January 13, 1824.

[87]*Louisiana Courier*, June 24, 1824. For Johnson's successful campaigning against his rivals, see, for example, Reuben Kemper to Josiah S. Johnston, March 18, 1824, in Johnston Papers.

[88]*Louisiana Advertiser*, December 4, 1823.

[89]Ibid., January 19, 20, 21, 1824.

[90]*Louisiana Gazette*, March 19, 1824.

[91]Ibid., June 28, 1824.

[92]Ibid., June 29, 1824; *Louisiana Courier*, June 28, 29, 30, 1824.

[93]*Louisiana Senate Journal*, 1824, p. 3.

[94]Isaac L. Baker to William S. Hamilton, June 15, 1824, in Hamilton Papers; John Clay to Josiah S. Johnston, November 30, 1824, in Johnston Papers; *Louisiana Gazette*, October 11, 1824.

[95]Walter H. Overton to Josiah S. Johnston, January 13, 1824, Martin Gordon to Johnston, March 10, 15, 1824, in Johnston Paper; Isaac L. Baker to William S. Hamilton, January 16, 1824, in Hamilton Papers.

[96]See Baker's complaint against their inactivity in the legislative caucus fight of May, 1823, in Isaac L. Baker to Andrew Jackson, May 3, 1823, in Jackson Papers.

[97]Isaac L. Baker to William S. Hamilton, July 25, 1823, in Hamilton Papers.

[98]Walter H. Overton to Josiah S. Johnston, November 22, 1824, John Linton to Johnston, November 14, 1824, in Johnston Papers.

[99]*Louisiana Gazette*, January 14, 17, February 7, 1823; *Louisiana Advertiser*, March 11, 1824; *St. Francisville Asylum*, May 8, 1824.

[100]T. S. Slocum to Josiah S. Johnston, December 8, 1824, Charles T. Scott to Johnston, July 24, 1824, in Johnston Papers; *Louisiana Gazette*, July 26, 1823.

[101]*Louisiana Gazette*, November 17, 1824.

[102]William L. Brent to Henry Clay, September 3, 1824, in Henry Clay Papers; James M. Bradford to Josiah S. Johnston, December 21, 1824, in Johnston Papers; *Louisiana Gazette*, May 5, 1824.

[103]*St. Francisville Asylum*, March 13, June 19, 1824; Alexander Porter to Josiah S. Johnston, April 3, 1824, in Johnston Papers.

[104]See the comments on this point in John Spencer Bassett, ed., *The Correspondence of Andrew Jackson*, 6 vols. (Washington, D. C., 1927-1935), 3:v.

[105]*Louisiana Courier*, July 28, August 2, 1824.

[106]*Louisiana Advertiser*, January 5, 1824; *Louisiana Gazette*, November 17, 1824.

[107]*Louisiana Gazette*, December 1, 1824; *Louisiana Journal*, March 4, 1824.

[108]Charles T. Scott to Josiah S. Johnston, July 24, 1824, in Johnston Papers; *Louisiana Gazette*, May 1, October 11, 1824; *St. Francisville Asylum*, August 16, 1823, April 3, 10, 17, June 26, July 10, 24, 1824; *L'Ami des Lois*, September 12, 1823, April 10, 1824; *New Orleans Mercantile Advertiser*, November 13, 1824.

[109]*Louisiana Gazette*, May 1, 1824; *St. Francisville Asylum*, July 3, 1824.

[110]*Louisiana Courier*, June 19, 1824.

[111]*Louisiana Gazette*, June 10, 1824.

[112]John B. Dawson to William S. Hamilton, June 29, 1824, in Hamilton Papers.

[113]*Louisiana Gazette*, June 7, 1824.

[114]Ibid., September 29, 1824; *St. Francisville Asylum*, May 8, 1824.

[115]*St. Francisville Asylum*, June 19, 1824.

[116]John B. Dawson to William S. Hamilton, June 29, 1824, in Hamilton Papers.

[117]Tregle, "Louisiana and the Tariff," 18 ff.

[118]Henry Clay to Josiah S. Johnston, October 2, 1824, in Johnston Papers; William L. Brent to Clay, September 3, 1824, in Henry Clay Papers.

[119]*Louisiana House Journal*, 1824, p. 113; *Louisiana Herald*, April 28, 1824; *Louisiana Journal*, February 5, 1824; *St. Francisville Asylum*, April 17, May 8, 29, July 10, 1824; *Louisiana Advertiser*, April 3, May 24, 27, 28, June 11, 1824; *Louisiana Gazette*, May 21, June 26, 1824.

[120]*Louisiana Gazette*, May 19, 1824.

[121]*Louisiana Courier*, June 11, 1824; *Louisiana Advertiser*, June 3, 1824.

[122]*Louisiana Gazette*, June 7, 1824.

[123]Ibid., June 24, 1824.

[124]Ibid., May 19, 20, June 8, July 1, 5, 1824; *Louisiana Courier*, June 14, 17, 1824; *St. Francisville Asylum*, June 19, 26, 1824; *Louisiana Advertiser*, May 24, 1824.

[125]John Sibley to Stephen Austin, July 8, 1824, in Barker, ed., *Austin Papers*, Pt. 1:849.

[126]Isaac Baker to William S. Hamilton, June 15, 1824, in Hamilton Papers.

[127]*Louisiana Gazette*, February 24, August 24, 1824; *St. Francisville Asylum*, April 17, 1824.

[128]*Louisiana Gazette*, June 29, July 3, 1824.

[129]Alexander Porter to Josiah S. Johnston, July 8, 1824, in Johnston Papers.

[130]John H. Johnston to Josiah S. Johnston, June 8, 1824, Walter H. Overton to Johnston, June 24, July 10, 1824, Reuben Kemper to Johnston, March 18, 1824, ibid.; Isaac L. Baker to William S. Hamilton, June 15, July 10, 1824, in Hamilton Papers.

[131]*Louisiana Gazette*, July 10, 1824; *Louisiana Journal*, July 22, 1824; Henry Clay to Josiah S. Johnston, August 31, 1824, in Johnston Papers.

[132]*St. Francisville Asylum*, July 10, 1824.

[133]Alexander Porter to Josiah S. Johnston, July 8, 1824, in Johnston Papers.

[134]*Louisiana Herald*, June 9, 16, 23, 20, 1824; Isaac Baker to Josiah S. Johnston, March 5, 1824, John H. Johnston to Johnston, June 19, July 15, 1824, Henry A. Bullard to Johnston, August 5, 1824, all in Johnston Papers.

[135]See, for example, D. Mallory to Josiah S. Johnston, November 4, 10, 1824, George M. McClure to Josephus B. Stuart, November 15, 1824, Stuart to Johnston, November 26, 1824, Henry Clay to Johnston, September 10,

1824, all in Johnston Papers; Harriet A. Weed, ed., *Autobiography of Thurlow Weed*, 2 vols. (Boston, 1883), 1:128-29; Glyndon Van Deusen, *The Life of Henry Clay* (Boston, 1937), 177.

[136]Alexander Porter to Josiah S. Johnston, September 15, 1824, John Linton to Johnston, November 14, 1824, in Johnston Papers.

[137]*Louisiana Gazette*, November 17, 19, 1824.

[138]*Louisiana Advertiser*, June 3, 1824; *St. Francisville Asylum*, November 13, 1824.

[139]John H. Johnston to Josiah S. Johnston, November 13, 1824, in Johnston Papers.

[140]L. S. Hazelton to Josiah S. Johnston, [November 23], 1824, Reuben Kemper to Johnston, November 27, 1824, John Clay to Johnston, November 30, 1824, Walter H. Overton to Johnston, November 22, 1824, ibid., David C. Ker to Andrew Jackson, November 23, 1824, in Jackson Papers; *Louisiana House Journal*, 1824, p. 8; *Louisiana Gazette*, November 23, 1824.

[141]John Clay to Josiah S. Johnston, November 30, 1824, in Johnston Papers.

[142]Henry Clay to Josiah S. Johnston, August 30, 1824, ibid.; Isaac L. Baker to William S. Hamilton, June 15, 1824, in Hamilton Papers; *Louisiana Gazette*, October 11, 1824.

[143]John Sibley to Josiah S. Johnston, January 2, 1825, in Johnston Papers.

[144]Weed, ed., *Autobiography of Thurlow Weed*, 1:128-29.

[145]Van Deusen, *Life of Henry Clay*, 177.

[146]John Clay to Josiah S. Johnston, November 30, 1824, in Johnston Papers.

[147]*L'Ami des Lois*, April 30, 1823; *Louisiana Advertiser*, April 20, July 18, 21, 1823.

[148]*Louisiana Gazette*, November 23, 1824.

[149]Ibid., December 14, 1824.

[150]John H. Johnston to Josiah S. Johnston, November 18, 1824, Henry Johnson to Johnston, November 25, 1824, in Johnston Papers.

[151]Isaac L. Baker to Josiah S. Johnston, December 21, 1824, ibid.

[152]*St. Francisville Asylum*, July 24, 1824; Alexander Porter to Josiah S. Johnston, September 15, 1824, L. S. Hazelton to Johnston, November 21, 1824, David C. Ker to Johnston, December 3, 1824, in Johnston Papers.

[153]Reuben Kemper to Josiah S. Johnston, November 27, 1824, Alexander Porter to Johnston, December 10, 31, 1824, January 10, 20, 1825, Nathaniel Cox to Johnston, December 10, 1824, L. S. Hazelton to Johnston, January 10, 1825, Walter H. Overton to Johnston, January 4, 1825, in Johnston Papers.

[154]Walter H. Overton to Josiah S. Johnston, October 29, 1824, January 4, 1825, Reuben Kemper to Johnston, November 27, 1824, Alexander Porter to Johnston, December 31, 1824, John H. Johnston to Johnston, December 21, 1824, John Moore to Johnston, January 10, 1825, ibid.

[155]David C. Ker to Josiah S. Johnston, December 3, 1824, James Sterrett to Johnston, February 1, 1825, ibid.

[156]*Louisiana House Journal*, 1824, p. 67; Henry Clay to Josiah S. Johnston, October 2, 1824, John Moore to Johnston, January 10, 1825, Walter H. Overton to Johnston, January 11, 1825, Nathaniel Cox to Johnston, December 10, 1824, Isaac L. Baker to Johnston, January 10, 1825, Alexander Porter to Johnston, January 20, 1825, Martin Gordon to Johnston, November 28, 1824, February 1, 1825, in Johnston Papers.

[157]Walter H. Overton to Josiah S. Johnston, January 11, 1825, in Johnston Papers.

[158]Henry A. Bullard to Josiah S. Johnston, December 21, 1824, James M. Bradford to Johnston, December 21, 1824, ibid.

[159]*Louisiana Gazette*, January 11, 1825.

[160]James M. Bradford to Josiah S. Johnston, January 15, 1825, in Johnston Papers; *Louisiana Gazette*, January 5, 1825.

[161]*Louisiana Gazette*, February 8, 1825.

[162]*Louisiana Journal*, March 24, 1825.

[163]*Louisiana Gazette*, February 28, 1825.

[164]John Pemberton to Andrew Jackson, February 15, 1825; Isaac L. Baker to Jackson, March 21, 1825, in Jackson Papers.

[165]*Louisiana Gazette*, March 5, 17, 30, 1825; *New Orleans Mercantile Advertiser*, March 17, 1825, *New Orleans Argus*, March 8, 10, 1825.

[166]*Natchitoches Courier*, April 4, 1825.

[167]*Louisiana Gazette*, February 28, March 11, 18, 25, 26, 1825.

[168]*Louisiana Courier*, April 5, 1825.

[169]*Louisiana Gazette*, April 19, 1825.

[170]Ibid., March 30, 1825.

[171]*New Orleans Mercantile Advertiser*, May 4, 1824. See also the claim of R. K. Call that Brent had replied to a query as to his choice in the House election with 'Vox populi, vox Dei,' thus giving Call the impression that Louisiana was safe for Jackson in James, *Andrew Jackson*, 416.

[172]*Louisiana Gazette*, March 11, 1825; Nathan Sargent, *Public Men and Events*, 2 vols. (Philadelphia, 1875), 1:75.

[173]William L. Brent to Henry Clay, September 3, 1824, in Henry Clay Papers.

[174]*Louisiana Journal*, May 5, 1825; *Louisiana Gazette*, April 7, 1825; *New Orleans Argus*, March 26, 1825.

[175]John Eaton to John Overton, April 3, 1825, in John Overton Papers, Tennessee Historical Society; *Louisiana Gazette*, March 8, 1825.

DEMOCRACY TRIUMPHANT*

Joseph G. Tregle, Jr.

The torrent of argument and debate flowing from the campaign of 1828 engulfed Louisiana and brought it for the first time in its history to a consuming involvement in a national election. Much of this excitement unquestionably derived from the disputed outcome of the preceding contest and from the personal relationships, good or bad, which tied so many Louisianians to Andrew Jackson. But to an even greater extent, perhaps, the state assembly in 1825 added immensely to this heightened popular participation in the political process by abolishing legislative choice of presidential electors and transferring the selection to the qualified voters of the state.[1] Edward Douglass White reported his assessment of how this affected the populace in a jocular note to Nicholas Trist which reflects a rather caustic view of the political sophistication of his neighbors:

> The influence of this fall has pressed hard on our biliary ducts, and another cause has helped to derange them in their function—politics—so called; for every man who has been told, and has faculties enough to remember the fact, that there are two men candidates for the presidency, considers himself a politician engrossed by politics. As for us we are for Fitz Jack, and the reasons are obvious—1. He lives nearer us; 2. He is a good fighter, which suits us, who are bellicose. 3. He knows nothing about the Science of Government; neither do we and therefore despise the knowledge and deem it hurtful. 4. We are hostile to all former usages in the United Sates, saving the one which tends to preservation, and Fitz Jack has some character in that way.—5. We are tired of the monotonous system, and want to change it: we are glad to find our brethren in London agree with us, and advise us to vote for Fitz Jack. 6. Davezac says the work of separation is begun, and that we shall make Fitz Jack emperor of the West. We can't all be Heroes, but it is still something to be Heroites. We are told all the folks in Virginia have feelings like our own. I hope it's true.[2]

The memories of popular reaction against the attempted caucus nomination in the 1824 campaign made political leaders wary of any such devices during the 1828 canvass,

*First published as Chapter 9 in Joseph G. Tregle, Jr., *Louisiana in the Age of Jackson: A Clash of Cultures and Personalities* (Baton Rouge: Louisiana State University Press, © 1999), 208-28. Reprinted with the kind permission of the author and the publisher.

legislators in January of 1827 rejecting caucus calls out of hand.[3] Emphasis shifted instead to public assemblies in every parish and town of the state, at which resolutions and recommendations tolled off the repetitious claims of virtue and vice to be found in the contending candidates. The scale and frequency of these meetings far exceeded anything comparable in 1824, giving them an especially impressive new organizational unity which for the first time indicated the beginning emergence of a modern political party system. Vigilance committees and committees of correspondence sprang up all over the state, dedicated to keeping their adherents both informed and loyal.[4] In no sense honorary or transient, they met regularly to rally their forces and to maintain disciplined support of their favorites, functioning down to ward units in the city of New Orleans.[5]

Centralized guidance of these new party activities also appeared at the state level for the first time in the 1828 campaign. In November of 1827 Adams delegates elected from each parish gathered in convention at Baton Rouge and elected Thomas Urquhart of New Orleans president, appointed a slate of five presidential elector candidates, and listened to Mazureau's scathing denunciation of the Jacksonians.[6] The General's backers held their own meeting in New Orleans late in January 1828, with 120 delegates from 27 of the state's 30 parishes in attendance, providing the audience for General Ripley's blast against the aristocracy of the Adams administration.[7]

The frenzy of the campaign allowed hardly a moment's peace throughout 1827 and 1828. January 8 and July 4 celebrations turned into rousing political rallies, with Jacksonians contributing especially aggressive and vocal excitement to the gatherings. Slidell, Davezac, General Robeson, Nathan Morse, and Ripley proved the most energetic of these oratorical minutemen, but friends and enemies duplicated their efforts all over the state.[8] In rough and tumble competition each side delighted particularly in seizing upon an opportunity to embarrass the opposition, with the Jacksonians again demonstrating greater adeptness at the game. When Commodore David Porter visited New Orleans in July of 1827, for example, to be honored at a public dinner in gratitude for his past naval services, both the Jackson and Adams camps agreed that no reference would be made to the quarrel with Adams which had caused Porter's resignation from the navy, or, for that matter, to any political issue whatsoever. Ignoring their pledge, the Jacksonians took control of the meeting, allowing their friends to launch noisy demonstrations at every mention of their hero's name, and forcing poor Porter to sit neglected through an evening of Jacksonian adulation.[9]

Activity begat optimism. Each month saw the champions of both sides more and more certain of eventual victory, though in their expressions of confidence, an occasional muted note of fear might indeed be heard. Alexander Porter watched somewhat uneasily as the campaign progressed, concerned because he perceived the Jacksonian ranks to be "composed of men who have reason to *wish for much*, and the stimulus of self interest gives great energy to their movements."[10] By late 1827, though still confident, he confessed a growing distress as campaign hysteria pushed the state to a level of excitement it had never before known. "A spirit of proscription is abroad, such as I never expected to see for a difference of opinion," he informed Johnston in yet another message. "I have been trying to rouse a *friend* of ours," he continued, with obvious reference to Governor Johnson, "who has great influence if he would exert it. If he thinks to escape by neutrality he is mistaken. He is marked already, and he will share the fate of every man who does not bow down before the idol and worship it."[11] Only Henry Clay seemed to be confident and without fears. "Louisiana, at this time" he told Edward Everett late in 1827, "is one of the safest and best organized states in the Union."[12]

Preoccupation with the presidential campaign became so intense that it dominated both the gubernatorial and congressional elections as well, a situation which would have hardly seemed possible only four years before. The gubernatorial campaign had actually begun immediately after Henry Johnson's inauguration in November of 1824, and the first two years of his administration gave every indication that the old issues would still prevail, with Americans and French lining up in opposing camps. Most Americans looked to Josiah Johnston as their only hope of uniting the several sectional factions in their ranks, planning to bring his name forward so early and with such backing that it might forestall the expected quadrennial emergence of General Thomas into the field.[13] Even such ardent Jacksonians as Isaac L. Baker, W. H. Overton, and Martin Gordon pledged to support that strategy, despite Johnston's known devotion to Clay,[14] and again it appeared as if Louisiana's ethnic fixation would isolate the state election process from national party concerns. As the presidential campaign grew more heated, however, a clear change of sentiment began to emerge, plainly confessed by Baker in a frank communication to Johnston in October of 1826. The administration party, Baker complained, had become so violent and proscriptive toward anyone not of their persuasion that Jacksonians felt they must "look to ourselves," and without a tremor Baker continued with open hints that many American voters in Attakapas now looked to the Jacksonian Marigny as their next gubernatorial candidate.[15]

Fully aware of these changing attitudes, Johnston held back from any open announcement of his candidacy for other reasons as well, chiefly because he knew the uncertainties of popular elections in Louisiana and much preferred the security of his Senate seat. "I am too old to be thrown out of public life," he advised his friends as early as 1825, thus preparing them for his final refusal to enter the race,[16] and though Porter and others continued to push his pretensions,[17] Johnston did not relent from his decision. By June of 1826 he had definitely taken himself out of the campaign.[18]

Even without him the field soon overflowed. As expected, Gurley and the Baton Rouge partisans of Philemon Thomas announced the old general's candidacy in April of 1826;[19] determined to erase the ignominy of his 1824 defeat, Marigny again roamed the countryside convinced that Jacksonians all over the state would rally to his support;[20] Henry S. Thibodaux offered from the Lafourche area, much to the delight of the Adams forces, who expected him to cut into the French vote of Marigny;[21] Bouligny took to the stump vigorously, apparently oblivious to the fact that he had practically no following;[22] Derbigny announced in August of 1827, hoping to attract a strong French-American Adams vote because of his reputation for moderation in the ethnic question;[23] and finally, with a French New Orleanian like Marigny utterly impossible to support, Florida Jacksonians united behind Thomas Butler.[24]

Meanwhile, a host of contenders girded for battle over the state's three congressional seats in a campaign completely unlike that of 1826 in its clear linkage to the presidential preferences of candidates. All three incumbents offered for reelection, Brent being opposed by Gen. W. H. Overton and Charles T. Scott, Gurley by Lafayette Saunders, and Livingston by Edward Douglass White. Gurley felt reasonably safe, Saunders having only recently come to Louisiana, and Brent and Livingston seemed to share an optimistic sense of security. In the case of these last two, confidence blithely ignored the facts. The closeness of his relationship to Jackson and the intensity of this dedication to the General's cause aroused Overton's previously dormant adherents, concentrating opposition to Brent in a way which neither Brownson nor Bullard had been capable of in 1826. As for Livingston, he now had to contend with one of the most popular men in the state.[25]

The climactic campaign year of 1828 opened on a note of nervous excitation which would be sustained with hardly a break until the great presidential question reached resolution in November. Clay's printed defense against the revived bargain and corruption charges of the Jacksonians reached the state shortly after the New Year, sent on by Johnston and others, to meet with immediate acerbic response.[26] It included sharp attacks upon Clay's critics, that by Brent couched in especially offensive language. The libels of Clay, he said, came from a frustrated group of fanatics, "headed by a military chief, without talents, and whose life is a history of immorality, bloodshed, and violation of the laws of God and of his country. . . . If Genl. Jackson does not establish his assertion (which he cannot), he ought to stand forth to the world, as a proven base calumniator, as unworthy of public or private confidence, and avoided by every man who has a respect for virtue and for Honor."[27]

So Brent had once again done violence to the Hero of New Orleans, and while Louisiana Jacksonians shook with rage, news from the east sent the Adams party, especially its French segment, into a temper of its own. This time the culprit was Livingston, who in addressing a Washington banquet on January 8 so praised Jackson's behavior in New Orleans in 1814-1815 as to seem insulting to the Louisiana French. On the same occasion, Gen. Robert Desha of Tennessee toasted Livingston as the "first and only *Honor* in the Louisiana pack," who "though beaten in the Presidential game, by the *Knave* from that state . . . shall shine conspicuously, while the *Knave* 'will stand before the world as a proven base calumniator, unworthy of public or private confidence, and avoided by every man who has respect for virtue and for honor.'"[28] Desha had thus thrown Brent's words "in his own teeth,"[29] with results that reverberated as far away as Louisiana itself.

Over and above all these flamboyant campaign dramatics, the Adams party recognized that their best hope of defeating Jackson lay in giving increasing and ever wider emphasis to the charge that his ungovernable temper, violent behavior, disdain for constitutional forms, and primitive ignorance of statecraft made him unsuitable for the office of president of the United States. It required little political insight to conclude that nothing better supported that representation than the supposed record of his behavior at New Orleans in 1814-1815. The Adams English-language press in the city had early on leaped to attack this vulnerability, led by John Gibson in the *Argus*, whose columns in July 1827 suggested that the next January 8 celebration should feature a great parade with banners portraying the constitution of the United States pierced by Jackson's sword, Judge Hall in prison, Louis Louaillier about to be shot, the Louisiana legislature driven from its hall, flames consuming the city of New Orleans, and the six Tennessee militiamen once executed by Jackson's order being led to the firing squad.[30]

The effectiveness of this kind of attack so alarmed Jackson's national committee leadership that they cast about desperately for some design to counteract its damaging impact. How better to strike back, the General's chief strategist, William B. Lewis, finally decided, than to have Jackson return to the very scene of his supposed greatest crimes, there to give the lie to the base charges against him, in the midst of a grateful populace who knew the truth of his services and heroism. Out of that decision came a well-crafted scenario which provided the climactic event of the 1828 campaign in the state.

In February 1827 the Louisiana legislature invited Jackson to be its guest in New Orleans on January 8, 1828, to join in celebration of his great victory on the plains of Chalmette. It is not clear if this move had in some fashion been engineered by Lewis or had simply been seized by him as a most welcome vehicle for the carrying out of his plan to counter the representations of Jackson as a violent misfit. In either case, it caught the Adams forces in the state completely off guard.[31] When Gen. Pierre Lacoste proposed this gesture of respect in the state senate, Jackson's opponents feared to resist the move, not wishing to appear spiteful or to drive voters to the General out of a sense of sympathy. Nor did they wish to give the impression of being so unsure of their strength that they would tremble at his presence in their capital. Relying on their control of the legislature, they decided to join in the invitation, boast of their magnanimity, and then take over the celebration themselves as proof that Jackson's visit could not be understood as any mark of political favor or sign of overwhelming support by the people of the state.[32] At this point the Jackson leaders committed a tactical blunder which almost spoiled their victory. Overjoyed at the ease of their success, they neglected to ask for any appropriation of state funds to receive the General or meet his expenses. On record as having joined in the invitation, the Adams men felt safe in rejecting all pleas for state money, forcing the Jacksonians to rely upon popular subscription to raise the funds to support Jackson's visit. Martin Gordon took the lead in that effort, but the Jacksonians suffered additional humiliation when many amused Adams men offered to help and added their names to the subscription list.[33]

But at least the visit had been assured, for Jackson quickly sent word that only the "interposition of Divine Providence" would keep him away from the celebration,[34] and now plans could be laid to wring the utmost political propaganda out of the event. Everything centered on using the January 8 celebration to convince the United States that Jackson's enemies had maliciously misrepresented his character and falsified the record of his behavior, as would be proved by the outpouring of admiration and respect bestowed upon him by the grateful people of Louisiana. "It is the first time our Legislature have given you any testimony of good feeling," Isaac Baker wrote his old chief, "and it will at once prostrate the Demagogues who have hitherto stifled the feeling of Louisiana in your behalf. The effect through the Union would be such as would dispose all to feel grateful for your manifold Services." Apparently with total seriousness, Baker then assured the General that if the Adams partisans dared label his visit "politics" the indignation of the Union would overwhelm them.[35]

On December 13, 1827, the steamship *Pocahontas* left New Orleans and headed toward Nashville to take on board the honored guest of Louisiana. Fog and murky nights delayed her passage while William B. Lewis fretted in Tennessee, fearful of some slip-up which might make useless the long weeks of planning. The "importance of the occasion requires absolute certainty with regard to our movements," he advised Jackson, and proceeded to instruct the General in alternate plans to be followed should the *Pocahontas* fail her deadline.[36] But the official escort finally arrived. Sick and uncomfortable, Jackson nonetheless set forth on the journey, issuing determined orders that no stops be made en route except at Natchez, where the New Orleans committee would meet him, for he thought thus to escape enemy charges of electioneering.[37]

Meanwhile in New Orleans celebrants paraded Nashville-grown "Jackson Beef" through the city streets and offered elk meat as a special delicacy of the occasion. At daybreak on January 8 a three-gun salute from the official steamboat cortege announced Jackson's arrival three miles above the city, answered by twenty-four blasts from the guns at the Place d'Armes—the festivities had begun. They would last for four days, beginning with the long procession of the eighteen boats through the mist and fog down to the hallowed plains of Chalmette, where the General answered the long and flowery welcomes with a justification of his martial-law rule during the days then being celebrated and rejoiced in the reunion as a "deep testimony" refuting the calumnies aimed at destroying his good name.[38]

His words carried particular significance, for they spelled out what would remain his unchanging and defiant justification of his actions during the critical days of the 1815 campaign:

> When I review the measures then adopted, and the circumstances with which we were surrounded, I think now as I did then, that they were necessary for the preservation of the country: without them that country would have been sacrificed. The substance of law which ordinarily governs the actions of society, was then suspended by necessity, by the controlling principle of self-preservation, so far as the course of military operations extended. The whole scope of those operations, according to the genius of our invaluable institutions, had for its object the substantial support of this great principle; to have for-

> borne in a case of unquestionable necessity would have resulted in a sacrifice of substance for form; constitution, laws, and all, would have been forever lost.[39]

Through the din of continuous salvos from Chalmette and the Place d'Armes, the party made its way back to New Orleans, landing at the levee fronting Marigny's estate, where Jackson marched ashore bareheaded to the acclaim of the throngs who massed along his way or hung dangling from windows, ship riggings, and roof tops. Père Antoine greeted him at the cathedral, where a choir intoned a "Te Deum" and the altar displayed a banner proclaiming VICTORIA A DEO ET JACKSON DATA. Cantatas, receptions, theatrical performances, balls, and banquets filled the four-day stay, until finally an exhausted General and his lady set out once again for the Hermitage.[40]

Behind them they left a city which for months would argue and debate the significance of his visit. From the conflicting reports it is impossible to reach any certain conclusion, for Adams observers all reported a coldness exhibited toward Jackson by all but those imported by the committee to swell the crowds and shout the huzzas, while just as unanimously Jacksonians rejoiced at the magnificent success of their venture. "On the very spot where you are charged with violating the Constitution," R. K. Call exulted to Jackson, "you have been hailed as its redeemer, and its champion."[41] To A. P. Hayne, everything "connected with the late wonderful celebration at New Orleans, now that it is over," appeared like a dream. "The World had never witnessed so glorious, so wonderful a celebration—never were *Gratitude & Patriotism* so happily united," he exclaimed in a congratulatory message to Jackson.[42]

Of all the commentaries on the celebration, none caused anything like the sensation produced by a series of articles sent to the *New York American* by that bitter critic of everything Jacksonian, Vincent Nolte. In a typically contemptuous vein, Nolte referred slurringly in these letters to various Jacksonian committeemen, calling one a "cabinet maker by trade," labeling another "a *successful bricklayer* alias architect," and heaping general ridicule on what he called sycophants trying to strut in the role of president-makers. His reports played right into the hands of Wagner, who jumped at this opportunity to resume his role as the great spokesman for social equality and respect for the workingman. Nolte's characterization of the Jacksonians as "low cartmen, dirty woodsawyers and contemptible bricklayers" provided the meat for endless columns in the *Advertiser*, which warned the "mechanics" and "all those who support themselves by the sweat of their brow to keep aloof from a faction, who, if they had the power, would convert them into hewers of wood and drawers of water for those spurious notables of the land."[43] John Slidell demanded a public apology from Nolte, and when the latter refused, the friendship of the two men shattered. More ferocious than Slidell, F. B. Ogden tried to kill Nolte in his home, but failed. As late as 1829, when the outspoken merchant made his last farewell to New Orleans, his friends guarded the way to his ship to prevent other attempts upon his life.[44]

The weeks between January and July of 1828 continued the rounds of ceaseless political activity. Shortly after Jackson's departure, his adherents assembled their state convention in New Orleans, where Ripley and others addressed themselves to the glorification of their cause while Marigny and Overton took on the more pragmatic task of committing the party to individual candidates in the congressional and gubernatorial races to avoid a scattering of their votes. But Scott's friends argued that this would be offensive to men who had remained loyal to the General for years, and the Florida delegates balked at giving up Butler for Marigny. The fiery Creole believed his gubernatorial chances had been greatly enhanced by his prominence during Jackson's visit, when he had presided at the major banquet in the General's honor, but now he began to grumble that the Florida men would make Derbigny governor and give Adams the vote of the state.[45]

Jackson spirits lifted considerably in April, when Denis Prieur swept to an easy victory over Anathole Peychaud in the New Orleans mayoral race and seven of the ten council seats also fell to supporters of the General's cause.[46] The municipal election had been largely waged along Adams-Jackson lines, but the administration forces pretended to see no indication here of the real presidential preferences of the people. Many extraneous factors had indeed influenced the mayoral campaign, chief among them the great personal popularity of Prieur and the equally profound antagonism against Peychaud because of his foreign French birth.[47] For Wagner, aristocracy provided the key again. "It was diverting to see the arch smile on the face of the laboring mechanic," he wrote, "when rejecting with a dry sneer a ticket proffered to him by a hand never before extended to him in token of friendship or with the frankness of equality."[48]

As the July elections approached, political leaders over the nation turned their eyes to Louisiana for some glimmer of light which might indicate the trend of public favor, for these contests introduced what would be a steady progression of important electoral decisions throughout the country, climaxing with the great presidential choice itself. Edward Everett advised his brother as early as March to watch carefully for the outcome of this "most important event" in Louisiana,[49] Brent felt that the November decision in the state would be fixed by the results of the July canvass,[50] and Alexander Porter predicted that success of the Adams forces in the summer campaigns would greatly influence later elections in Kentucky.[51]

With so much at stake, New Orleans became tremendously agitated and tense as the political battles raged toward their climax, radiating much excitement to the rural parishes as well. In February, fire destroyed the state house and the Pontalba mansion in the heart of the city, leading to disturbing reports of a phantom incendiary plotting to put the whole town to the torch.[52] The following month a rumor of Henry Clay's death spread dismay everywhere, adding a pall of darkness to an already cloudy scene.[53] Then in June John Gibson flooded the community with the inflammatory "coffin hand bills" depicting Jackson as a murderer for his execution of several militiamen under his command during the late war. Tempers now reached the breaking point. Sheltered young ladies came close to exchanging blows while furiously debating the question of Jackson's character, and one writer in the *Advertiser* moaned that the "ordinary courtesies of society are trampled upon, and in every circle dividing lines are drawn—harmony and good understanding are banished; and in their place are introduced topics calculated only to exasperate and offend."[54]

The politicos, meanwhile, steeled themselves for exhausting last efforts. Thibodaux had died of an abscessed liver in October, leading to a scramble for his votes in which Derbigny came off much the best.[55] The foreign Frenchman's strength seemed to grow in proportion to the malignity of the campaign, for his determination to stand as a moderate between the extremists of both the Adams-Jackson and the French-American quarrels appealed to many Louisianians frightened by the intensity of the political storms disturbing the community. Despite his moderation, moreover, he clearly benefited by being the only Adams man in the governor's race, while Jacksonian power still fragmented on the split between Butler and Marigny.[56] Not even the fever of fanatical Jacksonianism could prevail over old ethnic hatreds.

The congressional campaign presented contrasting studies in boundless exertion and comfortable indolence. Overton threw himself into his task with an energy even his friends found difficult to believe, while Brent remained listless at his post in Washington.[57] Much the same pattern prevailed in the Livingston-White contest, with the incumbent almost unbelievably careless of his own congressional future. Skillfully coached by Henry Johnson and Alexander Porter, White neglected his duties as city judge in New Orleans to conduct a lengthy tour of the Lafourche area, capitalizing on his old and steady friendships among the French population.[58] Livingston did nothing but urge Davezac and St. Romes to greater and greater efforts in the *Courier*, while he lolled in Washington and at Montgomery Place in New York, attentive only to his criminal code. He apparently felt that public recognition of his superiority over White made defeat by such a young upstart out of the question. A letter to his constituents in June announced his inability to return home for the elections because of the great press of his duties in Congress, and elaborated on his willingness to suffer such dangerous personal inconvenience for the good of those he represented. His references to White insultingly patronized and belittled his opponent, clearly implying that no person with sense could fail to understand the difference between his own genius and the shallow talents of a city judge.[59] At almost the same moment, he sent a note to Jackson describing his leisurely life at his sister's home in Red Hook, New York, making not a single reference to Louisiana campaigns. In the ease of his own optimistic security, he obviously cared little about the fate of his fellow Jacksonians at home.[60] But for the exertions of his relatives and the worried assistance of Wagner and Martin Gordon, Livingston would have had no campaign at all. As it was, the Jacksonian committees raised quite a clamor for the absent congressman, and it may well have been that Livingston relied on Wagner and Gordon not being able to abandon him in a campaign so vital to their own interests.[61] The Gurley-Saunders race presented problems of a wholly different character. Jacksonian strength clearly dominated in the Second District, but Saunders had so little personal appeal that even his friends made ready to concede his defeat.[62]

The July elections surpassed in excitement even the most exaggerated forecasts of the campaign. Confusion reigned from the opening of the polls, primarily because each side, with seemingly good cause, had come to believe absolutely that the other planned monstrous frauds to steal the election. As early as June the *Argus* charged the Jacksonians with buying large plots of ground which they then parceled out to their followers to qualify them as tax payers entitled to vote. The evasiveness of Wagner's denials convinced the Adams men that they had hit upon the truth,[63] and they made preparations of their own to prevent being swamped by what they called illegal voters. Two of the official election supervisors of Orleans Parish, Judges Preval and Pitot, nominally politically neutral, agreed to step down from their positions as commissioners, forcing the other eligible judges in the parish to serve in their place. But one of these was White, who clearly could not function in such a capacity, being himself a candidate. Governor Johnson hurriedly dispatched Derbigny to Donaldsonville to receive White's resignation, meanwhile signing an appointment for Felix Grima to fill White's place on the bench and round out the three-man election board. In the process he had guaranteed a pro-Adams majority on the panel of election judges, for Grima was not only a supporter of the president but a brother-in-law of Mazureau.

The plan soon took on clearer shape. No longer attorney general, Mazureau nonetheless commanded great respect as a legal authority, and his insistence persuaded the judges to disregard the tax rolls for 1828, declaring them invalid for having been made up by assessors appointed after the date stipulated by law. This meant, he argued, that the 1827 rolls must be used, which would result in the exclusion from the polls of the newly propertied Jacksonians, who naturally did not appear on the 1827 list. With the Mazureau opinion as their guide, the two pro-Adams election judges prepared to face the opposition.[64]

For the full three days of the election the Jacksonians performed near miracles to get their supporters to the polls. Twenty hacks and carriages coursed through the city streets, carrying the faithful to the voting site and trailing banners of blue silk blazoned with the motto, JACKSON AND THE PEOPLE. But at the polls the Adams judges held fast, refusing to accept some two hundred persons as legitimate voters. Slidell and Grymes protested each unfavorable decision with all the vigor they could command, though each felt near death from the Spanish dengue fever ravaging the city, a disease not fatal but so painful as to incapacitate its victims for weeks.

The Jacksonians had not come to all this with entirely clean hands. They relied essentially upon the unfinished state of the 1828 tax lists, hoping to push as many of their partisans through to the polls as possible, whether legitimate taxpayers or not. Many of the rejected clearly belonged to this class, and it would have been almost impossible for the election judges to have successfully denied the ballot to two hundred legitimate voters.[65] Outside the city, as always, a greater decorum prevailed, though passions could run high, as they did in Donaldsonville, where S. J. Tournillon, stepfather of the Trists, almost came to blows with E. D. White after reading a fiery pro-Livingston appeal in his presence.[66]

The results gave the Adams forces an overwhelming victory. Derbigny piled up such a vote over Butler and Marigny that his total exceeded their combined tally, leaving the disappointed Creole humiliated and angered by his poor third place showing.[67] Marigny's old hatred of the Florida section flared anew, for he thought himself betrayed by their support of Butler. "Je me vengerai en Novembre," he muttered to his friends in dark threats to abandon the Jacksonian cause itself, if that might allow him the pleasure of striking back at those who had once again thwarted his greatest ambition.[68] Old General Thomas, supposedly neutral to the end, finished last in the race.

The Jacksonians suffered staggering losses in the New Orleans legislative delegation as well, every seat going to the opposition, and only the solid support received in the Floridas prevented their being completely eclipsed in the assembly. Statewide, they managed to win six of the seventeen senate seats and twenty-one of the fifty in the house, with three of the members of that body being of uncertain party affiliation.[69]

Of the three Jacksonian congressional candidates, only W. H. Overton had been successful, in a victory largely attributable to William Brent's continued absence from the state. With the sale of his Louisiana lands shortly before the campaign, Brent became virtually a nonresident, loathed by the Jacksonians because of his violent attacks upon the General and detested personally by most of the men of his own party because of his slanders against Josiah Johnston.[70] As had been expected, Henry Gurley edged out Lafayette Saunders, though by a mere thirty votes, for despite his newness in Louisiana the young challenger profited from a large party following.[71] Edward D. White won the campaign's most decisive victory by capturing every parish but one in the district, polling 1,780 votes to Livingston's 1,173. The incumbent lost even his base in New Orleans, compelling proof of the collapse of his once strong Creole support.[72] Sectional and ethnic hatreds, together with the indolence of Livingston, had pretty well done the Jacksonians in.

With resounding cheers and editorial bombast, the preponderance of Adams supporters celebrated their splendid victory as a sure harbinger of repeated success in the November presidential elections. Some, however, cautioned against misplaced confidence. Happy at the success of his friends, Porter nonetheless warned Johnston that the July vote "must not be understood *by you* as indicative of the sentiments of the state on the Presidential election. Not a single one of our elections turned exclusively on it."[73] But it was clearly good politics to impress the opposite opinion upon observers in other parts of the nation, and the Adams press did its best, with some effect. Henry Lee, one of the General's trusted publicists, wrote to Jackson from New York that the "defeat of Mr. Livingston and the failure of our ticket in La. produced an unpleasant thrill in this quarter."[74] Even more upset, James A. Hamilton, son of the great treasury secretary, shared his anger with Van Buren in a note which revealed at least some insight into the Louisiana campaigns: "That creole Mongrel Louisiana has again stuck the fang of her ingratitude in the sides of her Benefactor by the late administration Triumph in that State. As it respects Livingston he almost deserves his fate, for his neglect of his Constituents & apathy to his own interests. There is always a Lion in the path to the Sluggard. It is what I expected & the result does not surprise me."[75]

Eventually, however, indignant complaints that the election had been stolen by the corrupt practices of the Adams men restored some confidence to Jackson's followers.[76] They still had November in which to redeem their cause. By August the recent defeat seemed important only as an object lesson highlighting their own errors. Baker repeatedly pushed W. S. Hamilton to greater efforts in the Floridas, the urgency of his language reflecting the new determination of the party: "Something must be done to counteract the plans of H. Johnson, Duralde & Co. for giving the vote of the State to Adams. . . . we are not organized. . . . You, Dawson, Butler, Hickey & Lawrence in the West [of the Floridas] must communicate often with Moore, Morgan, Goff, Penn, etc. in the East."[77] Moved by the same spirit, Ripley and Hennen spent most of their summer in active campaigning, while some of their imaginative colleagues busied themselves in mailing pamphlets to their neighbors bearing what purported to be the personal greetings of Jackson himself.[78]

Despite the warnings of Porter and others, overconfidence generated by their July successes almost drained the Adams party of energy during the last critical weeks of the campaign. Still primarily concerned with local elections, the French in the interior parishes simply relaxed after the great summer victory, to the dismay of the administration men who recognized them as the principal strength of the Adams party in the state.[79] "The struggle here will be fierce," an obviously distraught Porter advised Johnston. "The Jackson party," he lamented, "are more active than ever, and certainly if ever zeal and devotion merited success, theirs deserve it. Were it not for *one* or *two* persons in this state I know not what would become of the administration here."[80] Even carefully chosen T. J. Pew, Johnston's protégé as editor of the *Mercantile Advertiser* from whom so much had been expected, abandoned his post for a private trip which took him away from his paper for several months through the whole climax of the November canvass.[81]

Long before the day of decision arrived, the Jacksonian press mounted an intensive campaign urging its followers to verify their enrollment on the finally completed 1828 tax list to prevent a repetition of the July exclusions.[82] With Denis Prieur and the county sheriff on their side, they hoped this time to dominate the polls themselves. Their efforts redoubled with receipt early in November of the news of Jackson's great victory in Pennsylvania, which voted before Louisiana, and in a moment they covered the city with handbills announcing the tidings. Isaac Preston delivered one of his rousing speeches at a great party rally the following night, urging his fellow Louisianians to climb aboard the General's bandwagon, and for the next few days Wagner ran in review the whole argument which he and his colleagues had developed over the months in favor of the Hero of New Orleans. With a final effort he pleaded, "Louisianians! remember that Andrew Jackson is a man of the South, a slave holder, a cotton planter."[83] Belatedly, the Adams forces began to bestir themselves anew, with George Eustis presiding over a great administration meeting on the eve of the election and Gibson's *Argus* reciting once again the old and familiar sins attributed to the General.[84]

This time, victory belonged to the Hero of New Orleans. Sloughing off the indolence which had threatened them, the Adams camp brought its full force into the field, polling even more votes than they had won in the July canvass, and this despite the pressures of the rolling season which made so many demands on the time of sugar planters. But the Jacksonians had done their work even better since that summer defeat. Hundreds of additional voters now made their way to the polls, many newly enfranchised by the purchase of simple vehicle licenses made possible by party support, while the northern cotton parishes spilled forth other hundreds who had remained inert in the gubernatorial campaign. With Prieur and his cooperative sheriff controlling the polls in the capital, it was the Adams men who this time found difficulty in reaching the voting booth.[85]

Jackson carried all of Florida and every parish north of Red River save Avoyelles, plus Orleans, Iberville, West Baton Rouge, Lafayette, and Pointe Coupée. Adams won every major sugar parish except Iberville, but his popular vote of 4,076 fell short of Jackson's 4,603. Within the sugar parishes, predominantly Gallic in population, it would be difficult to single out the factor which most attracted them to Adams. No doubt a combination of factors swayed their vote—Duralde and the tariff had meant Clay and Adams. New Orleans had broken almost down the middle, 747 to 665 in favor of Jackson, while the heavily American cotton sector to the north had given an overwhelming preponderance to the victor.[86]

"I am almost mad with joy," an old friend of the General proclaimed in a hastily scrawled note informing Jackson that Louisiana had at last paid its debt of gratitude. "I thank God," he rejoiced, "that I have lived to see the downfall of the Yanky [*sic*] Dynasty!"[87] In the Floridas, cotton planters and "resin heels" joined in singing:

> To establish a monarchy was Johnny Q's intentions
> Whilst Clay as premier, was to serve the lads with pensions,
> Who could best defame our Hero by some unfounded tale
> Or, in supporting aristocracy; pen or tongue did never fail.
> Huzza, huzza, huzza, huzza, huzza!
> By unity like free-born men, we have won the day![88]

The Age of Jackson had begun.

Notes for "Democracy Triumphant"

[1]Moreau Lislet, ed., *A General Digest of the Acts of the Legislature of Louisiana Passed from the Year 1804 to 1827, Inclusive*, 2 vols. (New Orleans, 1828), 1:451.

[2]Edward D. White to Nicholas P. Trist, November 29, 1827, in Nicholas P. Trist Papers, Library of Congress (hereafter cited as Trist Papers).

[3]Alexander Porter to Josiah S. Johnston, January 27, 1827, in Josiah Stoddard Johnston Papers, Historical Society of Pennsylvania, Philadelphia, Penn. (hereafter cited as Johnston Papers); *Louisiana Advertiser*, January 25, 1827.

[4]*Louisiana Advertiser*, August 6, December 25, 28, 1827, January 5, 7, 8, 11, 15, 1828; *Louisiana Courier*, December 1, 1827; March 5, June 21, 24, 1828; *Baton Rouge Gazette*, July 14, 1827; *New Orleans Argus*, September 28, 1827, October 3, 17, 22, 24, 30, 31, November 15, 1827; *Natchitoches Courier*, July 17, September 1, 25, 1827.

[5]*New Orleans Argus*, March 29, October 20, 27, November 1, 1828.

[6]The five electors chosen were Jacques Villeré, Charles Bushnell, Andrew Le Blanc, Neuville Declouet, and Benjamin Morris, according to the *Baton Rouge Gazette*, November 10, 1827; *New Orleans Argus*, November 20, 1827.

[7]Chosen as Jacksonian electors were J. B. Plauché, Trasimond Landry, T. W. Scott, Alexandre Mouton, and Placide Bossier, who had undergone a substantial change of outlook since his 1824 horserace. *Louisiana Advertiser*, January 16, 1828. The Louisiana experience in the campaign was quite similar to that prevailing in most parts of the Union. See, for example, Culver H. Smith, "Propaganda Technique in the Jackson Campaign of 1828," in *East Tennessee Historical Society's Publications*, 6 (1934): 44-66; Erik M. Eriksson, "Official Newspaper Organs and the Campaign of 1828," in *Tennessee Magazine of History*, 8 (1924): 231-47.

[8]*Louisiana Advertiser*, July 6, 1827.

[9]Ibid., July 25, 1827; Maunsel White to Andrew Jackson, August 4, 1827, in Andrew Jackson Papers, Library of Congress (hereafter cited as Jackson Papers).

[10]Alexander Porter to Josiah S. Johnston, January 27, 1827, in Johnston Papers. See also John Slidell to Joel K. Poinsett, March 27, 1827, in Joel Poinsett Papers, Historical Society of Pennsylvania, Philadelphia, Penn.; Eleazar Ripley to John McNeil, April 30, 1827, in Miscellaneous Manuscripts, New York Historical Society.

[11]Alexander Porter to Josiah S. Johnston, December 8, 1827, in Johnston Papers.

[12]Henry Clay to Edward Everett, November 7, 1827, in Edward Everett Papers, Massachusetts Historical Society (hereafter cited as Everett Papers).

[13]L. S. Hazelton to Josiah S. Johnston, March 30, 1825, Henry A. Bullard to Johnston, October 23, 1825, John Linton to Johnston, November 24, 1825, Nathaniel Cox to Johnston, November 26, 1826, Alexander Porter to Johnston, April 11, 1826, in Johnston Papers.

[14]Isaac L. Baker to Josiah S. Johnston, November 1, 1825, Martin Gordon to Johnston, February 1, 1825, Walter H. Overton to Johnston, October 2, 1826, ibid.

[15]Isaac L. Baker to Josiah S. Johnston, October 5, 1826, ibid.

[16]Josiah S. Johnston to John Linton, October 9, 1825, ibid.

[17]Alexander Porter to Josiah S. Johnston, April 11, 14, 1826, ibid.

[18]Alexander Porter to Josiah S. Johnston, June 21, 1826, ibid.

[19]Alexander Porter to Josiah S. Johnston, April 14, 1826, ibid.; *Natchitoches Courier*, November 5, 1827; *Louisiana Advertiser*, June 29, 1827.

[20]*Louisiana Gazette*, April 6, 7, 10, 1826; *Baton Rouge Gazette*, February 2, 1827; Isaac L. Baker to Josiah S. Johnston, October 5, 1826, in Johnston Papers.

[21]Alexander Porter to Josiah S. Johnston, January 27, August 30, 1827, in Johnston Papers.

[22]Henry A. Bullard to Josiah S. Johnston, October 23, 1825, ibid; *Louisiana Courier*, June 15, 1827.

[23]Alexander Porter to Josiah S. Johnston, August 30, 1827, in Johnston Papers; *New Orleans Argus*, August 22, 1827.

[24]*Baton Rouge Gazette*, November 3, 17, 1827.

[25]*Louisiana Advertiser*, February 5, April 8, 1828; Alexander Porter to Josiah S. Johnston, May 21, 1828, in Johnston Papers.

[26]Henry A. Bullard to Josiah S. Johnston, January 10, 1828, in Johnston Papers.

[27]William L. Brent to [Tobias Watkins], June 4, 1827, Dominique Bouligny to Henry Clay, December 3, 1827, in Henry Clay Papers, Library of Congress.

[28]*New Orleans Argus*, February 12, 20, May 3, 6, 1828; *Louisiana Advertiser*, February 13, 1828; *Louisiana Courier*, February 11, 1828.

[29]Robert Desha to Andrew Jackson, January 21, 1828, in Jackson Papers.

[30]*New Orleans Argus*, July 18, 20, 1827.

[31]*Louisiana Advertiser*, February 27, 1827; *New Orleans Argus*, March 10, 1827.

[32]Alexander Porter to Josiah S. Johnston, January 9, 1828, in Johnston Papers; *New Orleans Argus*, June 6, July 18, 1827.

[33]*Louisiana Courier*, June 23, 25, September 11, 1827, March 22, 31, 1828; *New Orleans Argus*, November 24, 28, 29, 1827.

[34]Andrew Jackson to Henry Johnson, April 18, 1827, in Jackson Papers.

[35]Isaac L. Baker to Andrew Jackson, April 21, 1827, ibid.

[36]William B. Lewis to Andrew Jackson, December 24, 1827, ibid.

[37]Andrew Jackson to William B. Lewis, December 19, 25, 1827, in William B. Lewis Papers, New York Public Library.

[38]*Louisiana Advertiser*, December 29, 1827, January 8, 1828; *Louisiana Courier*, January 5, 7, 1828; Speech of Lucius C. Duncan at January 8, 1828, celebration in Jackson Papers.

[39]Jackson's Address to Citizens of New Orleans, January 8, 1828, Jackson Papers.

[40]*Louisiana Advertiser*, January 9, 14, 16, 21, 23, 1828; *Louisiana Courier*, January 10, 16, 18, 1828; *New Orleans Argus*, March 26, 1828.

[41]R. K. Call to Andrew Jackson, March 11, 1828, in Jackson Papers.

[42]A. P. Hayne to Andrew Jackson, March 12, 1828, ibid.

[43]Vincent Nolte, *Fifty Years in Both Hemispheres* (New York, 1854), 345; *Louisiana Advertiser*, March 10, 1826. See also, the *Advertiser*'s later discussions on March 12, May 26, June 5, 12, 28, 30, 1828.

[44]Nolte, *Fifty Years in Both Hemispheres*, 346-47.

[45]John Erwin to Josiah S. Johnston, January 16, 1828, Alexander Porter to Johnston, January 24, 1828, in Johnston Papers; *Louisiana Advertiser*, February 5, 1828.

[46]*Louisiana Courier*, April 8, 1828.

[47]T. J. Pew to Josiah S. Johnston, May 31, 1828, in Johnston Papers; *New Orleans Argus*, April 9, 11, May 13, 1828.

[48]*Louisiana Advertiser*, April 15, 1828.

[49]Edward Everett to [Alexander Everett], March 15, 1828, in Everett Papers.

[50]William L. Brent to James G. Taliaferro, May 9, 1828, in James G. Taliaferro Papers, Department of Archives, Louisiana State University, Baton Rouge, La.

[51]Alexander Porter to Johnston, May 21, 1828, in Johnston Papers.

[52]*New Orleans Argus*, February 4, 7, 9, 12, 1828.

[53]Ibid., March 26, 1828.

[54]Ibid., June 13, 1828; *Louisiana Advertiser*, June 11, August 23, 1828. Gibson publicly admitted the printing of the "coffin handbills." See *New Orleans Argus*, August 11, 1829. John Binns, *Recollections of the Life of John Binns* (Philadelphia, 1854), 246, describes the origins of these famous campaign items.

[55]*New Orleans Argus*, October 29, 1827; George Eustis to Josiah S. Johnston, October 31, 1827, Alexander Porter to Johnston, December 8, 1827, in Johnston Papers.

[56]George Eustis to Josiah S. Johnston, October 31, 1827, January 11, May 11, 1828, Alexander Porter to Johnston, December 8, 1827, James Hull to Johnston, June 3, 1828, Henry A. Bullard to Johnston, November 25, 1827, July 4, 1828, in Johnston Papers.

[57]John H. Johnston to Josiah S. Johnston, August 6, 1828, ibid.

[58]Alexander Porter to Josiah S. Johnston, April 16, May 21, 1828, ibid.

[59]*Louisiana Advertiser*, June 19, 1828; *Louisiana Courier*, June 3, 1828.

[60]Edward Livingston to Andrew Jackson, June 20, 1828, in Jackson Papers.

[61]Alexander Porter to Josiah S. Johnston, June 27, 1828, in Johnston Papers; *Louisiana Advertiser*, January 28, February 1, May 10, 19, 21, June 21, 23, 30, July 4, 1828; *Louisiana Courier*, June 3, 21, 23, 24, 26, 28, 1828; *New Orleans Argus*, February 12, 28, May 3, 6, 7, June 30, 1828.

[62]Alexander Porter to Josiah S. Johnston, June 27, 1827, 1828, in Johnston Papers.

[63]*New Orleans Argus*, June 7, 1828; *Louisiana Advertiser*, June 10, 1828.

[64]*Louisiana Advertiser*, July 7, 12, 15, August 21, 1828; *New Orleans Argus*, July 14, August 23, 1828.

[65]*Louisiana Advertiser*, July 15, 1828; *New Orleans Argus*, July 9, August 29, 1828; Richard Davidson to William S. Hamilton, August 15, 1827, in William S. Hamilton Papers, Department of Archives, Louisiana State University, Baton Rouge, La. (hereafter cited as Hamilton Papers).

[66]H. B. Trist to Nicholas P. Trist, August 20, 1828, in Nicholas P. Trist Papers, Library of Congress (hereafter cited as Trist Papers).

[67]*Louisiana House Journal*, 1828, p. 5.

[68]John H. Johnston to Josiah S. Johnston, August 6, 1828, in Johnston Papers.

[69]*New Orleans Argus*, July 29, 1828.

[70]John H. Johnston to Josiah S. Johnston, August 6, 1828, in Johnston Papers; Josiah Baker to Nicholas P. Trist, July 26, 1828, in Trist Papers.

[71]Lafayette Saunders to Andrew Jackson, July 18, 1828, in Jackson Papers.

[72]Alexander Porter to Josiah Johnston, March 7, July 19, 1828, in Johnston Papers.

[73]Alexander Porter to Josiah S. Johnston, July 27, 1828, ibid.

[74]Henry Lee to Andrew Jackson, August 13, 1828, in Jackson Papers.

[75]James Hamilton to Martin Van Buren, July 31, 1828, in Martin Van Buren Papers, Library of Congress.

[76]Lafayette Saunders to Andrew Jackson, July 18, 1828, Edward Livingston to Jackson, August 12, 1828, Henry Lee to Jackson, August 15, 1828, in Jackson Papers.

[77]Isaac L. Baker to William S. Hamilton, August 10, 1828, in Hamilton Papers.

[78]*New Orleans Argus*, October 22, 1828; *Louisiana Journal*, October 4, 1828.

[79]For an analysis of this support, see Alexander Porter to Josiah S. Johnston, April 16, June 27, July 27, in Johnston Papers.

[80]Alexander Porter to Josiah S. Johnston, September 20, 1828, ibid.

[81]T. J. Pew to Josiah S. Johnston, November 29, 1828, ibid.

[82]*Louisiana Courier*, October 13, 1828.

[83]Ibid., November 1, 3, 1828; *New Orleans Argus*, November 1, 1828; *Louisiana Advertiser*, November 4, 1828.

[84]*New Orleans Argus*, November 4, 1828.

[85]Ibid., November 4, 5, 6, 1828; *Louisiana Advertiser*, November 7, 1828.

[86]*Louisiana Courier*, November 25, 1828; Joseph G. Tregle, Jr., "Louisiana and the Tariff, 1816-1846," *Louisiana Historical Quarterly*, 25 (1942): 30-31.

[87]David C. Ker to Andrew Jackson, November 6, 11, 1828, in Jackson Papers.

[88]*St. Francisville Crisis*, November 22, 1828.

DEMOCRACY REGNANT*

Joseph G. Tregle, Jr.

"Now let our side come in—or let us never *labor* as I have labored!" an exuberant Louisiana Jacksonian exclaimed as he greeted the beginning of Old Hickory's tenure in the White House.[1] That frank expression of expectation mirrored a sentiment common to many in the Jacksonian fold anxious to enjoy the fruits of their momentous triumph. They gave little time now to talk of principle or usurpers and even less to an old pledge by Wagner that "Jackson has too much greatness of soul to imitate the poor, vindictive policy of Mr. Clay, in removing people from office because they differ from him in opinion."[2]

Instead, they joined the Jackson press in support of what they called the "doctrine of reform," urging the new president to effect the "complete political purgation" demanded by the people in the great victory of 1828. The Adams-Clay regime had polluted government service with corrupt and irresponsible men, ran the new theme, and Jackson must now be given the freedom to wipe away this ugliness from the American scene. Moreover, said Archibald Haralson of St. Francisville's *Florida Gazette*, the "President is the only person to judge of the means (provided always that they be constitutional) by which such an end is to be accomplished." Nor should the people ever complain, "for it is for their benefit that the act is done."[3] True to his preachments, Haralson did his best to aid reform by finding some federal job in which he might himself replace an enemy to republicanism, for after many years service to the Jacksonian cause, as he wrote his friend Thomas Butler, "My mouth is yet open."[4]

Many mouths opened in Louisiana when Jackson finally defeated Adams in the 1828 campaign, insistently seeking to be filled. Edward Livingston figured prominently among them, for it must have been galling to find himself turned out of office almost at the very moment of the General's triumph. He denied any great disappointment at his loss to White, but a note to Jackson shortly after that melancholy affair in July clearly meant to work on the sympathies of his old chief. Should the General be elected in November, it plainly implied, Livingston would be grateful to be remembered in the obscu-

*First published as Chapter 10 in Joseph G. Tregle, Jr., *Louisiana in the Age of Jackson: A Clash of Cultures and Personalities* (Baton Rouge: Louisiana State University Press, © 1999), 229-64. Reprinted with the kind permission of the author and the publisher.

rity of his Louisiana surroundings, from which, he sighed, it might have been better never to have emerged.[5]

His conduct during the presidential campaign actually gave him small claim on Jackson's gratitude. He had, in truth, essentially ignored the contest altogether, enjoying leisurely days at his sister's home during the fall of 1827, "quietly employed in preparing systems that will most probably never pass whoever may be president," while "you politicians," he wrote Johnston, "are exercising your electioneering talents."[6] In August of 1828, he did give a speech at Harrisburg, Pennsylvania, supporting the General, but only because his private professional duties required his presence in that city to check into an involved inheritance case.[7] Otherwise he confined his activities to speculations concerning New York affairs and to general advice sent on for Jackson's consideration. He contributed no more to the national victory than he had to the one in Louisiana, and that was very little indeed.[8]

Jackson's success in November, however, stimulated Livingston to a new burst of energy. Upon confirmation of Jackson's election he immediately set out for Louisiana to exploit the newfound power of his party, anxious to win the United States Senate seat held by Dominique Bouligny, whose term was soon due to expire. Intent upon reaching New Orleans before the legislature balloted in January of 1829, he stopped nowhere en route except at the Hermitage, where his short visit aroused conjectures that Jackson had chosen him to be the next secretary of state.[9] Ripley and others of his friends at home snapped up these rumors as a compelling reason for Louisiana Jacksonians to unite behind him for the Senate. Only then would the repudiation of July be cleared from his record, thus justifying Jackson in granting whatever place he might deign to bestow.[10]

The thing would require some doing, however, for the Louisiana legislature unquestionably remained under the control of the Clay faction. Both the *Advertiser* and the *Courier* jumped to build up a great noise for the returning Livingston, charting his journey homeward every day, until finally a sumptuous dinner at Davis's Ball Room welcomed him back to New Orleans. Excusing his absence from Washington as a service to many constituents who required his presence in the city to advise them on a vital legal problem, Livingston launched into one of the strangest political speeches of the new era, in effect declaring himself the only man capable of representing the state properly in the Senate. With a grateful nod to Gordon, he pledged his best efforts to get the United States to purchase the Orleans Navigation Company, "at a modest price."[11] Trying to help, Jacksonian members of the legislature attempted to cut the Clay faction's strength in the assembly by challenging the legitimacy of the New Orleans house delegation because of alleged fraud in the July elections, but the move got nowhere.[12]

Only a miracle could make Livingston a United States senator, Alexander Porter had once said, confident of the anti-Jacksonian strength in the assembly.[13] He had not reckoned with Henry Johnson. That glutton for office stepped down from the governorship in November 1828, and apparently feeling that Bouligny had simply been warming his Senate seat until his return, promptly announced for the latter's place. As the January election approached, the two rivals agreed to unite behind whichever of them won the higher vote on the legislature's first ballot, but when that proved to be Bouligny, Johnson brazenly refused to honor his pledge and remained in the race. Bouligny's outraged supporters threw their votes to Livingston out of sheer hatred for the ex-governor, giving him the senatorial seat and leaving a bewildered Henry A. Bullard to exclaim, "I have this day seen the most singular election ever known in the state."[14]

Livingston was not the only one who scrambled for a place in the new regime. Hardly a week after the election, David C. Ker wrote the General demanding the dismissal of Beverly Chew as collector of customs at New Orleans. Chew, it seems, had committed the unpardonable crime of opposing the president-elect, with a commitment "so virulent," Ker swore, "as even to refuse permission to us to hoist a flag on the church [of which he was a vestryman] or to have the bells rung on the 8th of January in honor of the day—because they could not celebrate that glorious victory without honoring also the Chief who atchieved it. . . . An early example ought to be made of this man." Ker and Gordon had a ready suggestion for Chew's successor—Gordon himself. By late 1828 the Virginian clearly stood out as one of the major figures in the Louisiana Jackson party, in large measure because of wealth accumulated through the hated Orleans Navigation Company. Wagner and the *Advertiser* jumped to his command; Livingston respected and feared his strength and money; Grymes, Preston, Ripley, and Slidell courted his favor. Now he sought truly commanding dominance by winning the collector's office, for as Ker pointed out to Jackson, the man who held that position could "wield at will the whole mercantile body" of New Orleans and go far toward establishing himself as the political boss of the community.[15] He had read Gordon's designs perfectly.

Unlike most leading Jacksonians in the state, Gordon could not claim a long or intimate relationship to the General, nor had he fought under him at Chalmette, for at the time of the Battle of New Orleans he had prudently retired to safer precincts of the Union.[16] It was not until late 1827, when he headed the committee planning Jackson's campaign trip to New Orleans, that Gordon actually traveled to Nashville to meet the old warrior, carrying with him a letter of introduction from Grymes.[17] Now again in December 1828 he set out for Washington with a double purpose in mind—to sell his Orleans Navigation Company to the government and to get the promise of Chew's job.[18]

His trip proved profitable indeed. By the time of his return to New Orleans in March 1829, Jackson had been inaugurated and the first federal appointments in Louisiana announced. They included two which Gordon had promoted, placing John Slidell in the United States attorney's post for the eastern district of Louisiana and John Nicholson in the office of United States marshal. Gordon strutted among his friends, proudly describing the intimacy of his contacts with the president while in Washington despite the crush of office seekers penning in the old man, and carefully cultivating the impression that national governmental patronage must now be sought only through him.[19]

In May his own appointment as collector verified those claims, reinforced shortly thereafter by the naming of Wagner as naval officer, Ker as postmaster, Preston as register of the land office, W. L. Robeson as receiver of public moneys, James McFarlane as surgeon of the United States marine hospital, and S. H. Harper as judge of the eastern district court, all of them members of Gordon's circle, if not altogether beholden to him.[20]

Such examples of so-called reform brought quick and angry response. The Louisiana French seethed at the dismissal of Cruzat and Dupuy from the jobs now given to Wagner and Ker, especially since the list of new appointments included not a single Creole,[21] while the unblushing political proscription applied against Chew and other Adams sympathizers gave even some Jacksonians uneasy pause.[22] Outraged friends convened a great public meeting to protest the removal of Chew, who had served as collector for eleven years and won praise as a "popular man and a good officer" even from such an avid Jacksonian as Lafayette Saunders.[23] Irritated by the fuss, the Jacksonians staged a gathering of their own a few nights later, where they reaffirmed the party doctrine of reform in resolutions which defended the recent dismissals as necessary because the enemies of Jackson had used patronage to prevent his coming into office, "without any regard to the decorum of official station, and in defiance of public opinion." They hailed Gordon as a "man of the people," once a "mechanic," who "had lent his body as a rampart to Jackson [while] the bullets whistled about his ears" at the Battle of New Orleans, though most people knew full well that he had been in Cincinnati on that great occasion.[24]

Responding to the loud clamor over removals, the Jacksonians dismissed much of the noise as proceeding from the camp of Clay partisans always ready to "lay hold of everything to excite opposition to the present administration."[25] But however much this might have convinced the general public, it did little to assuage mounting resentment against Gordon among powerful forces within the party itself. For the new list of appointments was barren not only of Creoles but of Florida Jacksonians as well. Haralson's mouth, together with those of many of his colleagues, remained still open, a disturbing fact which John B. Dawson brought quickly to the president's attention. "There is a voice from Florida," he wrote the General, "that whispers to you, that thus far you have overlooked her, and believe me sir, 'twas Florida that [gave] you this State. The noisy clamours of New Orleans may have told better abroad, but it was the silent work of modest and noiseless Patriotism in Florida that gave us victory."[26]

Complaints of neglect in the Floridas became so pervasive that the *Political Gridiron* of East Feliciana, fearful of party disunity, felt compelled to warn against reading anything significant into what it called the carping criticism of men who had little claim upon the president, but such an obvious gloss hardly sufficed to hide the truth.[27] Gordon's treatment of Col. William S. Hamilton, one of the General's most loyal and effective supports from the beginning of his political career, gave disturbing evidence of his determination to control everything Jacksonian within the state. Already grooming Ripley for Congress, the collector now moved to shift him back to the Floridas as the agent of the New Orleans clique in that strongly Jacksonian area. The success of this venture required removal of Hamilton from the scene, and Ripley urged the colonel to accept Gordon's offer of aid in acquiring the post of federal surveyor general for the territory south of

Tennessee. Knowing Hamilton's reluctance to assume an office located outside the state, Ripley pledged to have the surveyor's headquarters moved to Baton Rouge. But he advised Hamilton not to delay acceptance of the appointment, even if it meant settling in Mississippi while awaiting transfer of the post to Louisiana. The cautious Hamilton, however, declined to be trapped. He refused to accept the appointment without proof of its being shifted to Baton Rouge and finally determined that Ripley and Gordon had in fact made no attempt to relocate the office. Recognizing finally that the plan had simply been a device to get him out of the state and open a clear avenue to Congress for Ripley, the enraged Hamilton declined the post and sent off a biting report of the devious scheme to Jackson and his old schoolmate, John Eaton, loaded with venom against the "cold, selfish, and cunning" Yankee who had set to work "like a Burr or a Clay to manage and to master."[28] Clearly, Gordon meant to rule or ruin. With such a break in the Jacksonian ranks as early as 1829, the latter possibility seemed real indeed.

Meanwhile, the New Orleans Jacksonians luxuriated in their newfound ascendancy. With Prieur in the mayor's office and a majority of their adherents on the municipal council, they began to build an effective distribution of city patronage through contracts and control of the police force.[29] For his part, Gordon swept the collector's office clean of old appointees, replaced them with minions of his own,[30] and then turned to plague the secretary of the treasury with incessant demands that he be allowed to expand his staff. He insisted on an additional deputy collector; argued the necessity of appointing full-time inspectors year-round rather than only in the busy season; and urged the hiring of a corps of special watchers for the ships in port. An exasperated Secretary Ingham finally gave way to anger, bluntly informing Gordon that "I regret to be obliged to resist in this as in many other cases the incessant importunity for patronage; but it is indispensable that it should be understood from this place that offices are not made for the incumbents, but for the public." Unabashed, Gordon continued his badgering until Ingham ended the exchange by going directly to Jackson, whose threats to "apply the Correction" finally brought the collector to heel.[31]

Frustrations of this kind may well explain the collector's response to the visit of Anne Royall in his offices at just about the time of Ingham's rebuke. That roaming virago answered his blunt query as to her business with an equally blunt rejoinder that she had called to see how he was conducting his affairs. "No wild beast caught in a trap, looked more astonished," she later remarked, "and wrinkling his skinny face without speaking a word he stalked back again" to his desk.[32]

Far away in Washington, ensconced now in new senatorial dignity, Livingston had greater opportunities than ever before to realize the perquisites of office. Davezac he provided for with an appointment to assist William Pitt Preble in the discussions of the Maine border at The Hague,[33] and then for a time seriously considered accepting Jackson's offer to become minister to France. In a "long and gloomy" interview with Martin Van Buren in Philadelphia early in the new president's term, however, he gave the secretary of state to understand that he and his wife could not accept such a post while there remained any possibility that the Jackson administration would be so primitive in its "social phases" as to "lead to degradation and contempt in the eyes of foreigners and of good society in general." Van Buren took this to mean that the Livingstons foresaw the "probability that they would be the persons most exposed to annoyances at a foreign court, from any scandal that might obtain circulation upon that point." In May, Livingston declined the position, pleading the press of financial problems, but only a few days later he gave every indication of having changed his mind. By then it was too late. The post had gone to W. C. Rives of Virginia, much to Van Buren's satisfaction, for he had expressed definite opposition to Livingston from the beginning.[34] For the Louisianian it meant resigning himself to life as a United States senator.

At least this elevated position gave him his best chance to end at last the twenty-five-year-old judgment still pending against him in the New York federal courts. That tangled problem had not been simplified by his activities in New Orleans, becoming even more complicated as a consequence of its eventual connection to the intricate complexities of the batture controversy. By 1820 Livingston had won clear title to a major part of that extremely valuable property along the Faubourg Ste. Marie levee by compromise with the city of New Orleans and the "front proprietors" behind the embankment, but the United States in 1822 recorded its claim of $100,014.89 against him in the Louisiana federal courts and seized his batture lots to satisfy his government debt. Finally sold at auction, they left an unpaid balance against him of $9,511.47, a sum that the resourceful senator now sought to escape paying.

His reputation as a lawyer had not been won for nothing. He knew that certain of the seized lots had been released from the government lien by the federal attorney in order that they might be sold prior to the general auction to pay the cost of filling in the property as required by city ordinance. When this lifting of the lien on these few units had been announced, however, his private creditors won seizure of them in the state courts, resulting in a judgment ordering their sale to meet his local debts. Almost immediately the state supreme court reversed that judgment, but because no steps had been taken to stay the order of the sale, the lots passed into the hands of private buyers purchasing under affirmed clear title guaranteed by the state recorder of mortgages.[35]

There the matter stood until March 1829, when Livingston became a United States senator, John Slidell assumed office as federal attorney in New Orleans, and Samuel H. Harper donned his robes as judge of the eastern district court. Jacksonians all, they had little cause to complain of any inequities in distribution of the patronage. Slidell had a particularly close connection to Livingston, for the latter had carried his recommendations for the federal attorney's job to Washington in January and had been the first to inform him of his appointment. Now Livingston asked for help. Responding to his requests, Slidell brought suit against the purchaser of one of the lots sold by state court order, demanding payment of the $9,511.47 still outstanding against the senator. He argued that because the lifting of the lien was irregular, the property purchased by Daniel T. Walden remained subject to the United States claim upon Livingston, and although Walden had bought it with clear title from the state, Harper decided he must pay the amount demanded or surrender his lot to the government. Overruled even in his attempts to make Livingston at least a party to the suit, Walden finally capitulated and paid the $9,511.47. Proud of such success in one of his first ventures, Slidell hurried to inform the treasury department that this "finally disposes of the judgment against Mr. Livingston."[36] He also had paid his debt.

On October 6, 1829, Governor Derbigny died of injuries sustained a few days earlier when bolting horses had flung him from his carriage, plunging the state into a bizarre confusion over the gubernatorial succession which would have been the delight of later Savoyards. The Constitution of 1812 made no provision for a lieutenant governor but designated the president of the senate as the successor to the governor's office should any vacancy occur. In conformity to this principle, Arnaud Beauvais became governor upon Derbigny's death, but when the legislature met in January 1830 and the senate necessarily elected a new presiding officer, Jacques Dupré, many insisted that since Beauvais was no longer president of the upper chamber he must surrender his executive chair to Dupré, who was. When the chagrined Beauvais complied with these demands, the absurdity of countenancing an endless succession of presidents of the senate moving up to the governorship impelled the legislature to call for a special election in July to select a chief executive for a full four-year term.[37] So after a respite of only a few months, Louisiana faced anew the rigors of a major political campaign, and for the first time since the great victory of 1828 the Jacksonian forces could test the effectiveness of their organization in a contest on the state level.

Tempers already frayed by the nonsense of the gubernatorial succession grew increasingly testy as old ethnic disputes once again tended to confuse the political scene. Despite his inability to capture the governorship, Bernard Marigny, still muttering threats of vengeance against the Americans, had managed to generate a force more and more at odds with those hoping to build Louisiana political parties along lines which conformed to prevailing national norms. The "*creole feeling*," Porter reported to Johnston with his usual insight, kept "getting stronger every year and every day in the state."[38] By 1830, indeed, its strength fired the French-speaking citizens to a fixed commitment to approach the gubernatorial canvass as if Jackson and Clay had no relevance to the election. That determination, after all, simply reflected their long-standing conviction that the choice of state officers should be unrelated to national issues or personalities. Equally responsive to the ethnic imperative, some of the American leadership tried to commit members of their community to an agreement that the election would be waged on a no-party basis, allowing them to unite behind the strongest American candidate whatever his national party ties. But that kind of campaign inevitably spelled disaster for Jacksonian hopes of seizing control of the governorship, for the party's major strength unquestionably lay in the Florida Parishes, whose leaders had long ago demonstrated that even their dedication to Andrew Jackson could not bring them to support a French candidate for office, however strong his credentials. The Jacksonians consequently had no French-speaking champion to push forward to exploit the Creole feeling, for the memories of Marigny's humiliation in 1828 still burned among the natives in their ranks, none of whom wished to be a second victim on the altar of Florida prejudices. Even the consuming ambition of Marigny could not prod him into a battle which he knew he could not win.[39]

By contrast, this hardening of Gallic unity immeasurably strengthened the Clay forces in the state. Their support had always been grounded primarily in the French parishes, despite the absence of anything approaching complete Gallic loyalty to their cause. Thus they had no difficulty in finding strong native candidates who also shared their national political attachments, and to their relief the American segment of their party now revealed a significant if not complete willingness to support these French-speaking colleagues.[40] The major activating force behind this congealing unity unquestionably came from Clay himself, giving an ironic twist to a campaign supposedly free of national party overtones. He arrived in New Orleans early in 1830, at the very beginning of the contest, and quickly threw himself into meticulous direction of his camp's strategy, with an eye to 1832 as well as to the immediate problem. The greatest threat to his success lay in the possible fragmentation of the Gallic vote among Duralde, Beauvais, and A. B. Roman, all of whom had announced for the governorship. Such division could easily throw the victory to an American, and since Clay had effectively kept his own American supporters from entering the field, this would have been unquestionably an American Jacksonian.[41] With his usual willingness to sacrifice his own personal ambitions, Duralde virtually eliminated this danger by withdrawing his candidacy to throw his weight behind Roman, eventually joined by such ardent Gallic Jacksonians as Alexander Mouton, Placide Bossier, and Benjamin Metoyer. Some rumors even placed Denis Prieur in this alliance, while the traditionally pro-Creole *Louisiana Courier* made little attempt to keep up its pretense of neutrality in the conflict.[42]

These defections by no means exhausted the difficulties besetting the Jacksonians. Gordon could agree with the French on at least one thing—he wanted no Florida governor. His hold on the Louisiana Jackson party would have been seriously threatened by the victory of a man from the region which so bitterly resented its neglect in the patronage distribution he claimed to have managed. He also knew that Hamilton would almost certainly be the choice of the Florida Jacksonians for the governorship, and he had little doubt where he stood in that old campaigner's esteem after the manner in which he and Ripley had tried to maneuver him out of the state.

Without even bothering to check with him, Gordon, Ripley, Wagner, and Carleton announced Overton's candidacy in the *Louisiana Advertiser* immediately following the legislative call for the July election.[43] Compared to Hamilton, Overton represented in every respect a safer risk for the New Orleans faction, which knew full well that the more than normally inflamed rural resentment against the city made a choice of one of their own group an impossibility. At least he would owe his advancement to the Gordon wing of the party, and they in a sense could claim him as one of their protégés, something which would have been ridiculous in the case of Hamilton, with the massed Florida voters at his back.

For his part, Hamilton had no great confidence in his own electability, never underestimating the reality of Gordon's power, for all the resentment it might have engendered. The announcement of the coming election moved him to seek out the advice of Wagner, an old friend whose support he had won on earlier occasions. What, he asked Wagner, could Florida expect of the Gordon group in the ensuing campaign? Now even closer to Gordon than ever before, Wagner coolly lied to Hamilton that the collector had been in constant communication with Overton before the two men decided to bring the general's name forward only three days before receipt of the colonel's letter in New Orleans. Confident that Overton's chances of success made him the strongest possible candidate, Gordon felt compelled to support him, Wagner reported. Hamilton must have writhed at the patronizing tone of Wagner's final comment on the collector's position. "He long since expressed a wish tome and he now repeats it," the ex-editor turned naval officer wrote, "that you should be the successor of J. S. Johnston in the senate."[44]

Convinced now that he could expect no aid from Gordon, Hamilton might well have declined the poll had not other voices made themselves immediately heard. Hatred of Gordon and his White House clique, as that faction was now called by its enemies, so permeated the country parishes that it suddenly seemed possible that it might give Hamilton a united rural support from his party which could hardly have been foreseen. Isaac L. Baker volunteered his active aid in the prairies, assuring Hamilton that "Your being opposed by old Martin Gordon would only make me stick more close to you . . . he is playing the devil with our party and should be kept in check."[45] From his Florida compatriots, too, came renewed pledges of support, most of whom seemed to share Robert Haile's wish "to see a country candidate succeed above all measure, even if for no other reason than that it would sorely dissapoint [*sic*] a certain New Orleans Set, who arrogate so much to themselves, that not content with seizing and taking under their especial protection the affairs of General Jackson as connected with this state, [they] wish likewise to extend their hated influence over the whole government."[46] Equally anxious to put an American in the governor's chair, the old Adams partisans in the Floridas offered their aid to Hamilton too, though the colonel prudently placed no great reliance in their protests of friendship.[47]

Even in New Orleans Gordon's leadership stimulated some opposition, for not all city Jacksonians found it pleasing to trot at the collector's heels like faithful hounds. W. L. Robeson, Isaac Preston, and Samuel Spotts, the surveyor of the port, grew more and more critical of the White House phalanx at the very moment that some of the Clay Americans in the capital began to question their party's obvious determination to throw its weight behind Roman. Robeson and Richard Davidson, one of these disgruntled Clayites, did their best to keep Hamilton in the race, promising him at least some support in the metropolis.[48]

The greatest factor in upsetting Gordon's plans proved to be General Overton himself. Drafted by the White House set without his consent, Overton agreed to remain in the race only if he could be assured that the Florida wing of the party would back his candidacy. He had no desire to contend against his old friend Hamilton, and he seemed quite sincere in his pledge to step aside in the latter's favor should he ascertain that this was the wish of the Florida region.[49]

Dismayed at the possible crash of all his schemes, Gordon hit upon a stratagem designed at least to extricate himself from an embarrassing position should that indeed become necessary. He arranged a gathering for March 20 at Davis's Ball Room to choose delegates to a Donaldsonville meeting with Jacksonians from other parishes called to decide upon a single candidate for governor. But just prior to the session at Davis's, Gordon and his close followers met together at his home and there determined to push Overton no matter what the cost. If successful at Donaldsonville, well and good. If it proved impossible to put Overton across, then Gordon might still claim credit for advancing the plan by which a candidate had finally been agreed upon. Watching these tactics, Robeson refused to have anything to do with Gordon's proposals. Instead, he reported everything to Hamilton with a caustic observation concerning the White House clique. "I think it impolitic for them or for officers of the Federal Government to be interfering publicly in state politics," he complained. "Let them go to H---- their own way. Mr. G[ordon] is certainly laboring under severe mental derangements, or he must be politically speaking an unprincipled man."[50]

The Donaldsonville convention collapsed in complete failure. Only eight delegates appeared for the meeting, so insignificant a number that no sessions ever convened.[51] Overton had already become convinced that he could expect no support in the Floridas, and true to his pledge he retired from the race in favor of Hamilton, leaving Gordon completely abandoned.[52] The collector had, in effect, been essentially cut out of the campaign. The *Louisiana Advertiser* came forward in May with a halfhearted endorsement of *two* candidates, Hamilton and David Randall, who offered primarily in the hope of taking votes from Roman in the Lafourche area and along the coast, where he had something of a personal following. Except for this feeble gesture, however, and a few scattered attacks upon Roman as a defender and proponent of the protective tariff, the *Advertiser* remained singularly quiet throughout the ensuing campaign.[53]

The effectiveness of Clay and Duralde gave Roman an overwhelming victory. He carried most of the French parishes easily, losing but three to Beauvais and two to Randall, while Hamilton had difficulty even in some parts of Florida, actually dropping St. Tammany to his Creole rival. The New Orleans vote demonstrated clearly the disastrous consequences of the disarray in the city's Jacksonian ranks, giving Roman a total of 587, Beauvais 460, Hamilton 191, and Randall 3. The determining factor in all this, one of his disappointed backers, Benjamin F. Linton, told Hamilton, had been the guiding genius of Clay, working diligently from his base in the city. Despite the repeated declarations that ethnic loyalties would take precedence over national party affiliations in the race, Linton maintained, Clay kept his American followers solidly behind Roman, while the Jacksonians failed to give a comparable unified support to Hamilton. All told, the Clay candidates outpolled the Jacksonians 5,116 to 3,164.[54] But those who knew Louisiana politics best reminded the rest that no message as to presidential probabilities in 1832 should be read into the contest. The state had obviously not given up its attachment to a political system operating on two distinct levels—one local, one national—and each had its own dynamics.

For Jacksonians, the 1830 campaigns could only be seen as disastrous. In the congressional races, old Philemon Thomas had little trouble winning the seat recently vacated by Gurley, for again the Jacksonians split their ranks. Ripley had made his bid for the place with the blessing of Gordon and the *Louisiana Advertiser*, while the Floridians rallied behind Lafayette Saunders again to thwart this invasion of their region by an agent of the White House coterie. The angry blasts of the *Advertiser* that it "had expected better things" of Saunders only widened the breach and in effect insured Thomas's election.[55] Edward Douglass White continued so popular in the First District that no one offered against him, and in the western district Henry Adams Bullard finally succeeded in his political ambitions. Overton had decided not to seek reelection to Congress even before the gubernatorial issue arose, wishing to keep a closer watch on his still unsettled business affairs. He pledged his support to young P. A. Rost of Natchitoches, but his protégé's vigorous attempt to win favor as an avowed Jacksonian candidate could not offset his own personal liabilities. A foreign Frenchman to begin with, he committed the incredible blunder of voting in a legislative session against an apportionment bill which would have added strength to his own district. Against such competition even Bullard could win, giving the Adams men a clean sweep of the congressional seats.[56] At the same time, however, the legislative canvass assured a majority for the Jacksonians in the assembly. And in the New Orleans mayoral elections they also triumphed, but there their standard bearer had been Prieur, whose popularity notoriously transcended party loyalties.[57]

On the surface the Jacksonians seemed to accept their defeats placidly enough. Gordon maintained that he had not really been involved, a claim faithfully seconded by Maunsel White, a close confederate of the collector and Andrew Jackson's New Orleans factor. Shrugging off the recent elections as indicating no weakness of the *real* Jacksonian strength in the state, White reported to the president that his important Louisiana friends were "as true as steel but some who wished to get office by your popularity have been disappointed, and they deserved it." Then came the revealing final comment: "They were not our choice."[58]

But the impact of the 1830 failings could not really be dismissed so easily. Gordon's electoral humiliation intensified an earlier public embarrassment when various blunders on his part in interpreting certain trade regulations provoked a furious howl from the mercantile community and brought him another stinging rebuke from Secretary Ingham.[59] A week following Roman's victory, he was telling friends he had decided to give up the collector's post,[60] though he fixed no date for this action and his comments may well have been designed to provide a face-saving escape should his interim appointment to the office fail to receive Senate approval in the newly convened session.

Elsewhere, violence attending the campaign still agitated Ouachita Parish, climaxed by the killing of Gen. Ferdinand Morgan in a brawl resulting from charges by the Morehouse faction that Morgan had defrauded Jacksonian candidates by stuffing the ballot box during the canvass. The parish remained in an uproar for months, and when the accused came to trial, party hatreds seemed fully personalized in Bullard as chief prosecutor and Ripley as principal defense attorney. Acquittal of the defendant by what Bullard claimed to be a politically biased jury only exacerbated the tensions. "We are here now so effectually divided," one observer wrote Johnston, "that society does not exist for any one except with those of his side. The line of demarcation is traced with blood."[61]

The Floridas experienced no such bloody affray, but tempers flared and emotions ran high. "Florida failed to do her duty, & is forever disgraced," Alexander Barrow, one of the region's leading politicos, raged. "The Jackson party in Florida and I may say throughout the state," he ranted in a letter of sympathy to Hamilton, "deserve to be ruled forever hereafter by a rod of iron, and I wish from my soul that all *Americans* who voted for Roman were placed on his sugar farm under the lash of his drivers." If Louisiana was ever to have an American governor again, Archibald Haralson groused to Hamilton, "it will be by French sufferance. . . . I think the American population at the mercy of the French." He ended on a despairing note: "We may all say as much as we please about the practicability of uniting Florida in the support of any American candidate. It can't be done."[62] Most troubling and laden with prospects of continued Jacksonian failings, reports had it that even heretofore loyal Florida adherents to the American cause had defected to Roman, some going so far as to claim that Thomas Butler had begun to look more favorably upon Clay than Jackson and that he had indeed voted for the Creole against Hamilton. His defeat so embittered the colonel that he retreated into practical retirement after the election, though he kept up a busy conspiracy by letter with some of his cohorts, who engaged in stealthily checking old church records in the hope of proving Roman too young to meet the age requirement established for the governor's office by the constitution. All in all, 1830 had certainly been no time of glory for Louisiana Jacksonianism.[63]

The new year brought little promise of better things to come. January saw prodigious efforts to reunite the party for the defeat of Senator Johnston's bid for reelection, but again the doctrinaire Florida faction made success almost an impossibility. By insisting that Johnston's protariff record must constitute the main public issue in the contest they naturally drove sugar-area legislators to energetic moves of their own in Johnston's defense. The incumbent, moreover, had many personal friends among Jacksonians irritated by Florida efforts to whip their party into line behind J. B. Dawson. Again the Jacksonians failed, managing to gather but twenty-two votes for the iridescent Dawson against Johnston's twenty-nine. Dejected by yet another defeat, Robert Haile admitted to what must have been a general feeling among his colleagues. "I am," he confessed to Hamilton, "a good deal staggered with the virtual [collapse] of our party in this state."[64]

Upon an already weakened cause there now fell the confusion of the Peggy Eaton affair and the first real awareness of the inner tensions threatening the unity of the central Jacksonian forces. The trouble stemmed from the unwillingness of some Washingtonians to admit the secretary of war's wife to capital society because of alleged sexual immorality, despite her obvious place in the affections of the president. Jackson fumed at what he took to be an attack upon Peggy's reputation akin to that which his enemies had waged against his own Rachel in the stormy days of the election of 1828, when they had charged her with adultery because of her union with him before her first marriage had been legally dissolved. Floride Calhoun, wife of Vice-president John C. Calhoun, figured as a leader of the anti-Eaton protagonists, and the furor over the dispute soon drove a wedge between Jackson and the South Carolinian. Secretary of State Martin Van Buren, anxious to supplant Calhoun as heir apparent to the General, seized the opportunity to champion the Eatons and thus establish himself in the good graces of the president. Early rumors of a Calhoun-Van Buren split in the administration began to be heard in New Orleans in late January, but they aroused little interest. St. Romes in the *Louisiana Courier* tried to smooth over the reported quarrel as an insignificant difference between two ambitious men, making it quite obvious, however, that Calhoun as a Southerner certainly warranted greater trust than the crafty New Yorker. More cautious, the *Louisiana Advertiser* ignored the story until the position of the president could be more clearly understood, a wise move which saved it from the embarrassing gyrations forced upon St. Romes by the eventual revelations of the break between Jackson and his vice-president.[65] By July the *Courier* had come so far around as to label Calhoun "a malignant spirit," encouraging men to the same reckless attack upon helpless women as that turned upon Rachel Jackson herself in 1828.[66]

The strident quarrel over Peggy Eaton inflamed additional differences between Jackson and Calhoun which eventually resulted in dissolution of the cabinet, a development which threw a pall of depression over the once buoyant Jackson forces in the state.[67] Their enemies ridiculed the spectacle of St. Romes shifting ground with almost every issue of the *Courier*,[68] charged that the president had turned Washington into a brothel,[69] and noted with pleasure that even some of the oldest friends of the administration seemed shaken by the recent developments in the national capital.[70] Upset by the turn of events, Gordon and Henry Carleton launched a vigorous campaign to counteract the opposition propaganda by giving the *Washington Globe* a wider circulation in New Orleans, going so far as to visit all subscribers to the pro-Calhoun *United States Telegraph* to urge transfer of their subscriptions to the official Jacksonian organ.[71] Their efforts underscored an awareness of how seriously the party's local press had failed it in this critical period, with St. Romes increasingly incompetent and the *Advertiser* bereft of passion and fire since Wagner had left its editorship to take on public office.

Increasing bitterness surrounding the tariff and nullification controversies soon threatened to raise issues of even greater import than the embarrassments of the cabinet crisis and Eaton imbroglio. It must have been particularly disheartening for the Louisiana Jacksonians to realize that again they faced a situation laden with possibilities of disaster for their own cause far beyond those threatening their rivals. The difficulties sprang from the peculiar economy of the state, resting as it did upon the two great staples of cotton and sugar. Cultivators of the first shared the general Southern antipathy to the protective tariff system, while producers of the second felt their very existence to depend upon duties shielding them from the destructive competition of the West Indies. Associated with a national party generally considered hostile to the protective policy, Louisiana Jacksonians frequently felt the distrust of the sugar parishes, which regularly gave majorities to candidates friendly to Clay and his American System. Moreover, what support might have been won in the cotton parishes by an antitariff stand could hardly compensate for the enmity it engendered in the sugar regions, for the speculative fears of free trade proponents seldom matched in intensity the dread with which a sugar planter faced the prospect of a slash in the import duties on his commodity.[72]

The rising importance of the sugar industry to the Louisiana economy added substantially to the complexities of the problem. The total value of the state's annual production of sugar and molasses had forged ahead of that of the cotton crop of 1828,[73] and the turn of the new decade saw vast new acres opened to the cultivation of the cane.[74] At almost that very moment, rumors that the Jackson administration planned drastic reductions in the sugar duty spread fear and uncertainty through the industry.

Secretary of the Treasury Ingham in January 1830 circularized the planters for information on their operations and profits, stirring up memories in Louisiana of earlier warnings by Governor Beauvais and Henry Gurley that the 1830 sessions of Congress would inevitably witness an assault upon the sugar tariff.[75] Fearful of such attacks from the antitariff forces, the Louisiana sugar interests began to feel that they could no longer support the state's old policy of denouncing all protection except that on their own product. "We must join somebody," Alexander Porter remarked at the time, "neutral we cannot be."[76] Sensing the futility of trying to maintain an alliance with the Southern free traders, the Louisiana legislature finally took the full step toward partnership with the avowed protariff forces, and in March of 1830 the assembly passed an almost unanimous resolution in support of protectionism, declaring it harmless to the property of the South and pledging its support to "such measures as those that are contemplated by the law of 1828, on the tariff."[77]

Jacksonian attack upon the measure came immediately and forcefully, for it could hardly be considered anything other than a victory for Clay and a rebuke to their own tariff program. But later attempts in Congress to reduce the sugar duties vindicated the wisdom of the assembly's policy when Southern antitariff forces lined up solidly against the Louisiana staple.[78] Left with no other argument, the Jacksonians in the state could only maintain that all had been well until the legislature shifted position to join forces with Eastern manufacturers. Whatever fate now befell the sugar industry, they claimed, would be completely the responsibility of the Clay forces. Licking their wounds, they fell back to the old position that only the antiprotection policy of the Southern states truly secured the sugar tariff, because its duties had never formed part of the hated American System but derived from a constitutional application of the tariff-for-revenue doctrine.[79] Even they realized, however, that few sugar planters would accept such rationalization,[80] and Ripley told Bullard bluntly that it had become "the settled and determined policy of the Jackson party to break down the aristocracy of Louisiana, consisting of the sugar interest and the Banks—and that to punish Louisiana for committing itself on the subject of the tariff, the duty on sugar must and will be taken off." This had been a private warning, but it so shocked Bullard that he could find no other reply than "God have mercy on us."[81]

With the excitement of the cabinet dissolution almost certain to push the nullificationists to a more radical stance, the Louisiana Jacksonians had to tread very carefully between two extreme positions, trying to woo the sugar planters without appearing to embrace the American System and at the same time attempting to maintain the backing of the free-trade wing of the party without seeming to encourage the heresy of nullification. How they must have envied the Clay men their easy course of embracing the tariff and cursing the South Carolina aberration without reservation.

The reorganization of the cabinet produced yet another problem, for Livingston's ascendancy to the Department of State required Louisiana to select a senator to fill his place. Failure to put one of their own in the seat would leave Louisiana Jacksonians unrepresented in Congress, additional evidence of the decline of their fortunes at the very moment that the approaching 1832 campaign required at least some sign of their party's vitality in the state. Fearful that Governor Roman might fill the vacancy with a Clay partisan, they quickly demanded a special legislative session to make the choice, reminding Roman that any other procedure would be a marked insult to all those Jacksonians who had helped him win office.[82] With the governor's acceptance of their challenge, the campaign moved into full swing.[83] Taking advantage of the November timing of the session, which made it difficult for sugar planters to attend because of the rolling season, the Jacksonians decided to make the tariff a principal issue in their campaign strategy,[84] at the same time stressing a particular attraction of their candidate, Henry Carleton. The *Louisiana Advertiser* made much of this point, emphasizing Carleton's brother-in-law relationship to Livingston, now high in the official family of the president. "It would be madness," the *Advertiser* lectured the legislators, "to shut your eyes to advantages like these."[85]

But even with this clever strategy, things did not go well. A meeting called by the *Courier* and *Advertiser* to choose delegates to the Free Trade Convention in Philadelphia ended in a ludicrous rout of the antitariff forces. Clay men packed the hall, put Dr. A. E. McConnell in the chair, and howled with delight as he denounced Jackson for seeking a second term, reviled free traders as nullifiers, and adjourned the gathering until September 1, 1939.[86] Even the attempts to picture Gordon as the savior of the state's industry because he had recently exposed and halted the introduction of liquefied sugar into the nation under the duty-free label of "syrups" failed miserably when it turned out that White and Porter had for weeks warned the collector of the fraud without stirring him to the slightest action. He had moved only after finding an opening which allowed him to claim credit for ending the deception himself.[87]

The fatal blow to Jacksonian hopes of winning the Senate seat came, ironically enough, from Livingston himself. On the eve of the legislature's choice, with Jacksonians as far away as Natchitoches being dragged from sick beds to make the poll, word arrived in New Orleans of Davezac's appointment as *chargé d'affaires* to The Hague, and once again the old odor of nepotism which seemed to cling to the Livingston name ruined whatever chances Carleton might have had. A Jackson member of the legislature told Porter that "he supposed the next thing would be that Carleton if elected would go out minister to England or France, and Harry Lockett [another Livingston relative] be made one of the judges of the Sup. court of the U. States, and this he could not stomach."[88] Evidently other Jacksonians shared his disgust, for though their party had a majority in the assembly, Roman's secretary of state, George A. Waggaman, won the election by a substantial margin.[89] For the Jacksonians, 1832 looked bleak indeed.

Elsewhere in the Union, however, Jacksonian party prospects brightened day by day. Each month seemed to expose more clearly the basic weaknesses of Clay's position. Unacceptable to the South because of his tariff views, unable to shake Jackson's grip upon the West, and frankly uncertain as to the potential of the anti-Masonic movement growing in the East, Clay appeared to be continuously losing ground in his campaign for the White House. The victory of the Jacksonians in the Kentucky elections of 1831, followed closely by the anti-Masonic nomination of William Wirt, spelled disaster in the eyes of most of Clay's Louisiana friends, and Josiah Johnston's mail pouch grew heavier with predictions that if the Kentuckian remained in the race he would destroy his own party.[90]

Completely aware of his slipping fortunes, Clay had no desire to bind his friends to a fruitless campaign. At a gloomy conclave in Washington on December 7, 1831, he confessed that he thought his chances hopeless and urged withdrawal of his name from the contest. But when his followers could see no alternate candidate who might take his place, he agreed to continue the fight, primarily, as he told Edward Everett, because he had become convinced that his withdrawal would have toppled his faithful adherents from their control of state governments in places like Louisiana and Maryland.[91]

Reports of Clay's own pessimism must certainly have reached Louisiana through his family connections if in no other way, and after the long series of victories over their enemies in 1830 and 1831 the Clay party now faltered and proceeded to fall slowly apart. Duralde and his associates, normally the vitalizing spark of the Kentuckian's forces in the state, suddenly seemed to be paralyzed in the grip of a sense of futility, despondent and inactive.[92] To the ever watchful Porter they appeared "to have taken leave of their senses,"[93] while apprehensive opportunists such as T. J. Pew, editor of the *Mercantile Advertiser*, found their inertia clear warning of impending disaster. For Pew the remedy was simple enough—he deserted to the Jackson camp.[94]

The apathy and despair of their opponents gave new life to the once battered forces of the president. Soon after Pew's shift in loyalties, the editors of the *New Orleans Bee*, a rapidly growing publication once bitterly opposed to the administration,[95] also joined the growing coalition. Even the strident voice of Gibson now fell practically mute. As the Clay forces sank deeper into lethargy, Jacksonians all over the state met in enthusiastic gatherings to reaffirm their faith and to organize their strength for the coming electoral battles.[96] A boisterous party conclave in New Orleans early in January 1832 culminated in nominations of presidential electors and the choice of delegates to the Baltimore convention for the naming of Jackson's running mate. Van Buren and Martin Gordon won particular plaudits from the participants, with the collector receiving acclaim as the Hero of the Second Battle of New Orleans, as overgenerous reference to his role in blocking the importation of syrups to evade the sugar duty.[97]

Already thoroughly aroused from their earlier lassitude and ineffectiveness, Jacksonians joined together in even greater solidarity when the United States Senate, by the casting vote of John C. Calhoun, rejected Van Buren's appointment as ambassador to Great Britain. Storms of protest reminiscent of the 1825 charges of bargain and corruption once again reverberated throughout the nation, with the *Advertiser* cursing this victory of a "new coalition" as one designed to "degrade [our] chief magistrate in the eyes of his own country and of foreign nations."[98] Gordon broadcast his devotion to the president and his martyred defender with brilliant transparencies draped from the balcony of his home on Royal Street,[99] while the party faithful thronged to a public meeting in New Orleans called as a testimony of admiration for Van Buren.[100] Such acclaim completely drowned out the feeble praise for the Senate's action at a pitifully small anti-Van Buren demonstration staged by Clay sympathizers, evoking from a disgusted Porter the despondent admission that for men of his persuasion the political prospects seemed "more gloomy in this State, than I ever knew them."[101]

This impressive resurgence of strength and optimism in the state's Jacksonian ranks covered over what might have developed into a major break in the party. The Florida leaders of the administration forces had lost much of their enthusiasm for Jackson because of his refusal to bend to South Carolina's view of the Union as subordinate to a state's right to interpose its sovereignty between federal power and the citizenry. More and more this turned them to an open acceptance of John C. Calhoun as their true champion. W. H. Overton, meanwhile, had played a major part in the attack upon John Eaton, husband of the notorious Peggy, convinced in his own mind that the president had fallen under the spell of evil men dominated by the crafty Van Buren.[102] With all his sympathy for Calhoun, however, Overton had no leanings toward nullification, which clearly distinguished him from the Florida doctrinaires. Alexander Barrow, appalled at Jackson's admission that he considered protection perfectly constitutional, openly advocated nullification to the president's face during a conversation late in 1831. His comments in letters to Hamilton leave little doubt that the colonel as well as John B. Dawson shared these views, which Barrow defended as the original faith of 1798. Barrow actually considered embracing the doctrine openly and publicly in December 1831, but he recognized the dangers latent in such a course. "Dawson you know," he wrote to Hamilton, "is the declared candidate for the office of Governor and if . . . [he] was to come out in favor of the nullifiers, there is no telling what loss he would sustain by it."[103]

Outside the Florida Parishes the nullification doctrine attracted little support, a reality fully appreciated by those tempted to endorse it. By 1832 the Louisiana Jackson party's overwhelming commitment to the president's stand on national sovereignty made opposition futile and would almost certainly have ended Dawson's hopes for the governorship in 1834, a prospect particularly distasteful now that the future of the Jacksonians seemed so bright. Barrow and Dawson held their tongues.

Their silence attracted no great attention, for the passions once aroused by divisions on nullification and the tariff dissipated appreciably as 1832 wore on. The fiery attacks upon protectionism by the South Carolina nullifiers did much to swing Louisiana Jacksonians toward a defense of the system hardly distinguishable from that of the Clay party itself, and the tariff debates in Congress during the spring and summer stimulated the *Courier* and *Advertiser* to comments which they would have damned only a few months earlier.[104] No major difference emerged in the approaches of the two parties to the proposed Tariff of 1832, except for the greater Jacksonian push for acceptable compromise features in the measure. Gone now were the wonted attacks upon the tariff as a conspiracy to enrich eastern manufacturers, replaced by regular pronouncements in the *Advertiser* that the true Jacksonian creed had always recognized "free trade absurdities" as the tool of British economic colonialism. Those still clinging to antitariff principles common to Jacksonians only a few months previously found themselves damned as "those who pant for a 'solemn league and covenant' between Carolina nullifiers and English manufacturers."[105]

This remarkable blurring of party distinctions led to a demonstration of bipartisan accord which must have appeared like a dream to those who could remember 1825 and 1828. At a great antinullification meeting in New Orleans on June 17, 1832, leaders of both parties gathered to condemn the South Carolina doctrines convulsing the nation. The Jacksonians clearly meant to use the occasion to urge adoption of the proposed tariff compromises then pending in Congress, but when the Clay leaders threatened to withdraw rather than support any kind of reduction in duties, the two sides agreed to a simple blanket resolution condemning nullification as anarchy. Significantly, even some of the Jacksonians insisted that no concessions could be made in tariff adjustment until South Carolina renounced its heresy, a position most strongly held by the Gallic members of both parties who, Porter reported, "were all for marching off to S. Carolina and fighting."[106]

Passage of the Tariff of 1832 shortly thereafter eased the sectional antagonisms to a degree by providing for a modest reduction in most duties, although it clearly retained the principle of protection. Louisiana Jacksonians generally praised its more moderate schedules, and even the Clay faction eventually gave it their somewhat reluctant support, for loss of a half-cent total in the sugar rates seemed small enough price to pay for what everyone hoped might be a permanent tariff settlement. At least the Jacksonians had been brought to a point at which they no longer threatened destruction to the whole system of protective imposts. The Calhounites had been effectively silenced,[107] and the radical states' rights cause which had loomed so large in the first years of the Jacksonian movement found itself now without any major champion in Louisiana. From the Florida Parishes came no word of protest against the president. Clearly, no one determined to rule the state at the head of his party could afford to cast off Andrew Jackson as an ally. So Barrow and Dawson continued to hold their tongues.

This defusing of nullification and the tariff as issues in the coming campaign of 1832 left the Bank of the United States as the center of controversy around which the election would revolve. Essentially an imported disagreement in Louisiana, the quarrel over the rechartering of the financial giant would probably never have developed in the state without outside stimulus. Not that this made the consequences of the struggle any less real or important in the community. The New Orleans branch of the Second Bank of the United States served the whole Mississippi Valley, especially facilitating the solution of the complex exchange problems growing out of the position of New Orleans as the place to which the flood of Western produce came to be sold but not the place at which the West bought most of the things required to satisfy its own needs. By acting as the major channel through which bills of exchange finally found their way to the points of greatest need in the vast national marketing system, the New Orleans branch performed one of its most valuable services, at the same time filling the additional and equally important role of providing ready credit and discount services to the multifarious commercial interests of the metropolis.

The branch and its officers established such a record of efficiency and liberality in New Orleans that few found any reason to complain against it prior to the beginning of the titanic struggle between Jackson and the Bank's imperious president, Nicholas Biddle. Even in the long history of bitterness directed toward financial houses in the city by the planter class of the parishes, the national bank generally escaped any major criticism. Nor had there been any serious public sentiment against banks in principle in Louisiana during the pre-Jackson period, for one can discount the many attacks found in the press as the normal complaints of a society which generally felt that banks were not evil but too few and that favored citizens received special privileges in the parceling out of available funds. The anti-Jackson composition of the state's congressional delegation makes its vote in favor of rechartering the Bank in 1832 and 1834 in no way unusual, but that this position enjoyed wide sympathy back home seems confirmed by the extensive expressions of support Samuel Jaudon, the branch cashier, managed to drum up for the Bank from a broad spectrum of the community's mercantile and financial institutions. After Jackson's bank veto, Samuel H. Harper advised Secretary Taney that the banking houses of New Orleans represented a "mixed character" so far as their political attachments could be determined, and that the directors of only one of them had refused to sign a memorial recommending renewed charter of the Bank of the United States.[108]

There is no history of any antibanking or antibusiness bias even among the men who formed the nucleus of the Jackson party in the state. Martin Gordon, Isaac T. Preston, W. L. Robeson, James W. Breedlove, J. B. Plauché, William G. Hewes, William C. Withers, J. B. Labatut, S. W. Oakey, Harvey Elkin, Nathan Morse, Joseph Saul, Peter Laidlaw, Henry Lockett, Samuel Spotts, John Hagan, and many others, Jacksonians all, had a long record of being among the most active bank directors and businessmen of the community. Maunsel White as late as 1832 continued to serve as one of the branch bank's board of directors, a position earlier held by other prominent Jacksonians including Hewes, Hagan, and Gordon himself. Up in Rapides Parish, W. H. Overton, for all his dedication to Jackson, had considerable uneasiness about his old comrade's anti-Bank policy, which he ascribed to his having fallen under the spell of the evil Martin Van Buren. "I had hoped," he confided to Josiah S. Johnston, "that with slight modifications the charter of the bank would have been renewed & the interests & currency of the country remain in its present satisfactory state." In Washington, Edward Livingston apparently felt much the same. Before Jackson made opposition to the Bank a matter of party and personal loyalty, Livingston did everything he could to facilitate its salvation, on one occasion telling Charles J. Ingersoll, a Pennsylvania Jacksonian, that he "denounced all substitutes for the present Bank of the United States and every kind of other fiscal contrivance as absurd and impracticable," adding that he thought it "impossible to administer the Treasury of the United States without just such a Bank."[109]

Prior to Jackson's veto the Louisiana press more or less tended to ignore financial questions altogether. There had been some threats against banks and monied aristocracies, to be sure, but these had generally been of much the same type as Wagner's 1828 campaign against those supposedly antimechanic in sentiment, which meant that they stressed social snobbery as the great offending sin or else made completely unsupported assertions that aristocrats used the Bank of the United States to buy political control of the country.[110]

It was not until late May of 1832 that the Jacksonian press began to give any appreciable space to the great bank fight, and that primarily in the form of reprints from Francis P. Blair's *Washington Globe*. Local editors copied these with little additional comment for the most part, or contented themselves with observations typical of one in the *Advertiser*: "Thank God, that the American people are too intelligent to be led astray by the hirelings, and paid mercenaries of an ambitious aristocracy, who would be the *noblemen* of the land."[111] But one would look in vain for any analysis of flaws in the Bank's financial structure or for any explication of how its business practices did harm to the nation's economy or threatened the political freedoms of its people. It sufficed to know that Jackson found it necessary to do battle with the institution. That alone made it evil.

The president's insistence that the Bank was unconstitutional, financially despotic, and politically corrupt created an inevitable furor, and Louisiana learned that one of the principle complaints against Biddle and his associates charged them with deliberately using the New Orleans branch to drain capital from the West to the coffers of the East. Despite the unlikelihood that such claims had any basis in fact beyond the admitted and regular transfer from New Orleans of funds which had accumulated there through the Mexican trade,[112] the Louisiana Jacksonians seized upon the president's message outlining his reasons for the Bank veto as the greatest state paper since Washington's farewell address, happy that they now had something around which to wage their campaign.[113] Again they could go forth to crush the evil of Federalism, to do battle with aristocrats.

Despite an increase in the number of original articles in the Jacksonian press blasting Biddle's "Octopus," local papers came nowhere close to matching the veritable avalanche of print spewed out against the Bank in the columns of the administration's chief mouthpiece, the *Washington Globe.* Jacksonians outdid themselves in flooding the state with Blair's publication. One dismayed Clay supporter reported to Johnston that the mail to his small town in the Floridas had become so heavy because of the mass of *Globes* being delivered that the bag had to be carried slung on a pole between two men, whereas in earlier times a single clerk had been able to manage it easily under one arm. The "Extra Globes are sent gratis all over the country," he moaned. "You see them everywhere."[114]

In such fashion did Jackson's veto and Blair's pen succeed in inflaming Louisiana Jacksonianism against the Bank. Maunsel White, only recently a director of the New Orleans branch, not only bestowed lavish praise upon the president for striking at such a vicious economic tyrant but actually bestowed upon his blameless newborn son the name of Andrew Veto Jackson White.[115] Forced to act by the approaching end to the Bank's charter and the instability of the eastern financial market, already upset by the cholera epidemic raging in the nation, Biddle reluctantly ordered the New Orleans branch to curtail its discount and exchange services. The branch's compliance produced such financial hardship in the metropolis that by late August credit had almost completely dried up in the city, leaving even friends of the Bank to protest the severity of its curtailment. Biddle may well have hoped to demonstrate the value of his institution's services by making them unavailable, but if that had been his strategy it played instead right into the president's hands. In the eyes of many, the Bank's actions seemed to prove exactly what Jackson had always maintained—perhaps, they said, no private institution should be allowed in a republic to possess power to cause such distress at will. Further questions as to the Bank's propriety mounted with the *Advertiser*'s report that Josiah Johnston, one of its major Senate defenders, was indebted to the institution for as much as $36,000, clear evidence in the minds of some that such a loan must have constituted a subsidy for attack upon the president.[116]

The war upon the Bank in Louisiana came at a most opportune time for the Jacksonians, for it did not require them to defend a policy which would almost completely deprive the state of access to banking capital and services, as would have been true only a few years earlier. The new decade had seen a veritable rash of additional banks in the community, pushed by planters who hoped to play one house against the other and enthusiastically supported by businessmen in New Orleans anxious to link banking with internal improvement projects while they also tested the new device of using mortgages on urban property as pledges for stock. Between 1830 and 1833 chartered banks in the state other than the Bank of the United States increased from four to eleven, with a jump in capitalization from $9 million to $39 million. Curtailment of the Bank's functions in New Orleans produced serious distress, but these new financial establishments allowed the state to ride out the storm.[117]

In the face of such an explosion of Jacksonian vigor, the Clay forces had little chance to escape their own slough of despondency and inactivity. Not even the successful return of their three incumbent congressmen in the July elections revived their spirits, for as was so often true in Louisiana these contests once again swung primarily on personal factors and augured no success for Clay in November. Bullard defeated Alexandre Mouton, a young Creole handicapped by opposition from the powerful Dupré clan based more on family than political differences.[118] In the First District White had again gone unchallenged, and in the Floridas General Thomas repeated his victory over a Jacksonian opposition still divided by the pretensions of the Yankee from New Orleans, Eleazar Ripley.[119]

The last months of the campaign changed nothing. Clay was already defeated.

On the morning of October 25, 1832, Dr. James S. McFarlane pushed his way through a New Orleans crowd of early risers gathered around the still bodies of two men at Poydras Street and the levee. Uneasy but curious, they watched his quick inspection of the dead. then they broke in panic, scattering through the streets of the city, down to the Exchange, out to the faubourgs, carrying the terrifying news. The cholera had finally come to New Orleans.

By the next day death was rampant in the city, and as the disease began to radiate out into the parishes, mounting consternation spread with it. In ten days New Orleans lost one-tenth of is people, while the rest struggled through scenes of horror unparalleled even in this place of recurrent plague. The whole state plunged into a surrealist nightmare. Sheets of rain poured down from skies perpetually reddened by the blaze of great fires of burning "goudron" belching suffocating smoke designed to keep away infection. Cannon boomed constantly, day and night, in the hope that they might stir the air and waft away the sickness. The grim signs of death loomed everywhere—silent homes occupied only by the dead; stacks of corpses piled high one upon another, abandoned in cemeteries, burned in open lots, or dumped into great common graves in the enveloping swamps. There was nothing to do but wait. Some encased themselves in binding plasters of burgundy pitch, while others downed a so-called cholera preventative composed of "pure French brandy mixed with plenty of red pepper." But the disease had its way.[120]

In the very midst of this terror came the election of 1832; it is remarkable that anyone at all felt any interest in going to the polls. Many who went were dead before the counting of their ballots. It may well have made little difference in the outcome, considering the collapse of Clay's forces, but the cholera struck most viciously in those parishes of the Kentuckian's greatest strength. "No human exertion could get the French to the polls," Porter wrote to Johnston in explanation of the overwhelming Jackson victory,[121] and the returns bolster his findings. The total ballots cast in the rural sugar parishes fell far below normal, while the strong pro-Jackson region of Florida, relatively untouched by the disease, brought its full force to bear. The final tabulation gave Jackson 4,873 votes to Clay's 2,207, and once again the Hero of New Orleans had carried Louisiana.[122]

Under the circumstances of this peculiar campaign, abandoned almost from its start by Clay men, who felt their champion had been deserted elsewhere in the Union, and climaxing in the worst epidemic the state was ever to know, who could find in the election of 1832 any proof of the political or economic faith of Louisiana? Only one thing remained beyond dispute—the Jackson party had surpassed its rival in energy, spirit, and organization. Even without the cholera, victory almost certainly would have been theirs. It had turned not on issues clearly setting them apart from their opponents, but on the magnetism and will of Andrew Jackson.

Notes for "Democracy Regnant"

[1]William Haile to William S. Hamilton, May 20, 1829, in William S. Hamilton Papers, Department of Archives, Louisiana State University, Baton Rouge, La. (hereafter cited as Hamilton Papers).

[2]*Louisiana Advertiser*, March 26, 1827.

[3]*Florida Gazette* (St. Francisville), June 27, 1829.

[4]Archibald Haralson to Thomas Butler, December 29, 1828, in Thomas Butler Papers, Department of Archives, Louisiana State University, Baton Rouge, La. (hereafter cited as Butler Papers).

[5]Edward Livingston to Andrew Jackson, August 12, 1828, in Andrew Jackson Papers, Library of Congress (hereafter cited as Jackson Papers).

[6]Edward Livingston to Josiah S. Johnston, October 22, 1827, in Josiah Stoddard Johnston Papers, Historical Society of Pennsylvania, Philadelphia, Penn. (hereafter cited as Johnston Papers).

[7]*Louisiana Advertiser*, November 6, 1828.

[8]The claim of his biographer that Livingston was a major force in both these campaigns is insupportable in fact. Unfortunately, this glorification of Livingston permeates Hatcher's work. See his *Livingston*, 316, 218, 219.

[9]Gulian C. Verplank to Martin Van Buren, December 6, 1828, in Martin Van Buren Papers, Library of Congress (hereafter cited as Van Buren Papers); Edward Everett to Alexander Everett, December 15, 1828, in Edward Everett Papers, Massachusetts Historical Society (hereafter cited as Everett Papers).

[10]Archibald Haralson to Thomas Butler, December 29, 1828, in Butler Papers.

[11]*Louisiana Courier*, December 9, 11, 22, 1828; *Louisiana Advertiser*, December 6, 8, 9, 16, 22, 1828, January 12, 19, 1829.

[12]*New Orleans Argus*, December 2, 8, 1828.

[13]Alexander Porter to Josiah S. Johnston, July 27, 1828, in Johnston Papers.

[14]Henry A. Bullard to Josiah S. Johnston, January 12, 1829, John Erwin to Johnston, January 12, 1829, Alexander Porter to Johnston, January 13, 1829, ibid.

[15]David C. Ker to Andrew Jackson, November 15, 1828, in Jackson Papers.

[16]*Louisiana Courier*, October 22, 1831.

[17]John R. Grymes to Andrew Jackson, November 3, 1827, in Jackson Papers.

[18]Alexander Porter to Josiah S. Johnston, December 4, 1828, D. B. Morgan to Johnston, February 6, 1829, in Johnston Papers.

[19]Martin Gordon and Edward Livingston to Andrew Jackson, [January ?], 1829 (John Slidell file), Alfred Hennen to Lafayette Saunders, February 2, 1829 (Saunders file), Letters of Application and Recommendation During the Administration of Andrew Jackson, 1829-1837, in Record Group 59, General Records of the Department of State, National Archives (hereafter cited as RG 59, GRDS, NA); Joseph Saul to Andrew Jackson, March 31, 1829, in Jackson Papers.

[20]*Louisiana Courier*, May 13, 1829; *Louisiana Advertiser*, March 30, 1829.

[21]*New Orleans Argus*, May 20, 1829; W. C. C. Claiborne to Henry Clay, June 5, 1829, in Henry Clay Papers, Library of Congress (hereafter cited as Henry Clay Papers).

[22]*New Orleans Argus*, May 5, 1829, February 6, 1829, D. B. Morgan to Josiah S. Johnston, November 15, 28, 1829, in Johnston Papers; Dorothy C. Barck, ed., *Letters from John Pintard to His Daughter*, 4 vols., (New York, 1940), 3:81.

[23]*New Orleans Argus*, May 16, 19, 1829; *Louisiana Courier*, May 16, 1829; Lafayette Saunders to Martin Van Buren, May 8, 1829 (Beverly Chew file), Letters of Application and Recommendation During the Administration of Andrew Jackson, 1829-1837, in RG 59, GRDS, NA.

[24]*Louisiana Advertiser*, May 16, 18, 20, 1829; *New Orleans Argus*, May 20, 21, 1829; *Louisiana Courier*, May 20, 1829.

[25]Archibald Haralson to Andrew J. Donelson, August 18, 1829 (Haralson file), Letters of Application and Recommendation During the Administration of Andrew Jackson, 1829-1837, in RG 59, GRDS, NA.

[26]John D. Dawson to Andrew Jackson, May 26, 1829, ibid.

[27]Quoted in *New Orleans Argus*, July 28, 1829.

[28]Eleazar Ripley to William S. Hamilton, May 21, September 7, 1829, Alexander Barrow to Hamilton, October 28, 1829, Hamilton to J. P. Turner, November 25, 1829, Hamilton to Andrew Jackson, November 5, 1829 [rough draft]; Hamilton to George M. Graham, December 11, 1829, in Hamilton Papers.

[29]*New Orleans Argus*, May 25, 26, 27, 28, 29, 30, July 3, 18, October 1, 1829.

[30]*Louisiana Courier*, June 6, 1829.

[31]S. D. Ingham to Martin Gordon, October 28, November 12, December 21, 1829, February 12, March 19, 1830, Letter Books of Secretary's Correspondence with Collectors of Small Ports, in Record Group 56, General Records of the Department of the Treasury, National Archives (hereafter cited as RG 56, GRDT, NA).

[32]Anne Royall, *Mrs. Royall's Southern Tour; or, Second Series of the Black Book*, 3 vols. (Washington, D. C., 1830), 3:32.

[33]Edward Livingston to Andrew J. Donelson, April 19, 1829, in Andrew Jackson Donelson Papers, Library of Congress; William P. Preble to Martin Van Buren, July 6, 1829, Preble to Andrew Jackson, January 17, 1831 in Van Buren Papers.

[34]John C. Fitzpatrick, ed., *The Autobiography of Martin Van Buren. Annual Report of the American Historical Association for the Year 1918, Vol. II* (Washington, D. C., 1920), 229, 251-52, 259; James A. Hamilton, *Reminiscences* (New York, 1869), 138.

[35]*United States v. Daniel T. Walden*, Records of the Eastern District Court of Louisiana, Case #2670, 1829, Federal Records Center, Fort Worth, Tex.; John Slidell to Stephen Pleasanton, May 6, 1830, in John Slidell Letter Book, Howard-Tilton Memorial Library, Tulane University, New Orleans, La.; Sale to Daniel T. Walden, in Record Book 1, Conveyance Office, Parish of Orleans, 480.

[36]*United Sates v. Daniel T. Walden*, Records of the Eastern District Court of Louisiana; John Slidell to Stephen Pleasanton, July 18, 1829, in Lidell Letter Book, Howard-Tilton Memorial Library, Tulane University, New Orleans, La. For the difficulties encountered by Livingston in clearing the claim in the New York district attorney's office, see Hamilton, *Reminiscences*, 140. Even here Livingston's procedure was so irregular that Hamilton wrote: "It was a piece of jugglery with which I did not choose to be supposed to be connected."

[37]*New Orleans Argus*, October 13, 1829; Henry A. Bullard and Thomas Curry, eds., *A New Digest of the Statute Laws of the State of Louisiana* (New Orleans, 1842), 399.

[38]Alexander Porter to Josiah S. Johnston, January 23, 1830, in Johnston Papers.

[39]Alexander Porter to Josiah S. Johnston, February 25, 1830, ibid.; W. L. Robeson to W. S. Hamilton, February 6, 1830, in Hamilton Papers.

[40]T. J. Pew to Josiah S. Johnston, January 31, 1830, Alexander Porter to Johnston, March 10, 1830, in Johnston Papers, HSP; Benjamin F. Linton to William S. Hamilton, September 1, 1830, in Hamilton Papers.

[41]Henry Clay to Josiah S. Johnston, March 11, 1830, John H. Johnston to Johnston, February 28, 1830, in Johnston Papers; Benjamin F. Linton to William S. Hamilton, September 1, 1830, in Hamilton Papers.

[42]Henry Clay to James Brown, April 17, 1830; W. C .C. Claiborne to Clay, May 23, 1830, in Henry Clay Papers, LC; Richard Davidson to William S. Hamilton, February 4, 1830, John R. Dunn to Hamilton, April 12, 1830, John Nicholson to Hamilton, April 22, 1830, Charles A. Bullard to Hamilton, May 1, 1830, Alexander Mouton to Hamilton, June 1, 1830, in Hamilton Papers.

[43]Walter H. Overton to William S. Hamilton, March 5, 1830, P. K. Wagner to Hamilton, January 21, 1830, in Hamilton Papers; Alexander Porter to Josiah S. Johnston, February 10, 1830, in Johnston Papers.

[44]P. K. Wagner to William S. Hamilton, January 21, 1830, in Hamilton Papers.

[45]Isaac L. Baker to William S. Hamilton, April 18, 1830, ibid.

[46]Robert Haile to William S. Hamilton, January 27, 1830, ibid.

[47]Alexander Barrow to William S. Hamilton, January 25, 1830, John T. McNeill to Hamilton, January 25, 1830, ibid.

[48]W. L. Robeson to William S. Hamilton, February 6, 1830, Richard Davidson to Hamilton, April 9, 1830, ibid.

[49]Walter H. Overton to William S. Hamilton, March 5, 1830, ibid.

[50]W. L. Robeson to William S. Hamilton, March 21, April 20, 1830, ibid.

[51]M. G. Penn to William S. Hamilton, April 23, 1830, John J. Burk to Hamilton, April 25, 1830, W. Winfree to Hamilton, May 2, 1830, Montgomery Sloan to Hamilton, May 6, 1830, John T. McNeill to Hamilton, May 6, 1830, ibid.

[52]John R. Dunn to William S. Hamilton, April 12, 1830, ibid.; *Louisiana State Gazette and Creole* (Donaldsonville), May 15, 1830.

[53]*Louisiana Advertiser*, May 14, 1830; Montgomery Sloan to William S. Hamilton, May 6, 1830, in Hamilton Papers.

[54]*Louisiana House Journal*, 1831, p. 7; Benjamin F. Linton to W.S. Hamilton, September 1, 1830, in Hamilton Papers.

[55]*Louisiana Advertiser*, May 14, 1830; Lafayette Saunders to William S. Hamilton, November 4, 1829, Hamilton to Saunders, December 14, 1829, in Hamilton Papers.

[56]Alexander Porter to Josiah S. Johnston, February 10, 1830, Henry A. Bullard to Johnston, February 12, 1830, Thomas Curry to Johnston, March 30, 1830, in Johnston Papers; Walter H. Overton to William S. Hamilton, March 5, 1830, in Hamilton Papers; *Attakapas Gazette*, May 15, 1830.

[57]*New Orleans Argus*, April 6, 1830. As usual, both parties claimed control of the legislature at first, but by 1831 it was generally conceded that the Jacksonians had the edge. See Alexander Porter to Josiah S. Johnston, January 12, 1831, in Johnston Papers.

[58]Maunsel White to Andrew Jackson, January 29, 1831, in Jackson Papers.

[59]S. D. Ingham to Martin Gordon, March 18, 1830, Letter Books of Secretary's Correspondence with Collectors of Small Ports, in RG 56, GRDT, NA.

[60]Joseph Saul to Andrew Jackson, July 13, 1830, in Jackson Papers.

[61]Henry Bry to Josiah S. Johnston, December 24, 1830, Henry A. Bullard to Johnston, December 9, 1830, in Johnston Papers; F. A. McWilliams to William S. Hamilton, September 11, 1830, in Hamilton Papers; *Louisiana Advertiser*, January 5, 1831.

[62]Alexander Barrow to William S. Hamilton, July 12, 1830, Archibald Haralson to Hamilton, July 31, 1830, in Hamilton Papers.

[63]R. Davidson to W. S. Hamilton, April 9, 1830, Archibald Haralson to Hamilton, July 31, October 30, 1830, E. W. Taylor to Hamilton, October 13, 1830, John Nicholson to Hamilton, November 16, 1830, ibid.

[64]John H. Johnston to Josiah S. Johnston, January 8, 10, 11, 1831, Alexander Porter to Johnston, January 12, 1831, James Porter to Johnston, January 10, 1831, in Johnston Papers; Robert Haile to William S. Hamilton, January 19, 1831, in Hamilton Papers; *Louisiana Advertiser*, January 1, 6, 7, 8, 11, 1831; *Louisiana Courier*, December 2, 3, 1830; January 4, 11, 1831; *New Orleans Bee*, January 10, 1831.

[65]*Louisiana Courier*, January 27, March 7, 15, 29, April 28, May 4, 6, June 2, July 12, 20, 23, September 17, October 1, 1831; *Louisiana Advertiser*, May 11, June 20, July 3, November 15, 1831.

[66]*Louisiana Courier*, July 12, 20, 23, 1831.

[67]Alexander Porter to Henry Clay, June 10, 1831, in Henry Clay Papers; Porter to Josiah S. Johnston, September 2, 1831, in Johnston Papers.

[68]*New Orleans Mercantile Advertiser*, October 1, 1831.

[69]Ibid., August 13, 1831.

[70]Alexander Porter to Josiah S. Johnston, September 2, 1831, in Johnston Papers.

[71]*Louisiana Courier*, June 20, 1831.

[72]Joseph G. Tregle, Jr., "Louisiana and the Tariff, 1816-1846," *Louisiana Historical Quarterly*, 25 (1942): 48-53.

[73]Ibid., 57.

[74]See, for example, the *Southern Agriculturist*, 1 (1828): 236, 337; Edmund J. Forstall, *The Agricultural Productions of Louisiana* (New Orleans, 1845), 7.

[75]Tregle, "Louisiana and the Tariff," 58-59.

[76]Alexander Porter to Josiah S. Johnston, December 13, 1830, in Johnston Papers.

[77]*Louisiana Senate Journal*, 1830, p. 55; *Louisiana House Journal*, 1830, p. 70; Henry Clay to James Brown, April 17, 1830, in Henry Clay Papers; Clay to Josiah S. Johnston, March 11, 1830, in Calvin Colton, ed., *The Private Correspondence of Henry Clay* (New York, 1856), 255.

[78]Tregle, "Louisiana and the Tariff," 69.

[79]*Louisiana Courier*, November 6, 13, 15, December 22, 1830, February 17, March 10, May 19, August 27, September 17, 1831.

[80]D. B. Morgan to Josiah S. Johnston, December 4, 1830, in Johnston Papers; Wade Hampton to Goodhue and Co., February 6, 1831, in Wade Hampton Papers, Southern Historical Collection, University of North Carolina, Chapel Hill, N. C.; *Rémarques Sur la Culture de la Canne à Sucre, à la Louisiane, et Sur la Diminution des Droits Sur les Sucres Etrangers* (New Orleans, 1831), 8; *Letter of Mr. J. S. Johnston, of Louisiana, to a Gentleman in New York; In Reply to an Article of the Expediency of Reducing the Duty on Sugar* (n.p., n.d.), 5-8.

[81]Henry A. Bullard to Josiah S. Johnston, December 9, 1830, in Johnston Papers.

[82]*Louisiana Courier*, May 14, 1831.

[83]Ibid., October 1, 1831.

[84]Alexander Porter to Josiah S. Johnston, October 29, 1831, in Johnston Papers.

[85]*Louisiana Advertiser*, November 11, 1831.

[86]*Louisiana Courier*, September 3, 1831.

[87]Ibid., October 17, 22, 1831; Alexander Porter to Josiah S. Johnston, September 2, 1831, Martin Gordon to J. A. Barker, September 20, 1831, in Johnston Papers.

[88]Alexander Porter to Josiah S. Johnston, December 1, 1831, Charles A. Bullard to Johnston, November 12, 1831, in Johnston Papers.

[89]Alexander Porter to Josiah S. Johnston, December 1, 1831, ibid.

[90]Alexander Porter to Josiah S. Johnston, September 1, 1831, Charles A. Bullard to Johnston, November 12, 1831, Thomas Curry to Johnston, November 15, 1831, ibid.; *New Orleans Mercantile Advertiser*, November 15, 1831.

[91]Edward Everett to Alexander Everett, December 8, 1831, in Everett Papers.

[92]Thomas Curry to Josiah S. Johnston, January 26, 1832, in Johnston Papers.

[93]Alexander Porter to Josiah S. Johnston, March 18, 1832, ibid.

[94]Thomas Curry to Josiah S. Johnston, January 26, 1832, ibid.

[95]*New Orleans Bee*, January 11, 1833.

[96]*Louisiana Courier*, January 10, 13, 27, 1832.

[97]Ibid., January 10, 11, 1832; *Louisiana Advertiser*, January 13, 1832.

[98]*Louisiana Advertiser*, February 10, March 9, 1832; *Louisiana Courier*, February 10, March 5, 1832.

[99]*Louisiana Courier*, February 23, 1832.

[100]Ibid., March 5, 10, 1832; *Louisiana Advertiser*, March 9, 10, 1832.

[101]Alexander Porter to Josiah S. Johnston, March 18, 1832, Dr. Duncan to Johnston, April 17, 1831, Johnston Strawbridge to Johnston, May 12, 1832, in Johnston Papers.

[102]*Louisiana Advertiser*, September 6, 1832, December 6, 1834; Walter H. Overton to Josiah S. Johnston, April 29, 1832, in Johnston Papers.

[103]Alexander Barrow to William S. Hamilton, September 3, December 9, 1831, in Hamilton Papers.

[104]*Louisiana Advertiser*, May 28, June 29, August 21, 1832; *Louisiana Courier*, October 8, 1832.

[105]*Louisiana Advertiser*, August 21, 23, September 26, 1832.

[106]Ibid., June 29, 1832; *Louisiana Courier*, June 28, 1832; Alexander Porter to Josiah S. Johnston, June 17, 1832, in Johnston Papers.

[107]Tregle, "Louisiana and the Tariff," 90-92.

[108]T. P. Abernethy, "The Early Development of Commerce and Banking in Tennessee," *Mississippi Valley Historical Review*, 14 (1927): 371; Samuel Jaudon to Nicholas Biddle, February 11, 1832, in Nicholas Biddle Papers, Library of Congress (hereafter cited as Biddle Papers); "Memorial of the President and Directors of the Louisiana State Bank for the Rechartering of the Bank of the United States," *House Executive Documents*, 22nd Cong., 1st Sess., No. 153; "Memorial of the Bank of Orleans, for a Renewal of the Charter of the Bank of the United States," *House Executive Documents*, 22nd Cong., 1st Sess., No. 184; "Memorial of the New Orleans Canal and Banking Company for Renewal of the Charter of the Bank of the United States," *Senate Documents*, 22nd Cong., 1st Sess., No. 108; Samuel H. Harper to Roger B. Taney, October 23, 1833, Letters from Banks, in RG 56, GRDT, NA.

[109]W. H. Overton to Josiah S. Johnston, April 29, 1832, in Johnston Papers, HSP; Charles J. Ingersoll to Nicholas Biddle, February 10, 1832, in Biddle Papers. George D. Green in *Finance and Economic Development in the Old South: Louisiana Banking, 1804-1861* (Stanford, 1972), 219, disputes the assertion that the Bank quarrel constituted an "imported issue" in Louisiana and denies that any significance should attach to Jacksonian membership on the branch bank's board of directors, maintaining that such an interpretation "wrongly assumes that Jacksonians on the board of the New Orleans branch were therefore disloyal to the party." Actually, he continues, "Biddle appointed them at the suggestion of William Lewis, one of Jackson's 'kitchen cabinet,' in order to give political balance to the board." Green obviously misses the point here, which is that Maunsel White, Martin Gordon, and others friendly to the Bank before Jackson's veto saw nothing in their relationship to it at odds with loyalty to their party. The wrong assumption is Green's, that they presumably agreed to serve on the branch board only to please the president and William B. Lewis.

[110]See, for example, the typical comment of St. Romes in the *Louisiana Courier*, February 1, 1831.

[111]*Louisiana Advertiser*, August 11, 1832.

[112]*Debates in Congress*, 22nd Cong., 1st Sess., appendix, 39; Erik M. Eriksson, "Official Newspaper Organs and Jackson's Re-election, 1832," in *Tennessee Magazine of History*, 9 (1925): 55.

[113]Thomas G. Davidson to F. P. Blair, September 6, 1832, in Blair-Rives Papers, Library of Congress.

[114]D. B. Morgan to Josiah S. Johnston, October 13, 1832, in Johnston Papers.

[115]Maunsel White to Andrew Jackson, December 14, 1832, in Jackson Papers.

[116]John Linton to Josiah S. Johnston, October 5, 1832, in Johnston Papers; *Louisiana Advertiser*, September 25, October 16, 1832.

[117]S. A. Trufant, "Review of Banking in New Orleans, 1830-1840," *Publications of the Louisiana Historical Society*, 9 (1917): 32; Stephen Caldwell, *A Banking History of Louisiana* (Baton Rouge, 1935), 56-58; Green, *Finance and Economic Development in the Old South*, 22-23; Alexander Porter to Josiah S. Johnston, February 14, 1832, Thomas Butler to Johnston, February 23, 1832, L. Hodge Johnston, March 8, 1832, John Linton to Johnston, October 5, 1832, in Johnston Papers; *Louisiana Courier*, January 20, 1832.

[118]Thomas Curry to Josiah S. Johnston, May 6, 1832, in Johnston Papers.

[119]*Louisiana Courier*, July 6, 1832.

[120]For the plague of 1832, see Jo Ann Carrigan, *The Saffron Scourge: A History of Yellow Fever in Louisiana, 1796-1905* (Lafayette, La., 1994); Michel Halphen, *Mémoire sur le Cholera-morbus qui a Régné à la Nouvelle-Orléans en 1832* (Paris, 1833), 57; Thomas J. Spear, *Ancient and Modern New Orleans* (New Orleans, 1879), 34; H. B. Trist to Nicholas P. Trist, November 7, 1832, in Nicholas P. Trist Papers, Southern Historical Collection, University of North Carolina, Chapel Hill, N. C.; *New Orleans Bee*, November 4, 1834.

[121]Alexander Porter to Josiah S. Johnston, December 6, 1832, in Johnston Papers; see also Martin Gordon to William B. Lewis, November 12, 1832, in Miscellaneous Papers, Massachusetts Historical Society.

[122]*Louisiana Advertiser*, November 28, 1832.

DEMOCRACY DISCORDANT*

Joseph G. Tregle, Jr.

In all of his public life only one action by Edward Livingston ever met with the almost universal acclaim of the people of Louisiana. And yet as perversely ironic as it must have seemed, he could not claim it as his own. For what he had done was to fashion a state paper aimed at destroying the theory of nullification, and it bore the name of Andrew Jackson.

The proclamation embodying the president's reply to the South Carolina ordinance of nullification reached New Orleans on Christmas Day of 1832, amidst a wild mixture of terrible rains and bursts of thunder which seemed to underscore the temper of the great dispute. It produced excited and unreserved praise for the chief executive, with even his traditional enemies blessing his name. The archdefender of the Union, Alexander Porter, seemed almost converted to the ranks of the General as he gave thanks for Jackson's energy and "indomitable will,"[1] and others of like mind rushed plans for a great public meeting in New Orleans on January 2 to allow the people an opportunity to voice their support of the president's stand.[2]

As had been true in 1832, public sentiment against nullification united both Louisiana parties in opposition to the South Carolina doctrine. Dominique Bouligny presided over the January meeting; John R. Grymes helped draft the resolution declaring the Union an "indissoluble compact;" and Governor Roman reinforced these popular expressions with an official declaration to the state legislature which called upon Louisiana to honor her motto of "Justice, Union, and Confidence" with a pledge to "surround the President with all the force possible by expression of general approbation" of his actions.[3]

By now even the Florida nullifiers had somewhat modified their position, at least vocally if not in substance. When the legislature proceeded to consider Roman's recommendations, the committee to whom the question was referred voted unanimously in opposition to the South Carolina vision of the Union but divided as to the proper course to be pursued by the national government. One segment of the committee offered resolu-

*First published as Chapter 11 in Joseph G. Tregle, Jr., *Louisiana in the Age of Jackson: A Clash of Cultures and Personalities* (Baton Rouge: Louisiana State University Press, © 1999), 265-95. Reprinted with the kind permission of the author and the publisher.

tions which would have fully justified the complaints of the Southern states against the tariff and called for immediate reduction of duties to a revenue-only level. But this would have meant a repudiation of the 1830 resolutions in favor of the tariff of 1828, as well as a practical abandonment of the state's claims to protection of her sugar industry. Alert to the danger, the legislature turned back these attempts to damn the tariff along with nullification, and once again the state officially ratified its support of protection.[4]

Leadership in this antitariff campaign had been taken by the Florida Jacksonians and John R. Grymes, with the latter responsible for the major presentation of their arguments. It is difficult to deduce from the evidence exactly what doctrinal position Grymes held in this whole affair, for he could pronounce violent strictures against nullifiers, affirm the sanctity of the Union, and then, as on this occasion, attempt to prevent the inclusion of a condemnation of secession in the resolutions attacking nullification. But at least he voted in favor of reprobating both when the measure came to the test, which was more than Alexander Barrow and several of his fellow Florida delegates could bring themselves to do.[5] Clearly the nullification flame still flickered in the Florida area, but prudence again prevented any public acknowledgment of it by the leaders of the region. Too much was at stake in the coming attempt to win American control of the state to allow all to be lost in defense of an idea which had become so obviously hated by the majority of the citizens and which had been condemned by the man whose personality seemed destined to maintain its spell over the political affairs of the community.

Writing to Hamilton from New Orleans shortly after the defeat of the antitariff resolutions in the legislature, Alexander Barrow reported that he had tried to follow the colonel's advice to keep mum on his ideas concerning states' rights, but the debate on nullification forced him to drop a few observations on the issues in dispute. "I am now put under the ban," he complained, "and am denounced as a nullifier, as all are considered here nullifiers who do not laud the proclamation, and pronounce General Jackson to be immaculate." Clearly, his conflicting loyalties troubled him deeply. "I am no nullifier, as you know," Barrow protested, in a strange departure from many of his earlier comments to Hamilton, "but all my sympathies are with them, and as the nullifiers are contending against laws which are unconstitutional, unjust, oppressive and ruinous to the South, I never will consent to see them put down by military force." His final observation gives the key to the reluctance of his group to do more than sulk and complain against the wickedness of the tariff. "The popularity of Jackson is so overwhelming—the belief in his purity is so deeprooted—and the spirit of man worship is so prevalent," he wrote, that it appeared futile to resist.[6] Nullification had indeed aroused little sympathy in Louisiana. Public opinion remained so hostile to the doctrine that even men with the views of Barrow shied away from any open support of it, largely out of fear that they might be taken for secessionists.

Louisiana gave additional demonstration of its devotion to the Union with vigorous support of the Compromise Tariff of 1833, which provided for a gradual reduction of duties to a flat rate of 20 percent ad valorem over a ten-year period. As early as December 1832 Johnston had warned Porter that some such arrangement would be the only way to save the nation from schism, and Porter had replied in a fashion which would sum up the later reaction of the state in the face of the accomplished fact: "Be it so," was his comment. "It will nearly ruin me, and it will totally ruin others, but I trust we all have patriotism enough to bear this and much more for the sake of the Union."[7]

Porter's judgment of the feelings of his neighbors proved sound. The slash in the sugar duties at first induced what Governor Roman called "a kind of panic," but this soon subsided in the hope that the years would bring some measure of salvation to the industry. A sugar planter himself, Roman assured Johnston that the people recognized that no alternative to the compromise had been open to their congressional representatives—"we all agree," he remarked, "that you have done your best for the interest of the state."[8] But as early as 1834 the nullification threat had so dissipated that politics could produce the strange spectacle of a Florida antitariff candidate for governor belaboring his opponent for having voted to reduce duties on sugar in 1833 in order to save the Union.

The appearance of unity demonstrated by Louisiana Jacksonianism in the face of the nullification crisis quickly shattered on old ambitions. Democratic success in the election of 1832 once again emboldened Gordon to bid for complete mastery of his party under the General's banner, for now success might well mean political control of the state during at least the next four years. To attain that end he was willing to jeopardize the solidarity of the Jacksonian organization in the state.

No real cause of dissension threatened the party except Gordon's determination to have his colleagues accept his status as Andrew Jackson's alter ego in Louisiana. He ruled the custom house with a grip of iron, terrorizing merchants in his disfavor, demanding unquestioning obedience from his subordinates, and dispensing his patronage with a zeal which had already called down admonitions from the treasury department under Secretary Samuel D. Ingham.[9] Wagner, now naval officer of the port, served as his principal lieutenant, pandering to his notorious hypochondria and acting frequently as confidential secretary in the political maneuverings of the White House clique.

From the beginning of his tenure as collector, Gordon alienated many of his fellow Jacksonians, particularly W. L. Robeson, Isaac Preston, and Samuel Spotts, who resented his tyranny and blamed him for their party's rout in the disastrous gubernatorial campaign of 1830. Spotts seems especially to have incurred Gordon's wrath, their antagonisms frequently bubbling up in disputes over their respective duties in the custom house.[10] As surveyor of the port, Spotts exercised wide authority over inspectors, watchers, and other minor customs officials who generally owed their appointments to joint recommendation from his own office and that of the collector. Unlike Wagner, Spotts did not owe his job to Gordon's influence and always remained an outsider in the latter's eyes, to be spied upon, harassed at every turn, and pressed to accommodate Gordon's political and patronage demands.[11] Clearly, if the collector meant to retain his self-proclaimed role as the president's chief friend and adviser in Louisiana, he could brook no independence of action on the part of Spotts or any other federal officeholder in the state, countenance no resistance to his plans or to his will.

In some fashion not entirely clear, John Slidell transgressed against this majesty of the collector, suddenly to find himself a man marked for destruction. There is no proof, but a strong probability, that the misunderstanding had its roots in a situation which developed in September 1832, when three boatmen in the custom house service—Alexander Smith, James McFarlane, and William Whitney—seized the brig *Primero de Mahon* as she tried to smuggle cigars and rum into Louisiana. Gordon retained the informers' fee of $5,179.59 and later divided it with Spotts, Wagner, McFarlane, and Whitney, but refused to render any share to Smith. The latter protested in vain, for Wagner and the collector had forced Whitney to sign a false statement that Smith had not participated in the seizure of the brig. Unable to obtain redress in any other fashion, Smith finally sued Gordon for his share of the fee and won judgment against him in February 1834.[12]

No evidence links Slidell to this dispute, but Smith may well have enlisted his aid, for Thomas Slidell and Robert M. Carter served as his lawyers in the case, the first a brother to the federal attorney and the second his close friend and associate.[13] Whatever the cause, by December 1832 Gordon had determined that Slidell must be crushed. He made no overt break with his associate, however, leaving Slidell to grow increasingly puzzled by the collector's mounting coolness and refusal to cooperate in government cases requiring their joint action.[14] The breach soon became so wide that Slidell could ignore it no longer, especially since his appointment was to expire in March. On January 7, 1833, he wrote to the president requesting renewal of his commission and asking that any attacks upon him by Gordon be judged in the light of the known vindictiveness of the collector.[15] To Gordon himself Slidell the next day proposed an end at least to their official bickerings. "You have thought proper for reasons best known to yourself," he wrote the collector, "to change the friendly relations which have hitherto existed between us, but I wish you to understand that I am at all times prepared to give you every information in my power in any official matter upon which you may think fit to consult me." All he asked was an end to "captious correspondence."[16]

There was to be no placating the adamant Gordon. Already he had won Henry Carleton to his side in an alliance which assured support from Livingston, the only Louisiana Jacksonian in the national capital. Having thus cut Slidell off from any defense in Washington, he then demanded of President Jackson that he choose between his federal attorney and collector at New Orleans, since it was obvious that they could no longer work together in harmony, suggesting at the same time that Carleton would be the perfect choice to succeed his errant colleague.[17]

On March 15 Slidell received the news. He was not to be reappointed, Livingston's brother in law having been named in his place.[18] Taken completely by surprise, he soon managed to get an abashed Carleton to admit that the whole thing had been planned by

Gordon, thus confirming his fears of early January. He had received not a single complaint from the president nor the slightest sign of his impending dismissal.[19]

In a matter of days Jackson discovered himself in the middle of a noisy battle among his followers in Louisiana. Furious at the intrigue against him, Slidell enlisted the aid of practically every prominent Jacksonian in the state, and most of them affixed their signatures to a protest against his removal which charged bluntly that Gordon's attempts to dominate his Jacksonian colleagues spelled possible disaster for the party.[20] They forwarded a copy of the remonstrance to Martin Van Buren as well, in the hope, as Slidell wrote the vice-president, that he at least would be able to prevent the memorial from falling into the hands of the very people around Jackson who had furthered Gordon's plans. Slidell clearly meant to warn against Livingston. Determined to impress upon Van Buren the significance of what might appear on the surface a petty quarrel, he also took pains to make the ambitious vice-president recognize the personal stake he himself had in maintaining the unity of a party anxious to see him as Jackson's successor in the White House:

> To preserve its organization and moral force it is necessary to destroy an impression which has been gradually gaining ground and which my removal has served to confirm; that an individual of all others the most unpopular in this community, possesses in everything relating to Louisiana, a controlling influence with the president. This influence has been acquired by a course of persevering intrigue and by the systematic denunciation of everyone who may have the misfortune to excite the ire of Mr. Gordon and is boasted of by him in a tone calculated to degrade the president and disgust his warmest friends. The crisis has now arrived and the question must be decided, whether the single voice of Mr. Gordon is to be more potential at Washington than the expressed and unanimous wish of the whole party. . . . The occasion calls for frankness and I assure you with the utmost sincerity, that if this man be not put down, the party that has uniformly supported General Jackson must inevitably be broken up. . . . The harmony of the party cannot be affected by his dismissal, it must be destroyed and put down.[21]

But the wily Van Buren, in a position to observe Jackson's reaction to the remonstrance, sensed immediately the indiscretion of interfering in a matter which had so disturbed the president, and he brushed Slidell off with regrets that his letter had come too late for any corrective action.[22] The president had reason indeed to be agitated, for the petition in Slidell's favor carried the endorsement of several of his closest friends in Louisiana, like Maunsel White and J. B. Plauché, as well as those of Trasimond Landry, Sebastian Hiriart, and J. B. Labatut, all of whom had given long service to the general's cause and whose loyalty to his interest could hardly be challenged.[23]

Suddenly confronted with the realization that he had acted solely upon the charges of Gordon alone, Jackson reacted in typical Jacksonian fashion. Having done this, he never doubted for a moment that it was the right thing to have done. So now he had to write hastily to Gordon for some evidence of Slidell's misconduct which he might use to convince his Louisiana friends that the removal had been proper. "Send me a copy of your letter upon which I acted," he advised the collector, "with such a justification for your application for Mr. Slidell's being superceded as you have in your power, shewing the want of harmony between you and in what of his acts it consisted."[24] Slidell was clearly to be given no hearing at all.

The implacable Gordon needed no encouragement. Aware of the efforts in Slidell's behalf, he moved quickly to guarantee Jackson's continued support by a heavy-handed but nonetheless effective device. At what must have been the same moment that the Slidell memorial made its way to the president, the collector mailed a one-thousand-dollar donation to Francis P. Blair from himself and nine associates, to attest to their "support of the true Democratic and American principles proclaimed and acted upon by our illustrious chief magistrate."[25]

On the very day that the president sat drafting his own letter to Gordon announcing the arrival of the Slidell remonstrance, Blair hastened to the White House to report on Gordon's gift and to read to Jackson the letter which had accompanied it. As Blair repeated the message's encouragement to "go on—the friends of Jackson will support you," the General's eyes filled with gratitude. "Why . . . Mr. Blair," he said, "these friends of mine mean to pay back through you the thousand-dollar fine imposed on me at New Orleans," and he related the whole story with great gusto to Van Buren that evening at dinner. As for Blair, he was similarly affected. "I need not say to you," he wrote Gordon, "how deeply I feel the obligation I owe to you personally for the early and active part you took in my behalf. . . . it is easy to say you have given a support to the Globe, which has almost taken its burden off my shoulders."[26]

Such powerful friends at court soon stood Gordon in good stead. Late in March a committee of New Orleans merchants headed by W. L. Robeson drafted a petition to Secretary of the Treasury Louis McLane requesting the immediate removal of the collector because of his tyrannical and oppressive conduct in office.[27] Informing William B. Lewis of this attack, Gordon placed the blame for it squarely upon Slidell, and then widened the campaign to destroy his enemies by adding his old foe Spotts and John Nicholson, the United States marshal at New Orleans, to his list of those officeholders opposed to the best interests of the president. His move shows clearly the scatter-gun nature of his campaign and how well he understood Jackson's easily aroused paranoia:

> In a former communication to the President of the United States, I recommended the Same course with respect to the Surveyor [Spotts], namely that he ought not again to be nominated for that appointment, and earnestly recommended our very worthy and true friend, Col. H. D. Peire, to succeed him.
>
> Respecting Mr. Nicholson, I will remark that he had never given the President that support which he ought to have done; I have always considered him as a *disguised ennemy* [*sic*], and I may say with great truth, that he has opposed to the present Administration, *as far as he dared to go.* He has never, nor has Captain Spotts, ever contributed one cent towards the support of our Cause; they have always been found associating with our most vindictive, and malicious political enemies.[28]

Transmitting the letter to the president, Lewis advised Jackson that "Gordon, no doubt, is a good deal excited at the course of these gentlemen, but he is a true and sincere friend, and worth a regiment of *lukewarm* or *pretending* friends."[29] Jackson needed little encouragement to give Gordon the benefit of the doubt, having already instructed Secretary McLane to forward a copy of the charges against him to the collector, with the promise that "no opinion will be formed upon the subject until you shall have had full opportunity for defense."[30] The signers of the memorial were meanwhile advised that their complaints must be made in more specific form for any action upon them to be considered.[31]

While Robeson worked vigorously with his fellow merchants to draft the bill of indictment, Slidell and Spotts accumulated additional evidence of malpractice by Gordon, and in July and August 1833 a veritable barrage of accusations against the collector poured down upon the treasury department. They charged him with making false oaths against sea captains for personal reasons, demanding exorbitant storage and drayage fees not required by the treasury, and forcing merchants to have papers notarized by his brother-in-law despite their already proper form.[32] The most serious indictment alleged fraud involving the collector's paying excessive rent to himself for the use of one of his buildings as a storehouse even though he knew of the availability of United States property suitable to the purpose.[33]

The meager and obviously controversial evidence now available makes it impossible at this late date to decide the question of Gordon's guilt in these matters. But the weakness of his rejoinders to the accusations against him adds credibility to their accuracy. Only one deposition in the records actually denies the charges, the other letters and comments submitted in his behalf being simple avowals of friendship and confidence in his integrity.[34] Slidell and his associates continually urged Secretary Roger B. Taney to appoint a committee of inquiry to assess the complaints against Gordon and committed themselves to abide by its findings, but no such action was ever taken.[35] Increasingly irritated by the turmoil among his Louisiana partisans, Jackson moved to end the imbroglio by giving Gordon an indisputable sign of his support. When the collector advised the president in July that he would resign from office rather than continue to serve with Spotts, Jackson summarily dismissed the surveyor as well as Robeson as receiver of public moneys.[36] Unlike Gordon, they had been given no opportunity to defend themselves.

Slidell, meanwhile, had journeyed to Saratoga Springs to lay his own case personally before Van Buren, only to be told by the vice-president that an "acknowledgment of injustice on Jackson's part was out of the question." True to his promise, however, Van Buren did finally write the president to explain that Slidell would be satisfied with the offer of any public office "of sufficient respectability to wipe away the effect of what had been done, such as a chargé's," it being understood that he would decline accepting so as to devote full time to his private practice.[37] Not even this was to be granted him, for in November Gordon journeyed to Washington on official leave, determined to block any action against himself and to settle his account with Slidell as well. This time he was at least more specific in his claims, if no more generous with his proof. Jackson obviously welcomed this new confirmation of his own fairness in the matter, and hastened to advise Van Buren of these new developments:

> Mr. Gordon (Collector of New Orleans) is now here. From testimonials submitted Mr. Slidel[l] has imposed upon the Secretary of the Treasury and myself in his recommendation of an appraiser for the port of New Orleans—the man had been suspended as an inspector for intemperance twice and then permitted to resign. This is charged to be in the knowledge of Mr. Slidel[l]—it is stated further by Mr. Gordon that Slidel[l], Nicholson and Grimes are all Calhoun men and nullifiers . . . and he asserts that they all three are your and my bitter opponents at all their elections. . . .
>
> Knowing that you had a favourable opinion of Mr. Slidel[l] as well as myself this letter is written to put you on your guard against this man, that you may not break your shins over stools not in your way—and that you may be guarded in any communication you may happen to make with him.[38]

For Slidell this was the end. Nothing more came of the charges against Gordon, but Slidell, Spotts, and Robeson found themselves cast out without mercy, for what appears to have been the single sin of incurring the wrath of the collector. Gordon could with good reason now feel that his claims to special place in the confidence of the president had been vindicated. But he had yet to reckon with the United States Senate, and humiliation of members of his own party, however satisfying, could not give him that mastery of the state government which he so ardently craved. In the spring and summer of 1834, his victory over Slidell would seem evanescent indeed.

Although pure malice alone might have sufficed for Gordon's attacks upon Slidell and the many others in his disfavor, he unquestionably had much more at stake in the months following the campaign of 1832 than simple spiteful gratification. To the political dominance which he sought, he now added the additional goal of snatching up the scepter of financial power which he knew would fall for the hands of the Bank of the United States when Jackson removed the federal deposits from that institution. In short, his program for 1833-1834 looked forward to placing a successor of his own choosing in the governorship to succeed Roman, creation of his own bank in New Orleans, and winning for it the federal funds when these were removed from Biddle's "Monster." With such political patronage and financial power, he would indeed be master of the state.

That strategy had required as a first step the purging from his party of those who might challenge his claim to its leadership, and so Slidell, Spotts, Nicholson, and Robeson had been doomed. Meanwhile, as early as December 1832, he made it quite clear to Secretary McLane that great caution must be exercised should the federal deposits be transferred to some local institution. "We have already experienced the baneful influence of the Bank of the United States *using the funds of the General Government to affect political objects*," he explained, "and great care and circumspection will be necessary to guard against like evils being exercised by *Local Banks*, making *use of the same means for like purposes*."[39] Already active in the affairs of the Louisiana State Bank, Gordon in

January 1833 succeeded in establishing the Mechanics and Traders Bank of New Orleans, whose claims to the deposits he pushed in correspondence with members of Jackson's cabinet, his letters filled with condemnation of all competitors as enemies of the administration. Confident of his support in Washington, he boasted openly that he was certain to be allowed to handle the public funds when Jackson finally removed them from Biddle's clutches.[40]

While waiting for that happy occasion he could turn his attention to the coming state campaign of 1834. Gordon had learned much since the debacle of 1830, chiefly that the only hope of a Jacksonian victory in the gubernatorial race depended on a fusion of his White House set with the Florida leadership. Fortunately for his plans, a link between the two factions was not only available but practically panting for an opportunity to be of service. John B. Dawson had finally reached the minimum age required of Louisiana governors, and he now moved to take over command of a Florida Jacksonian party left without guidance by the crushing defeat of Hamilton in 1830. Unlike his old tutor, Dawson had firm ties to General Ripley despite the latter's Yankee origins. An association with Wagner growing out of Dawson's ownership of various newspapers in the Floridas paved the way to an understanding with Gordon, and as early as November 1831 Dawson announced his candidacy to succeed Roman.[41] Aware of the strength of a Gordon-Dawson coalition, the Clay forces turned to Edward Douglass White as their candidate, convinced that no other man in the state possessed a popularity so strong among both the French and American populations.[42]

Before the battle between Dawson and White could get up any momentum, however, the Jacksonian ranks shattered in the Gordon-Slidell feud early in 1833. Encouraged by the loud denunciation of his dismissal by so many of their colleagues, Slidell and his friends moved boldly to seize control of the Jacksonian leadership from the White House clique, fully convinced that they would be able to drive Gordon from office once they had made their case before Jackson and the treasury department. Their numbers were by no means insignificant, including as they did Slidell, Spotts, Robeson, Nicholson, and General Overton. But the full measure of their strength became evident in August 1833, when their recent acquisition of the *Louisiana Advertiser*, the state's leading Jacksonian newspaper, allowed them to bring forward Denis Prieur as their own candidate for governor.[43] Prieur had long been out of favor with Gordon, who had tried in 1832 to replace him in the New Orleans mayoralty with one of his own favorites, H. D. Peire.[44] Surviving that attack with ease, Prieur had announced for governor a few months later, but his candidacy had not been taken in any way seriously.[45] Now with Slidell and the enemies of Gordon united behind him, he became a threat of major importance, for aside from his famed personal drawing power, he might well exploit his newfound support to convince the Creole population that his chances of success were by no means illusory. Against two American candidates such as Dawson and White, a combination of disaffected Jacksonians and loyal Creoles could well prove irresistible. In addition, the likelihood that White would be a major contender suffered a serious blow from a tragic accident which almost removed him from the contest. The explosion of the Red River steamboat *Lioness* on May 18, 1833, snuffed out the life of Senator Josiah Johnston and so seriously injured White that it would be months before his recovery was assured.[46] In this state of uncertainty, Prieur's possibilities of victory could hardly be taken lightly.

The extent of Gordon's concern at this unexpected retaliation of his victims reveals itself starkly in the deluge of vilification which now poured down on Prieur from the organs of the White House clique. Chief among these, the *Louisiana Courier* and *Bee* of New Orleans abandoned earlier claims to independence from the internal quarrels of the party to launch strident onslaughts against Slidell and his associates. Their attack matched in brutality anything known in the many violent political wars which preceded it. They assailed Prieur as an ignorant city man who knew nothing of the problems of the rural countryside, as an immoral and corrupt figure in his private life, a venal dictator and bungling incompetent in his management of the affairs of the metropolis, and the pawn of "a petty-half-way-pretended-Jackson party, which is now in direct opposition to the President."[47]

This vicious onslaught simply replicated in large measure the tactics which Gordon had used so effectively against Slidell. Not once did it advance a single concrete example of how anyone on Gordon's enemies list had betrayed Jackson or his party. Nowhere did it proffer any explanation of why they should suddenly find themselves labeled with the favorite stamp of "aristocrat." Nothing was forthcoming, in short, but a continuous flood of denunciation and condemnation by unsupported assertion, all reflecting the primary article of Jacksonian faith as purveyed by the followers of the White House coterie: to refuse acknowledgment of Martin Gordon as the unchallenged leader of Louisiana Jacksonianism was to stand convicted as an enemy of the president and as a nabob who would spit upon the workingman.[48]

A second challenge to Gordon's leadership suddenly came unexpectedly from General Overton, once considered a pliable instrument of the collector's will but now in open rebellion. Overton had his eye on the Senate seat of the late Josiah Johnston, and since he had been one of the main signers of the anti-Gordon memorial sent to Jackson in Slidell's defense, he naturally held a high place on the collector's roll of traitors. Upon him too there now fell the full weight of the custom house press. "What folly!" cried the *Bee*. "Can it be that *Mr. Overton* has been so deceived by some half-a dozen *doubtful* friends of the Administration, as to take such a step, one that will bring upon him in the end, should he not resign, disgrace and humiliation?"[49] What Jacksonian could support Overton, the *Bee* demanded, when it was known that he "is in heart a Calhoun man, and a nullifier . . . as we have strong reasons to believe." Determined to cut Overton off from any support in Washington, Wagner, in typical subservience to Gordon, wrote Francis P. Blair to warn that "Col. O. is strongly attached to Mr. Calhoun and if elected to the senate would be inclined to support him and all his projects." Overton stood high in his estimation, Wagner assured Blair, proceeding then to suggest that "three or four lines in the Globe, written in a decided and positive tone, would fix his fate."[50]

Thus the summer and fall of 1833 reverberated with assaults upon Gordon's enemies from editors who remained singularly quiet about the charges against their own favorites. The *Bee*'s assertions that it possessed complete data refuting the charges made against the collector were never followed by publication of any of these supposed facts,[51] nor did any hint ever appear in its columns that Dawson's flirtation with nullification had been by all odds more serious than Overton's admitted attachment to Calhoun during the Eaton affair, a sympathy totally unrelated to the South Carolinian's constitutional theories.[52]

Gordon's spokesmen continued their slashing denunciation of Overton but could find no satisfactory candidate loyal to them to back in his place, which resulted in the bizarre exhibition of the supposedly official Jackson papers reviling the senatorial nominees of both parties with judicial impartiality. For however great their hatred of Overton, it paled into nothingness when compared to that which they felt for Alexander Porter, the Clay aspirant to the office. Not content to challenge his political ideas, the *Bee* labeled Porter as an ignorant alien unable to write good English and lacking eligibility for the office because he had never become a citizen of the United States. These were remarkable charges indeed in light of Porter's gifts as one of the most polished and witty correspondents of the state and his long tenure on the Louisiana Supreme Court, especially coming from men who had always proclaimed themselves the understanding friends of immigrants in their fight against "alien and sedition law aristocrats."[53]

Prieur, meanwhile, continued to add additional worries to the Gordon camp by remaining a candidate to succeed himself as head of the city government. Reelection had always been rather easy for an incumbent mayor, and the *Bee* charged Prieur with deliberately contriving to retain his city post long enough to use the New Orleans police to coerce votes in his favor in the gubernatorial contest.[54] As a countermeasure, the Gordon forces brought forth John H. Holland as their mayoral candidate, and then unleashed a vigorous assault disputing Prieur's eligibility for the office. In the midst of continuous reference to the incumbent's immorality, the *Bee* ran at its mast the legislative act of March 14, 1820, which required the mayor and recorder of New Orleans "to be chosen from among the citizens who are heads of families."[55] There could be no misunderstanding the meaning of this device, a clear allusion to the notorious fact that Prieur's only family consisted of his colored paramour and their children.

It is easy to imagine Gordon's fury—engaged as he was to the limit of his strength against Prieur, Overton, Slidell, and Porter—when in November 1833 Secretary Taney announced selection of the Union and Commercial Banks of New Orleans as the institutions chosen to receive the public deposits in Louisiana, bypassing the collector's Mechanics and Traders Bank completely.[56] Having clashed for one reason or another with all of Taney's predecessors, Gordon had never been a particular favorite at the treasury department, his political strength depending primarily upon the president and his personal advisors like Francis P. Blair and William B. Lewis. The reasons underlying Taney's choices remain obscure and may indeed have been based on judicious financial, rather than personal or political, considerations. With a cash capital of $7 million, the Union

Bank had been the major single force easing the financial tension in New Orleans in the fall of 1832, and its regulations restricting stockholders to citizens of the state presumably guarded against the kind of foreign influences charged against the Bank of the United States.[57] William G. Hewes, president of the Commercial Bank, had long identified with the Jackson party and labored diligently to persuade Taney that his institution deserved the deposits because of its semipublic character as provider of the city's water supply.[58] Hewes was also closely allied to William D. Lewis, cashier of the Girard Bank of Philadelphia, and Reuben M. Whitney, a onetime director of the Bank of the United States anxious to become coordinator of the pet-bank system, their scheme envisioning a partnership between the New Orleans and Philadelphia pets which might ensure financial stability when they became custodians of the public moneys. Taney always denied any connection to Whitney, but the irrepressible meddler clearly enjoyed close contact with those involved in decisions determining pet-bank selections, and his influence may well have proved profitable to Hewes and the Union Bank directors.[59]

To Gordon, Taney's action came as a humiliating and costly defeat. His oft-repeated boasts that Jackson would surely adopt his recommendations in the selection of the pet banks collapsed around him, and he now saw himself as the laughingstock of New Orleans. For he had long reviled the Union Bank as a tool of the friends of Henry Clay,[60] and now Hewes might be seen as yet another challenge to his Jackson party leadership. All the more embarrassing, when Taney's decision reached Louisiana it was widely known that Gordon was at that very moment in Washington attempting to make sure that his own bank became one of the pets while he clinched the destruction of his intraparty enemies. Particularly galling, the Union and Commercial Banks turned out to have been sponsored by his old foes, Slidell and Nicholson.[61]

The defeat at least gave him a ready-made explanation for Porter's victory in the Senate election in December. Overton had withdrawn from the race at the last moment, to paeans of praise from the *Bee*, which suddenly discovered in him a man whose talents and loyalty deserved the universal admiration of the people of Louisiana. The move bespoke no particular rapprochement with the Gordon faction; Overton, as in 1830, once again simply deferred to a man who seemed better able to guarantee Jacksonian victory, this time to Joseph Walker of Rapides, his own parish. But the sacrifice came too late to give much propulsion to Walker or to unify his badly divided party, and Porter carried the day.[62]

Not one to overlook an opportunity to point out how disaster followed upon rejection of his advice, Gordon immediately took up his pen not only to rage against those who had bested him in the pet-banks competition but to open the eyes of Jackson, Blair, and Lewis to another of their "hidden enemies," Roger B. Taney. The sole factor leading to the victory of Porter—"a foreigner by birth, an *alien* by the laws of our country," Gordon proclaimed in an angry note to Blair—was Taney's incredible appointments. Directors of the Union Bank he condemned as minions of Henry Clay, then blasted William G. Hewes as "the brother in Law of that immaculate George Poindexter [a United States senator from

Mississippi and one of Andrew Jackson's most hated enemies], under whose control, and at whose wink, he is the willing menial." "We are cursed with *Traitors* in our *Ranks*," he raged, but these might have been overcome, he maintained, had it not been for their "being supported—nay, cultivated by the effects produced on our party in the public Deposits. . . . We have been defeated but not conquered. . . . Believe me without hypocrisy or dissimulation."[63]

In a companion letter to William B. Lewis, these veiled accusations against Taney became more specific. As early as 1832, Gordon wrote, he had warned Secretary McLane of the "identical evils which have been fastened upon us by Mr. Taney." They had already lost the party a Senate seat, he observed, and would likely bring a Jacksonian defeat in the coming gubernatorial campaign, and yet Taney, he charged, continued to aggravate the problem by giving "countenance and support . . . to officers in the Customs at this port, who are politically opposed to us." In a closing move, he cast his net even wider. "When at Washington," he told Lewis, "I was a close observer of passing events, and I must now confess to you, that I observed much to be displeased and mortified with.—Individuals for whom you and the President entertain the highest regard, are in fact and in truth *not* your political friends."[64]

Thus it became Taney's turn to be read out of the party by Martin Gordon, obviously a dangerous man to cross. But some hope remained, in spite of Taney's "treachery." By late December the Slidell-Prieur faction had seen enough in the correspondence from Washington to convince them that their opposition to Gordon would prove fruitless, and that his position in the confidence of Jackson remained unshakable. Spotts was now dead,[65] Robeson removed from office, and Overton once again at peace with the White House clique. All at once the Prieur campaign simply collapsed. On December 18, 1833, John Gibson bought up its principal news organ, the *Louisiana Advertiser*, and promptly announced for White,[66] leaving Prieur to abandon his candidacy in January. The latter made no open truce with the Gordon faction, but in some fashion an agreement clearly had been reached between the opposing camps. Without the slightest embarrassment, the *Bee* welcomed the mayor back into the Jacksonian fold of which it was guardian, explaining unblushingly that Prieur had never been attacked in its columns for any personal defects but only because of the "false friends by whom he was surrounded."[67] In March, Holland withdrew from the mayoral campaign for "causes beyond my control,"[68] assuring the unopposed reelection of Prieur.[69]

Now the opposing camps could concentrate their forces for the climactic struggle between White and Dawson. In many ways it would be the most bitterly contested election of the Jacksonian period in Louisiana, at least equaling in intensity the presidential battle of 1828. For just as in that national contest, high stakes and passionate commitments pushed the rival partisans to extraordinary efforts. And just as in that earlier clash, the Jacksonians set out to fight what they claimed to be the all-important war of the people versus the aristocracy.

The opportunities to develop such a theme were many in 1834, and the Jacksonians missed none of them. By January the Bank of the United States had resumed its curtailment policy and once again money and credit became practically unavailable in Louisiana. At first the Jackson press simply refused to admit the existence of any hardship, ridiculing the reports of financial depression as the propaganda of those who would falsely maintain that removal of the deposits had brought ruin and economic suffering to the state.[70] But as the Bank continued to tighten its credit and discount activities in the early months of 1834, the painful consequences of that policy could no longer be denied. Many, some ardent Jacksonians among them, now concluded that the economic woes attendant upon the Bank's contraction had indeed been made inevitable by the president's rash removal of the deposits, and a great pro-Bank meeting gathered in New Orleans on February 19 to protest that policy, presided over by S. W. Oakey, a longtime supporter of the administration.[71]

As the economy grew more and more stringent, the administration press began to flood the country with the reams of oratory from Thomas Hart Benton and the *Globe* insisting that the Bank's worst crimes could be found in New Orleans, where thousands of dollars had reportedly been kept out of circulation or shipped to the East to create panic in the Mississippi valley and spread disaffection against Jackson's Bank policies. This led Democratic editors in Louisiana to belated recognition that the economic distress of 1834, instead of being denied, might be turned into the most dramatic argument against Biddle's hated institution.[72] Swearing vengeance against the "Monster" for needlessly producing this misery in the society, the *Courier* repeatedly claimed that those who supported such a cruel and irresponsible enemy of the people revealed themselves as the aristocrats against whom Jacksonians had always warned. "Who can show an instance of friendship extended on the part of the Bank to a poor man?" St. Romes demanded. "Banks are established for the benefit of the rich," he argued, with the final question: "Will the poor lend their aid to sustain and perpetuate an institution from which they can derive no advantage, and which threatens their liberties, by its extensive powers and the corrupting influence which it is enabled to exercise over the country, in the shape of bribery to one and influence to another? . . . Is it not better that the people should sustain the President, of whose honesty there can be no question, rather than side with an institution unknown to the constitution?"[73]

C. W. Duhy, editor of the *Merchant's Daily News* (New Orleans) and a onetime bitter enemy of Jackson who had been won over to the general's cause by the outright monetary bribes of H. B. Trist,[74] soon launched a campaign on the same tack, managing to bring the old anti-Federalist arguments of the Jacksonians completely up to date. Remnants of the old Federalist party, he warned, reenergized in the anti-Jackson camp, would restore the alien and sedition laws and "bind our interests, nay, our very thoughts, to the wheels of the political waggons driven by Webster and Biddle."[75]

Relishing their revived role as champions of the people, Jacksonian editors showed not the least embarrassment at the reminders of the opposition that Marigny, a prominent

Jacksonian, was at that very moment doing all in his power to push through the legislature a charter for his Citizen's Bank which would bind the state's credit to a bond issue of $12 million to facilitate the raising of capital for his purely private enterprise.[76] To this, as well as to pointed reminders of Gordon's long presidency of the notorious Orleans Navigation Company[77] and the extensive financial and commercial activity of Jacksonians like Maunsel White, J. B. Plauché, William G. Hewes, S. W. Oakey, and others, the *Courier* answered for its followers with the standard refrain: "The *Argus* seems to think that Aristocracy necessarily implies *wealth*. This is a great error. Aristocracy is a thing of the *head* and the *heart*, not of the *pocket* or the *purse*. . . . Now, everybody knows that Bernard Marigny is a democrat in theory and practice—that he had intermixed with, and has in fact been one of the people, from his earliest years—that he is plain and unostentatious in his manners, and that he pays as much deference to the poor as to the rich."[78] And when the puzzled defenders of White asked then if it were not well known that their candidate was loved for the friendliness of his manner and the simplicity of his life as contrasted to the gaudy effulgence of Dawson, the *Bee* seized upon this as the best proof of White's duplicity, that he should act like a democrat while harboring a hatred of the common man.[79]

So nebulous and empty of specifics were the arguments of the Jacksonians against the "aristocracy" of the Bank and its supporters that they scarcely deserve the name *arguments* at all. Skillfully contrived, they appealed to the jealousies and hatreds of the many who felt that their economic plight must indeed be the result of some conspiracy against them. Consistent or meaningful economic facts or demonstrations of how the Bank specifically injured the interests of the common Louisianian appear nowhere in this tangle of campaign oratory, whose recurrent theme could be summed up in one sentence: those for Jackson and Dawson were men of the people; those in the opposite camp were "aristocrats." This was not something to be explained, analyzed, or demonstrated. It sufficed simply to declaim it.[80]

Much more consequential than anything to be found in these pseudo-economic rantings, the Jacksonian assault upon the Constitution of 1812 as a document preserving the dominance of the "aristocracy" in the political life of the state addressed a clearly substantive issue. As early as January 1833 calls sounded in the legislature for a poll of the citizenry to ascertain their feelings on the matter of constitutional revision.[81] They failed of passage, but the argument remained alive in the months of the 1834 gubernatorial campaign. The Jacksonians generally favored abolition of the tax qualification for voting, reduction of the appointive powers of the governor, and a more equitable apportionment of representation in the state legislature.[82] All such demands had unquestionable legitimacy as integral components of a liberal democratic credo, a rise-of-the-common-man type rebellion against conservative public policy. But in this instance, given the political history of Gordon and Dawson, the purposes behind their advancement of these principles must be highly suspect. For them, more than being a matter of abstract political commitment, the question of constitutional change tied directly to the particular opportunity that each saw in the election of 1834. In Dawson's case, he clearly meant to use it to attract support of his candidacy from those sections of the state like north-central Louisiana and his own Florida Parishes, more and more restive under the political dominance secured to the Gallic southeastern region by the Constitution of 1812. Alliance with the formidable Gordon camp of New Orleans might well bring him to the governorship, in position to humble French pretensions and reorder the political dynamics of the state.

Like most New Orleanians, Gordon knew that both Gallic and American rural sections feared and indeed hated the city. The cosmopolitan population of the great metropolitan center made it essentially neutral in the ethnic rivalry between the Gallic southwest and the American parishes, its habitual course of action being totally with those sections that might best advance the city's own interest in a particular matter. Indeed, the ethnic contest had little importance to Gordon, whose main objective always centered on engineering whatever arrangement might secure for him the political supremacy he had so long sought. Being the principal factor in putting the Jacksonian Dawson in the governor's chair, in his judgment, would do precisely that. Indeed, no other course seemed open to him, for the pervasive attachment to Henry Clay in the southwestern sugar parishes made the likelihood of any combination between them and the New Orleans Jacksonian White House clique remote indeed. Aside from any ethnic considerations, moreover, proposals to revise the fundamental law might also strengthen his position in New Orleans by the promise of at least partially redressing the notorious inequities in legislative representation imposed on the great metropolitan center by the existent constitution. With such potential for advancing the ambitions of both Dawson and Gordon, constitutional reform became, therefore, a major rallying cry of the Jacksonian campaign in 1834.[83]

It lent itself particularly well to the strategy of attacking the E. D. White forces as elitists resistant to any change which might give greater political power to a larger number of Louisianians, the Jackson press constantly harping on how the Constitution of 1812 restricted the suffrage to those who paid taxes and limited officeholding to men of property. The *Louisiana Democrat* (Clinton) charged that "there is more aristocracy entwined in our State Constitution and Government, then in all the other states of the Union, but is also true that it is early doomed to be eradicated. The democracy are coming to the rescue." Not even the supposed iniquities of the Bank of the United States provided a better whipping boy for those who would claim to speak for the rights of the people.[84]

In his constant harangues in the *Merchant's Daily News*, Duhy made it inescapably clear where the Jacksonians perceived this aristocratic system to be most firmly entrenched. Avoiding any overt reference to Creole parishes of the state, he nonetheless claimed that aristocrats ruled "in districts where ignorance is the principal trait in the character of the population," imposing their will through parish judges, curates, sheriffs, and the influence of family ties. The power of these aristocrats, Duhy charged, rested in the archaic strictures which they had cemented into the Constitution of 1812, allowing them to maintain a "contempt for the masses of the people." He even managed to link together the two favorite Jacksonian targets: "Connected by a similarity of views, with the monied aristocracy throughout the Union, this faction has been emboldened of late by the successful efforts of the United States Bank in oppressing the middling classes and alarming the poor." And who, a writer to the *Bee* asked, had been most responsible for the aristocratic features of the Constitution of 1812? His answer: Alexander Porter. "*Will you*," he demanded, "*have Alexander Porter to reign over you*? If so, elect his pupil, his adopted child, his willing and obedient servant, Edward D. White!"[85]

The White camp responded to these attacks with arguments compounded of rather transparent rationalization and hardheaded analytical realism. The restrictions of the Constitution of 1812, they maintained, imposed such modest restraints on suffrage and officeholding that no man willing to work should feel burdened by them. Calls for universal suffrage and readjustment of legislative representation, according to this view, reflected no championing of expanded popular rights but aimed instead at enfranchising the indolent masses of the Florida Parishes, thus providing Dawson the electoral power needed to destroy the delicately structured ethnic balance built into the Constitution of 1812, which for more than twenty years had allowed the state's Gallic and American factions to live together in reasonable equity and harmony.[86] In direct appeal to Creole voters, the *New Orleans Argus* warned that a Dawson victory would mean shifting control of the state to their old American antagonists, with a consequent elimination of all French influences in the legislature and courts and a move of the state capital to the Florida Parishes. The end result would be to make French-speaking Louisianians "strangers in their own land."[87]

From the very beginning of the campaign the Jacksonians recognized that White's greatest strength lay in the Creole sections of the state and had begun to challenge his reputation as a particular favorite of the native population.[88] Aware of the ever present sensitivity of the Creole sugar parishes to any threat against their basic industry, from April 21, 1834, until the end of the election the *Bee* highlighted its masthead with the running line, "THINGS TO BE REMEMBERED AT THE POLLS. REMEMBER, that Edward D. White voted in favor of a law, calculated to bring distress and ruin upon the great flourishing interest of our state." And on the very eve of the balloting they exploited another opening which the always unpredictable White provided them. Jacksonian papers raised a great fuss over a report by Isaac Johnson that during a campaign visit to Bayou Sara, White had asked a friend if he was a Creole, pronouncing the word as "creowl." "No," the friend was said to have replied, "but I have a negro in my kitchen who is."[89] John Gibson in the *Louisiana Advertiser* and other White supporters at first denounced the story as totally false, stressing that its source, Johnson, was Dawson's brother-in-law, but their later attempts to characterize the incident as simply a "trifling pleasantry" tend to confirm that it actually happened.[90] But even that likelihood apparently did little harm to White's strength among the Creole population, most of them seemingly accepting the whole exchange as just more evidence of White's notorious strangeness. His behavior, in any case, may well have been adjudged harmless compared to that of Dawson, who at almost the same time had thrown himself into a campaign brawl at Donaldsonville with drawn dagger, but only, his defenders said, to restore order.[91]

In the more pedestrian routines of campaigning, the White camp dutifully extolled their candidate's record in Congress, stressing his efforts in the always troubling question of disputed land titles in the state and defending his vote for the Compromise Tariff of 1833 as actually protective of the Louisiana sugar industry rather than damaging to it as charged by the Democrats. They denounced his Jacksonian opponent as an enemy of internal improvements and a nullifier at heart, condemned the Jackson administration's war against the Bank of the United States as the destructive folly of an ignorant old man, and made much of the fact that even Dawson admitted opposing the removal of the deposits despite his conviction that the Bank of the United States should be dismantled.[92] For Dawson the man they had nothing but contempt, dismissing him as a "painted butterfly," limited in ability, and notoriously the pawn of Martin Gordon, the would-be "Pacha" and "viceroy" of the Jackson party in Louisiana.[93]

In all this storm of controversy, Dawson did indeed play a highly unusual part for a Louisiana politician: he said practically nothing for himself. His specific views on nullification, internal improvements, the tariff, and removal of the deposits remained largely unspoken, leaving it to Duhy, Robert J. Ker of the *Bee*, and St. Romes of the *Courier* to fill their pages with explanations of what they were "assured" Dawson really believed.[94] In obvious counterthrust to Jacksonian charges of Dawson's subservience to Gordon, they paraded White in the meantime as devoid of any ideas of his own, dependent in all things upon Alexander Porter, the aristocratic and foreign master who controlled all aspects of his candidacy.[95] For their part, White's supporters tried to blunt this attack by urging Irish voters to rally to his side as one of them, claiming his Hibernian ancestry as a guarantee of his attachment to their interests, but the effort never managed to gain much momentum.[96]

Rejection by the United States Senate of Gordon's reappointment as collector of the port provided additional tension in the last weeks of the campaign.[97] His great offense, the *Courier* proclaimed, "consists in his being a staunch democrat, and therefore an eyesore to the ruffle-shirt gentry. . . . What generous heart will not envy Mr. Gordon martyrdom?"[98] It was slightly more difficult to weep for Martin Gordon Jr., who at his father's rejection had been pushed forward unsuccessfully by the Jacksonians as a substitute, though not yet twenty-one.[99] The expostulations of the New Orleans Jackson press fed upon the effusions of the *Globe*, which trumpeted the praises of both Gordons as the firmest of the president's allies and mourned their fate as victims of Nicholas Biddle and New Orleans "smugglers," Blair's description of the merchants who had opposed his friend and financial patron.[100] Forced to keep pace with Blair, the *Bee* and *Courier* lashed themselves to ever more violent denunciations of those who opposed their champions.[101]

Nothing better captured the frequently mindless extremism of this campaign than the uproar that erupted upon the report that Mazureau had replied to the vigorous pro-Dawson speeches of Pierre Soulé with the charge that most Jacksonian votes could be purchased for a glass of whiskey. What more striking proof of the aristocratic tendencies of the White party could be found, cried the *Courier*, than this shameful attack upon the humble drink of the working man.[102] Even Marigny, ludicrously enough, felt impelled to appear before a Dawson gathering to declaim: "Those aristocrats who are moved by the love of personal interest, will be defeated, and triumphant democracy will be seen rising as they fall. . . . They believe that because they have a few bankers on their side, that they will have a majority. . . . In the great contest between Great Britain and the United States, who was it that triumphed? The drinkers of Bordeaux and Chateau Margaux, or the drinkers of whiskey? When the Bostonians repulsed John Bull, was Claret or Whiskey drank?"[103]

In New Orleans the election proved as hectic as the campaign itself. Burly Irish draymen blocked suspected White voters from the polls, with little interference from John Holland, the county's deputy sheriff, otherwise occupied as a Dawson poll commissioner. Both sides crowded their partisans into the narrow stairway leading to one of the polling booths where election judges had placed a barrier across the head of the stairs, narrowing the approach to the officials' desk, and as the crowd pushed and pulled to get their own men through the opening the whole mass frequently went crashing down to the bottom landing.[104]

The returns gave White an impressive victory, not only in New Orleans but throughout the state as well, showing him defeating his opponent by a vote of 6,065 to 4,149. He carried the city by a margin of 958 to 542 and every parish south of Red River except Plaquemines, while Dawson captured the Floridas and the Red River region except for Avoyelles and Concordia.[105] Jacksonians fared almost as badly in the congressional campaigns. Among them only Ripley won his race, profiting from predicted support in the traditional Jacksonian stronghold of the Floridas and the scattering of votes among three opposing candidates. In the First District, Henry Johnson took the seat vacated by White, defeating young Charles E. Gayarré in a campaign which saw the ex-governor courting his old Creole support by suddenly appearing regularly at mass, though not a Catholic. And in the western district Rice Garland won over the Jacksonian Joseph Walker.[106]

Sadly, the *Courier* surveyed the wreckage of Jacksonian hopes and blamed everything on "that humbug, the Deposites."[107] Little in the record would seem to support that judgment, a lame rationalization hardly convincing even to those who propounded it. The economic distress of 1834 had indeed affected rural parishes as well as the financial centers of New Orleans, leading Browse Trist to the conviction that White's victory "was owing in a great measure to it." But most observers seemed to agree that few followers of the General broke with his party on that issue.[108]

Distribution of the returns underlines the principal verity of this clangorous contest: no ascendancy of an aristocracy over the people, no victory of Chateau Margaux over whiskey, had much to do with the outcome. Behind all the various maneuverings and tactics, behind all the frenzied campaign rhetoric, the old and still vibrant question of Gallic or American rule continued to dominate the Louisiana political scene. The election of 1834 added to that abiding issue the even more inflaming consideration that in this campaign American victory would clearly have meant dominion over the state by Martin Gordon and his White House coterie. Secure in the protections of the Constitution of 1812, Gallic south Louisiana was simply not yet ready to submit to the invader.

Its successful resistance had in large measure been assured by what remained a besetting weakness of the Jacksonian cause, the constant unwillingness of its principle leaders to surrender individual ambition to party solidarity. The Dawson-Gordon alliance never managed to repair the breach of the Slidell-Prieur challenge in New Orleans, and even many of the candidate's closest Florida advisers remained clearly uncomfortable in their association with the collector and his White House clique. Old frictions between adherents of Dawson and General Ripley never completely dissipated, and the always smoldering antagonisms between Southerners and Yankees, Nullifiers and Unionists, prevented a united support of Dawson's candidacy even in those American precincts most important to him. The pine woods area of the eastern Florida Parishes, for example, harbored growing suspicion of the more affluent St. Francisville political leadership which he personalized. The wounds of internecine party conflict, especially those provoked by Gordon and his hacks, had cut deep—too deep to be easily forgotten.[109]

Buoyed by the joy of victory, White's supporters spent little time analyzing their success. In New Orleans a boisterous throng paraded through the city streets at the news of their triumph, bands blaring "The Rogue's March" before the home of St. Romes and intoning "The Dead March" before that of Jerome Bayon, publisher of the *Bee*. The following evening raucous crowds assembled outside Martin Gordon's residence on Royal Street to shout cries of "Whiskey! Whiskey!" and to rail at the dejected leader of the scattered Jacksonian forces.[110] Within, Gordon may well have listened and pondered his unhappy fate. The puzzle remained ever the same—Louisiana insisted on voting for Jackson but would have little to do with Jacksonians.

Notes for "Democracy Discordant"

[1]Alexander Porter to Josiah S. Johnston, December 26, 1832, in Josiah Stoddard Johnston Papers, Historical Society of Pennsylvania, Philadelphia, Penn. (hereafter cited as Johnston Papers); *Louisiana Courier*, December 26, 1832.

[2]*Louisiana Courier*, December 28, 1832.

[3]Ibid., January 3, 1833; *New Orleans Bee*, January 3, 1833; *Louisiana House Journal*, 1833, p. 4.

[4]*Louisiana House Journal*, 1833, pp. 42-44, 72-74.

[5]Ibid., 73-74.

[6]Alexander Barrow to William S. Hamilton, February 19, 1833, in William S. Hamilton Papers, Department of Archives, Louisiana State University, Baton Rouge, La. (hereafter cited as Hamilton Papers).

[7]Alexander Porter to Josiah S. Johnston, December 20, 1832, in Johnston Papers.

[8]A. B. Roman to Josiah S. Johnston, April 20, 1833, ibid.

[9]Edward Didier to S. D. Ingham, May 15, 1830 [copy], Collector's Letter Books of Correspondence Received, 1830, New Orleans; P. A. Rousseau to Samuel Spotts, April 3, 1833 [copy], Charges Against Custom House Officers, 1833-1841, both in Record Group 56, General Records of the Department of the Treasury, National Archives (hereafter cited as RG 56, GRDT, NA).

[10]Disputes between Gordon and Spotts are recorded in their correspondence with various secretaries of the treasury. See, for example, S. D. Ingham to Martin Gordon, March 19, 1830, Letter Books of Secretary's Correspondence with Collectors of Small Ports, Louis McLane to Gordon, April 21, 1833, McLane to Samuel Spotts, April 21, 1833, Letters Sent by the Secretary of the Treasury to Collectors of Customs, all ibid.

[11]Samuel Spotts to Louis McLane, April 4, 1833, Charges Against Custom House Officers, 1833-1841, ibid.

[12]*Alexander Smith v. Martin Gordon* (copy of parish court proceedings), ibid.

[13]Ibid.

[14]John Slidell to Martin Gordon, December 13, 1832, in Slidell Letter Book, Howard-Tilton Memorial Libray, Tulane University, New Orleans, La. (hereafter cited as Slidell Letter Book).

[15]John Slidell to Andrew Jackson, January 7, 1833, ibid.

[16]John Slidell to Martin Gordon, January 8, 1833, ibid.

[17]Andrew Jackson to Martin Gordon, April 9, 1833, in Andrew Jackson Papers, Library of Congress (hereafter cited as Jackson Papers); John Slidell to Henry Carleton, March 16, 17, 1833, in Slidell Letter Book.

[18]John Slidell to Henry Carleton, March 16, 1833, in Slidell Letter Book.

[19]John Slidell to Henry Carleton, March 17, 1833, ibid.

[20]John Slidell to Martin Van Buren, March 27, 1833, in Martin Van Buren Papers, Library of Congress (hereafter cited as Van Buren Papers); Andrew Jackson to Martin Gordon, April 9, 1833, in Jackson Papers.

[21]John Slidell to Martin Van Buren, March 27, 1833, in Van Buren Papers.

[22]Martin Van Buren to John Slidell, April 20, 1833, ibid.

[23]Andrew Jackson to Martin Gordon, April 9, 1833, in Jackson Papers; John Slidell to Martin Van Buren, March 27, 1833, in Van Buren Papers.

[24]Andrew Jackson to Martin Gordon, April 9, 1833, in Jackson Papers.

[25]F. P. Blair to Martin Gordon, April 11, 1833, in Miscellaneous Papers, New York Historical Society.

[26]Ibid.

[27]Committee of Signers of Memorial to Roger B. Taney, June 16, 1833, Charges Against Custom House Officers, 1833-1841, in RG 56, GRDT, NA.

[28]Martin Gordon to William B. Lewis, March 27, 1833, in Jackson Papers; for Nicholson's reactions to these charges, see John Nicholson to Andrew Jackson, April 8, 1833, Miscellaneous Letters Received, Secretary of State, in Record Group 59, General Records of the Department of State, National Archives.

[29]William B. Lewis to Andrew Jackson, April 26, 1833, in Jackson Papers.

[30]Louis McLane to Martin Gordon, April 16, 1833, McLane to Samuel Spotts, April 16, 1833, Secretary's Letter Books of Correspondence with Collectors of Small Ports, in RG 56, GRDT, NA.

[31]Committee of Signers of Memorial to Roger B. Taney, June 16, 1833, Charges Against Custom House Officers, 1833-1841, ibid.

[32]Memorial against Martin Gordon, ibid.

[33]R. F. Canfield to William J. Duane, August [?], 1833, ibid.

[34]Deposition of Charles J. Gow, November 1, 1833, ibid.

[35]John Slidell to Roger B. Taney, October 18, 1833, R. F. Canfield to Taney, December 28, 1833, ibid.

[36]Martin Gordon to Andrew Jackson, July 2, 1833, Letters from Collectors of Customs, in RG 56, GRDT, NA; *Louisiana Courier*, August 1, 1833; *New Orleans Bee*, February 1, 1834.

[37]Martin Van Buren to Andrew Jackson, August 6, 1833, in Van Buren Papers.

[38]Roger B. Taney to Martin Gordon, November 11, 1833, Letters to Collectors of Customs, in RG 56, GRDT, NA; Andrew Jackson to Martin Van Buren, November 19, 1833, in Van Buren Papers.

[39]Martin Gordon to Louis McLane, December 21, 1832, in Jackson Papers.

[40]*Louisiana Courier*, February 12, 1833; William L. Hodge to Josiah S. Johnston, January 1, 22, 1833, in Johnston Papers; Martin Gordon to Amos Kendall, October 15, 1833, Gordon to Roger B. Taney, November 22, 1833, Letters from Banks, in RG 56, GRDT, NA.

[41]*Baton Rouge Gazette*, November 26, 1831; *New Orleans Bee*, May 10, 1834.

[42]*Baton Rouge Gazette*, September 1, 1832.

[43]*Louisiana Courier*, August 10, 1833; *New Orleans Bee*, August 7, 1833.

[44]*Louisiana Advertiser*, March 31, April 5, July 21, 1832.

[45]*New Orleans Emporium*, November 26, 1832.

[46]*Louisiana Courier*, May 25, 1833.

[47]Ibid., August 29, 1833; *New Orleans Bee*, August 9, 14, 23, 26, 28, 30, 1833.

[48]See, for example, *Louisiana Courier*, August 10, 29, 1833; *New Orleans Bee*, July 8, 1833.

[49]*New Orleans Bee*, July 8, 1833.

[50]Ibid., August 7, 1833.

[51]Ibid., September 6, 1833.

[52]See Overton's comments on his feelings toward Calhoun in Walter H. Overton to Josiah S. Johnston, April 29, May 23, 1832, in Johnston Papers, and his observations on the Eaton affair in Walter H. Overton to John Overton, December 21, 1830, in John Overton Papers, Tennessee Historical Society (hereafter cited as Overton Papers); *Louisiana Advertiser*, September 5, 1832; *New Orleans Bee*, August 5, 1833.

[53]*New Orleans Bee*, December 7, 1833.

[54]Ibid., September 2, 1833.

[55]Ibid., October 4, 1833.

[56]Roger B. Taney to Martin Gordon, November 4, 1833, Letters to Collectors, in RG 56, GRDT, NA; *Louisiana Courier*, November 21, 1833.

[57]*Louisiana Courier*, January 9, 1833; Matthew Morgan to Louis McLane, December 21, 1832, Letters from Banks, in RG 56, GRDT, NA.

[58]William G. Hewes to Roger B. Taney, October 27, 1833, Letters from Banks, in RG 56, GRDT, NA; Hewes to George Poindexter, March 21, 1834, in John F. H. Claiborne Collection, Mississippi State Department of History and Archives.

[59]Reuben Whitney to William D. Lewis, November 2, 4, 5, 1833, in Lewis-Neilsen Letters, Historical Society of Pennsylvania, Philadelphia, Penn.; John M. McFaul, *The Politics of Jacksonian Finance* (Ithaca, 1972), 64-69; Carl Brent Swisher, *Roger B. Taney* (New York, 1935), 223, 244, 283. The extent of Whitney's involvement in the Treasury Department's review of possible pet bank choices in New Orleans is suggested in John A. Brown to Reuben M. Whitney, October 1, 1833, Letters from Banks, in RG 56, GRDT, NA.

[60]Roger B. Taney to Martin Gordon, November 4, 1833, Letters to Collectors, John Slidell to Taney, October 21, 1833, John Nicholson to Taney, October 29, 1833, Miscellaneous Letters Received, all in RG 56, GRDT, NA. Martin Gordon to F. P. Blair, December 13, 1833, in Jackson Papers.

[61]*New Orleans Bee*, December 6, 14, 1833; *Washington Globe*, December 30, 1833.

[62]Martin Gordon to F. P. Blair, December 13, 1833, in Jackson Papers.

[63]Martin Gordon to William B. Lewis, December 16, 1833, ibid.

[64]Martin Gordon to Andrew Jackson, December 14, 1833, ibid.

[65]*Louisiana Courier*, July 12, 1833.

[66]Ibid., December 23, 1833.

[67]*New Orleans Bee*, January 6, 1834.

[68]Ibid., March 17, 1834.

[69]Ibid., April 8, 1834.

[70]*Louisiana Courier*, February 10, 1834; *New Orleans Bee*, February 18, 1834.

[71]"Memorial of New Orleans Citizens," *Senate Documents*, 23rd Cong., 1st Sess., No. 187; "Memorial and Resolution of Tradesmen and Others of New Orleans," ibid., No. 188; *Louisiana Courier*, February 20, 1834.

[72]Thomas Hart Benton, *Thirty Years' View*, 2 vols. (New York, 1854), 1:465, 485, 541, 544; *Debates in Congress*, 23rd Cong., 1st Sess., 257-59, 702-15, 1007; *Washington Globe*, January 23, March 6, 10, April 1, 12, 1834; *United States Telegraph*, February 20, 1834; *Louisiana Courier*, February 20, 24, March 7, 8, 13, 1834; *New Orleans Bee*, March 14, April 5, 1834.

[73]*Louisiana Courier*, February 20, 24, 1834.

[74]H. B. Trist to Nicholas P. Trist, April 30, 1832, in Nicholas P. Trist Papers, Southern Historical Collection, University of North Carolina, Chapel Hill, N. C. (hereafter cited as Trist Papers).

[75]*Merchant's Daily News* (New Orleans), February 13, 1834.

[76]*Louisiana Advertiser*, February 12, 21, 18, March 7, 8, 11, 31, 1834; *Louisiana Courier*, February 18, 1834; *New Orleans Argus*, July 2, 1834.

[77]*Louisiana Advertiser*, June 2, 1834.

[78]*Louisiana Courier*, July 2, 1834.

[79]*New Orleans Bee*, June 21, 1834.

[80]See, for example, the speeches of Pierre Soulé and Alfred Hennen at the Dawson rally of June 7, 1834, in *New Orleans Bee*, June 9, 11, 1834.

[81]*Louisiana Senate Journal*, 1833, p. 11.

[82]*New Orleans Bee*, May 13, 30, July 2, 4, 1834; *Louisiana Advertiser*, June 26, 1834; *Merchant's Daily News*, April 24, June 27, 1834.

[83]*Merchant's Daily News*, April 24, June 27, 1834; *New Orleans Bee*, July 3, 4, 1834; *New Orleans Courier*, June 28, 1834.

[84]Reprinted in *New Orleans Bee*, May 13, 1834.

[85]*Merchant's Daily News*, February 13, 1834; *New Orleans Bee*, June 24, July 1, 1834.

[86]*New Orleans Argus*, July 8, 1834.

[87]Ibid., July 9, 1834.

[88]*Merchants' Daily News*, February 3, 1834.

[89]*Louisiana Courier*, July 4, 1834.

[90]*Louisiana Advertiser*, July 1, 3, 1834.

[91]*New Orleans Argus*, July 1, 1834; *Louisiana Advertiser*, June 21, 1834.

[92]*New Orleans Argus*, May 7, 1834.

[93]*Louisiana Advertiser*, February 12, 14, April 23, 25, June 30, 1834; *Baton Rouge Gazette*, May 3, 1834.

[94]*New Orleans Argus*, April 19, May 27, 1834; *Louisiana Advertiser*, January 15, May 2, 1834.

[95]See *New Orleans Bee*, May 30, 31, 1834; *Merchants' Daily News*, March 17, 24, May 13, 1834.

[96]*Louisiana Advertiser*, July 4, 1834; *New Orleans Bee*, May 2, 16, June 19, 1834; *New Orleans Argus*, June 5, 1834; Alexander Porter to J. Burton Harrison, June 9, 1834, in J. Burton Harrison Papers, Library of Congress; Wendell H. Stephenson, *Alexander Porter, Whig Planter of Old Louisiana* (Baton Rouge, 1934), 81-87.

[97]*New Orleans Bee*, June 16, 1834.

[98]*New Orleans Courier*, June 13, 1834.

[99]John Riddle to Roger B. Taney, June 24, 1834, in Levi Woodbury Papers, Library of Congress (hereafter cited as Woodbury Papers); *United States Telegraph*, May 31, June 5, 1834.

[100]*Washington Globe*, May 30, June 4, 11, July 10, 11, 1834.

[101]*New Orleans Bee*, June 16, 18, 1834; *New Orleans Courier*, June 16, 18, 1834.

[102]*New Orleans Courier*, June 28, 1834.

[103]Ibid., June 30, 1834.

[104]Ibid., July 9, 1834; *Louisiana Advertiser*, July 8, 9, 10, 1834.

[105]*Louisiana House Journal*, 1835, p. 10.

[106]*New Orleans Bee*, June 28, July 17, 1834.

[107]*New Orleans Courier*, July 11, 1834.

[108]H. B. Trist to Nicholas P. Trist, August 27, 1834, in Trist Papers; E. G. W. Butler to Thomas Butler, April 27, 1835, in Thomas Butler Papers, Department of Archives, Louisiana State University, Baton Rouge, La.

(hereafter cited as Butler Papers); Henry A. Bullard to Gulian C. Verplanck, January 18, 1834, in Gulian C. Verplank Papers, New York Historical Society; Maunsel White to Andrew Jackson, April 18, 1834, in Jackson Papers; William G. Hewes to George Poindexter, March 21, 1834, in John F. H. Claiborne Collection, Mississippi State Department of History and Archives; R. J. Walker to William C. Rives, July 17, 1837, in William C. Rives Papers, Library of Congress; *Baton Rouge Gazette*, June 21, 1834.

[109]*New Orleans Argus*, July 1, 1834; Lafayette Saunders to Thomas Butler, January 31, 1830, in Butler Papers; Eleazar W. Ripley to Levi Woodbury, January 25, 1835, in Woodbury Papers, in which Ripley blames "personal antipathies" within the party for Dawson's defeat, supports John Nicholson's retention as federal marshal, and subtly warns against letting Gordon sow seeds of further division in Jacksonian ranks.

[110]*New Orleans Courier*, July 11, 12, 1834; *New Orleans Bee*, July 14, 1834.

POLITICAL CORRUPTION IN THE EARLY REPUBLIC: LOUISIANA AS A CASE STUDY, 1829-1845*

Joseph G. Tregle, Jr.

In one of the more provocative assessments advanced in his multivolume biography of Andrew Jackson, Robert Remini argues that early on in the presidential campaign of 1824 the general became convinced of an overwhelming presence of fiscal dishonesty in the administration of James Monroe, a finding which Remini claims now to be validated by his own historical research. The Era of Good Feelings, he contends, "really deserves to be called the nation's first Era of Corruption."[1]

This judgment provides Remini a platform from which to launch his vision of a Jacksonian presidency sincerely committed to a policy of "reform and rotation" designed to root out those who had contributed to the despoiling of the public treasury during the preceding twelve years and to a systematic cycling of governmental office holders which would discourage defalcation in the future. Misrepresentation of these goals and tactics by enemies of Jackson at the time and by historians given to exaggerated evaluation in subsequent years had been responsible, Remini maintains, for the tradition of a Jacksonian administration wedded to an understanding of civic responsibility best articulated in the famous aphorism of William L. Marcy: "To the victor belong the spoils."[2]

Remini's Jackson strides across his pages as a president acutely conscious of the necessity for eternal vigilance in reviewing the performance of political appointees to guard against dereliction from the high ethical standards which he mandated. Indeed, says Remini, his "concern with honesty in government" approached the "nearly obsessive,"[3] leading one to believe that this demonic rectitude must surely have produced a radical change from the alleged corruption of the Monroe-Adams years.

Actually, Remini produces very little in the way of hard evidence to support his view that such was indeed the case. The existence of scandalous behavior in the ranks of public officials in the period from 1816 to 1828 need hardly be debated. From the first days of the republic, whether under Washington or Jefferson, dereliction from public trust occurred with regularity in the ranks of the Federalists and Republicans alike. Destruction

*First published in *Louisiana History*, 31 (1990): 125-39. Reprinted with the kind permission of the author and the Louisiana Historical Association.

of most of the early archives of the Treasury Department in the disastrous fire of April 1833 makes it essentially impossible, however, to measure the extent of such malfeasance during the Era of Good Feelings as compared to what followed it. But if one were to rely on the public appreciation of levels of behavior as recorded in the press and correspondence of the period, for example, the consensus seems to be that the Jacksonian "revolution" ushered in a time of political spoils and official misconduct more pronounced than anything known before. A check of what happened in Louisiana during those years tends to confirm the accuracy of contemporary judgment rather than that of Remini.

Those who had labored for the victory of Andrew Jackson in 1828, for example, knew exactly what they intended that triumph to bring with it. "Now let our side come in!" one Louisiana Jacksonian exulted in greeting the new administration, with no ambiguity as to the precise meaning of his jubilation.[4] And the new victors looked for immediate gratification. As early as December 1828, even before the general had established himself in office, grumbling began to circulate to the effect that the promised distribution of loaves and fishes failed to meet expectations. In the doleful phrase of one complainant to the party leadership, "My mouth is yet open!"[5]

A deeper sense of urgency, a greater intensity of demand suffuses this transition to full-fledged Jacksonian Democracy than anything found in previous administrations, with the possible exception of the one which ushered in another reform team in the Revolution of 1800. But that earlier clamor had been chastened by Jefferson's sensitivity to his own doctrinal commitment to fairness and the ethical precept that no honest man should be turned out of office for political opinion alone. Jackson professed similar principles, but brought to them a far less sophisticated appreciation of the subtleties of their application, blessed as he was with the happiest of faculties, a guileless and sincere ability to identify his own purposes with unchallengeable righteousness and moral integrity.

Henry Adams long ago pointed out the implications for civilization of the geometric multiplication in the production of energy, but we have had no comparable analysis of the impact upon society of the remarkable increase in the perception of possible avenues to wealth accompanying the Age of Jackson. Edward Pessen, it is true, insists that few poor men did in fact manage to graduate into the ranks of the wealthy during this uncertain "Rise of the Common Man," and his evidence remains strong and persuasive.[6] Be that as it may, the spirit of the age clearly reinforced a widening acceptance that possibilities of enrichment, at least, now seemed more ready to hand than ever before.

The confluence of new devices for getting from one place to another, new market opportunities in the burgeoning factory towns of the Industrial Revolution, new acres opening to cultivation in rewarding money crops—all of these gave to the period its restless, entrepreneurial character, imbuing it with that "on the make" spirit which envelops the entire era. These pressures clearly molded new approaches to public service at a time impossible with only the old, customary genteel leadership of Virginia dynasty days. There simply weren't enough gentlemen to go around.

Evidence of a more unbuttoned lifestyle after 1830 abounds in practically every level of American society. Standards of official conduct in legislative bodies, for example, became considerably more relaxed than they had been in the past. One caustic visitor to the Louisiana house of representatives in 1835 reported how "some members sat grouped around the fires in close divan, some supinely lolled at ease, while others very composedly sat with their legs thrown over the tables, their feet obliquely projected towards the speaker, and their behinds—like Ossian's moon round as the shields of my fathers—were placed vis-a-vis their comrades, as if they bore the *memento more* of *requiescat in pace*."[7]

By 1844, possibilities of violence in Congress had become so heightened that one member complained that he "really should not be surprised to have a bowie in my back any day of the week."[8] And when Reuben Whitney came in 1837 before a house hearing in Washington charged with contempt, two committee members, chairman Henry A. Wise of Virginia and Balie Peyton of Tennessee, brandished dirks and pistols and threatened to kill him on the spot if he moved quickly in a menacing way. The next year saw the death of Congressman Jonathan Cilley of Maine in a murderous rifle duel with his colleague William G. Graves of Kentucky, an encounter pushed to inescapable tragedy by the bloodthirsty Wise.[9]

At much the same time there began to appear that charming American gift for dressing up questionable official performance in deceptive garb. Willie Mangum, president pro tem of the senate in the early 1840s, for example, long brooded over the logical incongruity of placing the cost of the vast quantities of champagne swilled by his legislative associates under the budget for stationery, until finally he hit upon the inspired solution of consigning the jeroboams to the chamber's fuel account.[10] Lest it be thought that Mangum's difficulties grew from the predilections of Democratic cronies of Andrew Jackson, cut from the pattern of those who had trampled over settees and table tops to get at the liquid refreshments during the Hero's inauguration, it should be remembered that polished Whigs like Henry Clay and Daniel Webster owned the primary claim to especially elevated osmosis quotients.

Fittingly enough, the first demonstration of Jacksonian uses of power came from one of the most experienced practitioners in the entire nation, Edward Livingston. He had moved to the state in 1804, a refugee from the scandal attendant upon his having disgraced the sensitive Jefferson administration by his inability to replace some $43,000 in custom bond returns which he had subverted to his personal use while federal attorney in New York City. The story has been told elsewhere of how he and John Slidell in their new positions as United States senator and federal attorney for the eastern district of Louisiana, respectively, schemed successfully in 1829 to liquidate Livingston's twenty-five-year debt to the government by legal chicanery of magnificent imagination and unflinching moral turpitude.[11] Their collaboration, however, victimized private citizens of New Orleans, not the federal treasury, and accordingly falls outside the area of public corruption, whatever might be said of its ethical failings.

But the same kind of piratical exuberance marked the official conduct of a whole variety of political appointees in Jacksonian Louisiana, made incredibly easy by the accountability practices in place during the period. The real puzzle is how the federal government of the 1830s and 1840s ever managed to meet its financial obligations, dependent as it was upon revenues collected and held by hundreds of individuals working in a system of such lax and haphazard control as to be unbelievable to a modern observer.

The great preponderance of those who figure in this tale of delinquency, it must be noted, violated only departmental rules against defaulting in their accounts rather than criminal statutes against theft, a distinction of profound legal significance whatever might be said of its moral ambiguity. To understand why this was so and to place the malfeasance in proper historical setting requires a brief description of the accountability procedures employed by the federal government in the early national period, mechanisms dating largely from the leadership of Alexander Hamilton and strangely incompatible with our notions of that meticulous taskmaster.

All collectors of customs, federal attorneys, marshals, and special agents of the government reported their receipt of public funds directly to the first auditor of the treasury, who checked these quarterly returns for accuracy and conformity to law before sending them on to a final review by the first comptroller, who affirmed or corrected the balances in the officer's accounts and then directed the audits to the register of the treasury for recording. Additional regulations required collectors of public moneys to send reports of weekly and monthly receipts directly to the secretary of the treasury, primarily to give that officer an up-to-date view of the government's liquidity, not to provide a check on the honesty of the agents. By law, the quarterly reports to the first auditor came due three months following expiration of the period covered in the returns. Failure of an agent to balance his account within a reasonable time supposedly required the first comptroller to refer his records to the agent of the treasury, who would then instruct the federal attorney of the proper judicial district to file suit against the defaulter in federal court. Theoretically, this entire accountability and auditing process lay outside the responsibility of the secretary of the treasury, final determination of audits being left to the comptroller. By the 1830s, second, third, fourth, fifth, and sixth auditors monitored the affairs of the army and navy, the state department, Indian offices, and miscellaneous governmental bureaus, generally reporting directly to a second comptroller for final resolution of accounts. Officers called receivers of public moneys, responsible for the revenues from the sale of the public lands, reported first to the commissioner of the land office, with review by the second comptroller, while post office personnel directed their returns to a separate departmental accountant, subject to confirmation of the first auditor.[12]

In light of eventual developments, it is ironic that one of the most forceful passages in President Jackson's inaugural address flailed the laxity with which he considered this system to be administered, leading him to call for more energetic pursuit of those who proved delinquent in the settling of their accounts with the government.[13] Little came of this exhortation except the creation by Congress of the position of solicitor of the treasury to replace that of the old agent, establishing in the department an officer specifically trained in the law and responsible thereafter for prosecution of suits against defaulters.[14] But the solicitor's powers extended only to civil actions, and it was not until August 31, 1841, that Congress attempted to strengthen the system by providing for indictment on criminal perjury charges of officers who swore to false data in their financial returns.[15] Not even this protected against a delinquent who simply defaulted without lying about it.

An astonishing laxity and carelessness in administration made a weak system even worse, despite Jackson's scolding. The congressional inquiry into the frauds of Samuel Swartwout, collector at New York who made off with a million and a quarter dollars in public funds in 1838, revealed shocking lack of attention to his returns during the months that he regularly stole government revenues. The first auditor's recording of custom bonds deposited in the New York district fell several years behind current status, affording Swartwout his chief opportunity for escaping detection. The first auditor ignored as well the absence of proper vouchers to support disbursements, the first comptroller failed to look behind the surface records, and Secretary of the Treasury Levi Woodbury disclaimed any responsibility for his subordinates' accounts.[16] Nor did the Treasury profit from the lesson of Swartwout's performance. His immediate successor, Jesse Hoyt, proved even more audacious in his depredations and equally skillful in escaping discovery until it was too late to prevent enormous losses to the government. Compounding the Democratic administration's culpability in all this, Hoyt's penchant for thievery had long been notorious among his party colleagues. No less powerful a figure than Silas Wright, as close to Van Buren as any man, admitted that at the news of Hoyt's appointment he had "trembled . . . and felt chills," knowing as he did his colleague's "passion for accumulation without an honest equivalent."[17]

Some of this remarkable nonchalance to fiscal accountability may very well have been the result of the decrepitude of the men filling the offices of first auditor and first comptroller until 1836, Richard Harrison and Joseph Anderson, both of whom were advanced in seniority and senility at the time of their resignations, Harrison being then eighty-six and long notorious as a drunkard.[18] But relatively youthful successors did little if any better, as the Swartwout and Hoyt cases clearly demonstrated.

Given these conditions in Washington and the ever-present pressures of cupidity so highly developed in Louisiana during this period of her boomtime expansion, it is no wonder that the state figured prominently in the Jacksonian corruption sweepstakes. The irresistible seduction of loosely guarded federal funds, moreover, did not operate on Jacksonian party faithful alone. Whatever their claims to respectability, Whigs demonstrated an openness to gentlemanly thievery equal to that of their opponents whenever given the chance, as the following evidence will certify.

Unhappily for the reputation of Jacksonian dedication to the supposed principles of the Democratic faith in Louisiana, one of the first to fall afoul of the law was Peter K. Wagner, the party's unrivalled Ajax in the field of political journalism. His services as editor of the New Orleans *Louisiana Advertiser* in the campaign of 1828 had been prodigious, and this, added to his fawning sycophancy toward party chieftain Martin Gordon, had been sufficient to win him appointment as naval officer in the New Orleans Custom House in 1829.[19] No man had prated more piously the Jacksonian credo of service to the people, nor voiced more strident attacks upon Adams and Clay supporters as defenders of "Bargain and Corruption" aristocratically disdainful of common honesty. By 1832 his accounts showed a delinquency of more than three thousand dollars, but the forgiving treasury auditors did nothing and he won appointment to a second term in 1834, his surety bond of two thousand dollars signed by Gordon and his son, Martin Gordon, Jr.[20] The slow-moving treasury officers at last, in September of 1835, reported that a new examination of Wagner's accounts revealed that he had simply stopped making reports altogether in 1832, ballooning his delinquency to some $12,000. When called upon by Gordon for an explanation, Wagner packed his things at the office, left, and never returned.[21] Despite their clear responsibility as Wagner's securities, the Gordons blithely refused to pay the two thousand dollar bond liability, ignored a federal judgment against them, and used their connections in Washington to prevent any executive action to collect.[22] As late as 1868 the books of the treasury still carried them as "public debtors."[23]

In the very year of this fiasco and despite their contempt for judicial attempts at collection of the surety bond, the younger Gordon received appointment to Wagner's old position as naval officer by direct order of President Jackson, while his father snared the commission as agent for construction of the branch mint of the United States at New Orleans.[24] It took the government until 1841 before it could bring the elder Gordon to a final clearing of his accounts, in which he had been declared delinquent to the sum of $70,000 in 1836.[25] Adding rueful flavor to all this, the same documents preserving the record of Gordon's financial filibustering in the building of the branch mint include the government's pay voucher to William Strickland for designing and drawing the plans for the famous New Orleans landmark, generally acclaimed as a masterpiece of American architecture. It shows a payment in full of $300.[26]

True son of his father, the younger Gordon moved in 1836 from the naval post to that of cashier of the Union Bank, one of Jackson's pets, only to be expelled from that position in 1839 when some $50,000 disappeared from funds supposedly transferred by him to branch offices in the country parishes. To understandable inquiries, he blandly replied that he had bundled the money into plain packets and then dropped them into ordinary mail receptacles, taking no receipts and registering no bill numbers.[27]

Almost everything and everyone touched by the Gordons proved eventually to be tainted. Their close associate in designing the distribution of Jacksonian patronage in Louisiana in 1829, Dr. Robert Ker, had himself assumed the office of postmaster at New Orleans upon the opening of the general's administration. In no way discomfited by the knowledge that he would be eliminating from public service one of the very few Latin Creoles ever to hold federal office in the city, Ker, a prosperous physician, openly claimed the position as the spoils of war, and once ensconced promptly vacated the post for his son William.[28] The latter remained relatively quiescent in the bitter factional battles of the next decade and managed to hold on to his assignment until August 1839, when he confessed to a defalcation of over $93,000, a sum never recovered by the United States, which in 1854 abandoned its efforts to collect from his securities.[29]

On a per annum basis, Ker's successor, William McQueen, did even better, managing to divert $20,000 of government funds to his own pockets during the twelve months of his tenure. Again, despite sureties of the most impressive financial and social stature, like Christian Roselius, Louis Bringier, and Mandeville Marigny, the government failed to recover on McQueen's delinquency and wrote off his account as a "bad debt" in 1853.[30]

Should all this reinforce a rural assessment of New Orleans as a peculiarly and uniquely corrupt exception in an otherwise pristinely virtuous state, it must be noted that listed alongside Ker and McQueen in the folio of postal defaulters are Stuart B. Nunn, postmaster at Clinton; Newcomb Hunt at Thibodaux; Vincent Page at Alexandria; and William P. Jones at Natchitoches, from whose clutches the government tried vainly in 1837 and 1840 to retrieve sums ranging from $336.77 to over $4,000.[31] Country and city differed only in degree, not the nature, of their defalcations.

Another of the stalwarts of Gordon's "Custom House Coterie," John H. Holland contributed tremendously to the Jacksonian cause in Louisiana by virtue of his rank as grand master of the Masonic forces in New Orleans. A native of Connecticut, he had come to the area in 1801 as a youth of fifteen, steeping himself in the mores and culture of his new home until in the 1830s he could claim unrivaled knowledge of the city's history, personalities, and local customs.[32] When Jacksonian forces shattered in Louisiana over the fierce 1833 struggle for party control between adherents of Gordon and those of John Slidell, Holland threw his support to Gordon's successful Custom House faction, which quickly bounced Slidell out of his post as federal attorney and into an extended political exile with many of his friends. Holland replaced one of them, John Nicholson, as federal marshal for the eastern district of Louisiana in 1835, and the old story began anew.[33]

As marshal, Holland collected all fines and penalties imposed by federal courts in his jurisdiction, being responsible as well for moneys received from governmental seizures and foreclosures. By early 1839 President Van Buren and Secretary of the Treasury Woodbury began to receive clear warnings about confusion in Holland's accounts, soon followed by complaints from the federal attorney at New Orleans that he refused to respond to requests for information or to explain the total absence of any formal entries in the records of the court as to his receipts. Alexandre Mouton, a rising power in the state's Democratic ranks, finally wrote despairingly to Secretary of State John Forsyth that while he remained unsure as to the facts in Holland's case, swirling rumors in the city gave him grave concern, as well they might, for one reality spoke volumes on the point: Holland had just absconded to Texas, abandoning wife and children in his inability to produce $20,000 which he had appropriated to his private use from governmental funds.[34] At almost the same time, Thomas Shields, navy purser at New Orleans, died with a delinquency of $98,471 charged against his account. His surety, John K. Smith, confessed inability to make restitution, being insolvent and himself indebted to the government for a sum in excess of $28,000, the balance still outstanding in his own default as navy agent dating back to 1821.[35]

Those delinquent in their accounts reflected a wide range of temperaments in dealing with their superiors in Washington, none more winningly than Parish Childress, receiver of public moneys in St. Helena Parish. At first, Childress demonstrated something close to supercilious independence, writing to Woodbury in March 1836 to complain of being criticized for laxity in making his reports: "I, like others," he told the secretary, "am liable to make mistakes and neglect my duty; but I believe seldom, in comparison with others." Childress must have possessed a truly remarkable faculty for calm self-appraisal, for in February 1838, he was again revealing all to Woodbury: "In this, I . . . tender you my resignation as receiver of public moneys, being no longer worthy of the trust." He would appear to have been correct in this last judgment, at least, for as late as 1868 he had made no payment on the $12,000 which he had failed to deliver to the government.[36]

Even the somewhat saving grace of shame is absent from Richard M. Carter's part in this saga. He had managed to escape the vindictiveness of the Gordons toward friends of Slidell, rising in favor along with Slidell's brother Thomas as the more flexible Van Buren took over the presidential reins from an unforgiving Andrew Jackson. In his newly won office as receiver of public moneys, Carter began almost immediately upon his accession in 1837 to direct to his superiors in the land office a correspondence astonishing in its hectoring tone and expression of disdain for even the few rudimentary procedures of Washington's gentle bureaucracy. Perhaps his arrogance stemmed from knowledge that various of his immediate predecessors had for years been allowed to go without satisfactory of settlement of their accounts. The unseemly distemper of his communications prompted the land office to move against him more expeditiously than was customary, with peremptory demand for delivery of $124,597, which Carter had cavalierly neglected to pay over to the United States. Some cold solace remained—a federal court jury brought back a judgment against him of only $96,000. One of his sureties, Samuel Lockett, despite heroic legal resistance, finally surrendered the $25,000 which he had guaranteed by endorsing Carter's duty bond, victim also, it would seem, of his friend's unpopularity in Washington. With continuing hostility, the government seized large and valuable properties belonging to Carter in New Orleans and the rich Yazoo delta, but even these left a deficit which, with accumulated interest, had risen to $98,000 when it appears to have been written off in 1868.[37] Ever irrepressible, the impudent Carter reopened his testy correspondence with the government in 1843, demanding to be paid the proper fee for having assisted Balie Peyton, the federal attorney at New Orleans, in preparing the legal work required for seizure of the assets of the Banks of the United States the previous year.[38]

To round out the rural side of the account, lest New Orleans become again suspect as uniquely abandoned, it may be noted that at Opelousas during the 1830s and 1840s, various receivers like David L. Todd, Benjamin R. Rogers, John T. Daniel, A. H. Andrus, and Benjamin R. Gantt, each proved delinquent for sums usually in the thousands of dollars, as did Alexander G. Penn, receiver at St. Helena; Benjamin F. Linton, federal attorney for the western district of Louisiana; Benjamin Laurents, receiver at Natchitoches; Joseph Friend at Ouachita; and William McFarlane in the land district north of Red River.[39] One of the most disruptive of all these rural defaults came at the very end of the Jacksonian period, when Francis D. Newcomb, surveyor general of Louisiana from 1841 to 1845, with headquarters at Donaldsonville, stole sums of a vast amount difficult to determine, because he not only forged receipts for non-existent disbursements but threw the whole process of land sales into disorder by making off with almost the entire body of files and archives of his office, to the despair of his successor.[40]

The Whig part in this lupercalia has so far gone unmentioned, for until Van Buren's departure in 1841, they were guiltless of misbehavior, having enjoyed no office in which to perform it. Things changed altogether with the administrations of William Henry Harrison and John Tyler, Whig incumbency providing a demonstration of the nonpartisan nature of corruption, highlighted by the experience of the various collectors of customs at New Orleans from 1841 to 1845. Thomas Gibbs Morgan assumed the post late in 1841, to be succeeded by Greenberry Dorsey in 1843, Manuel Cucullu in early 1844, and Thomas G. Barrett a few months later in the same year. Without exception, they each had great difficulty in clearing their accounts, Morgan and Barrett eventually being adjudged public defaulters by the courts in the amounts of $14,000 and $40,000 respectively, none of which the government ever managed to recover.[41]

Surrounding this mischief in high places was a veritable swamp of petty and routine malefaction. Deposits in the branch mint at New Orleans regularly simply disappeared from the vaults, and it was common knowledge that weighers at the facility often flagrantly undervalued bullion presented there for assaying. An official inquiry into the confusion at the mint, conducted by Thomas Slidell in 1839, brought to light an almost ridiculous mismanagement of the office, revealing an absence of any security for the deposit vaults in a building which generally stood hopelessly exposed to plundering, doors and windows unlocked and unattended during the night. In a species of fraud particularly infuriating to employees of the Custom House, officers receiving specie to meet their payrolls frequently sold a fraction of it for practically worthless bank paper, paid their workers with the bills at par, and pocketed the remainder of the hard cash.[42]

The best that can be said for this miserable record of official corruption is that the private sector could lay little claim to any higher moral tone. Paul Lanusse, president of Planters Bank, and Bailley Blanchard, cashier, brought the institution to financial collapse by a series of frauds in 1829, leading Supreme Court Justice Alexander Porter to excoriate some of the state's wealthiest citizens, like Laurent Millaudon, Joseph Abat, and John Lanna, for their attempts to cover up the criminality of their bank's officers.[43] T. G. Joans, proprietor and editor of the prestigious *New Orleans Mercantile Advertiser,* in 1834 forged notes with the names of various well-known citizens, among them Mayor Denis Prieur, and absconded with a small fortune,[44] while Antoine Foucher, Jr., fabricated his father's name to swindle $200,000 in 1843, fleeing the city in which he had outstanding almost a half-million dollars in unsettled debts.[45]

The cumulative mass of this pile of dereliction is quite overwhelming when viewed in retrospect, perhaps more so than for those who experienced its particular parts seriatim. But from any perspective the data are of a quantity and of a substance that can hardly fail to astonish, especially considering that the historical record most certainly tells but a portion of the story. Six postmasters, a federal marshal, one naval officer, one navy purser, one federal attorney, one surveyor general, no fewer than ten receivers of public moneys, at least two collectors of customs—all despoilers of the public treasury in a period of a bare fifteen years, in one state. It is an imposing array, even more striking because countless others have been excluded from the listing by virtue of their eventual clearing of accounts years after they had come due. With typical Louisiana political cynicism, public opinion accepted as fact that many wrongdoers escaped their proper punishment. Reports circulated repeatedly, for example, that Collector James Breedlove, Gordon's successor, had accumulated his considerable fortune by exchanging governmental specie for bank paper to his own profit, though such accusations seem never to have been proved.[46]

In at least partial support of Remini's thesis of a Jacksonian dedication to reform of civil service fiscal responsibility, Matthew Crenson sees in the period of sincere attempt to professionalize governmental administration through a greater institutionalization of the Washington bureaucracy, largely the work of Amos Kendall.[47] But little in the record would seem to demonstrate that "nearly obsessive" concern for honesty in public service ascribed to Jackson by Remini, nor does the history of Jacksonian Louisiana do much to sustain the lingering myth of a modern falling away from a golden age of superior public morality in the early years of the Republic.

Notes for "Political Corruption in the Early Republic: Louisiana as a Case Study, 1829-1845"

[1]Robert Remini, *Andrew Jackson and the Course of American Freedom, 1822-1832* (New York, 1981), 12-14.

[2]Ibid., 183-85, 347.

[3]Ibid., 189.

[4]William Haile to William S. Hamilton, May 20, 1829, William S. Hamilton Papers, Department of Archives, Louisiana State University, Baton Rouge, La. (hereafter cited as LSU-BR).

[5]Archibald Haralson to Thomas Butler, December 29, 1828, Thomas Butler Papers, LSU-BR.

[6]Edward Pessen, *Riches, Class, and Power Before the Civil War* (Lexington, Mass., 1973), 73-151.

[7]*New Orleans Bee,* March 11, 1835.

[8]C. Winthrop to Edward Everett, March 27, 1844, Edward Everett Papers, Massachusetts Historical Society, Boston, Mass.

[9]Lawrence A. Gobright, *Recollections of Men and Things at Washington* (Philadelphia, 1869), 29-30.

[10][T. N. Parmelee], "Recollections of an Old Stager," *Harper's New Monthly Magazine,* 45 (1872): 603.

[11]Joseph G. Tregle, Jr., "The Political Apprenticeship of John Slidell," *Journal of Southern History,* 26 (1960): 57-70.

[12]This account is based upon reports and documents in various record groups of the National Archives, particularly Record Group 56, General Records of the Department of the Treasury; Record Group 59, Records of the Bureau of Accounts; Record Group 217, Records of the United States General Accounting Office; and Record Group 206, Records of the Solicitor of the Treasury. A useful summary of the developments of governmental control policies in public accounts may be found in *House Report 81,* 25 Cong., 2 Sess. (1837); *Senate Doc. 1,* 25 Cong., 2 Sess. (1837); and in the introduction to George S. Ulibarri, *Preliminary Inventory of the Records of the Solicitor of the Treasury* (Washington, D. C., 1968). See also Treasury Secretary Levi Woodbury's description of the process in *House Report 313,* 25 Cong., 3 Sess. (1839), 579-84.

[13]*Senate Journal,* 21 Cong., 1 Sess. (1829), 14; Stephen Pleasanton to Andrew Jackson, October 21, 1829, Letters on Debts and Suits, Records of the Solicitor of the Treasury, Record Group 206, National Archives.

[14]4 U. S. Stat., 414.

[15]5 U. S. Stat., 439.

[16]*House Doc. No. 13,* 25 Cong., 3 Sess. (1838), 29; *House Report No. 313,* 25 Cong., 3 Sess. (1839), 8ff, 282-83, 580.

[17]*House Doc. No. 212,* 27 Cong., 2 Sess. (1842); Wright to Benjamin F. Butler, February 27, 1841, Wright-Butler Letters, New York Public Library, New York City, N. Y.

[18]*House Report No. 313,* 25 Cong., 3 Sess. (1839), 584, 627, 632; David Campbell to his wife, June 3, 1829, as quoted in Marquis James, *Andrew Jackson* (New York, 1940), 499.

[19]*New Orleans Argus,* May 6, 13, 1829.

[20]*United States v. Peter K. Wagner,* Case No. 3666, United States Eastern District Court of Louisiana, 1836, Federal Records Center, Fort Worth, Texas; Martin Gordon to Andrew Jackson, October 2, 1835, Collectors of Customs Applications (Gordon file), General Records of the Department of the Treasury, Record Group 56, National Archives; Sureties for Bonds, Records of the Bureau of Accounts, 1789-1925, Record Group 39, National Archives; *Bee,* May 15, 1834.

[21]Joseph Anderson to Virgil Maxcy, September 21, 1835, Letters Received from First Comptroller (1820-1839), Records of the Solicitor of the Treasury, Record Group 206, National Archives; Andrew Jackson to Levi Woodbury, January 5, 1835; Martin Gordon to Woodbury, January 25, 1835; Gordon to Jackson, October 8, 1835, all in Miscellaneous Letters Received, General Records of the Department of the Treasury, Record Group 56, National Archives; *United States v. Nicholas Sinnot et al.,* Case 3684, United States Eastern District Court of Louisiana, 1838, Federal Records Center, Fort Worth, Texas.

[22]Virgil Maxcy to P. K. Lawrence, April 8, 1837, Letters on Debts and Suits, 1821-1869; Clerk's Returns, 1821-1929 (1838), both in Records of the Solicitor of the Treasury, Record Group 206, National Archives; *United States v. Martin Gordon, Sr., and Martin Gordon, Jr.,* Case 4363, United States Eastern District Court of Louisiana, 1838, Federal Records Center, Fort Worth, Tex.

[23]General Index of Public Debtors, 1820-1868 (1868), Records of the Solicitor of the Treasury, Record Group 206, National Archives.

[24]*Bee,* April 17, 1835; endorsement, Martin Gordon to Andrew Jackson, October 8, 1835, Miscellaneous Letters Received, General Records of the Department of the Treasury, Record Group 56, National Archives.

[25]Audits 72,293 (December 28, 1836) and 81,124 (February 17, 1841), Miscellaneous Treasury Accounts of the General Accounting Office, First Auditor's Reports, Records of the United States General Accounting Office, Record Group 217, National Archives.

[26]Ibid.

[27]Martin Gordon, Jr., to Andrew Jackson, March 22, 1836, Collectors of Customs Applications (Louisiana), General Records of the Department of the Treasury, Record Group 56, National Archives; Hore B. Trist to Nicholas P. Trist, April 18, 1839, Nicholas P. Trist Papers, Manuscript Division, Library of Congress.

[28]*Argus*, May 6, 13, 1829; *New Orleans Louisiana Courier*, June 30, 1829.

[29]Accounts Transmitted for Suit, Post Office, Records of the Solicitor of the Treasury, Record Group 206, National Archives.

[30]Ibid.

[31]Ibid.

[32]*Bee*, November 15, 1833; Anne Royall, *Mrs. Royall's Southern Tour: Or, the Second Edition of the Black Book*, 3 vols. (Washington, D. C., 1830), 3:35.

[33]Minute Book No. 8 (1835), United States Eastern District Court of Louisiana, Federal Records Center, Fort Worth, Tex.

[34]Duncan Hennen to Martin Van Buren, February 7, 1839; J. N. Barker to Levi Woodbury, February 7, 1839; Alexandre Mouton to John Forsyth, February 11, 1839, all in Letters of Application and Recommendation during the Administrations of Martin Van Buren, William Henry Harrison, and John Tyler, 1839-1845, General Records of the Department of State, Record Group 59, National Archives (National Archives microcopy #687); Thomas Slidell to H. D. Gilpin, February 6, 1839, Letters Received from Attorneys, Clerks of Court, and Marshals, 1810-1839; General Index of Public Debtors, 1820-1868, both in records of the Office of the Solicitor of the Treasury, Record Group 206, National Archives.

[35]*House Doc. No. 93*, 27 Cong., 2 Sess. (1841), 186.

[36]*House Doc. No. 122*, 25 Cong., 3 Sess. (1839); *House Doc. No. 313*, 25 Cong., 3 Sess. (1839), 198-99; *House Doc. No. 186*, 27 Cong., 2 Sess. (1842), 4.

[37]*House Doc. No. 198*, 27 Cong., 3 Sess. (1842), 94; judgments against Carter, June 11, 1839, February 21, 1842, Clerk's Returns, Records of the Solicitor of the Treasury, Record Group 206, National Archives; *United States v. Richard M. Carter*, Case 464; *United States* v. *Samuel Lockett*, Case 463, both United States Circuit Court, Eastern District of Louisiana, Federal Records Center, Fort Worth, Tex.; affidavit affirming Lockett's surrender of surety, June 24, 1839, Letters Received by First Comptroller from the Solicitor of the Treasury, Records of the United States General Accounting Office, Record Group 217, National Archives.

[38]Charles B. Penrose to Mandeville Marigny, July 29, 1841; Penrose to Balie Peyton, July 29, 1841, both in Letters on Debts and Suits, 1821-1869, Records of the Solicitor of the Treasury, Record Group 206, National Archives; Richard M. Carter to John C. Spencer, August 7, 1843; Balie Peyton to Spencer, June 9, 1843, both in Miscellaneous Letters Received, Secretary of the Treasury, General Records of the Department of the Treasury, Record Group 56, National Archives.

[39]*House Doc. No. 313*, 25 Cong., 3 Sess. (1839), 143, 144, 242-44; *House Doc. No. 186*, 27 Cong., 2 Sess. (1842), 3-4, 10.

[40]Thomas H. Blake to F. D. Newcomb, February 19, October 21, November 27, 1844; February 24, May 13, 1845, all in Letters Sent to Surveyors General, 1796-1901, Records of the General Land Office, Record Group 49, National Archives; audit 97,235, November 5, 1847 (Newcomb), Miscellaneous Treasury Accounts of the General Accounting Office, Record Group 217, National Archives; *United States v. F. D. Newcomb*, United

States Circuit Court Eastern District of Louisiana, Cases 1447, 1484, 1488, 1489, 1494, 1497, Federal Records Center, Fort Worth, Tex.

[41]Trully M. Wise to J. C. Spencer, May 23, 1843, Miscellaneous Letters Received, General Records of the Department of the Treasury, Record Group 56, National Archives; *House Ex. Doc. No. 68,* 30 Cong., 1 Sess. (1847), 58; audit 91,543 (Morgan), Miscellaneous Treasury Accounts of the General Accounting Office, First Auditor's Reports, Records of the United States General Accounting Office, Record Group 217, National Archives; *United States v. Thomas Barrett,* Cases 3735, 4087, 4114, 4153, 4198, 4200, 4212, United States Eastern District Court of Louisiana, 1854, Federal Records Center, Fort Worth, Tex.; General Index of Public Debtors, 1820-1868, Records of the Solicitor of the Treasury, Record Group 206, National Archives.

[42]Investigation of the New Orleans Branch Mint by Thomas Slidell, June 17-July 4, 1839; Herman Schroeder to Thomas Ewing, May 30, 1841, Miscellaneous Letters Received, both in General Records of the Department of the Treasury, Record Group 56, National Archives.

[43]*Louisiana Courier,* June 4, 1829; W. H. Dudley to James Colles, August 11, 1829, James Colles Correspondence, New York Public Library.

[44]*Bee,* March 18, 1834.

[45]Henry W. Palfrey to John Palfrey, May 10, 1843, Palfrey Family Papers, Houghton Library, Harvard University, Cambridge, Mass.

[46]William McCullogh to Levi Woodbury, May 23, 1838, Miscellaneous Letters Received, General Records of the Department of the Treasury, Record Group 56, National Archives; Hore Browse Trist to Nicholas P. Trist, January 4, 1840, Nicholas P. Trist Papers, Library of Congress.

[47]Matthew Crenson, *The Federal Machine: Beginnings of Bureaucracy in Jacksonian America* (Baltimore and London, 1975), 158-74.

PART III

Antebellum Politics, 1845-1861

THE LOUISIANA WHIGS*

William H. Adams

The Louisiana Whig party[1] was an integral part of the organization which evolved in part from the National Republican party in 1834. The new party was joined by dissident Democrats and others unhappy with Andrew Jackson's Democratic party. Jackson's attack on and subsequent destruction of the Bank of the United States outraged many of Louisiana's leaders. The 1833 Compromise Tariff, which was Henry Clay's device to settle the nullification crisis produced by the Tariff of 1832, brought a reduction in tariff protection so dear to the sugar planters' purse. Jackson's veto of the Maysville Road Bill made it clear that he opposed internal improvements at the expense of the federal government.

The sugar planters of south Louisiana, the merchants and bankers of the area, as well as less affluent citizens, felt that Andrew Jackson possessed too much power. This power, they felt, he was using to undermine the economic structure of south Louisiana, which, being built on sugar, needed tariff protection, a sound banking system on a national basis and internal improvements.

The National Republicans of Louisiana, soon to become Whigs, were generally opposed to South Carolina's threat to secede from the Union because of the Tariff of 1832. Yet Alexander Barrow, a future Whig leader, expressed what many Southerners must have felt when he wrote that although he was not a Nullifier, ". . . before I would take part in a crusade by the Yankees to put South Carolina to the sword, I would be hung for treason."[2] The Louisiana Whigs of 1834 expressed no fear that the institution of slavery might be attacked by members of the national organization, at least not then. The Nullification crisis forced Southern Whigs to decide for Union rather than sectionalism. Thus the program of the emerging Whig party was the program of the National Republican party, which in turn borrowed heavily from Henry Clay's American system outlined before Congress as early as 1816.[3] Referring to Jackson as King Andrew I, and his party as the Tories, the National Republicans began calling themselves the Whigs in 1834. They

*First published in *Louisiana History*, 15 (1974): 213-228. Reprinted with the kind permission of the Louisiana Historical Association.

hoped to elicit from the voters the kind of emotional response the label "democrat" received in making Jackson's party so popular.

It was during the controversy over these issues, the tariff, nullification, and Jackson's attack on the Bank of the United States, that Edward Douglass White announced his candidacy for the office of governor. He began his campaign as a National Republican, and was elected as a Whig party governor in 1834.[4] It was the first major victory for the national Whig party. White's opponent was John Barrow Dawson who, like White, was born in Nashville, Tennessee. Dawson was from West Feliciana Parish where he was a successful cotton planter. He also served in the legislature, was a parish judge, and a general in the state militia. He opposed the Bank of the United States, internal improvements, and supported the South Carolina Nullifiers.[5] Although the usual verbal attacks were launched by both sides, the issues were clear, and White defeated Dawson when he received nearly 60 percent of the popular vote, most of it in the sugar parishes and the city of New Orleans.[6]

The new governor was from Bayou Lafourche where he studied law in the Donaldsonville office of Alexander Porter before becoming a criminal judge in New Orleans. He then served three terms in Congress before his election as governor.

The new party was completely triumphant in 1834, for not only had the Whigs put White in the gubernatorial office, but the party had won a majority of seats in the state legislature and among the state's delegation in the national House of Representatives.[7]

This success in Louisiana's election of 1834 demonstrated a degree of Whig party unity that varied considerably during its twenty-year existence. Within two years of its 1834 victories the state party was divided by the national party's tactics in the presidential election. Martin Van Buren was the Democratic candidate in 1836, and the Whigs, considering him unbeatable in a one-to-one contest because he had Jackson's support, entered three candidates into the race. The Whigs thereby hoped to divide the electoral vote, prevent Van Buren from getting a majority, and thus elect a Whig president when the contest was submitted to the House of Representatives. The Whigs of Louisiana, confused by this manipulation, split their vote, with the result that Van Buren carried Louisiana by 225 votes. Hugh L. White received the majority of Whig votes cast in the state.[8]

Shortly after Van Buren's inauguration Whig predictions of an economic panic and depression were realized, and throughout 1837 and 1838 banks closed in New Orleans and other cities of the state.[9]

Despite the depression, the Whigs won the gubernatorial election of 1838 when André Bienvenu Roman defeated Denis Prieur, mayor of New Orleans. The Whig platform for this election advocated public education, internal improvements, and a protective tariff, but avoided the national bank issue.[10] Whigs also won a majority of seats in the state legislature. The party was committed to a policy of alleviating the depression and business conditions, which remained poor throughout 1839, and thus gave Whigs reason to believe they could elect a president in 1840.

William Henry Harrison, a military hero, carried the state and the nation to become the Whig party's first president, but died before the Whigs could enact their important legislation. The new president, John Tyler, a states-rights Democrat and the only senator to vote against Jackson's Force Bill, twice vetoed a new bank bill. His action caused Whigs throughout the nation to raise cries of anguish.[11]

The Whig legislature enacted a state banking law designed to stabilize currency and banking in Louisiana, and after several false starts, New Orleans banks first opened their doors for the exchange of paper notes, and then resumed specie payment on May 20, 1842. But within days, outraged citizens attacked and plundered the offices of four exchange brokers on Canal and Camp streets and troops were called out.[12] The depression grew worse in Louisiana, although the new tariff of 1842 alleviated the state's economic plight by raising the price of sugar, and payment was made in specie, not in paper money.[13]

The 1842 gubernatorial campaign was won by Alexandre Mouton, the Democrat, who defeated Henry Johnson by a majority of sixteen hundred votes.[14] The Whigs maintained a slim majority, nine votes on a joint ballot, in the state legislature, and two of the three congressmen, John Moore and Edward Douglass White, were Whigs.[15] Yet, in the next congressional elections all seats in the House were won by Democrats.

The Louisiana Whig party reached its zenith in 1842 and thereafter went into a slow decline. André Roman was the last of two Whig governors, but the party continued to elect congressmen and majorities in the state legislature, although Whig dominance in state politics weakened progressively after 1842.

The presidential campaign of 1844 was a contest between the Whig, Henry Clay, and the Democrat, James K. Polk. The issues at first were the usual concerns of the Whigs: the Bank, internal improvements, and the tariff. However, expansion in general, particularly the annexation of Texas, became the key issue in Louisiana. Clay visited Louisiana twice during the election year and was warmly received by his many friends, political supporters and family members. Clay had always been popular in the state, but his Raleigh letter stunned many of his Louisiana followers. It was printed in the *Daily Picayune,* May 5, 1844; in it the presidential candidate plainly opposed the annexation of Texas. James K. Polk, the Democratic candidate, favored the annexation of Texas and a great deal more. Although many Louisiana Whigs tried to minimize the annexation issue, it was the primary reason for Clay's loss of Louisiana's vote. Louisiana's Whig electors received 12,821 votes to 13,477 for the Democrats, a majority of 656 for Polk.[16] The voting pattern followed the usual lines: southern Louisiana and New Orleans were the strongholds of the Whig party while northern and southwestern Louisiana were carried by the Democrats.[17] Voting fraud in Plaquemines Parish, where the vote was for James K. Polk, insured that Louisiana's six electoral votes were counted for the new president.[18]

In response to a growing demand, the legislature created the Constitutional Convention of 1845. The demand came primarily from the Democrats who wanted to broaden the franchise so that all free white male adults could vote. In July 1843 the voters had overwhelmingly indicated they favored a constitutional convention. The convention, scheduled for August 1844, did not meet for business until January 1845 and then produced a new state charter decidedly inimical to Whig principles. The convention was composed of thirty-six Whigs, thirty-nine Democrats, one "non-partisan" and one "probable" Democrat. Fifty-six percent of the convention members were born outside Louisiana. Of these, thirty-two were born in the South, six in the North, and six outside the United States. Ten Whigs and twelve Democrats were planters; one member was a doctor, another a merchant, and several were classified as "employees."[19]

There was almost constant controversy in the convention. The end result was to broaden the franchise by abolishing the property qualification for voting and for holding public office. Now, all white male citizens twenty-one and over, who had resided in the state for two years, could vote. More public officials, formerly appointed, would now be elected, and state aid for banks or monopolies, or special charters, was pointedly prohibited. The new constitution expressed the Jacksonian trend toward greater participation in government by more voters, and the Jacksonian antipathy toward government-sponsored banks. The Whigs now had little chance to regain their former place of strength in state politics. Yet both Whigs and Democrats must have voted for final adoption because it was approved by a vote of 12,277 to 1,395.[20]

The Constitution of 1845 was to go into effect with a new administration and a new legislature in January 1846. William DeBuys, a New Orleanian, was nominated by the Whigs in a convention which adopted the motto, "Principles and not men."[21] Isaac Johnson, master of Troy Plantation in West Feliciana Parish, was nominated by the Democrats. The campaign was rather dull; the final tabulation of votes showed that Johnson received 12,629 and William DeBuys 10,138. Moreover, the Democrats had a clear majority in the legislature.[22]

State party strife was soon obscured by the war with Mexico, supported by leaders of both parties in Louisiana who were "exasperated" and "outraged" at the "obstinancy" of the Mexican government. As the war progressed and presidential politics emerged as an unforeseen product of the war, the Whigs won a majority of legislative seats in 1847. When the new legislature met in January 1848, however, it elected a Democrat, Pierre Soulé, to the United States Senate.

By that time Gen. Zachary Taylor had returned to his home in Baton Rouge and was coyly seeking the Whig party presidential nomination. Henry Clay was still a great favorite among the Whigs of Louisiana as well as the nation, and when the news of Taylor's nomination by the national convention meeting in Philadelphia reached New Orleans, there was a "general feeling of gratification," but not extreme elation.[23] Henry Clay refused to endorse the general because he felt Taylor was not a Whig and did not support Whig principles.[24] The Whigs had again endorsed a military hero, overlooking the true leaders of the national party in an effort to win the presidency. The Democrats nominated Lewis Cass of Michigan.

By 1848 the slavery issue was paramount. The Panic of 1837, and the ensuing depression which lasted until 1844 in some states, had passed. The bank issue was no longer important, the state banks had survived. The internal improvements issue was now reshaped by the desire for railroads, and Democrats as well as Whigs favored government aid for railroad construction. The tariff was working well so that the third plank of the Whig party platform was also no longer an issue. Perhaps Henry Clay was well advised when he wrote that he desired ". . . to remain henceforward in undisturbed tranquility and perfect repose."[25] Zachary Taylor and his running mate, Millard Fillmore, carried Louisiana by a majority of 2,847 votes.[26] Probably Taylor's campaign, based on a no-party and non-sectional theme, was the decisive factor in the election. Taylor must have appeared the safest candidate to the nation's voters, perhaps he would not rock the sectional boat. In New Orleans the young diarist, Samuel J. Peters, Jr., wrote on the day of Taylor's inauguration, "Thank God we are no longer under Locofoco rule." Within five months the youthful lawyer had changed his mind about Taylor and wrote, "The whole United States was never in a worse condition than they are in this present moment. President Taylor is detested by all."[27]

When he took office the major issue was the expansion of slavery into the territory acquired from Mexico. That issue was opened by the introduction of the Wilmot Proviso in 1846, and the issue was temporarily settled by Henry Clay's Compromise of 1850.

Hoping to ride General Taylor's coattails into office, the Louisiana Whigs held a state convention to nominate candidates for the 1849 general election. They chose Alexandre Declouet as their candidate for governor and Duncan Kenner for the office of lieutenant governor.[28] The Democrats nominated Joseph Walker for governor and John B. Plauché of New Orleans as his running mate.[29] The main issues of the campaign were an elective judiciary and improvement of water control facilities because of damage caused by recent flooding. Both parties favored the elective judiciary, and they both favored improvement in flood control facilities, thus the state issues were not conducive to a heated campaign. Joseph Walker was elected governor by a vote of 18,566 to 17,533 for Declouet. Walker's running mate, John Plauché, was elected lieutenant governor, defeating Duncan Kenner by a majority of 422 votes.[30] In the legislature the Whigs had won a majority of the house and the Democrats had control of the state senate. Three Democrats and one Whig, Charles Conrad, had been successful in the congressional elections. National issues were seldom mentioned in the political oratory of this election.[31]

Baton Rouge was the new state capital, and the records of the government were moved there on December 1, 1849. When the legislature convened there for the first time, outgoing Gov. Isaac Johnson delivered a farewell message, and Joseph Walker soon delivered his inaugural address. His address contained recommendations for an elective judiciary, improvements in the public-school system, a denunciation of the abolitionists, and the suggestion that the state send delegates to attend a convention in Nashville sponsored by Southerners to resist Northern "aggression."[32]

The legislature refused to send delegates to the Nashville convention, a decision attributed largely to Daniel Webster's Seventh of March speech on the Compromise of 1850.[33] The legislature adjourned in March and was accused of not having done any act "worthy of commendation."[34] President Taylor died in July, and although many citizens mourned his passing, Louisiana Whigs had been generally disappointed in a president they might claim as their own. He had not been particularly generous in the distribution of patronage to the state's Whig leaders and supporters, although many of them had played key roles in managing his presidential campaign. Moreover during the controversy over the Wilmot Proviso and other national issues which led to the Compromise of 1850, Taylor had not taken a position completely acceptable to Southerners.

His successor, Millard Fillmore, soon appointed Charles Conrad, a Louisiana congressman, to the cabinet as secretary of war.[35] In the special election called to fill Conrad's vacant seat, Henry Bullard, a staunch Whig, defeated the Democratic candidate, ex-governor Henry Johnson.[36]

In 1852 the state's political interest centered on the proposed constitution and the presidential election. The state's voters had voted overwhelmingly in favor of a proposed convention to write a new state charter. The Orleans vote reflected the state's mood: it was 5,490 for and 171 against the proposition.[37] The Whigs had taken the lead in advocating constitutional revision and were joined by most Democrats who voted in favor of the convention. The voters then selected delegates to attend the convention, and again the Whigs triumphed at the polls when the voters sent eighty-five Whigs and forty-five Democrats to the convention in July 1852.[38]

In drafting the new constitution the Whigs won a significant point when they succeeded in removing all restrictions on corporations, and allowed banks almost complete freedom to operate. The Whigs were also successful in advocating that total population be made the basis for determining representation in the legislature. This favored the rural parishes of southern Louisiana where the slave population was large and weakened the political force of the hill parishes where there was little slavery. In addition Orleans was limited to four senators, although it contained approximately one-fourth of the state's population. The new instrument made no distinction between a native-born and a naturalized citizen. Many offices formerly filled by appointment were now made elective, including all state judgeships.[39] Thus, when the new document was accepted by the voters on November 2, 1852, it was interpreted as a major Whig victory. For Louisiana Whigs, it was a bittersweet experience, for at the time they learned of the constitution's adoption, they also realized that their presidential candidate, Winfield Scott, had been defeated by Franklin Pierce.

The Compromise of 1850 brought to a climax the diverse issues creating disunity within the party for over fifteen years. Some Whig leaders were conscious of this discord and attempted in the early 1850s to create a Union party by merging the various elements of both major parties which supported the Compromise.[40]

With sectional discord rending the party in 1852, the selection of the Whig presidential candidate was of vital importance. Henry Clay and Daniel Webster were old, their views were well known, perhaps too well known. So the Whigs again nominated a military hero, probably because his political ideology was obscure, and the Whigs believed his military fame would be sufficient for his election. Perhaps all three Whig military hero-nominees for president were selected for that reason, plus the possibility that the Whig party always opposed a strong executive and believed it could control generals who became presidents.

Louisiana cast its electoral votes for Franklin Pierce in 1852, after his electors received 17,426 votes and those of Winfield Scott received 15,967 votes.[41] Nationwide, Scott carried only four states; the election was a Whig disaster. A *New Orleans Bee* editorial stated: "Defection has done its worse. The Whig Party is entitled to the signal honor of defeating itself through apathy and disaffection within the party."[42]

Shortly after the presidential election and the adoption of the new constitution, the two parties had to select candidates for a general election of officials who would inaugurate the new charter of government. The Whigs nominated Louis Bordelon for governor and John Ray for lieutenant governor.[43] The Democrats, in convention on December 1, 1852, nominated Paul Hébert for governor and W. W. Farmer for lieutenant governor.[44] In an election marked by indifference and listlessness, the Whigs were thoroughly defeated when Hébert and his ticket won election by substantial majorities.

The election returns gave Hébert a majority of 2,030 votes over his opponent, and the other candidates received greater or only slightly smaller majorities.[45] The voters sent seventeen Democrats and nine Whigs to the senate; in the house of representatives the Democrats captured fifty seats to forty-one for the Whigs.[46] Thus, on a joint ballot the Democrats had a majority of seventeen. A Whig journal took the results philosophically and reasoned that since the Democrats now favored internal improvements and a system of free banking, the defeat was no so bad after all for "a Rose will smell sweet by another name. . . ."[47]

The Whigs never recovered from their disastrous defeats of 1852. Although the party in Louisiana was responsible for calling the constitutional convention, and dominated the convention itself, they were unable to control the new state government by winning the general elections. Yet, the Whigs had finally achieved state aid for banking and aid for internal improvements, but only with help from Democrats.

Millard Fillmore's failure to receive the Whig party's nomination for president disenchanted many Louisiana Whigs who found themselves unable to support Winfield Scott. Third party movements tended to divide the disgruntled Whigs more than successful Democrats, although the Union party movement was not successful in Louisiana.

So, failure in both the national and state elections of 1852 shattered the Whig party. Underlying the local reasons for the party's demise, however, were the intense sectional disputes which erupted over the Compromise of 1850, and the introduction of the Kansas-Nebraska Act by Stephen A. Douglas. In June 1854 the *New Orleans Bee* editorialized that, in brief, "the party is disintegrated and disorganized."[48]

Some Whigs joined the state's Democratic party, and many more joined the nativist movement called the American party, or the Order of the Star Spangled Banner, and popularly known as the Know Nothing party. Thomas Greer Davidson, who quit the Whigs in 1852, gave his reason for joining the nativist movement in Louisiana as being dislike of "foreign influence" in the United States.[49] The Whigs had always been tainted with the brush of anti-foreign and anti-Catholic attitudes, and in their frustration of 1852 they naturally turned to the new party.

A nativist movement had begun in Louisiana as early as 1835 under the leadership of William Christy, and anti-foreign sentiment surfaced on a number of occasions thereafter. In 1835 Gov. Edward Douglass White was severely criticized for appointing naturalized citizens to public office, but he was a Whig governor.[50] When Carroll Parish Judge Felix Bosworth was impeached in 1840, the proceedings were based on accusations that he had been falsely issuing certificates which enabled foreigners to vote in state elections. Following this, resolutions were introduced in the 1840 session of the legislature calling upon Congress to prevent the immigration to the United States of alien undesirables.[51] Simultaneously, a Native American Association was formed in the state and worked to extend the period of naturalization from five to fourteen years.[52] A few years later Judge Benjamin Elliott of New Orleans was impeached for issuing landownership titles to foreigners so that they might vote, and in 1844 the Plaquemines Parish election fraud, which became a national scandal, involved the fraudulent voting of foreigners. Nativism was a strong factor in the constitutional conventions of 1845 and 1852. An editorial in the *Clinton Louisiana Democrat* noted: "Hardly has a twelve month rolled over our heads than from their state of power, of respectability and of worth, they have stopped to the embraces of *Know Nothingism.* Their name is now but a memento of the past and the flag of Henry Clay ingloriously trails in the dust."[53]

The Whigs had fallen at the apparent height of their power. In 1846 the Whigs won control of Congress, in 1848 they elected a president, and in 1850 they devised the compromise designed to cement the Union once and for all. Even in the 1852 presidential election, with a poor candidate, the party carried 46 percent of the nation's popular vote. Yet, after the 1854 congressional elections not one member of the Whig party was seated in Congress. The party was born in 1834 and was dead in 1854.

For two decades the Whigs were the party of respectability and frequently the majority. It was a nationwide, multi-interest party of New England mill owners and mill workers, property owners, intellectuals, Louisiana sugar planters, and Southern mountain folk. Its great leaders far outshined the Democrats. Daniel Webster and Henry Clay were the giants in Congress for a generation. Leader of the Southern Whigs was the brilliant Alexander Stephens who was later the vice president of the Confederacy. Horace Greeley, of the *New York Tribune,* and William H. Seward of New York led the party's anti-slavery faction, the so-called "conscience Whigs," whose beliefs were not appreciated in Louisiana.

Bad luck was a factor in the destruction of the Whig party; the aforementioned death of the two Whigs presidents caused confusion. Tyler was an anti-Jacksonian Democrat who should not have been on the Whig party ticket in 1840. Taylor would probably have vetoed the Compromise of 1850 had he lived, and his successor Millard Fillmore reversed his predecessor's policy and did his utmost in support of the Compromise, and still did not receive the nomination of the party in 1852.

There was always party dissension caused by personality conflicts and individual ambitions. Thus, Clay and Webster were rivals for the presidency and party leadership for many years, but did work together for Union. These and many other disputes reflected a healthy diversity within the Whig party that was a sign of strength, not weakness. Formed as a coalition of Andrew Jackson's enemies, the Whigs were not ideologues. Save for the unifying influence of devotion to the Union, the Whigs tolerated all shades of opinion, even welcoming both abolitionists and pro-slavery Southerners to their ranks. It is just this nonideological sort of party, not the doctrinaire one-interest party, that survives in American politics.

Still, the internal dissension of the Whigs was not really much worse than the divisions of the 1850s in the Democratic party, whose Northern and Southern wings were far less compatible than the Northern and Southern wings of the Whigs. The Union was splitting over the slavery question, and as the Union disintegrated so did the party system, but the Whig party totally disappeared while the Democratic party survived. The Democratic party split, North and South, but showed amazing resiliency and somehow emerged from the holocaust.

The Whigs tended to restrict their base to the Anglo-Saxon Protestant segment of the electorate, although many French Catholics of Louisiana were Whig party members. It was the kind of limitation that could only lead to grief. As the flow of Irish and German immigrants increased in the 1840s, the Whig party in Louisiana, as elsewhere, could not maintain its position of power. The new immigrant vote was solidly Democratic, and although the Whigs made overtures to the new vote, the overtures were not sincere.

The Whig party was essentially a parliamentary party, and in a political system keyed directly to the power and personality of the presidency, a parliamentary party is handicapped in national elections. Clay and Webster and other Whig party leaders failed to perceive how deeply the American electorate viewed the presidency as the center of politics. As congressional leaders they could not understand or accept the power of the president of the United States. So the Whigs won the White House only when they nominated a military hero, but the hero was elected not to achieve party leadership, only to secure the reins of government so that power could be transmitted from the presidency back to Congress.

It was Whig President Harrison who retorted to Clay, "Mr. Clay, you forget that I am President." It was Harrison who read the Webster-prepared inaugural address which clearly declared the president inferior to Congress.

The Whigs were also opposed to the expansion of the United States. President Tyler's secretary of war, Abel Upshur, negotiated an annexation treaty with Texas, and the treaty was defeated in the Senate when all the Whigs voted against it.[54] This was in 1844 when Clay, running for president, issued the Raleigh letter. The Whigs referred to the war with Mexico as "Mr. Polk's War," but then elected one of its heroes, Zachary Taylor, as president of the United States. The Whigs apparently believed in expansion of markets at home and abroad, and not in actual geographic expansion, at least in the 1840s. Or perhaps they believed geographic expansion westward would come in the natural course of events, and they did not wish to precipitate that expansion.

The Whigs were older and probably wealthier than the Democrats, although that conclusion is unsubstantiated by factual information. Whigs believed that participants in government, either as voters or officeholders, should have a stake in society, that is property. The Whigs opposed intervention in the affairs of foreign nations, and were appalled when Democrats talked of intervention in Hungary at the request of Kossuth. Whigs were more interested in national issues than local ones; were Anglophiles rather than anglophobes, and always advocated a more positive federal and state role in the economy. By the 1850s the Democrats were advocating the same economic policy by government at all levels.

The Whigs did hold a nominating convention in 1856, but their nominees were lost in the struggle between the Democratic party and the new Republican party. In retrospect, however, the Whigs of Louisiana had won a victory of sorts. The Democrats of 1852 adopted the internal improvements program, accepted the protective tariff, and provided a banking system that was adequate to the needs of the state.

So, the Whigs disappeared quickly after 1852. At least, briefly in the antebellum period, Louisiana was not "solid;" the Whig party of Louisiana existed when the two-party system was a vigorous aspect of the state's political life, and a true two-party system may again appear in Louisiana.

Notes for "The Louisiana Whigs"

[1]The presidential address and this article were taken from William H. Adams, *The Whig Party of Louisiana* (Lafayette, La., 1973). Unless otherwise indicated, footnotes cite the Department of Archives, Louisiana State University, Baton Rouge, La., for original sources.

[2]Hamilton Papers, letter from Alexander Barrow to William S. Hamilton, February 19, 1833.

[3]Clement Eaton, *Henry Clay and the Art of American Politics* (Boston, 1957), 43; Glyndon G. Van Deusen, *The Life of Henry Clay* (Boston, 1937), 132.

[4]Diedrich Ramke, "Edward Douglas White, Sr., Governor of Louisiana, 1835-1839," *Louisiana Historical Quarterly*, 19 (1936): 273-76.

[5]*New Orleans Advertiser*, May 13, 1834; *New Orleans Bee*, August 30, 1833; May 10, 1834.

[6]Perry Howard, *Political Tendencies in Louisiana* (Baton Rouge, 1957), 35.

[7]Mercer Papers, Howard-Tilton Memorial Library, Tulane University, New Orleans, La., letter from Henry Clay to William N. Mercer, August 13, 1834.

[8]*Niles to Weekly Register*, 51:1.

[9]*New Orleans Daily Picayune*, May 14, 18, 24, 27, 1837.

[10]*New Orleans Bee*, May 26, June 19, 1838.

[11]*Baton Rouge Gazette*, August 28, September 4, 1841; *New Orleans Morning Advertiser*, October 20, 1841; *New Orleans Daily Picayune*, August 31, 1841. Letter from Benjamin Ogle Taylor to Henry Clay, September 6, 1841, Clay Papers, Library of Congress.

[12]*New Orleans Daily Picayune*, May 21, 1842.

[13]*Baton Rouge Gazette*, October 1, 1842.

[14]*Louisiana Senate Journal*, 16 leg., 1 sess., 8.

[15]*Baton Rouge Gazette*, July 16, 1842; *Opelousas Gazette*, July 16, 1842; *New Orleans Daily Picayune*, July 21, 1842.

[16]*Baton Rouge Gazette*, August 31, 1844.

[17]*New Orleans Daily Picayune*, November 4, 29, December 4, 1844.

[18]Anonymous, "The Election Frauds in Plaquemines Parish, Louisiana," *Louisiana Historical Quarterly*, 10 (1927): 146-47, from the *New York Nation*, February 27, 1879.

[19]Ted Ferguson, "The Louisiana Constitution of 1845" (M.A. thesis, Louisiana State University, 1948), 62.

[20]*Baton Rouge Gazette*, November 8, 1845; *New Orleans Daily Picayune*, December 2, 1845.

[21]*Baton Rouge Gazette*, July 28, 1845.

[22]*Louisiana House Journal*, 1 leg., 1 sess., 7.

[23]*New Orleans Daily Picayune*, January 26, 1848.

[24]Letter from Henry Clay to Sargent S. Prentiss, April 12, 1848, Clay Papers.

[25]Ibid., letter to a committee of Louisville Citizens from Henry Clay, June 28, 1848.

[26]*New Orleans Weekly Delta*, December 14, 1848.

[27]S. J. Peters, Jr., Diary, Department of Archives, Louisiana State University, Baton Rouge, La., entries for March 4, August 12, 1849.

[28]*New Orleans Daily Picayune*, May 15, 1849.

[29]*New Orleans Weekly Delta*, July 9, 1849.

[30]*New Orleans Daily Picayune*, January 24, 1850.

[31]*New Orleans Weekly Delta*, September 3, 1849.

[32]*New Orleans Daily Crescent*, January 30, 1850; *Louisiana Senate Journal*, 3 leg., 1 sess., 22-25.

[33]*New Orleans Daily Delta*, March 21, April 4, 1850.

[34]*Plaquemine Southern Sentinel*, March 27, 1850.

[35]*New Orleans Daily Picayune*, August 2, 1850.

[36]Ibid., September 13, 1850.

[37]*New Orleans Daily Crescent*, April 13, 1852.

[38]*Plaquemine Southern Sentinel*, July 3, 1852.

[39]*New Orleans Daily Delta*, August 8, 1852. For the complete version of the 1852 Constitution, see *West's Louisiana Statutes Annotated*, part 3, vol. 3 (St. Paul, 1955), 544-63.

[40]*New Orleans Daily Delta*, November 26, 1852.

[41]*New Orleans Daily Picayune*, November 16, 1852.

[42]*New Orleans Bee*, November 4, 12, 1852.

[43]Ibid., October 9, 1852.

[44]*Plaquemine Southern Sentinel*, December 14, 1852.

[45]*New Orleans Weekly Delta*, January 16, 1853.

[46]*New Orleans Daily Picayune*, January 15, 1853.

[47]*Baton Rouge Gazette*, January 1, 1853.

[48]*New Orleans Bee*, June 10, 1854.

[49]*West Baton Rouge Capitolian Vis-A-Vis*, September 8, 1852.

[50]*Philadelphia National Gazette and Literary Register*, April 21, 1835.

[51]*New Orleans Daily Picayune*, February 11, 1840.

[52]*Baton Rouge Gazette*, February 15, 1840.

[53]*Clinton East Feliciana Democrat*, April 21, 1855.

[54]Lloyd C. Gardner, Walter F. LaFeber, Thomas J. McCormick, *Creation of the American Empire* (Chicago, 1973), 142.

THE CAMPAIGN OF 1856, AND THE SUPREMACY OF JOHN SLIDELL*

James K. Greer

In the year 1856, both spring and fall elections were of great importance. Interest in the spring elections concentrated on the struggle between the Know Nothings and the Democrats for control of New Orleans. The fall elections were of greater importance, and the struggle for power was marked by an attempt at a comeback on the part of the "old Line Whigs," an interesting struggle within the ranks of the Democracy, and the defeat of the "Americans" or Know Nothings. The activities of the Legislature and the spring election will be considered first.

The retiring Governor Hébert, called the attention of the legislature to the violence and bloodshed which had marked the recent November elections in New Orleans; and urged that the State adopt measures to prevent "bloodthirsty mobs" from over-aweing people at the polls.[1]

Governor Wickliffe's inaugural address dwelt on the same subject. He said, in part:

> This city has been too long misgoverned—too long the prey of political harpies and reckless office seekers, to admit of such a denial. Her present condition is a melancholy confirmation of the justice of the Governor's remarks . . . I recur to the scenes recently enacted in New Orleans with pain and humiliation; the polls disgraced by turbulence—ballot-boxes broken, men threatened, wounded and murdered, nor has bloodshed ceased since the election.[2]

Even with allowance for the fact that these executives were Democrats, it is hardly necessary to add that they would have hesitated to indulge in such statements, if there had not been much truth in their assertions and a general demand that their opinions be publicly recorded.

The conclusion of Governor Hébert's message touched on federal relations:

> The wild spirit of fanaticism which has, for many years, disturbed the repose of the country, has steadily increased in power and influence. It controls the councils of several

*First published in *Louisiana Historical Quarterly*, 13 (1930): 97-116. Reprinted with the kind permission of the Louisiana Historical Society.

> States, nullifies the laws of Congress enacted for the protection of our property, and resists the execution of them even to the shedding of blood. It has grown so powerful that it now aspires to control the Federal Legislature. The fact can no longer be concealed, however much it may be regretted. The slaveholding States are warned in time; they should be prepared for the issue. If it must come, the sooner the better. The time for concessions on our part and compromises has passed. If the Union cannot be maintained upon the just and wholesome principles of the Constitution, concessions and compromises will only retard its dissolution, not save it. They have had, thus far, no other result than to encourage attack and to increase the numbers of the abolitionists.[3]

Governor Wickliffe also touched on the encroachment of Southern rights by Congress. To protect herself from wrongs at the hands of the federal body, the South, he said, should never allow herself to be in the minority in the Senate as she was in the House.

The first several days of the session of the Legislature were spent in considering whether three Know Nothing senators elected in the recent election should be seated. Also, the position of sheriff of the parish of Orleans was being contested, although Joseph Hufty, Know Nothing, had been announced the victor. The result of the investigations was that Hufty was removed from office and the senate expelled the three Know Nothing Senators.[4] In New Orleans, the Know Nothings held an indignation meeting and passed resolutions eulogizing Hufty as a "martyr" and condemning the "tyranny" of the Legislature.[5] Naturally, the Know Nothing press condemned the investigation proceedings in both Senate and House as a "farce."[6] On the other hand, the Democrats talked of broken ballot boxes and legality,[7] to which the Know Nothings replied with veiled threats of what would happen in the spring election.[8]

But not all of the time of the Legislature was consumed with consideration of contested elections. Many private bills were passed, and two which affected New Orleans were hastened through despite the opposition of public opinion. Attempts had been made to get the last two legislatures to enact a registry law for New Orleans, for which the constitution provided. A bill was now introduced in the Senate which provided that the governor should appoint a "Register of Voters" for New Orleans, with a salary of $5,000 the first year, but subject to reduction thereafter. The naturalized citizen had to produce a certificate of naturalization or properly account for its loss before the registrar. Citizens naturalized in the parish could be registered upon certification of the clerk of the court where naturalization was granted. There were various other provisions of the bill designed to protect the city from the illegal voter. As an admission of willingness on the part of the Legislature to do something to protect the legal voter's interest, the bill was appreciated by the local press. But the project, not worked out by committee, which was presented primarily for purposes of discussion, failed to provide against possible corruption of the registering officials and other difficulties.[9]

Governor Wickliffe's inaugural address had pointed out that the frequent changes in the charter of New Orleans rendered its legislation intricate and confusing.[10] For instance, a bill had been introduced into and passed by the house of representatives, which provided that the debts of the old municipalities were made equally the debts of all the city; a subdivision of the principle of apportionment of the debt of the city, which had been agreed upon before consolidation could be secured. One city paper[11] hastened to protest that the city charter should be "let alone." Yet the same journal, a few days later, admitted that the charter did not require sufficient accountability to secure precision in public accounts in the administration of the Treasury. This admission followed a heavy default in the Treasury on the part of the city treasurer, William H. Garland.[12]

The amendments to the city charter and Registry laws passed the legislature, but it was realized that they would have to be amended because of imperfections due, at least in part, to hasty consideration.[13] The American party[14] continued its activities in 1856, and in January there were rumors that the organization was going to discard the ritual and the obligations in initiation of applicants and make the party an "open concern." No changes in the principles of the order were proposed, it was said, although knowledge of the actual proceedings of the state council's meeting, held in New Orleans, amounted to *nil*.[15] In the meantime, violence was continued. Innumerable assaults on respectable citizens occurred and the "purifiers" (a term of contempt applied by the opposition press to the Know Nothings) were held responsible. There was much complaint that the perpetrators, or at least nineteen-twentieths of them, escaped arrest.[16]

By the first of March, plans were being made by the political organizations of New Orleans, for the municipal election. Violence on the part of the Know Nothings, and malfeasance in office of officials under a Democratic city administration, resulted in the calling of "a meeting of the citizens of New Orleans," at Bank's Arcade on March 17th, to select a "Citizens Ticket" for the ensuing election.[17] The "call" stated that political parties would be ignored. A good crowd assembled and the meeting was being called to order when a group of men rushed forward, overturned the chairman's table, and pushed him from the stand.[18] Order was soon restored and organization was effected. But, in the meantime, many retired from the scene of the fracas. The outstanding Whigs and Democrats were among those who left, and they disclaimed any part in the nominations made or other proceedings, although they admitted signing the call for the assemblage.[19]

This affair caused Mayor Lewis to recommend to the common council an addition to the police force of one hundred and fifty men. Several of the papers of the city endorsed the proposition, but the *Daily Crescent,* an avowed Know Nothing journal,[20] vigorously protested[21] on the grounds of economy, the approach of the vacation season, and the adding of burdens to the duties of the new council. This paper argued that the end of the business season would see a departure of the vagabonds who caused much of the crime of the city, and criticised the mayor for having failed to first show efficiency with a small force.

The Know Nothings promised an economical, careful, and generally efficient city government if elected to office, while at the same time, they warned that "maladministration" would continue "if the Democratic party—or, rather the [John] Slidell portion of it—triumphs."[22] They charged all disorders to the Democrats because they had had the mayor and police during the two last years, 1854-1856, but were obliged to concede that with Know Nothing majorities in both boards of the common council, some responsibility devolved upon them.[23]

On election morning, one paper prophesied that the vote cast would be light and that the city would be again disgraced by riot and bloodshed, and observed that a majority of the barrooms had not obeyed the mayor's request to close.[24] The whole American ticket, headed by Charles M. Waterman, candidate for mayor, was elected.[25] The vote was very small, although Waterman's majority was very large. From eleven o'clock to the closing of the election booths, anarchy reigned. In two or three precincts, the naturalized citizens were debarred from voting,[26] while in some instances citizens were forced to give up their Democratic tickets and vote the Know Nothing.[27] The Democratic loss in votes since November was 2,196, while that of their opponents was only 325.[28] One city paper[29] estimated that about 6,000 electors out of more than 13,000 did not vote. But a Know Nothing journal[30] explained the smallness of the vote as being due to absence of legal voters from the city who were in the north on business and pleasure. A second reason assigned for the decreased vote of the Democrats was that the Democratic ticket was objectionable to [Pierre] Soulé and that his friends hardly cared to elevate the Slidell nominees.[31] In the third place, the Know Nothings said, many adopted citizens declined voting at all, while, lastly, probably one hundred "old line Whigs" stayed away altogether.

The local Know Nothing party organ[32] did not deny that members of its group were involved in the turbulence but placed the responsibility for the beginning of excesses at the feet of the "murderous Democratic Sicilians."[33] The Know Nothings hailed their success as a forecast of victory for [Millard] Fillmore in November. But the Democrats charged that they had been cheated[34] and planned to prevent a repetition of such an "obviously unfair" election. To this accusation of fraud, the Know Nothings rejoiced with reminders of the "Plaquemines fraud of 1844" and the State elections of 1853.[35]

An illustration of what happened in two or three precincts may be taken from what occurred in the Seventh. The normal Democratic majority in this precinct was approximately 300. At the November 1855, election, a total of 894 votes were cast. The Democratic vote now fell off by four hundred, and the Know Nothing majority was 243, while in November, an increase of only forty or fifty had been registered.[36]

The Democracy of the interior parishes looked upon the Democracy in the city as being "fettered, tied, powerless—chained," and urged energetic action in the *country* in November as a rebuke to city disorder.[37] But the minority group of the Democrats—the Souléites—claimed that the election showed that the people no longer had faith in the "Old Fogy Democracy"—the predominant officeholders.[38] Moreover, this faction said, the Democratic old fogies refused to listen to the "bold and original thinkers" of the party and persisted in doing nothing while the Know Nothing order was perfecting its local organization. So the election was regarded as a benefit to the party. It was admitted, also, that many Democrats had remained away from the polls in order that destruction would result and give opportunity for "reconstruction."[39] These opponents of the conservative Democracy argued that the party could assuredly be reconstructed, if the Democratic leaders would be "sincere," and would see to it that their creed was conservative in its objects but militant enough in its efforts.[40]

The presidential election was already in the mind of every voter, and the politicians early began to mention presidential possibilities, and then to call meetings for the selection of delegates to state conventions. [Franklin] Pierce had been condemned by the "progressive" or Soulé Democrats of the State as a failure, largely because he made no attempt to seize Cuba.[41] The *Delta* had named George Law of Pennsylvania as a probable choice, but later replaced him with Henry A. Wise of Virginia.[42] The "progressive," anti-"Old Fogy Democratic" groups held that [James] Buchanan, known to be Slidell's choice, could not be elected if nominated.[43]

The Democratic state convention met in Baton Rouge, and on March 11 appointed ten "consulting delegates" to the convention which was to meet in Cincinnati on the first Monday in June. The President of the Convention was also empowered to appoint twenty Democrats to act as the Central Executive Committee of the state until the meeting of the next state convention.[44]

In the convention a sharp conflict arose between the Soulé and Slidell followers as to whether [Stephen A.] Douglas or Buchanan possessed greater pretensions to the presidency.[45] One old Whig paper, which was not Know Nothing, and which evidently hoped for the discomfiture of Slidell, stated that Soulé represented the "progressive Democrats—Young America— . . . the spirit of filibusterism, . . . while Slidell's followers were 'old fogy'" and liked the spoils of office, but cared little for principle. It was claimed that Soulé's power lay among the country delegates who were usually out-maneuvered by those from the city; and charged that Slidell desired an appointment to the national convention in order to further his interests for the vice-presidency. It admitted, however, that the delegation to the national convention was equally divided between Pierce and Douglas.[46]

But the Democratic press at the scene of the Convention,[47] denied that Slidell had been defeated or that his preferences were mentioned or indicated in the convention. It was pointed out, too, that many of Slidell's political friends in the state were supporters of Douglas.[48] Seemingly of little significance, but worthy of remembrance, was the conclusion of these rival political papers. The *Bee* had remarked "what course Mr. Slidell will pursue is somewhat dubious,"[49] while the *Advocate* stated that the delegates at Baton Rouge seemed disposed to "act free from instructions, and (in choosing between Douglas and Buchanan) such knowledge only, of a preference as was familiar to them."[50]

It is hardly necessary to suggest that the Know Nothings, many of whom were "old Whigs," were frankly delighted at what they hoped would prove to be political discomfiture to one who had so long out-maneuvered them. If there should happen to be a further widening of the breach between the two factions of the Democracy, it would indeed be an occasion for joy.

The followers of Douglas now bravely took up the fight in his behalf, as they had done in 1852. They felt that Douglas's great cards—"Kansas-Nebraska and Nicaragua"—would win for him if he secured the nomination.[51] As Pierce's supposed attitude, previous to his election, on the Cuban question had won for him many votes in Louisiana[52] it was now thought that a similar position on Nicaragua would do the same for Douglas.[53] The Nicaraguan movement was growing, and Soulé was a favorite speaker[54] at the Central American meetings in New Orleans.

Before the meeting of the national conventions, [Judah P.] Benjamin announced that he was going over to the Democrats. Although many "old Whigs" had done the same, some of the Know Nothing papers expressed hot resentment at his act. The possible results of the change were vindictively belittled, but the same criticism stated that it "*does* come hard for men to be hit on the head with a stick of their own presenting."[55] It was observed by this time, the late spring, that Know Nothingism was losing ground in one of its strongholds in the last election, northwest Louisiana.[56] Hoping to arrest the drift to the Democrats the more conservative Know Nothings suggested to the Whigs that it would be better for them to remain independent than to sacrifice the fundamental doctrines of the Whig creed by accepting Democracy.[57] Such was the situation when national party organizations announced their nominees and campaigns began.

Of Buchanan, the "old Whigs" of the State felt that the Democrats had selected a man of great ability,—that they had "made a judicious choice."[58] An even more complimentary estimate was made by the more conservative Know Nothings, who held that the Democrats had put forward the strongest ticket possible. Pierce was impossible, and Douglas the favorite of a faction, who would have forfeited the support of the conservatives of the party.[59] Even the more radical Know Nothings agreed that Buchanan was not a "foe to despise," and conceded that he would receive "a respectable amount of old fogy support."[60] And [John C.] Breckinridge would strengthen the ticket from the ranks of the "Young Americans." The Democratic ratification meeting was participated in by both Buchanan and Douglas, Democrats, but it was quite evident that the latter did not do so with good grace.[61]

Reports of the deliberations of the national Democratic convention now reached Louisiana. Again, it was the conservative and radical Know Nothing papers that were first to report on what happened in the camp of the enemy. The apparent "defeat" of Slidell at Baton Rouge was turned into a victory at Cincinnati, to the astonishment of the *Bee*. Whereupon, it hastened to say that the votes of Louisiana's six delegates for Buchanan on the first ballot only proved "how extremely uncertain are the promises of uninstructed gentlemen, and it teaches a lesson to the Louisiana Democracy."[62]

However, an article that appeared in the *Daily Delta* of June 23, and which was quoted at length and commented upon by the *Daily Crescent* of June 24, gave a report of Slidell's control of the Louisiana delegation which may be given some credence. The article was signed "Close Observer" and evidently was written by one of the delegates from Louisiana who found himself in the minority at Cincinnati. The writer stated that the Louisiana delegation at Cincinnati, who were understood to be for Douglas, voted for Buchanan from the first, and secured the nomination of Breckinridge over John A. Quitman for vice-president. Soulé and Dr. Thomas Cottman and others formed a minority. The only effect upon the writer, so he claimed, was to create an intense admiration for Slidell as a political leader. Soulé, L. J. Sigur, Alexandre Mouton, and others, were blamed by the writer for their mismanagement of the delegates after leaving Baton Rouge.

The radical Know Nothings pretended to believe that such a published message was strong evidence that treason "against King Slidell" was contemplated, and sarcastically observed that the *Courier* should look into it.[63] But a bitter thought, admitted by the Know Nothings, which was intended to help their cause, was that Buchanan's election would mean the continued control of the Federal patronage by Slidell.[64]

The "progressive Democrats" were self-pityingly critical of the failure of the Louisiana delegation to support General Quitman for the Vice Presidency and thus gain Cuban liberation and the "revivification of New Orleans." The conduct of the Louisiana delegations was proof to them of the apathy of the state, and showed a disregard of the commonwealth's political dignity.[65] They did not oppose Buchanan, but held that he was not the best choice which the party could have made, yet suggested that he was the least of the "three evils,"—Fillmore, John Charles Fremont, and Buchanan.[66] Such a declaration was considered by many Democrats a "stab in the back" to the delegates,[67] and others, who were subscribers to the *Delta* wrote that "no good and true Democrat will turn against his party because he cannot get his favorite."[68]

By the latter part of August and early September, the campaign was well under way in the interior parishes.[69] A big Democratic mass meeting was held at Baton Rouge early in September at which thirty-five parishes were represented. A. S. Herron and T. Landry were leading figures in the meeting, which adopted resolutions endorsing the principles enunciated by the Cincinnati convention. Great political gatherings were held throughout the interior and reports of their proceedings uniformly agreed that "politics are raging."[70] Reports were numerous from the country papers that desertions from the ranks of the Know Nothings were continuing.[71] Colonel Pond, Know Nothing, and Thomas Greer Davidson, Democrat, both of the Third Congressional District, met in joint debate in which the chief point of difference between the speakers was the lack of justice to the South in the Nebraska bill, and a vindication of it, respectively.[72]

In the spring, some of the "Old Line Whigs" had cherished the hope that the Whig Party might be resuscitated, but the Old Whig editors smiled at the "delusion."[73] "Old Line Whig" meetings were held in some of the towns of the interior during the early summer, but they were participated in by Know Nothings to such an extent that they were not by any measure "Simon pure."[74] Still, incidental gatherings and conversations among the "Old Whigs" of New Orleans aroused sufficient interest for a meeting to be held on August 15. Their aims, as expressed in resolutions, strive for the "regeneration of the Whig party," and maintain an independent organization in the approaching presidential election.[75] Approximately one hundred men attended the meeting. Delegates were appointed to the Old Line Whig convention to be held at Baltimore.

Several weeks after the first meeting, there was held at the St. Charles Hotel a private meeting of Old Line Whigs to decide on the steps to take to unite the Whigs. A committee was appointed to prepare an address to the people of the state, and another on ways and means.[76] In keeping with their old policies, Old Whig journals now denounced "demagogues" who calculated the value of the Union and gave laudatory reviews of the great leaders of the past. Senator Slidell's letter of a few weeks past, to the secretary of the Democratic State Central Committee, in which it was declared that "if Fremont be elected, the Union cannot and ought not to be preserved," came in for much caustic denunciation by the same source.[77] But while his opponents professed to believe that Slidell had turned from his former views and embraced disunion doctrines, the prevalent opinion of the politically wise was that the letter was "for effect," that is, that Slidell wanted to create the impression that the choice of the South lay between Buchanan and disunion.[78] There is no doubt that Slidell was still a union man, and he had as yet taken no step which indicated inconsistency with his criticisms of the radicals, Robert Barnwell Rhett and William Yancey, in January 1852.[79]

On October 12, a mass meeting of Old Line Whigs was announced for the purpose of ratifying the proceedings and nominations of the Baltimore convention. "New Orleans should seize this occasion to show that the Whigs, who once numbered their thousands in her precincts, are not all dead yet, that they will follow the example of their brethren elsewhere," stated the *Daily Picayune* of October 12. The evening of October 14 saw a well attended Whig mass meeting on Canal Street. From a large platform erected in the center of the street, on which was a large banner with the inscription

> "The Whigs of the United States.
> The Life Guard of the Union Still Lives!"

Speeches were made, organization was perfected, and resolutions read. James P. Freret was made president. Harry T. Hays was the orator for the occasion, who spoke of the "treachery" of "the late Mr. Benjamin," and denied that the Whig party was dead. He ridiculed the idea that the issue of the campaign was North versus South and that Buchanan was the candidate of the South, which was a reference to the declaration of Slidell and his friend, John Perkins, of Louisiana.[80] So, the Old Line Whigs held that the way to preserve the union was to support the nominee (Fillmore) of the Baltimore convention.[81]

Speeches of Senator Benjamin, in New Orleans, during the last days of September, did much to enthuse the spirit of the Democracy of the city. His efforts centered on three leading ideas: first, that the abolitionists were guilty of a lack of national faith in the repeal of the Missouri Compromise instead of the Democrats; second, that the Know Nothing party was a "delusion" and that its nominee, Fillmore, did not deserve the support of Southern Whigs or Democrats; third, that members of the Democratic party alone stood by the constitution in defending the South in the recent Congressional struggle between North and South.[82]

Still the journal of the "progressive" Democrats, the *Delta,* could not resist the temptation to vent its spleen upon the Old Line Democracy when the occasion seemed to present itself. The *Delta* disapproved of Buchanan's nomination from the beginning, and after Breckinridge's Tippecanoe speech, it attempted to show that a difference existed between him and Governor Wickliffe on the subject of extension of slavery.[83] The Know Nothing press[84] also seized upon the apparent difference and both papers made the most of the opportunity by asserting that Governor Wickliffe had declared that the Democratic party of the State did not desire the extension of slavery.[85] Governor Wickliffe replied in a letter to the *Bee* in which he denied the statement attributed to him and stated that he endorsed fully Breckinridge's speech, in every respect, to the effect "that the Democratic party nowhere desired the strong arm of the Federal government outstretched to extend slavery. That non-intervention on the part of Congress was the doctrine of the Constitution, the Kansas-Nebraska bill, and our party."[86]

Expansion had been one of the two principal planks in the platform of the "progressive Democrats," in the spring. Some of them now called for contributions of men and money to assist Southern rights in Kansas, as well as the protection of private property there. A meeting was held at the St. Louis exchange, the first week in September, and a committee was appointed to recruit men and receive money, but the warmest advocates of the enterprise complained of little response.[87] The "Conservative Democracy" also expressed sympathy for "our Southern brethren" in Kansas, and asserted that it was the duty of the people of Louisiana, "*without distinction of party*," to aid them with "every legitimate and honorable support."[88] One or two enthusiasts declared their intentions of canvassing parts of the state for material aid.[89]

The attack of Brooks on Sumner was at first condemned by the "progressive Democratic" press as "Congressional bullying" and injurious to the Southern cause in Kansas, but was considered justifiable when all the circumstances were made known.[90] However, the Old Whig papers thought that the assault was wrong in principle and exceedingly impolitic. But, when the House of Representatives voted to expel Brooks, the act was resented as excessive of that body's jurisdiction and the vote was held to be purely "sectional."[91] After the transfer of the contest for Kansas from the territory to Congress, the Old Whigs of New Orleans looked upon the plan of Robert A. Toombs,[92] of Georgia, for a census and registration of voters, a constitutional convention, and admission under whatever constitution should be framed, as the most favorable method for putting an end to the controversy.

While the struggle over Kansas was being carried on in Congress, "Kansas meetings" were held in New Orleans for the purpose of furthering the cause of the pro-slavery people in that disputed territory. At Donaldsonville, on September 4, a meeting was held and a committee was appointed to obtain subscriptions among the planters "for the purpose of furnishing aid and assistance to the Southerners in Kansas." Two members of the committee canvassed one side of the river a few miles from New Orleans and reported the collection of $2,000.[93]

But it is not too much to say that, on the whole, Louisiana was apathetic toward the Kansas question. There was no expansion in that direction—no appeal was strong enough to induce the emigration of settlers who possessed slaves. People in New Orleans, for instance, talked Central America—not Kansas. Few had been to Kansas and it was not in the direction in which they thought their interests lay.

The "progressive" and "Old Fogy" Democrats had alike been interested in expansion southward for years, with the former constituting the ultra expansionists of the State. Hence, with the idea in mind of a revivified New Orleans as a leading commercial center of a Southern Confederacy, the "Union-stricken" *Bulletin* and the Old Line Whig supporters of Fillmore were wished a *bon voyage* for "Salt River."[94] At the same time General Walker was praised for making Nicaragua "a home for Southern men."[95]

The election was to be held on November 4. Several weeks previously, in hopes that a larger vote might be encouraged, voters were reminded that they must register.[96] The campaign in New Orleans was similar to that of 1848 and compared quite favorably with it in enthusiasm and public demonstrations. The returns showed that Buchanan carried 34 parishes to Fillmore's 14. Seven of these last had been "Whig" through every Presidential election since and including 1840 (or since their organization). They were Concordia, Morehouse, St. James, St. Mary, St. Martin, Terrebonne, and West Baton Rouge. Likewise, thirteen of the thirty-four parishes carried by Buchanan had always been Democratic, namely: Bienville, Calcasieu, Caldwell, Claiborne, De Soto, East Feliciana, Franklin, Jefferson, Lafayette, Livingston, Plaquemines, Sabine, St. Bernard, West Feliciana, and Winn.[97] Orleans Parish was carried by Fillmore by a majority of 2,983 votes out of a total of 7,933. In the whole state Fillmore received 20,709 and Buchanan 22,164.[98]

If the statements of several New Orleans papers are to be accepted there was much violence at the polls and the conduct of the election in general in that city. An Old Line Whig paper stated that the foreign-born voters were afraid to be seen in the vicinity of the polls, while, in some precincts, native Democrats were knocked down and prevented from casting their ballots.[99] Another journal[100] confirmed this statement, and added that fifty or sixty men, mounted on horses and disguised as Indians, galloped through the streets and frightened many voters from the election booths. The same journal affirmed that Buchanan should have carried the city by five hundred votes and that it was astonishing that Fillmore's vote was not larger than it was. One fourth of those who registered did not vote. The report concerning the disturbances at the polls which was made by the local organ of the Conservative Democrats[101] was not essentially different. While the newspaper spokesman for the "progressive Democrats"[102] largely blamed the disorganization of the party for the defeat, it declared that the election would have been a "burlesque" on the ballot box had it not been for the loss of two or three lives, but added that the election was less bloody than any that had been held during the past three years.[103]

Now that the election was over, some of the "progressives" among the Democrats who could never bring themselves to approve of Buchanan, resumed their advocacy of a Southern party. They held that the North would return with a united front in 1860, and that the Democrats would be weakened by the usual disadvantages of the party in power. Therefore, the South would have to make herself so strong in material progress, thorough domestic reforms, solidarity of social convictions, and unyielding political attitude that the Free Soilers would be held in check both by fear and interests. The main idea was to show ability to maintain independent to economic existence and to convince the North that the South could not be subdued except by means of military force.[104]

In keeping with this position, the proponents of the Southern party asserted that the principle of "State Rights" was growing weaker from day to day among the young who were becoming imbued with the "sentiment of unionism."[105] But while appealing for organization, they declared that the Southern party must ignore the political past and choose "the safest men as leaders."[106] Even some of the local papers which had been so strong for the "precious Union" were now advocating the encouragement of home enterprise to get rid of the depressing influence of the North and East "on the commerce of our city."

Despite the claim that the Southern party had established its nuclei in the state and that it was growing, the obvious fact was that the genesis of the agitation for such an organization in Louisiana was opposition to the "Old Fogy Democrats," ultra-expansion (southward) sentiment, and mis-apprehension of what the aims of the proposed party really were.[107] The Democratic press, joined by some of the "independents," accused the *Delta,* the Southern party champions, which had been shuffled out of the Democratic ranks recently on account of its position during the last political campaign, of now attempting to seize upon an issue which would enable it to recover some of its prestige.[108] The *True Delta,* now an "independent," openly ridiculed the idea of a Southern party.

During the final month of the year, with the election disposed of, discussion turned to the perennial problem of the commercial interests of New Orleans; this time the question of the labor supply of the state was debated briefly in some of the city papers.[109] One city paper suggested that white emigration to the state should be encouraged and that there was no danger of the demand for cotton exceeding the supply.[110] The *Delta* declared for more slaves, extension of slavery, and increase of cotton culture. It advocated the revival of the African slave trade[111] from the "conviction that the political requirements" demanded its revival. This position was supported by both political and economic arguments.[112] But a majority of the city papers that expressed themselves, either frowned upon or ridiculed the idea of reopening the slave trade.[113]

This position on the part of the Old Whig papers was consistent with their old policy of keeping down, in so far as possible, any agitation on the subject of slavery. But the *Delta* dwelt upon the alleged trouble caused earlier in the year by intercourse of free Negroes with the slaves and by whites who tampered with them. Visible results of intrigue among the Negroes amounted to the running away of Negroes by way of the Mississippi and Ohio rivers, robbery, and scattered rumors of attempted minor insurrections.[114]

Such were the political subjects which interested the people in 1856. The year had ended in a victory for the "conservative Democrats" and John Slidell had won and deserved the title of "the Warwick of America."[115] Buchanan's nomination was due to him more than to any other one politician.[116] The Know Nothing party had almost ceased to exist, except in a few scattered precincts in New Orleans. Even in these sections, many who disapproved of the violent methods of certain elements in the organization, withdrew from it. With chaos facing the remainder, they seemed to lose sight of their principles and to devote their efforts to furthering the aims of their office seekers.

Notes for "The Campaign of 1856, and the Supremacy of John Slidell"

[1]*Daily Picayune*, January 24, 1856; *Weekly Delta*, January 27, 1856.

[2]*Weekly Delta*, February 3, 1856. Methods established to cure this lawlessness are described in *Dart's Sketch of the Life and Times of J. B. Cotton*, Pamphlet, 1915.

[3]*Weekly Delta*, January 27, 1856.

[4]Ibid., March 30, 1856; *Daily Crescent*, March 27, 1856.

[5]Ibid., March 2, 1856.

[6]*Daily Crescent*, March 27, 1856.

[7]*Weekly Delta*, March 30; *Weekly Advocate*, February 16.

[8]Ibid., March 2, 1856.

[9]*Daily Picayune*, February 23, 24, 1856.

[10]*Weekly Delta*, February 3, 1856.

[11]*Daily Picayune*, February 29, 1856.

[12]Ibid., March 3, 1856. The *Weekly Advocate* of March 8 wanted to know what would be the end of this fresh example of "the beneficent influence" of the Know Nothing reforms in the city. This was not a fair statement. The *True Delta* was quoted in the same paper, as accrediting Garland and the sheriff of Orleans, with introducing Know Nothingism in New Orleans.

[13]Ibid., March 23, 1856.

[14]In 1856 the Know Nothings of 1855 called themselves the "American Party."

[15]*Daily Picayune*, January 20, 1856.

[16]*Weekly Delta*, February 3, 1856. The conservative Know Nothing and the anti-Know Nothing papers agreed that the police were doing nothing to preserve order in the city. It was hoped that the abolition of the Police Board and the reconcentration of all authority in the hands of the mayor would prove advantageous. (*Daily Picayune*, March 9.) The most sensational episode connected with the reign of Know Nothing violence in New Orleans was the attack upon Dennis Cocoran, one of the editors of the *Delta* and a man of thirty years' newspaper experience in the city. Cocoran claimed that he was "thugged" after leaving the St. Charles Hotel late one evening en route home. He accused F. A. Lumsden, of the *Picayune*, of having instigated the assault. Natu-

rally, the *Picayune* characterized the charge as "a base calumny." The attack occurred in mid-February, and the rival newspapers carried on a controversy until March 25, when the matter, which had been taken by Cocoran to the courts, was dismissed by Recorder Bright. Politics played a big part and it is hard to say just what the facts were. Certainly Cocoran was injured by someone. However, the Irish evidently did not permit the Know Nothings to do all the violence. For the affair see *Weekly Advocate*, February 16, 1856; *Weekly Delta*, February 17, 24, 1856; *Daily Picayune*, February 15, 17, March 6, 25, 1856.

[17]*Daily Picayune*, March 14, 1856.

[18]Ibid., March 18, 1856.

[19]Ibid., March 19, 1856.

[20]*New Orleans Daily Crescent*, May 26, 1856.

[21]See issue of April 1, 1856.

[22]*New Orleans Daily Crescent*, May 26, 1856.

[23]Ibid.

[24]*True Delta*, June 3, 1856.

[25]*Daily Picayune*, June 3, 1856.

[26]*Weekly Delta*, June 8, 1856.

[27]*Weekly Advocate*, June 14, 1856.

[28]Ibid., June 14, 1856.

[29]*True Delta*, June 5, 1856.

[30]*Daily Crescent*, June 5, 1856.

[31]There was probably some truth in this statement.

[32]*Daily Crescent.*

[33]Ibid., June 4, 1856.

[34]*Courier*, June 10, 1856.

[35]*Daily Crescent*, June 11, 1856.

[36]*Weekly Advocate*, June 14, 1856. An estimate of the Democratic majority in the Seventh precinct for the November 1855, election, made by the *Picayune* of November 7, 1855, was 213. (The ballot box had been broken in this election. The *Picayune* was a Know Nothing sheet.) The *Advocate's* figure of 243 for the Whig majority candidate, Waterman, is substantiated by the *Picayune* of June 3, 1856, but the latter journal ignores the charge of fraud, of course.

[37]Ibid.

[38]*Weekly Delta*, June 15, 1856. The Souléites refrained from voting in order to lessen the chances of the Slidell ticket. *Daily Crescent*, June 5, 1856.

[39]Ibid.

[40]Ibid.

[41]*Weekly Delta*, February 25, 1855.

[42]Ibid., March 11, April 8, September 30, 1855.

[43]Ibid., September 30, 1855.

[44]*Daily Picayune*, March 12, 1856.

[45]*Weekly Advocate*, March 15, 1856.

[46]*Bee*, March 15, 1856.

[47]*Weekly Advocate*, March 15, 1856.

[48]Ibid.

[49]*Bee*, March 15, 1856.

[50]*Weekly Advocate*, March 15, 1816.

[51]*Weekly Delta*, April 20, May 11, 1856.

[52]Ibid.

[53]However, neither favored acquisition by filibustering. Douglas flatly denounced Walker's system of filibustering. See William O. Scroggs, *Filibusters and Financiers: The Story of William Walker and His Associates* (New York, 1916; reissued 1969), 342, 350.

[54]Ibid.; *Weekly Delta*, May; *Daily Picayune*, April 30, 1856.

[55]*Daily Crescent*, May 12, 1856.

[56]*Weekly Advocate*, May 17, 1856.

[57]Ibid., May 31, 1856.

[58]*Daily Picayune*, June 10, 1856. Slidell was Buchanan's trusted personal friend and political manager. He noted the movements of Buchanan's enemies, and kept his chief informed. He advised Buchanan when to take a decided stand on the Kansas-Nebraska question, and in other ways, gave Buchanan the benefit of his political experience and astuteness. See Louis Martin Sears, *John Slidell* (Durham, 1925), 120-24.

[59]*Bee*, June 10, 1856.

[60]*Daily Crescent*, June 10, 1856.

[61]*Weekly Delta*, June 13, 1856. The following part of the *Delta's* report of a meeting of the regular Democrats is an example of the customary efforts of the Douglas faction to belittle the efforts of the other side:

The Democratic Ratification Meeting.—Moderately Numerous. Not Wildly Enthusiastic. Music Economical—Applause Ditto.

Judge Dunbar's Speech, more Peculiar than Acceptable.—Mr. Soulé Speaks. Mr. Villere Speaks.—General Cronan performs a telling episode.—Mr. Elmore concludes and the "unterrified" disperse.—Sic transit, &c.

Last night the long-expected Ratification meeting which was to gauge the sincerity of the Democracy of New Orleans, in its support of the nominees of the Cincinnati convention, came off amid a tolerable display of rockets, on Lafayette Square. An economical band played several patriotic airs; in due course of time the platform was occupied by several respectable gentlemen, and about eight o'clock some symptoms of a meeting were perceptible to an eager observer.—*Weekly Delta*, June 13, 1856.

[62]*Bee*, June 13, 1856.

[63]*Daily Crescent*, June 24, 1856.

[64]Ibid.

[65]*Weekly Delta*, July 13, 1856.

[66]Ibid., July 27, 1856.

[67]Ibid., August 3, 1856.

[68]Ibid., August 10, 1856.

[69]*Weekly Advocate*, August 23, 1856.

[70]*Daily Picayune*, September 13, 18, 1856; *Weekly Delta*, September 28, 1856.

[71]*Weekly Advocate*, September 20, October 4, 1856. This paper declared for the cause of the National Democrats. The former editor-in-chief had been succeeded by J. M. Taylor, who championed Buchanan's candidacy and led the assault against the Know Nothings with great spirit. *Weekly Delta*, November 21, 1857.

[72]Ibid., September 27, 1856.

[73]*Daily Picayune*, April 17, 1856.

[74]*Weekly Advocate*, July 19, 1856.

[75]*Daily Picayune*, September 7, 1856.

[76]Ibid., October 7, 1856.

[77]Ibid., October 8, 1856.

[78]*Bee*, quoted in *Weekly Advocate*, December 22, 1856.

[79]Slidell to Howell Cobb, New Orleans, January 28, 1852, in "The Correspondence of Toombs, Stephens, and Cobb," *Annual Report of the American Historical Association for 1911*, 11, 276.

[80]*Weekly Delta*, October 19, 1856.

[81]*Daily Picayune*, October 23, 1856.

[82]*Weekly Delta*, September 28, 1856.

[83]Ibid., October 12, 1856.

[84]*Bee*, October 1, 1856.

[85]*Weekly Advocate*, October 11, 1856.

[86]Quoted in *Weekly Advocate*, October 11, 1856.

[87]*Weekly Delta*, September 7, 1856.

[88]*Weekly Advocate*, October 11, 1856.

[89]*Weekly Delta*, October 12, 1856.

[90]Ibid., June 1, 1856.

[91]*Daily Picayune*, July 22, 1856.

[92]For Toombs's plan see Ulrich Bonnell Phillips, *The Life of Robert Toombs* (New York, 1968), 125.

[93]*Daily Picayune*, September 17, 1856.

[94]*Weekly Delta*, October 26, 1856. The *Delta* spoke, of course, for the ultra-expansionists, composed largely of Soulé's following.

[95]Ibid.

[96]*Daily Picayune*, September 28, 1856.

[97]Horace Greeley and John F. Cleveland, comp., *A Political Text-Book for 1860: Comprising a Brief View of Presidential Nominations and Elections* (New York, 1860), 232-33.

[98]*Weekly Delta*, November 30, 1856.

[99]*The Orleanian*, quoted in the *Weekly Advocate*.

[100]*True Delta*, November 8, 1856.

[101]*Courier*, quoted in *Weekly Advocate*, November 8, 1856.

[102]*Weekly Delta*.

[103]Ibid., November 9, 1856.

[104]*Weekly Delta*, November 16, 23, 1856.

[105]Ibid., November 30, 1856.

[106]Ibid.

[107]*Weekly Delta*, November 16, 23, 30, 1856, et seq., during November campaign.

[108]*Weekly Advocate*, November 29, 1856; *True Delta*, quoted in the *Weekly Delta*, December 7, 1856.

[109]*Creole* quoted in *Weekly Delta*, December 7, 1856.

[110]*Crescent*, December 7, 1856.

[111]*Weekly Delta*, December 14, 1856.

[112]Ibid. It said:

1st. Cotton can be raised only by African labor. . . . (Ridiculous, of course.)

2d. There can be no African labor unless it is slave labor—none, at least, of any genuine value and effect . . .

3d. The needs and necessities of the producing and slave-using States are gradually draining the border or breeding States, and Virginia cannot supply the demands for labor from cotton-cultivating headquarters much longer; so a source of *material* [*sic*] must be sought elsewhere. . . .

4th. Lord Palmerston, in one of the recent speeches, declared that the demand for cotton (as well as for negroes—one and the same thing) would soon exceed the supply . . .

5th. Slavery must be extended or it must perish—extended not only over new territory, but spread out and vigorously pushed into universal dissemination in the existing slave States.

We mean by this, our fifth assertion, that it is necessary to furnish poor men with the facilities for obtaining and owning slaves; that the Scotch *cresmatistic* political economy (as Sismundi calls it) is not the economy of the South . . .

6th. In a political point of view, the renewal of the African slave trade, or at all events a fearless and intelligent discussion of the subject, is a problem to be solved . . .

[113]*Bee*, December 7, 1856; *Bulletin*, December 14, 1856; *Crescent*, December 7, 28, 1856.

[114]*Weekly Picayune*, May 12, 1856; *Weekly Delta*, December 14, 1856.

[115]*Bee*, quoted in *Weekly Advocate*, December 22, 1856.

[116]Ibid.; E. M. Sears, *John Slidell*, 120-24.

THE GRAPPLE FOR POWER IN THE DEMOCRATIC PARTY IN LOUISIANA, 1859*

James K. Greer

The year 1859 saw a death grapple between [John] Slidell and [Pierre] Soulé for control of the state. Soulé openly avowed opposition to the administration and attempted to organize a new party composed of opposition Democrats and Know Nothings. The Senatorial election aroused keen interest at the opening of the year; but all other political contests were subordinated to the fight for dominance in the ranks of the one remaining organized party of the state.

Judah P. Benjamin's senatorial term was nearing its end, and a short contest was in prospect over his seat. The *Bee* had once denounced Benjamin's desertion from the Whig ranks to the Democracy, but it now praised the Jewish senator and his record in Congress.[1] The *Crescent* declared its intention of advocating the choice of the "proper man," regardless of geographical distinctions,[2] and predicted that Benjamin would be re-elected.[3] But the papers[4] of northern Louisiana became rather excited when it seemed that in the election of a senator, geographical questions were to be ignored.

The Democrats had a majority of twenty-five members in the assembly upon joint ballot. They spent two days in caucus before settling upon their candidate. North Louisiana wanted Sandidge, Gray was popular in the central part of the state, while Benjamin's standing had undoubtedly been injured by garbled accounts of his connection with the Houmas land question.[5] While the dominant party was finding it difficult to decide who should have the honors, the Americans waited—hopeless in their minority. On the first day, forty ballots were cast in the Democratic caucus, and no decision was reached. On the forty-second ballot, the vote stood: Benjamin 25; Sandidge 23; Gray 19; and Parham 1. There were seventy members in the caucus the afternoon of the second day, and Sandidge received thirty-five votes. Evidently some of the Benjamin men had cast votes for Sandidge, in order to get his supporters off their guard, or else were trading with them. Gray's friends called for an adjournment,[6] and a recess until 6 o'clock was taken.

Gray's supporters were evidently deceived by the scheme of Benjamin's friends, for they charged that a conspiracy existed to ignore Gray's claims. The friends of Gray con-

*First published in *Louisiana Historical Quarterly*, 13 (1930): 446-461. Reprinted with the kind permission the Louisiana Historical Society.

tended that they had been excluded from some conferences held between the Benjamin and Sandidge supporters, and refused to go back into caucus.[7] When the caucus re-assembled at 6 o'clock, only two of Gray's friends were present; Benjamin received twenty-six votes, and Sandidge twenty-three. When the house re-assembled it was announced that Benjamin was the nominee of the caucus. In the joint assembly, Benjamin and Gray were nominated. Benjamin received fifty-seven votes; Gray fifty, and Randell Hunt five. The contest was pronounced by the correspondent of the conservative *Picayune* as the "most excited contest ever held in Louisiana."[8] Benjamin received the Sandidge votes, of course, and those that had been given to Parham, while the Americans generally threw their votes to Gray.[9] Among the press which congratulated the people on the results of the election was the *Delta*, now favorable towards Benjamin, which thought that the victor would be vigilant of the wants of the commercial class, without overlooking "the great agricultural interests of the country."

The legislation of the session was almost entirely of a private nature, but some few matters of general interest were dealt with. Renewed agitation for the removal of the seat of government to New Orleans was silenced after the city council of that city failed to provide buildings for the legislature. Although an offer was made to share the rooms of the new courthouse, which was under construction, at "fair and equitable terms," the legislature had no desire for the status of a "tenant at will" and the discussion ceased.[10]

Much pressure was brought to bear on the assembly to restore the powers of nominating judges to the executive and to extend the term of office, with a salary commensurate with the dignity of the position.[11] Many had opposed the elective judiciary system from the beginning, and it was now denounced in the assembly as a failure, but no legislation was enacted concerning it.

The African Apprentice Bill which had been killed in the senate of the last session was again introduced in the House. At the previous session, the house had passed this measure, but now laid it upon the table by a vote of thirty-seven ayes to fourteen nays. This action, in the face of their previous record, was cited as proof that the people of Louisiana were true to the laws of their country.[12] There was gerrymandering by the legislature in the interest of the majority party, and to the disgust of those who were out of power.[13] The New Orleans politicians and press became excited when the census reports from the secretary of state's office showed a decrease in the population of the city, since 1853, from 153,000 to 117,000, and loudly declared this was evidence of a deliberate attempt to reduce the number of representatives from New Orleans from twenty-two to seventeen.[14]

Meanwhile, the time approached for the holding of the municipal election in New Orleans. The opponents of the Know-Nothing city administration were divided over the question again. But the *Courier* favored a regular Democratic ticket,[15] while the advocates of Independent nominations argued that this would divide and weaken the opposition to the city administration. In the end, the Democrats agreed to forego a regular ticket and united with their allies upon an "Independent Citizen's Ticket."[16] Nevertheless, their efforts were in vain, for street paving, tax collection, and other matters of the city business were left in the hands of the American candidates by a decided majority in the election.[17]

The voting was light; interest seemed to be lacking; and the election was quiet, generally, except in the First District. Here Independent tickets were destroyed at several polls and several fights occurred. J. L. Lewis, Superintendent of Elections, had a difficulty with one of the ticket destroyers, on Common Street, and was arrested for his participation in the affair.[18]

Interest in municipal politics was submerged by the general election campaigns. Dissension in the ranks of the Democrats had existed for some time, but early in 1859, purely personal issues gained ascendancy in the party.[19] Early in the year North Louisiana offered a candidate for governor when the *Attakapas Register*[20] and the *Franklin* (St. Mary) *Register*[21] nominated Thomas O. Moore, of Rapides Parish, "a disciple of the old Jackson school of Democracy,"[22] subject to the action of the Democratic convention. A strong feeling existed in that section that its interests had always been slighted in the selection of the more important officers and that it should now furnish the governor.

In the latter part of March, a correspondent of the *Weekly Advocate* headed a proposed Democratic state ticket with Moore for governor, whereupon the Know Nothing press of the same section[23] reiterated its statement that "King John" (Slidell) had planned the whole thing. Although Slidell's friends declared his "innocence" of the ticket and "ignorance of the author" of it, it is interesting to notice that the discontented Soulé Democrats made a similar charge through their organ, the *Daily True Delta*.[24] The disgruntled opposition claimed "that 'Houmas Slidell'"[25] would not allow the people to take care of their own affairs.[26] At the same time, North Louisiana was urged to stand forth in defense of its rights in the state convention and help rid the state of "cliques" of "Spurious Democrats."[27]

A call signed by one hundred and three names for a meeting at Odd Fellows' Hall, on April 4, to organize the Democratic party of Orleans Parish, and to prepare for the selection of Baton Rouge delegates, was published in the papers of New Orleans.[28] In these papers, there appeared a call of a meeting by the Democratic Central Committee for the same object. Evidently the first group was composed of combinations, including the Know Nothings, to form opposition to the Slidell forces.[29] The *Delta* pointed out that the "one hundred and three" could not establish a principle by which they were authorized to take direction of party affairs out of the hands of the state committee. If they meant division, they would probably achieve that.

No one had to hazard a guess that the "New-Liners"[30] and "Rip Sam"[31] were planning on the organization of a new party. That fact was established early in the spring by an address of Pierre Soulé. One paragraph of the address was:

> In Louisiana, as I conceive, we have to fight but against a single enemy: official interference and corruption. Partyisms are entombed in the history of the past. The American party, the Whig party exist no more as national or even state parties, though we may,

> at times, still see their shadows flit around our municipal halls and elective precincts. Their scattered fragments are in process of assimilation with the two factions into which the Democratic party is divided. We seek the alliance of none. But while our opponents, the federalists of the Democracy, strive to allure into their embrace, and openly curry favor with the most fanatic and unrelenting among those that were most ardent in their hostility to us, we can not but open our arms to such a desire, under the promptings of the loftiest impulses, to join our standard, and are willing to stand by our side and combat with us, in the cause of popular rights and popular independence.[32]

The leaders of the "New Liners" were Soulé, Clack, Maunsel White, and Dr. Choppin. The "New Liners" and the "Samuelites" had largely formed the list of signers to the public letter which had invited Douglas to New Orleans the previous December. Pierre Soulé, late "New Liner," and Christian Roselius, ancient Whig, were seen arm-in-arm on that occasion.[33] Thus, the followers of Sam were not regarded as ineligible material in the ranks of the proposed new organization, but were expected to take a prominent part.[34]

The meeting at Odd Fellows' Hall was held on April 4, and Clack, Soulé, and De Bow[35] spoke. One newspaper correspondent at the meeting, rather humorously reported that one set of "*miscreants*," led by John Slidell, had control of "Federal patronage," "which another set of miscreants belonging to Peter Soulé, . . . are anxious to get possession of."[36] It was the opinion of this correspondent that the "slaves," as "Soulé and the *True Delta* call them," would not exchange their present master (Slidell) "for a new one" (Soulé).[37] The National Democrats published notices requesting Democrats not to violate the usages of the party by attending a meeting not called by the proper authority.[38]

The "New Liners" meeting at Odd Fellows' Hall passed resolutions condemning: forming of a ticket before the state convention met; "dictators," "clans," and "cliques" in a republican community, etc. They also adopted a resolution which provided for the appointment of a committee of twenty-four to be called "The Democratic Executive Committee for the Parish of Orleans." Its duty was to give notices for the assembling of primary meetings which were to elect delegates to parish, district, and state conventions, and to direct the organization of the party within the parish.[39]

The first indication of activity on the part of the new organization was in the form of ten thousand copies of a card, on which appeared ". . . For Governor, Maj. Andrew S. Herron." Herron denied knowledge of the matter and declared he would only run for office as a nominee selected by a regular Democratic convention.[40] Meanwhile, the New Liners had called primary meetings in the several wards of the Parish of Orleans. Also, coalitions were being formed elsewhere between the "Purificators" and the Know Nothings. Such an organization was formally consummated at Plaquemine on April 22.[41]

During this time, the friends of Slidell denied that federal or state "Spoils" had contributed to or obstructed his progress. His success and strength, they asserted, lay in his always having been true to his party and loyal to his friends. Now that he was unshakable within the ranks, his enemies were trying to reach him by shaking the party itself to pieces.[42] Some Democrats said that the *True Delta*'s abuse had won him the friendship of men who were prejudiced against him.[43]

The "Old Liners" now raised the question how the new "true Democrats" of the city could avow the doctrine of Squatter Sovereignty and proclaim it as a part of the Democratic creed; and observed that should the state convention decide to admit delegates from the Odd Fellows' Hall group, it would be endorsing Squatter Sovereignty and assuming a position opposite to that of the States Rights men throughout the South. On the other hand, if the convention decided to take the true Southern Rights view, it would have to exclude the Odd Fellows' Hall delegation.[44] Furthermore, it was shown that not only was Soulé a follower of Douglas in previous years, but that he was the main spirit in Odd Fellows' Hall, where a resolution was passed asserting the right "of the public to regulate their domestic affairs, and shape their institutions in their own way."[45]

Slidell's supporters considered themselves authorized to state that Slidell was opposed to the "newly invented theory of Squatter Sovereignty," and conceded that Soulé represented that platform, while "orthodox principles of States Rights" were represented in Slidell.[46] "National" Democrats interpreted the visit of Douglas of the past winter as a bid for the electoral votes of Louisiana, but a failure, for Douglas could never look to or expect support from "the Democracy of Louisiana."[47]

In the meantime, the State Central Committee of the Democratic party designated May 16th as a proper time for the primary meetings in New Orleans. A large attendance was present and a fuller vote was cast than in the past four years. In some of the precincts of New Orleans, New Liners made opposition, but they carried only one—the ninth—by a vote of seventy-three to seventy. There were twenty-three precincts and Algiers in the New Orleans primaries.[48]

Just before the adjournment of the Legislature on March 18, its Democratic members suggested that the state convention be called the 25th of May. On March 25, the acting president of the Central Committee issued a call for a meeting of its members on April 2.

The Democratic state convention met in Baton Rouge on May 25th. The attendance was large. Many late Americans and Old Whigs, who had gone over to the Democrats and had been elected delegates in the May primaries, were observed in attendance and were accepted as good Democrats, besides the regular Democrats and the old sachems of the party. Both Old and New Liners made nominations for chairman of the convention, Pugh and Munday, respectively. Lieutenant-Governor Mouton suggested that both men should occupy the chair and appoint four members each as a Committee on Credentials and then toss "heads or tails" for the ninth member.[49] This was done; two secretaries were then selected. The Committee on Credentials finally reported the result of the vote to be: Pugh, 93; Munday, 90. The Old Liners had won, though the late Americans and late Old Whigs had strengthened the "New Liners."

The "New Liners" were discouraged by their defeat in the organization of the convention. Additional cause for worry came from the fact that Major Herron, who was their favorite for governor, was dissatisfied with their platform. A caucus was called, whereat

Soulé demanded that Herron endorse the preamble and resolutions of the Odd Fellows' Hall meeting. But others of the meeting thought these resolutions had done much harm and had injured Herron's chances. This show of disloyalty caused Soulé to become very indignant, and he withdrew from the meeting and soon returned to New Orleans. Herron and some of his friends decided, apparently, to transfer their support to another candidate,[50] since they did not also return to New Orleans.

Thomas O. Moore, of Rapides Parish, was nominated for governor by the regular Democrats. Other members of the ticket were: for Lieutenant-Governor, H. H. Hyams, of New Orleans; Secretary of State, P. D. Hardy, of St. Landry Parish; Auditor of Public Accounts, E. W. Robertson, of the Parish of Iberville; Treasurer, B. L. Dufreese, of Jackson Parish; Superintendent of Public Instruction, H. A. Avery, of East Baton Rouge Parish; Attorney General, Thos. J. Semmes, of New Orleans.[51]

The "new party" Democrats now wanted to know whether the "Slidellian mercenaries" or the northern Democracy were the true exponents of Democratic opinion.[52] Anti-Democrats in Moore's section declared the idea of making him governor was ridiculous, although he was a good plantation manager and a good citizen.[53] But when a paper of a neighboring state[54] described Soulé's reverse as a rout of "horse, foot, and dragoons," the *Weekly Advocate*[55] denied that there had been a trial of strength between Slidell and Soulé, as Soulé "had scarcely a body guard of supporters in the Convention."[56]

Know Nothing papers now began to try to create strife between the Creoles and the Democracy, by insisting that the Creole population had been insulted when they had not been given a place on the state ticket. The Democrats replied that the majority of the "Ancient Regime" in the state were Democrats, and that they could have had a Creole on the ticket if they had desired. The Democrats showed that old prejudice against North Louisiana on the part of the Creole, was being stirred by the "Samuelites."[57] They also had much to say about the lack of good faith on the part of their opponents. For example, Miles Taylor was elected candidate for Congress from the Second District by the New Liners, and the Old Liners accepted the nomination despite their disgust at having the New Orleans delegation excluded from the Convention.[58] But in the First Congressional District, the New Liners, although in the minority, would not live up to the creeds of the Democracy, although they claimed to be loyal, but maintained an independent organization. The same thing was true of St. Bernard Parish.

Despite the lack of an able chief to direct them, the disorganized Know Nothings struck at Slidell by appeals and denunciations of one sort or another. Douglas was compared with Buchanan to the disparagement of the latter,[59] pleas were made to the people to rise against "Slidell and his legions,"[60] and country parishes, with Know Nothings or opposition Democrats in the majority (there were only a few of these parishes), of North Louisiana were exacting pledges from their legislators-elect to support a country Democrat to succeed Slidell in the United States Senate.[61] In New Orleans, the aims of "Sam" were now largely confined to getting office.

The contest in the American clubs for the nomination for Congress from the First District was a close one. The contestants were C. D. Dreux, J. E. Bouligny, and Judge T. G. Hunt. The last named was a politician of the Old Whig school. But the American party had reached the point where it cared little for the chiefs of that party who grasped its skirts. The contest narrowed to Dreux and Bouligny, and the latter won the nomination by two votes.[62]

As we have seen, differences in motives and objects existing in the "Purificators" organization had been manifest since its beginning. At the state convention of the Democrats in Baton Rouge, the disagreement between Herron and Soulé brought the differences to a direct issue. Soulé, leader of the extreme branch of the Purificators, had left the convention, and Herron and the "moderates" remained. Later, the New Liners reassembled in New Orleans and the issue was again made. Soulé now proposed to organize a separate party and run a ticket against that named at Baton Rouge. At once, communication was opened with prominent citizens in the country in regard to using their names on a ticket, but the advances received slight attention. The "moderates" opposed this move.

Soon the "moderates" were "brought to taw" by the suggestion from the "extremists" that the division between Old and New Liners be increased by changing the name of the "States Rights Club" to "Douglas Club." Then the opponents of the extremists' policy and those who opposed the change of name divided; the majority decided to sustain the extremists, while the minority left the scene of their deliberations, grumbling that one political leader might be as dictatorial and domineering as another.[63] The minority resolved to abandon party leadership and one-man power.

In general, the American element of New Liners had allowed the discontented Democrats of the organization, as the leading spirits in the revolt, to take the lead. But those who had borne the brunt of leadership—chiefly Democrats—did not pass up an opportunity to put their allies on record, and at the same time cement stronger the bonds of common cause. A meeting which was characterized as an "Opposition Meeting" was advertised to be held at Lyceum Hall. There were only about a hundred and fifty at the assemblage, and the "Democratic" element was strangely absent. The chair made inquiries for prominent New Liners, whose presence had evidently been expected.[64] Resolutions were adopted which called for a general convention in New Orleans in September for the purpose of selecting an Opposition ticket for state officers. The coalition between the Know Nothings and the Purifiers was now perfected. It was composed, however, of the dissatisfied of both parties, who harmonized on opposition, although their hostility was directed toward different individuals.[65]

Appearances in early September indicated that the Democratic state ticket would meet no serious opposition in November;[66] but "Sam" seemed destined to carry Orleans Parish. For the past five years, Democratic organization had been unable to stand against the violent methods of the Know Nothings on election day. The same machinery which had defeated the Whigs did not function in the contests against this later opposition. Some 4,000 votes had ruled the parish and the Democratic party, although there were

13,000 registered voters. One explanation offered for this fact was that a party founded on great principles of national policy had no common ground on which to oppose a party that had become local in its aims and in its character.[67]

On the second Monday in September, the Opposition held its state convention in New Orleans. In a previous meeting, a committee had been appointed to select delegates to the Convention at which Opposition candidates for the state offices were to be nominated. When assembled, the convention included fifteen delegates—all Know Nothings. The interests of the city were guarded by having the majority of the delegates present from its confines. Four country parishes: Jefferson, Livingston, East Baton Rouge, and Rapides, were represented by a total of six delegates, one of whom was a proxy. "The other forty-four parishes of the state were not present in body, but were presumed to be in spirit."[68] An opposition ticket was named by acclamation, as follows:

For Governor, Thomas J. Wells, of Rapides.
For Lieutenant-Governor, John Ray, of Ouachita.
For Auditor, Adolphe Olivier, of St. Mary.
For Attorney General, Thomas J. Durant, of New Orleans.
For Treasurer, John Perkins, of East Baton Rouge.
For Secretary of State, Charles D. Dreux, of New Orleans.
For Superintendent of Public Education, R. H. Cuny, of Catahoula.[69]

One city paper[70] which printed the ticket reserved comments on the qualifications and claims of the nominees, from previous experience, until it learned whether the nominees would accept the honor tendered them.

The "*personnel*" of the Opposition state ticket was declared "irreproachable and worthy" by the old Know Nothing organ, the *Crescent*, although that paper disclaimed participation in any of the Opposition's activities.[71] A few days later, the same journal stated that the ticket was not being wildly acclaimed, although it affirmed that it was being well received.[72]

The regular Democrats decided upon a coalition in New Orleans with their old allies in the municipal elections, and succeeded in getting out what was termed locally the "Independent ticket."

Much attention was paid by the opposition to the fact that the Independent nominees were Old Line Whigs, regular Democrats, and former Know Nothings. They also revived the old story that Slidell's influence was back of the Independent ticket, and classified the parties in the state as "Administration" and "Anti-Administration."[73] But the Democrats reviewed the political events of the past few months and challenged their opponents to call the classification other than "opposition" and "Democrat."[74]

Country parishes also took up the contest. Conventions were called by the Opposition sympathizers and plans laid to assist the state ticket.[75] The parishes of St. Martin, Jackson, Ouachita, Terrebonne, Winn, and Ascension nominated candidates for the legislature or the parish offices on the Opposition ticket, or, in some cases, pledged Democratic candidates for the legislature to oppose Slidell's re-election to the Senate, by favoring a man from the country.[76] Federal state patronage, as directed by Slidell, came in for bitter denunciation at the hands of the Opposition of Madison[ville], Louisiana, and the St. Martinsville convention, held in the Parish of St. Martin.[77]

In the First Congressional District, there was much talk of calling upon Emile La Sère to stand for representative to Congress. Two candidates, Bouligny, Know Nothing, and Bienvenuee, of the "purifying" Democrats, were in the field, but La Sère, regular Democrat, had been a popular representative and his experience was an added recommendation, his supporters said.[78] An Independent candidate for Congress, Rufus Waples, came out against Miles Taylor, Democratic nominee for Congressional representative of the Second District. Taylor had been nominated by the New Liners, but the Administration Democrats had accepted the nomination, and now they fought the new entrant.[79]

In the city, the campaign grew interesting in October. The last night of September saw a long procession of the "Independent Americans" hold a meeting in Clay Square, in the Fourth District. This branch of the American party joined the Independents because the Know Nothings had degenerated into a group of office seekers, according to their own account.[80] The Creoles of the lower part of the city pledged themselves to stand by the Independents of the Fourth District. A few days later, open air meetings were announced by the "oppositionists," and the press of the city rejoiced at the appearance of a renewal of old time popular gatherings.[81]

But hopes for a return to campaign methods of former years were dashed by a resumption of the outrages of the past. Ruffians began to shoot, stab, and slug as of old, and the police made no arrests or granted "straw bail" in the few arrests that were made.[82] The Know Nothings made counter charges against the Democrats, and, having defended themselves in the premises, proceeded to ascribe the "Independent American" ticket to Slidell and the Federal appointees of New Orleans.[83] It was the old story and the election was near. The authorities charged that popular passions had been excited against them, but their assertions of innocence were not sustained by their police clerk records.[84]

A "Grand Mass Meeting of the Independents" held just before the end of October was a well attended and enthusiastic gathering. Dreux, Horner, and Cotton addressed the meeting on the history of the Know Nothings party which had deteriorated in aims during the past five years, and contrasted the "feeble faction" of the Democracy, which had followed Soulé, with the conservative branch of the Democratic party. Judge Cotton boldly named some of the gang who were hired by the Americans to do violence.[85]

Events in the country during the first days of October gave evidence of more political activity than was anticipated. Both parties were busily engaged in defending their respective tickets.[86] Only in parishes where there was no opposition was the situation described as quiet.[87] Slidell received some severe criticism at the hands of his rural opponents, one of which may be recounted, here, as quite novel. When Slidell secured appointments to Federal offices in New Orleans for two country gentlemen, he was blamed for taking them from rural life and exposing them to the corrupting influences of city life and office.[88]

Col. Thomas J. Wells,[89] Opposition candidate for governor, introduced personalities in his campaign for office, charging that any misrule of recent governors could be charged to "Slidellism." He was immediately brought up sharp by his opponents for descending to personal denunciation of his rivals and violating the properties, in a manner unbecoming a candidate for governor, and for not knowing that the last two governors were anti-Slidell men. The Opposition directed most of their attacks at Slidell, accusing him of mismanagement and of the inauguration of the "one-man power" in the New Orleans police system, by which the mayor appointed the police.

As election day was at hand, men and partisan journals bandied mutual charges of attempted fraud and incitement to violence. Returns from the election gave large majorities for the American ticket against the independents in the city, and against the Democrats in the congressional contest in the first district. Apprehensions of a recurrence of the usual outrages was given by the Democratic organs as a reason for the smallness of the vote[90]—about one-half the potential vote—in New Orleans; while the Americans' paper, the *Crescent*, assigned as reasons: the disgust of the people at "one man" rule which had been in the state for years, general insubordination to "a matchless manager," and dislike of the selfishness of the leaders.[91] The vote was less than 7,000 and should have reached, all agreed, 11,000, as the election was comparatively quiet. It can not be a great error to say that the meager vote was doubtless to be accounted for in large part to the terror which for the past several years had been instilled in the peaceable citizens, who did not care to risk life or limb in order to cast a ballot.

For Congress, the candidates for the First Congressional District were, as we have seen, Bouligny, Opposition; La Sère, Democrat; and Bienvenue, "Independent." Bouligny received 2,215 votes to La Sère's 1,796, and Bienvenue's 497. The Democrats charged that the Opposition managed to secure Bienvenue's nomination for the purpose of dividing the Democratic vote.[92] The Second and Third districts of Orleans, and Orleans right bank, gave heavy majorities for Bouligny. Especially was this true of the Third District (old Third Municipality), the home of the Know Nothing Clubs, which gave 904 votes for Bouligny to 493 for La Sère. Yet only about one-fourth of the voters of the First Congressional District cast their ballots. La Sère carried St. Bernard and Plaquemines by large majorities. Col. Maunsel White, enemy of Slidell and sugar planter, who was President of the Odd Fellows' Hall meeting, ran for Senatorial Representative of Plaquemines and Jefferson and polled only sixty votes.[93]

Against the Democratic state ticket, the Opposition brought itself into ridicule by its puny efforts, beginning with its state convention in New Orleans.[94] Undoubtedly, the Opposition's organizations of the state ticket in Orleans Parish were only for the purpose of strengthening their ticket in the parish. The Second, Third, and Fourth Congressional districts went Democratic by large majorities; Taylor, Davidson, and Landrum were the victors. Davidson, in the Third District, received 6,288 votes to Cannon's 726, while

Landrum, in the Fourth, defeated Jones, 8,823 to 3,220.[95] But Taylor defeated Nichols in the Second Congressional District by only 5,908 to 4,459. Still, Taylor carried all parishes except two, St. James and Terrebonne, and these were close. He received a splendid majority in the Fourth District of Orleans (old Lafayette), but lost the First District (old Second Municipality) by 300 votes.[96] The three chief Democratic candidates on the state ticket—governor, lieutenant governor, and secretary of state—received majorities of from eight to ten thousand votes.

As the year ended, the Opposition was making claims and overtures to the Democracy of the state in regard to its rights to be represented at the Democratic convention at Charleston, on the ground that they stood with the Democrats on the sectional question.[97] This appeal for the whole Opposition was interpreted by the Democrats as revealing a desire to support Douglas as a candidate of the South, and with Squatter Sovereignty for the platform. Neither for Douglas nor his platform "can the Southern Democracy unite with the Opposition," was the reply of the Democrats.[98]

Notes for "The Grapple for Power in the Democratic Party in Louisiana, 1859"

[1]*Bee*, quoted in *The Weekly Delta*, January 1, 1859.

[2]*Crescent*, quoted in *Weekly Delta*, January 8, 1859.

[3]Ibid., January 15, 1859.

[4]*Ouachita Registrar*, January 6, 1859, quoted in *Weekly Delta*, January 15, 1859.

[5]Pierce Butler, *Judah P. Benjamin* (1907, reprint ed.; New York, 1980), 170.

[6]*Daily Picayune*, January 25, 1859.

[7]Ibid.

[8]See also the account in Pierce Butler, *Judah P. Benjamin*, 170-172.

[9]*Weekly Delta*, January 29, 1859.

[10]Ibid., March 26, 1859.

[11]*Weekly Gazette*, October 8, 1858; *Weekly Picayune*, October 15, 1858; *Daily Picayune*, February 6, 1859.

[12]*New Orleans Bulletin*, March 13, 1859, quoted in *The Weekly Advocate*.

[13]*Daily Picayune*, February 20, 1859.

[14]Ibid., January 26, 27, 1859. Under the census of 1853, New Orleans had one fourth of the total number of representatives in the house, while the number of her senators was fixed at five by the constitution.

[15]Quoted in *Weekly Delta*, April 30, 1859.

[16]*Weekly Delta*, May 7, 1859.

[17]*Daily Picayune*, June 7, 1859.

[18]Ibid., June 7, 8, 1858.

[19]*Weekly Advocate*, February 13, 1859.

[20]Quoted in *Weekly Advocate*, February 13, 1859.

[21]Quoted in *Weekly Delta*, February 12, 1859.

[22]*Attakapas Register*.

[23]*Weekly Gazette* and *Comet*, February 6, 1859; *Weekly Advocate*, March 27, 1859.

[24]April 5. "He came poste haste from Washington before the adjournment of the Legislature to open house at the capitol and ply those arts none knew so well how to practice to make party subservient to his purposes; . . . During his stay there the state ticket which, the people of Louisiana were to be allowed to elect in November next, was formed by him." It is probable that Slidell tendered the governorship to North Louisiana in exchange for votes for Benjamin as United States senator.

[25]So-called from his participation in the Houmas land episode. Highlights on the "Houmas fraud," as Slidell's enemies termed it, were briefly: The Houmas land lay on the east side of the Mississippi, fifty miles above New Orleans, and contained several hundred thousand acres. A land claim to this tract was not approved by the government, at first, but a patent was later given, and settlers on the land were to be required to test their titles before the courts. The Supreme Court of Louisiana pronounced the patent void. Meantime Slidell bought a large share of the land and now sued for his purchase money. He lost the suit. But Benjamin, senator from Louisiana, got an amendment attached to a bill confirming land locations in Missouri, which confirmed the location of the "Houmas Claim." This legislation won money for Slidell, and dispossessed about five hundred settlers on the land. The settlers protested against the Missouri bill, and the Committee on Private Land Claims, despite the fact that Benjamin was chairman of the committee, suspended all action.—*Daily True Delta*, March 15, 1859.

But the rabidness of his accusers, Benjamin's reelection to the Senate the following January, and Slidell's private career, weigh heavily against the cries of fraud from his political enemies. Butler's *Judah P. Benjamin*, and Louis Martin Sears, *John Slidell* (Durham, N. C., 1925) offer a fair insight as to the probable facts in the case. Slidell's explanation of his acquisition of the land may be found in Sears, *John Slidell*, 165-166. These accounts are not fair to Slidell, but are given to show the venom of the opposition.

[26]*Daily True Delta*, April 3, 5, 1859.

[27]Ibid., April 3, 1859.

[28]*Daily Picayune*, April 2, 1859; also, *Delta*, etc.

[29]*Weekly Delta*, April 9, 1859. The *Delta* was no longer supporting the opposition. Since early in 1856, the *Delta* had opposed the political methods of the Know Nothings. Now Soulé was attempting an alliance with this group to strengthen what he hoped would prove more than mere opposition—a new party. Business interests of New Orleans had suffered for some four years from the nature of the political activities directed against the Democrats. *The True Delta*, on the other hand, was upholding the banner of the Opposition, and supporting Miles Taylor, who had endeavored because of political animus to prevent Slidell's securing valuable Congressional appropriations for the commercial good of the state. Such a combination of conditions evidently caused the *Delta* to pause and "take stock."

[30]Discontented Democrats opposed to the "Old Line Democrats."

[31]Know Nothings.

[32]*Weekly Delta*, April 9, 1859.

[33]Ibid.

[34]Ibid.

[35]R. R. Russell, in *Economic Aspects of Southern Sectionalism, 1840-1861*, criticizes De Bow as a thinker, and states, on page 140 of this work, that De Bow was an "Avowed disunionist" by August, 1857.

[36]*Weekly Advocate*, April 10, 1859.

[37]Ibid.

[38]*Weekly Delta*, April 9, 1859.

[39]*Weekly Delta*, April 9, 1859.

[40]Ibid., April 23, 1859.

[41]Ibid., April 30, 1859.

[42]*Weekly Advocate*, May 1, 1859.

[43]Ibid., May 8, 1859.

[44]*Weekly Delta*, May 7, 1859.

[45]*Weekly Delta*, May 14, 1859. The Conservative business men of New Orleans—largely Whigs—regarded "popular sovereignty" as a barren issue. Without labor or citizens from its section to people the territories, there was little use in protecting slavery in the territories. This was the view of the men who boomed the Bell-Everett ticket in 1860, and who now formed the remnant of the old Whig party. See the *Crescent*, September 22, 1859.

[46]Ibid.

[47]*Weekly Advocate*, February 10, 1859.

[48]Ibid., May 22, 1859, quoting the *Delta*. Algiers is opposite the Canal Street Docks, across the river.

[49]*Daily Picayune*, May 27, 1859; *Weekly Delta*, May 28, 1859.

[50]*Weekly Delta*, May 28, 1859. Slidell and Soulé's rival interests in 1856 may be said to have really begun the split in the party which affected it thereafter. Rural parish conventions at this time the spring of 1859, had no sympathy for Soulé, but neither were they over-loyal to Slidell. There were many who wanted the next senator to be from the country; they were called the "Bob Tails," while Slidell's supporters were termed by some the "Long Tails." Slidell had won out, in the election of Benjamin, but a wider margin would have been more comfortable.

[51]*Daily Picayune*, May 28, 1859.

[52]*True Delta*, June 4, 1859.

[53]*The American*, Alexandria, Louisiana, quoted in the *Weekly Delta*, June 18, 1859.

[54]*Charleston Mercury*, Charleston, S. C., quoted in *Weekly Delta*, June 18.

[55]June 19, 1859. National Democratic in politics.

[56]The large vote for Munday meant opposition to Slidell, but that opposition was not a personal following of Soulé.

[57]*Weekly Advocate*, July 3, 1859.

[58]*Weekly Delta*, July 23, 1859.

[59]*Weekly Crescent*, June 27, 1859.

[60]*Bee*, quoted in *Weekly Advocate*, July 31, 1859. The *Bee* was now a "conservatively Douglas" journal.

[61]*The Harrisonburg* (Catahoula) *Independent*, quoted in *Daily Picayune*, August 13, 1859.

[62]*Weekly Delta*, August 20, 1859.

[63]Ibid., August 27, 1859.

[64]*Weekly Delta*, August 27, 1859.

[65]*Weekly Advocate*, August 28, 1859. Undoubtedly true, as shown already, though from a hostile source.

[66]*Bee*, September 14, 1859.

[67]*Weekly Delta*, September 10, 1859.

[68]*Weekly Delta*, September 16, 1859. This account is from a hostile source, but accounts in other papers are not sufficiently positive to indict the account of the *Delta*.

[69]Ibid., September 17, 1859.

[70]Ibid.

[71]Ibid., September 17, 24, 1859.

[72]It is interesting to notice that the *Crescent* was openly advocating Douglas for the presidency. It argued that since the South had gained in Douglas' re-election to the Senate over Lincoln, that it would likewise gain in accepting him rather than having to accept the alternative—Seward. Lincoln was declared "the dirtiest and meanest Abolitionist alive. There is not an emotion of his heart, brain or soul, that is not unutterably filthy."—*Crescent*, September 20, 1859.

[73]*Bee*, and the *Crescent*, quoted in the *Weekly Delta*, October 1, 1859.

[74]*Weekly Delta*, October 1, 1859. It was observed that the *Crescent* was giving little aid to the Opposition, strange to say, and that the *True Delta* was quiet. See *Weekly Advocate*, October 2, 1859.

[75]The *St. Martinville Courier* of September 3, carried the following: "*Independent Convention.*—All the citizens of this parish, irrespective of party, who are opposed to the *Slidell State Ticket*, and who are interested in counteracting the corruption and intrigues of that man and of his confederates, are requested to meet at the Courthouse, in St. Martinsville [*sic*], on Wednesday, September 7."

[76]*Weekly Advocate*, September 24, 1859; *Daily Picayune*, September 27, 1859.

[77]*Weekly Delta*, September 24, 1859; *Daily Picayune*, September 27, 1859.

[78]*Weekly Delta*, October 8, 1859.

[79]Ibid.

[80]Ibid., October 1, 1859; *Bee*, quoted in *Weekly Delta*, October 1, 1859.

[81]*Weekly Delta*, October 22, 1859.

[82]*Weekly Delta*, October 29, 1859. The violence was probably not all on one side. Yet even the *Picayune's* daily city news items show that the Irish, etc., seemed to be getting the worst of encounters, on the whole.

[83]*Crescent*, October 25, 1859.

[84]*Weekly Delta*, October 29, 1859; *Courier*, quoted in the same.

[85]*Weekly Delta*, October 29, 1859. Bob Johnson, Forbes, Lockwood, and Strong were named by Judge Cotton as members of an organized stabbing and shooting gang.

[86]There had been a momentary lull in the agitation of the slavery question throughout the country, and many had hoped the subject would be allowed to rest. As a result of John Brown's raid upon Harper's Ferry, the topic

was suddenly renewed in every state. Even the most conservative Louisianians felt that the South would now have to depend upon herself.

The press of the state held John Brown to be an innocent man in comparison with the Beechers, Gerritt Smiths, and others who furnished the arms, money, and incited him to his deeds. The most serious thing was the proof that fanatics were ready to support such insurrections. But it was pointed out that those who wanted to ruin the South would probably not attempt it in that fashion. *Crescent*, October 26, 28, 1859. It was realized by most people, now, that they were facing fact—not theory.

[87]*Daily Picayune*, October 8, 11, 12, 1859.

[88]*Crescent*, quoting the *Richmond Journal*, in the *Weekly Delta*, October 22, 1859.

[89]Called the "planter turfman" by the *Courier*.

[90]*Weekly Delta*, November 12, 1859; *Courier*, November 8, 1859.

[91]*Crescent*, November 9, 1859.

[92]*Courier*, November 8, 1859.

[93]*Weekly Delta*, November 26, 1859.

[94]*Bulletin*, November 10, 1859.

[95]Greeley, *A Political Text-Book for 1860*, 243.

[96]Ibid.

[97]*Bee*, quoted in *Weekly Delta*, December 10, 1859; *Crescent*, December 12, 1859; also quoted in *Weekly Delta*, December 31, 1859.

[98]*Weekly Delta*, December 17, 1859.

"A PERFECT HELL ON EARTH:" A TIME OF TROUBLES IN THE REUNIFIED CITY, 1852-1861*

Dennis C. Rousey

When the English journalist William Howard Russell visited New Orleans in 1861, his itinerary included a tour of the parish prison. The parish criminal sheriff informed Russell that the city was "a perfect hell on earth, and that nothing would put an end to murders, manslaughters, and deadly assaults, till it was made penal to carry arms; but by law every American citizen may walk with an armory round his waist, if he likes. Bar-rooms, cock-tails, mint-juleps, gambling-houses, political discussions, and imperfect civilization do the rest."[1] Russell was one of many travelers to the Crescent City who remarked upon the incidence of violence there and the proclivity of New Orleanians to bear weapons. Certainly New Orleans was one of the most violent cities in the United States in the late antebellum period.

One conspicuous source of violence in this era was political conflict, especially between the nativist American party and the multiethnic coalition of Democrats. During the 1840s and early 1850s control of the police force had become an increasingly important issue in municipal politics because of its value as a source of patronage and its influence on elections. After the restoration of unitary government in the city in 1852, the police played an even larger role in the manipulation of elections and resorted more frequently to intimidation and violence. Although the first mayor of the rechartered city was a Whig, the Democrats achieved domination of the police by electing a majority of the members of the Board of Police, which controlled the force from 1853 to 1856. The American party organized and did battle at the polls in 1854-1855, and when its members failed to win a majority on the board, they arranged the impeachment of two Democrats and the substitution of men partial to their own party. Under the rule of the Know Nothings, the police force was reduced in size and funding, and most of the policemen who lost their jobs were foreign-born Democrats. The result was a force so woefully inade-

*First published as Chapter 3 in Dennis C. Rousey, *Policing the Southern City New Orleans, 1805-1899* (Baton Rouge: Louisiana State University Press, © 1996), 66-101. Reprinted with the kind permission of the author and the publisher.

quate to fight crime and maintain order and so abusive of the electoral process that a vigilance committee seized the city in 1858 in a brief and unsuccessful attempt to end what many people considered a reign of terror.

New Orleans shared turbulent ethnic politics with other American cities of the period. Several municipal governments attempted to reform their law enforcement systems in these years. One of the most widespread reforms was the integration of once-separate organizations, usually the day police and night watch, into a single entity with a unified chain of command. New York City had led the country by doing so in 1845, and Boston, Philadelphia, Chicago, Charleston, St. Louis, and Richmond were among those that followed in the 1850s. New Orleans had integrated the day and night forces by 1840 but did not consolidate the three municipalities' police forces until the legislature reunified the city in 1852. New Orleans also tinkered with other common nationwide reforms of the period, such as installing a police telegraph system and creating a "rogues' gallery" stocked with daguerreotypes of prominent career criminals, and it considered the "northern" reform of adopting a police uniform. In characteristically unique fashion, the New Orleans city government—which had uniformed its police force during the period 1805-1836—decided to reuniform the police in 1855 and then rescinded the order before it was put into effect. New Orleans also shared the national problem of increasingly available lethal weaponry, especially the proliferation of revolvers; a state statute forbade the carrying of concealed weapons and at least one mayor tried to enforce that law, but policemen began to carry deadly weapons and usually kept them concealed.[2]

Under the new city charter of 1852, the authority to set regulations for the police department and to appoint its personnel was vested in the mayor, subject to the advice and consent of the Board of Aldermen. This departed from the system of dispersed authority that had prevailed under the partition government, and it made partisan control of the police almost completely dependent on the party affiliation of the mayor. The new charter also created the office of chief of police, subordinate to the mayor.[3] For this post Mayor Abdil Crossman chose a fellow Whig, John Youenes, who had served nine years as captain of the First Municipality police.[4] Youenes, however, held the job for only one year. The city's Democrats procured a charter amendment from the legislature which removed the police from mayoral control and gave that authority to a Board of Police. The mayor served as presiding officer of the board but cast only one of five votes, the other four coming from the city's recorders, each of whom represented a district. Three of the four recorders were Democrats and so constituted a majority of the board. In April 1853, they elected as chief an Irish-born policeman, Stephen O'Leary, who had fifteen years of police experience in the old Second Municipality. While applicants for the force thronged the corridors of city hall, the board overrode the mayor's objections and appointed a largely new group of men to serve under O'Leary.[5]

It was during O'Leary's tenure as police chief that police became involved in the first serious political violence of the 1850s. Complaints of electoral fraud tainted elections in

May and November 1853, but both elections were peaceful, and neither Whigs nor Democrats found fault with the police.[6] When the American party presented a slate of candidates in the regular municipal election in March 1854, however, the polling turned violent. In one precinct a band of armed men destroyed a ballot box. The local press reported accusations that policemen led groups of men from one poll to another to vote "early and often" and permitted and abetted the intimidation of Know Nothing supporters. Two Irish-born policemen were killed in the fray. After the second slaying, the nativist *Daily Crescent* claimed the policemen had been trying to prevent a qualified voter from casting a ballot, whereas the Democratic *Daily True Delta* alleged that he had been courageously preserving the peace from nativist outrages. Police Chief Stephen O'Leary was among those wounded in the electoral combat.[7]

When O'Leary's term as chief expired in the spring of 1854, the Board of Police appointed William James to succeed him. James quickly made enemies on the board by vigorously enforcing the laws respecting gambling, taverns, and dance halls, consequently increasing the city's license revenues fivefold in just one year. The Board of Police did more than sack James; it abolished the office of chief of police, thereby giving each recorder more control over the police in his district.[8]

Despite the formal consolidation of the police in 1852, the department had continued to resemble four police forces rather than one. The establishment of the Board of Police had exacerbated this tendency, making the recorders "like despots in their respective districts," according to the *Daily True Delta.* The *Daily Crescent* concurred, asserting that "as at present organized, the police force of this city is divided and local." The editorial suggested a remedy: "the police should be organized on a different footing altogether. It should be the police of a consolidated city, and not a district one; there should be but one head to it, who should be held responsible for its acts." The recorders customarily selected the police for their own districts. When the Board of Police rejected the nominees of Recorder H. M. Summers for partisan reasons in April 1854, he protested that "I desired and expected to exercise the previously-conceded right of selecting the entire police of my district."[9]

After only one month a district court judge ruled the excision of the office of police chief illegal and the board was forced to restore the office. But during that month, in a week-long battle in the streets between the Democrats and the Know Nothings, the police proved almost totally ineffectual at restoring peace. The riots were triggered by the arrest on September 9 of Henry T. Sherman, who was allegedly brutalized by the police who took him into custody. A group of fifty to sixty Know Nothings assaulted the police station where Sherman was incarcerated, and two Irish policemen suffered gunshot wounds. A police lieutenant found former chief O'Leary carrying a shotgun and confiscated the weapon. Several days later he was found by police to be armed again and was arrested for carrying a concealed weapon.[10]

When the rioting continued after September 9, the police could not restore order. One detachment marched away from a riot in Tchoupitoulas Street when they received a misdirected order; another detachment stood idly by as a band of armed men passed. Three night policemen in the First District ran away from a pair of pursuers only to be overtaken and embarrassed to find that they had run from two day policemen who were coming on duty. A display of military force by a small militia unit failed to halt the violence, and the mayor eventually felt compelled to swear in a special citizen police force of about 250 men, who succeeded where the regular police had not. A few regular policemen did their duty and acquitted themselves honorably during the Sherman riots, but as a whole the force failed miserably.[11]

Democratic control of the police force ended six months later. The American party had won a majority of the Board of Assistant Aldermen in 1854, and in the municipal election of March 1855, it secured control of both branches of the Common Council. The Democrats accused the Know Nothings of excluding naturalized citizens from voting in the election, but to no avail. Even though the Democrats still held a majority on the Board of Police, the Know Nothings maneuvered into control of the board by impeaching the two Democratic recorders, Clement Ramos and Peter Seuzeneau. Chief William James, who had been restored to his post by judicial order shortly after the Sherman riots in September 1854, charged the two magistrates with malfeasance for permitting their subordinates to receive fees for issuing passes and bonds to blacks and for releasing from jail a policeman who was being held for interfering with the election. The Common Council responded to Chief James's accusations by impeaching Ramos and Seuzeneau before the Board of Police made its annual appointment of the force. Although the two Democrats were eventually vindicated in court and restored to their offices, they were replaced in the interim by American party loyalists.[12]

Democratic protests against the impeachment proved fruitless. One of the Know Nothing acting recorders expressed his willingness to table the police appointments, but the others pressed ahead and the board appointed a new police force over the objection of the lone Democrat, Mayor John Lewis. Even though Chief James had brought charges against Ramos and Seuzeneau he lost his post because he was a Democrat and was replaced by Alexander F. Moynan.[13]

Moynan commanded a radically altered police department. Even before the American party had won control of the Board of Police, its leaders used their Common Council majorities to enact a new police ordinance, reducing the force from 450 to 265 men. The Americans sought to limit other traditional expenditures throughout the municipal government so as to channel money to railroad construction. In July 1855, Chief Moynan attempted to requisition a ream of paper and a few pens, but the comptroller denied the request because it first had to be endorsed by the Common Council's finance committee. The *Daily Picayune* commented, "The police are busily engaged in scraping up backs of old letters and stray pieces of blank paper for present purposes, and will have to continue doing so till the next meeting of the Financial Committee." Because of its determination to invest in new transportation projects the new administration could not meet many of the city's other expenses. The public school teachers sued the city for payment of back salary and forced the sale of the police department's two paddy wagons, the Red Maria and Black Maria, at public auction. The buyer of the Marias acquired them at half their original cost to the city and promptly informed the police department that he would be willing to hire out the wagons.[14]

When the Know Nothings scaled down the police force, most of the men who lost their jobs were immigrants (see Table I). The Board of Police substantially nativized the department, though some foreign-born men remained. Almost every immigrant group lost part of its 1850 share of policemen in the reorganization of 1855. When the American party recast the ethnic composition of the police department, the Irish probably made up about 20 percent of the white adult male population of the city, but they received only 10 percent of the appointments in 1855. Five years later, the situation had not changed much; immigrants were underrepresented on the police and the Irish still held close to 10 percent of jobs (see Table II). The struggle in New Orleans between Democrats and Know Nothings was roughly paralleled in most other American cities of the period, though in some places the Democrats were more successful in meeting the American party challenge, and the level of violence varied considerably from one place to another. A survey of fifteen other southern cities indicates that in 1860 the Irish were substantially overrepresented in six and underrepresented in eight, with nearly proportionate representation in one (see Table III).

Immigrant policemen who lost their jobs were bitter. One dismissed policeman, William Gotts, reapplied for police work in the early 1860s describing himself as "at one time a Police Officer appointed by the Democrats but removed by the *Know Nothings* when the[y] got into power." Another longtime policemen, John Gallagher, wrote in condemnation of the Know Nothings: "I am an Irish man by Birth, I am an American by choice, constitutionally a Jeffersonian, I am a man of Family[,] I hold the Thugs in utter abhorence."[15]

TABLE I

Nativities of the Police in 1850 and 1855

	1850 %	1855 %	No.
Native-born	37.7	76.8	129
Louisiana	28.7	53.0	89
Other slave states	3.7	9.5	16
Pa., N. J., N. Y.	4.1	8.3	14
New England	1.1	3.6	6
Midwest	0	2.4	4

	1850 %	1855 %	No.
Foreign-born	62.3	23.2	39
Ireland	32.1	10.1	17
Germany	16.0	3.0	5
France	4.1	1.8	3
Italy	1.9	0.6	1
Britain	1.1	3.6	6
Other	7.1	4.1	7
Total	100.0	100.0	168

Sources: Census of 1850, RG 29, NA; New Orleans Death Certificates; newspaper obituaries.

The drastic reduction in police personnel caused serious problems. Chief Moynan notified the Board of Police in December 1855, that "this meagre force is inadequate to the wants of the city, and in consequence, I am compelled to leave a very large portion of the city entirely without any watchmen; and on those streets which have watchmen, the beats are necessarily so long that depredations can be committed before they can walk the extent of their beats and return." Citizens had complained "very justly," Moynan said, of being unable to find a policeman when they needed one. His proposal called for doubling the size of the force and returning to the use of a boat police to protect steamboats and other shipping in the river from thievery. The grand jury issued a report in agreement with the chief, suggesting an additional 250 policemen be hired. The *New Orleans Bee*, which supported the Know Nothing retrenchment in other departments, editorialized in behalf of an increased police budget, deeming an undersized police force a "sordid and ill-judged economy." Mayor John Lewis concurred that the department was under-manned, but the Common Council allowed only 50 new policemen and did not increase the force again for two years. Additions to the department thereafter brought the total number of policemen back to about 450 men in 1860, still proportionately smaller than the force had been in the early 1850s (the city's population in 1850 was 116,000 but had swelled to 169,000 by 1860, though part of the increase came from the annexation of Lafayette).[16]

TABLE II
Nativities of the Police in 1860

	Police		White Adult Males (sample)	
	%	No.	%	No.
Native-born	72.2	268	28.0	1,160
Louisiana	46.4	172	11.2	463
Other slave states	8.9	33	7.0	291

Pa., N. J., N. Y.	12.4	46	6.1	255
New England	2.7	10	2.5	105
Midwest	1.9	7	1.0	42
Other	0	0	0.1	4
Foreign-born	27.8	103	72.0	2,990
Ireland	10.8	40	24.7	1,023
Germany	5.9	22	22.5	935
France	2.7	10	12.4	514
Spain	1.9	7	2.0	84
Italy	0.5	2	1.5	62
Britain	3.2	12	4.2	174
Other	2.7	10	4.8	198
Totals	100	371	100	4,150

Source: Census of 1860, RG 29, NA.

The police remained politically partisan and controversial during the latter 1850s, still under American party control. Occasionally policemen faced punishment for abuse of the electoral process. Two members of the force were brought before the Board of Police on charges of interfering in an election in June 1855; one received a ten-day suspension for committing assault at the polls, but the other was reinstated without punishment. More complaints were forthcoming after the November 1855 election, when a Democratic newspaper accused two policemen of participating in a nativist assault against a preelection parade of Democrats. During the voting, outbreaks of violence occurred in four precincts, resulting in two deaths and destruction of two ballot boxes. The Know Nothings systematically excluded from the polls voters who had been naturalized during the courts' summer recess as well as any whose naturalizations had been processed in the First District court. Democrats complained that the police tolerated the intimidation of some voters and actively participated in violence against others. Mayor John Lewis roundly condemned the police for failing to execute warrants against men charged with offenses stemming from the election violence even though their identities were well known. He urged the chief of police to bring all offenders within the department to justice or, he warned, he would do so himself.[17]

The mayor's appeal for a housecleaning had little effect. As a Democrat, he was a political outsider in the Know Nothing administration, and his efforts were frustrated by the Board of Police, the Common Council, and the police department itself. The Democratic state legislature and governor removed one obstacle by abolishing the Board of Police in February 1856, and attempted to restrain American party electoral abuses by enacting a voter registration law creating a Democratic-controlled election commission for the city in 1857, but the entrenchment of the Americans in municipal government prevented any substantial reforms. Abolition of the board restored control of the police to the mayor, a situation Lewis had little chance to enjoy, for he surrendered his office to a Know Nothing, Charles Waterman, in June 1856. In the election that put Waterman in the mayor's office, voter turnout was light because the Know Nothings excluded many Democrats from voting. Armed men held the polls in three precincts throughout the day. Once exchange of gunfire resulted in the deaths of two Sicilian immigrants. At least four policemen were beaten during the polling, and that night a majority of the policemen in three of the city's four districts absented themselves from duty and absences ran above normal in the remaining district.[18]

Newly elected Mayor Waterman reappointed Alexander Moynan as chief of police. Moynan had stepped down from the office in March 1856, after being arrested for assaulting and threatening to kill one of his own policemen. The complainant claimed that the chief had referred to him as a "d----d Irish son of ---------," threatened to kill all the Irishmen in the city, and employed a knife and brass knuckles as proof of the sincerity of his words. (Similar bigotry was displayed by one of his lieutenants, who was reported by an Irish policeman to have said that "the Board of Police were appointing a parcel of damned Irish and Dutch, and a set of thieves on the police," and by one of his patrolmen, who killed a German immigrant after calling him a "d-----d Dutch son of a b------ch.") Moynan served as chief again until December 1856, when he resigned and was replaced by Henry Forno. Forno had at one time been captain of the guard in the old Second Municipality and during the 1850s had worked occasionally for the governor in extraditing fugitives.[19]

Mayor Waterman promised to reform the police by appointing the sober and industrious men without respect to party membership or place of birth, but he failed to create a nonpartisan police. The police made their typically controversial showing in the November election of 1856. A police lieutenant attempted to quell a disturbance at one location, failed and was wounded for his trouble, and then quit the scene, declaring that the disorder had grown too great to handle. One policeman attempting to arrest a man who had broken a table at a polling station found himself single-handedly engaged because other policemen at the scene refused to help him. If even a fraction of the complaints against the police were true, most stood by and did nothing in the presence of violence.[20]

Election days remained tumultuous into 1858. The last major episode of political violence of the decade came in June 1858, before and during a municipal election. Running against the regular American party ticket was an Independent organization, led by propertied merchant Know Nothings, who resented their loss of power to the labor wing of the party, and supported by many Democrats. They chose as their mayoral candidate P. G. T. Beauregard, a popular figure in the city (and later to become a general in the Confederate army). On June 3, 1858, four days before the election, a group of men calling themselves the Vigilance Committee, apparently for the most part Democrats, seized the state arsenal at Jackson Square as well as the police headquarters. They announced their intention to rid the city of thugs and ensure a fair election.[21]

Mayor Waterman convened the Common Council but declined to disperse the vigilantes by force. Waterman went to Jackson Square to negotiate with the vigilantes and, after refusing their demand that they be appointed as a special police force for the election, called out the militia. Maj. Gen. John Lewis (the former Democratic mayor) reported that the 150 men who could be mustered were insufficient to retake the arsenal. Neither Waterman nor anyone else seems to have expected the regular police to deal with the crisis, though many of them remained on duty during the early days of the siege. On June 4, Mayor Waterman agreed to appoint the vigilantes as special policemen without pay until the election was over. An armed and angry mob opposed to the Vigilance Committee marched toward Jackson Square but retreated when faced there with an imposing barricade and frightened by a single stray gunshot. A citizens' group disclaiming any connection with the vigilantes endorsed the agreement with Waterman, and several officials and civic leaders spoke to anti-vigilante mobs to restrain them from storming Jackson Square. Mayor Waterman delegated the task of swearing in the special police to Recorder Gerard Stith (the Know Nothing candidate for mayor) but rescinded his action when two lawyers advised him the delegation of authority was illegal. Stith ignored the rescinding order, and the men already sworn in served as specials at the election. The Common Council impeached Waterman, and H. M. Summers became acting mayor. Chief of Police Henry Forno abandoned his post and retired to his home in the country.[22]

Acting Mayor Summers appointed Jonathan A. Jacquess as a temporary chief of police, and his force joined the special police on election day. The only casualties during the siege were several members of the Vigilance Committee who were accidentally shot by their own people, leaving four of them dead. After the election had ended in victory for the Know Nothings, the vigilantes peacefully evacuated Jackson Square and the special police retired from the streets.[23]

The new Know Nothing mayor, Gerard Stith, appointed as chief of police Thomas E. Adams, a businessman and member of the state legislature, who served for the next two years. Mayor Stith was remarkably candid about the political role of the police, acknowledging that "the force is mainly constituted of men favorable to the principles which are professed by the American Party" and asserting that the "efficiency of the department requires that the men who compose it, so long as they take a part and feel an interest in politics, should sympathize with the chief in political opinion." But Stith sought to limit the influence of political partiality on police appointments, noting that the force did include "many . . . adopted citizens" and that "political brawlers, and those who would make their injudicious activity at the polls a passport to office, have not been preferred." As proof that merit was important, he noted that 269 men had been dismissed from the force during the first fifteen months of his administration. Stith castigated the New Orleans police for their political involvement, describing the "entire police organization of the city" as "radically wrong" and recommending that they be made independent of municipal politics and placed under the authority of the state legislature. Such a change took place in New York in 1857, in Baltimore, St. Louis, and Kansas City in the early 1860s, and in other cities later. It did not happen in New Orleans until 1868, and like the other cities in which the state took control of their police forces, the reform changed the party that controlled the police but did not extricate the police from politics.[24]

After June 1858, election days ceased to be times of bloodletting and terror, at least for a while. The American party held such complete control of municipal government—despite being defunct at the state and national levels—that the Democrats, hobbled as well by a deep split within their party, had difficulty turning out voters. As one Democratic newspaper reported in April 1861, "It is now becoming a trite remark that in our city the quietest days of the year are those on which elections are held." Thus elections had become peaceful and their outcome predictable.[25]

Policemen in New Orleans lived and worked in a world of chronic and pervasive violence. Few other cities in the United States in the 1850s could have matched the level of violence in New Orleans; indeed, the Crescent City may well have been the darkest stain on the butcher's apron. Virtually the dueling capital of the South, a major headquarters for career criminals, site of some of the most intense ethnic strife in the country, New Orleans earned a reputation as one of the most dangerous places in America.

Widespread carrying of revolvers, duckfoot and pepperbox pistols, knives, and slungshots was routine in New Orleans (a slungshot was a lead ball connected by a wire to a short wooden handle—a pocket-sized, unspiked version of the deadly medieval morningstar). An Englishman traveling in the United States at midcentury, Edward Sullivan, encountered this practice in the Crescent City, where he attended one of the renowned quadroon balls. "These balls take place," Sullivan reported,

> in a large saloon: at the entrance, where you pay half a dollar, you are requested to leave your *implements*, by which is meant your bowie-knife and revolvers; and you leave them as you would your overcoat on going to the opera, and get a ticket with their number, and on the way out they are returned to you. You hear the pistol and bowie-knife keeper in the arms-room call out, "No. 46—a six-barreled repeater." "No. 100—one eight-barrelled revolver, and bowie knife with a deaths'-head and cross-bones cut on the handle." "No. 95—a brace of double-barrels." All this is done as naturally as possible, and you see fellows fasten on their knives and pistols as coolly as if they were trying on a comforter or putting on a coat.
>
> As I was going up stairs, after getting my ticket, and replying to the quiet request, "whether I would leave my arms," that I had none to leave, I was stopped and searched from head to foot by a policeman, who, I suppose, fancied it impossible that I should be altogether without arms. Notwithstanding all this care murders and duels are of weekly occurrence at these balls, and during my stay at New Orleans there were three. There are more murders here than in any other city in the union.[26]

The invention of the revolver and its circulation into widespread ownership provided Americans from the late 1830s onward with a lethal weapon well adapted to urban use. It was more reliable in wet weather than the flintlock; the percussion system of ignition was united in one mechanism with a rotating cylinder to permit five or six shots in rapid succession. The user was limited only by the speed with which he could cock the hammer and pull the trigger and his accuracy in aiming the piece. The device did have mechanical deficiencies. It was prone to accidental discharge and misfire, the crude sights allowed a large error in aiming, and the black powder that propelled the separate lead bullet corroded the chambers when the gun was left loaded for any length of time. Most models were, however, small enough to be concealed upon the person.[27]

New Orleans policemen armed themselves with revolvers in the 1850s, in violation of the law and in response to the arming of the public. During the 1840s policemen armed only with spontoons or clubs had frequently confronted citizens carrying firearms. Officer James Norton of the First Municipality was shot to death in 1840 while attempting to execute a warrant, and in the scuffle his partner, Thomas McGovern, was stabbed several times. Eight years later policeman John Foster was found floating in the Claiborne Canal, dead of a gunshot wound received in the line of duty. Other police officers were shot but, like Thomas Hennessey in 1847, survived. Yet others, including Corporal Petard of the Third Municipality, were fired on without suffering wounds or death. Working under such conditions placed a considerable demand on policemen's courage. The temptation to look or run the other way when faced by armed opponents must have been strong. Some did resist the temptation. A night policeman named Kruse in 1840 interceded in a domestic quarrel to wrestle a gun away from an irate husband and was fortunate enough to avoid injury. In 1844 the captain of the guard in the Second Municipality, J. L. Winter, captured in a swamp outside of the city a murder suspect who was armed with "one of Colts revolving pistols."[28]

The burgeoning political conflict of the 1850s and the proliferation of revolvers in private ownership made it increasingly unrealistic for the public or the city's governors to expect the police to arm themselves less formidably than their opponents. In September 1854, the *Daily True Delta* observed that "it is all nonsense to expect a police armed with batons only, to disperse mobs of ruffians conscious of impunity for their crimes, and armed to the teeth with murderous weapons." Mayor John Lewis addressed the Common Council the following month to request limited authority to arm the police: "The propriety, also, under certain exigencies, of arming the force merits due consideration; at present the law forbids their being armed. In cases like those which have recently occurred, it is hardly fair to require unarmed men to march up and quell a mob or riot, and be met by an array of deadly weapons in the hands of their opponents."[29]

But the police had already taken the matter into their own hands. At the trial of a policeman indicted for murder, Chief of Police William James testified that during the September, 1854, riots following the arrest of Henry Sherman, "it was usual for the police to carry arms. Witness [James] had several times given orders to the police to carry arms when sent on some special duty." The new practice took root despite its illegality. A policeman who carried a concealed weapon—and most apparently did conceal their guns, knives, and slungshots—broke the law just as surely as other citizens who did so, for the statute covering the offense exempted no one. The punishment for a first offense was lenient: until March, 1855, a maximum fine of fifty dollars and thereafter one month in jail or a maximum fine of five hundred dollars. In September 1855, Mayor Lewis wrote to Chief of Police Alexander Moynan that "inasmuch as it is reported that members of the police department in this city are in the habit of carrying concealed weapons, and there being no law permitting them to do so, I direct that you issue peremptory orders, commanding a cessation of the practice in the department."[30]

This order proved ineffectual, and Lewis soon showed at least a partial change of heart. When he swore in special policemen for the municipal election in June 1856, he advised them to arm themselves before reporting for duty at the polls. Despite its illegality, the revolver became a basic tool of the policeman's trade during the remainder of the decade. Knives and slungshots also found their way into the waistbands and pockets of some policemen. In 1854 a policeman was dismissed from the force for drawing a knife on his sergeant, and two others were brought up on charges for resorting to knives in 1856. When policeman W. Oscar Somers was murdered on his levee beat in 1860, his partner, Peter McMullen, testified that Somers carried a "Colt's five shooter" and a slungshot, the same armament borne by McMullen. "When the officers go upon the Levee," observed McMullen, "they have to be like arsenals."[31]

Police adoption of firearms led to accidents. Lacking any training in safety or marksmanship, members of the police force had no claim to technical mastery of their guns. In one instance, a police officer accidentally shot his partner in the head, killing him, when the two men broke into a room to make an arrest while carrying cocked revolvers. A former policeman who was sitting in a coffee house in November 1859, lost his life when accidentally shot by a day police officer. Another policeman drew his revolver to stop a brawl and shot an innocent bystander by mistake. One unfortunate member of the river police patrol attempted to pull a gun from underneath a boat seat and fatally wounded himself when he caught the hammer on a projection and involuntarily discharged the piece.[32]

Deliberate misuse of firearms also became a serious problem. In 1854 policeman Michael Nugent dispatched a man he believed to be trifling with his wife by shooting him in the head. In that same year, one of the chief's special officers (special officers performed detective duties) drew his revolver on a militia captain without identifying himself as a policeman. The special officer lost his job but was subsequently reappointed to the force and came before the Board of Police again the following year for drawing a gun and threatening to shoot a butcher in one of the city's meat markets. He escaped punishment on the charge, but another policeman who drew his gun to settle a dispute was dismissed from the force. One policeman attempted to shoot the sergeant but was clubbed and sent to the hospital by the roundsman. Two officers were arrested in 1856 for beating and shooting a citizen, but their poor marksmanship kept them from being charged with murder, manslaughter, or mayhem. During a gun battle between a policeman and a private citizen in Canal Street, the latter discharged five shots without harming his opponent, while the policeman fired two ineffectual shots before his revolver misfired and jammed.[33]

Mere possession of a revolver did not confer safety on the carrier. It put policemen on the same footing as a large segment of the public, who commonly carried deadly weapons. The custom was not new, but it posed even greater danger to life and health because of the increase in political and ethnic strife and the greater availability of efficient lethal weaponry. The state legislature in 1855 enacted a slightly stricter law against carrying concealed weapons. But in his report for 1856, the state attorney general observed that the number of crimes of violence was growing. In the four years 1857-1860, at least 225 criminal homicides were committed in New Orleans, an annual rate of about 35 per 100,000 of population. (In Philadelphia and in Boston it was about 7.5 during the years 1855-1859.) In the latter half of the 1850s, the attorney general complained about the crime in New Orleans, stating that the police force was ineffective, witnesses to crimes were frequently afraid to testify, too many people were exempted from jury service, jurors received no per diem compensation and were called for too many days of service, the recorders' courts failed to keep written records of testimony in preliminary hearings, and the district attorney's office was grossly undermanned and overworked. As a consequence, the criminal justice system was not very effective at catching or prosecuting murder suspects; of the murders committed during 1857-1859, only 21.5 percent were resolved by conviction on a charge of either murder or manslaughter.[34]

The police suffered in this violent environment. At least seven policemen were murdered while on duty from 1854 through 1860. John and William Mocler died of wounds received in the election riots of March 1854. John Dunn was stabbed to death at the polls the following year. In 1856 Alexander Algeo was shot in the head and died, leaving a widow and two children. When police officer Gustave Lafferanderie was stabbed to death in 1860, he also left a family without a breadwinner. W. Oscar Somers was murdered in May of the same year, and James McIntosh was killed in December.[35]

Over a period of four years, at least eight policemen received gunshot wounds which they survived. One of them was the same Gustave Lafferanderie who would be killed in 1860; he was shot in the thigh in 1856 while wrestling a pistol away from a man he was attempting to arrest. Others encountered pistol-wielding assailants with less dire consequences, and still others were threatened with being shot. Knife-wielding assailants were also a danger. In the same four-year period, at least seven policemen were stabbed while on the job without fatal results. Many others were beaten in the course of their work. One former policeman narrowly escaped being hanged in revenge for an arrest he had made while on the force; a bystander intervened to rescue him from three assailants. An assault could be charged with indignity as well as danger, as one officer discovered when he became the target for "slops, urine and other filthy matter" thrown by five individuals while he stood on the corner of Julia and Levee streets.[36]

Some of the men who joined the police force brought with them a taste for violence that was fed by their work. Several policemen of the 1850s stood trial for murder. Antoine Cambre, a native of Plaquemines Parish and formerly a carpenter, was a Know Nothing appointee in 1855. Cambre also worked as a ballroom watchman (a notorious occupation because ballrooms were linked to many illegal activities). In 1859 he shot and killed a German lamplighter whom he mistook for another man with whom he had a score to settle. He was subsequently convicted of murder and sentenced to death. Cambre cheated the hangman by dying of a fever in prison. He shared a cell with Eugene Adams, another former policeman, who had been convicted in the stabbing murder of one man not long after having shot another. Adams was rumored to be willing to offer evidence in another murder case but was soon thereafter found in his cell dead of poison.[37]

One of the most gruesome cases of the decade involved police officer Jean Gros. Gros slipped into the room in which his free quadroon mistress lay sleeping beside her six-year-old son and shot her through the head with his pistol. The result was, according to a newspaper account, that "one side of the head was blown off and the bed and wall bespattered with bone, hair and brains, while a stream of gore had run down upon the floor in pools." Gros escaped by cab and was presumed by the police to have left the city. Six months later, the murdered woman's mother noticed him sitting in a house as she walked past one Saturday evening. She turned her head away and walked to the corner, then ran to a police station. Three officers returned with her and made the arrest, but he was eventually released and the district attorney entered a *nolle prosequi* in the case.[38]

One of the most enduring men of violent appetite who served on the police force was Arthur Guerin, a native of New Orleans. He lost his job as a policeman in 1855 after knifing two men, and in the two months thereafter he was arrested once for stabbing a man, once for assaulting a girl, and once for shooting a man in the back. He managed to stay out of prison, however, and in subsequent years was acquitted of murder on three occasions. He died in a courtroom in 1871, shot to death by a deputy sheriff who claimed Guerin had menaced him. Another policeman came to grief in a courtroom in 1856. Nathaniel McCann, known as "Old Hardweather" to his compatriots, was dismissed from the force and sought out a recorder to plead for reinstatement. When the magistrate refused to hear the case any further, McCann shot him in the neck with a pistol, but a policeman seized the gun and clubbed McCann to the floor. Another particularly serious offender on the police force was John Poole. Poole struck a black man in 1853, and his victim fell into the water and drowned, resulting in a murder charge against Poole.[39]

Other policemen were prosecuted or at least arrested for serious crimes. A policeman who committed robbery was nearly charged with murder when his victim died soon after the robbery; the coroner ruled that pneumonia was the cause of death, so the policeman faced only a count of robbery. A former police lieutenant, who had once been shot by Eugene Adams, was himself arrested for shooting two men. In 1857 the chief of police and his special officers, acting on a tip, lay in wait outside the home of a widow in the fourth district, expecting a burglary. When four burglars appeared shortly after midnight, the police fired on the men, wounding one in the thigh. The others escaped, but the wounded man proved to be a member of the police force.[40]

Violent behavior characterized the lives of many policemen in a variety of other ways. In one instance, two policemen were arrested by their commanding officer for attempting to fight a duel. Another time, a police captain was accused of participating in a lynching in Biloxi, Mississippi. Leaving the police department did not end a man's violent behavior. Several former policemen were arrested in 1854 in a plot to drown an active member of the force. Others died in the streets or in coffee houses as participants in brawls and shooting affrays. Less severe episodes of violence were legion. In a sample of cases covering a twenty-one-month period during 1854-1856, the Board of Police adjudicated forty-three cases of assault, assault and battery, or brutality by policemen, dismissing thirteen of the accused from the force and penalizing nine others with fines or loss of rank. Almost certainly many instances of police misuse of force never eventuated in any formal charges, or went unreported.[41]

The problem of violence in New Orleans was multifaceted and complex, deriving from many sources. New Orleans was a large city—the most populous in the Deep South—and perhaps more ethnically diverse than any other in the United States (though certainly New York, St. Louis, and Milwaukee were also diverse). It was a major port with many trade relationships with Latin America and second only to New York as a port of entry for immigrants in the 1850s. It had a large transient population of sailors, boatmen, and commercial travelers, and once the danger of yellow fever in the late summer and early autumn was over, the city experienced a large seasonal influx of population, including many professional criminals. As a Southern city, New Orleans had problems distinctive to the region. The institution of slavery helped brutalize the sensibilities of whites. Widely prevailing notions of masculine honor spurred gentlemen and workingmen alike to retributive acts of violence, in formal duels and informal brawls, whenever they perceived any slight or insult. Prickly personalities more readily indulged in bellicose behavior when or after visiting one of the city's thousands of saloons and coffee houses that dispensed alcoholic beverages. The large number of men who went about formidably armed made affrays more likely to result in deaths or serious injuries.[42]

To ameliorate the problem of violence to any substantial degree would have required state and municipal policies—and perhaps federal policies as well—for which there was not enough political or community support in the 1850s. Similarly, any realistic strategy to restrict or prohibit police use of arms would have necessitated a comparable policy to limit or prohibit ownership and carrying of firearms by all citizens, which was a political impossibility. With the exception of some decline in the level of political conflict, violence remained largely untouched by government policy in New Orleans in the late antebellum period.

The formal law and the public generally expected the police to catch criminals and suppress crime, to maintain order, and to render emergency aid to the victims of crime, accident, and misfortune. The crime-fighting role was perhaps the most dramatic of these—although maintaining order could sometimes become a spectacle—but most police work fell into the latter two categories. For a policeman to catch a criminal in the act was a rare and usually celebrated event. On one occasion, a policeman observed a black man stealing a thousand-dollar bill that had been dropped by a white man who was intoxicated and half asleep. The officer gave chase and after a long run captured the thief and restored the bank note to its owner. Long pursuits sometimes occurred, and New Orleans policemen made several arrests after tracking their prey to remote parts of Louisiana or, in one case, all the way to Illinois. Premeditated crimes were, however, very difficult to stop and their perpetrators very elusive. Policemen who succeeded in making arrests in such cases had to learn the skills of a detective, using informants, promising leniency for confessions, coercing and intimidating potential informants, and identifying the likeliest suspects from discernible patterns of criminal behavior.[43]

As maintainers of order, the police enforced a host of laws and ordinances proscribing public intoxication, disturbing the peace, vagrancy, and other minor offenses. They devoted considerably more time to this category of enforcement than to more serious crimes. Strikes, riots, traffic control, and Mardi Gras celebrations all fell within the police purview of keeping order. Riots were the most extreme form of disorder and often exposed the weaknesses in police training, organization, and discipline.[44]

A regionally distinctive example of the police responsibility for preserving order was the problem of slavery. Slaves had more laws to violate than did whites or free people of color, for they were forbidden to congregate in cabarets, buy liquor, gamble, walk the streets after curfew, rent rooms, or even move about without a pass. In addition to the normal police patrolling to curb such offenses, in one instance a police sergeant disguised himself as an African American to capture a cabaret keeper in the act of selling liquor to slaves. The fear of slave insurrection lay behind the plethora of legal restrictions on bondsmen, and the press was quick to congratulate policemen who claimed to have nipped an uprising in the bud.[45]

Maintaining the "moral" order of society (a nebulous notion) was also one of their tasks. The police made arrests for simple intoxication, gambling, prostitution, and circulation of "obscene and improper" publications. They even arrested women for wearing men's clothing. Enforcement of the laws against gambling and prostitution offered immense opportunity for malfeasance. The exact extent of clandestine corruption can only be a matter for conjecture, but the occasional scandals and grand jury reports of extensive networks of graft suggest that the problem was huge and remained largely unremedied.[46]

The police also helped the needy. Policemen transported the sick and injured to Charity Hospital, attempted to prevent suicides, and responded to emergencies. In one instance, a police corporal pulled a drunken man from a rapidly filling gutter during a rainstorm, saving him from drowning. They were also called upon to succor lost children and find their families. The police played a major role as a primitive relief agency, sheltering the homeless in the city's jails, where men and women lodged and fed (minimally) without charge or penalty and in large numbers during inclement weather.[47]

Although arrest data are notoriously biased and fragmentary indicators of police activity, a compilation of arrest reports from the 1850s suggests some of its dimensions (see Table III). Most involved minor offenses related to maintaining order. Intoxication, disturbing the peace, vagrancy, suspicion, and minor assaults accounted for about two-thirds of all arrests, and arrests for slavery-related offenses constituted an additional one-eighth of the total. The gravest violations, murder and other serious violent crimes, were less than one-twentieth of all arrests and, when added to professional crimes for profit, barely exceeded one-tenth. In addition, a total of 2,505 persons, mostly overnight lodgers, received help from the police from November 1853, through January 1856. Most official police activity involved routine transactions.

If arrests had been equally shared among policemen, each man would have made about forty-seven per year in the mid-1850s. During the summer and early autumn the population of the city fell to its annual nadir, and arrests dropped accordingly. Few women were arrested except for gambling and prostitution. Females accounted for only 17.1 percent of all arrests, but they constituted 71.1 percent of those in the gambling-prostitution category—and almost all prostitution-related arrestees were women. In 1850-51, 25.3 percent of those arrested in the First and Third municipalities were slaves or free persons of color, with slaves predominating over free blacks by slightly better than two to one. (African Americans made up 30.8 percent of the 1850 population of these two districts.)[48]

TABLE III
Police Arrests, November, 1853 - January, 1856

Offense	% of Total Arrests	No. of Arrests
Intoxication and disturbing the peace	39.3	19,363
Vagrancy and suspicion	17.8	8,786
Assault and battery, other minor crimes of violence	13.3	6,542
Slavery-related offenses	12.4	6,090
Professional crimes for profit	7.5	3,669
Serious crimes of violence, excluding murder	3.2	1,567
Gambling and prostitution	1.4	675
Murder-related offenses	0.3	124
Other unclassified	4.8	2,436
Totals	100.0	49,252

Sources: Daily Picayune, June 15, December 12, 15, 1854, January 7, February 24, March 18, April 22, May 12, 1855; Police Board Records.

Evidence regarding the nativity of arrestees in this period is very sparse. The federal census for 1850 included the inmates of the First Municipality jail: the Irish were highly overrepresented, natives slightly overrepresented, and immigrants other than Irish very underrepresented.[49]

Some arrests involved a highly controversial form of police activity—misconduct. When a police officer was accused of wrongdoing, his supervisors suspended him temporarily, and if the charge was serious, his case would be heard before the Board of Police during the years 1853-1856 or by the mayor in the other years of the period. The number of temporary suspensions was staggering, two or three per policeman each year, but between two-thirds and four-fifths of these suspensions did not lead to trial before the board. Yet even the minority of cases that came to trial revealed a glaring incidence of delinquency. During the year before the Know Nothings came to power, more than one-fourth of the police force was dismissed for cause and one-sixth more received punishment by spending additional time under suspension before being retained.[50]

Derelictions of duty constituted the largest category of offenses. These included standing, sitting, lying down, or sleeping on the beat; drinking on the job; and other forms of neglect. This class of offenses also drew the second highest proportion of dismissals. Abuse of authority was the next most numerous category and included brutality, interference in elections, extortion, and other forms of misfeasance and malfeasance. Disruption of the chain of command was a distant third in numerical rank but was the type of offense most likely to result in dismissal from the force. It included disobedience, insubordination, improper treatment of patrolmen by supervisors, and intrapolice assaults. Incidents of misbehavior off duty (or "conduct unbecoming a police officer") were fewer than disruptions of the chain of command.[51]

The records of police delinquency indicate that Irish policemen were substantially more likely to be brought before the Board of Police than were others. They were, however, slightly less likely to be dismissed from the force than other men on trial, both before and after the American party had consolidated its power over the police department in May 1855.[52]

One source of problematic behavior was the city's failure to train its policemen. One police chief made a brief effort to offer guidance to his men. When Chief Stephen O'Leary's force went on duty for the first time in May 1853, he lectured the men on the responsibilities of their job. O'Leary "explained what he conceived to be the best method of carrying" out the "minor details of police duties" and discouraged brutality and religious or national prejudices. Although the first manual for policemen was issued in 1852, no apparent effort was made to ensure that they were familiar with its contents.[53]

Most new appointees to the force first became supernumeraries. This was a probationary status; the supernumerary officers worked as substitutes for absentees among the regulars. These men were required to report for roll call daily but only occasionally got the chance to work. "In my present situation," wrote one supernumerary in the early 1860s, "I work only a few days in the month and barely earn enough to get through life."

Another wrote that "as a Supernumary I cannot gain a livelihood." Several men complained of their inability to earn enough to support their families. One man went so far as to assert that the "system of supernumeraries is a humbug, by reducing the men to the level of serfs."[54]

Policemen received no sick pay except by special dispensation of the Common Council, and they could not look forward to pensions. Turnover of personnel was high, ranging from 30 to 60 percent annually among the regulars, though by 1860-1861 the rate had dripped to 17 percent. Absenteeism was also high, running between 13 and 20 percent. Although many men served on the force for a short period, some persisted for years, often discontinuously, and so constituted a core of experienced veterans. They were probably the best policemen in some ways, but they also had the greatest opportunity to partake of graft. For most, policing was a short-term occupation. Untrained, they impressed their individuality on the beat in a highly informal, personalized style.[55]

Their economic status may also have had a significant influence on policemen's behavior. Most fell below the white population median in wealth and income but came from or soon achieved a status materially above the bottom rungs of the socioeconomic ladder. Patrolmen received a salary of $45 per month from 1852 to 1855 and $50 thereafter. The daily wage of $1.50 to $1.70 was more than the $1.00 to $1.50 earned by day laborers. Patrolmen's compensation was below that of carpenters, which was $2.30 and up, and longshoremen, who made between $2.50 and $3.00 per diem. Policemen were subject to less seasonal unemployment than day laborers and many skilled laborers, however, and had opportunities for illegal compensation through graft. Barring illness, injury, or a change in administration, their standard of living surpassed that of day laborers.[56]

Policemen were about as likely as any white adult male to own as much as $100 of personal property, but only a few owned real estate. Supervisory officers fared better than patrolmen: sergeants earned $55 to $58 per month, lieutenants $55 to $83, captains $75 to $100, and the chief $167. Several chiefs of police were modestly prosperous. The first chief of the period, John Youenes, was assessed for tax purposes on real estate worth $6,670 and two slaves valued at a total of $1,000. William James appeared in the tax books with $1,500 in real estate and one slave worth $600. Henry Forno, the chief who left the city during the Vigilance Committee crisis of 1858, owned real estate with a taxable value of $4,500 in 1852 and in 1856 held $1,500 plus slaves assessed at $1,000 altogether. He also owned a home outside the city that was not subject to municipal taxation. Other supervisory officers below the rank of chief also owned real estate.[57]

The case histories of a few men suggest that those with education tended to rise more than other men. Formal schooling was not, however, the surest route to upward mobility in the police department. Political favors and personal influence were extremely valuable in furthering a career. During the early 1860s, for example, several applicants for police jobs were endorsed by influential men under whom they had previously served, including former mayor Gerard Stith, former chief of police John Youenes, and businessman-politician Benjamin F. Flanders. Membership in a volunteer fire company could also boost a career. One police application included a recommendation from a city assessor, who asserted that the candidate's "appointment would be acceptable he having been a regular fireman of Louisiana Co. No. 10 in which company he became exempt after Seven or Eight years since." Further evidence of the value of belonging to a fire company can be found in a sample of the 1855 Know Nothing appointees, at least 21 percent and perhaps considerably more of whom were members of fire companies.[58]

Politics clearly influenced the police department, but some people—perhaps many—were displeased by that influence. Civil service was not adopted in New Orleans until 1889, but even in the 1850s there was support for a nonpartisan merit principle. In 1854, Mayor John Lewis and Recorder H. M. Summers advocated hiring on merit. Mayor Charles Waterman offered a brief and ineffectual plea in 1856 for the eradication of the "political features" of the force. His successor, Gerard Stith, advanced a more forceful—though ineffectual—proposal for reform in 1858, arguing for the economic benefit of a nonpartisan police department: "If a law should be enacted by the Legislature making the tenure of office dependent on good behavior and peculiar efficiency, thus elevating the present mere temporary appointments into the dignity of a profession, and securing as officers only such as had proved to possess special qualifications for their duties, it might be possible to accomplish more good with a small police force." Making policemen independent of the results of municipal elections would, he advised, remove the incentive to favor members of their own party. Both the *Louisiana Courier*, a Democratic paper, and the moderately Know Nothing *Daily Picayune* endorsed Stith's recommendation. Stith repeated this recommendation in 1859, but again to no avail.[59]

Reform proponents debated the most effective way to reduce partisan influence on the police. Calling the police department the most abused of municipal institutions, the *Daily True Delta* in 1859 branded both the mayoral and police board systems of control as failures. "Whatever party may possess the power, so long as it is deposited as at present, will prostitute it to its own advancement and perpetuation of its rule in office." Mayor Stith suggested electing a board of police commissioners composed of two persons from each ward. Noting that this inevitably meant two persons of the party then in power, the *Daily Delta* argued for a board of commissioners to be appointed by the governor or the legislature. Support for this proposal came also from the *Daily True Delta*, which stressed the success of the English system of commissioners appointed by the national government. The state legislature eventually produced a police reform bill that would create a board of commissioners, but not until January 1862, and its effect was undercut by the Union occupation in April of that year.[60]

Their involvement in politics was not the only complaint about the police. The parish grand jury as well as several newspapers objected to their inefficiency and their entanglement in a web of corruption. In 1854 the grand jury found that there was "every reason to believe that there has been a general system of dishonesty and peculation carried on for some time past in the First District at least." Gambling dens and bordellos operated in defiance of the law and on such a large scale as to require police protection. Another common complaint against the police was simple inefficiency: they caught too few criminals. Also, some people found the police to be uncooperative in working with other departments of city government.[61]

Reform efforts were largely ineffectual in this period. A minor reform, putting the police back into uniforms, seemed about to succeed in the middle of the decade. The ordinance that led to the reorganization of 1855 also authorized the mayor to provide uniforms for the force. After a considerable delay, the mayor ordered the chief of police to have the day force outfitted in a blue frock coat, with standing collar and metal buttons.[62]

The Common Council objected to the expense of the uniforms, said they were too conspicuous, and complained about purchasing city-owned uniforms for a force whose personnel changed frequently. The aldermen considered the crescent badge a sufficient symbol of police authority, but some of the men refused to display it. In other cities, especially New York and Philadelphia, policemen disliked wearing a uniform because, according to the New York correspondent for the *New Orleans Bee*, it was a "kind of dishonorable livery." Police resisted uniforms and even badges because an obvious and distinctive uniform would make shirking more difficult. Renewed attempts in the Crescent City to adopt a police uniform in 1858 and again in 1860 failed as well.[63]

A few minor reforms did occur in the late antebellum period. Chief Stephen O'Leary had begun a rogues' gallery of daguerreotypes of professional criminals as early as 1853, but the project withered without an appropriation of funds from the Common Council. When the council refused to authorize money for the purpose in 1858, Chief Thomas Adams began daguerreotyping prominent criminals at his own expense. The council finally funded the operation beginning in February 1860. A few months later, the city completed and put into service a fire alarm and police telegraph system. It was more valuable to firefighting than policing because it merely allowed the several district stations to communicate directly with one another and made no provision for emergency signals from citizens to police or from beat patrolmen to the station.[64]

These small reforms did little to improve the quality of policing in New Orleans.[65] Ironically, the most popular reform of this period was achieved by the state legislature: the consolidation of the police forces of the three formerly independent municipalities and the city of Lafayette as part the formal reunification and expansion of the city of New Orleans. But at the end of this period the police force satisfied only a narrow segment of the public—for the most part white nativists—and them only partially. Recruited from the ranks of the American party; commanded by stridently partisan politicians; subject to only intermittent supervision on the job; lacking training, sick pay, pensions, attractive salaries, compensation for experience, and a uniform to emphasize the official character of their role, the police continued to display an individualistic, partisan, and frequently abusive style of operation.

Notes for "A Perfect Hell on Earth:" A Time of Troubles in the Reunified City, 1852-1861"

[1]William Howard Russell, *My Diary North and South* (Boston, 1863), 244.

[2]James F. Richardson, *Urban Police in the United States* (London, 1974), 19-34; David R. Johnson, *American Law Enforcement: A History* (St. Louis, 1981), 17-33; Samuel Walker, *Popular Justice: A History of American Criminal Justice* (New York, 1980), 59-65; Allen Steinberg, *The Transformation of Criminal Justice: Philadelphia, 1800-1880* (Chapel Hill, 1989), 119-82; Roger Lane, *Policing the City: Boston, 1822-1885* (Cambridge, Mass., 1967), 37-105.

[3]*Daily Picayune*, February 29, 1852; *Acts of Louisiana*, 1852, pp. 42-57.

[4]For opposition to the appointment of Youenes, see *Daily Crescent*, April 27, 1852. Youenes was about thirty-five when appointed as chief. He ran unsuccessfully for coroner as a Whig in November 1853, held the post of city fire warden in the late 1850s, supported the presidential candidacy of John Bell in 1860, and served as an artillery officer in the Confederate army. The U. S. census listed his birthplace as Louisiana, but his death certificate showed his birthplace as Holland (New Orleans Death Certificates, 63, 82; Andrew B. Booth, comp., *Records of Louisiana Confederate Soldiers and Louisiana Confederate Commands* (New Orleans, 1920); *Daily Picayune*, April 15, 1852, February 21, 1856, February 21, 1875; *Daily Delta*, November 9, 1853; *Daily Crescent*, July 2, 1860; *Bee*, August 9, 1860.

[5]*Daily Picayune*, April 28, 1853; *Daily True Delta*, April 28, May 3, 1853; *Daily Orleanian*, April 4, 1854; *Daily Crescent*, November 1, 1853; *Louisiana Courier*, October 21, 1853; *Acts of Louisiana*, 1853, pp. 79-83. O'Leary served as an infantry captain in the Confederate army (Booth, comp., *Records of Louisiana Confederate Soldiers*). Although O'Leary was the first Irish-born chief of police for the entire city, Daniel Kennedy of County Limerick, Ireland, had become captain of the city guard in the Third Municipality in 1848—the first Irishman to hold the highest police rank possible in that period (New Orleans Death Certificates, 57, 511; *Daily Picayune*, March 26, 1873.

[6]*Daily True Delta*, November 3, 1852, May 17, 1853; *Daily Picayune*, March 24, 1852, November 10, 1853; *Daily Crescent*, November 5, 1852, November 3, 8, 1853; *Daily Delta*, November 4, 1852; *Louisiana Courier*, October 21, November 7, 1853.

[7]*Louisiana Courier*, March 28-31, 1854; *Daily True Delta*, March 29, 1854; *Daily Crescent*, March 28, 1854; *Daily Picayune*, March 28, 1854; *Daily Delta*, March 28, 1854.

[8]James, a native of New Orleans, was thirty-two years old when he became chief. He had served as chief deputy sheriff of Orleans Parish during the late 1840s under then sheriff John Lewis (*Daily Picayune*, August 27-28, September 1-3, 1854; *Daily True Delta*, August 26, 1854; *Times Democrat*, May 22, 1908).

[9]*Daily True Delta*, August 26, October 4, 1854; *Daily Crescent*, October 5, 1854; *Bee*, April 24, 1854; Police Board Records, New Orleans Public Library (hereafter cited as NOPL), April 15, 18, 1854.

[10]*Daily True Delta*, September 12-21, 1854; *Louisiana Courier*, September 12-20, 1854; *Daily Picayune*, September 11, 1854.

[11]*Daily True Delta*, September 14, 17, 1854; *Louisiana Courier*, September 13, 1854; *Daily Crescent*, September 11-21, 1854; *Daily Picayune*, September 12, 16, 17, 19, 1854.

[12]James was a Democrat, though his party compatriots subsequently branded him a turncoat for his role in the impeachment of Ramos and Seuzeneau (*Daily Crescent*, September 22, 1854; *Louisiana Courier*, March 26, 27, 1855; *Daily Picayune*, September 21, 1854, March 25-27, April 10, 1855; Police Board Records, September 21, 1854). The Common Council, which was the legislative branch of city government, had two chambers: a Board of Aldermen with eleven members and a Board of Assistant Aldermen with twenty-four members. In 1856, the membership of the boards was reduced to nine and fifteen, respectively (*Acts of Louisiana*, 1852, pp. 42-55, and 1856, pp. 136-37).

[13]*Daily Picayune*, April 10, 12, 13, 22, 1855; *Daily True Delta*, April 13, 15, 17, 18, 20, 21, 1855; *Louisiana Courier*, April 10, 13, 1855; *Bee*, April 12, 1855.

[14]Ordinances and Resolutions of the Common Council, NOPL, No. 2100, April 5, 1855; *Daily Picayune*, July 22, September 17, 18, October 23, 1855.

[15]Applications for Positions as Police Officers, 1862-65, for William Gotts and John Gallagher, Records of U. S. Army Continental Commands, 1821-1920, Part I, No. 1852, Record Group 393, National Archives (hereafter cited as RG 393, NA).

[16]Police Board Records, March 8, December 6, 1855; *Bee*, December 12, 1855; *Daily Picayune*, April 23, 1856; *Daily True Delta*, April 23, 1856; *The Seventh Census of the United States: 1850* (Washington, D. C., 1853), 474; *Population of the United States in 1860* (Washington, D. C., 1864), 195.

[17]*Daily Picayune*, August 31, November 6, 7, 1855; *Louisiana Courier*, November 4, 6, 8, 1855; *Commercial Bulletin*, November 8, 1855; *Daily Crescent*, November 7, 8, 1855; *Daily True Delta*, November 7, 1855; Police Board Records, August 30, November 20, 1855.

[18]Police Board Records, November 22, 1855; *Daily Picayune*, November 23, 1855, February 24, March 8, June 3, 4, 14, 1856; *Daily True Delta*, June 3, 1856; *Louisiana Courier*, June 3, 4, 1856; *Acts of Louisiana*, 1856, pp. 19-20, 131-36; Leon Cyprian Soulé, *The Know Nothing Party in New Orleans: A Reappraisal* (Baton Rouge, 1961), 86-90. Soulé's is the best overall account of the American party in New Orleans.

[19]Moynan may have been influenced to resign by the death of his wife in June 1856. He later served as a private in the Confederate army and died in 1864 (*Daily Picayune*, March 14, June 16, 1856; *Louisiana Courier*, March 25, June 17, December 14, 17, 1856, April 10, 1859; *Daily True Delta*, March 6, 1856; *Bee*, March 25, 31, December 17, 1856; Police Board Records, June 28, August 23, 1855, *Acts of Louisiana*, 1853, p. 171, and 1854, p. 133; Booth, comp., *Records of Louisiana Confederate Soldiers*).

[20]*Daily Picayune*, June 18, November 4, 5, 1856; *Louisiana Courier*, June 19, November 5-7, 1856; *Bee*, November 4-6, 1856.

[21]*Louisiana Courier*, November 3, 1857, June 5, 1858; *Daily Picayune*, November 3, 1857; *Daily True Delta*, November 3, 4, 1857, June 3-5, 8, 1858; *Bee*, June 4, 5, 7, 1858; Earl F. Niehaus, *The Irish in New Orleans, 1800-1860* (Baton Rouge, 1965), 96.

[22]*Communication of Charles M. Waterman, Mayor of the City of New Orleans, to the Board of Assistant Aldermen, and Their Action Thereon* (*June 18, 1858*) (New Orleans, 1858); *Daily Picayune*, June 5, 7, 8, 1858; *Louisiana Courier*, June 6, 8, 1858; *Daily Crescent*, June 7, 1858. Forno, a native of Charleston, South Carolina, distinguished himself in the Mexican War and as a colonel in the Confederate army, so lack of courage seems an unlikely explanation for his behavior in this instance. A rumor circulated in the city to the effect that he had accepted a bribe to withdraw. In any event, he died after the Civil War as the result of a locomotive boiler explosion (*Daily Crescent*, February 2, 3, 5, 1866; *Daily Picayune*, February 1-4, 1866; Soulé, *Know Nothing Party in New Orleans*, 94-104).

[23]*Daily Crescent*, June 8, 1858; *Bee*, June 8, 9, 1858.

[24]*Louisiana Courier*, June 22, 1858; *Daily Picayune*, October 12, 1859; Richardson, *Urban Police*, 38-40.

[25]*Bee*, April 2, 1861.

[26]Edward Sullivan, *Rambles and Scrambles in North and South America* (London, 1852), 223-25. Comparative generalizations about the level of violent crime in nineteenth-century America are necessarily somewhat tentative and conjectural because reliable statistical evidence from that period is sparse and very difficult to find. The available quantitative and literary evidence does suggest that New Orleans had a very high level of violent crime in the 1850s, however, probably more than any other large city in the United States. Among Southern cities, the incidence of political violence was probably also high in Baltimore and Louisville. See Charles E. Deusner, "The Know Nothing Riots in Louisville," *Register of the Kentucky Historical Society*, 61 (1963): 122-

47; Wallace S. Hutcheon, Jr., "The Louisville Riots of August, 1855," *Register of the Kentucky Historical Society*, 69 (1971): 150-72; Jean H. Baker, *Ambivalent Americans: The Know Nothing Party in Maryland* (Baltimore, 1977).

[27]For a discussion of revolvers, see Lee Kennett and James LaVerne Anderson, *The Gun in America: The Origins of a National Dilemma* (Westport, Conn., 1975), 89-90; Charles T. Haven and Frank A. Belden, *A History of the Cold Revolver and the Other Arms Made by Colt's Patent Fire Arms Manufacturing Company from 1836 to 1940* (New York, 1940), 17-82; Arcadi Gluckman, *United States Martial Pistols and Revolvers* (Harrisburg, Pa., 1960), 91-93, 153-210; Frederick Wilkinson, *Antique Firearms* (Garden City, N. Y., 1969), 180-88.

Regarding the custom of carrying weapons, see Dr. Thomas L. Nichols, *Forty Years of American* Life, 2 vols. (London, 1864), 1:184-86; George Vandenhoff, *Leaves from an Actor's Note-Book; with Reminiscences and Chit-Chat of the Green-Room and the Stage, in England and America* (New York, 1860), 206-207; Charles Mackay, *Life and Liberty in America; or, Sketches of a Tour in the United States and Canada, in 1857-8*, 2 vols. (London, 1859), 1:173; J. Benwell, *An Englishman's Travels' in America: His Observations of Life and Manners in the Free and Slave States* (London, 1853), 113-16; Alex Mackay, *The Western World; or, Travels in the United States in 1846-47*, 2 vols. (Philadelphia, 1849), 2:88-89; Henry Benjamin Whipple, *Bishop Whipple's Southern Diary, 1843-1844*, ed. Lester B. Shippee (Minneapolis, 1937), 115; Louis Fitzgerald Tasistro, *Random Shots and Southern Breezes, Containing Critical Remarks on the Southern States and Southern Institutions, with Semi-Serious Observations on Men and Manners*, 2 vols. (New York, 1842), 1:229-30, 2:36-37; Duke of Saxe-Weimar Eisenach Bernhard, *Travels Through North America, During the Years 1825 and 1826*, 2 vols. (Philadelphia, 1828), 2:61, 70-71; Joseph Holt Ingraham, *The South-West: By a Yankee*, 2 vols. (New York, 1835), 1:90, 208; Henry Bradshaw Fearon, *Sketches of America*, 2d ed. (1818; reprint ed., New York, 1969), 275.

[28]*Bee*, December 25, 1840; Messages of the Mayors to the First Municipality Council, March 13, 1848; Charity Hospital Admission Books, April 5, 1847; Reports of the Day and Night Police of the Third Municipality, October 22-23, 1840 (Night Watch), November 21, 1849 (Day Police); *Daily Picayune*, May 26, 1851; Ordinances and Resolutions of the Third Municipality Council, August 11, 1851; Reports of the Day and Night Police of the Second Municipality, July 6, 1844 (Day Police).

[29]*Daily True Delta*, September 14, 1854; *Daily Picayune*, October 6, 1854.

[30]*Daily Picayune*, September 17, 1855, October 13, 1854; *Louisiana Courier*, September 19, 1855; *Acts of Louisiana*, 1813, pp. 172-74, 1855, pp. 131, 146, 1858, pp. 32-33; *The Consolidation and Revision of the Statutes of the State, of a General Nature*, comp. Levi Pierce, Miles Taylor, and William W. King (New Orleans, 1852), 187. According to a Louisiana appellate decision in 1856, even partial concealment was illegal (*State v. J. T. Smith*, 11 Louisiana Annual Reports 633 [1856]).

[31]*Bee*, June 3, 1856, October 12, 1860, January 17, 1861; *Daily True Delta*, June 28, 1860.

[32]*Daily Picayune*, August 2, 1856; *Commercial Bulletin*, August 2, 1856; *Louisiana Courier*, June 12, 1856, June 7, 1859; Charity Hospital Admission Books, June 11, 1858. The police manual issued in 1852 (and apparently never revised during the 1850s) offered only brief and vague guidance about the use of force and made no reference to the possibility that the police might employ firearms. It advised that the policeman "must never use his club, except in the most urgent case of self defense," and that when endeavoring to arrest or disperse rioters "force will not be resorted to until it become absolutely necessary, but when necessary must be exercised to the degree required" (*Rules and Regulations for the General Government of the Police Department of the City of New Orleans* [New Orleans, 1852], 30, 48-49).

[33]*Daily Picayune*, October 8, 13, 1854, October 18, 26, 1855, February 14, 28, 1856; *Bee*, March 18, 1856; *Daily Delta*, November 14, 1859; *Louisiana Courier*, November 9, 1858; Police Board Records, August 10, 1854, June 14, 1855; Record of Inquests and Views, Coroner's Office, 1844-90, microfilm, NOPL, 9, 664.

[34]For the period 1892-1900, the homicide rate for New Orleans averaged 14 per 100,000 population, and for metropolitan New Orleans during the years 1965-72 it averaged about 13 per 100,000; *Annual Report of Board of Police Commissioners and Superintendent of Police*, 1892-1900; *New Orleans Police Department 1973*

Annual Report (Metairie, La., [1974?]); Roger Lane, *Violent Death in the City: Suicide, Accident, and Murder in Nineteenth-Century Philadelphia* (London, 1979), 71; Theodore N. Ferdinand, "The Criminal Patterns of Boston Since 1849," *American Journal of Sociology*, 73 (1967): 89; First District Court, Parish of Orleans, Docket Books, 1857-59, Minute Books, 1857-59, NOPL; *Report of the Attorney General to the Legislature of the State of Louisiana*, 1854, pp. 1-3, 1856, pp. 3-5, 1857, pp. 6-11, 1858, pp. 3-7; *Annual Report of the Attorney General to the Legislature of the State of Louisiana*, 1855, pp. 4-7, 1859, pp. 4-5, 1860, p. 7, 1861, pp. 3-5, 11.

Another suggestive indicator of the incidence of violence in New Orleans can be found in arrest rates for assault and assault and battery. The annual arrest rate for these minor crimes of violence in Boston in 1856 was 84.2 per 10,000 population, whereas the annual rate for New Orleans for the years 1854-56 was more than twice as high at 194.4 per 10,000. Because the Boston police seem to have been more efficient and vigorous than the police in New Orleans, and because both private citizens and policemen in the Crescent City were more likely than Bostonians to treat assaults as affairs of honor to be settled privately without the intervention of the police and the courts, it is likely that the real differential in the rates of minor violence between the two cities was even greater than that indicated by the nominal arrest rates; for arrest data, see *Daily Picayune*, June 15, December 12, 15, 1854, January 7, February 24, March 18, April 22, May 12, 1855; Police Board Reports, May, 1855-January, 1856; and Lane, *Policing the City*, 230-31.

[35]*Daily True Delta*, March 28, 1855; *Commercial Bulletin*, March 26, 27, 1856; *Louisiana Courier*, March 20, 1856, *Daily Picayune*, March 29, 1854, June 13, 1855; *Bee*, March 19, 1856, December 24, 1860, January 10, March 4, 25, 1861; Messages of the Mayors to the City Council, December 26, 1860; Record of Inquests, 8:171, 173, 12:58, 16:137, 343; *State v. Rosana Chilarri*, First District Court, Docket Books, Case No. 15095, acquitted May 2, 1861; *State v. John Mulholland and Peter McCabe*, First District Court, Minute Books, Case No. 14535, sentenced December 24, 1860, to hang.

[36]Ordinances and Resolutions of the Common Council, No. 3338, April 9, 1857; Charity Hospital Admission Books, December 27, 1857, February 20, May 3, 1858, May 27, October 8, 23, 1859, May 29, June 4, 1860; *Daily True Delta*, April 24, 1855; *Daily Crescent*, November 8, 1859; *Daily Picayune*, August 24, October 25, 1855, June 15, 23, August 28, 1856, January 3, 1860; *Bee*, April 8, 9, June 3, 1856, July 27, 1857.

[37]*Daily True Delta*, July 3, 1860; *Louisiana Courier*, April 10, 1859; *Bee*, June 21, August 8, 1860; Record of Inquests, 16:179; *State v. Antoine Cambre*, First District Court, Minute Books, Case No. 14369, sentenced July 2, 1860, to hang; *State v. Eugene Pepe alias Eugene Adams*, First District Court, Docket Books, Case No. 14066, sentenced June 14, 1860, to hang.

[38]*Bee*, April 23, 1860; Record of Inquests, 15:386; *State v. Jean Gros*, First District Court, Minute Books, Case No. 14514, *nolle prosequi*, December 20, 1861.

[39]*Daily Picayune*, December 24, 1849, October 16, 1853, October 12, 1855, February 17, 1856, August 26, 1871; *State v. Arthur Guerin*, First District Court, Docket Books, Case No. 12868, *nolle prosequi*, December 20, 1857. John Poole was acquitted of murder (*Annual Report of the Attorney General to the Legislature of the State of Louisiana*, 1855, p. 17).

[40]*Louisiana Courier*, April 12, 1857; *Daily Picayune*, October 7, 1857; *Bee*, January 30, February 1, 1861.

[41]Police Board Records, 1854-56; *Daily Crescent*, September 11, 1854, March 5, 1860; *Deutsche Zeitung*, May 5, 6, 1856; *Commercial Bulletin*, June 28, July 8, 1855; *Daily Picayune*, August 9, 10, 13, 15, 1850, February 2, August 2, October 18, 1854, September 13, 1855, July 25, 1856, February 13, 1858.

[42]New Orleans had a relatively large concentration of white men in the high-crime-age cohort of twenty to forty years who lived without the stabilizing and convincing influence of wives and families. In the Crescent City in 1850 the number of white males twenty to forty years old per 100 white women in the same age bracket was 167 to 100, while the ratio was 93 men per 100 women in Philadelphia County (Pennsylvania), 92 per 100 in Suffolk County (the Massachusetts county consisting mostly of Boston), and 100 to 100 in New York County (which consisted almost entirely of New York City). By 1860, the disparity had diminished somewhat but still remained substantial: New Orleans had 113 men per 100 women, Philadelphia had 88 per 100, Suffolk County

had 88 per 100, and New York had 89 per 100 (*Seventh Census*, 48, 88-90, 154-55, 466-67; *Population of the United States in 1860*, 188, 218, 322, 406). On honor and violence, see Edward L. Ayers, *Vengeance and Justice: Crime and Punishment in the 19th-Century American South* (New York, 1984), 9-33, 266-76; Bertram Wyatt-Brown, *Southern Honor: Ethics and Behavior in the Old South* (New York, 1982), 350-401.

[43]Police Board Records, November 29, 30, 1855; *Daily Picayune*, August 22, 1850, June 4, 13, September 6, 1855; *Louisiana Courier*, November 18, 1858; *Bee*, January 19, February 15, March 6, 1861.

[44]*Daily Picayune*, April 13, 1852, August 1, 2, 1854; *Daily Crescent*, August 1, 1854; *Daily True Delta*, August 1, 1854; *Bee*, February 14, 1861.

[45]*Daily Picayune*, June 16, 1853, October 30, November 1, 1855.

[46]*Daily Picayune*, November 3, 1855, February 22, 24, March 11, July 30, 1856. Richard Tansey, "Prostitution and Politics in Antebellum New Orleans," *Southern Studies*, 17 (1980): 449-79, and Richard Randall Tansey, "Economic Expansion and Urban Disorder in Antebellum New Orleans" (Ph.D. dissertation, University of Texas at Austin, 1981), 37-79, describe the failure of efforts to curb prostitution in the late 1840s and 1850s, noting that politicians from the Democratic, Whig, and American parties permitted brothels to operate largely unhindered. The Know Nothings did try in 1857 to restrict prostitution to multiple-story bordellos because some of their constituents complained that single-story houses of prostitution were driving down property values, but even this restriction was quickly defeated by brothel managers and landlords.

[47]*Daily Picayune*, August 24, September 7, 1850, January 13, August 17, November 29, 1855, March 13, 1856, June 9, 1858, January 1, 1860; *Bee*, January 3, 1861.

[48]Messages of the Mayors of the First Municipality Council, December 1, 1850, November 17, 1851; Messages of the Mayors to the Third Municipality Council, December 16, 1850. The percentage of arrestees who were black is a weighted average for two years of First Municipality data and one year for the Third Municipality, and the general population comparison percentage is also a weighted average. The arrest report of the Second Municipality police for the year ending June 30, 1851, did not include data about black arrestees (*Bee*, October 1, 1851). The average number of arrests per policeman of 47 per year was neither very large nor small; in the years 1868-77, the average varied from as high as 62 to as low as 38; in the 1890s it ranged from a low of 67 to a high of 105; and in 1973, the average was 32 (*Annual Report of the Board of Metropolitan Police to the Governor of Louisiana*, 1868/69-1873/74; *Annual Report of Board of Police Commissioners and Superintendent of Police*, 1891-1900; *New Orleans Police Department 1973 Annual Report.*

[49]Census of 1850, RG 29, NA. The jail population included 61.1 percent illiterates. It may, however, have somewhat overrepresented the poor, who were less likely to make bail or be released on their own recognizance.

[50]Dismissals from the force in the 1940s amounted to a mere 0.2 percent annually and in the years 1965-69 ran between 1.1 and 1.5 percent per annum. In the latter period, total complaints against policemen averaged one-third to one-half of one complaint per man annually, and not all complaints led to even temporary suspension (Police Board Records, 1854-56; Bruce Smith, *The New Orleans Police Survey* [New Orleans, 1946], 35; International Association of Chiefs of Police, Field Operations Division, *A Survey of the Police Department: New Orleans, Louisiana* [Gaithersburg, Md., 1971], 136; *Daily Picayune*, December 12, 1854).

[51]Of the 672 cases adjudicated by the Board of Police between April 1854, and February 1856, 59.2 percent involved charges of dereliction of duty, 17.4 percent abuses of authority, 7.2 percent violations of the chain of command, and 5.5 percent conduct unbecoming a police officer; 1.2 percent were for other specified offenses and 9.5 percent unspecified offenses. Charges of violating the chain of command led to dismissal from the force of 33.0 percent of the men charged, followed by dismissal of 30.8 percent of those charged with dereliction of duty. 21.6 percent of those accused of conduct unbecoming a police officer, and 18.4 percent of the men charged with abuses of authority (Police Board Records, 1854-56).

[52]Irish policemen were overrepresented among those tried by the Board of Police, both before and after the Know Nothings gained control of the board. During the period April 1854 - April 1855, Irishmen held about 26 percent of police jobs but constituted approximately 40 percent of the accused; between May 1855, and February 1856, the Irish accounted for roughly 10 percent of the police force but about 21 percent of those tried by the board. But Irish policemen brought up on charges were somewhat less likely than other policemen to be dismissed from the force. Between April 1854, and April 1855, 35 percent of Irish policemen tried by the board were fired for cause, while 37 percent of other accused policemen were terminated; for the period May 1855, to February 1856, the dismissal rate for the accused Irish policemen was 14 percent, and for other policemen before the board on charges it was 22 percent. Thus, although the American party members of the board were evidently less willing to employ Irish or other immigrant officers, they do not appear to have judged accused Irish policemen more harshly than men from other ethnic backgrounds. The dismissal rates after the Know Nothings gained control of the board were markedly lower than under the Democrats, suggesting that the Know Nothing board was less likely than its Democratic predecessors to respond to complaints about police misconduct with the most severe administrative punishment of dismissal.

[53]*Daily True Delta*, May 3, 1853.

[54]Applications for Positions as Police Officers, for A. Hoff, John Sass, Henry Hoff, Henry Parr, Joseph Nunnemacher, and George Washington Hopkins, RG 393, NA.

[55]The turnover data do not include the change in personnel as a consequence of annual reappointments. These figures describe turnover only among the full-time policemen, not the supernumeraries. If supernumeraries were included, the turnover rates would be much higher. Supernumeraries are not included to allow comparison with the turnover rates of 1840-52, for which no information about supernumerary turnover was available (turnover calculated from Police Board Records, 1854-56, and Personnel Records of the Police Department, 1856-61, NOPL). Absenteeism in the 1940s was 4.5 percent, twice the average for police departments with strict medical discipline (absenteeism estimated from the Reports of the Third District Police, 1855-56 and 1860, NOPL, and for the 1940s see Smith, *New Orleans Police Survey*, 39).

[56]Ordinances and Resolutions of the Common Council, No. 2100, April 5, 1855; *Daily Picayune*, May 14, 1852; *Daily True Delta*, August 1, 1854; *Statistical View of the United States*, 164.

[57]In 1860, 35.3 percent of the police force owned as much as $100 in personal property, while 34.6 percent of a control sample of the white adult male population held at least that much personality. But the mean value of the personal property of policemen was less than for the control sample—$400 for the former and $2,445 for the latter. Age was not the reason for the disparity, for an age-specific analysis shows lower values for policemen in every ten year age bracket from twenty-one through seventy. In 1850, 9.9 percent of policemen owned realty and in 1860, 8.7 percent; the control sample of white adult males revealed 10.0 percent to be owners of real estate in 1850 and 11.6 percent in 1860. But the mean values of realty for the police were lower than for the control sample—$2,149 for the police in 1850 and $11,143 for the control sample, and $1,427 for the police in 1860 compared with $8,792 for the control sample. An age-specific analysis shows that age differences did not cause the disparity between police and the control sample. The 1850 sample consisted of 4,566 white adult males drawn from the Census of 1850, RG 29, NA. The 1860 sample consisted of 4,566 white adult males drawn from the Census of 1860, RG 29, NA. Tax information came from Tax Registers and Ledgers, City of New Orleans, 1852-1860, NOPL.

[58]Applications for Positions as Police Officers, for Wendover and Smart, Anthony Vierira, Augustus Miller, and Jacob Lieser, RG 393, NA. Fire company sample information is derived from newspaper obituaries for former members of the Know Nothing force. For an example of political influence on one policeman's career, see obituary for Patrick Creagh, *Daily Picayune*, November 14, 1903; Creagh left the police department after a short term of service and subsequently held a multitude of political offices. Formal education probably helped Thomas N. Boylan get a rapid start in his career as a policeman, and he eventually rose to become superintendent of police; see his obituary, *Daily Picayune*, May 20, 1902. Although literacy was a nominal requirement to become a policeman, census records showed four illiterate men on the force in 1860 (about 1 percent of the force), and nine illiterates in 1850 (about 3 percent of the force). In 1841, 7 percent of the city guardsmen in the

Third Municipality were unable to sign the payroll (Pay List of the Day Police, Night Watchmen, and Lamplighters). The actual number of functional illiterates was probably higher than any of these figures suggest. For policemen who could speak neither French nor English, see Police Board Records, August 23, 1855. In 1850, 70.5 percent of the police force was 40 years of age or younger, while the mean and median ages were 34.6 years and 28.9 years, respectively. In 1860, 74.8 percent were 40 or younger, the mean age was 35.3, and the median was 32.9 (Censuses of 1850 and 1860, Orleans Parish). In 1970, 80 percent of the police were 40 or younger (International Association of Chiefs of Police, *Survey of the Police Department*).

[59]*Daily Picayune*, June 30, July 16, 1858; *Louisiana Courier*, June 20, 1858; *Message of Gerard Stith, Mayor of the City of New Orleans, to the Common Council* (New Orleans, 1858), 13.

[60]*Daily True Delta*, November 1, 1859, February 15, 1860, January 19, 1862; *Daily Delta*, January 17, 19, 1860, January 18, 1862.

[61]Police Board Records, August 31, 1854, June 21, July 19, 1855, February 14, 1856; *Louisiana Courier*, May 7, 1857, May 30, 1858, November 2, 1859; *Daily True Delta*, April 4, 1855; *Daily Crescent*, March 24, 1854, October 31, 1859; *Daily Picayune*, February 4, April 30, 1854, March 30, 1855.

[62]Journal of the Proceedings of the Board of Assistant Aldermen, NOPL, October 9, 1855; *Bee*, October 10, 1855; *Daily Picayune*, July 16, August 20, 1856.

[63]Journal of the Proceedings of the Board of Assistant Aldermen, October 16, 1855; Messages of the Mayors to the City Council, June 26, October 2, 1860; *Bee*, October 20, 1853, October 24, 1855, March 27, June 27, 1860; *Commercial Bulletin*, July 8, 1858; *Daily Delta*, June 27, 1860; *Daily True Delta*, July 11, 1860.

[64]Ordinances of the Common Council, No. 4974, February 18, 1860; *Daily Crescent*, May 19, 1853; *Louisiana Courier*, November 13, 21, 1858; *Bee*, June 6, 1860; *Daily Picayune*, April 6, 1853; *Daily True Delta*, June 7, 1860.

[65]Neither the Democrats nor the American party cared much about improving the condition of the city's jails. In 1854, the Orleans Parish Grand Jury complained that the Third District lockup was dilapidated and the prisoners needed blankets, the city surveyor reported that the principal police jail needed extensive repair, and the chief of police called the First District lockup a disgrace to the city. Two years later the mayor and chief of police both asserted that the Third District lockup was in poor condition (the chief said that "it would fall into the river if not repaired"), and the Grand Jury called it the "Black Hole of New Orleans." The Grand Jury also reported that both the boys' and girls' houses of refuge were old and unfit structures, that the main police jail was filthy and the prisoners were underfed, that the city workhouse was a fire hazard, and that the inmates of the parish prison were overcrowded and needed more food. The Second District lockup had cells exposed to the elements, and at least one prisoner died in the winter of 1860-61. When William Howard Russell visited the parish prison in 1861, he reported overcrowding, intermingling of serious and minor offenders, "wretched cells," and a "stench . . . so vile that I could not proceed further," and denounced the whole as "a disgraceful institution" (*Daily Picayune*, February 4, April 30, June 8, November 26, 1854, April 23, August 6, 1856, January 4, 1860; *Daily Crescent*, November 8, 1852; *Bee*, April 5, 1856; Russell, *My Diary North and South*, 245-48).

THE SUDDEN COLLAPSE OF THE LOUISIANA WHIG PARTY*

John M. Sacher

The federal system of the United States complicates the task of understanding the collapse of the Whig party in the 1850s. The national party, reflecting the political structure of the country itself, was a conglomeration of not necessarily compatible state organizations that gathered every four years to nominate a presidential candidate. In the intervening years, and to a significant extent even in presidential election years, the state parties had extensive autonomy, even though they were part of a national organization. Michael F. Holt—who has described the collapse of the Whig party as "mysterious" and unique in U. S. political history—provides a framework for understanding the disappearance of the Whig party: "[T]he real story of the political reorganization of the 1850s is to be found in individual states with their varying conditions." In this view, the weight of forces at the state and national levels must be balanced, or, as J. Mills Thornton contends, "state history must give form to national history, just as national history contributes to forming state history."[1] The national Whig party's disappearance resulted from its failure in individual states. Collapse at the state level does not necessarily imply the complete disappearance of the party but instead can be defined as the reduction of a majority or at least a fully competitive Whig party to an ineffectual, moribund minority. As the Whig party disintegrated in the individual states, the national party lost vitality; and as the national party weakened, remaining state parties became more vulnerable. Timing of the party's collapse in a given state varied according to the state's political climate and the vigor of the national party, factors that were interrelated. Only by focusing on the interplay between national and state issues can the puzzle of the breakup of each state's Whig party be solved.

Louisiana offers a particularly useful example for studying the interaction between national and state issues in the Whig party's demise. Because of issues at both levels of the federal system, Louisiana had one of the South's most vibrant Whig parties.[2] In the Pelican State, Henry Clay's American System was especially popular. The state's sugar cane industry required a tariff to remain viable; its extensive network of rivers and

*First published in *The Journal of Southern History*, 65 (1999): 221-48.

swamps led to a strong interest in internal improvements; and New Orleans's role as an import-export center encouraged many to support a national bank. Louisiana's south-central sugar bowl region formed the backbone of the state's Whig party, and its parishes provided Whig candidates with majorities in almost every gubernatorial and presidential contest from the party's formation in the 1830s forward. The Whig party's strength, however, was not limited to this area. New Orleans and its surrounding parishes could also be relied upon for support, as could the north Louisiana riverine parishes, which contained some of the nation's highest concentrations of slaves. Conversely, the Whig party very seldom mustered a majority in the rest of Northern Louisiana or in the Florida Parishes—those east of the Mississippi and north of New Orleans. The Whig party's program had little attraction for the cotton-growing, Anglo-Saxon, Protestant Democratic party loyalists in either of these regions.

Not only did the Whig party's association with an activist national government have an allure in Louisiana, but also, in the early 1850s, two other developments—one national and one state—benefited Louisiana Whigs. They profited from supporting the national Compromise of 1850, which they contended protected both slavery and the union. They branded Democratic opponents of the compromise—particularly Louisiana Senator Pierre Soulé—as dis-Unionists. At the state level, the Whig party profited from its call for a convention to revise the unpopular Constitution of 1845. In 1852 this stance helped the Whigs achieve their greatest legislative majority and enabled them to control the convention that was called to rewrite the constitution.

These triumphs were ephemeral. Just as events at both the national and state levels had advanced the Louisiana Whig party's fortunes, they also contributed to an abrupt reversal. The national Whig party's nomination of Winfield Scott for the presidency in 1852 demonstrated to the majority of Southern Whigs that the Northern wing of their party could no longer be trusted on the slavery question. After 1852, primarily because of divisions over slavery, the national Whig party never again nominated a presidential candidate. Louisiana Whigs were hurt by the national party's failings, and at home they were injured by their own success. By the end of the year Louisiana Democrats had accepted the Whig program of activist government, as exemplified by the constitution of 1852, and significant partisan differences disappeared. The weakening of the national party when combined with the successful resolution of questions at the state level dealt the Louisiana Whig party a crushing blow. The party could no longer present itself as a defender of slavery nor did it have viable issues to distinguish it from the Democrats. In the state elections of December 1852, the Democrats overwhelmed the Whigs, and the Whig party never again mounted a serious challenge in Louisiana.

An examination of the downfall of the Louisiana Whig party in 1852 demonstrates how an analysis of the interplay between national and state issues may be beneficial in understanding the collapse of the Southern Whig party. More broadly, this study illustrates the importance of studying antebellum Southern politics from the perspective of individual states. In the antebellum period, each state's reaction to national events was shaped by its own unique political conditions. Louisiana, as the lower South state with the strongest Whig party, offers a particularly useful lens through which to view national events. Also, since Louisianans in 1852 were "compelled to have a perfect war of politics throughout the year," including municipal, statewide, and national contests, there is ample opportunity to gauge the electoral pulse of the Louisiana Whigs at any given time.[3]

The Whig party of Louisiana first appeared in the 1830s and from the outset demonstrated its political strength. The party represented a combination of National Republicans and those who opposed Andrew Jackson or local Democratic groups. Whig candidates were elected governor in 1834 and 1838 and claimed a majority in all but one of the state legislatures that met from 1838 until their party's collapse in 1853. In addition, in presidential elections the party captured the state for William Henry Harrison in 1840 and for native-son Zachary Taylor in 1848.

Nevertheless, Louisiana Whigs did not experience unqualified success during the 1840s. Whig candidates were defeated in the governor's races during that decade, and the party, predominately because of an 1843 Whig gerrymander that backfired, controlled only one of the state's four congressional districts. Though the party had a majority in the state legislature, the narrowness of this majority, tension between legislators of different ethnic groups, voter fraud, and lack of strict Whig party discipline led to the selection of Whigs as United States senators on only four of eight occasions in the 1840s.[4]

In Louisiana in the 1840s and early 1850s, the Whigs and the Democrats offered the voters a clear choice. Louisiana Whigs championed the positive liberal state: the idea that government activism played a beneficial role in society. They advocated government aid to banks, railroads, and other internal improvement projects and served as champions of the protective tariff for the state's sugar industry. As the party of regulated liberty in Louisiana, Whigs stressed the rule of law and the danger of licentiousness. This fear of anarchy contributed to their opposition to the expansion of suffrage, especially if it allowed immigrants easier access to the ballot. During the antebellum period, New Orleans served as one of the chief entrepôts for European immigrants, a situation that had no parallel in the rest of the South. Whig resistance to this influx led to much more nativism than was found in other Southern Whig parties.[5]

In 1844, when Louisiana voters elected a convention to rewrite the state's 1812 constitution, they rejected the Whig view of active government. The Democrats controlled the convention, and the new charter articulated their vision of government. The 1845 document epitomized Louisiana Democrats' concept of the negative liberal state: the idea that society would prosper most with the least government interference. The convention prohibited state aid to corporations, state-sponsored internal improvements, and a state debt greater than one hundred thousand dollars. It also severely restricted the ability to form corporations and limited the life of both corporations and monopolies, while forbidding the incorporation of new banks in the state. Additionally, the constitution instituted universal white manhood suffrage and eliminated the substantial property requirements for officeholders.[6]

William H. Adams, in *The Whig Party in Louisiana,* argued that "the adoption of the new [1845] constitution would ultimately mean the [Whig] party's demise." The charter, however, did not weaken the Whigs but actually provided them with an opportunity to reinvigorate their party. Voters had ratified the constitution primarily because it was an improvement on the 1812 charter; or, in the colorful prose of a North Louisiana Whig, as they "would take a leaky boat when in the power of pirates." Louisianians, especially those living in New Orleans, rapidly grew disenchanted with the document's restrictive economic provisions, which, according to historian Wayne M. Everard, "contained features that were unsuitable to the political and economic milieu of antebellum Louisiana."[7] Whigs capitalized on the increasing discontent among businessmen, who complained of the "shackles and fetters" that had been placed on commerce.[8] Portraying themselves as agents of change, Whigs championed constitutional reform. In 1851 the party included in its platform for the state legislative elections a plank calling for a constitutional convention, while the Democrats, who were divided on the issue, did not. The *New Orleans Daily Picayune* correctly described pro-convention sentiment as "nearly unanimous," and the Whigs swept to their largest majority in the legislature, where they immediately used their control to elect New Orleans Whig Judah P. Benjamin to the United States Senate. Benefiting from reform sentiment and the party's identification with the Compromise of 1850, they also captured two of the state's four congressional seats for the first time.[9]

Thus, as the Whigs entered 1852, they had every reason to feel confident of success. The initial battle between the Democrats and Whigs occurred in the New Orleans municipal elections on March 22. Leaders of both parties acknowledged the importance of this campaign as a litmus test of their relative strengths. Democratic stalwart John Slidell contended that "if we succeed we shall carry the state in November." Speaking at a Whig meeting the night before the city elections, Senator-elect Benjamin concurred in the magnitude of the New Orleans elections and in their significance to the national contest. Additionally, the preamble to the resolutions adopted by this Whig gathering emphasized that the success of the Whig party in the city election "will insure a Whig Convention, a Whig Constitution, a Whig legislature, and the vote of the state for a Whig president."[10]

Political conflict in the Crescent City could not be separated from its traditional Creole-American power struggle. From 1836 to 1852 animosity among the city's ethnic groups had led to the physical division of the city into three virtually autonomous municipalities. In February 1852 the legislature mandated consolidation, calling for a March election to unify the city under a single board of aldermen. Prior to 1852, ethnicity and personality had shaped New Orleans elections, but with consolidation, the historic Creole-American contest took on more of the form of partisan politics. Leon C. Soulé, in his study of New Orleans politics, asserts that consolidation saw "the emergence of the political party as the dominant factor in municipal politics." Within the city, the strength of the Whig party came from the First District and from Lafayette—the American sections—and Democratic support came from the Second and Third Districts—the Creole and immigrant regions.[11]

At first glance, the municipal campaign appeared to be an unqualified Whig success: The party elected the mayor, treasurer, comptroller, and a majority of the board of aldermen. Upon further examination, however, the election exposed chinks in the party armor: Partisan attachments in the city were not solidified, and a third-party movement emerged. Samuel J. Peters, a prominent city Whig, observed that "Mr. James Robb got up an independent ticket with a view to injure (it is said) the Whig party. . . . the Whigs will not forget it though [the independent's] efforts prove[d] of little use." Robb, a Whig state senator and Louisiana's most prominent railroad promoter, represented a faction that considered commercial advancement more important than partisan affiliation. Claiming to represent business interests, the independent reform movement's leaders charged that old parties existed only for patronage purposes. The independent party's success is difficult to gauge, for though they elected seven of the city's twelve aldermen, all of their victorious candidates were also either Whig or Democratic nominees.[12]

A month after the city election, in a referendum marred by poor turnout, Louisiana voters called for a constitutional convention. Discussing the selection of delegates to the convention, the *Daily Picayune* stated, "The interest in these questions is not mixed up with the ordinary topics of party electioneering." The people and the parties disagreed with this sentiment and instead concurred with the *Plaquemine Southern Sentinel* that "electing delegates irrespective of their politics . . . is a moral impossibility."[13] The Whigs benefited from their party's unified position in favor of a convention, while the Democrats suffered from their internal division on this matter. In the June election, the Whigs achieved a triumph, which the partisan press labelled "UNPARALLELED" and "A TALL WHIG VICTORY," as they captured a majority of approximately 30 to 40 of the 125 contested seats.[14] W. W. Pugh, a Democratic delegate, lamented that the results left his party in a position in which it could "only object to disagreeable measure, without having the power to interpose any obstacle." The Whig victory was particularly impressive in commercial New Orleans, where the party captured twenty-six of the twenty-seven seats.[15]

The convention assembled on July 5, 1852, with the Whigs using their overwhelming majority to write a constitution based on their party platform of positive government: state aid to business and internal improvements, more liberal banking laws, and public education. The Whigs succeeded in legalizing state government purchase of stock in internal improvement projects, an article that Pugh saw as the "one great and controlling desire of the whigs of N. Orleans" and decried as "graft . . . solely for the promotion . . . of speculators." They also passed measures that raised the maximum state debt from one hundred thousand to eight million dollars, permitted free banking—the formation of banks with either general or special laws—and removed limits on the life of corporations and monopolies. Delegates who were not Whigs also favored these measures, and the constitution passed by an overwhelming 98-to-8 vote. Many of them probably agreed with R. A. Hargis's assessment, "I vote *yes,* not because I like the new Constitution in all of its details, but because I like it better than the Constitution of 1845."[16]

Whig papers were ecstatic about the proposed constitution, and the Baton Rouge *Gazette* exclaimed that the Whigs "now have it in our power to place Louisiana beyond the reach of Locofocoism and to retain its government in our hands for years to come."[17] The constitution still had to be ratified by the electorate, and opposition to the document soon developed over an issue that had nothing to do with the Whigs' primary goals. The charter included an article that based representation in both houses of the legislature upon total population, with slaves counting the same as free people. Thus, a parish with one thousand whites and nine thousand blacks would have the same representation as one with ten thousand whites and no slaves. In the antebellum period, no other Southern state used this basis of representation in both houses of the legislature.

Residents of parishes, including Orleans, with low concentrations of slaves objected to this measure, which would create a nobility of planters and, according to a convention delegate, would "place the African and the white man on a level."[18] In seizing upon this issue in their opposition to the constitution, the Democrats acted disingenuously because the article merely extended to both houses of the legislature the method of apportionment that the 1845 constitution, which had been written by the Democrats, had used for the state senate. Basing legislative representation upon total population emerged in the convention not as a partisan measure but as a sectional compromise among the parishes with high slave concentrations, those with low slave concentrations, and New Orleans. The Whig delegates from New Orleans supported this measure by a vote of sixteen to ten because they feared that any other method would include a limit on the number of legislators from the city, while the total population method placed no ceiling on the size of any parish's delegation. Some parishes with low concentrations of slaves supported the compromise because, for the first time in Louisiana history, its state constitution guaranteed each parish a representative in the legislature.[19]

Supporters of the constitution tried to avoid this controversy by reminding voters that "the choice is between the old and new Constitution. It is not, whether you entirely approve both, but which do you prefer." The voters apparently agreed with this argument and on November 2 accepted the constitution by a vote of 19,286 to 16,004.[20] Ironically, the Whig-authored 1852 constitution, not the 1845 constitution written by the Democrats, directly contributed to the Whig party's downfall in Louisiana. As Michael Holt writes, "The Whig party . . . continued to exist only so long as it remained a credible opposition party, that is, only so long as it provided clear alternatives to the Democrats."[21] Since 1845 the Whigs of Louisiana had used their advocacy of constitutional revision to create a clear alternative to the Democrats. With the revision issue no longer salient, the Whigs would have to find a new method to differentiate their party from the Democrats in the eyes of the electorate. The Whigs would also have to defend the constitution, and its total population clause greatly restricted their room for maneuver and exposed them to charges of being anti-democratic.

In 1852 the Whig party in Louisiana faced challenges on three levels—local, state, and national. That year marked the last time a nationwide Whig party contested the presidency. On November 2, the day that Louisiana approved the Whig-written constitution, Winfield Scott, the Whig presidential candidate, lost the state to Democrat Franklin Pierce, who received 51.9 percent of the 35,902 ballots cast. Although the *New Orleans Bee* considered Scott's 254-42 defeat in the electoral college "disastrous," it proclaimed that, in Louisiana, the Whigs were "barely beaten" and had "not been routed . . . and shattered into fragments."[22]

The Whig party in Louisiana had reason to be proud of its performance. In comparison with the rest of the South, and especially the lower South, Louisiana's Whigs performed magnificently. In the South as a whole, Scott received only 42.5 percent of the vote, and in the lower South that percentage fell to 34.9 percent. Of the Southern states, Scott won only in Tennessee and performed respectably only in Louisiana and North Carolina, the home of William A. Graham, the Whig vice presidential candidate. The defeat in the region appeared even worse when compared with Zachary Taylor's showing in 1848. Scott received 56,925 (or 43.2 percent) fewer popular votes than Taylor received in the six lower South states. These voters, however, did not abandon the Whig standard in order to vote for Pierce but instead remained at home on election day. Total turnout in the lower South fell 49,874 votes, nearly equaling the decline in the Whig vote.[23]

Louisiana's situation differed significantly from the other states of the lower South. In Louisiana, the Whig vote declined by less than seven percent between 1848 and 1852, and in 1848 Taylor's Louisiana vote undoubtedly benefited from his residency in the state. Even more surprisingly, voter turnout in Louisiana actually increased by 2,036 between 1848 and 1852. This increase probably resulted from the presidential election coinciding with the important vote on the ratification of the constitution. Scott's performance in Louisiana leads to two questions. First, if the Whigs in Louisiana were so powerful, then why did Scott lose the state? Second, why did Louisiana's voters go to the polls and support Scott so strongly in comparison with those in the rest of the lower South?

Poor political calculations by Louisiana Whig leaders explain why Scott lost the state. Throughout early 1852 the Whigs thoroughly convinced themselves that "the South will make the candidate of the [national] convention," and many discounted the possibility of being forced to campaign for Scott in the fall.[24] They refused to believe that the Northern Whigs would force such an unpalatable candidate upon them. Zachary Taylor's presidency had left Louisiana Whigs skeptical about war heroes and friends of New York Free Soiler William H. Seward—two categories into which Scott fit. His silence on the Compromise of 1850 also contributed to Southern Whigs' distaste, and one of them went so far as to contend that the nomination of Scott would "annihilate the Whig party here." The first choice of Louisiana and the rest of the South was the incumbent Millard Fillmore. As E. B. Carr proclaimed in a letter to his congressman, "There has not been a better President since the days of Madison," and another Louisiana Whig agreed that "Fillmore is our strongest man."[25] This praise resulted primarily from Fillmore's backing the Compromise of 1850, which had significant Southern support, and his enforcement of the Fugitive Slave Act. Louisiana Democratic kingpin John Slidell acknowledged, "If Fillmore be the Whig candidate we shall have a very even and doubtful contest in this state."[26]

In advocating Millard Fillmore's nomination, Louisiana Whigs attacked Winfield Scott and disparaged his commitment to the South. A Whig partisan asserted, "I doubt if there is a Southern state which could be induced to vote for him." Nevertheless, Southern Whigs faced a difficult task. While demonstrating to the North their strong disapproval of Scott's candidacy, they had to leave the door open if Scott became the national nominee. An editorial in the *New Orleans Bee,* a Whig newspaper, illustrates the difficulty of clarifying their position: "The *Bee* has never said that no Southern Whig can or should support Genl. SCOTT . . . What we have said, once, twice, and twenty times was that Southern Whigs would not and could not support Genl. SCOTT unless his opinions touching Slavery and the Compromise should be distinctly known, and should accord with the South."[27]

At the June national Whig convention held in Baltimore, Scott obtained the party's nomination on the fifty-third ballot, having received few Southern votes and none from Louisiana's delegation.[28] Not surprisingly, Louisiana Whigs reacted unenthusiastically. According to the *Plaquemine Southern Sentinel,* "that he [Scott] has previously been distrusted by Southern Whigs . . . cannot be denied," and the *New Orleans Commercial Bulletin,* describing its own editorial position, reported that it was "not a volunteer recruit under the standard of General SCOTT." Senator Benjamin, speaking at a ratification meeting, admitted that he had opposed Scott's nomination but had changed his mind with the candidate's acceptance of the party platform. Two of the six members of the Whig electoral slate not only resigned from the ticket but also announced that they would support the Democrat nominee, Franklin Pierce.[29]

In the November 1852 election, some Louisiana Whigs defected from the party, and others simply did not vote for either candidate. No account of the 1852 presidential campaign fails to mention the significant drop in turnout from 1848 to 1852, especially in the South. There are three explanations for this Southern apathy: (1) Whigs who believed that Scott was unsound on the Compromise of 1850 refused to vote for him, (2) those who concluded that Scott had no chance to win chose not to waste their vote, and (3) some voters detected no difference between the two parties and consequently saw no reason to vote. The *Daily Picayune* observed that the Whigs and Democrats stood "upon precisely the same ground" and that the campaign had been "without excitement." This reflected a nationwide trend in 1852. According to Michael Holt, "the perceived congruence between Democrats and Whigs fostered widespread public apathy and alienation from *both* parties."[30]

To overcome this apathy and repeat their 1848 victory, Louisiana Whigs first had to put their own political house in order and explain how they could move from excoriating Scott in the spring to supporting him in the fall. In order to accomplish this task, they chose to emphasize that Scott and his Northern supporters—not Southern Whigs—had changed their positions. The Whig leadership attempted to raise the spirits of the party's rank and file through a series of barbecues, pole raisings, and ratification meetings. Describing the fall campaign season, an East Feliciana Parish Whig asserted that "at present my *business* is attending barbecues, torchlight processions, etc." At these events Whigs dismissed their earlier anti-Scott declarations by saying that they had spoken of an old Gen. Winfield Scott—a candidate who had been silent on the Compromise of 1850. In contrast, the new Scott had accepted the Whig platform, was no longer a friend of the Free Soil Whigs, and was instead a champion of the compromise and, therefore, of the South.[31]

The powerful appeal of the compromise in the South actually weakened the Whigs in Mississippi, Alabama, and Georgia, where Union parties developed. Formed in 1850, Union parties accepted the compromise as a final settlement and eschewed traditional party labels.[32] Because of the complex interaction of state and national politics, no Union party developed in Louisiana. In Louisiana, the heated debate on constitutional reform in the early 1850s and solid support for the Whig party's programs enabled the Whigs to maintain their strong position in the state without merging with disaffected Democrats. All attempts to form a Union party failed, and at least one Louisiana Whig leader "thought it bad policy to try to establish a compromise party."[33]

The ability of the Louisiana Whig party to withstand the threat of Unionism partially resulted from the strength of its traditional appeal in the state. Its state platform not only stressed the Compromise of 1850 as the "final settlement" of the nation's sectional problems but also—unlike platforms in other Southern states—maintained a commitment to the customary Whig program. This plan included support of a high tariff to guard against "competition of half-paid[,] half-fed foreign paupers" and of government aid for internal improvements.[34] A Whig editor declared, "If you want your rivers and harbors improved vote for SCOTT." According to another partisan, Franklin Pierce's views opposing federal aid to internal improvements would soon become common knowledge, despite the Democrats' hope that their candidate's opinions would remain unknown.[35] In contrast, the Democrats' division on the compromise weakened their platform. As John Slidell lamented, "a very great majority of our party approved of the compromise; yet those who were opposed are sufficiently numerous to make our defeat certain in any contest when their support shall be withheld." Louisiana Democratic Senator Pierre Soulé, Slidell's chief rival for control of the party, was among the leading opponents of the measure in Congress.[36]

Louisiana Whigs turned to a traditional Southern political tactic and accused their opponents of being abolitionists or at least tools of the abolitionists. During the campaign, the *Plaquemine Southern Sentinel* and the *New Orleans Bee* carried quotations beneath their mastheads contrasting the candidates' stances on slavery. Attributed to Pierce, the first two quotes included, "I consider slavery a social and political evil" and "I loathe it [the fugitive slave law]." In the third quote, Scott counters, "I am dead for the

Constitution—dead for the Union—dead for the Compromise."[37] While the Whigs' examination of Pierce's statements exposed him as an abolitionist, their reexamination of Scott's writings revealed that he was opposed to interference with the South's peculiar institution. Whig planter Joseph Moore admitted that he had initially opposed Scott, but "on hearing of his nomination, I examined myself the grounds upon which were based the charges of faithlessness to the South, and I have found that the conclusion drawn from them is entirely erroneous."[38]

Though traditionally the Louisiana Whigs had ties to nativism, they decided to change their message in 1852 in order to capture for Scott the growing Irish vote in New Orleans. As part of their campaign the Whigs accused Franklin Pierce of nativism and anti-Catholicism. These messages had their best Southern potential in Louisiana because of its large Catholic population and its significant immigrant population.[39] Louisiana Whigs focused on the ban against Catholics holding office in Pierce's home state of New Hampshire. According to the *Bee,* "When religious liberty needed a champion General Pierce was found—wanting." Regarding nativism, Louisiana Whigs found themselves in the same position that they were on the compromise. After accusing Scott of nativism earlier in the year, they now tried to portray him as a friend of immigrants in contrast to the nativist Franklin Pierce. Unable to find any direct evidence that Pierce opposed immigration, the Whig papers in New Orleans improvised by revealing his Anglophilia, which they contended demonstrated his dislike of Irish immigrants.[40]

While Louisiana Whigs had opposed Winfield Scott's nomination at the national convention, they suppressed their disappointment and campaigned vigorously for him. They were, however, unable to overcome completely the distrust and apathy of enough Whigs to capture Louisiana's electoral votes. In the aftermath of Scott's defeat and the passage of the state constitution on the same day, Louisiana Whigs entered their final campaign of 1852. Under the new constitution, a governor, lieutenant governor, secretary of state, treasurer, and the entire 127-member legislature would be elected on December 27. Despite the national rout of General Scott, many Louisiana Whigs remained optimistic. Whig journals throughout the state stressed that party members should focus on the great Whig constitutional victory, not on Scott's defeat. Whig newspapers urged "Exult then in your triumph—you have a Constitution which will soon go into operation" and reassured their readers that "the Whig party is at this day as strong as ever." While acknowledging that as many as three thousand Louisiana Whigs had refused to vote for Scott, the papers emphasized that this abstention did not signal irreparable damage to the party. Instead, they declared that "we will be enabled to show Locofocoism, that while the Whigs slumbered in November, they awoke in December, like a giant refreshed with sleep."[41]

Disputing these positive prognoses of the Whig party's political health, the Democratic *New Orleans Louisiana Courier* proudly quoted the *New York Tribune*'s assertion that "*the whig party* [is] *not merely* DISCOMFITTED *but* ANNIHILATED," adding that Whig partisans "talk about the re-organization of the whig party! Why, the whig party is dead." Even some Whig editors admitted that the party had been severely wounded by its performance in November. The *Franklin Planters' Banner* feared that the Whigs would be so downcast that they would "let the approaching election go by default." The Whig leadership apparently shared this apathy, and the December campaign lacked the abundance of barbecues, processions, and meetings that had marked the presidential contest.[42]

Part of this lethargy can be attributed to Louisiana Whigs' sensitivity to national issues, especially the slavery question. Throughout the South, including Louisiana, all political parties presented themselves as the best defenders of slavery in the national arena. Winfield Scott's perceived unsoundness on the slavery question was a primary explanation for his disastrous performance throughout the region. While the Whig party's traditional appeals may have worked better in Louisiana than elsewhere in the South, Louisiana Whigs were as sensitive to the slavery issue as their sectional allies. They, too, feared that Free Soilers had corrupted the Northern wing of their party and made it unreliable on the slavery issue.

The Louisiana Whig party had demonstrated its commitment to the South and its institutions earlier in the year when its two representatives had joined nine other Southerners in abandoning the national caucus. The caucus had assembled in April 1852 in order to establish a site and date for the presidential convention, but Southern Whigs called for it also to affirm the Compromise of 1850. When this motion was ruled out of order, eleven Southerners walked out and subsequently issued the Southern Whig Address stressing that in the South in 1852 only a single important issue remained: the Compromise of 1850. Furthermore, at the national convention, held in June, a delegate from Louisiana initiated the demand for writing the platform prior to selecting nominees, and Louisiana Whigs voted unanimously for Millard Fillmore on all fifty-three ballots. Thus, the state's Whig leaders, aware that their fellow Southerners had rebuked Scott and the Whig party as unsound on the slavery issue, realized that they faced an uphill battle to convince the rank and file to continue to rally around the name *Whig*.[43]

Unfortunately for Louisiana Whigs, the decline of the national Whig party occurred simultaneously with the disappearance of the Whigs' foremost state-level issue—constitutional revision. After the ratification of the constitution in November, Whigs could no longer use their advocacy of constitutional change to differentiate themselves from Democrats. Writing three years after the campaign, independent New Orleans politician Charles Gayarré asserted that in December 1852 the Whigs and Democrats "looked like twin brothers struggling for the love of . . . 'popularity.'" Discussing the host of state constitutional revisions in this period, Michael Holt argues that this "was a classic case where political parties benefited much more from the conflict over an issue than from its peaceful resolution." In Louisiana, this "peaceful resolution" occurred when the Democrats accepted the 1852 constitution and joined the Whigs in promoting a more activist government.[44]

The Whigs' first opportunity to demonstrate that their party still possessed political vigor and differed from the Democrats came at the state nominating convention on November 29. The president of the convention declared that the Whigs were "a party which although apparently conquered was never subdued." Despite his optimism, the party's weakness immediately surfaced. Twenty-six of the forty-eight parishes, mainly from the Northern regions, sent no delegates, and the three top candidates for governor declined consideration. Congressman John Moore instructed his proponents to withhold his name from consideration, and later an ally congratulated Moore on not being nominated. The convention instead selected an unspectacular but loyal partisan, state auditor Louis Bordelon.[45]

In contrast, the Democratic gathering two days later on December 1 proceeded smoothly. Only six parishes had no representation, and, on the first ballot, the delegates overwhelmingly selected sugar planter Paul Hébert as the party's gubernatorial nominee. Hébert's nomination was a brilliant political stroke because, at the constitutional convention earlier in the year, he had signed the constitution but had voted against the unpopular total population clause. Arguing against the measure, Hébert had asserted that "the only true democratic basis of Representation" was the number of qualified electors. Also, learning from their mistake of November 1851, when their failure to issue a platform contributed to their defeat, the Democrats advanced a strong party platform declaring that they stood in favor of free banking, internal improvements, public education, and amendment of the total population basis of representation. As the *Daily Delta* observed, the Democrats had "reversed positions with the whigs. They have at last awoke to the necessity of laying down a platform of State Reform."[46]

At the same time, the Whigs—who in the November 1851 elections had used a pro-Compromise of 1850 and strong pro-convention platform to catapult them to a large legislative majority—forgot this lesson and failed to define their program in 1852. While the *Bee* argued that "the Whigs established their platform two years ago, when locofocoism was afraid to open its lips," a more logical reason for the absence of a platform lay in party disagreement over the total population clause. If the party were to present a platform, it would have to take a stand on the constitution and thus, at least implicitly, on this constitutional issue. In some parts of the state, especially New Orleans, a plank supporting the clause would have meant political suicide, but formal objection to part of a constitution that the Whigs claimed sole credit for would have caused political embarrassment for many other Whigs.[47]

While sidestepping the issue of representation, the Whigs proudly accepted the rest of the 1852 constitution as their own. They asserted that the constitution was the work of a Whig-controlled convention and had been opposed by the Democrats. According to the *Bee*'s editor, the Whig party had secured its passage against the opposition of the Democratic party including its current slate of candidates. He added that a Whig electoral defeat now "would be like beginning to build a house, and not finishing it."[48] Furthermore, addressing the Democrats' pro-constitution platform, another Whig editor contended that the Democrats were "running Whig principles into the ground." Democrat John Slidell admitted that "popular will is in favor of a cooperation on the part of the state in public improvement" and that his party "will carry it out in a proper spirit."[49]

Thus, by December, both Louisiana parties had come to champion an activist government. The *Baton Rouge Gazette* proclaimed that Louisiana was "whig to the back bone."[50] Ironically, while the Whigs had been the primary advocates of these measures, they suffered more from the convergence of political views. The Whigs had used these issues to revitalize their party after passage of the 1845 constitution and to suppress all talk of forming a Union party in 1850. But, as the measures lost their salience, the Whig party lost some of its vigorous backing, particularly in New Orleans. At the constitutional convention in July, the city's delegation, which comprised twenty-six Whigs and only one Democrat, demonstrated its strong support for the Whig program. By December, however, the Whigs could no longer use the same issues to distinguish between their party and the Democrats. The Democratic party, however, had found a point on which to differentiate itself from the Whig party—formal opposition to the total population clause.

Having worked so hard for the passage of the constitution, many New Orleans Whigs wished to retire from the political scene and reap the benefits of their labors. Difficulties that the Whigs had in finding candidates in New Orleans—where "it is asking a great deal of a man of business to absent himself from New Orleans during the busiest period of the year"—illustrate this change in attitude. In 1852 not only did the party have to settle for its fourth choice as gubernatorial candidate but also four potential senate candidates declined their nominations. The *Bee*'s editor declared, "it is no easy matter to find four capable gentlemen willing . . . to surrender the claims of their business avocations in the behests of party."[51] James Robb, who had served as a Whig in the previous state senate, now viewed his political work as complete. Considered "first, last, and always a banker," Robb wanted to return to his business interests. After being assured by John Slidell that his prospective Democratic opponent would support the new constitution, Robb rejected his Whig renomination to the state senate.[52]

The difficulty in finding men to accept nomination for state office was not limited to the senate or to the Whig party. In an article entitled "The City of Declinations," the independent *Daily Delta* declared, "at least half the gentlemen who were originally nominated [in New Orleans] have declined." The Democrats, however, did not suffer as much as the Whigs, for they had fewer refusals and handled their nominating process with greater political acumen. Unlike the Whigs, the Democrats explored a man's interest in holding office before formally nominating him and therefore did not suffer the Whigs' embarrassment of frequently having to change their mastheads when nominees declined to run. Declinations also hurt the Whig party more than the Democratic party because of the political climate in which they occurred. At a time when the national Whig party was seen as teetering on the verge of collapse, Louisiana Whigs could not afford any sign that they were part of this trend. In the state campaign, the party was attempting to do everything in its power to show both its members and its opponents that it still possessed political vitality.[53]

Not only were the Whigs in New Orleans hindered by refusals to run on their ticket, but their attempts to attract immigrant voters in the presidential election also backfired. With the consolidation of the city, the traditional Creole-American struggle took the form of partisan politics, and the First District—the American, anti-Creole, anti-immigrant section—supported the Whigs. Nativists in Louisiana traditionally gravitated toward the Whig party, which supported stricter naturalization requirements and used its best efforts to keep immigrants from voting. The American section of New Orleans was interested in suppressing, not co-opting, the Irish vote. Thus, the Whig party's appeal to the Irish in the presidential campaign probably cost the Whigs more support than it gained. In the city's First District, General Scott won but with only 51.1 percent of the vote, while the Whig constitution captured 65.5 percent in the district. In a futile effort to secure immigrant votes, the Whigs abandoned nativism, one of their most potent weapons in New Orleans.[54]

The results of the December 27 election confirmed the Whigs' worst nightmares as "Locofocoism . . . triumphed to its heart's content." Paul Hébert defeated Louis Bordelon in the race for governor, and, likewise, Democrats triumphed in the battle for the other five statewide elective positions. Even more devastating for the Whigs, their representation in the state legislature fell from between 55 and 60 percent to 38 percent. Since the appearance of the Whig party in the mid-1830s, neither party had ever been reduced to such a minority presence in the state capitol.[55]

Election results in New Orleans provide the key to understanding the Whig defeat. Orleans Parish cast only 4,244 of its 9,751 votes in the governor's race—43.5 percent—for Louis Bordelon, the Whig candidate. The city's support of the Democratic party stands out even more when its legislative delegation is examined. With the Democrats capturing all four senate seats and nineteen of the parish's twenty-seven representative races, the *Bee* lamented that "the loss in New Orleans [was] too great to be overcome by our gains in the interior." This Democratic victory stands in stark contrast to previous Whig triumphs in the city. In earlier gubernatorial and presidential elections, the Whigs had only once before received less than 48.8 percent of the vote in Orleans Parish. In the prior legislature, three of the city's four senators were Whigs as were eighteen of the city's twenty-five representatives. In 1852 the Whigs swept the municipal elections and overwhelmingly controlled the city's delegation to the constitutional convention. And, in November the city favored the adoption of the Whig constitution—5,463 to 3,832, and even Scott performed respectably in the city, garnering 49.4 percent of the vote.[56]

The *Plaquemine Southern Sentinel* commented, "It would take a man with a wise head to account correctly for the political vagaries of New Orleans." The weakness of the Whig party in New Orleans, however, can be explained and was evident as early as the municipal elections of March when the independent reform movement appeared. The actions of this group demonstrated that partisan attachments in the city, especially among Whigs, were not solidly fixed. Scott's poor performance in the presidential election reinforced the idea that voters in New Orleans had lost some of their enthusiasm for the Whig party. Additionally, Whig effort to win immigrant support alienated many of the party's traditional supporters. Furthermore, Democratic use of the new constitution's total population provision especially hurt the Whigs in Orleans Parish, which would suffer more than any other from its enactment. In 1850 the parish contained 39.8 percent of the state's white population but only 25.2 percent of its total population. The *Louisiana Courier*'s unceasing efforts to remind voters of this disparity and the avowal of Democrats to remove the total population clause helped ensure a solid Democratic turnout, which contrasted sharply with Whig apathy.[57]

The newspapers offered a broad spectrum of reactions to the Whig defeat. Comparison with the Whig national disaster in November could not be avoided, and, according to one Whig stalwart, "Nothing else could be expected so soon after the election of General Pierce." The *Southern Sentinel* lamented, "Similar to the sweeping current of destruction which swallowed up the Whigs on the 2d of November last throughout nearly the entire country, is the flood which submerged them in this State, undoubtedly, on Monday last." The Democratic *Louisiana Courier* concurred that the people had punished the Whigs for "their alliance with Sewardism in the national contest." The collapse of the Whig party throughout the nation left many Louisiana Whigs with the impression that the party was dead, and this perception contributed to their reluctance to campaign actively in December. Trying to put a more positive spin on the results, some Whigs insisted that the Democrats had won only by adopting Whig principles. The *Baton Rouge Gazette* chose to take this optimistic approach when assessing the Democratic victors, "so long as they will support that portion [internal improvements and banks] of their platform . . . we are satisfied, believing as we do that a *rose will smell as sweet by another name*."[58]

The devastating December 1852 state election was not the last campaign of the Louisiana Whig party, but, after this setback, it became a powerless minority. In March 1853 the Whigs suffered a tremendous defeat in the New Orleans municipal races, and the state judicial elections of April also resulted in a Democratic triumph. Furthermore, at the party's August convention, efforts to regroup failed when only seven of forty-eight parishes sent delegates. The party had no strength left except in the Second Congressional District, the pro-tariff sugar parishes, which sent a Whig to the House of Representatives in 1853. By 1854 even staunch partisan journals admitted that the Louisiana Whig party was dead.[59]

What had caused this abrupt collapse of the Louisiana Whig party? Between 1850 and 1852, issues on both the national and state levels changed, and the Louisiana Whig party suffered from these alterations. At the state level, the acceptance of the positive liberal state by both parties led to the search for new issues to distinguish between them. On the national level, slavery disrupted the Whig party, especially at the presidential nominating convention, and caused a schism between Northern and Southern Whiggery. The failure of the Louisiana Whig party to address its altered political circumstances and the concentration of these changes in the later months of 1852 contributed to the speed of the Louisiana Whig party's collapse.

At the state level, the Whigs attempted to display their handiwork, the constitution of 1852, in order to convince voters that a significant difference remained between the two parties. Not only did the Democratic acceptance of the constitution weaken this appeal, but also the Whigs discovered that criticizing the 1845 constitution was simpler than defending their own program. The Whigs' division on the total population clause of the 1852 constitution created confusion at the state convention and undermined their December campaign. That article left the Whigs vulnerable to the Democratic label of them as an aristocratic party of wealthy slaveholders trying to subvert democracy. Democrats seized the total population clause as the issue that sharply distinguished them from the Whigs and could catapult them back into control of the state.

Agreement between the Democrats and the Whigs on the necessity of an activist government did not signal the end of two-party politics in Louisiana. In the antebellum South, as Marc W. Kruman succinctly observes in his study of North Carolina, "voters demanded not only solutions, but conflict itself." After the Whigs' disastrous performance at the end of 1852, this conflict quickly changed from a battle between Democrats and Whigs to a contest between Democrats and Know Nothings. In Louisiana, the Know Nothings' anti-immigrant message had particular resonance. With the highest percentage of foreign-born residents of any state in the South, Louisiana has been described as "a veritable hotbed of nativism." Running on a platform of reform and nativism, the Know Nothing party achieved a surprising victory in the New Orleans municipal elections in March 1854. The party followed this success with victories in several other local races and narrow losses in the gubernatorial election of 1855 and the presidential contest of 1856.[60]

Some historians have contended that Know Nothingism in the South was "Whiggery in disguise," and Louisiana Democrats labeled the Know Nothing party "a Whig Trick."[61] This explanation is too simplistic. The bulk of the Know Nothing party did consist of former Whigs, both because many had an affinity for nativism and because they found joining the Democratic party anathema. At the same time, however, the party was not simply a Whig surrogate. Know Nothings proudly pointed out that they included four former Democrats on their state ticket in 1855 and that ex-Democratic congressman Charles Gayarré had enlisted in the party. Some Democrats became Know Nothings, and by the same token some prominent Whigs, including Senator Judah P. Benjamin, refused to join the Know Nothings and became Democrats instead. Both the defection of Democrats into the Know Nothing party and the presence of former Whigs in the Democratic party belie a one-to-one correspondence between Whigs and Know Nothings.[62]

The growth of the Louisiana Know Nothing party proved that contestable issues still existed in the state in the 1850s. More important, the sudden appearance and the strength of the Know Nothings raises the question of why they and not the Whigs were able to exploit nativism. The Whig party had traditionally been the party of Louisiana's nativists. In the 1840s Whigs had opposed the expansion of suffrage partly because it would enable more immigrants to vote, and they claimed that they were defeated at the polls by immigrants who, at the behest of Democrats, voted illegally. In New Orleans, Whig voters resided primarily in the anti-immigrant American district of the city, and the party was weakest in the Creole and immigrant districts. In their 1852 presidential campaign, in an unsuccessful effort to attract immigrant votes, Louisiana Whigs abandoned their nativist message, but this did not preclude a return to nativism later.[63]

Explaining why Know Nothings replaced Whigs in Louisiana confirms the importance of studying antebellum politics from both state and national perspectives. The Know Nothings' appeal demonstrates not only that nativism was a readily available issue with which to oppose the Democrats but also that this topic still attracted many Louisiana Whigs. Therefore, the reason that the Whigs did not employ nativism in an attempt to resurrect the party in the 1850s cannot be found solely at the state level. Furthermore, the Whigs' inability to articulate partisan differences in late 1852 and early 1853 may partly account for the collapse of the party, but this failure is by no means the whole story of its disappearance. The status of the national parties must also be examined in order to untangle the mystery of the Whigs' abrupt demise.

The viability of political parties in the antebellum South was based upon their ability to defend the South and slavery in a national arena. The presidential election in November 1852 indicated that the Whig party had virtually ceased as an organized political force in most Southern states. No longer trusting each other on the slavery question, the Southern and Northern members of the Whig party began to look for other political parties; however, as long as a state Whig party could exploit state-level issues, it could survive. In Louisiana, the passage of the 1852 constitution marked the disappearance of the Whigs' most salient issue, suddenly leaving the Whig party vulnerable. Nativists in Louisiana saw the national Know Nothing party with its ability to represent the South in the national arena as a much more attractive channel for their nativism than a moribund Whig party.

The Louisiana Whig party was a victim of both its success within the state and its failure as a national party. Neither situation alone can explain the timing of the Louisiana Whig party's stunning reversal in December 1852. By the end of 1852, Louisiana Democrats had adopted the Whig party's positive political program including state aid to internal improvements and free banking. Therefore, at the state level, the Whigs had won the ideological battle but lost the partisan war. The disappearance of the partisan differences on the role of the government had unsettled both of Louisiana's political parties. For the Whigs, unfortunately, this disruption occurred simultaneously with a severe sectional schism in the national party. The interaction between these national and state events left the Whigs helpless and resulted in the sudden collapse of the party in Louisiana.

Though state political parties in the antebellum South were almost completely autonomous, their internal politics did not occur in a vacuum. National events, such as Winfield Scott's disastrous performance in the 1852 presidential election, influenced their fortunes. Such national incidents, however, did not affect all states in the same manner.

The response of each state party to national events depended upon its own political vigor. Each state cannot be studied simply in terms of its internal affairs or exclusively in terms of national events. Instead, the interaction between a state's particular issues and national affairs must be analyzed in order to understand antebellum politics.

Notes for "The Sudden Collapse of the Louisiana Whig Party"

[1]Michael F. Holt, *The Political Crisis of the 1850s* (New York and other cities, 1978), 14 (quotation); Holt, "The Mysterious Disappearance of the American Whig Party," in Holt, *Political Parties and American Political Development from the Age of Jackson to the Age of Lincoln* (Baton Rouge, 1992), 237-64; and J. Mills Thornton, *Politics and Power in a Slave Society: Alabama, 1800-1861* (Baton Rouge and London, 1978), xvi (quotation). U. B. Phillips and Arthur C. Cole in their early-twentieth-century studies of the Southern Whigs proposed that sectional division over the slavery issue caused an irreparable rift between the Southern and Northern wings of the party. Ulrich B. Phillips, "The Southern Whigs, 1834-1854," in Guy Stanton Ford, ed., *Essays in American History Dedicated to Frederick Jackson Turner* (New York, 1910), 203-29; and Arthur C. Cole, *The Whig Party in the South* (Washington, 1913). More recently, scholars have concluded that this explanation often focuses more on the approaching Civil War than on the events of the 1850s. In place of sectionalism, some historians have suggested that "[m]ore than any other factor, the rise of ethnocultural issues destroyed the second party system" or that the system collapsed not because of the parties' differences but because of their similarities. These arguments coincided with a number of state studies that analyzed the intertwining of local, state, and national issues in the Whig party's collapse. Meanwhile, other scholars have continued to stress the idea that slavery was the most important political issue in the antebellum South. Joel H. Silbey, "The Civil War Synthesis in American Political History," *Civil War History,* 10 (1964): 130-40; Lee Benson, *The Concept of Jacksonian Democracy: New York as a Test Case* (Princeton, 1961); and William E. Gienapp, *The Origins of the Republican Party, 1852-1856* (New York and Oxford, 1987), 66 (quotation). Southern state-level studies of antebellum politics include Thornton, *Politics and Power in a Slave Society* (Alabama); Thomas E. Jeffrey, *State Parties and National Politics: North Carolina, 1815-1861* (Athens, Ga., and London, 1989); and Paul H. Bergeron, *Antebellum Politics in Tennessee* (Lexington, Ky., 1982). For a study that emphasizes slavery see William J. Cooper, Jr., *The South and the Politics of Slavery, 1828-1856* (Baton Rouge, 1978). For purposes of this work the South consists of the states that seceded from the union, and the lower South comprises Louisiana, Texas, Mississippi, Alabama, Georgia, and Florida. South Carolina has been excluded from both groups because it possessed neither a competitive two-party system nor popular presidential elections. While in every other state the electorate voted for presidential electors, in South Carolina the legislature chose them.

[2]Previous studies of the Louisiana Whig party include William H. Adams, *The Whig Party of Louisiana,* The University of Southwestern Louisiana History Series, no. 6 (Lafayette, La., 1973); and Leslie M. Norton, "A History of the Whig Party in Louisiana" (Ph.D. dissertation, Louisiana State University, 1940). For a study of Louisiana's antebellum politics that stresses national issues see James K. Greer, "Louisiana Politics, 1845-1861" (Ph. D. dissertation, University of Texas, 1927). For a broader study of Louisiana politics see Perry H. Howard, *Political Tendencies in Louisiana* (Baton Rouge, 1971). Howard's understanding of the Whig party's collapse is limited by his placement of the presidential and legislative elections of 1852 in the wrong chronological order. He contends that the presidential results copied the preceding state campaign. The presidential election, however, took place in November and the state election did not occur until the end of December (pp. 57-58).

[3]William C. Carr to John Moore, July 13, 1852, David Weeks Papers, Louisiana and Lower Mississippi Valley Collections, Louisiana State University, Baton Rouge, La. (hereafter referred to as LLMVC).

[4]Adams, *Whig Party of Louisiana,* 41-116 and 180; Norton, "History of the Whig Party in Louisiana," 47-102; and Charles G. Sellers, Jr., "Who Were the Southern Whigs?" *American Historical Review,* 59 (1954): 335-46. Sellers emphasizes the role of banking and financial issues in the genesis of Southern Whig parties, even asserting that in Louisiana "Whiggery was simply National Republicanism continued under a new name" (344).

[5]For a discussion of the positive and negative views of governmental power of Whigs and Democrats see Benson, *Concept of Jacksonian Democracy,* 86-109; Harry L. Watson, *Liberty and Power: The Politics of Jacksonian America* (New York, 1900), 231-53; Ronald P. Formisano, *The Transformation of Political Culture: Massachusetts Parties, 1790s-1840s* (New York and Oxford, 1983), 268-74; Richard L. McCormick, *The Party Period and Public Policy: American Politics from the Age of Jackson to the Progressive Era* (New York and Oxford, 1986), 164-66; and Thomas Brown, "The Southern Whigs and Economic Development," in Brown, *Politics and Statesmanship: Essays on the American Whig Party* (New York, 1985), 170-88.

[6]Judith K. Schafer, "Reform or Experiment? The Louisiana Constitution of 1845," in Warren M. Billings and Edward F. Haas, eds., *In Search of Fundamental Law: Louisiana's Constitutions, 1812-1974* (Lafayette, La., 1993), 21-36; and Ted Ferguson, "The Louisiana Constitution of 1845" (M.A. thesis, Louisiana State University, 1948).

[7]Adams, *Whig Party of Louisiana,* 149; Henry W. Huntington to James G. Taliaferro, June 23, 1845, James G. Taliaferro Papers, LLMVC (second quotation); and Wayne M. Everard, "Louisiana's 'Whig' Constitution Revisited: The Constitution of 1852," in Billings and Haas, eds., *In Search of Fundamental Law,* 37-51 (quotation on 37). Perry Howard concurs with Adams's assessment that the Louisiana Whig party peaked in strength in 1844-1845 (Howard, *Political Tendencies in Louisiana,* 53-55); and Leslie Norton contends that the Whigs were "in a state of decline" after 1848 (Norton, "History of the Whig Party in Louisiana," 305).

[8]George D. Green, *Finance and Economic Development in the Old South: Louisiana Banking 1804-1861* (Stanford, Calif., 1972), 131-33; and *New Orleans Commercial Bulletin,* March 22, 1852 (quotation).

[9]*New Orleans Daily Picayune,* January 21, 1852. Ascertaining the exact partisan breakdown in the Louisiana legislature is impossible, but for 1852 the Whig majority is estimated at between 15 and 18 out of 129 total members. See also Norton, "History of the Whig Party in Louisiana," 335-37.

[10]John Slidell to James Buchanan, March 19, 1852, James Buchanan Papers, Historical Society of Pennsylvania, Philadelphia, microfilm, reel 18 (hereafter cited as James Buchanan Papers); Whig meeting preamble in *New Orleans Commercial Bulletin,* March 22, 1852; and *New Orleans Daily Delta,* March 21, 1852, 5.

[11]Leon C. Soulé, "The Creole-American Struggle in New Orleans Politics, 1850-1862," *Louisiana Historical Quarterly,* 40 (1957): 54-83 (quotation on 61).

[12]*New Orleans Daily Delta,* March 12, 1852; Samuel J. Peters, Jr., Diary, March 23, 1852, LLMVC; and Harry H. Evans, "James Robb, Banker and Pioneer Railroad Builder of Ante-Bellum Louisiana," *Louisiana Historical Quarterly,* 23 (1940): 191-93. For election results see *New Orleans Daily Picayune,* March 24, 1852; ibid., March 20, 1852 (independent ticket); *New Orleans Commercial Bulletin,* March 8, 1852 (Whig ticket); and *New Orleans Louisiana Courier,* March 13, 1852 (Democratic ticket).

[13]The April referendum passed 10,080 to 2,672. *New Orleans Daily Picayune,* May 12, 1852; and *Plaquemine Southern Sentinel,* May 1, 1852.

[14]*New Orleans Commercial Bulletin,* June 16, 1852 (first quotation); and *New Orleans Bee,* June 15, 1852 (second quotation). Election results in *New Orleans Commercial Bulletin,* June 15, 1852. The exact partisan breakdown is impossible to ascertain because newspapers disagreed on the party affiliation of some of delegates, and some names in the newspapers do not correspond with those in attendance at the convention.

[15]W. W. Pugh to Josephine N. Pugh, July 5, 1852, Pugh Family Papers, Center for American History, University of Texas at Austin, microfilm Records of Antebellum Southern Plantations, Series G, Part 1, reel 5 (hereafter cited as Pugh Family Papers).

[16]W. W. Pugh to Josephine N. Pugh, July 11, 1852 (second quotation) and July 28, 1852 (first quotation), Pugh Family Papers, microfilm, reel 5; *Journal of the Convention to Form a New Constitution for the State of Louisiana* (New Orleans, 1852), 91-99 (text of the constitution), 99 (vote on constitution), 100 (Hargis quotation); and Everard, "Louisiana's 'Whig' Constitution Revisited," 37-51. Whigs voted in favor of the constitution 77-0 and Democrats supported it 21-8. See *Journal of the Convention,* 5-6, for the vote on the president of the conven-

tion, which is an index to the partisan makeup of the convention. The *New Orleans Daily Picayune*, July 6, 1852, asserts that the vote was strictly partisan. Everard objected to the depiction of the 1852 constitution as a Whig measure, arguing that many Democrats sustained it. Though many Democrats supported constitutional revision, as a party they were at best ambivalent, while the Whigs were adamant in their demands for change.

[17]*Baton Rouge Gazette*, July 10, 1852.

[18]*Journal of the Convention*, 100.

[19]For vote on total population see *Journal of the Convention*, 65. Whigs voted 51 to 19 in favor of the total population basis, and Democrats supported it 25 to 22.

[20]*New Orleans Daily Delta*, November 2, 1852 (quotation). Results by parish in *New Orleans Bee*, November 24, 1852.

[21]Holt, "Mysterious Disappearance of the American Whig Party," 244.

[22]Presidential election returns from Burnham, *Presidential Ballots*, 254-57; and *New Orleans Bee*, November 4, 1852 (first quotation), and November 12, 1852 (second and third quotations).

[23]Burnham, *Presidential Ballots*, 245-57.

[24]*New Orleans Daily Picayune*, March 31, 1852.

[25]William H. Sparks to John Moore, May 17, 1852 (first quotation), E. B. Carr to Moore, April 9, 1852 (second quotation), and John Ray to Moore, February 11, 1852 (third quotation), all in David Weeks Papers, LLMVC.

[26]John Slidell to James Buchanan, May 22, 1852, James Buchanan Papers, reel 18.

[27]E. B. Carr to John Moore, April 9, 1852, David Weeks Papers, LLMVC; and *New Orleans Bee*, March 18, 1852.

[28]Accounts of the national convention can be found in Cole, *Whig Party in the South*, 245-59; *South and the Politics of Slavery*, 326-30; and William E. Gienapp, "The Whig Party, the Compromise of 1850, and the Nomination of Winfield Scott," *Presidential Studies Quarterly*, 14 (1984): 399-415. Of Scott's 159 votes on the fifty-third ballot only 11 came from the South—8 from Virginia and 3 from Tennessee. Cole, *Whig Party in the South*, 255.

[29]*Plaquemine Southern Sentinel*, June 26, 1852; *New Orleans Commercial Bulletin*, June 23, 1852; *New Orleans Louisiana Courier*, June 24, 1852; and Pierce Butler, *Judah P. Benjamin* (Philadelphia, 1906), 104.

[30]*New Orleans Daily Picayune*, September 9, 1852; and Holt, "Mysterious Disappearance of the American Whig Party," 246. Other descriptions of apathy can be found in Norton, "History of the Whig Party in Louisiana," 332-35; Cole, *Whig Party in the South*, 265; Gienapp, *Origins of the Republican Party*, 20; and Cooper, *South and the Politics of Slavery*, 341.

[31]Charles McVea to J. E. Elam, October 25, 1852, James Elam Letterbook, LLMVC. For attempts by the Whigs to overcome this apathy and support their national ticket see *New Orleans Bee*, July 2, 1852; Plaquemine *Southern Sentinel*, October 9, 1852; *New Orleans Daily Delta*, October 30, 1852; and W. Forshey to John Moore, August 25, David Weeks Papers, LLMVC.

[32]For a discussion of Union parties in the South see Cooper, *South and the Politics of Slavery*, 304-20; Cole, *Whig Party in the South*, 183-203; and Thornton, *Politics and Power in a Slave Society*, 165-200.

[33]*Whig Party of Louisiana*, 223; and John Ray to John Moore, February 11, 1852, David Weeks Papers, LLMVC (quotation).

[34]Proceedings of the Whig state convention in the *Baton Rouge Gazette*, March 20, 1852 (platform printed on p. 2, c. 3). For a discussion of the absence of traditional Whig measures in Southern platforms of 1852 see Cole, *Whig Party in the South*, 219-21.

[35]*West Baton Rouge Capitolian Vis-A-Vis,* October 27, 1852 (quotation); "Mr. Pierce on Harbor and River Improvements," *Baton Rouge Gazette,* July 3, 1852; and A. F. Rightor to Andrew McCollam, June 20, 1852, Andrew McCollam Papers, Southern Historical Collection, Manuscripts Department, Library of the University of North Carolina at Chapel Hill, microfilm, Records of Antebellum Southern Plantations, Series J, Part 5, reel 3 (hereafter cited as Andrew McCollam Papers).

[36]John Slidell to Howell Cobb, January 28, 1852, in U. B. Phillips, ed., "The Correspondence of Robert Toombs, Alexander H. Stephens, and Howell Cobb," *American Historical Association, Annual Report,* 2 (1911): 276.

[37]For quotations see issues of *Plaquemine Southern Sentinel,* and *New Orleans Bee,* September 1852 through November 1852. For the Southern Whig party's use of the slavery issue against Pierce see Cooper, *South and the Politics of Slavery,* 332-40.

[38]Joseph Moore to John Moore, August 21, 1852, David Weeks Papers, LLMVC.

[39]J. D. B. De Bow, *Statistical View of the United States . . . Being a Compendium of the Seventh Census* ([Washington, 1854]), 45, 61, 133, 136-37. Louisiana had fifty-five Roman Catholic churches with a seating capacity of 37,780, and a white foreign-born population of 67,308 representing 26.3 percent of the state's white population. The related numbers in Alabama were five, 5,200, and 7,498 and 1.76 percent; in Mississippi nine, 3,250, and 4,782 and 1.61 percent; in Georgia eight, 4,250, and 6,452 and 1.24 percent.

[40]*New Orleans Bee,* August 17, 1852. For charges of nativism against Pierce see Larry Gara, *The Presidency of Franklin Pierce* (Lawrence, Kans., 1991), 38-40; and Gienapp, *Origins of the Republican Party,* 21-25. For Pierce's Anglophilia see *Plaquemine Southern Sentinel,* September 11 and 18, 1852; and Samuel J. Peters, Jr., Diary, October 30, 1852, LLMVC.

[41]*Baton Rouge Gazette,* November 6, 1852 (first quotation); *New Orleans Bee,* November 30 (second quotation) and November 13 (third quotation), 1852.

[42]*New Orleans Louisiana Courier,* November 30, 1852; and *Franklin Planter's Banner,* December 25, 1852.

[43]Text of the Southern Whig Address in *Baton Rouge Gazette,* May 15, 1852; Gienapp, "Whig Party, the Compromise of 1850, and the Nomination of Winfield Scott," 401-2; Cole, *Whig Party of the South,* 236-38 and 246. For Louisiana Whigs praising Congressman John Moore's withdrawal from the caucus see *Baton Rouge Gazette,* May 1, 1852; and W. G. Wilson to John Moore, May 12, 1852, and unknown to Moore, May 17, 1852, David Weeks Papers, LLMVC. See Adams, *Whig Party of Louisiana,* 229-31.

[44]Charles E. A. Gayarré, *Address to the People of Louisiana on the State of Parties* (New Orleans, 1855), 2; and Holt, *Political Crisis of the 1850s,* 107.

[45]Official Proceedings of the Whig convention printed in *New Orleans Bee,* December 3, 1852; B. H. Payne to John Moore, December 11, 1852, and W. F. Weeks to Moore, January 4, 1853, David Weeks Papers, LLMVC.

[46]*Journal of the Convention to Form a New Constitution,* 65-66, 100 (quotation on 66); Democratic platform in *New Orleans Louisiana Courier,* December 26, 1852; and *New Orleans Daily Delta,* December 4 (quotation), and 15, 1852.

[47]*New Orleans Bee,* December 8, 1852; and *Plaquemine Southern Sentinel,* December 18, 1852. For an example of the difficulties and confusion that the total population clause caused see *West Baton Rouge Capitolian Vis-A-Vis,* December 22, 1852. This Whig newspaper feebly alleged that the clause was not a Whig measure but a Democratic trick to get the constitution rejected. Every New Orleans paper regardless of political allegiance opposed the total population clause during this campaign.

[48]*New Orleans Bee,* December 6, 20, 22, and 23 (quotation), 1852.

[49]*West Baton Rouge Capitolian Vis-A-Vis,* December 8, 1852; and John Slidell to James Robb, December 3, 1852, James Robb Papers, Williams Research Center, Historic New Orleans Collection.

[50]*Baton Rouge Gazette,* December 25, 1852.

[51]*New Orleans Daily Delta,* December 7, 1852 (first quotation); and *New Orleans Bee,* November 26, 1852 (second quotation), December 3, 1852.

[52]Evans, "James Robb, Banker and Pioneer Railroad Builder of Ante-Bellum Louisiana," 243; and John Slidell to James Robb, December 3, 1852, James Robb Papers.

[53]*New Orleans Daily Delta,* December 7 and 16 (quotation), 1852. For Whig declinations outside New Orleans see G. F. Connely to Andrew McCollam, December 14, 1852, Andrew McCollam Papers, reel 3.

[54]*New Orleans Bee,* November 3, 1852 (for figures on votes on the constitution and on the president); and Earl F. Niehaus, *The Irish in New Orleans, 1800-1860* (Baton Rouge, 1965), 84-88.

[55]*Franklin Planters' Banner,* February 17, 1853 (quotation). According to official election results in the *New Orleans Louisiana Courier,* January 22, 1853, the statewide election figures were Hébert (the Democrat), 17,813 defeating Bordelon (the Whig), 15,781. Estimates of the Democrats' legislative majority appear in *New Orleans Louisiana Courier,* January 6 and 11, 1853; *New Orleans Daily Delta,* January 6 and 12, 1853.

[56]*New Orleans Bee,* December 29, 1852, and January 5, 1853 (quotation). In 1846 the Whig gubernatorial nominee had received 46.1 percent of the vote in Orleans Parish.

[57]*Plaquemine Southern Sentinel,* January 1, 1853; and De Bow, *Statistical View of the United States . . . Being a Compendium of the Seventh Census,* 487.

[58]W. F. Weeks to John Moore, January 4, 1853, David Weeks Papers, LLMVC; *Plaquemine Southern Sentinel,* January 1, 1853; *New Orleans Louisiana Courier,* January 11, 1853; and *Baton Rouge Gazette,* January 1, 1853.

[59]*Plaquemine Southern Sentinel,* August 13, 1853; and Adams, *Whig Party of Louisiana,* 246-64.

[60]Marc W. Kruman, *Parties and Politics in North Carolina, 1836-1865* (Baton Rouge and London, 1983), 141. For the success of Louisiana's Know Nothing party see Marius Carriere, Jr., "The Know Nothing Movement in Louisiana" (Ph.D. dissertation, Louisiana State University, 1977); and Carriere, "Anti-Catholicism, Nativism, and Louisiana Politics in the 1850s," *Louisiana History,* 35 (1994): 455-74; and W. Darrell Overdyke, *The Know-Nothing Party in the South* (Baton Rouge, 1950), 13 (second quotation), 45-72, and 91-126.

[61]For a discussion of historians viewing Know Nothingism as a Whig disguise see Carriere, "Know Nothing Movement in Louisiana," 1-4 (first quotation on 4). For Democrats' accusations see ibid., 95 (second quotation).

[62]Carriere, "Know Nothing Movement in Louisiana," 95-98; and Butler, *Judah P. Benjamin,* 151.

[63]Leon C. Soulé, *The Know Nothing Party in New Orleans: A Reappraisal* (Baton Rouge, 1961), 39-58.

THE BEGINNINGS OF SAM[1]*

Leon Cyprian Soulé

The high-water mark for the Democratic party in New Orleans came in 1853. The sectional conflict, reopened during the consolidation struggle, caused the second (Creole) and the third (Creole-immigrant) districts to join forces under the Democratic banner. For nearly two years the coalition worked, effectively overriding the Americans.

In the aldermanic elections of 1853 the Democrats of the second and third districts sufficiently organized to gain complete control of the city council. In this off-year contest they elected seven aldermen and twenty-one assistant aldermen. The Whig press looked forward with fear and trembling; events proved their foreboding justified.[2]

The new council was quick to press its advantage over the American Whig mayor. Members of the Democratic party in the city influenced fellow Democrats in the state legislature to amend the city charter of 1852, which gave to the mayor complete authority over the police force. According to the amendments this responsibility was now vested in a police board composed of the mayor and the four recorders, each with one vote. The Democrats controlled the five-man board, since it contained only two Whigs—the mayor, and the recorder of the fourth district.[3]

Repercussions from the act were most strongly felt a year later in the municipal elections of 1854. The board then comprised four Democrats and one Whig, Recorder H. M. Summers from the first district. Summers was completely stymied, even to the point of not being able to choose the policemen for his district, as was the custom. He resigned in protest, and the council appointed a Democrat, George Y. Bright, to take his place. The result was the emergence of a Democratic police force, a valuable asset to that party at election time.[4]

Again working through the state legislature, the Democrats tightened their grip in April 1853, by striking from the city charter the provision which required that a member of the council remain out of office for six months before he could be elected to any other city position. The reason for this move was partisan. Soon there was to be a vacancy in one of the recorderships, and the Democrats had chosen a man to fill it. The stumbling

*First published as Chapter 3 in *The Know Nothing Party in New Orleans: A Reappraisal* (Baton Rouge, Louisiana Historical Association, 1962), 39-60. Reprinted with the kind permission of the Louisiana Historical Association.

block was the city charter. Despite the opposition of the mayor and his Whig supporters, it was suitably amended and the Democrats elected C. Ramos, a Creole from the second district.

The apex of the Democratic party's attempt to entrench itself as the dominant political power in New Orleans was the proposal in November 1853, of a so-called health ordinance to establish the position of public health officer for the city. This official was to have been paid $6,000 a year, a salary greater than that of any public servant in the state except the chief justice of the supreme court. His control of patronage through the appointing power would have been greater than that of the governor. The police would have been subject to his requirements, and he was to have complete jurisdiction over the removal of dilapidated buildings and similar projects. His time of office was to last until May of 1856. Positive that this was another attempt by the Democrats to provide a political plum for one of the faithful, the Whigs campaigned vigorously against it.[5] The board of assistant aldermen passed the health ordinance by a vote of eleven to three but decided that it could not become law since it involved an appropriation of more than $1,000. According to the charter, such appropriations required a majority vote of the twenty-six members of the assistant board. When the ordinance was tabled,[6] the Whigs breathed a sigh of relief, for they feared that the Democratic board might go on creating positions until every member had been provided for, to the complete depletion of the city treasury.

Complaints about streets indicated that parties were aligning by districts. Whereas eight months earlier the streets had been clean and orderly, by June of 1853 they were described as festering and filthy, especially between Poydras and Canal, the heart of the American district.[7] The growing deadlock between the Whig executive and Democratic council was evident when the Whig controller, James Jolles, was accused of neglect of city sanitation. Jolles insisted that, although his weekly reports to the council showed that the street contractors were doing nothing, the board had taken no action. Instead, the Democratic council had infuriated the American section by laying a plank road on Prytania Street, even though the residents had signed a petition protesting its construction as incommodious and unhealthful. The controller's language was strong to the point of being abusive, and the council considered impeachment. They never took action, however, and he served out his term.[8]

The Americans presented a petition to the council to move the polling places from the "coffee-houses," as many of the city's saloons were called, to fire stations and school houses. It was met with derision by the Democratic council, who scornfully recommended submitting it to the educational committee. The Whigs retorted angrily that the Democrats were merely afraid of losing the votes of their immigrant political allies.[9]

The New Orleans press clearly reflected the swirl and flow of political currents as the two major parties formed along nationalistic lines. The *Daily Crescent*, published in the first district and traditionally representing American interests, fell in behind the Whigs and, after their demise, behind their successor, the American or Know Nothing party. The *Louisiana Courier* was published in French as well as in English in the second district. Representing the Creoles, it consistently supported the Democrats.[10] Emile La Sère, the owner, was one of the leaders of the Democratic party in the state.[11] The *Daily Orleanian*, also published in French and English, represented primarily the immigrants of the third district. It was generally Democratic in sympathy, but not so strongly partisan as the other two. In these newspapers, which were the organs of expression in the districts in which they were printed, the Democratic position soon became synonymous with the Creole point of view, while the Whig program and later that of the Know Nothings, was identified with American interests.

By 1853 the Americans knew that, even though their numbers were increasing rapidly and the American district was growing apace, they would never be able to catch up with the mounting tide of immigrants from Ireland and Germany who were pouring annually into New Orleans. As these immigrants coalesced politically with the Creoles, the Americans increasingly realized that the control of the city which they had sought by consolidation had slipped away from them. They struck at this coalition by denouncing naturalized citizens and attempting to hinder foreigners from becoming naturalized so that they could vote. Americans warned of the threat of foreign domination over the city; Creoles in reply called upon the immigrants to beware of the Americans.[12] E. J. Carrell, an American candidate for district attorney in 1853, was defeated by the appearance of an anonymous notice accusing him of Creole and foreign sympathies. His public denials were of no avail, and he lost the Whig vote.[13]

Doubtless it was the Creole-foreign alignment which forced the Americans into complete political organization. The Americans had long recognized the infiltration of the local Democratic party by the immigrants, though the influx of foreigners was by no means unique to New Orleans. All of the major American cities, and especially the seaports, were faced with this problem. From the councilmanic elections of 1853 until the outbreak of the Civil War the constant cry of the American press was against the illegal use of the foreign vote by the Democrats, and the whole brunt of American political action was to suppress what they considered an illegal vote. Election statistics after 1852 show that by and large the second (Creole) district turned to the Democratic party in order to use these foreign votes to fight their opponents—the Americans.

The supreme court justice election of April 1853 offers an excellent example of how the second (Creole) and third (immigrant) districts worked together to defeat the first (American). The candidates were Christian Roselius, a German-born American Whig, and Thomas Slidell, brother of John Slidell, chief of the Democratic party. Through intermarriage and by association the Slidells were both linked with the Creoles. The strategy followed by the Democrats was to accuse Roselius of being nativist in sympathy. The Democratic Creole press stressed this point, while the American press attempted to refute it in editorial after editorial. Speeches of Roselius from the constitutional convention of 1852 were quoted in order to prove that he had been proforeign in his attitudes toward getting the qualifications for voting reduced in order to help the immigrant or naturalized citizen. This was true. Nevertheless, papers like the *Louisiana Courier* constantly pressed the point that Roselius was against all immigrants and that to vote for him was to put a man on the bench who was inimical to their interests. In attempting to counteract this propaganda the *Daily Crescent* stressed the reason Roselius had been such an outstanding lawyer—he was a self-made man and had risen from nothing. Such a man as Thomas Slidell, on the other hand, had been born into affluence and had every opportunity to better himself.[14]

The Democratic strategy was successful and Slidell was elected over Roselius. The results furnish clear evidence that Slidell won because of the Creole-immigrant coalition. In the first (American) district the returns were 1,546 for Slidell and 2,137 for Roselius, who won by a majority of 591. In the second (Creole) district Slidell received 1,569 votes and Roselius 1,246—a majority of 323 for Slidell. In the third (immigrant) district Slidell got 828 votes and Roselius 523—a majority of 305 for Slidell. In the fourth district Slidell led by 18 votes out of a total of 206. Slidell carried the city by fifty-five votes. The combination of Creoles and immigrants within the Democratic party gave him the victory.

The Whig Americans attributed their loss of the election to two activities by the Democrat Creoles: the purchase of votes and the smearing of Roselius as a nativist. Influenced by this charge against the Whig candidate, immigrant voters had joined with the Creoles to bring victory to the Democratic party.[15]

About six weeks after the supreme court election the *Daily Crescent* virtually acknowledged the death of its party. A rumor had been circulating ever since the last presidential election that the Whigs were dying. Firmly denying the charge at first, the editor ended in admitting the disintegration of the party and re-emphasized the virtue of the Whig principles and the need for some new organization. In truth the day of the Whigs was over. The city was virtually abandoned to the Democratic party, in which American interests were so little represented.[16]

The joint strength of the second and third districts increased daily. With the Whig party in pieces, the Americans struck frantically at the coalition's source of power—the mounting tide of immigrants. As the fall election of 1853 for members of the state legislature and parish offices approached, the Americans continued to hammer away at the flagrant and fraudulent use the Democrats were making of the immigrant vote. It was reported that the sixth district court actually had to be closed for a few days in order to bring up the minutes. They were lagging because of the number of applications for naturalization papers, most of them illegal. The Democrats staunchly denied these allegations.[17]

As in the spring municipal elections of 1853, so in the fall, the Creole-immigrant coalition functioned well. The Democrats won all offices elected on a city-wide basis. In the race for sheriff their candidate, Bernard Marigny, beat his Whig opponent, James Freret, by 2,474 votes. In the American district the Whigs had majorities, but these were again offset in the Creole and immigrant sections. In the contest for state representatives, Americans placed some Whig candidates, for they were elected by district. But state senators, chosen on a city-wide basis, were all Democrats, as were the two congressmen elected from the New Orleans area.[18]

Americans were embittered that this election drew the largest vote ever cast, despite the depopulation of the city during the recent yellow fever epidemic. Even the noncommittal *Daily Picayune* wryly commented on the increase in an article entitled, "The Growth of New Orleans," contrasting the vote of 9,865 cast in the mayoralty contest of 1852, a very spirited election, with the 12,876 cast in 1853. With biting sarcasm the *Picayune* calculated that at this rate New Orleans would have 700,000 people by April 1, 1862. While the article did not explicitly say so, the implication was strong that the Democrats won by the use of many fraudulent votes.[19]

The most important reason advanced by the Americans to explain the landslide of the Democrats was that the Democrat-controlled municipal council had appointed none but "loco-foco Democrats" to be inspectors, and they in turn counted only Democratic votes. Dominating the council was tantamount to controlling elections at the state and national level, and therefore the party in power on the council virtually determined the outcome of these elections.[20]

The year 1853 closed with the Democrats practically in complete control of New Orleans politics at all levels. The Whig party had succeeded in electing only a few members to the state legislature from the first district. The demoralized condition of their party left the Americans in a state of despair. With the electorate almost completely determined by the Democrats and the members of that party largely representative of downtown New Orleans, the uptown portion of the city was becoming politically inarticulate.

To the Americans 1854 was at first but a continuation of the same dismal situation of 1853. A grand jury report showed that many prisoners had not been placed on the court dockets; convicted lawbreakers either were not put in jail or were released from charges that were not bailable. In some cases bonds had been accepted when the security was known to be no good. The weak registration law, recently passed by the legislature, was almost worthless since noncompliance was not a bar to voting. Naturalization frauds continued daily. According to the Americans the Irish were organized into bands by the Democrats and marched to the polls to vote, where hand-picked Irish Democratic inspectors and election officials permitted them to vote without question. Plural voting was rampant, and the protest of the citizenry had no effect.[21] At the bottom of the Americans' inability to gain a fair share in the voice of government was this use by the Democrats of the ever-mounting foreign or immigrant vote.

With the demise of the Whig party nationally[22] its anti-immigrant elements found outlet in a revival of the Native American party, a strongly nationalistic organization which had been briefly active during the 1840s. Now called the Know Nothing party, its basic principles were antiforeignism and anti-Roman Catholicism. The new party increased rapidly and had branches or wigwams throughout the United States. The year 1854 witnessed notable successes for the Know Nothings in many parts of the country. In Massachusetts they elected a governor, and they won control in Delaware also. In

New York they polled 122,000 votes for governor, although they did not succeed in electing their candidate. The national congressional elections saw seventy-five Know Nothing congressmen seated.[23]

As the New Orleans city election of 1854 approached, the American press began to speak in favor of a new political force, the Independent Reform party. A notice appeared in the local press on March 14, 1854: "In order to secure Public Reform in our Municipal affairs, in a economical and thorough administration of our city government . . . the undersigned hereby call a City Convention to assemble on Lafayette Square on Thursday evening, March 16, 1854, at six o'clock, for the purpose of nominating irrespective of Party some of our best and most capable citizens to fill the various charter offices."[24] Of approximately six hundred signers less than fifteen had French names.[25]

Some Democrats immediately concluded that this was nothing more than the Whig party trying to resuscitate itself.[26] Many Creoles, however, identified it as the Know Nothings (Native Americans) in disguise. The Americans did not deny this but replied, "Bodysnatchers should not be afraid of ghosts," explaining that a party that raised whole graveyards to vote should not be afraid of rumors about the Know Nothings.[27] The *Propagateur Catholique* publicly announced that the movement was Know Nothing inspired and warned Catholics not to join. The publication did not "believe that any Creole would be willing to degrade himself by such an act of apostacy."[28]

At the same time that the Reformers ran their announcement of the mass meeting in Lafayette Square, there appeared in the *Daily True Delta* a lengthy exposé of the Know Nothing organization in New Orleans.

> The objects of the 'Know Nothings,' are two-fold—part religious, part political; and the ends aimed at the disfranchisement of adopted citizens, and their exclusion from office, and perpetual war upon the Catholic religion. With these for cardinal principles, the qualifications for membership and brotherhood are easily determined.
>
> *1st.* The applicant for admission to a 'wigwam,' must be a native born citizen, of native born parents, and not of the Catholic religion.
>
> *2nd.* To renounce all previously entertained political leanings, and co-operate exclusively with the new order.
>
> *3rd.* To hold neither political, civil, nor religious intercourse with any person who is Catholic; but, on the contrary, to use all available means to abolish political and religious privileges he may at present enjoy.
>
> *4th.* That he will not vote for any man for office who is not a native citizen of the United States, or who may be disposed, if elected, to place any foreigner or Catholic in any office of emolument or trust—the latter not being, in the opinion of 'Know Nothings,' a credible witness, in any case, save where the oath is administered by his priest.
>
> The 'pass words' and 'signs' for admission into the 'wigwam' of the 'Know Nothings,' are as follows: The applicant raps at the outer door an indefinite number of times, asking at the close, in a low, whispering voice, 'What meets here, today, (or night, as the case may be)?' The interrogated immediately replies, 'I don't know,' to which the applicant for admission responds, 'I am one,' and forthwith is admitted to a second door, at which he

gives four distinct raps, when the door being opened, he whispers to its attendant, 'Thirteen,' and then advances into the body of the lodge.

If disposed to leave before the adjournment of the Lodge, the member leaving salutes the President, then the Vice President, by first placing his right hand on his heart, then letting it fall to his side, whispering to the guardian as he retires 'thirteen.'

If a member requires the assistance of a brother when mixing promiscuously with the public, he places the right forefinger upon the left eye-brow, as if in the act of scratching, looking directly at the person whose attention he desires to attract, when, if the person be a member, he is bound to respond immediately by a similar sign. If it be desired to know of a stranger whether he is of the initiated, on shaking hands with him the middle finger is placed upon the lowest joint of his little finger, next the wrist, with a gentle pressure; when, if he be a member, he will ask 'Where did you get that?' to which he will rejoin, 'I don't know;' and the querist will end by replying 'I don't know either.'

Nothing concerning the association is to be committed to writing, or published; and the most profound silence and secrecy are to be observed by every 'Know Nothing' outside; but every thing inside the Wigwam is imparted indiscriminately to members.

Every member, on admission, swears by holding up his right hand, and pleages [*sic*] himself to do all in his power to put down foreign influence, and particularly the Catholic religion, and in no case to vote for any person for any office who is not a 'native American citizen;' and no one, with some exceptions, is eligible to membership, unless he and both of his parents are native born.

There are several Lodges, or Wigwams, at this time open—one, presided over by a Mr. H---ty, assembles in a room in the Mechanics' Institute, and another holds its meetings at No. 9, New Basin.[29] There are three degrees to be taken by members, between each, intervals of three weeks must occur.

The New York Missionary who came here to organize the 'Know Nothings' is styled 'Judge Advocate,' and he is charged with like duties in every other city in this section.

As no records are kept, or publications made by the association, the plan of notifying members of any emergency requiring their speedy assembling is by scattering small square pieces of white paper over the banquettes and public thoroughfares, and by nailing them to posts, doors, or other places accessible to the public.[30]

The Americans defended their independent party on the ground that its purposes were to keep out those who would use parties for their own advantage and to cast off partisan shackles. They charged that the Democratic party perpetuated its power by corralling the immigrant vote and maintaining grog shops as polling places in order to keep decent people away. It was not right for a city the size of New Orleans to be governed by a comparative handful of foreigners who were ignorant of its laws and hardly spoke its language. The poor people should support law and order more than the rich, Americans maintained, for the rich could afford to buy protection, but the poor man could not. Instead of studying our institutions and waiting a while to take an active part, these Irish immigrants rushed headlong into politics as fast as they landed, aiding disorder and illegality. "The country must at last, . . . treat them as aliens," proclaimed the *Daily Crescent*, "if they will persist in not being Americans, nothing but Americans, and entitled to no more than all other Americans, even after being honestly naturalized."[31] The indignation of the "sons of the soil" was roused. The issue was drawn.

On March 22 the Democratic Creole *Louisiana Courier* openly stated that the American *Crescent* was one of the warmest friends of the Know Nothings and warned the foreign and Catholic elements of the city to beware. The *Crescent* insisted that there was no political nor religious question at stake, but a matter of justice and correction of misrule. But already in the American press there was practically open warfare against foreigners and Catholics.[32] At first the Americans pretended that the Independent movement was not a political party. They professed always to have considered parties in city government as "fooleries and abominations"[33] and could see no relation at all between national parties and municipal affairs. It was senseless to keep the same party in power on the local level because it was in power in Washington. What was the relation between men in Washington and the streets, levees, and gutters of New Orleans? Federal politics could not put out a fire or catch a thief or a housebreaker, or cleanse the town and prevent yellow fever. "Quit your party politics, gentlemen! and go to work, not like factionists, but like men and citizens!"[34]

While vigorously denouncing parties, the Americans were urging utmost support of one. No longer able to use the Whig party as a means of opposition because of its national disintegration, they found the new nativist movement ideally suited to their purpose, for it struck at the very basis of the Creoles' local political power. When questioned about their former stand against independent movements, the Americans simply replied that they had changed their minds.[35] But the truth was that in 1852 the term "Independent" had meant Democrat (or Creole), while in 1854 the term "Independent" meant American.

In its inception the Know Nothing party was anti-Catholic as well as anti-immigrant in New Orleans. The Creoles labeled it "the anti-Catholic Native American movement."[36] The Catholics on the ticket were explained as a Know Nothing bid for the Whig vote below Canal Street. The party knew that it could not have the support of the lower sections' former Whigs without renominating officials such as Pilié and DeBuys, that no ticket could be formed without bearing the names of Creoles, by birth and by baptism Catholic. Though antiforeign, anti-Catholic, and anti-Creole in sentiment, the Know Nothing party by this method succeeded in drawing some members from those sections.[37]

The Germans, who for the most part were not Catholic, rejected the Know Nothing party solely on its anti-immigrant basis. They immediately recognized the Independent Reform ticket of 1854 as the Know Nothing party and saw "in the principles of the Democratic party the best surety for defeating the enemies of the people." They appealed, therefore, "urgently to all German citizens of New Orleans, to vote at the next municipal election the whole Democratic ticket, without any exception."[38]

The Creole-immigrant combination worked well again in the municipal election of 1854; the Democratic party drew its strength almost wholly from those sections of the city inhabited by these two groups. The Know Nothing vote was concentrated in the first, or American, district, while the fourth district, Lafayette, was divided between both parties, to the keen disappointment of the Americans. The "Irish channel" probably accounted for much of the Democratic vote in that section.

Democrat John L. Lewis, an old resident of the city who was closely associated with the Creoles, was elected mayor in 1854. His strength lay completely in the second, third, and fourth districts. In the first district the Independent Reform candidate, J. W. Breedlove, polled the sizable majority of five hundred votes; and all of the Independent's candidates for alderman won easily. The other districts elected all of the Democratic candidates except three assistant aldermen. The Democratic vote in the second (Creole) district was larger than it had been in 1852, demonstrating that many of the erstwhile Creole Whigs had switched to the Democratic party in an attempt to defeat the Americans.[39]

In all districts there were minorities, but the majority supported the party which represented its sectional interests. In the American sector immigrants in the "Irish channel" rejected the Know Nothing party and chose to stay with the Democrats. Similarly many of the former Creole Whigs, unable to bring themselves to join Democratic ranks, had no other choice than the American party. There were also people like Charles Gayarré, a Democrat, who went over to the Know Nothing party in protest. He had personal grievances against the ruling clique of his party and did not approve of their fraudulent use of the immigrant vote.[40]

On election day, March 27, 1854, an incident occurred which set a pattern for much of the rest of the decade. Violence at one of the polls resulted in a stabbing. It had been rumored that the Democrats were going to march bands of voters from poll to poll and vote them over and over again in order to swell the Democratic numbers. The Independent Reform movement had been formed to stop this sort of thing; it was determined to do so. One of the polls to be attacked by these Democratic bands was the seventh precinct in the first ward of the first district, located at the O'Donnell ballroom at the corner of Circus (Rampart) and Poydras streets. Because of a rumor about much fraudulent voting there, the Independents decided to watch that poll carefully. According to the Know Nothings, twenty men who had already voted at the fourth precinct appeared at O'Donnell's and demanded to vote again. When they were refused, a fracas followed in which one man was stabbed in the back. The group was chased away, and it was said when the poll closed that the precinct's vote was 932, but the next morning it was announced as 1,400.[41] The party in power was accused of having done everything it could to get rid of the Independents who were challenging these illegal votes.[42]

A similar incident occurred about seven o'clock on election night. A band of men proceeded to a seventh ward poll after it had been called to their attention that no Reform men were witnessing the counting of the ballots. They requested admittance but were refused, whereupon they battered open the door and were met by several pistol shots. No one was killed, but the chief of police, Stephen O'Leary, was wounded. At about four in the morning the rooms where the ballot boxes of the seventh ward had been deposited were broken into and their contents scattered in the street. The *Daily Crescent* reported several rows of a similar nature.[43]

In another instance in the seventh ward the Democrats, fearing they had lost the election there, seized control of many of the boxes and proceeded to count the ballots. The mob in front of the poll, where no Independent commissioner was allowed to participate in the counting, learned that 750 more votes had been cast than there were registered voters in the ward. The mob destroyed the ballot box.[44] Other cases were reported in which Irish Democrats forcibly took possession of the boxes. A city policeman was charged with breaking into one of the polling places and literally throwing out the Independent commissioners. It was said that enough fraudulent ballots were known at a few precincts to question majorities everywhere else. The common council had ceased legislating, the recorders had not heard any cases, and their police had left their thief-catching, "piously consigning our city to the care of God," while they took to electioneering.[45] The results of the election were not contested, however, except where the ballot boxes were destroyed. In these instances new elections were held, which resulted in Independent Reform victories.[46]

Both parties were accused of abducting sailors from ships or boarding houses and of forcing or paying them to vote. By this means a band of fifty or a hundred men could readily be procured to vote at any precinct in the city.[47] Apparently the Democrats got the Irish to do their dirty work, as it was always they who came in for the heaviest criticism. All of the commissioners and police in the districts where trouble occurred were said to be Irish, the illegal votes were supposedly cast by the Irish, and all of the lawbreaking was attributed to them. Yet election statistics indicate that the Creoles must have been their partners in crime, for the same candidates who carried the Irish immigrant districts also won in the Creole-populated precincts.[48]

Though the Americans had made inroads on the Democratic control of the municipal government, they by no means controlled the situation, even in their own district. It was after the 1854 municipal election that first district Recorder H. M. Summers resigned from the Democratic controlled police board because he was blocked in choosing policemen for his own district. The police force was an important part of the election machinery and without it no party's power could be complete.

By September of 1854 New Orleans had become the scene of bloody riots, assassinations, brawls, and street fights, chiefly between the immigrants and the Know Nothings. Armed gangs paraded through the streets after nightfall looking for encounters. Allegedly the trouble originated during the first week of September when a man killed a dog, and the owner demanded the watchman to arrest the man. When the watchman refused to do this, the indignation of the injured person's neighbors touched off the riot that was to last for many days in New Orleans. Participants were mostly professional hoodsmen and half-grown boys; watchmen prowled the streets at night armed with muskets and joined the gangs of ruffians.[49] The days were peaceful, but the hours of nightfall were utterly disorderly. Men were attacked, beaten, and shot down; houses were gutted; and half-drunk armed bands paraded through the streets with threats and cries. It was said that the police not only failed to discourage these riots but actually participated in them.[50]

On one occasion Mayor Lewis, making a patrol of the city during the riot, at midnight encountered the former chief of police, Stephen O'Leary, armed with a musket and far from his home. The mayor finally persuaded him to give up his musket, although when O'Leary called the next day to collect it he spoke insultingly to Lewis.[51] Accounts were published of respectable men and women who were shot at on their own verandas by the ruffians. Wild rumors circulated that the Americans were out to burn the Catholic churches and to slaughter Catholics generally. Most of the initiative in these outbreaks seems to have been taken by the foreigners, especially the Irish. Even the Democratic mayor attempted to disperse crowds of Irishmen by telling them that Americans were not contemplating an attack.[52]

After a week of such rioting the mayor was finally obliged to recognize the inefficiency of the police force in dealing with the situation. He issued a proclamation calling for the enrollment of private citizens as a special civil police and placed a curfew of 8:00 p.m. on the entire city. About 250 citizens answered the call; divided into squads, they patrolled the city so effectively that a precarious peace was finally restored.[53] This newly formed police force arrested several of the ruffians, including O'Leary, who was charged with engaging in the riots, leading persons to commit acts of violence, and constantly carrying concealed weapons. He posted bond and was released.[54]

The Americans severely criticized the Democratic administration, and even Mayor Lewis admitted that the police were divided and sectional. A single head was lacking, and there was much insubordination. The mayor thought the police department should be consolidated with one person at the head, with full responsibility.[55] These riots, while not the occasion of an election, marked the first bloody encounter between the Know Nothings and the Democrats. The sectional nature which the parties had assumed was revealed when the *Louisiana Courier* remarked that "it was unsafe for a citizen to appear in the streets above Canal street, unless he was recognized as a Whig or as one of the fraternity."[56]

Political activity for 1854 ended on November 17 with a seemingly unimportant election for a state senator and two state representatives. The following excerpt, however, shows that no longer would the Americans consider any election unimportant: "Little things grow out of great ones—oaks from acorns [*sic*]. If these primary elections are attended to, the great ones will go right; for in our government there is the same intimate connection between the different parts, that there is in a nice piece of machinery. The municipal elections are the smaller wheels, and the more easily moved. If they go right, all goes right; but if they are out of gear no amount of steam or patriotism can make a fitting compensation. Let the little wheels, therefore, be attended to. Let *every* man vote on every occasion."[57]

In this election the Democratic party was positively identified as anti-American. Of its candidates, the American *Creole*[58] said, "It is . . . their peculiar praise that they do not sympathize with Americans. This is significant of the position they occupy, and the agencies invoked to secure success."[59]

Apparently the "little wheels" were well oiled. In this election all of the Democratic candidates lost for the first time in two years. The reason for the Know Nothing victory was best expressed by the Democratic *Louisiana Courier*: "Their perfect organization, and thorough concert of action, gave them extraordinary facilities for bringing their adherents to the polls." The use of knives and pistols to control the polls was an equally contributing factor, according to the Creoles.[60]

Not only did the Democrats lose, they lost by heavy majorities. Their candidate for state senator received 1,565 votes, while the Know Nothing drew 3,830 votes. In the election for house members both candidates were from the American district. The contest in the first representative district resulted in 355 for the Know Nothing and 212 for the Democrat; in the fourth the Democrat received 146 to his opponent's 290.[61]

By 1852 the American section of New Orleans was willing to reunify the city provided its interests were sufficiently protected. From the Americans' point of view, the other two sections had brought New Orleans to the verge of bankruptcy. Incorporating the town of Lafayette gave the Americans room for growth. In the years immediately after consolidation the immigrant vote there was sometimes larger than the American, and the Creoles won the foreigners over to their Democratic coalition. The Americans, finding themselves without an organization after the Whig party's dissolution, faced political oblivion. Events called for immediate and decisive action. The revival of the Native American party, with its anti-immigrant plank, furnished them a ready weapon with which to fight their way to political domination.

Notes for "The Beginnings of Sam"

[1]"Sam" was the symbol used by the Know Nothing party in all of its campaigns. Whenever Know Nothings appeared in great numbers at political rallies or during elections, "Sam" was said to have appeared.

[2]*Daily Crescent*, March 29, 1853.

[3]Ibid., November 1, 1853. This was the last time the first (American) district had a Democratic recorder.

[4]Ibid., April 12, 25, October 11, 15, 1854; *Louisiana Courier*, October 21, 1853.

[5]*Daily Crescent*, April 20, November 25, 29, 1853. See the *Louisiana Courier*, November 25 and 29, 1853, for Democratic justification of the measure.

[6]*Daily Crescent*, December 21, 1853. The board and the assistant board of aldermen were comparable to the two houses of Congress. An ordinance passed by one had to be approved by the other before becoming law.

[7]Ibid., June 3, July 1, November 25, 1853.

[8]Ibid., July 21, 22, 23, 1853; *Commercial Bulletin*, July 22, 25, 1853; *Louisiana Courier*, July 23, 1853.

[9]*Daily Crescent*, October 31, 1853; *Commercial Bulletin*, October 31, 1853.

[10]*Daily Crescent*, January 7, 1851.

[11]W. Darrell Overdyke, *The Know Nothing Party in the South* (Baton Rouge, 1950), 23.

[12]*Daily Crescent*, October 26, 1853, March 21, 1854; *Louisiana Courier*, March 22, 1854.

[13]*Daily Crescent*, May 23, 24, 1853.

[14]Ibid., April 4, 11, 1853; *Commercial Bulletin*, April 4, 1853; *Louisiana Courier*, April 2, 3, 1853.

[15]*Daily Crescent*, April 5, 7, 1853; *Commercial Bulletin*, April 8, 1853.

[16]*Daily Crescent*, May 24, 1853.

[17]Ibid., October 18, 19, 21, 1853; *Louisiana Courier*, October 20, 22, 23, 25, 1853.

[18]*Daily Picayune*, November 9, 1853; *Daily Crescent*, November 10, 1853.

[19]*Daily Picayune*, November 11, 1853.

[20]*Daily Crescent*, November 8, 11, 1853; *Louisiana Courier*, November 11, 1853.

[21]Overdyke, "History of the American Party in Louisiana," *Know Nothing Party*, 257.

[22]The last Whig candidate for president was Gen. Winfield Scott, who ran in 1852. Locally and statewide, 1853 was the last year in which the Whig party made nominations.

[23]Follet, "The History of the Know Nothing Party in Louisiana," 24.

[24]Ibid., 21-22; *Commercial Bulletin*, March 14, 16, 1854.

[25]*Daily Orleanian*, March 15, 1854.

[26]*Louisiana Courier*, March 15, 1854.

[27]*Daily Crescent*, March 16, 1854. The Democrats had often been accused of voting the dead.

[28]*Louisiana Courier*, March 19, 1854, quoting the *Propagateur Catholique*.

[29]Both of these locations were uptown.

[30]*Daily True Delta*, March 15, 1854.

[31]*Daily Crescent*, March 21, 1854.

[32]Ibid., March 23, 1854.

[33]Ibid., March 16, 1854.

[34]Ibid., February 27, 1854. See also, *Commercial Bulletin*, March 17, 22, 24, 1854.

[35]*Daily Crescent*, March 20, 1854.

[36]Follet, "The History of the Know Nothing Party in Louisiana," 19.

[37]*Louisiana Courier*, March 23, 27, 1854; Robert Clemens Reinders, "The Louisiana American Party and the Catholic Church," *Mid-America*, 40 (New Series, 29 [1958]): 218 and passim.

[38]*Louisiana Courier*, March 25, 1854; *Die Deutsche Zeitung*, March 25, 1854.

[39]*Daily Picayune*, March 29, 1854.

[40]Henry P. Dart, ed., "Autobiography of Charles Gayarré," *Louisiana Historical Quarterly*, 12 (1929): 13; *Daily Crescent*, November 5, 1854. Gayarré had been passed over as the party's choice for nominee for congressman in 1853.

[41]Follet, "The History of the Know Nothing Party in Louisiana," 21-22.

[42]*Daily Crescent*, March 28, 1854; *Commercial Bulletin*, March 28, 1854; *Louisiana Courier*, March 28, 29, 30, 1854.

[43]*Daily Crescent,* March 28, 1854; *Commercial Bulletin*, March 29, 1854.

[44]Overdyke, "History of the American Party in Louisiana," *Know Nothing Party*, 258. The *Louisiana Courier* of March 31, 1854, defended the Democratic tabulation in the seventh ward.

[45]*Daily Crescent*, March 28, 29, 1854.

[46]Follet, "The History of the Know Nothing Party in Louisiana," 22.

[47]*Daily True Delta*, April 16, 1854; Follet, "The History of the Know Nothing Party in Louisiana," 58-59.

[48]*Daily Crescent*, March 30, 1854.

[49]Follet, "The History of the Know Nothing Party in Louisiana," 23.

[50]*Daily Crescent*, September 12, 14, 1854; *Louisiana Courier*, September 15, 1854.

[51]*Daily Crescent*, September 16, 1854, quoting from the *Daily Delta*.

[52]Overdyke, "History of the American Party in Louisiana," *Know Nothing Party*, 259; *Daily Crescent*, September 18, 1854; *Commercial Bulletin*, September 16, 1854; *Louisiana Courier*, September 17, 1854.

[53]*Daily Crescent*, September 18, 1854; *Commercial Bulletin*, September 18, 1854; *Louisiana Courier*, September 20, 1854.

[54]*Daily Crescent*, September 19, 1854.

[55]Ibid., October 5, 1854; *Commercial Bulletin*, September 14, October 3, 1854. This was how it was before 1853 when the mayor was head of the police department, but the Democrats in 1853 changed the control of the police from the mayor to a board in order to deprive the Whig mayor of his authority. Their plan now backfired on them.

[56]*Louisiana Courier*, September 26, 1854.

[57]*Daily Crescent*, November 27, 1854; *Semi-Weekly Creole*, November 25, 1854.

[58]The *Creole* was a small sheet which was rabidly pro-American.

[59]*Louisiana Courier*, November 26, 1854, quoting from the *Creole*.

[60]*Louisiana Courier*, November 29, 1854.

[61]*Daily Crescent*, November 28, 1854.

POLITICAL STRIFE IN NEW ORLEANS*

Samuel Wilson, Jr., Patricia Brady, and Lynn D. Adams

May 18 [1858] 76° 80° 80°

Pleasant from the South West, after a terribly hot night, and unimaginable myriads of musquitoes. Floating clouds.

Strong efforts are being made by the best men in the city to draw out Major Beauregard as an independent candidate for the "Mayoralty" but he cannot serve without resigning his honorable position in the army, which he is unwilling to do. The dispatches from headquarters to that effect are positive. And the Major's "ultimatum" today equally peremptory, acknowledging the compliment but declining the overtures, for *him* to abandon a distinguished military for precarious civil & political career would be to verify the line in Dante. "Vai ch'entrate agni speranza lusciate."[1]. . .

May 20 [1858] 77° 81° 82°

Hot dry & dusty. Pleasant air from North West. . . .

The Department Telegraphs Major Beauregard that he can retain his superintendency at the New Custom House if elected Mayor. He will no doubt yield to pressure and consent to run. At least so he tells me this morning, if the guarantees that he requires are made satisfactory. This morning he handed me his notes of an address to the "Committee of nomination" defining his views in very firm and decided language, and I put them into complete shape ready for presentation before I left the office at 3.

After dinner Emily Tommy & I & the rest took the omnibus to the Gretna Ferry, crossed the river, and a pleasant walk of 1/2 a mile on the Levee brought us to the great "Bell crevasse" which has been pouring its relentless flood, for more than a month, into the opposite country, which now lies buried under a brown, soaking deluge as far as the eye can penetrate thro' the woods and many a weary mile beyond. The "crevasse" itself is several hundred feet wide, and the river rushes thro' the opening with terrific force,

*First published in *Queen of the South, New Orleans, 1853-1862: The Journal of Thomas K. Wharton* (New Orleans: Historic New Orleans Collection, © 1999), excerpts from 2-196. Reprinted with the kind permission of the authors, publisher, and the Manuscripts and Archives Division, New York Public Library, Astor, Lenox and Tilden Foundations.

assuming the general appearance of "rapids" on northern rivers in all respects except the want of clearness & lucidity in the current. Quite a number of familiar faces from the city had been, like ourselves, attracted to the spot. And fishermen were there with their landing nets scooping up myriads of shrimps and the large coarse varieties of fish which abound in the river. About an hour before we got there two men had been drawn into the furious torrent and have not been seen since. On Monday last, it is said, two others shared the same fate, and another was drowned a few days after the break first occurred by missing his footing on the edge of the vortex. So that life, as well as millions of money-value has been sacrificed to this fatal flood. We reached home about dark, tired indeed, but amply repaid by our visit to the "Bell Crevasse."

The idea of closing it is now wholly abandoned. The fall of the River alone can do it. Efforts, however, are still being made at the "Labranche crevasse," 12 miles above, under the direction of our Mr. J. Roy.

May 21 [1858] 76° 80° 81°

Hot, dry, & dusty. Pleasant breeze from the North East. . . .

Major Beauregard deep in with Committee men &c. &c. preparatory to running for the Mayoralty. A dispatch from the Department says that he can retain his Superintendency at the Custom House if elected but will have to resign his military Commission. After dinner I found that two of the foundations of Posts for inclined Plane had been put in with only 5 Brick base instead of 6 so I had them taken out again. Outside walls levelled up to ceiling joists.

May 25 [1858] 79° 82° 82°

Fine & breezy. Bright sunshine. South East wind. Every thing sparkling & flushed with color after the rain.

Found Mr. Huyghe at the building at 9. He misunderstood the decision fixing the front sill course at 2" & the rear at 4" above the Banquette, instead of 1" and 3" as he at first proposed. Says he thought the additional inch was to be taken out of the height of the floor above the sill course, which the contract fixes at 7 inches on both fronts. I told him that I would accept 6" on both fronts for the height of floor at the top of the 4 Foot slope, and orders were immediately given accordingly. This figure (6") is the height called for by Mr. Whitehead in an appendix to the Contract, at my suggestion. Committee waited on the Major this morning on the subject of the Mayoralty and a large meeting will convene at the St. Charles this evening. . . .

May 26 [1858] 80° 78° 82°

Pleasant air from the South East. Rains 11 to 1.

The meeting at the St. Charles last evening was an enthusiastic one and Major Beauregard's nomination for Mayor is now formally made and accepted. The press comes out warmly in his favor this morning, that is, the "Delta." The other papers have not spoken out yet. . . .

June 2 [1858] 82° 84° 84°

Hot, dry & dusty. South East wind.

At the building at 9. Copper gutters nearly finished. Slating & cornice going on rapidly and the Flooring of second story commenced. At the office the approaching election is an absorbing theme. Those who never talked politics before are eloquent now. The independent movement is spreading with giant strides, and Major Beauregard's success is considered certain. . . .

June 4 [1858] 82° 84° 83°

Hot, dry, and dusty. South East wind. Shower at 9 and again at 3 1/2. . . .

At the Building every thing goes on well. Exciting times down town. At 1 o'clock an armed force went down to attack the entrenchments of the Vigilance Committee but wisely retreated without striking a blow. An attack also was threatened at the Custom House, but our small force was immediately put under arms, and with Major Beauregard at the head, not a man could have entered the building alive. But one shot was fired at the building and that apparently in bravado. In the meantime the Mayor entered into an arrangement with the "Vigilance Committee," which it is probable will immediately restore order and confidence. Went down to the warehouse after dinner. Every thing going on well at the Building. Then went to Lafayette Square, the gathering ground of the "Thugs" &c. and found all quiet. Got an extra "Delta" down Camp Street, giving in general terms the arrangements made for the restoration of complete order & security throughout the city and then returned home to supper. Heavy rain at noon.

June 5 [1858] 80° 79° 82°

Showers in the night. Pleasant this morning, but hot, with South East wind.

The "Vigilance Committee" under the command of Capt. Jos. K. Duncan have achieved a signal tho' thus far bloodless triumph. They number now fully a thousand men, occupying an entrenchment absolutely impregnable to any of our "civic military" bodies, no matter how numerous, and still more so to undisciplined lawless ruffians. Every thing is arranged with the most scientific skill, & the whole organization is like clockwork. The Mayor and Major Genl. Lewis (Superintendent of Elections) waited upon the "Committee" yesterday at the Arsenal, and signed a Treaty with them accepting their services as a special Police for at least 5 days to come, and legalizing their acts for the entire extirpation of "ruffianism" and "thuggery" from the city. They to retain their organization complete, and full possession of their stronghold as now, until a post equally advantageous shall be selected. Thus the triumph of law and order, and the *will* of the best part of this long suffering community, is at length guaranteed, and bright prospects open out before. The terrorism of the last 3 years is virtually at an end. The assailants dared not, with all their hardihood, rush upon certain destruction as they would have done had they attacked yesterday. Called at the Warehouse at 9. Found the error that I complained of in the chimneys corrected. The header in front of chimney breast on the north side has been put in as directed, but the objectionable post in the framing of the inclined Plane remains untouched. I told Mr. Huyghe that I should insist upon compliance with my notification. At the office and down town things are altogether too stirring to write about with pleasure. Did not get home to dinner till between 4 and 5. . .

June 6 [1858] 81° 83° 85°

Sunday. Hot and sunny. West wind.

The Plot thickens. The city council late last night impeached and deposed the Mayor, and appointed H. M. Summers (Ex-Recorder) to act pro Tem. In the meantime the Vigilance Organization is complete, numbering 1,200 men within the lines, thoroughly trained, and ready for action. Besides strong bodies diffused thro' the city, important arrests of notorious ruffians are also being made. All of which tend to rivet the hopes of perfect quiet & security in the voting tomorrow. Major Beauregard's address appears in all the papers this morning, shewing his entire freedom from all political bias whatever in accepting his nomination. Mr. Duncan preached an admirable sermon on the text "and when he beheld the city he wept over it." Painting eloquently showing the *then* prosperous condition of Jerusalem and her *then* approaching doom, and shewing the sorrow which should fill every Christian bosom when he sees a large city around him full of wickedness, and the exertions he ought to make to save those around him from their certain spiritual doom if unrepentent. At 5 went down in the omnibus to the Custom House to get my "registry." Found the building occupied by a detachment of United States troops, and in the office Major Beauregard & Mr. Penn, entertaining the commanding officers & several friends. Remained a short time and then returned by Lafayette Square, the head quarters of the opposition, which I found strictly guarded by artillery, and the usual crowd around the Hall. I understand a reckless attack was made upon the "Vigilants" last night which was attended with the loss of 3 or 4 lives, tho' the accounts varied. . . .

June 7 [1858] 81° 85° 80°

Hot and clear. Wind due South. Clouds gathered at 9 and refreshing showers fell at intervals thro' the day.

This is the day of the great struggle. I was at the Polls at 8 and voted. Met a good many friends and talked over prospects &c. for half an hour. Mr. Reid was there just from the Custom House, and reported that no work would be done owing to its occupancy by United States troops, and, of course, no office business. So I returned home and went to work on a drawing for the Warehouses. Finished that by 11 then put the flower borders in good condition, and just finished when a smart shower put an end to all out door work. The Vigilance Committee have failed to yield the protection promised, but as far as I have seen up to this hour (12 o'clock) it has not been needed. And the rain now falling will throw some little cold water on the heated passions of the more belligerent contestants. But the palpable imperfection of the general arrangements throws a dark shadow on the prospects of Major Beauregard. The "American" party seemed in possession of the polls where I voted this morning and there were no tickets to be had for the "Independent" party. Those of us who voted that ticket either went provided, or obtained them from others who had a number in their possession. On inquiry I found that Mr. Marks who was entrusted by the Executive Committee with the tickets for our Precinct had not been able to find a man bold enough to take charge of a stand for their distribution. After a heavy shower at 3 the sun came out bright and I went round to the Polls at our precinct. Every thing in excellent order, and the hour of closing (4 o'clock) then near. The voting close. I then took the omnibus to the Custom House. Remained there awhile and on my return the Polls had closed, with a result at our precinct of 100 for the Major, against 91 for Stith.[2] From all that I could learn below things have been conducted with uniform quiet thro' the day. Upon the whole [th]is has been the *calmest* Election day ever known in this city.

June 8 [1858] 80° 83° 83°

Hot and clear. Wind due South. Thunder shower at P.M.

The result of the Election is now known. Mr. Stith's majority over Major Beauregard is estimated at 290. Chiefly attributable, it is said, to the defective arrangements of the "Independent Executive Committee."

Read all the papers before breakfast, with their varied expressions of chagrin or triumph. Men, however, will now return to their customary employments, and the wheels of the city government will again move on. The only exception seems to be the "Vigilance Committee" which still retains its organization at the Arsenal according to the Papers. Called at the Building at 9 and found every thing going on well. At the Custom [House] the military are still on duty but the works went on as usual, and Major Beauregard smiles over his defeat. The "Vigilants" it appears disbanded early this morning and the Police are hunting them down every where, about 50 arrests are said to have been made. Both the "Independent" and "Vigilance" measures have resulted in the most disastrous defeat. But it is to be hoped that a general salutary impression has been produced. The formidable and intense display of public feeling which has prevailed for the last 10 days will show the officers-elect that broad, wide-open, glaring eye of the Public is upon them and will inspire them with the most scrupulous caution in all their movements. . . .

June 9 [1858] 81° 83° 82°

Very pleasant weather with fresh air from the South.

Things have settled down again to their normal condition. The arrests made of Vigilants yesterday were unsupported by suitable affidavits & the parties soon dismissed. The general effect will be salutary, an awful & mysterious warning to the fiends who have heretofore been employed for party purposes and sufferred to go unpunished. Many, I am told, have left the city for other fields of "labor"! . . .

I ver[il]y believe that in any other city of the Union the bloodshed would have been frightful. But the tone of feeling in New Orleans is of a higher character than is found elsewhere, and I have the utmost confidence in it. And as a proof of it I have gone about during these exciting two weeks just the same as ever without carrying any means of defense of any description, not even a pocket knife. . . .

At 10 o'clock the Drum called the troops into rank, and they withdrew from the Building in admirable order, and proceeded to the Steamer for head quarters at Baton Rouge. . . .

Notes for "Political Strife in New Orleans"

[1]"Abandon hope all who enter here."

[2]Gerard Stith (1821-1880) was mayor of New Orleans from 1858 to 1860. He also served on the city council (1854-1856, 1860-1862) and as city recorder (1856-1858). New Orleans City Directory 1859; *Dictionary of Louisiana Biography*, ed. Glenn R. Conrad (Lafayette, La., 1988).

PART IV

Political Leadership

THE TRANSCENDENT EGO*

Joseph G. Tregle, Jr.

Through this maze of passionate hatred and icy calculation there passed a cadre of political leaders as colorful and variegated as any to be found elsewhere in the Union. In the natural fashion of men, they responded to the geographic, ethnic, and traditional loyalties which were their inheritance, but they shaped these, as is also the wont of men, to their own individual propensities. Neither issues, political philosophies, nor commitments could be really dominant in the climate of aggrandizement which pervaded the Louisiana of the early nineteenth century. Those basic dividing themes already described—ethnic and regional differences—figured largely as vehicles to serve the purposes of individual egos striving for personal ascendancy or as screens behind which to blur the lines of personal ambition. The necessities of politics nonetheless grouped the state's prominent men according to sectional localities. In the prairie region, despite its position as a stronghold of the Gallic interest, strangely few French leaders emerged in the 1820s as major figures in their own right. Most of the patriarchs, such as Neuville Declouet, Agricole Fusilier, Michel Broussard, Louis Guidry, Valéry Martin, and Charles Olivier, preferred to remain close to their flocks, following the lead of their more skilled compatriots in New Orleans.

The Americans in the area proved not nearly so self-effacing. Most vocal of them all and American at least by adoption, Alexander Porter could claim prominence both as a jurist and politician. Born in County Tyrone, Ireland, in 1786, Porter had come to the United States in 1801 after the Irish hanged his father as a spy for the British. Following a brief sojourn in Nashville he moved to St. Martinville in 1810, soon to become an active member of the convention which drafted the Constitution of 1812. Settling finally on a handsome estate at Oak Lawn on Bayou Teche, he busied himself with sugar planting and his duties as associate justice of the Louisiana Supreme Court, to which he had been appointed in 1821.

Judicial status did nothing to diminish Porter's love for politics, and probably no man of his generation in Louisiana cast a more searching eye over the activities of his col-

*First published as Chapter 6 in Joseph G. Tregle, Jr., *Louisiana in Age of Jackson: A Clash of Cultures and Personalities* (Baton Rouge: Louisiana State University Press, © 1999), 98-130. Reprinted with the kind permission of the author and the publisher.

leagues or reported on their doings with greater charm and obvious delight. Witty and urbane despite a limited schooling, he pretended to no great love for mankind in the mass, though bound to many associates in warm and abiding friendship. Impatient with stupidity or dullness, he could be brusque and curt to those he thought to be wasting his time. Such arrogance seldom extended to his servants, if reports are true, and to his guests he proved the most charming of hosts. Presiding over a table sumptuous even for Louisiana, he delighted in hours spent discussing Shakespeare, Byron, and Scott, his speech tinted by the light brogue which was never to leave him. A firm champion of strong central powers in government and a warm admirer of Henry Clay, one of whose sons studied law in his offices, he looked upon the federal compact as a sacred covenant. Governor Troup's behavior in the Georgia-Creek controversy struck him as so prejudicial to national integrity that he wrote his friend Josiah Johnston that the very name of the Union should be held in the same awe as that which the Jews gave to the word Jehovah. A haughty pride seems to have been his greatest fault, one which led him to almost universal criticism of his colleagues. The French he thought unreliable, stupid, and ignorant of the real meanings of republicanism, while many of his American colleagues he judged to be concerned only with corruption and thievery.[1]

Opposed to him in bitter enmity, his brother-in-law, young Isaac L. Baker of St. Martinville, had an equally developed capacity for critical appraisal of his contemporaries. They shared nothing except a love for politics and a willingness to commit themselves to paper. Baker threw himself into every political fray with an intensity and fervor which shook him as much as the consumptive coughs which spilled blood from his lungs. His ambition yielded place only to his capacity to hate, and his letters overflow with recriminations of one sort or another against most of the leading political figures of the day, as he tried to promote the victory of American candidates lucky enough to escape his list of cravens. "Yankees," anti-Jacksonians, the French—in short, all who disagreed with him—he put down as either "mad or corrupt."[2]

One of those who inspired Baker's special wrath—supposedly for ruining his chances of marriage to a politically desirable Creole belle—William Leigh Brent, also of St. Martinville, generated strife seemingly everywhere he went. A native of Maryland, Brent had come to Louisiana in 1809 as attorney for the western district of the Territory of Orleans. Sent to Congress in 1823, he played a peculiar role in the political quarrels of his day. Gigantic in size and a close friend of Henry Clay, he was continually involved in a swirl of controversy, disliked and distrusted even by those who steadfastly supported him. In a strange reversal of the usual attitudes of the time, his strength appeared to lie in his almost habitual absence from the state, for the many shafts of his enemies fell harmlessly to the ground, averted from their target by a wall of public determination to refuse final judgment on a man not present to defend himself.[3]

Farther to the east, in the domain of Bayou Lafourche, political power concentrated almost completely in the person of one man, Henry Schuyler Thibodaux. Hailed by his neighbors as the "Founder of Terrebonne Parish" and *pére* of the whole Lafourche community, he defied classification in any of the political categories of the state. Born in Albany, New York, in 1769, he combined in himself both French Canadian and American ancestry, and when he arrived in Louisiana in 1794 after a youth spent in Scotland, he immediately adapted to the cultural pattern of the Spanish colony. The coming of the Americans after 1803 allowed him to exploit his New York origins as well, and he deliberately sought to hold a middle position in the ethnic wars of the period. When this proved to be not always possible, Thibodaux generally cast his lot with the French. As the *pére* of Lafourche, it would have been difficult to do otherwise.[4]

Almost a counterpart of Thibodaux in some ways, Edward Douglass White also chose the Lafourche area as the base for his political career, though his early meanderings found him settled in various parts of the state. Three years after his birth in Nashville in 1795, White came to Louisiana when his father, Dr. James White, a former superintendent of Indian affairs in the government of the Confederation, migrated to the Spanish colony. He began his law practice at Donaldsonville, moved to New Orleans as judge of the city court in 1825, and in 1828 retired to his sugar plantation on Bayou Lafourche to campaign for Congress. Like Thibodaux, he in large measure represented both populations, for while unquestionably an American, his early life in the prairies and along the bayous had made him at home among the Gallic population, and his command of French and Spanish helped win him acceptance by them beyond that generally accorded those of his ethnic identity. Many of his contemporaries, indeed, actually thought him to be a legitimate member of the Creole community. Aside from his favored position, his greatest asset seems to have been a tenderness and attractiveness of demeanor sufficient to disarm even his most decided political opponents. An obviously complex and puzzling man, his winsome nature nonetheless had a darker side easily aroused to violence (he once drew a dagger against a critic at a polling booth, shouting "I want to kill him!"). Even his closest friends, like Judge Porter, admitted the eccentricities of his lifestyle, but their wide notoriety seemingly resulted, regrettably, in their not being spelled out for the historical record. Most of his associates obviously thought him slightly mad, but whatever his aberrations, they apparently yielded to his ingratiating charm, for as Duff Green remarked when told of his escape from death in a steamboat explosion, no public official in his memory had "more endeared himself to his numerous friends, than this excellent and amiable man."[5]

The pattern of powerful but not too obtrusive patriarchs characterized the coast as well, though here a spokesman for the Gallic cause, such as Sebastian Hiriart or Arnaud Beauvais, would occasionally make himself heard. Of them all, A. B. Roman of St. James clearly stood preeminent. Son of a wealthy cattleman of Attakapas, as a youth he moved with his family to St. James Parish, settling on a sugar plantation whose profits enabled the boy to study at St. Mary's College in Baltimore. Master of a sugar estate of his own while still in his early twenties, Roman rose rapidly in Louisiana politics, going to the state house of representatives in 1818, where he quickly became speaker of the assembly. Discreet and moderate in address, he possessed a fixity of purpose which often rose "even to obstinacy," his most frequently noted characteristic, joined to a deliberate behavior almost "rigidly formal and conventional in the ordinary affairs of everyday life." Alexander Everett found him totally devoid of conversation and surrounded by a wife and children equally solemn and taciturn, surprisingly lacking in "French vivacity." These were hardly attributes of a sort to arouse any committed or spontaneous following. But young Roman's undoubted talents and almost frightening dedication to purpose made him so clearly the jewel of the Creole population that leadership rested on him almost as a natural garment.[6]

Only a short distance from the Roman estate, Willow Island Plantation at Donaldsonville served as the Louisiana base of the widely connected Trist brothers. Nicholas, the older of the two, remained but seldom on his Louisiana holdings, more at home in the Virginia halls of his wife's family, the Randolphs, or the Washington chambers of Andrew Jackson, whom he served for a while as private secretary. His contacts with the state remained close, however, kept alive by a steady flow of letters from his sibling Hore Browse Trist at Willow Island. Browse married into the wealthy Bringier family and maintained a sharp watch on the political currents of his neighborhood. Small and quick of wit, he kept active in the state's Jacksonian faction but never rose to a status of major importance, prizing as he did his own leisure and the competing pleasures of his beloved Greek and Latin library. But the breadth of his associations, through Nicholas, the Bringiers, and Edward Livingston, whose wife was his godmother and in whose home he had been raised, made him always at least someone to consider in Louisiana affairs.[7]

Probably the most successful of the Donaldsonville politicos, Henry Johnson channeled his prodigious energy and ambition into a highly successful progress from a district judgeship to the United States Senate and finally to the governorship of the state. A native Virginian, his life revolved around politics, and he pursued it with a dedication and businesslike efficiency profoundly irritating to many of his less successful competitors. A prodigious letter writer, he kept the Washington mail pouches to Louisiana heavy with correspondence. Industry, indeed, appears to have been his greatest virtue, for he possessed little profundity or imagination and nurtured a professional caution which made Alexander Porter observe that he must have shared the sentiment of a favorite dramatic character that "the world is wicked . . . and the fewer people we praise in it the better." Insistence upon political place, moreover, could become wearisome after a while, and Johnson's insatiable thirst for office frequently proved a disturbing factor in the political planning of the day.[8]

In the Red River parishes, with a population fed by steady migration from other sections of the Union, American leadership easily dominated the political scene. The stubborn temper and determined conviction characteristic of the neighborhood had no better exemplar than Gen. Walter Hampton Overton, a Virginian by birth who had made his way to Louisiana after sojourns in North Carolina and Tennessee. A professional army man, his gallantry as commander of Forts St. Philip and Jackson during the Battle of New Orleans had won him considerable fame, and upon retiring form the service he had settled in Alexandria in Rapides Parish to combine the life of planter and major general in the state militia. The stirrings of the Jacksonian movement aroused him to political activity despite a crippling "inflammatory rheumatism" which often confined him to bed, for he had long ago determined to crush what appeared to him Yankee conspiracies to bend the great agricultural interests of the state to the will of the "minor forces" of manufacturing. Loud and gruff, he bore little of the conspirator stripe himself. But he clung fast to his principles, always ready to fight.[9]

One of the Yankee plotters Overton so feared, Henry Adams Bullard joined General Jackson at least in convictions of incontestable personal infallibility. A native of Massachusetts, Bullard had attended Groton and Harvard, where only a student row kept him from receiving his master of arts degree. Study of law in Boston and Philadelphia left him so restless that he joined the ill-fated Texas invasion of José Alvarez Toledo in 1813, winding up penniless in Louisiana the following year. Possessed of not even a single book and endowed with nothing, as he said, but "Yankee obstinacy of purpose," he began to practice law in Natchitoches and Alexandria. His success eventually proved so great that he soon concluded that only his love for politics kept him from becoming the highest figure at the Louisiana bar, a happy condition which "I owe all to myself," he confided to his old friend Amos Lawrence. Such brashness did not attract any overwhelming political success, though it did not prevent his eventual rise to Congress. Recurrent attacks of gout frequently propelled his naturally morose temperament into "harsh and . . . petulant" irascibility, confining him to his chambers to curse the cultural sterility of his frontier home and pine for someone who might discourse with him on the beauties of Tasso and Shakespeare. Handsome in person and gifted with a musical voice, he regretted most that he could not be the equal of his great idol, Daniel Webster. Abandoning his first love of politics, he would spend his last years on the bench of the Louisiana Supreme Court.[10]

Perhaps the most able of the Red River leaders, Josiah Stoddard Johnston joined to his many talents an equanimity of character which makes him almost colorless against the backdrop of Bullard and Overton. Also Yankee born, he left his native Connecticut at the age of six for the Kentucky frontier, moving on to Louisiana and entering the practice of law in 1805 at Alexandria, which he would represent in the territorial legislature from that year to 1812, when he became a district judge under the new state constitution. Sent to Congress in 1821, after one term he lost his seat to William Leigh Brent in a bitter campaign, but returned to Washington as a senator in 1824 to serve in that capacity until his death ten years later. His soundness of judgment and evenness of temper made him a valuable ally of Henry Clay. Their association transcended that of political captain and lieutenant and grew into a firm personal friendship so close that Johnston acted as one of Clay's seconds in his famous duel with John Randolph. Gifted with an exceptional memory which often made him appear dogmatic, Johnston busied himself especially with economic questions in Congress, his services to Louisiana as defender of her interests in tariff affairs winning him a respect more widespread than that accorded most of his colleagues. An undeviating party loyalist, he nonetheless managed to preserve the reputation of an honest man.[11]

That family politics might exist outside the circle of the Gallic community found striking confirmation in the Morgan clan of Ouachita Parish. Headed by Ferdinand Morgan, they controlled practically every office in their county. The chieftain held rank as brigadier general in the militia and served in the state senate; one brother presided as parish judge; and a second functioned as sheriff. Two brothers-in-law to the Morgans, Gen. John Hughes and Henry Bry, Jr., filled the Monroe postmastership. The tribe used their power ruthlessly, stealing elections by fraud and resorting to violence whenever necessary to keep their enemies, particularly the Morehouse family, in submission.[12]

With a record of factional violence almost equal to that of Ouachita, the Florida Parishes provided the political base of many of the most powerful and colorful of the American standard-bearers of the stormy 1820s and 1830s. Grand old man of the region, Gen. Philemon Thomas of Baton Rouge had won his laurels as a hero of the American Revolution and leader of the West Florida rebellion against the Spanish in 1810. He first visited Louisiana as early as 1784, when he steered a flatboat loaded with Kentucky produce down to New Orleans, a voyage he liked to imagine as having begun that interior trade destined one day to enrich the whole state. Following his permanent move to Baton Rouge in 1805, Thomas gave many years of service to his community as a major general in the militia, as a member of the state's house and senate, and eventually as a national congressman. The one job Thomas wanted most continued to escape him. Ardent champion of the American faction, he launched repeated campaigns for the governorship, his flaming red hair and huge frame becoming one of the most familiar sights in the Louisiana hustings. Sure in his own mind that his years and experience entitled him to that post, he almost childishly failed to see how frequently his enemies used him for no other purpose than to split the vote of the Florida Parishes. In some ways he seemed a pathetic remnant of the past, unable to grasp the meaning of events, puzzled by political thrusting and parrying which he thought devious, cowardly, and dishonest. In the untutored spelling and style which characterized his correspondence, the old general finally confessed his bewilderment in a letter to Amos Lawrence as he sat through one indecisive meeting of Congress after another in the spring of 1834: "Little did I cave think to live to se the day I now se - the people mite at least have weighted untill the old farthers had been moved from this world to a nother, where thay might have been at peas. . . . I much fear the suns is more ame than there farthers. . . . It makes my old blood run hot through eavery vain." Nonetheless, his simplicity and sincerity won him the love of most of his fellow citizens, and his long and fruitful service gave him an unchallenged place of honor in the state. But it was never to win him the governorship.[13]

From his estate near St. Francisville, called the Cottage, another Floridian frequently went forth to contest with Thomas for the support of the American voters of the state. A native Pennsylvanian, Thomas Butler moved to the Felicianas in 1811 to become in quick succession an affluent planter, judge of the parish, and representative in Congress from

1818 to 1821. A onetime association with Aaron Burr threatened to curtail his political advancement, a disability which he countered by frankly admitting the relationship but insisting that like so many others he had thought Burr engaged simply in a campaign against Mexico. Unfortunately, he found it considerably more difficult to dispel a common impression that indolence figured as one of the judge's more pronounced characteristics. But as with Thomas, no campaign of the 1820s or early 1830s proceeded far without some consideration being given to the master of the Cottage.[14]

"Whenever I hear everybody speak well of a man, I set him down as a damn'd rascal," Thomas B. Robertson once shouted in summing up his opinion of a particularly troublesome rival. Vain to a fault, Robertson prided himself upon being descended from the Indian chief Powhatan, and as if this conferred upon him some peculiar nobility, he seemed to feel, as Alexander Porter put it, that other men were not "made *with* him, but *for* him." He had indeed done well in life, progressing steadily from the office of secretary of the Territory of Orleans to a seat in Congress, the state governorship, and finally, in 1824, to the post of United States district judge. In the process he became the owner of two plantations in the Baton Rouge area and the husband of Lelia Skipwith, daughter of Fulwar Skipwith, one of the heroes of the West Florida rebellion.

Success came to Robertson as no surprise, for he considered himself a master politician, gifted with great acumen and a keen logical mind. In truth, he did command a considerable degree of ability and could express himself in a virile and straightforward style of address. But he was his own set of values. Envious, suspicious, emotional, and proud, he remained blind to any but his own point of view, frequently flying into a rage at the slightest opposition. Seldom burdened by any great sense of responsibility, he once allowed charges of negligence to be brought against a parish judge for failure to report election returns to him while governor, coming forward only after the impeachment trial had begun to announce to the astonished legislature that "thanks to God and His prophets," he had by accident finally found the missing returns in the bed of his hound bitch. His faith in his own emotional and intuitive responses extended even into his public attitudes, and he once startled Porter by a violent harangue against a recent Supreme Court decision, which he called the greatest bit of sophistry he had ever read. He could not point it out, he sputtered, as Porter demanded to know of what the sophistry consisted—he just felt it! For such a man, politics had no mysteries.[15]

One of his closest associates, Henry H. Gurley, a Connecticut Yankee, often found himself accused by enemies of being more Robertson's hireling than friend. Like Brent, Gurley spent most of his time outside the state, serving as congressman from 1823 to 1831. And as with Brent, his role in the disputed presidential election of 1824-25 would make him for a while a storm center in Louisiana politics.[16]

Considerably younger than any of these men and a bitter foe of Robertson, John Barrow Dawson provided the state a one-man parade of contradictions. Related to the extensive and influential Barrow clan of the Felicianas, though born in Tennessee, he strengthened these family advantages by marriage to Margaret, sister of another prominent figure of the Florida region, Isaac Johnson. A husband at seventeen, young Dawson boasted of his masculine precocity and flaunted his skill with the pistols, offering to sever a hair with his shot or spilt the ball on a knife blade. Yet in appearance and mannerisms he appeared almost effeminate, garbing himself in dazzling colors which won him a reputation as a "painted butterfly." His letters reveal a mind of unquestionable shallowness hiding a vain and pompous desire to appear learned and philosophical. He filled them with gushy quotation and vaulting apostrophe, and, more disturbing, with pleadings and sentiments which might almost be taken for the cajoleries addressed by a woman to a reluctant swain. These may well have been simple affectations, for no one at the time seems to have questioned his manliness, something which the political mores of the day would have had no hesitation in accepting had it been worthwhile. By his own appraisal, malignant hatred was the worst trait of his character, a judgment supported by his many envenomed attacks upon his enemies. He assailed one rival as being possessed of a "heart of the genuine Yankee clay," composed primarily of "cunning, management, dissimulation, and arrogance," and these antipathies on occasion moved him to actual physical violence. A confirmed agrarian, he found the city always alluring; an aristocrat in taste, he cast himself as the self-proclaimed enemy of aristocracy.[17]

Something of a political and intellectual guardian to Dawson, William S. Hamilton displayed none of the flagrant excesses of his protégé. A graduate of the state university of his native North Carolina, he continued his studies at Princeton before entering a military career which eventually brought him to New Orleans in 1809 as judge advocate of the Army of the Mississippi. He resigned his commission in 1812 to settle in St. Francisville, but war saw him once again in service along the Canadian border, where his skills so impressed James Monroe that he won command of the riflemen dispatched to scatter the Hartford Convention. A strict disciplinarian, he carried his military love for regularity and precision into his private life when he again retired to the Floridas in 1816 to practice law and eventually to establish himself as a planter. Cautious and reserved by comparison to the impetuous and fluttery Dawson, Hamilton's philosophical bent of mind won the admiration and confidence of myriad friends. Eventually he turned seriously to politics, until its treacheries proved too much even for his philosopher's spirit and soldier's stomach.[18]

If French leadership seemed comparatively weak in the country parishes, it commanded truly prodigious strength in the city of New Orleans. Most able of the Gallic spokesmen, Etienne Mazureau accordingly became the most hated and feared by the Americans. Born in France about 1777, he came to New Orleans in his early twenties, married into the prominent Creole family of the Grimas, and set about to develop a reputation for great legal attainments and oratorical power, which he proposed to use to make himself the great chieftain of the French cause in Louisiana. Almost constantly in public service as secretary of state, state legislator, or attorney general, Mazureau tried incessantly to identify the interests of the ancienne population with those of the foreign French, succeeding at least to the extent of calling down upon himself the most bitter curses of those Americans who saw him as the archfiend of the foreign faction trying to subvert Louisiana.

Short and rotund, with jet black hair and quick, dark eyes, Mazureau arrogantly exploited his manifold powers and moved with a constant air of command, delighting in ridiculing the common law and all things Anglo-American. His face reflected his emotions perfectly, cheery and bright when he engaged in the witty and rapid pleasantries of which he was capable, dark and disdainful when he found himself questioned or opposed. Then he could be startlingly violent in speech, his enormous head thrown back, nostrils pinched in contempt, and his deep voice thundering out in endless sound. His vanity knew no bounds, and in the terribly digressive and ornate style which he favored he was forever proclaiming on the countless scholarly and military fields over which he asserted mastery. Gentleness and affection he hoarded for his private life as husband and father.[19]

Second only to Mazureau in the hierarchy of Gallic leadership, Louis Moreau Lislet also belonged to the foreign French community, having come to Louisiana from Saint-Domingue, where he had been born at Cap Français in 1767. "Everything [seemed] soft in him," Charles Gayarré recalled in a later day, "even his bones. His flesh [was] tremulous, like blancmange or jelly, and as yielding under the touch." But within that gelatinous hulk dwelled a mind of adamantine genius. He was an "index to all legal learning," said one of his contemporaries, "a walking library, containing the pandects, institutes and edicts of Rome, the Partidas, *autos* and *fueros* of Spain, the ordinances of France and . . . everything that was ever written on the Civil law." These extraordinary powers he placed willingly in the service of the struggle to preserve Louisiana for the French, and yet, though he might frequently be found masterminding the strategic moves of his faction, he possessed none of the searing intensity of the younger Mazureau. A natural good humor made him always open to compromise, and he frequently proved capable of changing position without torturing his ego. Perhaps the personal tragedy of an insane daughter who divorced her husband, abandoned her children, and fell under the spell of a depraved paramour left the father with a clearer perception of what gave meaning to his life.[20]

Another of the impressive legal scholars of Louisiana, Justice François-Xavier Martin paired his exceptional judicial genius with an eccentricity notable even in a community which came almost to accept the bizarre as normal. He had left his native France for Martinique as a youth of eighteen, moving eventually to North Carolina, where he served in the legislature and produced a history of the state. In 1810 he arrived in New Orleans, and after a brief spell as attorney general, took the seat on the state supreme court which would be his place of greatest fame. Of all mankind, said John R. Grymes, Martin was the one best suited to be a judge, being "all head and no heart." He had no prejudices, no amusements, no wife, and no friends—nothing, seemingly, but an unquenchable thirst for knowledge and recurrent seizures of ambition to be sent to the United States Senate. No one doubted his mental qualifications for the post. He often demonstrated his prodigious memory with endless recitations from Horace, and his legendary analytical powers allowed him to knife through the most tangled legal questions to produce decisions remarkable for their clarity, precision, and conciseness. As he had done for North Carolina, so also did he produce for Louisiana a history of her growth and progress from colonial days through the great victory over the British in 1815.

Yet Martin generated hatred among many in New Orleans comparable to what a colleague called "Choctaw vengeance," for his tenure on the court threatened to be permanent. His peculiarities made him vulnerable to attack, it being easy to ridicule the old man whose short figure with its thick neck and massive head became one of the famous sights of New Orleans. An extreme miser, he could be seen each morning at the French Market, shabby and tattered, pinching and feeling everything in the stalls and always deciding on refuse meat and vegetables so that his expenditures would not exceed thirty cents a day. His sight failed him as he aged, leaving him almost blind by 1826. As his debility became more and more pronounced he tended to retire even more from social contracts, but he remained, at least negatively, always a factor in the politics of the state. Many coveted his job.[21]

Pierre Derbigny and Pierre Soulé also figured as mainstays of the foreign French faction. A former French nobleman, Derbigny had fled the Terror in 1793, and after a brief stay in Saint-Domingue roamed over the United States before settling in Louisiana in 1797. Governor Claiborne found him an "ultra-Frenchman" in 1804 and feared that he might be subversive to American control of the area, but by the 1820s Derbigny had established himself as one of the most moderate men in the community, so much so that he was to be the only foreign Frenchman ever to serve as governor of the state.[22]

Soulé understood nothing of moderation. After a turbulent early career, highlighted by rebellious flight from a Jesuit seminary and authorship of virulent newspaper attacks upon the restored Bourbons, he settled briefly in England after being expelled from France, then moved on to the West Indies, Baltimore, and New Orleans. Only twenty-five when he arrived in Louisiana in 1825, he soon rounded up letters of introduction to Andrew Jackson and departed to be a guest at the Hermitage, Jackson's estate near Nashville, supposedly to improve his English. By 1828 he was back in New Orleans as a student and eventual associate of Moreau Lislet, and in 1830 he began a tempestuous term on the city council. Some saw in him a striking resemblance to Napoleon, an impression which he took great pains to cultivate. He wore his raven hair long on his shoulders, framing penetrating black eyes set in a handsome face. With this striking countenance and vibrant voice he proceeded to act to the hilt the role of fiery spokesman for everything French, with a command of language thoroughly competent in English and brilliant in his native tongue. As much as any one influence could, his fiery partisanship inflamed old ethnic hatreds once again in the New Orleans of the 1830s.[23]

The richest man in New Orleans by repute and the greatest champion of the Creole cause in the state by his own declaration, Bernard Marigny grew up in the midst of luxury, the pampered favorite of the affluent family of the de Marigny de Mandevilles, whose noble lineage once allowed them to play host to Louis Philippe when that prince's wanderings brought him to New Orleans in 1798. As a gesture to republicanism Marigny dropped the aristocratic trappings of his name after the Purchase, as he and his family had long since dropped most of the substance of their noble traditions. But he could never forgo parading his wealth, talking of his family heritage, reminding everyone of his grandfather and great-grandfather, and swearing "by the ashes of his ancestors." The sense of ownership so dominated him that it became almost an obsession—he converted his vast New Orleans holdings below the Esplanade into the Faubourg Marigny; stamped J'APPARTIENS À M. BERNARD MARIGNY on the great silver bell which guarded his country estate of Mandeville across Lake Pontchartrain; and burned his initials into the breasts of his slaves. Master of so much, he insisted upon being master of everything, and he fought passionately to become political ruler of his native state. He loathed both Americans and foreign French as intruders in the domain of the ancienne population, and he matched his hatred with a jealous animosity toward any other Creole who might dispute his leadership.

From the very beginning of the American domination Marigny fought for Creole control of Louisiana, seizing every means to cripple the Faubourg Ste. Marie and to crush the American power of Red River and the Floridas. His behavior during the British invasion had been so ambivalent as to raise real doubts as to his loyalty to the Union, and his critics frequently charged that he would have willingly surrendered New Orleans to the English had this been the only way to save his property from destruction. By 1822 his anger and pique at being continually kept from the power he coveted reached such a pitch that he decided to renounce Louisiana forever and sailed away for France after publishing a vicious "Good Evening" farewell piece in the New Orleans press reviling the whole population for their failure to accept his guidance. The next year he was back, having been unable, apparently, to find the position and prestige he sought in Europe, and determined once again to create it for himself at home.

With limited education and lacking the superior talents of the foreign French leaders, Marigny offered little to the people except a hatred of outsiders. Yet his vanity knew no bounds. He claimed to possess "in the highest degree every vice of a gentleman" and so admired his own oratorical powers that he saw nothing unusual in proposing himself to the city council as the principal speaker at the funeral services mourning the death of Jefferson. Inactivity or silence seemed impossible for him. He was ever on the move, impatient and reckless of ceremony, emitting constant sound, whether in word, song, or the peculiar chuckling laugh which accompanied the creation of the many puns which provided his major intellectual delight. "Creole of the Creoles" he has been called by some, a title which he would have accepted as his due. But wealth, name, and unremitting political struggle never managed to gain for Marigny the political ascendancy which he also felt to be his by right. It remained something he found impossible to understand or to forgive.[24]

Many of Marigny's most vicious attacks centered on Jacques Villeré, the first Creole governor of Louisiana and successor to Claiborne, in no small part because of the admiration and affection felt for that gentle and courtly man in most quarters of the state. In

Marigny's eyes, Villeré had committed the unforgivable sin of trying to work with the Americans, a fault made all the worse by his status as a highly successful contender for Creole leadership. By the 1820s, however, Villeré began to show his years, having been born in 1761, and his always modest abilities proved hardly sufficient to meet the growing complexities of Louisiana politics.[25]

The Creole community obviously expected much more from Denis Prieur, a young New Orleans favorite of the ancienne population who rose rapidly in the late 1820s to become almost a fixture as mayor of the metropolis. He was technically one of the foreign French, having been born in Saint-Domingue in 1791, but his residence in the state since infancy made him a Creole in every sense but that of actual qualification. Handsome and gallant, he could be almost irresistible in his personal charm, and even the quarrelsome and termagant Anne Royall found herself completely captivated by his round, sunburned face, "silken voice and dove-like eye." Awareness of his many gifts made Prieur frequently careless in his actions. Impetuous and tactless, he many times committed himself to extreme positions on slight evidence, and he defied public censure by living in open concubinage with Harriet Rolls, a free woman of color who became the mother of his several children. Lacking in education and frequently yielding to what seems to have been an innate laziness, his actual accomplishments never fulfilled his great promise. But he remained the darling of the city, with a popularity impervious to fate or his many and varied indiscretions.[26]

With a popularity even greater than that of Prieur, Martin Duralde stood at the very apex of the Creole hierarchy, his political influence enhanced by family ties reaching into practically every quarter of the state. The son-in-law of Henry Clay, Duralde had access to national leaders as well, while his highly remunerative position as recorder of mortgages in New Orleans provided a financial base independent of his notoriously naïve business sense. But his real power flowed as much from the attractiveness of his character as from any family connections or political offices. Simple and unassuming in manner, unaggressive and trusting in professional relationships, he enjoyed high favor all over the state, so much so that some said he might easily have won for himself any office in the gift of the people. Position beyond that of recorder of mortgages he never sought, however, seemingly immobilized by self-doubts as to his own abilities and by an awareness that in the eyes of many of his American associates he was "an amiable good man, little removed from idiocy & totally incapable of performing the duties properly of the most simple office." Yet his unquestioned stature among the Creole population made him a constant factor in any formulation of Louisiana politics in his day.[27]

The political prominence which Duralde shied from found an eager suitor in yet another native Louisianian, Dominique Bouligny, who would be successful at least to the extent of rising to the Senate of the United States. Despite an impressive appearance which caused Mrs. Royall to call him "one of the most noble and majestic looking men in Congress," Bouligny remained perhaps the most ineffectual and obscure of all the Louisiana political figures of the period. He sat mute during most of his term in Washington, and one gets the definite impression that this disturbed no one at home. Seemingly few people had much interest in anything he might have chosen to say.[28]

Between these foreign-French and Creole leaders of New Orleans on one side and the American group on the other stood the imposing figure of Edward Livingston, unable to be identified completely with one or the other. In this, as in almost everything else, Livingston had but one major attachment: himself. There can be no doubt as to his high place in the history of jurisprudence. Roscoe Pound claimed that "Livingston will be held the great jurist of nineteenth-century America and one to rank with Bentham" among English-speaking peoples.[29] His legal genius generated the monumental Louisiana Civil Code, drafted with the aid of Moreau Lislet and Derbigny in 1825, and the visionary criminal code which won him the plaudits of scholars all over the world, though it was never adopted by the state.[30]

But many students of legal history have tended to confuse Livingston the codifier with Livingston the politician and man. One sees him as a great "democratic nationalist,"[31] and another claims that "Livingston assailed the leadership principle and energetically devoted himself to establishing a democratic unity of theory and practice through his conception of permanent legislation. Thus he leaps into the center of the world stage and becomes a principal and heroic personality in the decisive struggles which are taking place in our time."[32] Even his most recent biographer, a professional historian, has been unwilling or unable to look behind this figure of the printed word to find the Livingston his contemporaries knew.[33] These last recognized him for what he was—a legal scholar who had no rival, a lawyer who had no superior, and a man who had no apparent concern for personal integrity. He seemed incapable of thinking in terms of anything but his own advantage, his own enrichment, his own fame, or his own convenience, and even his great creative work was sullied by the stock-jobbing tactics with which he tried to sell his talents to the state and federal governments.

One perceptive acquaintance found him "unsocial and soulless, with every attribute of mind to be admired, without one quality of the heart to be loved."[34] His correspondence is unique, even for his day, for he seldom wrote except to ask for favors, publicize his latest accomplishment, or plot a profitable move against the unwary. Yet even while in public office he shamelessly ignored requests made upon his own time, and over and over again one reads in the letters of others such comments as, "from Livingston I have received no answer."[35] Old friends in need he could push aside with callous indifference, refusing on one occasion to offer even minor aid to a desperately destitute woman in whose home he had once been regularly received and honored.[36] Insistent upon his own rights to what was often a cruel degree, he ignored his public responsibilities at pleasure, frequently scorning to keep his own levees and roads in repair as required by law.[37] Such obstacles yielded to the effectiveness of his great legal skills, which enabled him to pursue a relentless grasping for wealth with a craftiness which, when added to an indifference to all considerations of equity, made his name one of the most hated and feared in the whole community.[38]

His rise to public prominence had its full measure of triumph and despair. A member of the powerful Livingston clan of New York, he graduated from the College of New Jersey (now Princeton) in 1781, won admission to the New York bar in 1785, and in 1794 became a member of the United States House of Representatives, where he soon distinguished himself as an ardent Democratic Republican.[39] Aaron Burr became his particular favorite, and only the adjurations of his older brother, Chancellor Robert R. Livingston, together with those of Alexander Hamilton, seem to have dissuaded him from honoring a pledge to give that problematic leader his House vote in the contested presidential election of 1800. As with so much else in his life, confusion and mystery still surround the exact role which he played in the final resolution of that question. The only thing certain is that his vote went finally to Jefferson, and that in 1801 the recipient of that support named him federal attorney for the southern district of New York.[40]

Early in his public career Livingston's sybaritic lifestyle earned him the sobriquet "Beau Ned," and his princely tastes soon had him deep in trouble as he joined to his new federal assignment the concurrent office of mayor of the city of New York, bestowed on him by the favor of Gov. George Clinton. To his obvious discomfort, Secretary of State Albert Gallatin in 1802 began to hear rumors of delinquencies in Livingston's accounts, which by the summer of 1803 so convinced him of the new federal attorney's peculation that he urged Jefferson to prosecute him criminally, but the reluctant president settled for replacement in office. Given that option, Livingston resigned his post with a federal judgment of some $100,000 against his name, and for the rest of his life he and his followers tried repeatedly to brush away charges that he had diverted public moneys to his private use.[41] He eventually insisted that his only fault had been lack of oversight of his subordinates, placing the blame for the shortages in his accounts on an unnamed clerk, while his defenders proffered many, often conflicting, versions of what had happened. But an audit of his returns by the General Accounting Office in 1832, the absence of any contemporary suggestion of an agent's involvement, and the unqualified acknowledgment of his culpability in family correspondence of the period make Livingston's personal guilt essentially a certainty.[42]

Thus it was that in 1804 he brought himself to Louisiana, to a life new in locale and surroundings but hardly stripped of old habits and predilections. He was forty years old, tall and robust, with high shoulders which gave him an awkward, ungainly appearance. Large gray eyes, restless and constantly searching, looked out from beneath his highly arched brow, which curved far back to meet his deep black hair. He had one hundred dollars in cash and a letter of credit for one thousand more.[43] In a remarkably short time he was one of the richest men in the territory.

Livingston plunged into the affairs of his new home with fierce dedication. In a matter of months he had launched speculations of ever widening scope, at the same time engaging in political activities which made Jefferson, Gallatin, and Governor Claiborne suspect him of inciting trouble for the government of the United States.[44] As early as September 1804 he represented the Baron de Bastrop in his attempts to gain federal recognition of vast land grants in the Ouachita River area which were as suspect as they were extensive, and in some mysterious manner which seems not to have cost him a cent, he managed rapidly to acquire title in his own name to six-tenths of the Bastrop lands.[45] Livingston's onetime hero, Aaron Burr, also had extensive claims in the same area, and when Gen. James Wilkinson terrified New Orleans in 1807 with his electrifying charges of a conspiracy against the city and nation headed by Burr, Livingston found himself singled out as one of the supposed agents of the conspirators. There is little which can be said with certainty about Burr's true objectives, and Livingston's complicity in his plotting, whatever it involved, has certainly never been proved. The questions posed by Wilkinson and others did, however, raise myriad doubts.[46]

With an energy as restless as his eye, Livingston pursued his fortune in haste. He collected handsome fees from the notorious Laffites to plead their defense against piracy charges, or rather, he sent his partner, John R. Grymes, to collect them, for timidity kept him away from the pirate kingdom at Barataria.[47] Together with Grymes he likewise sought to preserve the monopoly granted by the territorial legislature to Robert Fulton and Robert Livingston, allowing them exclusive rights "to navigate all vessels propelled by fire and steam on the rivers in said Territory." Even Livingston could not prevail against the determination of Henry M. Shreve to contest this grant, however, and when attempts to separate Shreve from any legal advice by buying up the services of all the lawyers in New Orleans failed, the grantees moved to offer the stubborn river captain one-half of the monopoly if he would advise his counsel to plead their case in such a fashion as to guarantee a verdict favorable to the franchise. Shreve refused even this, and the monopoly claims finally collapsed shortly thereafter.[48]

Livingston's attempts to clear the federal court judgment against his name demonstrated dramatically the extraordinary sharpness and scope of his talents. He had little interest in paying out actual cash, but his ingenuity found in the growing needs of the American navy after 1815 a possible easy solution to his problem. In 1816 he contracted with the United States government to deliver a large quantity of live oak timber to proper naval ports, the price agreed upon, remarkably enough, being precisely sufficient to wipe out his government debt. His extensive plans included the cutting of a live oak stand on the eastern side of the Mississippi at Fort Darby near Bayou Terre aux Boeufs, but upon what right he proposed to claim this timber remained unclear to examining government inspectors. Unfortunately for his hopes, his agents failed him, and the government voided the contracts in 1818.[49]

All these disappointments meant little, however, in the light of his success in the monumental batture controversy. The intricacies of that complex legal struggle defy any simple explication. Suffice it to say that shortly after his arrival in New Orleans, Livingston successfully defended the claims of Jean Gravier to the tremendously valuable alluvial soil deposited by the Mississippi between the water's edge and the levee before the Faubourg Ste. Marie in a series of brilliant arguments which destroyed conflicting claims by the city corporation and the so-called front proprietors who held title along the old levee line. In usual clouded fashion, he emerged from this litigation with a large share of the lands whose title he had cleared for Gravier, only to find himself faced by the opposition of his avenging angel, Thomas Jefferson, whose agents seized the property as having always belonged to the federal government under international law. In the strenuous legal battle which ensued, Livingston carried his cause to success before the United States Supreme Court, but in the 1820s the United States had what seemed to be the final word when it appropriated his confirmed batture lots under a lien issuing from the old judgment against him in New York. He managed to salvage enough from the ensuing contest to clear his debt, but his relentless attempts to rewin what had been lost to the government continued for the remainder of his days, and much of his later activity in Jacksonian politics can be understood only in the light of this consuming determination.[50]

His political influence kept pace with his rising personal fortunes. Since his arrival in Louisiana he had sensed the value of alliance with the native population, leading him during the troubled days of territorial status to take a prominent role in attacking the policies of Jefferson and Claiborne which had seemed so restrictive and hateful to the Creole group. He fought for a more liberal interpretation of the Treaty of 1803, drafted petitions for statehood, and organized relief for the impoverished Cuban and Saint-Domingan émigrés who had found refuge in Louisiana. With statehood finally won, he lent his great talents to defense of French traditions of jurisprudence, his authorship of the civil code winning for him the unqualified gratitude of the old population, as did his successful fight for federal court procedures likely to preserve Gallic predominance in the empaneling of Louisiana juries.[51] Not even his defense of Jackson before the court of Judge Dominick Hall in the dispute arising from the General's imposition of martial law during the 1814-1815 crisis weakened his position, for many Louisianians could understand the difficulties of that arduous time and willingly acknowledged Livingston's services before and during the great battle.

It was in his private life, however, that Livingston forged the strongest bonds tying him to the French faction in Louisiana. His first wife had succumbed to the constrictions of diphtheria in 1801, forcing him to find a home for his three children with a brother, John R. Livingston. They had not accompanied him on his trip into exile, and it was shortly after his arrival in New Orleans that he met and married Madame Louise Moreau de Lassy, whose life at nineteen had already been filled with violence and tragedy. A native of Saint-Domingue, she had married her first husband at thirteen; at sixteen she was a widow and mother of three children who died in infancy. The slave insurrection on the island took the lives of her father, grandmother, and two brothers, and scattered the remnants of the family. She finally made her way safely to New Orleans, joined eventually by her mother, an infant sister, and an older brother whom she worshiped, Auguste Davezac.

In the summer of 1805 she married Edward Livingston at a midnight ceremony in the chapel of the Ursuline Convent, and in 1806 gave birth to their only child, Coralie, or Cora, who grew to be her mother's great passion and her father's chief delight. The family closely identified with the French society of New Orleans, Madame Livingston presiding at regular soirees and dinners, where she loved to chatter in English and French over her newest literary interests or present her relative Jules Davezac, first president of the Collège d'Orléans, in readings from his poetry. Here Auguste would frequently display his oratorical talents in rehearsing appeals for the relief of Greece or in praise of some classical hero, and here Livingston himself seems to have been able to relax in an easy and affectionate relationship unknown in his public or professional life. Both his wife and daughter clearly adored him. His letters to Cora and the other children, models of sensitive and loving respect for their individuality and integrity as persons, reflect a side of the man totally at odds with his public record.[52]

But even within this warm and apparently exemplary family circle there existed something hidden, some sordid and unwholesome private climate which seems to have gathered around him. Few people knew the Livingstons better, for example, than Nicholas and Browse Trist. They had grown up under the Livingston roof, felt unquestionable attachment and gratitude to the couple, and generally identified with Edward's political positions. But when their stepfather considered on one occasion sending their half sister Mary to live with the Livingstons at her mother's death, the two brothers immediately joined in protest. Deeply troubled, Nicholas wrote his fiancée that his stepfather had become so fascinated by Cora that he would have his own daughter patterned after her, completely forgetting, he feared, "that Mrs. Livingston was notoriously a woman of intrigue; and the very *last* of all her acquaintances to whom Mary's mother would have entrusted her. . . . I had rather see my sister stung by a rattlesnake, than not be able to place the most implicit faith in her virtue and purity; which I could not do, were she brought up by Mrs. L."[53] His suspicions extended just as strongly to young Cora,[54] and it is unlikely that they stemmed from any simple puritanical misunderstanding of the Gallic temperament. The mother of the Trists had married a native Louisianian, as had Browse himself. This was no indictment of a group. Even Aglae, the young sister of Mrs. Livingston, seems to have shared her notoriety, and John Sibley once wrote to his daughter, the wife of Senator Johnston, that Aglae "will do to associate with Mrs. Eaton. I presume you have heard of her."[55] Sibley's allusion was to Peggy, spouse of John Eaton, Jackson's secretary of war. A great favorite of the General, she found herself nonetheless ostracized by a large portion of Washington society because of alleged sexual immorality.

If these suggestions of moral failing in the women of his household remained in some fashion hidden from Livingston, he could hardly have been blind to the reputation enjoyed by his brother-in-law, Auguste. Davezac had attached himself to the coattails of Livingston from the very beginning of their association, to become what Vincent Nolte called "factotum" to his more celebrated relative.[56] He worked with Livingston to embarrass Claiborne at every turn, leaving that harassed man to damn Davezac as the moving spirit behind the *Magic Lantern*, a paper boosting Burr and attempting, swore the governor, to "write down" every friend to the United States in Louisiana.[57] Trained in the law by Livingston himself, Davezac became his tutor's chief lieutenant, aiding him in his causes, living in his home, dashing off fulsome anonymous articles for the local press extolling the great virtues, services, and genius of his patron. Nolte, who loathed them both, maintains flatly that Davezac "made himself almost indispensable to [Livingston], in hunting up the evidence among the family papers of the French planters, and in procuring witnesses who were ready at all times to swear to anything that might be required of them."[58] In his own right, he made something of a reputation for himself as an effective criminal attorney, placing more reliance in his athletic oratory than in any profound knowledge of the law,[59] and winning renown of a sort on the municipal council for his pyrotechnics as defender of what he called the "bosom of the city," the old French Quarter, against the encroachments of the American faubourg.

Small and dapper, with a squinting eye and a face which sparkled with a "geniality bordering on sensualism," he reminded one observer of a "coarse and obscene" satyr,[60] an impression of moral depravity shared by a large part of the community. William Brent described him as "infamous, degraded and beastly;" Henry Johnson as "a man of talents, but of notorious bad character;"[61] and his vice, whatever it was, seems to have so appalled his contemporaries that no one ventured to spell it out on paper even to the closest of friends. Jackson's nephew, Andrew Jackson Donelson, received warning from one correspondent that Davezac "is in decidedly bad standing among his own neighbors. . . . I have no reference whatever to Mr. D.'s pecuniary concerns—my remarks apply to his moral character."[62] And Nicholas Trist once puzzled over a cryptic message from his brother-in-law in Boston to the effect that "Majr. Davezac of New Orleans is here; how I wish I knew whether he is a friend of yours; he is said to be an --------."[63] These attacks upon his character apparently worried Davezac not at all, his greater concern centering on perpetual monetary problems which frequently confined him to city limits as a public debtor.[64]

Marriage to Mrs. Livingston's younger sister tied yet another prominent New Orleanian, Henry Carleton, to the eminent jurist's family circle. An accomplished legal scholar in his own right, Carleton brought to his partnership with Livingston and Davezac a reputation for honesty and probity unknown to the other two. Unlike his partners, moreover, Carleton possessed a gentleness and sweetness of manner which made him one of the most beloved men in New Orleans society. He rarely enjoyed good health, a burden which might explain his eventual impatience with politics and the law. Forswearing the struggles of his earlier days, he would finally spend the last years of his life in Philadelphia, studying and writing on philosophy and religion.[65]

Also prominent in American circles of capital, Alfred Hennen enjoyed a reputation as the best scholar in Louisiana, famed as a linguist, book collector, and barrister. A massive and sturdy man, with a great head of gray hair and florid complexion, he radiated serenity and good humor. Secretary of the State Bible Society, a model of old-fashioned piety and rigid politeness, he wore his hair in a short queue as late as 1866 and abstained absolutely from all forms of alcohol. He injected a rare moral tone into New Orleans politics, an influence unfortunately minimized, despite his scholarship, by the limitations of a mind steeped in rigid formalism and such fanatical religiosity that in early life his family feared it might cost him his sanity.[66]

Isaac T. Preston shared Hennen's reputation for good humor and dignity of manner, and like him ranked as one of the first members of the New Orleans bar. A native of Virginia and a graduate of Yale, he captained a volunteer company in the War of 1812, carrying over into his later life a military stride and manner which went well with his tall and heavy figure. Plain and deliberate, he often gave a first impression of being slow and indolent in thought and address, but as he warmed to his subject his mind snapped fast to its purpose, his speech flowing in easy exposition of clear and impressive logic. In many respects he championed a political program more liberal than anything acceptable to his Jacksonian colleagues, focusing particularly on democratization of civic rights.[67]

Whatever Hennen and Preston might have lacked in fire and color, John R. Grymes possessed in more abundance than could be comfortable in any man. Even with his close friends in a private circle, "he spoke, he looked, he was the great man. He was great in his frivolities, great in his burlesques, great in his humor, great in common conversation; the great lawyer, the great orator, the great blackguard, and the great companion, the great beau, and the great spendthrift; in nothing was he little." Kin to John Randolph and himself a Virginian, he was one of those men, said an associate, "who leap into manhood without the probation of youth," and at twenty-two he already enjoyed an extensive practice and fame as an eminent member of the bar.[68]

There was hardly a natural endowment which he did not enjoy in full measure. One finds the word *beautiful* in descriptions of him by practically everyone who has left them, and to these physical gifts he joined a superb intellect, a mastery of speech and logic, and a command of wit and sarcasm the envy of his associates. And yet, something in him was deformed and twisted, something which he alone could see, and which made himself and all the world revolting in his eyes. Perhaps he sensed that with all his powers he lacked some mysterious force which would have made it possible for him to exploit them to the fullest. With all his great talents, he never managed to do great things. And so he turned from himself and sought to find in the company of men some proof that greatness was a lie and that all mankind deserved to be despised. He could never be alone, yet remained the loneliest of men. Rarely in his office, he roamed the streets by day and the social centers by night, a great diner, a model of fashion, and a habitué of the ball. A self-confessed libertine, Grymes professed a disdain for all women, though he never complained against his wife, and continued to claim and support her after she fled from him—no one knew why—to live on Staten Island. Ridicule and contempt he wielded as favorite weapons against the world, but even in this he could not be what he claimed. For his scorn remained ever impersonal; he raged against mankind, yet was profligate in generosity to his fellow men. Money to him had no value. He made fortunes, occasionally by very dubious means, and was always penniless, and it was said that he "owed everybody, loaned to everybody, gave to everybody, and paid nobody."[69]

The one regret to which he ever admitted was his inability to sit in the United States Senate, there to range himself against the great Webster, to test his skills in opposition to those he could not deny. But he lacked the funds, he said, to make the venture. He would go to the Senate in style or not at all, and so he slipped ever deeper into morose complaint against a society which he felt had paid him poorly, more poorly than even he deserved. Thus he went his way, brilliantly entertaining to those he pretended to despise; ridiculing knowledge and claiming to know everything; always at apparent ease, and always in a ferment of inner doubt. "He was at war with himself," said Sparks, "and consequently with all the world."[70]

In his later life Grymes looked back with nostalgic pleasure to the many times he had pitted his drinking prowess against that of John Slidell at the sumptuous Elkin's Club on Bayou St. John near Lake Pontchartrain. Slidell was a latecomer to Louisiana compared to Grymes, having arrived in New Orleans around 1821. They must have found much to talk about during their long, bibulous sessions, for gossip had it that Slidell had fled his native New York after wounding the manager of the Park Theatre in a duel which resulted from the impresario's discovery that the young man had forgotten the "distinctions usually maintained between the bed chambers of gay bachelors and dosy husbands."[71]

Whatever his past indiscretions, he put them behind him after his settlement in his new home, and though his bouts at Elkin's testify to the persistence of his love for the social life, they never seriously interfered with his ambition for political and economic advancement. He adjusted well to his new environment, with a fluent command of French gained during his legal studies on the Continent, and soon won attention at the bar and in the hustings for his shrewd and strong-minded intelligence. Possessed of none of the oratorical brilliance of Grymes and reserved even in conversation, his strength lay in his steadfast dedication to purpose and his willingness to bend his whole energy to its realization.[72]

John H. Holland and Gen. Eleazar Ripley came from even farther reaches of the Union, figuring prominently in the New England Yankee community of the city. Holland had moved to New Orleans from Connecticut in 1801 as a boy of fifteen, but retained so strongly the impress of his native origins that all through life many persons mistook him for an Englishman. Portly and robust, with a round, fair face and blue eyes, he won renown as the unchallenged authority on his adopted city, about which admirers claimed he knew anything and everything. This fund of information and his position as leader of the Masonic movement in New Orleans added greatly to his political influence.[73]

Eleazar Ripley had no exclusive connection to any part of the state. He first settled in the Floridas at the little town of Jackson after a brilliant career in the army, which saw him decorated for gallantry at the Battles of Chippewa, Niagara, and Fort Erie. His efficiency, regrettably, did not match his heroism, and his retirement from service in 1820 while commander of the troops at New Orleans came just in time to save Secretary of War John C. Calhoun the embarrassment of having to act on Andrew Jackson's demands that corrective actions be taken against him.[74] A man of considerable versatility, he could also look back upon an even earlier political career, which had taken him from his native New Hampshire and Dartmouth College to law practice in Maine, the Massachusetts senate, and the speakership of the Massachusetts house of representatives in 1811.

In the mid-1820s Ripley moved to join the New Orleans bar and to plunge himself into the political life of the metropolis. A commanding figure, he stood well over six feet in height, heavy without being fleshy, and with a ruddy complexion and blue eyes which won immediate attention. In youth his hair had been deep auburn in color, but now in his middle age it clustered in thinning yellow ringlets above his high forehead. A wound suffered at the Battle of Fort Erie froze his neck in rigid and unbending posture, keeping him in almost constant pain and making him frequently irascible and contentious, though by nature he seemed genuinely friendly and convivial. Bombastic and florid in address, delighting in great figures of speech and hyperbole, he generally performed poorly in debate, though he was not lacking in fundamental intelligence. In all, he remained a rather pathetic man, ambitious and active, but pursued by the fear which few knew, that his endless suffering would one day unhinge his mind. From his wife he extracted the promise that she would never permit him to die in an asylum.[75]

Finally, there was Martin Gordon, originally of Virginia, a mysterious man who would make himself perhaps the most dominant figure in Jacksonian Louisiana and whose name has been practically ignored in the chronicles of the state. Unlike most of his political colleagues, he had no legal training and figured in none of the dramatic courtroom scenes of his day. Nor did he ever become governor, congressman, or senator, and perhaps this accounts to some degree for the obscurity which has been his lot. But it is a fate completely undeserved, for Gordon in his time ranked as one of the wealthiest and most successful of New Orleans business leaders, president of the immensely powerful Orleans Navigation Company, and a dominant force in the politics of his day. He surrounded himself with all the influence that great wealth could buy, deploying its seductions and his own innate craftiness in pursuit of the power he so desperately craved. Only the waspish Mrs. Royall has left us any description of him, and though her account is obviously one inspired by distaste, it so fits what his own actions suggest that perhaps it does him no injustice. To her he appeared to have "just been imported from the antipodes. . . . He was old, ugly, gangling, rawboned, stoop-shouldered, with a yellow, greenish, long stringy face, and cat eye; his iron countenance would appall the Pink himself, a great Russian bear . . . [and] monster of clownishness." Appealing he might not have been, but noteworthy he certainly was, and no other Louisianian ranked higher in the esteem and confidence of Andrew Jackson.[76]

Notes for "The Transcendent Ego"

[1]*Biographical Directory of the American Congress, 1774-1927* (Washington, D. C., 1928); Charles Daubeny, *Journal of a Tour Through the United States and in Canada, Made During the Years 1837-1838* (Oxford, 1843), 144; Margaret Hall, *The Aristocratic Journey* (New York, 1931), 254; W. H. Sparks, *The Memories of Fifty Years* (Philadelphia, 1870), 418; William K. Dart, "The Justices of the Supreme Court," *Louisiana His-*

torical Quarterly, 4 (1921): 115; Alexander Porter to Josiah S. Johnston, November 16, 1825, in Josiah Stoddard Johnston Papers, Historical Society of Pennsylvania, Philadelphia, Penn. (Hereafter cited as Johnston Papers); Henry Clay, Jr., autobiographical note dated November 27, 1840, in Henry Clay Papers, King Library, University of Kentucky.

[2]Isaac L. Baker to William S. Hamilton, July 25, 1823, in William S. Hamilton Papers, Department of Archives, Louisiana State University, Baton Rouge, La. (hereafter cited as Hamilton Papers); Alexander Porter to Josiah S. Johnston, December 13, 1826, in Johnston Papers.

[3]*Biographical Directory of the American Congress*; Anne Royall, *Letters from Alabama* (Washington, D. C., 1830), 186; Isaac L. Baker to William S. Hamilton, July 25, 1823, in Hamilton Papers; John H. Johnston to Josiah S. Johnston, June 19, 1824, Alexander Porter to Josiah S. Johnston, November 27, 1826, in Johnston Papers.

[4]A. Meynier, Jr., *Louisiana Biographies* (New Orleans, 1882), 11; *La Fourche Gazette*, July 29, 1826.

[5]*Biographical Directory of the American Congress*; Diedrich Ramke, "Edward Douglas [*sic*] White, Sr., Governor of Louisiana, 1835-1839," *Louisiana Historical Quarterly*, 19 (1936): 275-81; Sparks, *Memories of Fifty Years*, 460; Alexander Porter to J. Burton Harrison, March 8, 1835, in J. Burton Harrison Papers, Library of Congress; Alexander Porter to Josiah Stoddard Johnston, September 20, 1828, in Johnston Papers; Lafayette Saunders to Andrew Jackson, July 18, 1828, in Andrew Jackson Papers, Library of Congress (hereafter cited as Jackson Papers); *United States Telegraph* (Washington, D. C.), June 12, 1833. Some anecdotal indications of White's idiosyncrasies may be found in George M. Wharton, *New Orleans Sketch Book* (Philadelphia, 1852), 106, and the *Louisiana Courier*, July 1, 1834.

[6]Cyprien Dufour, "Local Sketches," *Louisiana Historical Quarterly*, 14 (1931): 399; Edward Everett Diary, March 14, 1841, in Edward Everett Papers, Massachusetts Historical Society (hereafter cited as Edward Everett Papers); Edward Everett to Lucretia Everett, March 5, 1841, in Alexander Everett Papers, Massachusetts Historical Society.

[7]H. B. Trist to Mrs. Edward Livingston, February 5, 1829, in Nicholas P. Trist Papers, Library of Congress (hereafter cited as Trist Papers, LC); H. B. Trist to Nicholas P. Trist, August 17, 1834, in Nicholas P. Trist Papers, Southern Historical Collection, University of North Carolina, Chapel Hill, N. C. (hereafter cited as Trist Papers, UNC).

[8]*Biographical Directory of the American Congress*; *St. Francisville Asylum*, November 1, 1823; Alexander Porter to Josiah S. Johnston, January 12, 1827, in Johnston Papers.

[9]*Biographical Directory of the American Congress*; Walter H. Overton to Josiah S. Johnston, December 1, 1825, January 17, 1829, in Johnston Papers.

[10]*Biographical Directory of the American Congress*; W. H. Ivy, "The Late Henry A. Bullard," *DeBow's Review*, 12 (1852): 56; "Memoir of the Honorable Henry A. Bullard, LLD," *Louisiana Historical Quarterly*, 19 (1936): 18; Dora Bonquois, "The Career of Henry Adams Bullard, Louisiana Jurist, Legislator, and Educator," *Louisiana Historical Quarterly*, 23 (1940): 999-1002; Henry A. Bullard to Amos Lawrence, January 29, 1832, in Amos Lawrence Papers, Massachusetts Historical Society.

[11]*Biographical Directory of the American Congress*; *New Orleans Bee*, September 30, 1830.

[12]*Louisiana Advertiser*, January 5, 1831, April 14, 1832.

[13]*Biographical Dictionary of the American Congress*; M. L. Bonham, "A Conversation with the Granddaughters of Gen. Philemon Thomas," *Proceedings of the Historical Society of East and West Baton Rouge*, 1 (1917): 48; Francis Robertson, "The Will of Gen. Philemon Thomas," *Proceedings of the Historical Society of East and West Baton Rouge*, 2 (1917): 27, *Louisiana Gazette*, March 24, 26, 1824; Philemon Thomas to Amos Lawrence, March 3, 1834, in A. A. Lawrence Papers, Massachusetts Historical Society.

[14]*Biographical Directory of the American Congress*, Louise Butler, "West Feliciana: A Glimpse of Its History," *Louisiana Historical Quarterly*, 7 (1924): 103; *Louisiana Gazette*, March 18, 29, 1824.

[15]Meynier, Jr., *Louisiana Biographies*, 10; *Louisiana Gazette*, January 10, 1823; Isaac L. Baker to Josiah S. Johnston, November 11, 1822, Alexander Porter to Johnston, December 23, 1825, February 15, April 4, 21, 1826, in Johnston Papers; John B. Dawson to William S. Hamilton, April 6, 1825, in Hamilton Papers.

[16]*Biographical Directory of the American Congress.*

[17]Ibid.; Elrie Robinson, *Early Feliciana Politics* (St. Francisville, 1936), 21, 30, 57; *St. Francisville Asylum*, August 16, 1823; *Louisiana Journal*, May 18, 1826; *Louisiana Advertiser*, February 14, 19, 1834; *Merchants' Daily News*, April 16, 1834; John B. Dawson to William S. Hamilton, June 29, 1824, April 6, 1825, in Hamilton Papers.

[18]*Louisiana Advertiser*, June 18, 1830.

[19]Henry S. Foote, *The Bench and Bar of South and Southwest* (St. Louis, 1876), 194; Sparks, *Memories of Fifty Years*, 430; Charles Gayarré, "The New Orleans Bench and Bar in 1823," in *The Louisiana Book*, ed. Thomas McCaleb (New Orleans, 1894), 55; Dufour, "Local Sketches," 233-34; G. W. Pearson, "Alexis de Tocqueville in New Orleans," *Franco-American Review*, 1 (1936): 34; Edward Everett Diary, May 5, 1829, in Edward Everett Papers; Alexander Porter to Josiah S. Johnston, December 20, 1825, in Johnston Papers; *Louisiana Advertiser*, May 7, 17, 1826, November 13, 1827; *Louisiana Courier*, May 25, 1849.

[20]Gayarré, "New Orleans Bench and Bar," 68; *Louisiana Courier*, June 22, 1830.

[21]Sparks, *Memories of Fifty Years*, 410; Henry A. Bullard, "A Discourse on the Life, Character, and Writings of the Hon. François-Xavier Martin, LLD.," *Louisiana Historical Quarterly*, 19 (1936): 46; Alexander Porter to Josiah S. Johnston, January 5, 1831, in Johnston Papers; *Louisiana Gazette*, January 16, 1823.

[22]Meynier, *Louisiana Biographies*, 13; Clarence Carter, ed., *The Territory of Orleans* (Washington, D. C., 1948), 9:12, 312.

[23]*Biographical Directory of the American Congress*; Foote, *Bench and Bar of South and Southwest*, 201; John S. Whitaker, *Sketches of Life and Character in Louisiana* (New Orleans, 1847), 13; Dufour, "Local Sketches," 230; *Louisiana Courier*, August 26, 1828; Auguste Davezac to Andrew Jackson, April 11, 1825, in Jackson Papers; Arthur Freeman, "The Early Career of Pierre Soulé," *Louisiana Historical Quarterly*, 15 (1942): 972-80.

[24]Dufour, "Local Sketches," 397; Whitaker, *Life and Character in Louisiana*, 83; Edward L. Tinker, *The Palingenesis of Craps* (New York, 1933), n.p.; "Andrew Jackson and Judge D. A. Hall (Report of the Committee of Inquiry of the Military Measures Executed against the Legislature of Louisiana, Dec. 28, 1814)," *Louisiana Historical Quarterly*, 9 (1926): 236; Bernard Marigny, "Reflections on the Campaign of Gen. Andrew Jackson in Louisiana in 1814 and 1815," *Louisiana Historical Quarterly*, 6 (1923): 68; Ferdinand de Feriet to Janica de Feriet, November 21, 1823, in Feriet Family Papers, Howard-Tilton Memorial Library, Tulane University, New Orleans, La.; *L'Ami des Lois*, February 24, 1825, August 19, 1826; *Louisiana Advertiser*, November 1, 1827, July 4, 1834.

[25]Alcée Fortier, *History of Louisiana* (New York, 1904), III, 184; *St. Francisville Asylum*, July 3, 1824; *Louisiana Gazette*, June 28, 1824; Alexander Porter to Josiah S. Johnston, February 15, 1826, in Johnston Papers.

[26]Anne Royall, *Mrs. Royall's Southern Tour, or Second Series of the Black Book*, 3 vols. (Washington, D. C., 1830), 3:34; Benjamin Lundy, *The Life, Travels, and Opinions of Benjamin Lundy* (Philadelphia, 1847), 114; J. Merchant to James K. Polk, October 14, 1845, in James K. Polk Papers, Library of Congress; Denis Prieur Succession (#13,392), in Orleans Parish Second District Court Succession Records, 1846-1880, New Orleans Public Library.

[27]Etienne Mazureau to Henry Clay, September 19, 1825, Clay to James Brown, April 17, 1830, W. C. C. Claiborne to Clay, December 4, 1834, all in Henry Clay Papers, Library of Congress; Henry Johnson to Josiah S.

Johnston, December 10, 1825, in Johnston Papers; William Christy to John Tyler, April 13, 1841 (Christy file), Letters of Application and Recommendation During the Administrations of William Henry Harrison and John Tyler, in Record Group 59, General Records of the Department of State, National Archives.

[28]Royall, *Letters from Alabama*, 178; Carter, ed., *Territory of Orleans*, 526.

[29]Roscoe Pound, *The Formative Era of American Law* (Boston, 1938), 167.

[30]William B. Hatcher, *Edward Livingston* (Baton Rouge, 1940), 464-66.

[31]Rufus Harris in foreword to Pound, *Formative Era of American Law*, 14.

[32]Mitchell Franklin, "Concerning the Historic Importance of Edward Livingston," *Tulane Law Review*, 11 (1937): 204.

[33]Regrettably, the adulatory approach of Hatcher's biography and of Charles H. Hunt's *The Life of Edward Livingston* (New York, 1864) makes them of little value.

[34]Sparks, *Memories of Fifty Years*, 428.

[35]See, for example, Edward Livingston to Martin Van Buren, March 17, 1829, Livingston to Nicholas P. Trist, October 16, November 7, 1830, all in Trist Papers, LC; Thomas F. Hunt to William S. Hamilton, July 26, 1829, in Hamilton Papers.

[36]Mrs. R. Blodget to Harrison Gray Otis, October 30, 1824, in Harrison Gray Otis Papers, Massachusetts Historical Society.

[37]*Louisiana Advertiser*, December 29, 1823; *Louisiana Gazette*, November 24, 1823, January 28, 1826.

[38]See, for example, the record of his litigation in *Edward Livingston v. Benjamin Story*, United States Eastern District Court of Louisiana, Case #3380, 1834, in Federal Records Center, Fort Worth, Tex.; *Livingston v. Cornell*, 2 Martin (O.S.), 281-96; *Livingston v. Story*, 11 Peters, 351; *Story v. Livingston*, 13 Peters, 351; *Morgan v. Livingston*, Case #1373, all in *Conspicuous Cases in the United States District Court of Louisiana*, Compiled by the Survey of Federal Archives in Louisiana (New Orleans, 1940); *New Orleans Argus*, July 1, 1828.

[39]For Livingston's family connections and early congressional career, see Alfred E. Young, *The Democratic Republicans of New York: The Origins, 1763-1797* (Chapel Hill, N.C., 1963), passim.

[40]Details of Livingston's role in the election of 1800 may be found in William O. Lynch, *Fifty Years of Party Warfare* (Indianapolis, 1931), 119, 135; Noble E. Cunningham, *The Jeffersonian Republicans: The Formation of Party Organization, 1789-1801* (Chapel Hill, N. C., 1957), 243-44; and Milton Lomask, *Aaron Burr: The Years from Princeton to Vice-President, 1756-1805* (New York, 1979), 278, 281, 287-88. Robert R. Livingston's part in committing his brother's vote to Jefferson in 1801 may well have been determined by the crafty Virginian's hint of advancement for Edward in a letter offering the chancellor the post of secretary of the navy should he indeed win the presidency. His associates in the new administration, Jefferson promised, would be highly acceptable to him, "one of them, whom you cannot mistake, peculiarly so." Thomas Jefferson to Robert R. Livingston, December 12, 1800, in Robert R. Livingston Papers, Museum of the City of New York.

[41]Dixon Wecter, *The Saga of American Society* (New York, 1937), 56, 89; Albert Gallatin to Thomas Jefferson, July 24, 1802, June 16, August 11, 1803, in Thomas Jefferson Papers, Library of Congress. The *New Orleans Argus*, June 30, 1828, prints four different defenses offered by Livingston's friends against the New York fraud charges. See also Auguste Davezac, "Fragments of Unpublished Reminiscences of Edward Livingston, "*United States Magazine and Democratic Review*, 8 (1840): 376.

[42]Edward Livingston, "Address to the People of the United States on the Measures Pursued by the Executive with Respect to the Batture at New Orleans," in *American State Papers, Public Lands*, 2:19. Strangely, this self-serving, unsubstantiated version of events has been uncritically accepted by a wide range of historians, including James Parton, George Dargo, John Niven, George Dangerfield, and the authors of the entries in the

Dictionary of American Biography and *A Dictionary of Louisiana Biography*. The more circumspect Dumas Malone in his *Jefferson the President: First Term, 1801-1805* (Boston, 1970), 358, simply mentions Livingston's "troubles in New York, on which I pass no judgment here." The Livingston audit is Number 51,742, dated July 11, 1832, in Record Group 217, Miscellaneous Treasury Accounts of the General Accounting Office, 1790-1894, National Archives. The pertinent Livingston family letters include those to Robert R. Livingston from John R. Livingston, September 10, 1803, January 12, 1804, John Armstrong, February 7, 1804, and Edward himself, May 6, 1804, all in the Robert R. Livingston Papers, New York Historical Society.

[43]Sparks, *Memories of Fifty Years*, 428; Alexander Walker, *Jackson and New Orleans* (New York, 1856), 17; Carleton Hunt, "Life and Service of Edward Livingston," Louisiana Bar Association *Proceedings* (1903), 18.

[44]Carter, ed., *Territory of Orleans*, 348, 512.

[45]*United States v. The Mayor, Aldermen, and Inhabitants of the Cities of Philadelphia and New Orleans*, 11 Howard, 609-61; James Wilkinson, *Wilkinson, Solider and Pioneer* (New Orleans, 1935), 120-24; Carter, ed., *Territory of Orleans*, 294; Dunbar Rowland, ed., *The Official Letter Books of W. C. C. Claiborne 1801-1816*, 6 vols. (Jackson, Miss, 1917), 6:91, 156.

[46]Wilkinson, *Wilkinson*, 122-24; Carter, ed., *Territory of Orleans*, 489; Ira Flory, Jr., "Edward Livingston's Place in Louisiana Law," *Louisiana Historical Quarterly*, 19 (1936): 336; James Winston, ed., "A Faithful Picture of the Political Situation in New Orleans at the Close of the Last and the Beginning of the Present Year, 1807," *Louisiana Historical Quarterly*, 11 (1928): 390.

[47]Charles Gayarré, "Historical Sketch of Pierre and Jean Lafitte," *Magazine of American History*, 10 (1883): 295.

[48]J. Fair Hardin, "The First Great Western River Captain," *Louisiana Historical Quarterly*, 10 (1927): 32; Caroline S. Pfaff, "Henry Miller Shreve," *Louisiana Historical Quarterly*, 10 (1927): 218-19.

[49]"Contracts for the Year 1816" and "Increase of the Navy," in *American State Papers, Naval Affairs*, 1:431, 482, 553; Walter Prichard, Fred Kniffin, and Clair Brown, "Southern Louisiana and Southern Alabama in 1819: The Journal of James Leander Cathcart," *Louisiana Historical Quarterly*, 27 (1945): 885.

[50]*Edward Livingston v. F. J. LeBreton Dorgenois* (Case 675), *Benjamin Morgan v. Edward Livingston* (Case 1373), *L. B. McCarty v. Edward Livingston* (Case 1374), all in *Conspicuous Cases in the United States District Court of Louisiana*; Edward Livingston, *An Answer to Mr. Jefferson's Justification of His Conduct in the Case of the New Orleans Batture* (Philadelphia, 1813), 15; *Louisiana Gazette*, January 17, February 6, December 12, 1821; Francis P. Burns, "The Graviers and the Faubourg Ste. Marie," *Louisiana Historical Quarterly*, 22 (1939): 414-15.

[51]*L'Ami des Lois*, October 12, 1822; *New Orleans Argus*, June 21, 1826; *Louisiana Advertiser*, November 17, 1823.

[52]Louise Livingston Hunt, *Memoir of Mrs. Edward Livingston* (New York, 1886), 13-50; Elizabeth F. Ellet, *Court Circles of the Republic* (New York, 1869), 213-17. The extensive letters of Livingston to his children may be found in the Edward Livingston Papers, Firestone Library, Princeton University, Princeton, N. J.

[53]Nicholas P. Trist to Virginia Randolph, February 9, 1823 in Trist Papers, UNC.

[54]Nicholas P. Trist to Virginia Randolph, May 20, 1823, ibid.

[55]John Sibley to Ann Eliza Johnston, October 23, 1831, in Johnston Papers.

[56]Vincent Nolte, *Fifty Years in Both Hemispheres* (New York, 1854), 89.

[57]Rowland, ed., *Letter Books of Claiborne*, 4:167.

[58]Nolte, *Fifty Years in Both Hemispheres*, 89.

[59]H. B. Trist to Nicholas P. Trist, May 18, 1825, in Trist Papers, UNC; Foote, *Bench and Bar of South and Southwest*, 194.

[60]Foote, *Bench and Bar of South and Southwest*, 194.

[61]William L. Brent to Henry Clay, September 17, 1829, in Clay Papers; Henry Johnson to J. F. H. Claiborne, May 4, 1860, in J. F. H. Claiborne Collection, Southern Historical Collection, University of North Carolina, Chapel Hill, N. C.

[62]J. J. McLanahan to Andrew J. Donelson, July 21, 1829, in Andrew Jackson Donelson Papers, Library of Congress.

[63]Joseph Coolidge to Nicholas P. Trist, July 16, 1829, in Trist Papers, LC.

[64]Auguste Davezac to Nicholas P. Trist, July 27, 1829, H. B. Trist to Nicholas P. Trist, August 3, 1829, ibid.

[65]Foote, *Bench and Bar of South and Southwest*, 194; Dart, "Justices of the Supreme Court," 116.

[66]Alfred Hennen to Mrs. James Hennen, July 22, 1803, in Hennen-Jennings Papers, Department of Archives, Louisiana State University, Baton Rouge, La. See also Foote, *Bench and Bar of South and Southwest*, 195; Edward Everett Diary, May 6, 1829, in Edward Everett Papers; Gayarré, "New Orleans Bench and Bar," 69; W. O. Hart, "The Bible in Louisiana a Century Ago," *Publications of the Louisiana Historical Society*, 9 (1916); Whitaker, *Life and Character in Louisiana*, 5; James S. Zacharie, "New Orleans—Its Old Streets and Places," *Publications of the Louisiana Historical Society*, 2 (1902), Pt. 3:65.

[67]Dart, "Justices of the Supreme Court," 118; Dufour, "Local Sketches," 537; Whitaker, *Life and Character in Louisiana*, 9.

[68]Sparks, *Memories of Fifty Years*, 432.

[69]Ibid.

[70]Ibid.; Foote, *Bench and Bar of South and Southwest*, 197; Gayarré, "New Orleans Bench and Bar," 62; Whitaker, *Life and Character in Louisiana*, 8-9.

[71]*New Orleans Daily True Delta*, April 4, 1858.

[72]William Coleman, *Historical Sketch Book and Guide to New Orleans* (New Orleans, 1885), 93; Charles R. Craig, "John Slidell, Louisiana Politico, 1793-1847" (M.A. thesis, Tulane University, 1948), 5-6; Foote, *Bench and Bar of South and Southwest*, 202; Whitaker, *Life and Character in Louisiana*, 66.

[73]Royall, *Southern Tour*, 3:35; *New Orleans Bee*, November 15, 1833.

[74]Andrew Jackson to John C. Calhoun, January 17, 1820, in John S. Bassett, ed., *The Correspondence of Andrew Jackson*, 6 vols. (Washington, D. C., 1927-35), 3:9; Calhoun to Jackson, January 22, 1820, in Jackson Papers, LC.

[75]*Louisiana Advertiser*, October 23, 1829, May 14, 1820; Foote, *Bench and Bar of South and Southwest*, 196; Royall, *Southern Tour*, 3:93; Charles R. Corning, "Eleazar Wheelock Ripley" (Typescript, Louisiana State Museum, n.d.), passim.

[76]Whitaker, *Life and Character in Louisiana*, 80; Royall, *Southern Tour*, 3:32.

ALEXANDRE MOUTON: GOVERNOR, 1843-1846*

Judith F. Gentry

Mouton, Alexandre (b. Attakapas district [Lafayette Parish], Louisiana, November 18, 1804; d. Vermilionville [Lafayette], Louisiana, February 12, 1885), state legislator, speaker of the Louisiana House of Representatives, United States senator, governor, and chairman of the Louisiana Secession Convention. The sixth child of Jean Mouton and Marie Marthe Bordat, Mouton was born on his family's plantation on Bayou Carencro. Both his parents were of Acadian origin, and his father was considered the founder of Vermilionville (modern Lafayette). In 1820, Mouton was graduated from Georgetown College, in Washington, D. C.; he then read law in the offices of Charles Antoine and Edward Simon, of St. Martinville, and was admitted to the bar in 1825. After practicing law for a few years, Mouton turned his attention to the cultivation of cotton and sugar cane on Ile Copale Plantation, which his father had given him as a wedding present. In 1826, Mouton married Celia Rousseau, granddaughter of Jacques Dupré, a wealthy cattle rancher in the Opelousas region and a prominent local politician; they had five children before Celia died. In 1842, he married Emma Kitchell Gardner; they had six children.

Although the prairie and bayou sugarcane region was later a stronghold of the Whig party, Mouton became a supporter of the Jacksonian Democrats and rose to prominence within his party. He served as a Democratic presidential elector in 1828, 1832, and 1836, and represented Louisiana at the Democratic national conventions in 1856 and 1860. He served in the lower house of the Louisiana legislature from 1826 to 1832—the last two years as speaker of the house—and again from 1836 to 1837. As a legislator, he supported internal improvements and the chartering of banks, and encouraged the rapid sale of federal lands in Louisiana. In 1832, he cast the tie-breaking vote in favor of chartering the Union Bank of Louisiana, which was designed to make credit available to rural areas through eight branches; the state guaranteed the bonds of the bank in order to facilitate their sale in Europe. In 1834, Mouton became president of the bank's Vermilionville branch.

*First published in Joseph G. Dawson, III, *The Louisiana Governors: From Iberville to Edwards* (Baton Rouge: Louisiana State University Press, © 1990), 118-122. Reprinted with the kind permission of the author and publisher.

Mouton was elected by the state legislature to the United States Senate in 1837 and served until 1842. As a strong Jacksonian senator from Louisiana, he gave attention to better mail service, the settlement of land claims, the more rapid sale of federal lands in Louisiana, the distribution to the state of a portion of the proceeds from the sale of federal lands, and the support of internal improvement projects in Louisiana by the federal government. He opposed rechartering the Bank of the United States, and he was against the protective tariff.

In 1842, at the request of Democratic party leaders in Louisiana, Mouton resigned from the Senate in order to run for the governorship of the state. The Democrats were criticizing the Whigs for the economic difficulties the state was experiencing. Hardships associated with the depression that had begun in 1837 intensified in 1842. The legislature passed the Bank Act of 1842, intended to maintain the fiscal integrity of the state's economy. Subsequently, however, nine of Louisiana's fourteen banks went into liquidation, resulting in a serious shortage of money and credit. The state owed $1.2 million in short-term debt to the banks and had additional millions of dollars of long-term debt and other obligations.

Mouton won the election with 60 percent of the popular vote and on January 30, 1843, took the oath as the first Democratic governor of Louisiana. In office, Mouton developed controversial economic policies for Louisiana—including balancing the budget in a time of economic depression. Whereas Governor André Bienvenu Roman had pursued a policy of frugality and urged tax increases, Mouton further reduced state expenditures and liquidated state assets in order to balance the budget and meet bond obligations without raising taxes. He sold all the bank stock held by the state and applied the proceeds of the sales to the short-term debts of the state to the banks. He also sold steamboats, equipment, and slaves owned by the state, which had been employed since 1834 under a program inaugurated by Roman to remove the Red River raft and make other internal improvements. In contrast to his actions as a legislator, Mouton as governor opposed virtually all expenditures for internal improvements. He initiated a program of leasing out the state penitentiary with its labor and textile machinery, in order to relieve the state of the cost of operating the system. He supported limitations on state borrowing and advocated using all state income to pay the debt, except for proceeds of the sale of public lands dedicated to education.

In the 1842 gubernatorial campaign and during Mouton's governorship, the Democrats supported the calling of a constitutional convention. Along with many Democrats, Mouton favored the removal of property qualifications for suffrage and officeholding, and the election of all local officials and most judges. The two required referenda were conducted while Mouton was governor, delegates to the convention were elected, and a new constitution was written and ratified by the voters in 1845. A majority of the delegates were Democrats, but a radical-conservative split among Democrats allowed a Whig—conservative Democratic alliance to wield influence. Consequently, Mouton was unable to exert the influence in the convention that he might have, and several of the provisions of the Constitution of 1845 bore the mark of many compromises.

After his governorship, Mouton retired to the life of a sugar planter and railroad promoter. In 1851, he became vice-president of the newly formed New Orleans, Algiers, Attakapas, and Opelousas Railroad.

As a member of the Louisiana delegation to the national Democratic convention in 1860, Mouton presented the resolution that demanded the right for slaveowners to take slaves into any territory of the United States; when the motion was rejected, he joined in the walkout by Deep South Democrats. A supporter of immediate secession, he was elected to the Louisiana Secession Convention, for which the delegates chose him chairman. Mouton stood for election to the senate of the Confederate States of America but was defeated. During the Civil War, he was arrested by, and once had to flee from, Union troops, who used Ile Copale Plantation as a headquarters and burned the sugar mill and other work buildings. As a result of the Union victory, Mouton's 120 slaves were freed. The destruction and economic hardship of the war years contributed to Mouton's declining wealth, although he continued to own the 1,900 acres that Ile Copale comprised.

* * *

Mouton's decision to balance the state budget during a time of depression had important political and economic consequences, intensifying the hard times and making recovery difficult. The decrease in bank-note circulation necessitated by his policies caused a severe contraction of money and credit. Mouton, however, was acting in accordance with the best financial and economic understanding of the day. Balancing the budget was not a party issue; both Whigs and most Democrats were committed to that goal. Mouton left the governorship with a $225,000 surplus for his last year of office (compared with a $200,000 deficit for the year before he took office) and a significantly reduced state debt. But his stringent fiscal retrenchment was only partially responsible for the improved financial condition of the state government. The most important cause was the general economic recovery, a development Mouton's programs had retarded rather than advanced.

Perhaps the most important accomplishment of Mouton's term was the writing of the Constitution of 1845. This new constitution reflected a strong North-South split in the state, and indicated some anticity bias against New Orleans. Although the property requirements for suffrage and officeholding were eliminated, provisions designed to maintain political control by wealthy planters were introduced. For the first time, the state senate was to be apportioned on the basis of total population—including voteless slaves—and New Orleans was to be limited to no more than one-eighth of the membership. The design was to give the slaveholding parishes, with their greater total population, more votes in the state senate than the northern, hill-country parishes and the city of

New Orleans. A two-year residence requirement for voting, instead of the previous one-year requirement, would delay the enfranchisement of recently arrived men from other states and newly arrived, generally poor, immigrants from abroad. The proponents of democratic reform was successful, however, in providing for the direct election of the governor by the voters and the election of most local officials. The reapportionment in the Constitution of 1845 reduced the power of the French-speaking Roman Catholics of South Louisiana, who were an overwhelming majority of the state's population when the Constitution of 1812 had been written. The new charter also provided for regular reapportionment in the future.

Furthermore, the Constitution of 1845 included restrictions on state aid to economic enterprise, as well as limitations on borrowing. It prohibited the legislature from granting any monopoly for more than twenty years, from incorporating or renewing the charters of any banks, and from guaranteeing the bonds of any person, corporation, or body politic. The legislature was prohibited from incurring debts totaling more than $100,000 without providing for the taxes necessary to extinguish the debt. It was required to establish a free public-education system, but the limitations on going into debt and the restrictions against guaranteeing the bonds of any body politic made it difficult to comply with that mandate.

Both Whigs and Democrats were dissatisfied with the Constitution of 1845. Both parties mildly supported the ratification of the new constitution, but both also proved willing to call a new constitutional convention only seven years later. Thus Mouton's support for the Constitution of 1845 had created only a short-lived state charter.

DUNCAN F. KENNER: WHIG LEADER*

Craig A. Bauer

Within weeks of the popular vote on the adoption of the state's new constitution in 1845, campaigning began for the legislature and other state offices. Among the many candidates for elected office was Duncan Kenner, who entered the race for the state senate seat for Ascension Parish. Kenner actually was the incumbent. In 1844, when everyone's interest was focused upon the effort to bring about constitutional reform and the selection of representatives for the convention, Kenner had not only won a seat at the convention but also to the legislature as a senator. Because the latter met concurrently with the constitutional convention, only passing interest was given to the legislative assemblage by either its members or the people of the state.[1]

Because the new legislature would have much to say about the implementation of the new constitution, Louisianians viewed the 1846 elections with more seriousness and interest than usual. As with most campaigns for political office in antebellum Louisiana, the election was hard fought. Candidates attracted much public attention as they stumped their districts speaking either to large audiences at mass meetings or talking individually with residents with whom they came in contact. Office seekers either traveled alone or in groups; on occasion candidates for the same office journeyed together and took turns in speaking to their constituents. At times campaigns even took on the look of a traveling minstrel show as the candidates joked, played pranks on each other, told stories, and sang songs to their audiences.[2]

In the campaign the Democrats were determined to build on the Jacksonian theme of the needs of the common man versus the wants of the privileged, whereas the Whigs endorsed the undistinguished motto of "principles and not men" as their campaign theme. To get their point across the Democrats attacked the Whigs for supporting the tariff, which, they claimed, led to the accumulation of vast wealth for the few. To the voters the election became a struggle between "monopoly and privilege and money on the one hand, and justice, common sense, and the rights of the masses on the other."[3] The Democrats' efforts succeeded in putting the Whigs on the defensive and forced them to center their

*First published as Chapter 6 in *A Leader Among Peers: The Life and Times of Duncan Farrar Kenner* (Lafayette, La.: Center for Louisiana Studies, © 1993), 112-130. Reprinted with the kind permission of the author and the publisher.

campaign efforts around defending the tariff and limply denouncing their opponents as anti-tariff politicians.

The Democratic strategy worked. Isaac Johnson, the Democratic gubernatorial candidate, defeated his Whig opponent in thirty of Louisiana's forty-five parishes. Even in Kenner's home parish of Ascension, where the tariff was looked upon favorably because of the area's sugar economy, the Democrats made a strong showing. In a letter to William Minor in Natchez a short time after the vote and before he knew all of the statewide results, Kenner glumly wrote: "the elections have been very animated, but I have carried my election by eight votes—two democratic representatives were elected from our parish—one by two and one by four votes—the parish went democratic for governor and lieutenant governor—by thirty for the first and sixty for the second." He concluded with the lament that "our defeat throughout the state will be overwhelming." Fortunately for his party, things did not turn out quite as badly as Kenner predicted. Though they lost the executive office and the Democrats held a two-vote majority in the senate, the Whigs were able to win a majority of three seats in the house of representatives. Furthermore, the new Democratic governor was a member of the predominantly Anglo-American West Feliciana aristocracy who did not act as a strict party man. Hence, over the period of his administration there were relatively few changes between the new Democrats and the old Whigs.[4]

The new legislature met in early February 1846, and began the process of activating the new constitution. Though much of the work dealt with routine and uncontroversial issues, one of the most hotly debated subjects at the session was the constitutional provision which required the removal of the state capital from New Orleans. Those who supported the effort criticized the length of the legislative sessions held in the Crescent City. They speculated that the many distractions found in the city kept the lawmakers from concentrating on their legislative duties. Adding to the heat of the debate was the fact that nearly every city in the state had supporters in the legislature seeking the new capital. Of the various communities mentioned as an alternative location for the capital, Baton Rouge, St. Francisville, and Donaldsonville were the leading contenders. Kenner pushed hard for Donaldsonville, the parish seat of his home parish of Ascension. He pointed out to his colleagues that Donaldsonville was conveniently located and was accessible from nearly every section of the state. In spite of his efforts, Kenner's arguments in favor of Donaldsonville went unheeded by the legislature. Once before, in 1830, the capital had briefly been moved from the Crescent City to Donaldsonville. That experience had been such a fiasco that Kenner's appeal for the establishment of the capital in his home district stood little chance for success. After much debate, Baton Rouge was elected as the new capital.[5]

In the spring, constitutional reform and state politics were overshadowed by national events. Paramount among these national issues was the war with Mexico. Fueled by the expansionist mood of the country and by President James K. Polk's assertions that the Mexicans had invaded our territory and had "shed American blood upon . . . American soil," Congress declared war against Mexico on May 13, 1846. With the outbreak of hostilities between the two nations, war fever spread quickly throughout Louisiana. Even before the president sent his war message to Congress, Kenner and his colleagues in the legislature appropriated $100,000 for the purpose of equipping regiments of volunteers from Louisiana to be placed at the call of Gen. Zachary Taylor at the war front. In addition to sponsoring the funding for what he called the "Louisiana Legion," Kenner later proposed to tender General Taylor a sword in recognition of his valiant service in the Mexican conflict. His motion was unanimously adopted.[6]

The war with Mexico was not the only national issue to receive the attention of state legislators. The American effort to expand its territorial holdings into the Southwest was but one goal of the proponents of Manifest Destiny. From the beginning of his administration, President Polk had pressed the American claim to all of Oregon. Though the president received strong support for his position from the states of the Old Northwest, the great majority of the members of Congress, both Democrats and Whigs, favored a settlement of the Oregon dispute with Britain on the basis of a partition of the territory at the forty-ninth parallel. Southerners in particular were not interested in vast territorial additions to the Pacific Northwest, and they feared taking any action which might endanger British markets for their agricultural surplus. However, as in the case of his support for the war with Mexico, Kenner demonstrated the depth of his nationalistic feelings and his independent political thought by strongly supporting the doctrine of Manifest Destiny—a stand which was in support of a Democrat president and in opposition to the majority of his fellow Whigs around the country. In an address to the legislature he embraced Polk's efforts to secure the whole of Oregon. On the basis of priority of exploration, Kenner declared that the claim of the United States to the boundary 54' 40" was unquestionable.[7]

It did not take long, however, for the novelty of the international situation to wear off and for the legislature to return its attention to implementing the terms of the new constitution. In early 1847 the question of education and the new constitution came before the state lawmakers. Louisiana Secretary of State Charles Gayarré reported to the legislature on the "precarious existence" of the state's educational system. He warned that its "days [were] numbered" and that quick action was needed by the legislature. As was the case at the recent constitutional convention, Kenner was in the forefront of the drive to bring about the needed educational reforms. His effort to improve the system by introducing a bill to "establish free school throughout the state" won Kenner the praise of a New Orleans paper, which expressed pleasure that at least one legislator was making an effort to put into effect the educational reforms mandated by the constitution.[8]

Sometimes referred to by the press as the "Kenner Bill," the proposal for free schools throughout Louisiana was eventually passed during the session. Though the issue was not a partisan one, the debate on education was sometimes punctuated with long-winded discussions of parochial issues. One such discussion involved Kenner and concerned the choice of a location for a state university. As he had at the constitutional convention when he resisted the efforts to keep the capital in the Crescent City, Kenner also thought that the state's largest city was not a good choice for the location of a university. He claimed that locating a university in New Orleans would expose its young students to the varied diversions of urban life which would negatively affect their concentration and possibly undermine the desire of some for an education. Kenner's rather provincial argument against the establishment of a university in the state's largest city did not go unanswered. One of the more effective replies came from the *Daily Delta,* a newspaper which on occasion had positive things to say about Kenner. It stated that "we regret to see so intelligent and patriotic a gentleman, and legislator as Mr. Kenner . . . discouraging a university in New Orleans." The paper went on to point out that the most prestigious and flourishing colleges in the world were to be found in the largest cities. The paper argued that a large city offered the added security of a large police force which might be needed to control unruly students. Finally, the *Delta* ended its remarks on the subject by making the point that New Orleans had had a medical school for some time without any of Kenner's predicted consequences having taken place.[9]

Kenner's colleagues in the legislature failed to agree with him on this issue. As authorized by the constitution, the state appropriated revenues for the establishment in New Orleans of the University of Louisiana, which it was hoped would have colleges of medicine, law, natural sciences, and literature. Though the new university's schools of medicine and law were successful, those of literature and natural sciences never developed because of insufficient operating funds. The university remained in existence until the outbreak of the Civil War. Despite his unhappiness over the location of the university, Kenner continued his activism for years as one of the chief supporters of a free public school system for Louisiana.[10]

Throughout his legislative career, Kenner applied himself to the task at hand. Whether it was a major issue such as constitutional reform or simple petitions or relief from his constituents, he diligently sought to have his position on an issue accepted by his colleagues. His skill on the floor of the legislature, along with his ability as a speaker, his good judgment, and his thorough knowledge and mastery of the workings of the legislative committee system, all brought Kenner recognition not only from his fellow lawmakers but also from people and politicians throughout the state. Among the honors be stowed upon the legislator was his selection in 1847 as vice-president of the Bar Association of New Orleans.[11]

The most significant acknowledgment of Kenner's rising political stature came in 1848 when the Whig party turned to him as its nominee for one of the most important political offices in the state. The tenure of United States Senator Henry Johnson was drawing to a close, and both the Whigs and Democrats hoped to replace the senator with one of their own.

Since the state legislature then chose United States senators, it appeared that, because the Whigs now held a narrow majority of two votes on a joint legislative ballot, they had the advantage. However, because of the lack of party unity which Louisiana's Whigs sometimes displayed on crucial votes, there was much public interest and political concern over the outcome of the contest. The *New Orleans Daily Delta* reported that "the town is agog about the election," while the Whig paper, the *Baton Rouge Gazette,* publicly voiced concern over the lack of party unity.[12] The paper commented that:

> On former occasions, we have seen the mortifying spectacle of a legislature of Louisiana, with a Whig majority, electing a Democratic Senator, in consequence of local feeling or personal preference. It is time that the Whig party of Louisiana should adopt a system of [more] rigid discipline, than heretofore [has] been practiced in the ranks, and we are glad to perceive a growing disposition to do so.[13]

Unfortunately for Kenner and the Whigs, when the legislature met in late January to choose Louisiana's new United States senator, the worst fears of the *Gazette's* editor and the party faithful were realized. In an effort to keep their party members in line, the Whigs used the Democrats' custom of the caucus to choose a single nominee to support for the office. When they met on January 20 there were several individuals interested in the Senate seat. On the first ballot Judah P. Benjamin received 25 votes; Kenner, 24; Randell Hunt, 9; Henry Johnson, 2; and candidate James Elam received no votes. On the second ballot only the top two vote-getters remained in the race. Kenner picked up most of the votes of the first ballot's losing candidates and thus captured the nomination with 36 votes to Benjamin's 26. Meanwhile, the Democrats selected Kenner's acquaintance and former employer John Slidell as their nominee. They also agreed, however, to turn to Pierre Soulé after the second ballot by the legislature if Slidell was unable to win the nomination at the outset.[14]

There was an interval of several days between the time of Kenner's selection as the Whig nominee and the actual election by the legislature. This time was a period of considerable speculation and anxiety over the outcome of this major political contest between the two parties. Public interest in the race was intense. Though there was much interest over who would be the Democratic nominee, for that party did not caucus until the very night before the election, there also continued to be considerable speculation among state political leaders and the public over the question of whether the Whigs could hold their members in line to vote for their nominee.[15]

The issue was finally resolved when, at 12:20 p.m. on January 24, 1848, the legislature met in the hall of the state house of representatives to choose a new United States senator. Tension was great. The reporter for the *Daily Delta* noted the mood when he wrote: "The house hall was densely crowded, many . . . distinguished citizens were in attendance, and the important event was about to transpire. Anxiety and painful suspense were depicted on many countenances."[16]

As soon as the assembly was called to order, Kenner and his Whig allies realized that they were going to have problems. As the house clerk called the roll of the members present, all but one responded. Isaac A. Myles, a Whig from Washington Parish, failed to answer the call. His absence caused a great sensation, for without Myles's presence the joint assembly consisted of 129 members, with sixty-five votes needed to win. Realizing that their prospect for victory was substantially lessened without Myles, the Whigs attempted to strengthen their position with a parliamentary procedure. They protested the right of Senator John Bell of Orleans Parish to vote in the election because the senate at that time was investigating his right to sit in the senate. However, after only limited debate, the Democrat president of the senate dismissed the Whig protest, claiming that it violated the rules of the meeting.[17]

When the assembly returned to the matter at hand, the nomination process for the senate race was completed. John Bell, having successfully avoided the Whig challenge, was given the honor of nominating the Democratic nominee, John Slidell. Kenner's name was placed into consideration by his friend and political ally, Christopher Adams of Iberville Parish. When the balloting started, Kenner attempted to break some of the tension in the hall by playfully hesitating to cast his own ballot for himself as if he had second thoughts. The mood in the room, however, quickly became more serious when Maunsel White, Democratic senator from Plaquemines, threw his vote away by casting for an un-nominated individual. Unfortunately for Kenner and the Whigs, White's defection from Slidell did not help them, for Representative Baldwin of Sabine Parish, who had been considered a member of the Whig camp, cast his vote for Slidell. Hence the first ballot ended with Kenner receiving a total of sixty-four votes (fifteen in the senate and forty-nine in the house) and his opponent earning an equal number (one more than Kenner in the senate and one less in the house).[18]

A second vote was taken with the same results. With an obvious deadlock in place, the Whigs attempted to break off the contest by moving to discontinue to joint session. After heated debate, the senate withdrew to its chamber where the Whigs again renewed their efforts to challenge Bell's right to take part in the election. When their efforts proved futile and motions to adjourn the senate and the house also failed, the two legislative houses reassembled together.[19]

Considerable behind-the-scenes maneuvering had taken place while the two houses caucused. The Democrats now moved to break the impasse. Senator Bell, who had been in the center of so much of the day's events, rose and nominated Pierre Soulé for the office in question. Events moved quickly. Slidell, who was not pleased with the move to replace him with Soulé and who would from that time on be a bitter political enemy of the new Democratic nominee, nevertheless remained a loyal party man and threw his support behind Soulé. With the political momentum now in their favor, the Democrats pushed for a new vote. There was little that Kenner and his supporters could do. Five individuals who had cast their votes against Slidell in the first round of voting now shifted their support to Soulé. They included the Democrat Maunsel White and four Whigs, Senators Felix Garcia and William Parham and house members Bienvenue and Watkins. Only one Slidell voter named Baldwin switched his support to Kenner. Thus, the final vote for the United States Senate seat was sixty-eight votes (nineteen in the Senate and forty-nine in the House) for Soulé to sixty-one for Kenner (thirteen in the upper house and forty-eight in the lower).[20]

The vote of the legislature ended Kenner's chance for a seat in Congress; however, it did not stop the controversy and speculation which had engulfed the campaign from its start. Not unexpectedly, the surprise election of Soulé caused much consternation throughout the state, with the Whigs denouncing and the Democrats lauding the results. The Whig press in particular was not pleased. One Whig editor commented that "it would require a more astute Oedipus than him of old to account for the means by which the Democrats have elected a U. S. Senator . . . with a clear Whig majority of two."[21] The most bitter comments concerning the Whig disaster were reserved for those Whigs who had not supported their party's nominee. The *New Orleans Bulletin* bitterly attacked the party traitors and concluded that, "As for Isaac A. Myles . . . we think it will be fortunate for his fame, if some accident has removed him from this to a better world, as no less excuse will be satisfaction for his mysterious absence." The paper went on to castigate the other turncoats with the comment that "Baldwin's voting for Slidell and not for Soulé showed his illegal bargain ended with the former."[22] The *Baton Rouge Gazette* expressed a similar view with the comment that, "If he [Kenner] is not a U. S. Senator now in the stead of Pierre Soulé, it is because he was incapable of doing what he considered wrong in consequence of the treachery of William S. Parham."[23]

While the Whig press viciously assailed its opponents and those individuals responsible for their party's defeat, the Democratic press reveled in its victory by lauding Soulé's success. In caustic language typical of the political papers of the time, the *Democratic Advocate* of Baton Rouge even belittled the defeated candidate's vote for himself by commenting that "Kenner was driven to the alternative of voting for himself, a rather delicate matter, and in pressure he did it as timidly as a Miss, the first time she whispered yes."[24]

Many Whigs considered the election to have been stolen from them. As noted earlier, there was much conjecture in the period leading up to the vote that something was going to happen which would give the election to the Democrats. The *Daily Picayune* even published before the election an anonymous letter in which the author reported that he had heard two Democrats, one of whom was a legislator, "say very confidentially that the Democrats would elect a United States Senator." The unnamed writer went on to question whether any Whig legislators would publicly vote for a Democrat or if "any of them [would] be sick . . . and not attend." Observing "that in times past money has effected wonders," the *Picayune's* anonymous correspondent concluded, somewhat expectantly, that the Whigs would simply have to wait to see "who are the Judases."[25]

With so many in the state holding a similar belief to that of the *Picayune's* writer and with the furor over the Whig setback growing, several legislators who had unexpectedly voted for the Democratic nominee instead of Kenner scrambled to explain their position to their colleagues and constituents. On the day following the election, Senator Parham addressed the senate and defended his vote by claiming that he had determined that a victory by Kenner was impossible because of Whig dissension. Originally he had expected Kenner to win, as every Whig at their party caucus promised to stand by the nominee. However, when it was rumored about an hour before the vote that Myles was absent, he concluded that something would happen to deny the Whigs their one-vote majority. During the actual voting, when the Whig Baldwin voted for Slidell and Kenner was unable to gather enough votes for victory on two ballots, he decided that something had to be done to deny the race to Slidell. After unsuccessfully trying to get another Whig candidate into the race, he informed one of the Democratic leaders that he would vote for Soulé. He then approached Kenner, telling him that the only way to keep Slidell from winning would be to divide the Democrats. Kenner replied that "perhaps it was a trick on the part of the opposite party" to get Soulé elected. Parham claimed that at that time he did not know of anyone else who would vote for Soulé, whom he considered a man of ability and a true patriot, by Slidell's defeat rather than Slidell's victory by Kenner's defeat.[26]

After explaining his own actions, Parham then concluded his remarks by commenting on the motives of two other legislators who had crossed party lines in the election. Echoing the popular sentiment of the day, Parham declared that he, along with many others, "believed that improper means had been used, both in procuring the absence of Mr. Myles and getting Mr. Baldwin to vote against Mr. Kenner," and he hoped that through a proper investigation the truth of the matter would be revealed.[27]

Parham's defense was followed by similar ones by Garcia in the senate and Watkins in the house. Both claimed that they had switched their vote from Kenner to Soulé only because they believed that the former had lost his chance of winning and they wanted to take steps to prevent Slidell from being elected. However, despite their pleas for understanding from their colleagues, bad feelings remained. Many of Kenner's supporters did not accept their explanations and did not mind letting them know of their unhappiness. For example, when Parham was challenged on his vote by Senator Martin, the discussion between the two legislators on the floor of the senate became so heated that the exchange of coarse and vulgar epithets soon led to the trading of physical blows between the two lawmakers.[28]

The question of what really led to the Whigs' unexpected loss in the senate race became even more clouded when Representative Jones of Jefferson Parish openly accused the absent Isaac A. Myles of Washington Parish of fraud. In a written statement to the house, he claimed that Myles had told him on the Saturday before the Monday election that he had been offered four Negroes not to vote for a Whig for United States senator. Jones urged that a committee be appointed to investigate the alleged corruption. Disclaiming any knowledge of the affair, Democrats seconded the motion and voted with the Whigs to form an investigative committee.[29]

When the "Myles Committee" began to gather its evidence it quickly became evident that it would be difficult to discern what had really happened in the election. Each of the legislators whose votes for U. S. senator had seemed questionable was called to explain his action. Most explained away their actions with vague political excuses. However, testimony was given which tended to exonerate Myles of the charges that he had accepted a bribe not to be present when the vote was taken. An individual identified only as Colonel Staples reported to the committee that he had introduced Myles to Slidell and that afterwards he had heard him express great satisfaction for Slidell. He also testified that after the election he spoke with Myles and asked him if the rumors about his taking a bribe were based upon fact. Myles replied that he had not been bribed. The only thing offered him, he explained to Staples, was a promise by the speaker of the house to place him on any committee he might select. The speaker later denied any ulterior motive in making the offer.[30]

Some of the most unexpected testimony before the committee occurred when Jones was called before the group to repeat his accusation about Myles. After hearing his comments and those of others who had knowledge of the events leading up to the vote for U. S. senator, the committee reached the following conclusion:

> A few days before the election, Jones went to the gentleman who was considered the choice of the democratic party, and told him he was no great shakes of a whig anyhow—he was too liberal for his party—that his parish, he believed, was democratic—that he would not on any terms vote for . . . the probable candidates of the whigs—that he was poor and sickly, and his health would be benefitted and his life prolonged by a visit to Cuba.[31]

With the accuser thus becoming the accused and with additional testimony from other witnesses which revealed that legislators other than just Jones and Myles were involved in making deals during the senate election, the "Myles Committee" was unable or unwilling to give a definitive report of wrongdoing in the election. Instead, it reported on March 7 that, from the evidence reviewed, the committee did not "feel authorized to report any breach of privilege [had] been committed." According to the committee, offers of the same type had been made to others in the house, as well as to Myles, and in their judgment the offers were considered to be "perfectly in accordance with parliamentary usage." They did, however, believe that part of the evidence was of such a nature that a written report was needed. The committee's report was quickly adopted by the legislature, and, with public interest waning, the issue was allowed to die without any real penalties being assessed against those individuals involved in the scandal.[32]

Despite their disappointing defeat in the senatorial race, Kenner and his Whig colleagues were able to come away from the election with the satisfaction of knowing that the Democrats' victory was not won without cost. For although they had entered the election as allies, Slidell and Soulé, the two most important leaders in the Louisiana Democratic Party, became bitter political rivals as a result of the contest. The surprising turn of events which denied victory to Slidell so affected him that he became the determined and implacable foe of Soulé for political control of Louisiana. The rivalry between the two

Democrats remained a central theme in the state's politics up to the eve of the Civil War.[33]

Louisiana's Whigs quickly put the senatorial election behind them and began to look forward to the next political contest, the presidential race in the fall of the year. Both state and national Whig leaders' hopes ran high for victory. Borrowing from the Democratic tradition which had given the country the Jackson presidency, the Whigs turned to a public hero, Gen. Zachary Taylor, who could exploit his military fame to obtain the presidency. A Mexican War hero, Taylor was a Louisiana planter who owned more than one hundred slaves and had never been a member of the Whig party nor had ever voted in a presidential election. His Democratic opponent, Lewis Cass of Michigan, was also a general in the war with Mexico and was a politician who had always tried to placate the South. Whereas the Whigs did not bother with a platform, the Democrats supported the American involvement in Mexico and declared that the federal government had no right to meddle with slavery. The campaign was largely one of ambiguities and personalities and ended with Taylor narrowly winning in both Louisiana and the nation. The Democratic defeat nationally was the result of a strong third party showing in New York by the Free Soil ticket headed by former president Martin Van Buren. In Louisiana, Taylor carried the state with 54.6 percent of the vote by doing extremely well in the planter areas of both cotton and sugar country.[34]

Their victory in the presidential election gave the Whigs in Louisiana high hopes for success in the next state election contest with the Democrats. Within a few weeks, the enthusiasm and confidence of the Whigs was reinforced when the party won a smashing victory in the New Orleans municipal elections. In light of these successes, Louisiana's Whigs began to set their sights on the state's upcoming gubernatorial campaign. Confident of their chances for victory, the Whigs began to review carefully their prospective candidates for the state's highest office. Among those prominently mentioned were Bannon Thibodaux, the only Louisiana Whig in Congress; Judah P. Benjamin; Alexander Bullitt, editor of the *Daily Picayune;* and Kenner, who was now looked upon as a spokesman for the state's country Whigs.[35]

Although on the surface things looked promising for the party, beneath the public image party unity was beginning to show some strain. Many of the old "setfast" Whigs, as distinguished from the younger and more liberal members, were disgruntled with President Taylor's failure to reward supporters from his home state with appointments to federal office. But the dissatisfaction of the "setfasts" went beyond that which they directed towards the president. They also found it increasingly difficult to agree with the younger and newer members of the party, who were more practical, vigorous, energetic, and adaptable to change. In spite of their success in recent elections, the lack of agreement between the old and new factions of the party did not bode well for the Whigs.[36]

When the state nominating convention met in Baton Rouge, more than three hundred delegates took part. Though several other individuals had been mentioned as likely candidates, the delegates, after only two ballots, nominated Alexandre Declouet for governor. The convention then selected Kenner as its nominee for the office of lieutenant governor. Despite its consensus on a choice of nominees, the convention reflected the developing factionalism which was beginning to afflict the party. When the young Whigs sponsored a resolution calling for the election of the state judiciary and denouncing the Democrats for appointing corrupt judges, the older "setfast" party members opposed any such change in the system. Though he personally liked the system of election, Kenner sided with the conservatives and opposed the proposal for political reasons because he thought it was unwise to antagonize the politically powerful state judiciary. Joining with Kenner and the conservatives, the majority of the delegates voted down the measure. Despite the convention's vote on the issue, the question of electing judges became an important issue during the ensuing campaign, with both parties, ironically, supporting and claiming it as their own.[37]

Opposing Declouet and Kenner were the Democratic nominees, Joseph Walker for governor and John B. Plauché for lieutenant governor. Like the Whigs, the Democrats also had problems between the older and young members of the party. Both groups agreed upon Walker as their nominee, but only after he agreed to be true to the principles of the party. This unusual requirement was added because it was well known that Walker had many friends who were Whigs, and the Democrats wanted to avoid a repetition of the behavior of the previous Democratic governor, Isaac Johnson, who had irritated many of his party's faithful by appointing Whigs to office.[38]

The campaign itself was distinguished by a lack of major issues between the two parties. For the most part, the Democrats attempted to make the point that their party represented progress and that the Whigs favored holding on to the current evils rather than entertaining measures of reform and experimentation. In the rural sections of the state the Democrats depicted their party as seeking to protect the people against the encroachment of the moneyed interests, whereas the Whig party's chief goal and purpose was to acquire wealth. On the other hand, the Whigs continually alluded to their ties with President Taylor. They also attempted to use the issue of naturalization of foreigners as a point against the Democrats by showing that Declouet had opposed making the naturalization laws more restrictive while a member of the senate. During most of the campaign, however, the issues raised in the respective party platforms were subordinated to bitter personal attacks by the candidates against each other. Kenner, for example, on several occasions attacked his Democratic counterpart for having only a limited knowledge of English which he claimed would limit the French-speaking Plauché from working effectively with the members of the senate.[39]

As the campaign continued and the parties and nominees exchanged charges and countercharges, both political camps were criticized by the press and by other observers for conducting a campaign devoid of principles and apparently aimed only at acquiring power and the taste of victory. The absence of clearly defined issues caused much public interest to be directed to the peripheries of the campaign, such as the public meetings, parades, club organizations, and songs, all of which were designed to enliven the campaign as election day neared. Clubs such as the Kenner Guards and Declouet Rangers and their Democrat counterparts played important roles in stirring up public support for their favorite candidates.[40]

In the antebellum South there were generally two types of successful politicians—the aristocratic type represented by Kenner and the folksy, demagogic type who duped unsophisticated rural voters by imitating the language and manners of the common man and by telling jokes. Among those who appealed to the feelings of the common man was Kenner's running mate. At rallies he would frequently belittle Joseph Walker, his Democratic opponent, by singing the familiar tune "The Ranger's Lament for Poor Old Joe," the chorus of which ran:

> Take off the saddle from his back,
> Pull down the fodder from his rack;
> There is no more run in poor old Joe—
> Turn him out to grass and let him go.[41]

Possessing a keen sense of humor, Kenner was not above poking a little fun at his political opponents during his campaign speeches, as demonstrated by his comments during the 1849 race about his opponent's poor mastery of English. For the most part, however, Kenner's reserved and undemonstrative temperament and his refined manners kept him from adopting many of the garish campaign techniques of some of the South's more flamboyant politicians. Despite his intelligence and sense of humor, his speech-making ability never matched the level of talent he demonstrated in mastering the intricacies of the legislative process. Though usually well received by his audience, Kenner's speeches were not equal to those of Louisiana's most brilliant politicians—for example, the Kenner family's friend Etienne Mazureau, who reportedly gave speeches which ran up to six hours in length.[42]

Of the many political gatherings that occurred during the campaign, one of the largest and most elaborate took place in New Orleans on the eve of the election. The Whigs of the city hosted a barbecue at the plantation home of Judge Joachim Bermudez on Gentilly Road. Six thousand persons attended and took part in the festivities. The Declouet Rangers and Kenner Guards were present along with many of the area's most prominent Whigs. Tables overflowed with roasted meats, and caskets of claret and ale were consumed while several bands played lively music under hundreds of political banners and symbols. Handbills were distributed to remind everyone present to vote for the party ticket on election day. Several of the notable Whigs who were present gave speeches; however, it was Kenner's oration which most affected the crowd. The press reported that upon his appearance there was a burst of enthusiasm, for Kenner was highly esteemed by his political friends and was a warm favorite of the party's supporters. In his address to the crowd Kenner gave his standard campaign speech. He reviewed the work of the campaign and mentioned the success of the Whigs in electing Taylor. He warned about the possibility of a let-down after such a great victory but added that, judging from the enthu-

enthusiasm of the people present, the upcoming vote held great promise for the Whig nominees. Before ending his remarks, Kenner commented briefly on the controversy which had arisen over his comments concerning his opponent's poor command of English. To those in the opposition party who took exception to his observations, Kenner stated he had been guided in his comments by earlier remarks on the subject by none other than Gen. Joseph Walker, the Democratic gubernatorial nominee.[43]

The large and raucous campaign rallies, which were by then a mainstay of Louisiana elections, continued up until the very eve of the vote. The balloting took place on Monday, November 5, 1849, and was one of the most active ever to take place in the state during the antebellum period. The results of the election took some time to tally, but when all the votes were counted, the Democrats had won victories in the races for the state's two highest offices. With 51.4 percent of the vote, Walker had narrowly defeated Declouet by a little more than a thousand votes, 18,566 for the Democrat to 17,533 for the Whig. Kenner did a little better than his running mate by losing the lieutenant governorship to Plauché by a vote of 18,200 to 17,385, or a margin of 815 votes. The greatest support for the Democrats came from the interior sections of the state, where the small farmers dominated, and from Orleans Parish. The Whig candidates not only did well in their traditional strongholds, such as Lafourche and the sugar lands along the Mississippi, but they also carried many of the cotton plantation parishes in the northern part of the state. The unity between the two planter groups in support of Whiggery was such that the election nearly turned in favor of Declouet and Kenner. The salient factor in the results was the vote in Orleans Parish, where many of the Democrats who had deserted their party in the recent presidential race to vote for Taylor returned to support their party's choices in the 1849 gubernatorial contest.[44]

In spite of the disappointing loss, Kenner continued to play a central role in the course of Whig politics in Louisiana. Within months of the end of the gubernatorial election, the voters of the southeastern portion of the state were faced with a special election to fill the vacancy left in the Second Congressional District when Charles Conrad resigned his seat in Congress to accept an appointment to the president's cabinet as secretary of war. At first Kenner was mentioned in the Whig press as the logical candidate for the party's nomination. But he let it be known that he did not want the nomination, although he was concerned about who would receive it.[45]

The contest for the nomination was between the "Country" and "City" factions of the Louisiana Whig Party. Though the larger geographical portion of the district was rural and allied with the "Country Whigs," the populated areas of Jefferson Parish—Algiers, which was located directly across the Mississippi River from the Vieux Carré section of New Orleans, and the city's Second Municipality—were centers of strength for the "City Whigs." Before the Whigs met in convention to choose their nominee for the race, the "City Whigs" united behind the candidacy of Theodore Hunt. They also were able to get assurances of support for their man from several of the country delegates to the convention. With this extra help, the New Orleans area delegates were primed for victory.[46]

Not wanting to see the urban Whigs acquire additional influence at the expense of their own power base, Kenner and several of his "Country Whig" colleagues moved to deny the "City Whigs" their expected victory. The key to victory centered on what technique would be used in counting the votes in the convention. The urban Whigs expected to use the ratio which had been used at the last Whig gubernatorial convention. Known as the "numerical basis," the plan called for votes to be allotted according to the number of Whig voters in each parish. With the population concentrated in their area, the advantage of this plan for the "City Whigs" was obvious. Kenner maneuvered to undercut the plan of the city delegates by substituting a plan of his own. Labeled the "legislative basis," Kenner's plan called for convention votes to be based upon an area's legislative representation. For example, under the "numerical basis," Jefferson Parish with the town of Lafayette would have received seven votes in the convention; by contrast, under Kenner's "legislative basis," this parish adjacent to New Orleans and a "City Whig" stronghold would get only three votes.[47]

Caught off guard by the surprise move by Kenner and the country delegates to undermine their alliance, the city delegates reacted with outrage and claimed that the country delegates were going back on an agreement which had been reached between the two groups at the gubernatorial convention of 1849. Kenner and other opponents of the numerical plan responded with a plea designed to win back the votes of those country delegates who had earlier promised to support the city plan. They contended that the basic issue was simply a struggle for power between the city and country and that the country delegates needed to unite in order to protect their minority rights in the party. The conflict was finally resolved when the city representatives were assured that the country group only wanted to make the point of their minority rights and that they held no animosity towards the city's candidate for the nomination, Theodore Hunt. The question was called and voted upon, and Kenner's proposal was accepted.[48]

The convention then turned its attention to the selection of a nominee. Since the rural Whigs had gotten their way on the representation issue, the party's "City Whigs" expected their candidate to be selected. The "Country Whigs," however, having gained additional strength from their victory on the representation issue, were unwilling to concede the nomination to their urban opponents. Instead of uniting behind Theodore Hunt, the city's candidate, the convention permitted the names of several individuals to be placed before the group for consideration. This effectively diluted the strength of the "City Whig" faction. Realizing that they were about to lose their chance to have their candidate chosen, the "City Whigs" called a brief recess and appealed directly to the various country delegates who had earlier promised support for the city candidate to redeem their pledge. With control of the nomination in their grasp, the rural Whigs ignored the pleas of the New Orleans area delegates and supported the "Country" candidate, Henry A. Bullard. When the convention reconvened, Bullard was awarded the nomination on the second ballot. Stunned by their defeat, the city delegates fiercely denounced the "Country Whigs" for their political subterfuge and legerdemain. Kenner's plan had worked. He had not only successfully denied the "City" faction of the party the congressional nomination that they at one time had in their pocket, but in one brief encounter he had also managed to undercut his opponents' base of support and had made them, as one New Orleans paper reported, "as weak and impotent as Sampson was after he had lost his locks."[49]

In spite of their anger over being "chiselled" by the "Country Whigs" on the nomination, the "City Whigs" pledged their support for the convention's nominee. Although hard feelings between the two Whig factions continued, their efforts in support of Bullard proved successful and he was able to defeat the Democratic nominee, Henry Johnson, in the congressional election. Unfortunately for the "Country Whigs," their victory was short-lived, for Bullard did not live long after winning election to Congress. With his death, affairs returned to their status before the Bullard nominating convention. With the memory of their defeat in the previous convention and how it was orchestrated fresh in their minds, the urban Whigs were determined to regain some of the ground they had lost to their country opponents. Because of the announced defection of several delegates who had supported his position at the previous convention, Kenner realized that the odds were against his being able to repeat his control of events at the new meeting.[50]

When the convention met, the "City Whigs" had on their agenda a re-examination of the controversy over the "numerical" and "legislative" allotment of delegates. When the "Country Whigs" approached the issue with an open mind and amicably agreed to accept the "numerical" basis, much of the tension between the two factions of the party evaporated. The new harmonious relations between the state's Whigs carried over to the selection of the nominee. For, although the "City Whigs" had a preferred candidate for the nomination, they went along with the choice of the rural delegates, and J. Aristide Landry of Ascension Parish was nominated by acclamation. Hence, despite the reversal on the issue of the allotment of delegates, Kenner's sagacity in both conventions strengthened his position in the power structure of the Louisiana Whig Party and placed him in the forefront of the "Country" faction of the party.[51]

Kenner's leadership position in the party placed him at the top of the list of possible candidates for important upcoming elections. When the Whigs turned their attention to the selection of a nominee for the impending United States Senate race in which the incumbent was a Democrat, Kenner was among those individuals most frequently named by the Whig press as a possible party nominee. However, his lack of support among the urban Whigs caused him to be passed over for the nomination. An unexpectedly strong showing by the Whigs in the 1851 general election in New Orleans gave the "City Whigs" an edge in party strength and threw the nomination to one of Kenner's opponents. At the party caucus in which the senate nominee was chosen, there were three major candidates—Kenner, Judah P. Benjamin, and Randall Hunt. Benjamin was selected on the second ballot, receiving thirty-seven votes to Kenner's nineteen and eleven for Hunt. The Whig's recent gain in strength in local elections also added to their power in the legislature. Thus, when the senatorial election took place in the lawmaking body, Benjamin defeated the Democratic incumbent, Solomon Downs, by twelve votes.[52]

Thus, despite his rise to the pinnacle of power and respect among the wealthy agrarian faction of the Louisiana Whig Party, Kenner was unable to marshal behind him the support of a majority of his party. Because of this failure to unite his party behind him, Kenner never achieved his goal of a statewide political office for which he labored so long.

Notes for "Duncan F. Kenner: Whig Leader"

[1]George Mitchell, "The Ante-Bellum Political Career of Duncan Farrar Kenner" (M.A. thesis, Louisiana State University, 1936), 26-28.

[2]James Kimmins Greer, "Louisiana Politics, 1845-1861," *Louisiana Historical Quarterly,* 12 (1929): 417; Edwin Adams Davis, *Louisiana: A Narrative History,* 3rd ed. (Baton Rouge, 1971), 192.

[3]Quoted in William H. Adams, *The Whig Party of Louisiana* (Lafayette, 1973), 151.

[4]Duncan Farrar Kenner to William Minor, January 22, 1846, Duncan Farrar Kenner Papers, Department of Archives, Louisiana State University, Baton Rouge, La.; Perry H. Howard, *Political Tendencies in Louisiana* (Baton Rouge, 1971), 54-55.

[5]*Daily Picayune,* February 18, 1846; *Baton Rouge Gazette,* February 21, 1846.

[6]T. Harry Williams, *The History of American Wars from 1745 to 1818* (New York, 1981), 155; *Journal of the Senate of the State of Louisiana, Session 1846-47—Continued* (New Orleans), 42, 110-11; *Daily Picayune,* May 2, 1846; Davis, *Louisiana,* 196.

[7]Frederick Merk, *History of the Westward Movement* (New York, 1978), 325-26, 363-64; *Louisiana Senate Journal, 1846,* 6; Clement Eaton, *A History of the Old South,* 2nd ed. (New York, 1966), 331.

[8]*Louisiana State Journal, 1847,* 11-14, 54-58; *New Orleans Daily Delta,* February 10, 1847.

[9]*Daily Delta,* January 30, 1847.

[10]Davis, *Louisiana,* 217; Mitchell, "Ante-Bellum Political Career," 39.

[11]Edwin L. Jewell, *Crescent City Illustrated: The Commercial, Social, Political and General History of New Orleans* (New Orleans, 1873), n.p.; Herman de Bachellé Seebold, *Old Louisiana Plantation Homes and Family Trees,* 2 vols. (New Orleans, 1941), 2:87; Arthur Freeman, "Early Career of Pierre Soulé," *Louisiana Historical Quarterly,* 25 (1942): 1086.

[12]Adams, *Whig Party of Louisiana,* 160, *Daily Delta,* January 16, 1848.

[13]*Baton Rouge Gazette,* November 20, 1847.

[14]Freeman, "Early Career of Pierre Soulé," 1095.

[15]Mitchell, "Ante-Bellum Political Career," 42.

[16]*New Orleans Weekly Delta,* January 31, 1848.

[17]Freeman, "Early Career of Pierre Soulé," 1094-96; Mitchell, "Ante-Bellum Political Career," 43-44.

[18]Freeman, "Early Career of Pierre Soulé," 1095-96; *Daily Delta,* January 25, 1848; Adams, *Whig Party of Louisiana,* 161.

[19]Freeman, "Early Career of Pierre Soulé," 1096; Mitchell, "Ante-Bellum Political Career," 46-47.

[20]Freeman, "Early Career of Pierre Soulé," 1096; Adams, *Whig Party of Louisiana,* 161-62.

[21]Quoted in Freeman, "Early Career of Pierre Soulé," 1096.

[22]Quoted in *Daily Delta,* January 26, 1848.

[23]*Baton Rouge Gazette,* July 17, 1852.

[24]Quoted in Mitchell, "Ante-Bellum Political Career," 46.

[25]Ibid., 43.

[26]*Louisiana Senate Journal, 1848,* 38-39; Freeman, "Early Career of Pierre Soulé," 1098-99.

[27]*Louisiana Senate Journal, 1848,* 38-39.

[28]Freeman, "Early Career of Pierre Soulé," 1100.

[29]Greer, "Louisiana Politics," 557-58.

[30]Mitchell, "Ante-Bellum Political Career," 56; Freeman, "Early Career of Pierre Soulé," 1103.

[31]*Daily Delta,* February 2, 1848.

[32]Greer, "Louisiana Politics," 558; *Daily Picayune,* January 8, 1848.

[33]Freeman, "Early Career of Pierre Soulé," 1104-5.

[34]Howard, *Political Tendencies,* 56-57; David M. Potter, *The Impending Crisis, 1848-1861* (New York, 1976), 82-83.

[35]Adams, *Whig Party of Louisiana,* 184.

[36]Greer, "Louisiana Politics," 564, 566.

[37]Ibid., 566-67; Adams, *Whig Party of Louisiana,* 185.

[38]Adams, *Whig Party of Louisiana,* 186.

[39]Ibid., 188-189; Mitchell, "Ante-Bellum Political Career," 59, 62; Greer, "Louisiana Politics," 567.

[40]Ibid., 190; Mitchell, "Ante-Bellum Political Career," 59-60.

[41]Eaton, *Davis,* 90; Davis, *Louisiana,* 192-93.

[42]Davis, *Louisiana,* 192; Jewel, *Crescent City Illustrated,* 11; "Kenner's Mission to Europe," *Tyler's Quarterly Historical and Genealogical Magazine,* 4 (1923): 27.

[43]*Daily Picayune,* October 30, 1849; Mitchell, "Ante-Bellum Political Career," 61-62.

[44]Howard, *Political Tendencies,* 57; Adams, *Whig Party of Louisiana,* 191-92; Mitchell, "Ante-Bellum Political Career," 64-65.

[45]Mitchell, "Ante-Bellum Political Career," 67.

[46]Ibid., 68.

[47]Ibid., 69.

[48]Ibid., 70-71.

[49]*Weekly Delta,* September 16, 1850; Mitchell, "Ante-Bellum Political Career," 71-72.

[50]Mitchell, "Ante-Bellum Political Career," 73-75.

[51]Ibid., 73-76.

[52]Ibid., 79, 85.

ISAAC JOHNSON: GOVERNOR, 1846-1850*

Carolyn E. De Latte

Johnson, Isaac (b. West Feliciana Parish, Louisiana, November 1, 1803; d. New Orleans, Louisiana, March 15, 1853), state legislator, state judge, governor, and state attorney general. Johnson, fourth of the numerous progeny of John Hunter Johnson and Thenia Munson, was born at his father's plantation, Troy. The influential Johnson clan had been established by his grandfather, who had come to the area from England in the 1770s. Johnson's father played a leading role in the West Florida Rebellion, prospered as a successful lawyer and planter, and served the parish as sheriff and judge.

Surrounded by many brothers, sisters, and cousins, young Johnson spent his childhood at Troy Plantation. The Feliciana of his youth was a frontier where riding, hunting, and shooting absorbed the attention of all males, whether young or old, and owners of large estates were plagued by a shortage of labor, a lack of ready cash, and an abundance of debts. Private tutors attended to his early education, and later he probably read law under the supervision of his father and his uncle, Joseph E. Johnson. In 1828, Johnson began to practice law, and in the same year, he married Charlotte McDermott. Shortly afterward, he joined his uncle and his brother William in a partnership. The Johnson firm prospered, and Johnson's legal reputation spread throughout the Felicianas.

Johnson soon became involved in local politics in the Democratic party, and in 1833, he won a seat in the Louisiana State Assembly. At the end of his term, he returned to his law practice until he was appointed judge of the third district court in 1839, a post he held with one brief interruption until he received the Democratic nomination for governor in 1845. The Whig party selected William De Buys to oppose Johnson. In a campaign marked by an unresponsive electorate and the absence of the usual personal invective, the "boy of Feliciana," as the phrase the opposition coined to emphasize Johnson's youth and inexperience described him, defeated De Buys on January 19, 1846, by a margin of 2,491 votes.

*First published in Joseph G. Dawson, III, *The Louisiana Governors: From Iberville to Edwards* (Baton Rouge: Louisiana State University Press, © 1990), 122-126. Reprinted with the kind permission of the author and the publisher.

Johnson's administration was filled with political turmoil. Implementing the new state constitution that had been ratified in 1845 was a large undertaking and caused acrimonious debates over matters large and small. The inaugural ceremony, held February 12, 1846, itself occasioned the first difficulty to confront the new governor. Some maintained that Johnson had taken an improper oath and therefore was not legally governor of the state. Hardly had the courts attended to that matter—in Johnson's favor—than the ancient feud between city and country erupted over the removal of the capital from New Orleans. In a similar way, debates over the Public School Law and over providing appropriations to implement that legislation caused internal political divisions. Johnson was consistently concerned about the state of education in Louisiana.

At the same time, political attention focused upon the war between the United States and Mexico (1846-1848), after which the controversy over the expansion of slavery in the new territories became heated. Johnson, like most Louisianians, responded enthusiastically to the war with Mexico. Indeed, he advocated annexing all of Mexico. His ardor cooled considerably when he was bombarded with complaints from Louisiana's soldiers, who maintained that they had not been paid and that they had no funds to return home. Johnson engaged in a sharp exchange with the United States Army's paymaster general, and he criticized the federal government for not sharing the expenses for equipping the state's militia. Throughout the troubled years of his administration, the governor upheld a strict interpretation of the constitution and states' rights, and he vehemently denounced the Wilmot Proviso, a resolution introduced in Congress by the Pennsylvania congressman David Wilmot to prohibit slavery in the territories obtained from Mexico.

More important, Johnson faced a difficult political situation in Louisiana. By 1846, the fortunes of the Democratic party were on the rise. After years of frustration, party leaders such as John Slidell had succeeded in molding a disciplined organization. Yet their efforts seemed worthless when "Taylor Democrats" (supporters of Gen. Zachary Taylor) carried the state for the Whigs in the 1848 presidential election and factional disputes within the party threatened to deprive it of gains so recently made. Johnson's leadership proved a disappointment to Democratic party leaders. An affable man who enjoyed being popular, he could not accept the tenets of strict party discipline. He appointed Whigs to office, much to the chagrin of Democratic leaders and much to the delight of the opposition. By 1848, Johnson was out of favor with the party chieftains who had secured his election.

In addition to the difficulties of his office, Johnson had to contend with a personal tragedy during his administration. In 1847, Charlotte Johnson died, leaving the governor with three children to raise. Johnson married again, but his second marriage appears to have been based upon convenience rather than geniune affection.

In 1849, Johnson and the principal state officials moved to the new capital in Baton Rouge, and when the legislature met there in 1850, the governor delivered his final message. He requested funds for the repair and construction of levees damaged in the severe flood of 1849, and he took great pleasure in reporting an increased enrollment in the state's public schools. He retired from office on January 28, 1850.

Johnson's retirement from public life was short. On February 15, 1850, Gov. Joseph M. Walker, his successor, appointed him attorney general of Louisiana. He served as the state's top legal officer for two years, and he represented the state well in a number of important cases. In 1852, he again returned to his estate in West Feliciana, where it appeared he would retire for good. In 1853, however, Johnson announced his candidacy for associate justice on the state supreme court and again embarked upon the campaign trail. Johnson was not to see the results of his election, because before it took place, he suffered a heart attack and died in his room at the Verandah Hotel, in New Orleans. Burial ceremonies at Troy, West Feliciana, were hardly completed when tragedy again struck the Johnson family. For later in the same year his two sons were stricken with yellow fever and died.

* * *

Johnson was only forty-three years old when he became Louisiana's chief executive. Although an impressive physical figure with an open, easygoing manner, Johnson had little political experience and few of the qualities essential in a decisive politician or strong executive leader. During his brief tenure in the state legislature, he did not participate in any of the heated debates. Nor did he seek reelection when his term ended in 1835. As governor, he rapidly succeeded in alienating leaders of his own Democratic party by giving patronage appointments to rival Whigs. Political confrontations and the give-and-take of debate held little fascination for him. He was more comfortable preparing a legal brief or defining or ruling on a point of law. A Louisiana facsimile of President and Chief Justice William Howard Taft, Johnson had talents and interests that were legal rather than political.

Unquestionably, Johnson was a fine lawyer. It was from the bench of the third judicial district court that Johnson's reputation and popularity originated, prompting Democrats to select him as the party's gubernatorial nominee in 1845. Indeed, Johnson died amid a campaign to secure a seat on the state supreme court—a post he would almost surely have won had he lived.

Although Johnson was more judge than politician, Louisiana made progress during his administration. Health conditions improved, school attendance and the population increased, and prosperity grew apace. And Johnson's contemporaries, whether friend or foe, appraised him as a man of unquestionable honesty and integrity.

THOMAS O. MOORE: CONFEDERATE GOVERNOR, 1860-1864*

Arthur W. Bergeron, Jr.

Moore, Thomas Overton (b. Sampson County, North Carolina, April 10, 1804; d. near Alexandria, Louisiana, June 25, 1876), state representative, state senator, and governor. Moore attended schools in Sampson County, North Carolina, and apparently aided his father in running their plantation. At the age of twenty-five, he moved to Rapides Parish, Louisiana, to live with an uncle, Walter H. Overton. The next year, 1830, Moore married Bethiah Jane Leonard, and their union produced five children. He managed Overton's sugar plantation for several years and eventually purchased property of his own. In time, Moore's landholdings increased until he became one of the leading planters in the state. Early, he developed an interest in local politics and served several terms on the parish police jury. In 1848, the people of Rapides Parish elected him to the state house of representatives. He ran successfully for a seat in the state senate in 1856. During his time in the state legislature, he served as a supporter of Gov. Joseph M. Walker, another planter from Rapides Parish. Upon Walker's death, Moore became head of the Democratic party in central Louisiana.

John Slidell, head of the regular faction of the state Democratic party, chose Moore as his faction's gubernatorial candidate in 1859. The opposition faction, led by Pierre Soulé, nominated Thomas Jefferson Wells, a native of Rapides Parish. Moore defeated Wells by a vote of 24,434 to 15,587 and took the oath as governor on January 23, 1860.

The growing sectional crisis dominated Moore's early months in office. When the national Democratic party's convention split into northern and southern wings at Charleston, South Carolina, he threw his support to the ticket headed by states' rights advocate John C. Breckinridge, of Kentucky. Moore's considerable influence aided Breckinridge in carrying Louisiana in the 1860 presidential election. The election of the Republican candidate, Abraham Lincoln, however, caused Moore to recommend that the legislature call a convention to decide what course the state would follow. Prior to the convening of the convention, Moore ordered the state militia to seize all federal military installations in

*First published in Joseph G. Dawson, III, *The Louisiana Governors: From Iberville to Edwards* (Baton Rouge: Louisiana State University Press, © 1990), 138-141. Reprinted with the kind permission of the author and the publisher.

Louisiana. When the convention met in January 1861, its members voted to approve an ordinance of secession. Moore soon appointed Braxton Bragg as a brigadier general to head a state army authorized by the legislature. Moore recognized the need for cooperation among the Southern states in secession, and he strongly supported the formation of the Confederate States of America, which the Louisiana legislature voted to join in March 1861.

Moore encouraged the organization of local defense companies throughout the state and established supply depots and food-processing plants at several locations. The Confederate president, Jefferson Davis, asked Louisiana to supply three thousand men for the Confederate army, and with the outbreak of war after the bombardment of Fort Sumter, in Charleston, South Carolina (April 12-13, 1861), Moore asked for an additional five thousand men to respond to the president's call.

New Orleans was the South's largest financial center, and its banks held a large reserve of gold and silver. Moore asked the banks in the Crescent City to halt payments in specie and ordered them to begin using Confederate treasury notes. He urged Confederate authorities to establish a strong defense system for New Orleans, which he realized would be a major target for attack by United States military forces.

As Moore feared, the Federals, under Flag Officer David G. Farragut, mounted an attack against New Orleans, which fell in April 1862. Baton Rouge also came under Federal assault. Therefore, in May 1862, Moore moved the state capital to Opelousas; later he moved it to Shreveport. After a short stay at Camp Moore, near Tangipahoa, the governor went to Opelousas to direct the state's war effort. From there, he issued an appeal for continued resistance, even though no organized military force remained in the part of the state west of the Mississippi. He called out the state militia to do active duty until regular Confederate units could reach south Louisiana, and he began organizing companies of partisan rangers. Moore issued orders forbidding trade with the enemy and mandating the burning of cotton that might fall into hostile hands. The Confederate War Department ordered Maj. Gen. Richard Taylor to assume command of all military forces in western Louisiana in July 1862. Moore cooperated with Taylor in every way he could. He persuaded the legislature to appropriate money for the construction of defensive fortifications and to provide slave labor to aid in the construction. The legislature created a state guard to be filled by men exempt from conscription. This guard would serve as reinforcements to Taylor's regular Confederate army when needed. Moore also obtained legislation to provide support for families whose men were in the army or had died or been disabled in service.

In January 1864, Moore relinquished the governor's chair to Henry Watkins Allen and retired to his plantation south of Alexandria. A Federal raid up the Red River in the spring of that year forced Moore and his family to become refugees. Union soldiers burned Moore's plantation home and many of its buildings in May 1864. At the end of the war, Moore again had to flee, because the Union government of the state had ordered his arrest. Moore, Allen, and a number of other former Confederate officials went to

Mexico. Moore did not remain there long but made his way to Havana. Eventually, Pres. Andrew Johnson granted him a full pardon, allowing him to return to his home. During the remaining years of his life, he attempted to rebuild his fortunes as a planter but kept clear of any involvement in politics.

* * *

Some historians have viewed Moore as a puppet or tool of Slidell in the secession crisis. Moore's political philosophy made him acceptable to the Slidell faction, but his record of support for the idea of secession probably contradicts the idea that he was merely a pawn. Moore recognized very early that for secession to be valid, the Southern states would have to cooperate in forming a new national government. He worked with the Confederate States authorities in forwarding men and supplies to threatened areas, sometimes to the detriment of the defenses of his own state.

Moore's constant warnings about the vulnerability of New Orleans and the lower Mississippi to Federal attack went unheeded by the Confederate high command. He recognized the geographical, political, and economic importance of the Crescent City to the new nation and did not make his requests for aid out of narrow, local interest. Federal occupation of New Orleans and Baton Rouge and enemy incursions into the rich parishes along the Mississippi made Moore's job as governor extremely difficult.

In contrast to Governors Zebulon Vance, of North Carolina, and Joe Brown of Georgia, Moore firmly supported President Jefferson Davis and the Confederate government. He did not hesitate to apply to President Davis for authority to declare martial law in his own Rapides and several other parishes to quell Union sympathies. Moore supported enforcement of the Confederate Conscription Act and aided in establishing camps of instruction in north and south Louisiana. He recognized the effects of Union control of the Mississippi and became one of the first officials to request a unified military command over the states west of the river. Contemporary accounts attest to Moore's genuine concern for the well-being not only of the soldiers in the field but the families they left at home.

Beset by numerous difficulties and obstacles, Moore performed his job as well as could be expected under trying circumstances.

PART V

Secession

BISHOP PALMER'S THANKSGIVING DAY ADDRESS*

Haskell Monroe

No man is born in Charleston and reared in the Carolina Low Country, without developing a strong Southern heritage. Such was the case of Benjamin Morgan Palmer, born in 1818 of Puritan ancestry, for he was a true son of South Carolina civilization. His entire academic career was marked by high achievement, at Amherst, where he began a long friendship with Henry Ward Beecher, at the University of Georgia, where he was noted for oratory and scholarship, and at Columbia Seminary. Here the young theologian came under the influence of the most profound theologian of the period among Southern Presbyterians, James Henley Thornwell. From the time he entered the Seminary in 1839, he attracted the attention of the faculty for his mental capacity, his tenacity, and the strength of his conviction on any point. Upon completion of the Seminary course, he succeeded Thornwell as minister at the First Presbyterian Church in the capital city of South Carolina.

Numerous calls to other congregations and seminary posts came to him. Finally in 1856 after great deliberation and hesitation the members of his presbytery and synod consented to his acceptance of a call to the First Presbyterian Church of New Orleans, a congregation of some 350 communicants. A few months after his arrival this congregation dedicated the impressive Gothic sanctuary on South Street, facing Lafayette Square. He soon attracted favorable attention to his ministry because of the increase of membership in his church, his decision to remain in the city during the yellow fever epidemic of 1858, and for his brilliant sermons.[1]

By 1860 the congregation included more than five hundred members, the third largest Presbyterian congregation in the South.[2] But Palmer preached regularly to hundreds who were not members of his own flock, for travellers in New Orleans crowded his sanctuary. Sunday morning crowds frequently strained the seating capacity of the large building and many thought his messages were among the best Protestant sermons in the Mississippi Valley. Certainly he was one of the most admired members of the clergy in the

*First published in *Louisiana History*, 4 (1963): 105-118. Reprinted with the kind permission of the author and the Louisiana Historical Association.

city and was second only to Thornwell in influence among Presbyterians in the South. His fame drew numerous calls, including a New York City pastorate in the late spring of 1860, and the chair of Practical Theology at Princeton Seminary the same year.[3] When he declined all of these proposals, Southerners of many denominational affiliations expressed satisfaction, for the section thought it needed its best minds at home during the increasing heat of the sectional debate.

During the heated presidential campaign of 1860, Palmer expressed no public sentiments, but his opinions indicated he desired no compromise with the abolitionists or their political allies. Many of his Louisiana neighbors agreed with him, but their economic ties with the upper Mississippi Valley were the lifeblood of the merchants of New Orleans. With Carolinians and Georgians chanting for secession, men in New Orleans were measuring state rights with the yardstick of economics. A large minority of Louisianians was sympathetic to the ideas of Stephen A. Douglas, the candidate of the Northern Democrats, but a plurality supported John C. Breckinridge, who defended the South with more extreme arguments. John Bell, the candidate of the Constitutional Union party which hoped to bridge the widening gap between the sections, had a particularly strong following among the voters of the New Orleans area.

Although Breckinridge carried Louisiana in the 1860 vote, his total was more than five thousand votes shy of a majority, and in the region near the Crescent City, he ran third. Bell carried Orleans and Jefferson parishes, while Douglas was second in both of these parishes plus Plaquemines as well. In Orleans the combined vote of Bell and Douglas, the two most conciliatory of the four candidates in the race, was more than three times the Breckinridge total.[4]

Such an indication of non-extremism in the largest city of the South worried secessionists. Without New Orleans there could be no unified South, for along her wharves crowded the produce of many states. Even Lincoln's victory at the polls and the imminent Republican assumption of power did not quickly frighten the mass of citizens in New Orleans. "Our wrongs are prospective rather than real," said one paper, which called for a Congress which would obstruct Lincoln's anti-Southern measures.[5] But while some spoke with optimism, militia units began to muster and practice their military arts. The situation was confused, tense, and hyper-explosive. In such a time Gov. Thomas O. Moore thought it wise to proclaim Thursday, November 29, as a "day of Thanksgiving and Worship to Almighty God." Perhaps the Father of Men could assist His children in arranging their affairs.

As the appointed day approached, the economic prospects of the New Orleans markets were dismal. The local financial journal reported "operations have been restricted in every branch of trade," mentioned a "heavy decline" in sugar prices, and saw few rays of hope for the immediate future. Meanwhile, a "Southern Rights Association" formed with many expressions of animosity against the hated anti-slavery voices of the North. Such events led one correspondent to report "events are fast hastening to some definite action here. . . . The times are those of momentous interest, and we can hardly tell from day to day what any may bring forth."[6]

Although the entertainment of the pre-Christmas season in 1860 was outwardly joyous and the opera was reported to be going "full blast," careful observers were aware of the dangers of the time. The *New Orleans True Witness,* the Presbyterian paper for the Southwest, spoke for these observers when it appealed to the electors to vote for "some known patriot and truly national man; and thus restore peace;" to Southerners "to reflect calmly, soberly, honestly;" and to the people of God to "Pray for your country."[7]

No man with the temperament of Ben Palmer could long remain silent in such a situation. His native South Carolina was preparing for secession and other states were moving swiftly to follow her lead. He could not imagine that Louisiana would remain behind. The call for the Thanksgiving service seemed to him the proper time to speak out on the issues before the people.

Rumors persisted that Robert Toombs, the well-known Georgia fire-eater, had come to the city to encourage the latent secessionists. Supposedly he was not pleased with the results and turned to Palmer for assistance.[8] Thus, the politician and preacher were said to have joined causes. With all his fervor, Palmer labored over the Thanksgiving sermon. According to his custom he paced his study as he formed ideas he planned to pour out to the congregation on November 29. This was to be no ordinary homiletic exercise, for this would be his first sally into the realm of political combat. He was determined to use all his pulpit arts to defend the cause of the South.

Thanksgiving was a beautiful day in the city. The *Daily Crescent* called it a "perfectly delicious day," and it was a bright and warm municipal holiday. Most sanctuaries held special services, like the First Presbyterian Church, at eleven o'clock. Businesses closed, so streets were quiet and most of the persons seen about were moving to the church of their choice. A few individuals expected messages which might give special insight to the problems of the day and some had heard that Palmer's sermon was filled with fire and already in type.[9]

In the sanctuary the crowd waited in hushed silence for the appearance of Palmer. Every eye watched him as he walked to the lectern and arranged his carefully written sermon. Perhaps the visitor first noticed the diminutive stature of this man. He was small and slender, with square shoulders, which made him seem taller when he emphasized the message of a sermon. There was an abundant mop of dark brown hair on his head and a matching beard. His mouth was unusually large and yet he did not seem to require personal attractions to command the respect of the audience, for as he approached the pulpit, he appeared to have a quality which carried attention away from the physical man to the thoughts of this man.[10]

After the usual opening formalities Palmer began his sermon. The crown hushed as he read the twentieth verse of Psalm XCIV: "Shall the throne of iniquity have fellowship with thee, which frameth mischief by a law?" To this, he added the seventh verse of Obadiah: "All the men of thy confederacy have brought thee even to the border; the men that were at peace with thee have deceived thee, and prevailed against thee; they that ate [*sic*] thy bread have laid a snare under thee; there is no understanding in him."

With this ominous beginning the pastor noted the day of thanksgiving, but commented sadly that no time of joy was at hand because "that which all men dreaded, but against which all men hoped, has been realized; and in the triumph of a sectional minority we are compelled to read the probable doom of our once happy and united confederacy." He thought the crisis at hand had no previous counterpart, and the "virtue, the patriotism and the purity of the country" was to be put to a "crucifying test."[11]

Lest anyone forget, the minister reminded his audience that he had never "intermeddled with political questions" before, nor attempted to influence any man's political attitude. But during the recent presidential campaign, he said he had realized the imminence of the crisis and considered, "with solitary and prayerful thought," the message he was now delivering. A time of decision was at hand. No one could retreat with honor. "At a juncture so solemn as the present," he proclaimed, "with the destiny of a great people waiting upon the decision of an hour, it is not lawful to be still. Whoever may have influence to shape public opinion, at such a time must lend it, or prove faithless to a trust as solemn as any to be accounted for at the bar of God."[12]

In Palmer's opinion the conflict was rooted in "morals and religion." This was so, he believed, because of the trust "providentially committed" to the South—the trust "*to conserve and to perpetuate the institution of domestic slavery as now existing*." Any legislative attempt to alter the status of the peculiar institution would tamper with godly prerogatives.

Southerners were obligated to the task of "conserving and transmitting the system of slavery with the freest scope for its natural development and extension," because of their duties to themselves, to the Negroes, to the world, and to God Himself. Without the land and the "serfs," as Palmer labelled the slaves, the Southern way of life would disappear. In his opinion, no other method of labor could accomplish the same results, for "any other than a tropical race must faint and wither beneath a tropical sun."

As he spoke of the institution of slavery, the Presbyterian divine indicated that he clearly believed it was sanctioned throughout the Scriptures. Here were two peoples living in peaceful harmony, tilling the rich soil of Dixie in contentment, while he termed the "teeming population" of the North suffered "with an eternal friction between the grades of their society." For a quarter of a century the abolitionists had waged their "unrighteous assault" against slavery. These men who sought to loosen the bonds of black to white in the South were the real enemies of the Negro, Palmer declared, since Southerners "know better than others that every attribute of their character fits them for dependence and servitude. By nature the most affectionate and loyal of all races beneath the sun, they are also the most helpless."[13]

If emancipation should come to these people, the whole world could not handle the problem, he argued. "Freedom would be their doom," for the slaves were but children. As such they leaned on their masters "for protection, for counsel, and for blessing." This committed the Southerner to conserve the institution in order to spare the world the agonies of emancipation, and to perpetuate the material production of Southern agriculture. Even the North should not fail to realize its stake in the produce from the plantations. This idea recalled the scripture from Obadiah and the minister noted what he believed to be the almost self-damaging cries of outsiders against slavery. Textile cities everywhere could not exist without the cotton of the Gulf States, he cried, particularly those of the English Midlands. With a thunderous voice, he echoed, "Strike now a blow at this system of labor and the world itself totters at the stroke."[14]

Nearing the mid-point of his remarks, the strong-willed minister faced an intrigued audience. His words were carefully measured, each phrase containing precisely the desired amount of venom for the enemies of Dixie and yet still overflowing with entreaties for defense of the Southern way of life. Throughout the sermon, he read entirely from prepared manuscript, using no gestures, no asides or anecdotes. Instead, he captured the imagination and expectancy of his audience with the spark of his emotion and the fire of his words.

Most significant of all the issues in this struggle, Palmer assured his Southern neighbors, was the fact that "*we defend the cause of God and religion.*" He thought the "abolition spirit . . . undeniably atheistic." This movement had sought to disguise its course in a cloak of "human rights." "Availing itself of the morbid and misdirected sympathies of men, it has entrapped weak consciences in the meshes of its treachery," Palmer asserted, "and now, at last, has seated its high priest on the throne, clad in the black garments of discord and schism."[15]

To this Presbyterian the present cries presented a situation similar to the godlessness of the French Revolution. No one could turn aside. To the South alone fell the duty of defending what he termed "the cause of all religion and truth." In this battle the South must oppose a power which warred on laws and compacts, "against Sabbaths and sanctuaries, against the family, the state, and the church." In such a contest, who could refuse the challenge? Who would not join in a Christian phalanx to wipe out such a scourge?

Once more he repeated the theme of the duty to preserve the existing system of domestic servitude, and now added the related idea of the right of slave owners to carry their chattels "wherever Providence and nature may carry" them. Perhaps conflict might result, but the sons of Dixie would not shrink from their mission. They would never surrender their duty nor their rights. Not till "the last man has fallen behind the last rampart," did he feel the South would desert her heritage.[16]

Palmer explained that he had seen the emerging crisis for many years. Using the word "fanaticism" to describe the movement against slavery, he placed all blame at the feet of the Yankees. Soon the sectional party would seek to dominate the minority region of the South, he warned. With words such as "despotism" and "unprincipled democracy" hurled like verbal grenades at the audience, Palmer sadly concluded that the "Union of our forefathers is already gone." There was now more cause for separation than in 1776. As for Lincoln, the little minister thought him "nearly as impotent for good as he is competent for evil." With such a man at the head of the Republican party, the time of talking was past.

"Decide either way, it is the moment of our destiny," he thundered. "If the South bows before this throne, she accepts the decree of restriction and ultimate extinction, which is made the condition of her homage." The people must reclaim their delegated powers and then mutually pledge "to uphold and perpetuate what they cannot resign without dishonor and palpable ruin." Only in this way could the true union of the founding fathers be saved and perhaps the conservatives of the North might yet crush what he called the "abolition hydra."[17]

Yet, he was fearful that a peaceful solution was no longer possible. The cause of peace must be an object of prayer, but the faint-hearted must not shrink if battle was in the offing. The moment was brief and fleeting. Hesitation might doom the ancestry of the South forever. "If she will arise in her majesty," Palmer proclaimed, "and speak now as with the voice of one man, she will roll back for all time, the curse that is upon her." Failure to do so now would bring the cruel fate of Saint-Domingue, where bloody insurrection had taken the lives of many whites, to Louisiana in a quarter of a century. The children of the present audience would be driven homeless across the land.

As he closed, Palmer stated his personal credo for the land he loved: "It only remains to say, that whatsoever be the fortunes of the South, I accept them for my own. Born upon her soil, of a father thus born before me—from an ancestry that occupied it while yet it was a part of England's possession—she is in every sense, my mother. I shall die upon her bosom—she shall know no peril, but it is my peril—no conflict, but it is my conflict—and no abyss of ruin in which I shall not share her fall. May the Lord God cover her head in this her day of battle."[18]

As the last word faded away, the audience rose in silence and filed out of the sanctuary. Many had been surprised by the boldness of the pastor. No one spoke on leaving the church, for these required thought—and prayer. A few men indicated their disapproval, but most seemed deep in contemplation. Soon, however, the words took their effect. One listener summarized the sermon as having "confirmed and strengthened those who were in doubt." Soon the populace reacted and an eyewitness wrote: "The drums beat and the bugles sounded; for New Orleans was shouting for secession."[19]

Before many people could join in this shouting, Palmer's words came off the printing presses. Soon after concluding his sermon he received written communications from two groups of men. Ten from his own congregation informed him simply that they thought "it should be read by every citizen of the United States" and wanted to print 30,000 copies, but a more numerous group of citizens indicated their desire to print the sermon so the community might read "an argument squarely up to the occasion" and the nation might study and ponder the "opinions of a representative man." Palmer thought the two communications indicated true interest and thus consented to publication of his address, "with the earnest desire that it may contribute something toward rallying our whole people to the issue that is upon us."[20]

Other ministers had spoken on the Thanksgiving occasion, but none of their sermons produced the impact of Palmer's words. All the citizenry discussed his war-cry that afternoon and night. Hardly another topic of conversation was to be heard in the city. He had spoken the quiet desires of many silent hearts.

The local newspapers immediately began to reprint and comment on the sermon. Among the major New Orleans sheets, the Unionist *Picayune* was apparently the only one to avoid mention of the Presbyterian's call for action. Instead, this paper commented on the comparative quiet of the holiday among the police courts and noted that even pickpockets had taken the day off. The *Delta* commended the "manly and patriotic position" taken by Palmer, and later added that the address was "sacramental in its fervor" and "above compliment." The *Crescent* believed the sermon "so full of sense, reason and truth, coupled with text and Holy Writ," that the congregation was wise to spread the sermon over the Union. Meanwhile, the *Bee* considered it a "masterly discourse," and most of the papers reprinted the sermon in full. The *Delta* alone carried it three times.[21]

The near unanimity of praise for this stirring endorsement of slavery and secession drowned out all other local sentiments. Papers continued their commendation as they frequently referred to the sermon. One editor wrote that "a more cogent, exhaustive, logical and impressive production of not greater length we never met with," and another argued that the quality of the message justified bringing a secular topic into the pulpit. Within a week of its delivery, the *Daily Delta* informed its readers that it had printed more than 30,000 copies of the message, which were available throughout the city.[22]

Soon the news of the daring cry for Southern action spread throughout the plantation region. Neighbors in Mississippi were particularly pleased with Palmer's attitudes. So strong were these words of truth, thought a Natchez sheet, that the sermon "ought to be printed in letters of gold and spread wide-cast among the people." Another Mississippi paper believed that now there was proof of the revolutionary maxim that "resistance to tyranny is obedience to God." But the news did not halt in the Mississippi Valley. Papers all over the South noted the sermon and referred to it as proof of the changing emphasis in the movement for Southern rights.[23]

Among fellow Presbyterians, Palmer attracted a wide audience. Upriver in Baton River the minister discovered he was unable to persuade his congregation to support national unity after they read Palmer's words. Although the *Central Presbyterian,* published in Richmond, remained silent on the subject, the other three denominational sheets in the South commended the reports they heard from New Orleans. In South Carolina the *Southern Presbyterian* thought the address had been an "able, eloquent and patriotic" statement of the duty of the Southern people in regard to the "present conflict between the North and South." North Carolinians were not quite as enthusiastic, but still liked the vigorous defense of slavery. In New Orleans the *True Witness* maintained a careful silence on the sectional issues, but revealed a definite affinity for Palmer's words by printing many copies of the sermon for distribution.[24]

Only in the border areas and in the North, did observers criticize this cry for action. In Virginia, for instance, some thought this was "an able and conclusive argument," but one minister believed the sermon was so far removed from reality as to have been intended only to frighten the Yankees.[25] Beyond Mason and Dixon's Line, the criticism was loud and angry. Editors joined in condemnation and some of the leading clergymen of the denomination pronounced their shock at the extremity of the arguments of the little man from New Orleans. They charged him with inciting "unbecoming excitement" and related evils which might result in bloodshed.[26]

The vigorous minister was not to be deterred, however, from his dedication to the South and her cause. By the end of the year he was a famous personage, in demand for speeches and recognized as an outstanding voice of the Southern rights movement. His sermons appeared regularly in New Orleans newspapers. Perhaps 50,000 copies of the Thanksgiving sermon were distributed in the city alone, and soon it seemed to contemporaries that the mass of the people had become converted to his political opinions. Even a Northern critic admitted the man of God "had carried the mass of his hearers captive."[27]

But Palmer's hopes were not yet satisfied. He continued to lend his voice to the rising chorus of secessionists. Like many others he was delighted with the announcement of an election on January 7 of delegates to a convention to consider taking Louisiana out of the Union. Perhaps the results of this election in New Orleans offer some indication of the effectiveness of the Thanksgiving sermon. Although the secessionists polled only a small majority in the state, not very different from the outcome of the presidential vote two months earlier, there was a remarkable change in Orleans Parish, where the "immediate secessionists" won fifteen of twenty seats in the convention.[28] Nowhere else was the sudden transformation so evident, but nowhere else had people heard such a call for militant action. Perhaps he had been a decisive factor in moving the city to disunion.

A few contemporaries attempted to define the role of this man in the movements during the winter of 1860-1861. One, a Northern rival, thought Palmer a prime force in the creation of a Southern nation. The unionist pastor, who sought to overcome the secessionists in Baton Rouge, found the New Orleans minister had swept the state toward disunion. He was the first prominent Southern churchman to call for vigorous action and secession. After his stirring call to arms, others echoed his sentiments. Still, it remained for a Crescent City editor to evaluate the man's accomplishments, a few months later: "The Rev. Dr. Palmer . . . whose inspiring eloquence has rendered him the most efficient recruiting officer for our army in the state . . . has done more for the cause of secession in this state than any other man."[29]

Notes for "Bishop Palmer's Thanksgiving Day Address"

[1]Thomas Cary Johnson, *The Life and Letters of Benjamin Morgan Palmer* (Richmond, 1906); John Miller Wells, *Southern Presbyterian Worthies* (Richmond, 1936), 141-52; Benjamin Morgan Palmer, "An Historical Paper on . . . Presbyterianism in New Orleans," in John R. Hutchinson, *Reminiscences, Sketches and Addresses selected from My Papers during a Ministry of Forty-Five Years . . .* (Houston, 1874), 147-68.

[2]*Minutes of the General Assembly of the Presbyterian Church in the Confederate States of America* (Columbia, S. C., 1863), 202.

[3](St. Louis) *Presbyterian,* quoted in *New Orleans True Witness,* May 5, June 30, 1860; (Fayetteville) *North Carolina Presbyterian,* June 30, 1860.

[4]For a review of the 1860 campaign in Louisiana see Jefferson Davis Bragg, *Louisiana in the Confederacy* (Baton Rouge, 1941), 6-12, and Ollinger Crenshaw, *The Slave States in the Presidential Election of 1860* (Baltimore, 1955), 492. The state totals were: Breckinridge, 22,681; Bell, 20,204; Douglas, 7,625. In Orleans Parish the vote was: Bell, 5,215; Douglas, 2,998; Breckinridge, 2,645. W. Dean Burnham, *Presidential Ballots, 1836-1892* (Baltimore, 1955), 492.

[5]*New Orleans Bee,* November 8, 1860.

[6]*New Orleans Price Current,* November 21, 24, 28, 1860; "Soto," New Orleans, to editor, November 24, 1860, printed in *Charleston Daily Courier,* November 30, 1860.

[7]*True Witness,* November 24, 1860.

[8]R. L. Stanton, *The Church and the Rebellion: A Consideration of the Rebellion against the Government of the United States; and the Agency of the Church, North and South, in Relation Thereto* (New York, 1864), 163-65; Lewis G. Vander Velde, *The Presbyterian Churches and the Federal Union, 1861-1869* (Cambridge, 1932), 31. No information has been found to substantiate this rumor of collaboration between Palmer and Toombs.

[9]*New Orleans Daily Crescent,* November 30, 1860 (incorrectly dated November 29 on title page). No information has been found to lend credence to a report that the *True Delta* had the sermon in type by the night of November 28; Daniel W. Fisher, *A Human Life. An Autobiography with Excurses* (New York, 1909), 121-22.

[10]Ella Gertrude (Clanton) Thomas Journals, 3:44 (December 31, 1861), Duke University, Durham, N. C.; Johnson, *Palmer,* 170; Eugene Daniel, *In Memory of Reverend Benjamin Morgan Palmer, D.D.* (n. p., n. d.), 13; Robert Q. Mallard, "Personal Reminiscences of Rev. Benjamin Morgan Palmer, D.D., LL.D.," *Union Seminary Magazine,* 14 (1902-1903): 110-19; "Recollection of Dr. B. M. Palmer," in Thomas Cary Johnson Papers, Union Seminary, Richmond, Va.

[11]Benjamin Morgan Palmer, *The South: Her Peril and Her Duty. A Discourse delivered in the First Presbyterian Church, New Orleans, on Thursday, November 29, 1860* (New Orleans, 1860), 3-4.

[12]Ibid., 5.

[13]Ibid., 6-8.

[14]Ibid., 9-10.

[15]Ibid.

[16]Ibid., 11.

[17]Ibid., 12-15.

[18]Ibid., 15-16. Although a number of sources indicate the sermon lasted two hours, the sixteen printed versions would not require more than forty minutes to read.

[19]Unknown writer to Thomas Cary Johnson, June 9, 1904, Josiah Stoddard Johnson Papers, Historical Society of Pennsylvania, Philadelphia, Penn.; statement of William O. Rogers quoted in Johnson, *Palmer,* 219-20.

[20]Palmer, *The South,* 2.

[21]*New Orleans Daily Picayune,* November 30, 1860; *New Orleans Daily Delta,* November 30, 1860; *New Orleans Sunday Delta,* December 2, 1860; *New Orleans Daily Crescent,* November 30, 1860; *New Orleans Bee,* December 5, 1860.

[22]*New Orleans Daily Delta,* December 2, 4, 1860; *New Orleans Daily Crescent,* December 3, 1860.

[23]*Natchez Free-Trader,* December 4, 1860; *Jackson Weekly Mississippian,* December 12, 1860; *Charleston Daily Courier,* December 7, 10, 1860.

[24]"Autobiography of Thaddeus McRae," 35, typescript, Historical Foundation of the Presbyterian and Reformed Churches, Montreat, N. C.; James M. Green, Macon, Ga., to R. N. Gourdin, December 15, 1860, R. N. Gourdin Papers, Emory University, Atlanta, Ga.; *Columbia Southern Presbyterian,* December 15, 1860; *Fayetteville North Carolina Presbyterian,* January 26, 1861; *New Orleans True Witness,* December 1, 1860.

[25]John S. Wise, *The End of an Era* (New York, 1899), 145-46; William S. White, Lexington, Va., to John S. Watt, December 13, 1860, in Henry M. White, ed., *Rev. William S. White, D.D., and His Times, 1800-1873* (Richmond, 1891), 169-70.

[26]*Chicago Presbyterian Expositor,* quoted in *Columbia Southern Presbyterian,* January 5, 1861; *Princeton Review,* quoted in ibid., March 9, 1861; *Cincinnati Presbytere,* quoted in ibid., December 29, 1860; Stanton, *Church and the Rebellion,* 163-70.

[27]J. H. Harrison, New Orleans, to Robert J. Breckinridge, December 29, 1860, Breckinridge Papers, Manuscripts Division, Library of Congress; Stanton, *Church and the Rebellion,* 164. Five different printings of the sermon in pamphlet form have been found: *Thanksgiving Sermon, delivered at the First Presbyterian Church, New Orleans, on Thursday, December* [November] *29, 1860, by Rev. B. M. Palmer, D.D.* (New York, 1861); *Slavery and Divine Trust—The Duty of the South to Preserve and Perpetuate the Institution As It Now Exists* (New York, 1861?); *The Rights of the South Defended in the Pulpit: By B. M. Palmer, D.D., and W. T. Leacock, D.D., of New Orleans* (Mobile, 1860); Benjamin Morgan Palmer, *Thanksgiving Sermon Delivered in the First Presbyterian Church, New Orleans, on Thursday, Nov. 29th, 1860* (Milledgeville, Ga., 1860); Benjamin Morgan Palmer, *The South: Her Peril and Her Duty. A Discourse Delivered in the First Presbyterian Church, New Orleans, on Thursday, November 29, 1860* (New Orleans, 1860). The address was printed in full in many newspapers. Those reprintings which have been located are: *Southern Presbyterian Review,* 12 (1860-61): 860-69; *Columbia Southern Presbyterian,* December 22, 1860; *New Orleans True Witness,* December 1, 1860; *New Orleans Daily Delta,* December 1, 2, 4, 1860; *New Orleans Daily Crescent,* December 3, 1860; *Jackson Mississippian,* December 12, 1860. When the latter paper printed the sermon, it indicated that numerous Mississippi papers had done likewise.

[28]*Daily Picayune,* January 9, 1861.

[29]Stanton, *Church and the Rebellion,* 163-70; "Autobiography of McRae," 35.

"SECESSION MEANS DISUNION," A SPEECH BY PIERRE SOULÉ*

Waldo W. Braden

Pierre Soulé (1801-1870), lawyer, U. S. Senator (1847, 1849-1853), U. S. minister to Spain (1853-1855), and prominent Louisiana politician, played an important role in Louisiana politics during the 1860 presidential campaign as a supporter of Stephen A. Douglas.

At the national Democratic Convention which met at Charleston, South Carolina, April 23 to May 3, 1860, many Southern delegates including those from Louisiana objected to the control of the Douglasites and consequently withdrew from the convention. Following the disruption of the meeting, the old Louisiana Democratic State Convention reconvened in Baton Rouge, and the majority endorsed the actions of their delegates and recommissioned them to go to Baltimore where the Democrats were to reconvene. Under the leadership of Soulé, the Douglasites met at Donaldsonville, June 6, 1860, and named their own delegation. This action brought wide recognition to Soulé, who became a hero of the Douglas clan.

When they reconvened, the Democrats had to choose between the two delegations from Louisiana as well as from Alabama. Determined to punish John Slidell of Louisiana and William Yancey of Alabama, prime movers in the Charleston bolt, the Douglas majority seated the Douglas delegates in both cases, causing a second secession.

On June 23, the day after he was seated, Soulé addressed the convention before casting the vote of his delegation for Douglas. Apparently the audience looked forward with considerable anticipation to his remarks. The *Baltimore Republican* reported that "loud cries were made for Mr. Soulé. The whole body rose and amid the waving of hats and deafening shouts that gentleman rose in the centre of the area and proceeded . . . to make a calm and dignified address. . . . When the chair announced . . . that his time had expired . . . on motion of Mr. Ryder, of New York, he was allowed to go on by unanimous consent."

*First published in *Louisiana History*, 6 (1965): 77-82. Reprinted with the kind permission of the Louisiana Historical Association.

Murat Halstead referred to this presentation as "the speech of the Convention." He described the Louisianian as follows:

> His rolling, glittering, eagle eye. Napoleonic head and face, sharp voice, with a margin of French accent, and piercing intense earnestness of manner, commanded profound attention, and fascinated all who saw and heard. His speech was a brilliant and noble effort, and was rapturously applauded to the echo. The effect of this speech was to greatly animate and reassure the friends of Douglas.[1]

The speech probably was delivered extemporaneously and transcribed by a reporter. It remains one of the few extant speeches which Soulé delivered outside of the Senate. The text given below appeared in the *Baltimore American*, June 23, 1860. It was also printed in full in the *New York Times*, June 25, 1860, with only minor variations in style. Halstead quoted about 250 words from the version appearing in the *American* and also summarized a small portion. The editor has corrected only obvious typographical errors.

Mr. President, I am appalled, truly appalled, by the expectations which the welcome which has been extended to me seems to signify. I am the last man in this Convention from whom anything deserving these manifestations could be expected; and it is at once with a deep feeling of gratitude for what kindness there was in them, and of great diffidence, that I attempt to address you on this solemn, most momentous occasion. Be not afraid, however, that I shall trespass long upon your kindness and your attention; but a few remarks from me will lay the foundation for the vote which I shall cast for the noble State which I have the honor in part to represent in this body.

I have not been at all discouraged by the emotion which has been attempted to be created in this body, by those whose have seceded from it. We, from the farthest South, were prepared; we had heard around us the rumors which were to be initiatory of the exit which you have witnessed on this day, and we knew that the conspiracy which had been brooding for months past, would break out on this occasion, and for the purposes which are obvious to every member. Sirs, there are in political life men who, when once honored by popular favor, consider that the favor has become to them an inalienable property, and who cling to it as something that can no longer be wrested from their hands—political fossils so much encrusted in office that there is hardly any power that can extract them. [Applause.] They saw that the popular voice was clearly manifesting to this glorious nation who was to be her next ruler. More than eight or ten months before this convention assembled, the name of that future ruler of these States had been thrown into the canvass and was before the people. Instead of bringing a candidate to oppose him; instead of creating before the people issues upon which the choice of the nation could be enlightened; instead of the principles discussed, what have we seen? An unrelenting war against the individual presumed to be the favorite of the nation—[applause] a war waged by an army of unprincipled and unscrupulous politicians, leagued with a power which could not be exerted on their side without disgracing itself and disgracing the nation. [Renewed applause]

When the Convention assembled at Charleston the idea had not yet struck their minds that a movement of the nature of the one which had been effected could be based upon the doctrines of the distinguished gentleman from Alabama [Mr. Yancey], who has fathered this secession. It was presumed by these political intriguers outside of the Convention who were manoeuvering the measures through by which the destruction of the Democratic party was to be effected—it was presumed by them that it would be their power, after raising the storm, to master and guide it. But it will be found before 48 hours have elapsed, that in that storm they are bound eventually to sink and disappear. [Laud applause.] For it is idle for Southern men to disguise the true object of that movement. Secession from the Democratic party can be nothing else than a disruption of that party at the every moment when the hopes of the whole nation are hanging upon its continuity in power. [Applause.] Secession is a word intended to conceal another word of more significancy.

If secession was to find an echo among the people of this great confederacy, then no longer could this Republic boast that the structure which our fathers erected with so much sacrifice and so much toil, was a noble experiment. Secession must beget disunion. Upon what pretence has secession been predicted? I will not do those distinguished gentlemen who stepped out of this room this morning the injustice to suppose that they truly parted from you because of your having decided the question of internal organization in a manner that did not agree with their views. They may give this as a pretence—they may use it as a cloak to cover their desertion from the party—but the truth cannot be disguised; whether deluded or not, they are tools in the hands of intriguers, and their course must necessarily tend to disunion. [Applause.] Sirs, it is said they carry with them out of this Convention the sympathies of the South. Believe it not. [Renewed applause.] Believe it not. And I have in my own experience in the past, certain strong reasons why I cannot bring my mind to the supposition that the South, under present circumstances can respond to that movement, and I will briefly lay them before you.

In 1849 and 1850 when California was about being admitted into this Union, the South rose against her admission, passed resolutions upon resolutions, and impressed upon the men of the North that if the outrage was perpetrated she would secede from the Union. Many of us who were then representatives of the South in the national councils, believing that the South was in earnest, and considering ourselves bound to follow in her footsteps, fought the battle, not with the view of creating the contingency contemplated, but to defend the rights of the South and oppose the introduction of California into the councils of the nation. That at that time was to the South a great wrong and creating great danger, because not only was California coming into the Union with a constitution obliterating the Missouri Compromise; not only was she coming into the Union without having passed through the ordeal of Territorial existence; not only was she coming into the Union organized by the military forces of the federal government, but her entrance into the Union was going to destroy that power of numbers, which was the last bulwark of our protection in the Senate. [In] the higher house of Congress we fought against that wrong; we engaged in the battle to maintain our rights to the last. But when the question came to the last, one after the other, we saw the States of the South receding from their position, disowning every effort we had made to maintain our rights—and let me say with sorrow, dragging us into the very gutter for the very devotion we had shown them.

And why did the South do this? There is no ungrateful heart at the South. It could not be that she was inclined to disown the service of those who had stood by her to the last. But it was because she considered, and truly considered, that even an impending wrong was not to be put in the scale with the preservation of this glorious confederacy. [Great Applause.] And we, in obedience to their wishes, out of deference to their conventions, surrendered; we considered that we were in duty bound to abide by our own decisions; and perhaps it may not be improper for me here to refer to the considerations upon which those decisions were predicted. The only compensation which the South could find in the measures generally known as compromise measures, was the doctrine of non-intervention then claimed. [Applause] That was the only boon offered us in those days as a compensation for the great sacrifice which was asked at our hands, and the South accepted the compromise, and the compromise became the law of the nation, certainly of the party, as far as the question of slavery was concerned.

I am surprised at the extreme sensitiveness exhibited by men of the South at this day upon that question of non-intervention. John C. Calhoun, when the famous compromise tendered by Mr. Clayton, of Delaware was being discussed in the United States Senate—John C. Calhoun considered that the proffer to place in the hands of one federal tribunal the question of the extent of power in the Territories was to the South a sufficient guaranty to make acceptable the compromise tendered; and when Calhoun could stand a Southern man need not fear to stand. [Applause.]

I have said, in the very unconnected remarks, I have had the honor to submit to you, that *secession* means *disunion*; and I will go on to show upon what considerations that opinion of mine is predicated. What is the question at issue? On the other hand, Northern abolitionists claim intervention for the purpose of excluding slavery from the Territories. On the other hand, Southern men claim intervention on the part of Congress for the purpose of protecting slavery in the Territories. Now I ask Southern gentlemen, here and elsewhere, are you serious, when the battle is thus drawn—when the lines are thus drawn out—when the whole strength of the North is combined with the great strength on the part of the West, to exclude slavery from the Territories—are you, my friends of the South, in earnest, when you ask to submit the protection of your property to the keeping of such men as may be sent from the North and West to constitute the majority in your Congress? There is not a paper in the South which is not teeming with denunciations, that Congress has become a rotten body that the majority in both houses in heart and to all intents and purposes, opposed to slavery; and yet these men, who set up the pretension of being the exclusive friends of slavery at the South, ask that the protection of slavery shall be put in the keeping of that very power which is represented as being bent upon its destruction. [Applause]

I say whatever be the views they take of the manner in which that power might eventually be exerted, from the moment that power is recognized as existing in Congress, from that moment there is not a Southern heart which does not beat to the conviction that slavery is gone. And if that should be the ultimatum of the issue, is the South ready for it? Have they prepared their armor? Are they ready for battle? Sirs, they are not; and the reason is very obvious. The gentlemen who have seceded from this convention know that the masses of their people at home will not respond to the call which they make upon them. And the best proof of it is that in no State whose delegations have seceded did the seceders call a fair Convention of the people to put to the test the innovation which they have attempted. [Applause.]

I perceive that I have detained the Convention longer than I had intended, [cries of "go on," "go on"] and my own strength is nearly exhausted. Mr. President, though Louisiana is mindful of what she owes to her sisters of the South, and is ever ready to act in concert with them when actual oppression shall call for actual resistance, still Louisiana is unwilling to risk her future and the future of this Union upon impracticable issues and purely theoretical abstractions. [Applause.] She cannot be so far oblivious of the past and recent services as to disown that fearless and indomitable champion of popular rights and state equality—him, who in that great and memorable struggle which in his own State initiated that war which has been waged against him so unrelentingly—him, who has vindicated the rights of the South so victoriously against infuriated opponents; him, who will yet enable us to triumph over the enemies of the South, the Black Republicans who are arrayed against us. Louisiana casts her entire vote for Stephen A. Douglas, of Illinois. [Vociferous cheers and applause.]

Notes for "'Secession Means Disunion,' A Speech by Pierre Soulé"

[1]Murat Halstead, *Caucuses of 1860, A History of the National Political Convention of the Current Presidential Campaign being a Complete Record of the Business of All on Conventions* (Columbus, 1860), 206-207.

THE LONG LOST RETURNS: THE CANDIDATES AND THEIR TOTALS IN LOUISIANA'S SECESSION ELECTION*

Charles B. Dew

What was probably the most important election ever held in Louisiana took place in January 1861. On the seventh of that month the state's eligible voters chose delegates to a state convention that would decide whether or not Louisiana should leave the Union. The Secessionist forces evidently won this election since a majority of the delegates who ultimately took seats in the convention voted for the secession ordinance and subsequently took the state into the Confederacy.[1] And yet both contemporary observers and historians of the Louisiana secession movement have expressed serious doubt that the radicals really did carry the state in the 1861 election.[2] The primary cause of this uncertainty was, and remains, the fact that state authorities refused to release the official returns of the election or even to publish a full list of the candidates. The question of who really won the Louisiana secession election has recently been answered, however. The complete parish returns, containing the names of both winning and losing candidates and the vote polled by each, have been discovered, and they are presented here in full for the first time.

Although scholars have had one incomplete and unsatisfactory set of returns with which to work, the official count could not be found. All that was available was an unofficial tabulation published in the *New Orleans Daily Delta*, a leading Secessionist newspaper, almost three months after the election.[3] According to the *Daily Delta*'s figures, the radical immediate secessionists had carried the state over the more moderate Cooperationists by a vote of 20,448 to 17,296.[4] One historian, John R. Ficklen, seeking firmer evidence than that provided by the *Daily Delta*, was informed by the Louisiana secretary of state in 1903 "that the returns of this election are not in his office, and that if they exist they are in Washington."[5] Ficklen was given an excellent lead, but he evidently did not press his inquiries beyond this point because he failed to come up with the returns.

*First published in *Louisiana History*, 10 (1969): 353-369. Reprinted with the kind permission of the author and the Louisiana Historical Association.

Other historians have had no better luck than Ficklen. Students of the secession movement at both the national and the state level have bemoaned the fact that so much of their analysis of the Louisiana situation has had to rest on partial and unreliable returns.[6] Typical of their comments are those of Ralph A. Wooster in his excellent study of the Southern secession conventions. "Unfortunately," he observes, "there exists no complete list of candidates in the race, most sources simply giving the names of the winners."[7] As a result, Wooster, who did a detailed statistical profile of the members of the Louisiana convention, could not do the same thing for the losing candidates simply because he did not know who they were.[8]

When the Louisiana secretary of state reported in 1903 that the returns might be in Washington, he probably knew that the records in question had been taken from the state after the fall of the Confederacy. In the summer of 1865 Gen. Nathaniel P. Banks had ordered the seizure of the Louisiana Confederate archives, and a large body of state records had been confiscated by the federals and sent to the War Department in Washington. After the National Archives were organized in 1934, the War Department turned the Louisiana records, including the secession election returns, over to that agency, and there they remained until the federal government sent the entire "rebel archives" back to the state in 1961. These materials are now on deposit at the State Archives and Records Commission in Baton Rouge.[9]

Since the secession election was conducted on the same basis as a regular legislative canvass, there were two classes of candidates in the race. The representative candidates, as the name indicates, ran in the representative districts, which were set up on the basis of individual parishes;[10] the senatorial candidates were chosen by voters in the state senatorial districts, which almost always were composed of more than one parish.[11] As a result, the vote was posted on the official returns in two separate columns, and it is presented here in this fashion.

Table I gives the representative and the senatorial vote for each candidate in each parish. The sources for this table are what appear to be the original returns as they came in to the Louisiana secretary of state from parish officials, properly witnessed and certified as true and correct by the local sheriff, as required by state law. In addition to presenting the vote, Table I shows the number of seats to be filled, lists the parishes comprising the senatorial districts, and indicates who won the various races. An attempt has also been made to ascertain the affiliations of the various candidates (S—Immediate Secessionist; S?—probably Immediate Secessionist; C—Co-operationist, including those men of various shades of opinion who were opposed to immediate secession; C?—probably Co-operationist; ?—position unknown).

Determining the positions of the winning candidates was usually a fairly simple matter, since their votes on key roll calls in the convention indicate whether they were for or against immediate secession.[12] The stand of the losing candidates was more difficult to discover. In a few instances, the manuscript returns designate "Secessionist" and "Co-operationist" or "Unionist." In most cases, however, the affiliations of the defeated candidates were found by checking accounts of local political meetings that appeared in the New Orleans and Baton Rouge press prior to January 7 and by examining the reports of parish races that were published in the weeks following the election. The *New Orleans Daily Picayune*, the *New Orleans Daily Delta*, the *New Orleans Daily Crescent*, and the *Baton Rouge Daily Advocate* were found most useful in this regard.

Occasionally, classifying the candidates proved to be a hard task even when a considerable amount of information could be found. The case of Judge Thomas W. Scott, a prominent planter and large slaveholder who ran in the representative race in East Feliciana Parish, is exceptional, but it illustrates the nature of the problem.[13] The moderate *New Orleans Daily Picayune* reported in late December 1860 that Scott and William Patterson, another candidate from East Feliciana, "declared themselves opposed to separate state action looking to secession, and in favor of a convention of all the Southern States."[14] Shortly after the election, the *Daily Picayune* again listed Scott, a winner in East Feliciana, as a Co-operationist.[15] The radical *Baton Rouge Daily Advocate*, however, reported on January 8, 1861, that Scott was on both the Secessionist and Co-operationist tickets but was, in fact, in favor of immediate secession. The same paper on January 20 repeated its claim that Scott was a radical and called Patterson a Co-operationist. When Scott went to the convention in Baton Rouge in late January, he perversely refused to clear up the confusion; on four key roll calls in the convention, he voted with the Secessionists on two and with the Co-operationists on the other two. Ralph A. Wooster classifies the seventy-three-year-old Scott, the oldest member of the convention, as a Co-operationist.[16] It seemed more accurate, however, to compromise and call him a Secessionist/Co-operationist, an imprecise but, in this case, an apparently appropriate label. Fortunately, Scott is the only candidate who presents such a thoroughly complicated picture.

In addition to telling us who all of the candidates were, the manuscript returns confirm the fact that the immediate secessionists won a majority of the popular vote. Their margin of victory, however, was not as large as that claimed by the *Daily Delta* in March 1861. According to the published returns, the Secessionists polled 20,488 votes while the Co-operationists captured 17,296, giving the radical ticket a statewide majority of 3,152. But the actual returns show that in the representative races, the vote was 20,557 Secessionist versus 18,651 Co-operationist, a difference of 1,906. When the totals are figured on the basis of the senatorial districts, probably the fairest test since there were fewer unopposed candidates in these races, the margin is even narrower. Here the results show the Secessionists winning 20,214 votes, the Co-operationists 18,451, for a radical majority of only 1,763.[17]

The Secessionists could legitimately lay claim to at least a tenuous popular majority for their subsequent course of action, but that support was less impressive than the radicals wanted, or were willing, to admit. The narrow margin of their victory in the convention election was probably a major reason why the disunionist forces, in clear violation of the state constitution, refused to submit the ordinance of secession to the voters for ratification.[18] On the basis of very recent evidence, the risk may well have appeared too high to Louisiana's Secessionists in 1861.

Table I
LOUISIANA SECESSION ELECTION
January 7, 1861

Manuscript Parish Returns
(*indicates candidates who won seats in the convention)

ASCENSION

Senatorial District (2 seats)
(Ascension, Assumption Terrebonne)

Candidate	Votes
R. L. Gibson (S)	174
E. J. McCall (S)	261
Robert C. Martin (C)*	458
Adolphe Verret (C)*	370

Parish Representative (2 seats)

Candidate	Votes
L. D. Nichols (S)	258
D. F. Kenner (S)	234
Thomas Cottman (C)*	422
Edward Duffel (C)*	348

ASSUMPTION

Senatorial District (2 seats)
(Ascension, Assumption, Terrebonne)

Candidate	Votes
R. L. Gibson (S)	83
E. J. McCall (S)	29
Robert C. Martin (C)*	597
Adolphe Verret (C)*	501

Parish Representative (2 seats)

Edmond L. Melancon (C)*
Walter Pugh (C)*
(both unopposed; no vote given)

AVOYELLES

Senatorial District (2 seats)
(Avoyelles, Pointe Coupée, West Feliciana)

Candidate	Votes
Abraham M. Gray (S)*	637
B. B. Simms (S)	485
Charles D. Stewart (S)*	240
Robert J. Barrow (S)	112

Parish Representative (2 seats)

Candidate	Votes
Aristide Barbin (S)*	384
Fenelon Cannon (S)*	605
F. B. Coco (S)	326
R. Windes (C)	162

BIENVILLE

Senatorial District (1 seat)
(Bienville, Bossier)

Robert Hodges (S)* 553
Calvin Leary (C) 213

Parish Representative
(1 seat)

Felix Lewis (S)* 547
James B. Head (C) 213

BOSSIER

Senatorial District (1 seat)
(Bienville, Bossier)

Robert Hodges (S)* 408
Calvin Leary (C) 374

Parish Representative
(2 seats)

Thomas J. Caldwell (S)* 407
Henderson M.
McFarland (S)* 402
John M. Sandige (C) 372
E. W. Hodges (C) 379

CADDO

Senatorial District (2 seats)
(Caddo, DeSoto,
Natchitoches, Sabine)

Henry Marshall (S)* 747
Benjamin L. Hodge (S)* 745
James G. Campbell (C) 122
Thomas H. Patterson (C) 119

Parish Representative
(2 seats)

George Williamson (S)* 751
Leon D. Marks (S)* 731
Joseph C. Beall (C) 123
Joseph B. Thompson (C) 122

CALCASIEU

Senatorial District (2 seats)
(Calcasieu, Lafayette,
St. Landry)

Alexandre Mouton (S)* 240
Lucius J. Dupré (S)* 245
Alexis O. Guidry (C) 3
François Robin (C) 8
John E. King (C?) 5

Parish Representative
(1 seat)

William E. Gill (S)* 152
William L. Carnes (S?) 45
Zadoc Mumford (S?) 47

CALDWELL

Senatorial District (1 seat)
(Caldwell, Catahoula, Winn)

Jacob Humble (S) 128
Wade H. Hough (C)* 248

Parish Representative
(1 seat)

John T. Simons (S) 130
Cicero C. Meredith (C)* 248

CARROLL

Senatorial District (1 seat)
(Carroll, Franklin)

Mark Valentine (S)* 530
S. C. Floyd (C) 181

Parish Representative
(2 seats)

Edward Sparrow (S)* 548
John H. Martin (S)* 510
Hugh Short (C?) 214
John Bishop (C?) 178

CATAHOULA

Senatorial District (1 seat)
(Caldwell, Catahoula, Winn)

Jacob Humble (S) 333
Wade H. Hough (C)* 599

Parish Representative
(1 seat)

Henry J. Peck (S) 335
James G. Taliaferro (C)* 595

CLAIBORNE

Senatorial District (1 seat)

J. Barrow (S) 636
John L. Lewis (C)* 912

Parish Representative
(2 seats)

A. C. Hill (S) 658
E. H. Fay (S) 644
James M. Thomasson (C)* 896
Nelson J. Scott (C)* 895

CONCORDIA

Senatorial District (2 seats)
(Concordia, Madison, Tensas)

John Perkins, Jr. (S)* 210
Lemuel P. Conner (S)* 193
A. T. Welch (C) 58
John Routh (C)[19] 1

Parish Representative
(2 seats)

Joseph E. Miller (S)* 193
Zebulon York (S)* 198
Charles Crossgrove (C) 56
Isaac Lum (C) 52

DeSOTO

Senatorial District (2 seats)
(Caddo, DeSoto, Natchitoches
Sabine)

Henry Marshall (S)* 680
Benjamin L. Hodge (S)* 666
James G. Campbell (C) 51
Thomas H. Patterson (C) 50

Parish Representative
(2 seats)

Joseph B. Elam (S)* 666
Y. W. Graves (S)* 660
J. H. Eastham (C) 49
W. A. Sharp (C) 50

EAST BATON ROUGE

Senatorial District (2 seats)
(East Baton Rouge, East
Feliciana, West Baton Rouge)

A. G. Carter (S) 264
E. W. Robertson (S) 274
Andrew S. Herron (C)* 864
James O. Fuqua (C)* 828

Parish Representative
(2 seats)

Tom Bynum (S) 292
Bertrand Haralson (S) 263
William S. Pike (C)* 848
I. Ambrose Williams (C)* 837

EAST FELICIANA

Senatorial District (2 seats)
(East Baton Rouge, East
Feliciana, West Baton Rouge)

A. G. Carter (S) 231
E. W. Robertson (S) 222
Andrew S. Herron (C)* 390
James O. Fuqua (C)* 404

Parish Representative
(2 seats)

J. J. Smith (S) 222
Jno. M. Roberts (S?) 3
Thomas W. Scott (C/S)* 595
William Patterson (C)* 405

FRANKLIN

Senatorial District (1 seat)
(Carroll, Franklin)

Mark Valentine (S)* 273
S. C. Floyd (C) 206

Parish Representative
(1 seat)

Allen Bonair (S)* 272
W. B. Grayson (C) 204

IBERVILLE

Senatorial District (1 seat)

Augustus Talbot (S)* 390
Joseph A. Breaux (C) 329

Parish Representative
(2 seats)

Theodore Johnston (S)* 381
Edward G. W. Butler (S)* 323
Charles A. Bruslé (S) 187
Gervais Schlatre (C) 319
Charles Kleinpeter (C) 251

JACKSON

Senatorial District (1 seat)
(Jackson, Union)

William M. Kidd (S)* 546
C. Buchanan (C?) 170

Parish Representative
(1 seat)

William B. Warren (S)* 415
O. S. Lane (C) 345

JEFFERSON

Senatorial District (2 seats)
(Jefferson, Orleans, right bank,
Plaquemines, St. Bernard)
Charles J. Villeré (S) 245
E. Warren Moise (S) 127
Fergus Gardére (C)* 902
Charles Bienvenu (C)* 732

Parish Representative
(2 seats)
J. J. Land (S) 207
A. N. Ogden, Sr. (S) 207
Christian Roselius (C)* 820
C. Théodule Lagroue (C)* 809

LAFAYETTE

Senatorial District (2 seats)
(Calcasieu, Lafayette,
St. Landry)
Alexandre Mouton (S)* 448
Lucius J. Dupré (S)* 391
Alexis O. Guidry (C) 91
François Robin (C) 29

Parish Representative
(1 seat)
Michael E. Girard (S)* 452
(unopposed)

LAFOURCHE

Senatorial District (1 seat)
(Lafourche, St. Charles)
Louis Bush (C)* 877
Richard Taylor (S)[20] 1

Parish Representative
(2 seats)
George S. Guion (S?) 456
L. C. Aubert (S?) 168
J. Scrudder Perkins (C)* 534
Caleb J. Tucker (C)* 481

LIVINGSTON

Senatorial District (1 seat)
(Livingston, St. Helena, St.
Tammany, Washington)
Hardy Richardson (S)* 231
Cade D. Strickland, Sr. (C) 88
T. G. Davidson (?) 6
W. E. Walker (?) 6

Parish Representative
(1 seat)
William A. Davidson (S)* 197
William Akers (C) 140
P. H. Spear (?) 1

MADISON

Senatorial District (2 seats)
(Concordia, Madison, Tensas)
John Perkins, Jr. (S)* 232
Lemuel P. Conner (S)* 226
(both unopposed)

Parish Representative
(2 seats)
Claiborne C. Briscoe (S)* 226
William R. Peck (S)* 229
Scattering (C)[21] 117

MOREHOUSE

Senatorial District (1 seat) (Morehouse, Ouachita)		*Parish Representative* (1 seat)	
Jacob B. Matthews (S)	376	Robert B. Todd (S)*	374
Horace M. Polk (C)*	283	A. J. Bobo (C)	283

NATCHITOCHES

Senatorial District (2 seats) (Caddo, DeSoto, Natchitoches, Sabine)		*Parish Representative* (2 seats)	
Benjamin L. Hodge (S)*	556	John W. Butler (S)	544
Henry Marshall (S)*	547	Phanor Prudhomme (S)	547
James G. Campbell (C)	621	A. H. Pierson (C)*	620
Thomas H. Patterson (C)	613	Jules Sompayrac (C)*	625

ORLEANS, LEFT BANK

Senatorial District (5 seats)	
Peter E. Bonford (S)*	4,321
Felix Labatut (S)*	4,327
William R. Adams (S)*	4,277
Thomas H. Kennedy (S)*	4,321
J. J. Michel (S)*	4,286
Thomas J. Durant (C)	3,918
Randall Hunt (C)	3,940
Pierre Soulé (C)	3,848
C. Dufour (C)	3,963
Benjamin F. Jonas (C)	3,902

Parish Representative (20 seats)	
1st District	
Thomas J. Semmes (S)*	493
Isaac M. Marks (S)*	477
Benjamin S. Tappan (S)*	509
George M. Pinckard (C)	357
Samuel H. Torrey (C)	333
Robert H. Marr (C)	337
L. N. Larre (?)	102
2nd District	
Daniel W. Adams (S)	517
A. F. Axson (S)	509
Joseph Ad. Rozier (C)*	533
W. T. Stocker (C)*	529
Scattering	7
3rd District	
A. H. Gladden (S)*	824
James McCloskey (S)*	833
Robert W. Estlin (S)*	829
John B. Slawson (S)*	828
Gilbert S. Hawkins (C)	715
Josiah Cole (C)	718
L. F. Generes (C)	711
George S. Lacey (C)	709
Scattering	7

Parish Representative, Orleans, Left Bank (cont'd)

4th District

M. O. H. Norton (S)* 441
Edmond J. Forstall (C) 229
Scattering 5

5th District

Joseph Hernandez (S)* 588
Bernard Avegno (S)* 550
Emile Hiriart (C) 266
Charles Deléry (C) 292

6th District

John Pemberton (S)* 259
A. Abadie (C) 219
Jules Lavergne (?) 121

7th District

W. C. C. Claiborne (S) 203
Daniel Edwards (S) 180
George Clark (C)* 263
Edward Bermudez (C)* 284

8th District

John G. Eustis (S) 77
C. Octave LeBlanc (C)* 317
Scattering 1

9th District

P. Sever Wiltz (S)* 293
J. McLean (C) 143

10th District

William R. Miles (S)* 654
William M. Perkins (S)* 643
Alexander Walker (S)* 608
M. Musson (C) 569
Alfred Phillips (C) 591
D. S. Dewees (C) 567
Scattering 5

ORLEANS, RIGHT BANK

Senatorial District (2 seats)
(Jefferson, Orleans, right bank,
Plaquemines, St. Bernard)

E. Warren Moise (S) 66
Charles J. Villeré (S) 86
Fergus Gardére (C)* 350
Charles Bienvenu (C)* 317
J. Desames (?) 1

Parish Representative
(1 seat)

John McGee (S) 77
George W. Lewis (C)* 177
N. Trépagnier (C?) 163

OUACHITA

Senatorial District (1 seat)
(Morehouse, Ouachita)

Jacob B. Matthews (S) 316
Horace M. Polk (C)* 420

Parish Representative
(1 seat)

R. W. Richardson (S) 316
Isaiah Garrett (C)* 418

PLAQUEMINES

Senatorial District (2 seats)
(Jefferson, Orleans, right bank,
Plaquemines, St. Bernard)

Charles J. Villeré (S) 109
E. Warren Moise (S) 123
Fergus Gardére (C)* 408
Charles Bienvenu (C)* 220

Parish Representative
(2 seats)

Joseph B.
Wilkinson, Jr. (S)* 229
Effingham Lawrence (S)* 223
Galveston B. Egan (C) 220
Auguste Lesseps (C) 221
Auguste Reggio (?) 1

POINTE COUPÉE

Senatorial District (2 seats)
(Avoyelles, Pointe Coupée,
West Feliciana)

Charles D. Stewart (S)* 546
Abraham M. Gray (S)* 334
Robert J. Barrow (S) 261
B. B. Simms (S) 199
M. Courtney (C?) 1

Parish Representative
(2 seats)

Auguste Provosty (S)* 546
Samuel W. McKneely (S)* 482
Jacob C. Vanwickle (C) 224
John H. Seibert (C) 208
Ebenezer Cooley (S)[22] 31

RAPIDES

Senatorial District (1 seat)

John K. Elgee (S)* 933
(unopposed)

Parish Representative (3 seats)

Thomas C. Manning (S)* 772
William W. Smart (S)* 729
Lewis E. Texada (S)* 736
L. A. Stafford (C) 416
Josiah Chambers (C) 249
W. W. Whittington (C) 395

SABINE

Senatorial District (2 seats)
(Caddo, DeSoto, Natchitoches, Sabine)

Henry Marshall (S)* 149
Benjamin L. Hodge (S)* 145
Thomas H. Patterson (C) 339
James G. Campbell (C) 334

Parish Representative (1 seat)

Edward C. Davidson (C)* 421
(unopposed)

ST. BERNARD

Senatorial District (2 seats)
(Jefferson, Orleans, right bank, Plaquemines, St. Bernard)

Charles J. Villeré (S) 197
E. Warren Moise (S) 79
Charles Bienvenu (C)* 105
Fergus Gardére (C)* 41

Parish Representative (1 seat)

Antoine Marrero (S)* 169
Philippe Toca (C)......................... 43

ST. CHARLES

Senatorial District (1 seat)
(Lafourche, St. Charles)

Louis Bush (C)* 49
Lartigue Mongrue (C?) 43

Parish Representative (1 seat)

Richard Taylor (S)* 78
(unopposed)

ST. HELENA

Senatorial District (1 seat)
(Livingston, St. Helena, St. Tammany, Washington)

Hardy Richardson (S)* 184
Cade D. Strickland, Sr. (C) 285

Parish Representative (1 seat)

Warren A. Grice (S) 192
James A. Williams (C)* 288

ST. JAMES

Senatorial District (1 seat)
(St. James, St. John the Baptist)
J. H. Loughborough (S) 61
A. B. Roman (C)* 509

Parish Representative
(2 seats)
L. L. Armant (S) 73
H. C. Colomb (S) 64
J. K. Gaudet (C)* 500
Louis L. LeBourgeois (C)* 500

ST. JOHN THE BAPTIST

Senatorial District (1 seat)
(St. James, St. John the Baptist)
J. H. Loughborough (S) 66
A. B. Roman (C)* 289

Parish Representative
(1 seat)
P. A. St. Martin (S) 66
Samuel Hollingsworth (C) 290

ST. LANDRY

Senatorial District (2 seats)
(Calcasieu, Lafayette,
St. Landry)
Alexandre Mouton (S)* 941
Lucius J. Dupré (S)* 891
Alexis O. Guidry (C) 850
François Robin (C) 803

Parish Representative
(4 seats)
John A. Taylor (S)* 974
Walthal Burton (S)* 906
William H. Spencer (S) 793
Raphael J. Smith, Jr. (S) 810
Caleb L. Swayze (C)* 922
Thomas A. Cook (C)* 899
John E. King (C) 889
Daniel Gobert (C) 739

ST. MARTIN

Senatorial District (1 seat)
(St. Martin, Vermilion)
Alexandre Declouet (S)* 723
Edgard E. Voorhies (C) 172

Parish Representative
(2 seats)
John Moore (S)* 658
Alcibiade De Blanc (S)* 743
E. W. Fuller (C) 213
S. Belden (C) 169

ST. MARY

Senatorial District (1 seat)
(St. Mary)
G. Laclaire Fuselier (S)* 448
William T. Palfrey (C) 423

Parish Representative
(2 seats)
Jules G. Olivier (S)* 453
Washington M. Smith (S)* 444
Henry J. Saunders (C) 425
Joseph D. Olivier (C) 412

ST. TAMMANY

Senatorial District (1 seat)
(Livingston, St. Helena,
St. Tammany, Washington)
Hardy Richardson (S)* 254
Cade D. Strickland, Sr. (C) 133

Parish Representative
(1 seat)
Jules LeBlanc (S) 193
Sidney S. Conner (C)* 221

TENSAS

Senatorial District (2 seats)
(Concordia, Madison, Tensas)
Lemuel P. Conner (S)* 256
John Perkins, Jr. (S)* 250
(unopposed)

Parish Representative
(2 seats)
Samuel W. Dorsey (S)* 248
William D. Anderson (S)* 242
John Routh (C) 33

TERREBONNE

Senatorial District (2 seats)
(Ascension, Assumption,
Terrebonne)
R. L. Gibson (S) 390
E. J. McCall (S) 319
Adolphe Verret (C)* 503
Robert C. Martin (C)* 473

Parish Representative
(2 seats)
D. S. Cage (S) 427
F. S. Goode (S) 408
Andrew McCollom (C)* 478
Gilmore F. Connelly (C)* 469

UNION

Senatorial District (1 seat)
(Jackson, Union)
William M. Kidd (S) 377
C. Buchanan (C?) 217

Parish Representative
(2 seats)
Sidney H. Griffin (S)* 555
William C. Carr (S)* 417
W. C. Andrews (C?) 117
Samuel Robertson (C?) 24
Scattering 5

VERMILION

Senatorial District (1 seat)
(St. Martin, Vermilion)

Alexandre Declouet (S) 275
Edgard E. Voorhies (C) 38
Albert Voorhies (C?) 38

Parish Representative (1 seat)

Daniel O'Bryan (S)* 247
J. B. Theall (C) 65

WASHINGTON

Senatorial District (1 seat)
(Livingston, St. Helena, St. Tammany, Washington)

Hardy Richardson (S)* 276
Cade D. Strickland, Sr. (C) 120

Parish Representative (1 seat)

John Wadsworth (S) 193
Nehemiah Magee (C)* 196

WEST BATON ROUGE

Senatorial District (2 seats)
(East Baton Rouge, East Feliciana, West Baton Rouge)

A. G. Carter (S) 88
E. W. Robertson (S) 88
Andrew S. Herron (C)* 234
James O. Fuqua (C)* 235

Parish Representative (1 seat)

William B. Robertson (S?) 57
Nathaniel W. Pope (C)* 263

WEST FELICIANA

Senatorial District (2 seats)
(Avoyelles, Pointe Coupée, West Feliciana)

Abraham M. Gray (S)* 221
Charles D. Stewart (S)* 217
Robert J. Barrow (S) 81
B. B. Simms (S) 55

Parish Representative (2 seats)

William R. Barrow, Sr. (S)* 233
John T. Towles (S)* 231
John B. Wederstrandt (C) 32

WINN

Senatorial District (1 seat)
(Caldwell, Catahoula, Winn)

Jacob Humble (S) 66
Wade H. Hough (C)* 505
D. Meredith (?) 7

Parish Representative (1 seat)

John D. Strother (S) 88
David Pierson (C)* 507
John Frazier (?) 11

Notes for "The Long Lost Returns: The Candidates and Their Totals in Louisiana's Secession Election"

[1]Although the ordinance of secession was adopted by a vote of 113 to 17, the radicals did not dominate the convention as thoroughly as this vote indicates. Ralph A. Wooster finds that the Immediate Secessionists held 80 seats while their opponents controlled 50; see his *The Secession Conventions of the South* (Princeton, 1962), 106.

[2]For a discussion of this aspect of the election controversy, see Charles B. Dew, "Who Won the Secession Election in Louisiana?," *Journal of Southern History*, 36 (1970): 18-32.

[3]*New Orleans Daily Delta*, March 27, 28, 1861. These returns gave a Secessionist and a Co-operationist vote for each parish but did not list the candidates by name or give the totals polled by individual winning and losing candidates.

[4]The Immediate Secessionists advocated prompt, unqualified withdrawal from the Union and represented the most radical position. Their opponents were divided into three groups, but all three campaigned under one banner, Co-operationist, in an effort to prevent an Immediate Secessionist victory: the Co-operationists per se, who, as a delaying tactic, supported a program of joint secession of all the slave states; the Conditional Unionists, who favored a convention of the slaveholding states which would submit the South's grievances to the North, with secession following if the North refused to meet their demands; and the straightout Unconditional Unionists, who opposed secession under any circumstances. In this paper, Co-operationist is used collectively and refers to all those elements opposed to the Immediate Secessionist position.

[5]John Rose Ficklen, *History of Reconstruction in Louisiana (Through 1868)* (Baltimore, 1910), 16n.

[6]Ibid., 21-24; James Kimmins Greer, "Louisiana Politics, 1845-1861," *Louisiana Historical Quarterly*, 13 (1930): 640; Roger W. Shugg, *Origins of Class Struggle in Louisiana: A Social History of White Farmers and Laborers during Slavery and After, 1840-1875* (Baton Rouge, La., 1939), 163-64; Willie Malvin Caskey, *Secession and Restoration of Louisiana* (Baton Rouge, La., 1938), 25; David M. Potter, *Lincoln and His Party in the Secession Crisis* (New Haven, 1942), 214; Allan Nevins, *The Emergence of Lincoln*, 2 vols. (New York, 1950), 2:421; Avery O. Craven, *The Growth of Southern Nationalism, 1848-1861* ([Baton Rouge], 1953), 375; Wooster, *Secession Conventions*, 104n.

[7]Wooster, *Secession Conventions*, 104n.

[8]Ibid., 101-20; Ralph Wooster, "The Louisiana Secession Convention," *Louisiana Historical Quarterly*, 34 (1951): 103-33.

[9]The returns are also available in Records of the Louisiana State Government, 1850-88, National Archives Microfilm Publications, M-359, roll 9.

[10]Every parish was entitled to at least one representative; Orleans Parish (left bank) elected twenty, the largest number chosen by a single parish.

[11]The only single-parish senatorial districts were Claiborne, Iberville, Orleans (left bank), Rapides, and St. Mary.

[12]The crucial roll calls are discussed in Wooster, *Secession Conventions*, 107-11; the individual roll call votes are recorded in the *Official Journal of the Proceedings of the Convention of the State of Louisiana* (New Orleans, 1861).

[13]Scott owned a plantation of more than 2,300 acres and held 107 slaves in 1860; see Joseph K. Menn, *The Large Slaveholders of Louisiana—1860* (New Orleans, 1964), 222-23.

[14]*New Orleans Daily Picayune*, December 27, 1860.

[15]Ibid., January 12, 1861.

[16]Wooster, "Louisiana Secession Convention," 128.

[17]For a comparison of the published and the manuscript returns, see Dew, "Who Won the Secession Election."

[18]The refusal to hold a ratification election on the ordinance is discussed in Roger W. Shugg, "A Suppressed Co-operationist Protest Against Secession," *Louisiana Historical Quarterly*, 19 (1936): 199-203.

[19]See Tensas Parish returns.

[20]See St. Charles Parish returns.

[21]The *New Orleans Daily Picayune*, December 26, 1860, reported that Dr. James Foster had been nominated as an "anti-secession" candidate in Madison Parish. The same paper noted on January 11, 1861, that Briscoe and Peck, the Secessionist representative candidates, had been elected without opposition. Since the vote for the Secessionist representative and senatorial candidates is almost exactly the same, it seems logical to assume that most, if not all, of these 117 scattered votes were Co-operationist voters looking for a candidate after Foster dropped out of the race.

[22]Withdrew from the race in favor of Auguste Provosty; see *Baton Rouge Daily Advocate*, January 8, 1861.

THE SECESSION CONVENTIONS OF THE SOUTH: LOUISIANA*

Ralph A. Wooster

Secession was never as popular in Louisiana as in her sister states of the lower South, as the state seemed bound to the Union by social and economic ties. The tariff protected her sugar industry from foreign competition, the Mississippi Valley fed her commerce, and many of her leading citizens were natives of the northern states.[1] The secession movement of the early 1850s found little sympathy in Louisiana,[2] and as late as the presidential campaign of 1860 there were strong elements within the state opposed to any disruption of the Union. In that year a bitter contest had been waged by the supporters of John C. Breckinridge, Stephen A. Douglas, and John Bell for Louisiana's electoral vote. Although the state's electoral votes went into the Breckinridge column, no candidate obtained a majority of the popular vote. Breckinridge received 22,681, compared with 20,204 for Bell and 7,625 for Douglas. As Bell and Douglas were pledged to upholding the Union, the results of the election may be taken to indicate that a majority of Louisianians in November 1860 opposed radical or drastic measures for guaranteeing Southern rights.[3]

Following the election of Lincoln, however, sentiment in Louisiana underwent a change. The factions that made up the strong Bell support in the presidential election seemed to feel that compromise with a Republican administration was impossible. Sentiment for secession grew, accompanied by the formation of military clubs and units throughout the state. Gov. Thomas O. Moore therefore issued a call for a special session of the state legislature to consider the situation.[4]

On December 10, 1860, the state legislature met in Baton Rouge in answer to Governor Moore's call. In his inaugural message, Moore declared the election of a "Black Republican" to be an outrage, and recommended that a special convention be called to determine the future relations of Louisiana with the federal government.[5] This recommendation was immediately drawn up in the form of a bill for an election on January 7 of delegates to a state convention to be held in Baton Rouge on January 23, 1861. After

*First published as Chapter 7 in Ralph Wooster, *The Secession Conventions of the South* (Princeton, N. J.: Princeton University Press, © 1962) 101-120. Reprinted with the kind permission of the author and publisher.

slight debate, the bill was passed without amendment and approved by the governor December 12, 1860; the framework for secession had been laid.[6]

By the first days of the new year, South Carolina had already left the Union, and December elections had indicated that other slave states of the lower South would follow in the early part of January. Even in Louisiana the contest was not over secession; that seemed a foregone conclusion. The real issue was rather over the method of secession. One group, known as the "Co-operationists," favored withdrawal from the Union, but in the form of united Southern action. The other group, the "immediate secessionists," favored withdrawal by separate state action without delay. Another faction, which may be labeled "Conditional Unionists," opposed any disruption of the Union until a last effort at compromise, preferably by constitutional amendments guaranteeing protection of Southern rights, had been attempted. The "Conditional Unionist" group was so small, however, that its members combined with the "Co-operationist" faction and campaigned under that label. Thus, there were only two tickets in the campaign—"Co-operationists" and "immediate secessionists."[7]

The result of the election of January 7 was a sweeping victory for the immediate secessionists. In New Orleans, formerly a stronghold of moderate sentiment, twenty of the twenty-five elected delegates were avowed separate state actionists. In the entire state, eighty secessionist delegates and forty-four Co-operationists were elected, while six delegates were listed as doubtful.[8] The popular vote in the state was 20,448 for immediate secessionists and 17,296 for their Co-operationist opponents.[9]

On Wednesday, January 23, 1861, the special convention to consider federal relations convened at Baton Rouge.[10] Composed of ninety-nine delegates elected from state representative districts, and thirty-one delegates elected from senatorial districts, the convention included former United States Senator and ex-Governor Alexandre Mouton; former United States Congressmen John Moore and John Perkins, Jr.; and ex-Governor André B. Roman. In attendance, also, was young Richard Taylor, son of Zachary Taylor; and great planters of the state, such as Edward Sparrow and John Martin of Carroll, and C. Laclaire Fuselier and Alexandre Declouet of St. Martin. By no means all the delegates to the convention were great planters or experienced statesmen; indeed, several had no prior political experience and no established position in the economic and social life of the state.

In years of age, the membership of the Louisiana convention averaged 42.5 years (median 43 years), and was thus a middle-aged group. Fifty-one of the delegates, or 39.2 percent of the convention, were aged 40-49 years; while thirty-seven members, or 28.5 percent of the entire body, were aged 30-39 years. Seven members were younger than 30 years of age and twenty-three delegates were above the 50-year mark. The ages ranged from 21-year-old David Pierson of Winn to 73-year-old Thomas W. Scott of East Feliciana.[11]

In respect to place of birth, forty-seven of the members, or 36.2 percent of the convention, were native sons of Louisiana. Of the seventy-two delegates born outside the state, ten came from South Carolina, eight from Mississippi, seven each from New York and Tennessee, six each from Kentucky and Georgia, four each from Maryland and Virginia, and two from North Carolina. The states of Arkansas, Indiana, New Jersey, Pennsylvania, Massachusetts, and Alabama each contributed one native, as did also the District of Columbia. Nine members of the convention were born outside the United States—four born in Ireland, two each in Germany and France, and one in England.[12]

The predominance of planters and farmers in the convention was evident as fifty-one members, or 38.9 percent of the total group, were listed as planter or farmer in the 1860 census. Thirty-nine members, or 30.0 percent of the total convention, were lawyers. Seven members were public officials,[13] five were physicians, four were merchants, four were commission merchant, and two were editors. One delegate listed his occupation as "omnibus," another as "adjuster of averages," another as an exchange broker, and another as president of an insurance company. One member was an overseer, two were planter-lawyers, and one was a farmer-lawyer.[14]

TABLE 1

Louisiana Secession Convention Occupations

Occupation Of Delegate	*Conditional Unionists*	*Coopera-tionists*	*Immediate Secessionists*	*Total*
Lawyer	8	7	24	39
Planter	5	5	26	36
Farmer	2	7	6	15
Public Official	2	3	2	7
Physician	3	1	1	5
Merchant			4	4
Com. Merchant	1		3	4
Planter-Lawyer			2	2
Editor		1	1	2
Farmer-Lawyer			1	1
Omnibus			1	1
Broker			1	1
Insurance			1	1
Adjuster of Aver.	1			1
Overseer	1			1
Unknown	1	2	7	10
	----	----	-----	------
Total	24	26	80	130

In real property the one hundred and twenty delegates for whom information is available possessed an average of $74,587.50. Because the holdings of a few wealthy delegates such as John H. Martin and Edward Sparrow of Carroll, with $374,500 and $665,500 respectively, J. Kleber Gaudet of St. James, with $450,000, and John Perkins, Jr., of Madison, with $500,000, ran the average up very high, the median holding of $30,000 is doubtless a more accurate indication of the wealth of the typical delegate. In personal property the one hundred and fourteen delegates for whom information is available had an average of $54,690.23, but the median was only $20,000 for the convention. Even so, the wealth of the delegates to the Louisiana convention, with $50,000 as the median and $129,277.73 as the average, was still high and indicates unmistakably the position of the average delegate in the society of his state.[15]

One hundred and seven of the one hundred and thirty members of the convention were slaveholders in 1860. The average and the median holdings were far apart, the average being 46.3 slaves per delegate and the median only twelve. The accompanying table (Table 3) shows that fifty-five members or 42.4 percent of the convention held 20 slaves or more in 1860, and were thus in the planter class; thirty-six of them held 50 slaves or more, and nineteen held 100 or more.[16]

TABLE 2
Louisiana Secession Convention Property Holding

Amount of Property Held by Delegate	*Conditional Unionists*	*Coopera-tionists*	*Immediate Secessionists*	*Total*
	Real Property			
Under $5,000	6	5	11	22
$5,000 and under $25,000	6	8	19	33
$25,000 and under $74,587 (Average)	6	6	15	27
$74,587 and under $200,000	4	5	17	26
$200,000 and over		1	11	12
Total	22	25	73	120
	Personal Property*			
Under $5,000	11	5	16	32
$5,000 and under $25,000	2	4	24	30
$25,000 and under $52,690 (Average)	2	6	11	19
$52,690 and under $100,000	2	5	4	11
$100,000 and under $200,000	3	4	9	16
$200,000 and over	1		5	6
Total	21	24	69	114

*Personal property was not listed in census enumeration for R. C. Martin, Lemuel Conner, Joseph E. Miller, Edward Bermudez, J. B. Wilkinson, and Richard Taylor; yet their slaveholding indicates personal property, hence they are not included in this table.

Upon the assembly of the convention at Baton Rouge on January 23, 1861, the first order of business was the election of a presiding officer. Alexandre Mouton, senatorial delegate from Lafayette Parish and a separate state actionist, was elected president over Isaiah Garrett, a Co-operationist from Ouachita Parish, by an 81 to 43 vote.[17] The secessionists had promptly illustrated that they were the majority party of the Louisiana convention.

After he assumed the chair, President Mouton received a motion from S. W. Dorsey of Tensas that a committee of fifteen members be appointed "to prepare and report as soon as possible an ordinance providing for the withdrawal of the State of Louisiana from the present Federal Union, with a view to the establishment of a new confederacy to be composed of seceding states." The immediate secessionists, led by Alexandre Walker and John Moore, regarded this proposal with suspicion, and succeeded in getting the words "with the view to the establishment of a new confederacy . . ." dropped from the resolution, thus making it a plain instruction to prepare a secession ordinance.[18] The Committee of Fifteen immediately received for consideration ordinances from delegates John Moore, William R. Miles, and Mark Valentine. All of them provided for immediate withdrawal from the Union. Next day Chairman John Perkins, Jr., reported on behalf of the committee an ordinance of secession. Before the vote upon this ordinance Joseph A. Rozier, a lawyer from New Orleans, offered a substitute providing that "all slaveholding states be invited to assemble in convention at Nashville on February 25th to take into consideration the relations which the slaveholding states shall hereafter occupy to the General Government and the other states of the Union; to determine what amendments of the Constitution of the United States are necessary. . . ."[19]

TABLE 3

Louisiana Secession Convention Slaveholding

Slaves held By Delegate	*Conditional Unionists*	*Coopera-tionists*	*Immediate Secessionists*	*Total*
None	5	4	14	23
1 and under 10	8	5	20	19
10 and under 20	2	5	12	19
20 and under 30	3	1	3	7
30 and under 40			7	7
40 and under 50		3	2	5
50 and under 70	2	2	4	8
70 and under 100	3	1	5	9
100 and under 200	1	5	4	10
200 and under 300			7	7
300 and under 500			2	2
	----	----	----	-----
Total	21	24	69	114

The Rozier resolution can thus be classified as one of "conditional union." It would have the Southern states stay in the Union if certain basic concessions were made. Should these concessions not be forthcoming, then the South would consider secession. Sponsored by the ultra-conservative faction, the motion was a last attempt to save the Union from disruption. On Friday, January 25, the Rozier resolution was defeated, by a vote of 24 to 106, thus crushing any real hope of the Conditional Unionists.[20]

The defeat of Rozier's Conditional Unionist proposal prompted James O. Fuqua, lawyer and small slaveholder from East Feliciana, to offer another substitute for the Perkins ordinance of secession. The Fuqua substitute called for acceptance of an invitation by Alabama to meet for consideration of a union of the slaveholding states, and would have delayed secession until after consultation with the other Southern states. This proposal had the support of both the Co-operationists, whose position it represented, and the Conditional Unionists, who accepted it as the best measure they could now hope to have passed.[21] Again the immediate secessionists held firm, and by a 74 to 47 vote defeated the Fuqua substitute.[22]

Once Fuqua's Co-operationist motion had been defeated, the convention turned again to consideration of the Perkins secession ordinance. A final plea for less immediate action was entered by Charles Bienvenu of New Orleans, who moved that secession not be effective until ratified by a vote of the people. This resolution, the last united attempt by the Unionists and Co-operationists to halt the tide of secession, was defeated by a 45 to 84 roll-call vote.[23] The ordinance of secession was then voted upon and passed by a 113 to 17 count. President Mouton declared "the connection between the State of Louisiana and the Federal Union dissolved, and that it is a free, sovereign, and independent power."[24] The governor of the state, Thomas O. Moore, and several high-ranking state officials marched into the hall bearing a flag of the state; and a prayer was offered for divine guidance. The ties with the Union had been broken.[25]

The leader of the seventeen delegates who opposed final passage of the secession ordinance was James G. Taliaferro, a sixty-year-old lawyer from Catahoula. He entered a sharp protest against the secession proceedings, declaring that "the act of dissolving the ties which connect Louisiana with the Federal Union is a revolutionary act, that this Convention is, of itself, without legitimate power to perform. . . ." The convention, however, refused to enter the protest upon the pages of the journal.[26]

Following the passage of the secession ordinance, the convention, which had by now moved to New Orleans,[27] proceeded to consider the matter of relations with the other Southern states. Upon a motion by John Perkins, Jr., an ordinance was passed providing for the appointment of six delegates to the convention called at Montgomery, Alabama, for formation of a new confederacy. On the next day, Perkins and Alexandre Declouet were selected by the convention as delegates at large, and Charles M. Conrad, Henry Marshall, Duncan Kenner, and Edward M. Sparrow as delegates upon a representative-district basis.[28]

The completion of the Confederate constitution by the Montgomery group provided the Louisiana convention with its last important task—ratification of that document. A motion that the constitution be submitted to the people of the state for approval was defeated by a twenty-six to seventy-four vote, and the convention then voted 109 to 7 to ratify the constitution of the Confederacy.[29] After five days devoted to questions of redistricting, new oaths of office for public officials, a new judiciary system, and payment of officials, the secession convention, its work completed, adjourned on March 26, 1861.[30]

To understand properly the work of the Louisiana convention, it is necessary to study the characteristics of the delegates comprising the three factions in the convention. Classifying the twenty-four members who voted for the Rozier motion as Conditional Unionists, the twenty-six who voted for the Fuqua motion but against Rozier's as Co-operationists, and all others as immediate secessionists, we find that in years of age the Conditional Unionists, with an average of 44.5 years (median 45.5), were the oldest group present. Second were the immediate secessionists with an average of 43.7 years (median 43), followed by the Co-operationists, whose average age was 40.3 years (median 40 years). If the two non-immediate-secessionist factions were combined, however, their average was about that of the immediate secessionists. Evidently age made little difference in determining opposition or support of separate state action in the Louisiana convention.

Regarding place of birth, all three factions had a plurality of native-born Louisianians. Nine of them favored Conditional union, thirteen favored cooperation, and twenty-five favored immediate secession. If the two non-immediate-secessionist factions were combined, the vote of native Louisianians at the convention would be twenty-five to twenty-two in favor of separate state action. However, this majority is a good deal smaller proportionally than the majority of the entire convention for immediate action; hence, it appears that native-born Louisianians were less inclined to support secession than were their companions born in other states. The same statement applies to the delegates of South Carolina birth, among whom five opposed and five supported separate state action. On the other hand, delegates who were born New Yorkers favored immediate secession by a six to one vote, Georgians by a four to two vote, and Irish by a four to 0 vote. Delegates born in Tennessee, Virginia, Maryland, North Carolina, and France were pretty evenly divided. The delegates born in Germany (two), Pennsylvania (one), and England (one) opposed separate state action.

The occupation of a delegate evidently had little to do with his position regarding secession. The lawyers and planters and farmers comprised the majority of each faction in the convention. Twenty-four lawyers were secessionists, eight were Conditional Unionists, and seven were Co-operationists. The other occupational groups were distributed proportionally among the three factions. Exceptions were the four merchants, all of whom voted for secession, and the five physicians, three of whom favored conditional union.[31]

The average total property holding of the immediate secessionist was considerably more than that of his Co-operationist and Unionist opponent. The secessionist group had a $153,622.54 average for total property, compared to the $108,159.78 and $72,744.97 averages for the Co-operationists and Unionists respectively. The high average wealth of the secessionists, however, owed much to the presence among them of several extremely wealthy individuals. If the median holding is considered, the property holding of the Co-operationists, with $59,900, is nearly as high as that of the secessionists, which was $60,250. The Conditional Unionist group had a median of only $19,500.[32]

The average slaveholding of the immediate secessionists was likewise higher than that of their opponents. The secessionist average holding was 56.5 slaves, compared to 39.9 and 26.1 for the Co-operationists and Unionists respectively. Again the average is deceptive, however, and the median holding probably is more reliable. Here, the Co-operationist group, whose median slaveholding was seventeen slaves, ranks above both the secessionists and Unionists, whose averages were twelve and nine slaves respectively. Fourteen members of the secessionist group, or 17.5 percent, were not found in the census as slaveholders. Only four Co-operationists, or 15.4 percent of the group, were non-slaveholders, while five Unionists, or 20.8 percent, were in this category. Thirty-four secessionists, twelve Co-operationists, and nine Unionists held twenty slaves or more in 1860. Nine of the secessionists owned 200 slaves; not a single Co-operationist or Unionist owned that many slaves.

Analysis of the personal characteristics has illustrated that the secessionists and their opponents in the convention were in many ways similar. In age both the typical secessionist and his opponents were in their early forties. Both were slaveholders, and both secessionist and non-secessionist groups were dominated by planters and lawyers. Except for the fact that the immediate secessionists comprised most of the extremely large property owners and slaveholders, there was actually little difference in the non-political characteristics of the several groups of delegates in the convention.

Evidently what determined the vote of a delegate in the Louisiana body was not his own characteristics, but the characteristics of the particular parish that he represented in the convention. It will, therefore, be instructive to examine the types of parishes to see which were represented in the convention by Unionists, which by Co-operationists, and which by immediate secessionists.[33]

Delegates representing the sugar parishes of Louisiana tended to favor delay more than did delegates from the other areas of the state. Of the sixteen parishes producing more sugar than cotton in 1859, six elected Co-operationist delegates, and two elected Conditional Unionist delegations. The sugar parishes were thus split over separate state action, eight parishes to eight. Too, it may be noted that in the election for convention delegates three other sugar parishes were carried by the immediate secessionists by only the most narrow margin.[34] It may be speculated that the sugar planters of the state felt that the advantages derived from the protection afforded by the tariff were considerable, and were on that account reluctant to disrupt the Union.

TABLE 4
Louisiana Sugar Parishes and Secession

Voters of Parish Delegation In the Convention of 1861	*Sugar Parishes**	*Other Parishes*	*Total*
Conditional Union	2	6	8
Cooperation	6	2	8
Immediate Secession	8	16	24
Divided		7	7
	-----	-----	-----
Total	16	31	47

*Includes parishes of Ascension, Assumption, East Baton Rouge, Iberville, Jefferson, Lafourche, Plaquemines, Pointe Coupée, St. Bernard, St. Charles, St. James, St. John the Baptist, St. Martin, St. Mary, Terrebonne, and West Baton Rouge. These sixteen parishes produced more pounds of sugar cane than pounds of cotton in 1859. The parish of New Orleans also produced more sugar than cotton, but since the amount was so small that it could not properly be called a sugar parish, it is not included in this table.

In per capita wealth the parishes electing immediate secessionists ranked higher than the Conditional Unionist and Co-operationist parishes. Only one Co-operationist parish, and no Conditional Unionist parish, had a per capita wealth of $5,000 or above in 1860, whereas eight secessionist parishes ranked that high. Among the parishes in which the per capita wealth was $3,000 but below $5,000, two were represented by Unionists in the 1861 convention, one by Co-operationists, and two by secessionists. Thus, of parishes with a per capita wealth of $3,000 or above, ten were immediate secessionists and four non-separate state actionists.[35]

As would be expected from the per capita-wealth distribution, the secessionist parishes were the larger slaveholding parishes in 1860. It is true that in the twenty-four black parishes (50 percent or more slave) the division between immediate secessionist and opponents was pretty even—they elected to the convention ten separate state actionist delegations, five Unionist, five Co-operationist, and four divided. But among these "black" parishes those that were secessionist had a much higher slave population than did the other parishes. The seven parishes of the state wherein over 75 percent of the total population was slave were all represented by separate state actionists in the 1861 convention.[36]

TABLE 5
Slave Population in Louisiana Parishes, 1860

	VOTE OF COUNTY DELEGATION IN CONVENTION				
Percentage Of Slaves in Total Population	*Conditional Unionists*	*Cooperationists*	*Immediate Secessionists*	*Divided*	*Total*
Less than 12.5%				1	1
12.5%and less than 25%		2			2
25% and less than 37.5 %	2		3	2	7
37.5% and less than 50%	1	1	4	1	7
50% and less than 62.5%	4	3	5	2	14
62.5% and less than 75%	1	2	5	2	10
75% and over			7		2
	-----	-----	-----	-----	-----
Total	8	8	24	8	48

Little difference can be found in the political background of the secessionist, the Conditional Unionist, and the Co-operationist parishes. The Democratic party by 1860 had a firm grip on Louisiana politics, and a majority of the parishes had supported the nominee of that party in the recent presidential elections.[37] Indeed, twenty had supported the Democratic nominee in all of the four preceding presidential elections. Ten of these were represented by immediate secessionist delegates in the 1861 convention, four by Unionists, three by Co-operationists, and three by divided delegations. This ratio is about that of the state as a whole, and indicates little correlation one way or the other between Democratic tradition and secessionist sentiment. The same want of correlation holds true in the nine parishes which supported the Democratic nominee in three of the four presidential elections. These counties elected four secessionist, two Conditional Unionist, two Co-operationist, and one divided delegation to the convention of 1861.

The old Whig parishes were likewise pretty evenly divided over the matter of immediate secession. To be sure, the two parishes, West Baton Rouge and St. James, that had cast a majority of their popular votes against the Democratic nominee in the four preceding elections were both Co-operationist in 1861.[38] But nine other parishes that had cast a majority of votes for the opposition candidate (Whig in 1848 and 1852; American in 1856; Constitutional Union in 1860) in three of the four elections were represented in the convention by five secessionist, two Conditional Unionist, and two divided delegations.[39] Eight other Louisiana parishes had supported the opposition ticket in two of the four elections; only two of these were Co-operationist in the convention, four were secessionist, and two had divided delegations. It seems evident that long-term political preferences played little part in determining the position of a parish in the secession crisis of 1861.

If attention is centered on the election of 1860 alone, however, there seems to be a relationship between the votes for the presidential candidates and attitudes toward secession. The nine parishes that cast a plurality of votes for John Bell in 1860 leaned away from separate state action. Four were Co-operationist, two were Unionist, and two were divided in the secession crisis. Only one, Madison, favored separate state action, and did so by an overwhelming 5-1 margin in the election for convention delegates. One of the divided parishes was Orleans, which cast nineteen of its twenty-six votes in the convention for immediate secession. Two of the three parishes carried by Stephen A. Douglas were Co-operationist in the convention and one was a Conditional Unionist. In each case over 70 percent of the parish's vote had been cast against immediate secessionists in the election for convention delegates. Twenty-two of the thirty-six Breckinridge parishes were represented by immediate secessionists in 1861, five by Conditional Unionists, three by Co-operationists, and six by divided delegations.[40]

This analysis of Louisiana parishes affords certain conclusions regarding the secession movement of 1861 in that state. The parishes supporting immediate secession were the heavily slave-populated cotton-producing parishes in which per capita wealth was the highest in the state. These parishes felt the economic system of the South could best be preserved outside of the Union. Opposing immediate disruption of the Union were half of the rich sugar parishes of Southern Louisiana. Combined with them in opposition to immediate secession were several less wealthy parishes in northern Louisiana whose inhabitants believed that they had little to gain by disruption of the Union.[41] These two groups opposed separate state action, but to no avail. Already five sister Southern states had seceded from the Union and the secessionist spirit was strong enough to defeat the more cautious Co-operationists and Unionists and carry Louisiana out of the Union and into the Confederacy.

Notes for "The Secession Convention of the South: Louisiana"

[1]Roger W. Shugg, *Origins of Class Struggle in Louisiana: A Social History of White Farmers and Laborers During Slavery and After, 1849-1875* (Baton Rouge, 1939), 157.

[2]For the story of Louisiana and the 1850 secession movement, see M. J. White, "Louisiana and the Secession Movement of the Early Fifties," Mississippi Valley Historical Association *Proceedings*, 8 (1914-1915): 278-88.

[3]For the campaign in full, see Jefferson Davis Bragg, *Louisiana in the Confederacy* (Baton Rouge, 1941), 1-20; Willie M. Caskey, *Secession and Restoration of Louisiana* (Baton Rouge, 1938), 1-15; James K. Greer, *Louisiana Politics, 1845-1861* (Baton Rouge, 1930), 221-47; Mary Lilla McLure, "The Elections of 1860 in Louisiana," *Louisiana Historical Quarterly*, 9 (1926): 602-702.

[4]That Governor Moore was under the influence of the powerful John Slidell, United States senator from Louisiana, seems evident. Slidell had hitherto been a moderate who felt the South might rule through control of the Democratic party, but with Lincoln's election saw no alternative to secession. Shugg, *Origins of Class Struggle*, 161-62, calls Moore a "puppet" of Slidell.

[5]"Inaugural Address of Gov. Thomas O. Moore," *Documents of the 1st Session of the Fifth Legislature of the State of Louisiana* (Baton Rouge, 1860), 5-6.

[6]Greer, *Louisiana Politics*, 247-48. Shugg, *Origins of Class Struggle*, 161-62, notes that the legislature acted in an illegal manner, as the Constitution of 1852 required that the question of a convention be submitted to a popular referendum.

[7]Caskey, *Secession and Restoration*, 20-21.

[8]Bragg, *Louisiana in the Confederacy*, 26; Caskey, *Secession and Restoration*, 26-28; Greer, *Louisiana Politics*, 260-61; *New Orleans Daily Picayune*, January 11, 18, 15, 1861. Unfortunately, there exists no complete list of candidates in the race, most sources simply giving the names of the winners. Shugg, *Origins of Class Struggle*, 163, does not accept the returns printed in newspapers for the period. He seems to be of the opinion that the Co-operationists actually carried the state. The present writer accepts the returns given in the above sources as authentic.

[9]Bragg, *Louisiana in the Confederacy*, believes that the fact that 12,776 votes less were cast in this election than in the presidential election 2 months earlier was a protest of these voters against secession. The present writer does not agree with this assumption.

[10]*Proceedings of the Louisiana State Convention (in English and French) Together with the Ordinances Passed by Said Convention (in Both Languages) and the Constitution of the State as Amended* (New Orleans, 1861), 3. Cited hereafter as *Proceedings of Convention.*

[11]Based on information obtained from the manuscript returns of the Eighth Census of United States, 1860, Schedule 1, Free Inhabitants. The ages for 12 delegates were not determined by the writer.

[12]Ibid.

[13]Four court clerks, one state representative, one sheriff, and one United States officer comprised this group.

[14]See Table 1.

[15]See Table 2.

[16]See Table 3. Largest slaveholder present was William R. Barrow, who held 432 slaves in 1860.

[17]*Proceedings of Convention*, 5; *New Orleans Daily Picayune*, January 24, 1861. The official journal gives a bare sketch of events, while the debates are published in full in the *Daily Picayune.*

[18]*Proceedings of Convention*, 5-6.

[19]Ibid., 15-16. On the afternoon that the Rozier motion was presented, a message from Gov. Thomas O. Moore was read to the convention. The convention then passed, by a 119 to 5 vote, a resolution approving the governor's action in seizing Federal property. The mover of the resolution was a Co-operationist, Louis Bush of Lafourche Parish. C. C. Meredith, David Pierson, Joseph Rozier, W. T. Stocker, and James Taliaferro—all strong unionists—voted in the negative.

[20]Ibid.

[21]Exceptions were James Taliaferro, William E. Gill, and William W. Smart, who voted for the Rozier motion, but refused to support Fuqua's substitute.

[22]*Proceedings of Convention*, 16, gives the vote as 47 to 73, which most historians have accepted, but examination of the delegates' vote will show that a 74-vote count was recorded against the Fuqua resolution. The 47 voting in the affirmative included 21 members who had supported the 26 who had voted against the Rozier conditional union motion. The 26 properly constitute the Co-operationists at the convention.

[23]Ibid., 17, gives the figure 43 to 84, but an examination of the vote will show it to be a 45 to 85 vote. With several exceptions, this was a partisan vote, with the immediate secessionists opposing any such delay.

[24]Ibid., 18.

[25]For a description of this ceremony, see *New Orleans Daily Picayune*, January 26, 1861. The formal signing of the ordinance took place immediately. All but 9 delegates signed.

[26]Taliaferro's protest, originally published in the *New Orleans Daily Crescent*, January 31, 1861, may be found in Roger W. Shugg, "A Suppressed Co-operationist Protest Against Secession," *Louisiana Historical Quarterly*, 19 (1936): 199-203; and Bragg, *Louisiana in the Confederacy*, 30-31.

[27]Necessitated by the convening state legislature at Baton Rouge for its regular session. The ordinance of secession was passed on January 26, the last day the convention met in Baton Rouge.

[28]*Proceedings of Convention*, 20-23.

[29]Ibid., 75-76. Voting in the negative were Bienvenu, Lewis, Rozier, and Stocker, all of Orleans, Garrett of Ouachita, Roselius of Jefferson, and Taliaferro of Catahoula. These 7 were among the 17 who had voted against final passage of secession. Eight of the others now voted for ratification of the Constitution. Two were absent.

[30]Ibid., 92.

[31]A study of the manuscript returns for Schedule No. 4, Productions of Agriculture (originals located at the Library of Duke University, Durham, N. C.; microfilm copy at the Library of the University of Texas), U. S. Census, 1860; and P. A. Champomier, *Statement of the Sugar Crop of Louisiana, 1859-1860* (New Orleans, 1860), reveals that the ratio of sugar cane producers and cotton growers in 1859 is similar to that of the 3 factions in the whole convention. For example, 5 Conditional unionists, 6 Co-operationists, and 14 secessionists were found as growers of sugar cane in 1859. Five unionists, 9 Co-operationists, and 27 secessionists were listed as growing cotton in 1859. It should be noted that 10 secessionists, and not a single non-secessionist, produced over 300 bales of cotton in that year.

[32]See Table 2 for the variations in property-holding. Note that only one Co-operationist had above $200,000 in personal property, whereas 11 secessionists had above $200,000 in real property and 5 above $200,000 in personal property.

[33]In analysis of parishes represented by secessionists and non-secessionists, a senatorial delegate is considered as representing only the parish of his residence. It would be more correct to consider him as representing all the parishes in his district, but to do so is impracticable in analysis of the present type.

[34]The non-sugar parishes, mainly cotton-producing areas, were predominantly favorable to separate state action. Sixteen elected secessionists, 6 elected unionists, 2 elected Co-operationists, and 7 elected divided delegations. Classification as sugar parishes and non-sugar parishes is based upon Eighth Census of United States, 1860, Vol. 3, *Agriculture* (Washington, 1864), 66-69. See Table 4.

[35]Based on Eighth Census of United States, 1860, Vol. 1, *Population* (Washington, 1864), 194, and Vol. 4, *Statistics* (Washington, 1866), 303.

[36]Two Louisiana parishes, Tensas and Concordia, were over 90 percent slave in 1860.

[37]In 1848 the Whig nominee, Zachary Taylor, a resident of Louisiana, carried the state, but in the elections of 1852, 1856, and 1860 the Democratic nominees received a plurality of votes cast.

[38]Both had returned overwhelming margins for the Co-operationist ticket in the election for convention delegates. Returns in the *New Orleans Weekly Delta*, January 19, 1861, show 509 votes for the Co-operationists as against 73 votes for the secessionists in St. James, and 120 Co-operationist and no secessionist votes in West Baton Rouge.

[39]An analysis of the vote cast in these parishes in the actual election for convention delegates shows that in 3 such parishes the secessionists polled better than 70 percent of the vote, in 2 parishes the opposition to secession polled better than 70 percent of the vote, 2 were carried by the secessionists by a close margin, and 2 by the Co-operationists by a close margin.

[40]Perry H. Howard, *Political Tendencies in Louisiana, 1815-1952* (Baton Rouge, 1957), 62-64, compares the vote in the presidential election of 1860 with that for convention delegates and concludes that where the presidential vote was extremely close the voters later supported Co-operationists. For example, he notes that the 8 parishes with a close Breckinridge plurality later supported Co-operationists in the election for convention delegates.

[41]Unfortunately, there appears to be no way, short of a count of names in the manuscript census returns, to determine the percentage of Creoles in parish populations. The writer is inclined to believe that parishes with a large Creole population tended to oppose separate state action more than did the other parishes of the state.

Index